CW01464435

Latin Fict

The Latin novel is an area which has precipitated a great deal of study in the last two decades, but the focus of past attention has tended to centre on the novels of Petronius and Apuleius. This comprehensive and innovative study redefines the limits of the Roman novel, setting it in a broader context.

Latin Fiction provides a chronological study of the Roman novel from the Classical period to the Middle Ages, exploring its development and the continuity of Latin culture up to the early modern period. Among the texts considered are:

- Petronius, *Satyrica* and *Cena Trimalchionis*
- Apuleius, *Metamorphosis* (*The Golden Ass*)
- *The History of Apollonius King of Tyre*
- The Trojan tales of Darius Phrygius and Dictys Cretensis
- The Latin Alexander
- Hagiographic fiction

Medieval interpretation of 'Cupid and Psyche', *Apollonius of Tyre* and the *Alexander Romance.*

Editor: **Heinz Hofmann** is Professor of Latin at the University of Tübingen. He is co-editor, with M. Zimmermann, of the *Groningen Colloquia on the Novel*.

Latin Fiction

The Latin Novel in Context

Heinz Hofmann

Routledge
Taylor & Francis Group
LONDON AND NEW YORK

First published 1999
by Routledge
11 New Fetter Lane, London EC4P 4EE

Simultaneously published in the USA and Canada
by Routledge
29 West 35th Street, New York, NY 10001

Routledge is an imprint of the Taylor & Francis Group

First published in paperback 2004

Typeset in Garamond by RefineCatch Limited, Bungay, Suffolk
Printed and bound in Great Britain by
MPG Books Ltd, Bodmin, Cornwall

British Library Cataloguing in Publication Data
A catalogue record for this book is available from the British Library

Library of Congress Cataloging in Publication Data
A catalog record for this book has been requested

ISBN 0–415–14722–0

CONTENTS

CONTRIBUTORS

Graham Anderson is Professor of Classics at the University of Kent at Canterbury. He has published on the ancient novel and the literature of the Second Sophistic and is author of *Eros Sophistes: Ancient Novelists at Play* (Chico, CA 1982), *Ancient Fiction: the Novel in the Graeco-Roman World* (London 1984) and *Philostratus: Biography and Belles-Lettres in the Third Century A.D.* (London 1986). Currently he is engaged in a study of folk- and fairytales in antiquity.

Elizabeth Archibald is Associate Professor of English at the University of Victoria in British Columbia, Canada. She has published on the reception of the *Historia Apolloni* and on Renaissance literature and is the author of *Apollonius of Tyre: Medieval and Renaissance Themes and Variations* (Cambridge: D.S. Brewer, 1991).

John Bodel is Professor of Classics at Rutgers University in New Brunswick, NJ. He has published on Petronius and Roman literature and is author of *Freedmen in the 'Satyricon' of Petronius* (Ann Arbor: University of Michigan, 1984). Currently he is at work on a study of funerals and undertakers in the Roman world.

Robert H.F. Carver is Lecturer in Renaissance Literature in the Department of English Studies at the University of Durham. He is currently completing a book on the reception of Apuleius during the Middle Ages and the Renaissance.

Catherine Connors is Associate Professor of Classics at the University of Washington, Seattle and the author of *Petronius the Poet: Verse and Literary Tradition in the Satyricon* (Cambridge University Press, 1998).

Heinz Hofmann was Professor of Latin at the University of Groningen (in the Netherlands) between 1982 and 1993 where he was a member of the Research Group on Apuleius and in 1986 inaugurated the meetings of the 'Groningen Colloquia on the Novel'. Since 1993 he has been Professor of Latin at the University of Tübingen (Germany). He is editor of the

Groningen Colloquia on the Novel (vol. 1 ff., 1988 ff.) – since vol. 7, 1996, together with M. Zimmerman – and published, among numerous studies mainly on topics of late antiquity and Neo-Latin, also several articles on Apuleius.

Gerlinde Huber-Rebenich is Professor of Latin literature of the Middle Ages and Neo-Latin at the Friedrich-Schiller-Universität of Jena. She has worked on the reception of ancient novella motives and Ovid's *Metamorphoses* and is author of *Das Motiv der 'Witwe von Ephesus' in lateinischen Texten der Antike und des Mittelalters* (Tübingen: Gunter Narr, 1990).

Hugh J. Mason is Associate Professor and Undergraduate Coordinator in the Department of Classics at the University of Toronto. He has published articles on Apuleius, Longus and the history and topography of Lesbos. Other scholarly interests include the Venetian composer Tommaso Albinoni and the modern Greek novelist Stratis Myrivilis.

Stefan Merkle is Lecturer in the Department of Classics at the University of Munich. He has published on Ovid and the Trojan narratives of late antiquity and is author of *Die 'Ephemeris belli Troiani' des Diktys von Kreta* (Frankfurt/M. etc.: Lang, 1989). Currently he is completing a monograph on Phaedrus' books of fables.

Claudio Moreschini is Professor of Latin Literature at the University of Pisa. His principal area of study has been Apuleius, including his philosophical works, as well as Hermeticism and the philosophy of the Church Fathers. He is the author of *Apuleio il platonismo* (Florence: S. Olschki, 1978), *Apuleio, La magia* (Milan: Rizzoli, 1990) and Apuleio, *La novela di Amore e Psiche* (Padua: Editoriale Programma). He also edited the critical edition of *Apuleius, De philosophia libri* for the Bibliotheca Teubriesana (Leipzig, 1991).

Gerald N. Sandy is Professor of Classics at the University of British Columbia in Vancouver and has specialized in the study of ancient Greek and Latin prose fiction and of the classical heritage in France. He is author of a monograph on Heliodorus (Boston: Twayne Publishers, 1982) and of *The Greek World of Apuleius: Apuleius and the Second Sophistic* (Leiden: Brill, 1997).

Gareth Schmeling is Distinguished Professor of Classics at the University of Florida at Gainesville. He is author of several books on the ancient novel, among which are monographs on Chariton (Boston: Twayne Publishers, 1974) and Xenophon of Ephesus (Boston: Twayne Publishers, 1980), and has compiled *A Bibliography on Petronius* (Leiden: Brill, 1977); he made a critical edition of the *Historia Apollonii regis Tyri* for the Bibliotheca Teubneriana (Leipzig, 1988) and is editor of *The Novel in the Ancient World* (Leiden: Brill, 1996), and of *The Petronian Society Newsletter* (1970 ff.).

Nancy Shumate is Associate Professor of Classical Languages and Literatures at Smith College in Northampton, Massachusetts. She has published mainly on Apuleius and is the author of *Crisis and Conversion in Apuleius' Metamorphoses* (Ann Arbor: University of Michigan, 1996).

Richard Stoneman is a Senior Editor at Routledge and an Honorary Fellow of the University of Exeter. He is the author of the Penguin translation of the *Alexander Romance*, and is preparing a commentary on the Greek and Latin recensions of the *Alexander Romance* for Mondadori.

PREFACE

In the course of the broadening of the traditional canon of ancient literature, genres and periods which have been rather neglected so far are receiving more attention and interest from students of Latin literature. One of the genres profiting from this new orientation is the Latin novel and related texts of Latin fiction as, for instance, historiographic, biographic, and hagiographic fiction.

It is the purpose of this volume to take up the present discussion on various aspects and problems of the Latin novel while providing the student with a synoptic treatment of the most important works of Latin fiction from the first until the sixth century AD and to sketch the heritage of Latin fiction through the Middle Ages until the rediscovery of the main texts of the Latin novels in the fourteenth and fifteenth centuries AD and the various ways of their exegesis and adaptation in the Early Modern period. In this sense *Latin Fiction* serves both as a first introduction to the subject also for those who are not yet acquainted with the texts of Latin fiction written between the first and fifteenth centuries AD, and as a textbook for university courses on the Latin novel and the various aspects of its later reception through the early Renaissance.

The volume is conceived as a companion volume to *Greek Fiction: The Greek Novel in Context*, edited by J.R. Morgan and Richard Stoneman and published by Routledge in 1994. Its authors – some of them already known as contributors to *Greek Fiction* – have collaborated to map another large terrain of ancient and medieval fictional writing and to enable the student to see the full extent of Latin fiction through the centuries and to open a way to a critical reading and fuller understanding of the relevant texts either in the Latin original or in translation.

INTRODUCTION

Heinz Hofmann

I

In comparison with the Greek novels the texts of the Latin novel which are known to us are rather limited: In Greek literature we have the tight corpus of the five extant 'ideal' love romances by Chariton, Xenophon of Ephesus, Achilles Tatius, Longus, and Heliodorus.[1] Moreover we know of quite a few novels whose fragments are preserved on papyrus and which allow us to get at least a rough idea of their contents;[2] this knowledge is supported by some mosaics dating from the second and third centuries AD and showing scenes from two lost Greek novels.[3] Finally we have a number of texts both extant and in fragments which do not belong to the type of the 'ideal' love romance but which contain various adventure stories and comparable fictional narratives and are being subsumed under the genre of the novel where they form the group of the so-called 'fringe novels' (cf. Holzberg 1996a).

In Latin literature we only know three novels proper: Petronius' *Satyrica*, Apuleius' *Metamorphoses*, and the *Historia Apollonii regis Tyri*. We also know of another text by Apuleius which presumably was a novel entitled *Hermagoras* and from which a few quotations are transmitted.[4] But we do not have a single Latin papyrus with fragments from a Latin novel: this is mainly because, thanks to the favourable climatic and geological circumstances, the bulk of ancient papyri was preserved and found in Egypt which belonged to the Greek-speaking part of the Roman Empire so that with a few exceptions all papyri contain Greek texts. Even the papyri carbonized in the *Villa dei papiri* in Herculaneum during the eruption of Mt Vesuvius in AD 79 are almost exclusively Greek, testifying the interest of the owner of the villa in Greek – mainly Epicurean – philosophy. As a consequence, there are no other authors and fragments of Latin novels known which may be compared with the extant complete texts and fragments of Greek novels. On the other hand there are some texts which belong to the group of 'fringe novels' – the Trojan narratives by Dictys and Dares and the Latin versions of the *Alexander Romance* – and there are quite a number of Lives of Saints and Apocryphal

Acts of Apostles which may, as their Greek counterparts, be considered as hagiographic fiction mainly written for the purpose of entertainment and edification of a Christian audience.

II

Like Roman literature in general, the samples of Latin novel too are adaptations from Greek literature. Very early, in the second half of the third century BC, Roman authors turned to Greek literature, which they considered superior both formally and aesthetically to the literary forms of their native Italy, and tried to translate and adapt Greek genres to the Latin language. The comedies of Plautus and Terence, the poems and tragedies of Ennius and other early Roman writers are proof of the dependence of the system of Roman literary genres from Greek models: even the first work of Roman literature, the *Odusia* of Livius Andronicus, was an abbreviated translation of Homer's *Odyssey*. Horace's famous line *Graecia capta ferum victorem cepit et artes / intulit agresti Latio*, 'Conquered Greece in its turn has conquered the brute victor and introduced arts and civilization into rural Latium' (*Epistle* 2, 1, 156 f.) is also valid for the Roman novel: Petronius' *Satyrica* have been recognized for a long time as a witty and parodying adaptation of the central elements and action of an 'ideal' Greek love romance (Heinze 1899; cf. Sandy 1994: 140f.), and this insight has been confirmed by recent papyrus finds with fragments of two Greek novels – *A Phoenician Story* by Lollianus and the so-called *Iolaus*-novel[5] – which have many traits in common with the *Satyrica* so that the *Iolaus* papyrus even was published under the title 'A Greek *Satyricon?*' (Parsons 1971). Apuleius' *Metamorphoses* is an enlarged translation and adaptation of the Greek *Metamorphoses* of an unknown author (according to some scholars, by Lucian of Samosata) of which an abridged version under the title *Lucius or the Ass* is transmitted among the writings of the sophist and rhetor Lucian of Samosata of the second century AD (see Chapter 6 by H. Mason, this volume). Finally *The History of Apollonius King of Tyre* very much smacks of a Greek romance though no papyrus has yet been found that can without doubt be identified as part of a Greek *Apollonius*-novel (see Chapter 9 by G. Schmeling, this volume). Papyrus fragments of a Greek *Ephemeris of the Trojan War* have been discovered in 1907 (cf. Merkle 1989: 22ff., 243ff. and his Chapter 10 in this volume), and scholars agree that there must have been a Greek Dares although no fragments have yet been found which can with certainty be identified as the Greek model of the *Acta diurna belli Troiani* (cf. Beschorner 1992: 8ff., 231ff. and Chapter 10 by S. Merkle, this volume). Of the *Alexander Romance* numerous Greek recensions are transmitted (cf. Chapter 11 by Richard Stoneman, this volume), and the same is true of the Apocryphal Acts of Apostles and most of the Latin Lives of Saints (cf. Chapter 12 by G. Huber-Rebenich, this volume), and even of another 'fringe' text, the *Life of Apollonius of Tyana* by Philostratus (cf. Bowie 1994, 187ff.), it is known that it was translated into Latin by Virius Nicomachus Flavianus († 394), a leading member of the pagan senatorial aristocracy in Rome.

Nevertheless the Latin novel developed into a genre in its own right, and of varied literary form, although the 'novel proper' is extant in three representatives only – Petronius' *Satyrica*, Apuleius' *Metamorphoses*, and *The History of Apollonius King of Tyre* – and even here one scholar has recently questioned again the character of the *Satyrica* as 'novel' and tried to describe it exclusively in terms of Menippean Satire (cf. Adamietz 1987, 1995). These and similar attempts to re-define the genre of texts commonly labelled as 'novels' reveal the problem of the existence in antiquity of a genre comparable with the genre 'novel' current since the seventeenth and eighteenth centuries – a problem that posed itself right at the beginning of the serious study of the ancient novel in the second half of the nineteenth century (cf. Rohde 1876). The novels and other fictional texts discussed in this volume cover a broad spectrum of Latin fiction: apart from the *Satyrica*, also *The History of Apollonius King of Tyre* contains some poems which give it a touch of Menippean Satire or prosimetrum, i.e., prose interspersed with verse (cf. Relihan 1993: 49ff., 91ff.; Dronke 1994; Pabst 1994). Historiography and biography are present in the various versions of the *Alexander Romance*, but also in the Apocryphal Acts of Apostles and the Lives of Saints: These texts in their turn draw heavily on the model of the *Acts of the Apostles*, commonly attributed to St Luke, which form part of the earliest New Testament canon, and try to capture their audience by combining edification with suspense and excitement when they narrate the most incredible adventures of the new heroes of faith and chastity. This process of adaptation and reworking of earlier novel texts even went so far that Lives of fictive saints have been composed entirely from the material of pagan romances: a good example is the coptic fragment of a *Life of St Parthenope* from the ninth or tenth century AD which has been known so far only from an Arabic version (*Life of St Bartānūbā*) where the holy virgin Parthenope experiences similar adventures and sufferings as the heroine of the Greek romance of Metiochus and Parthenope (first century BC) which we mainly know from three papyrus fragments.[6]

III

It has become evident that, on the one hand, the various kinds of ancient fiction both Greek and Latin cover a wide range of topics and literary forms and that their authors drew their inspiration from different literary genres and motifs and opened new provinces of writing. On the other hand it is true that ancient literary criticism developed no 'theory' of the novel and that the genre is simply neglected in the treatises on poetics and rhetorics; as a consequence neither in Greek nor in Latin was a specific term coined for that genre in spite of the existence of quite a few texts which modern critics assign to that genre. Several reasons can be adduced to explain this phenomenon.

First, the system of literary genres was developed by scholars working at the famous library in Alexandria in the third and second century BC. We know this best from the Roman rhetor Quintilian who, towards the end of the first century AD, wrote a lengthy 'Introduction to the Study of Rhetoric' (*Institutio oratoria*) where in Book X he gave a survey of the existent genres of Greek and Roman literature in both poetry and prose (*Inst. or.* 10, 1, 46–131). These scholars had fixed the canon of literary genres once for ever, and since then no new additions had been made, the only exception being Roman Satire which was still unknown to the Greek philologists in Alexandria and of which Quintilian proudly remarked *satura quidem tota nostra est*, 'satire, at any rate, is completely our own', i.e., satire as a literary genre is entirely a Roman achievement.[7] But he does not mention Petronius' *Satyrica* even within the genre of satire although he praises M. Terentius Varro at length for his Menippean Satires (*Inst. or.* 10, 1, 95). The genre of the novel which for the first time occurs towards the end of the second or early in the first century BC, was too late to be taken into account by the Alexandrian scholars and has never since found access into rhetorical handbooks.

Second, the pedigree of the ancient novel is rooted in several other genres of Greek literature (cf. Perry 1967; Hägg 1983: 109ff.; Holzberg 1996a). It resembles closest Hellenistic historiography of the fourth and third century BC which developed many marvellous and fictitious traits. Notorious are the *Persian Stories* of Ctesias, the historiography around Alexander the Great (Callisthenes, Nearchus, Cleitophon, Onesicritus), and fantastic travel stories like those of Euhemerus, Iambulus or Antonius Diogenes (cf. Stoneman 1994; Holzberg 1996b). It is no wonder, therefore, that these texts belong in a broader sense to what we call ancient novels and romances or longer fictional prose narratives. Another important tradition was that of the so-called 'Milesian Tales', a nebulous Greek prose genre attributed to a certain Aristides (about 100 BC) which was notorious for its erotic lasciviousness and is often thought of as utterly pornographic (cf. Perry 1967: 90ff.; Harrison 1998). Its function as model for Petronius and Apuleius is acknowledged by both authors in the *Satyrica* and the *Metamorphoses* respectively. They obviously used Aristides' collection not only for several tales of sensational and lubricious character within their novels (for instance, the 'Widow of Ephesus' and the 'Youth of Pergamum' in the *Satyrica* or the 'Tale of Thelyphron' in Book II, the adultery stories in Book IX and the episode of the 'Matron of Corinth' in Book X of the *Metamorphoses*) but also for the overall narrative structure of their novels as first-person narratives with inserted tales.[8]

Third, in spite of the literary and aesthetic endeavours of the authors of the ancient novel and their considerable artistic and narrative skills, and in spite of the growing appreciation of the genre by modern scholars and critics, novels in antiquity had a low reputation among educated readers. Proof are a few scattered remarks of some authors of late antiquity whose judgement is rather derogatory. In Latin literature we know of two such remarks: the first is to be found in the *Life of Clodius Albinus*[9] in the so-called *Historia Augusta*, a collection of biographies of Roman emperors from Hadrian (117–138) to Carus and his sons Carinus and Numerianus (283/4) written towards the end of the fourth century AD, where Septimus Severus is quoted with the remark that Clodius had been considered by many people as a lettered man but as a matter of fact he spent his life reading the African 'Milesian Tales' of his compatriot Apuleius and similar nonsense (*... neniis quibusdam anilibus occupatus inter Milesias Punicas Apulei sui et ludicra litteraria consenesceret*).[10] The second one occurs in the fifth-century commentary by Macrobius on Cicero's 'Dream of Scipio', the closing section of his treatise *On the Republic*. There Macrobius compares the 'Dream of Scipio' with the 'Myth of Er' at the end of Plato's *Republic* and deals with the problem of why Cicero chose a dream and not a myth as final set-piece of his philosophical dialogue. Macrobius renders the Greek term 'myth' (*mythos*) with the Latin word *fabula* ('story') for which he also uses the equivalents *figmentum* ('fiction'), *genus figmenti* ('kind of fiction' or 'fictional genre'), *mendacium* (Latin translation of Greek *pseudos* – literally 'lie' – which in literary contexts means 'fiction' as well). Then he discusses the term *fabula* whose etymology (from *fari*) according to him acknowledges the falsity of the stories it tells, and declares that those *fabulae* serve two purposes: 'either merely to gratify the ear or to encourage the reader to good works'.[11] The first aim he sees achieved in 'the comedies of Menander and his imitators, or the narratives replete with imaginary doings of lovers (*argumenta fictis casibus amatorum referta*) in which Petronius Arbiter so freely indulged and with which Apuleius, astonishingly, sometimes amused himself. A philosophical treatise avoids this whole category of fables that promise only to gratify the ear and relegates it to children's nurseries.'

With the word *argumenta* ('narratives') Macrobius refers to the theory and classification of narratives which we encounter in the rhetorical handbooks as, for instance, in the anonymous *Rhetorica ad Herennium* or in Cicero's *De inventione* ('How to Find Material for a Speech'), both dating from about 81/80 BC.[12] There three types of narratives are distinguished: apart from two types which occur in legal speeches there is a third type which has nothing to do with legal cases but is written for pleasure and entertainment. In the latter case there are again three different sorts of narratives which can be distinguished according to the degree of their truth: the *fabula*, i.e., the contents of the ancient epics and tragedies, is neither true (*verum*) nor probable (*verisimile*), the *historia*, i.e., historical narrative, is true (*verum*), and the *argumentum*, i.e., a fictional narrative which nevertheless could have happened in this form (*ficta res quae tamen fieri potuit*) as, for instance, the contents of a comedy, is probable or likely (*verisimile*).

This classification of narratives according to their truth ultimately goes back to the difference between poetry and historiography as stated by

Aristotle in Chapter 9 of his *Poetics* (1451 a 36 ff.) – an important passage for the concept of fictionality in antiquity.[13] It is evident that both comedy and what Macrobius with a reference to Petronius and Apuleius calls *fabulae* and what we are used to call novels, are narratives of the *argumentum* type, i.e., fictional narratives which nevertheless could have happened in this form, in contrast to the mythological narratives in epic poetry or in Greek tragedies where the divine machinery is in action and other incredible things happen. So the Latin novel did, after all, find a modest place in ancient discussions even if its evaluation was negative.[14]

IV

The audience of the Latin novels is broadly speaking the same as that of the Greek novels, and this is true for all texts of Latin fiction, also for historiographic and hagiographic fiction. It certainly was a consumer literature but not a mass literature because, as J. Morgan rightly observed, 'mass literacy never existed in the ancient world'.[15] Literacy in antiquity was always limited to a small minority, and those capable of reading longer literary texts were only a small group within those who possessed a certain knowledge of reading and writing for official and administrative purposes.[16] More important than reading literary texts was therefore listening to their authors and recitators: the performance of literature in the public through the authors themselves or specialized groups of performing artists who were organized in unions formed an integral part of cultural life in antiquity (Engels and Hofmann 1997a: 46ff.). In particular, the representatives of the so-called Second Sophistic, those wandering poets and declamators like Lucian of Samosata and Maximus of Tyre, Dio Chrysostomus and Aelius Aristides, Favorinus of Arles and Apuleius, who gave 'recitals' of their own texts in the theatres and odeons, the market-places and colonnades, the gymnasia and baths, the municipal buildings and imperial palaces, were the main mediators of literature and also of Latin and Greek fiction. We know, for instance, from Apuleius, this 'ultimate word artist' (Fantham 1996: 252), that he recited speeches and poems of his own in both languages, Latin and Greek, in the theatre in Carthage and elsewhere in the Greek and Roman world, and not only speeches and poems, but also his philosophical works on Socrates and Plato and his novel *The Golden Ass*, whose single books not only fill a papyrus roll (*volumen*) of average length, but form also a convenient discourse for a public lecture of about 60 to 90 minutes.[17] Literary communication among Christians worked in similar ways. There must have been many Christians who were not able to *read* the adventures of Paulus and Thecla, Petrus and Clemens, Malchus and Hilarion, but must have enjoyed themselves tremendously when listening to someone who was reading, or almost performing, these texts to them.

V

Latin novels, as has been stated above, are few, but Latin fiction in the broad sense as it is understood here abounds in texts. Therefore the contributions in the present volume discuss not only the three novels proper – Petronius' *Satyrica*, Apuleius' *Metamorphoses* or *The Golden Ass* and *The History of Apollonius King of Tyre* –, but pay also special attention to their Greek models and the inserted tales which are often, as in the case of the tale of Cupid and Psyche, miniature novels or novellas in their own right. In addition there is the huge mass of 'historical novels', including the Trojan narratives of Dares and Dictys and the numerous recensions of the *Alexander Romance*, truly a *texte vivant*, oscillating between the more historically conceived *History of Alexander the Great* by Q. Curtius Rufus and the quite fictitious adventures of Alexander's encounters with the Brahmans and other gurus, peoples and monsters reported in later novelistic texts. Saints and martyrs as the new heroes of the ancient world turning Christian found their way into Latin fiction by the third and fourth century: as they received their share of the adventures of the heroes and heroines in 'classical' fiction, they occupy a corresponding space in the later pages of ancient fiction and, consequently, also in this volume. This inclusion of Christian fiction in a volume on Latin fiction need no longer be defended nowadays after we have achieved the insight that both Christian and non-Christian texts are products of one and the same culture and derive ultimately from one and the same concept of art, literature and the life which is mirrored in them.

The history of Latin fiction, however, did not stop in the sixth or seventh century when the European world began to change from antiquity into the Middle Ages. It is true that the two main texts of Latin fiction – Petronius' *Satyrica* and Apuleius' *Metamorphoses* – disappeared from the bookshelves of readers and scholars and lay buried in the dust of monastic libraries where nobody looked after them: a complete copy of the *Satyrica* must still have been available somewhere in the Loire Valley in France at least in the eighth or ninth century, since from it some monks made those longer and shorter excerpts (including the *Cena Trimalchionis*) which have survived and have been discovered since the fifteenth century item by item and pieced together to form what we today can read as the remains of the *Satyrica*. Apuleius' novel was forgotten very early in the sixth century – St Augustine is the last author to cite *The Golden Ass*, in his *De civitate dei* (18, 18) – but knowledge of the tale of Cupid and Psyche which forms the centrepiece of the novel survived thanks to the allegorizing interpretation of Fulgentius.[18] A rich medieval tradition includes also *The History of Apollonius King of Tyre* which is not only preserved in some hundred manuscripts written between the ninth and fifteenth centuries, but exists also in numerous translations and adaptations in both Latin and vernacular, prose and verse. The same is true of the *Alexander Romance* which circulated in dozens of recensions, translations and adaptations, satisfying the desire for adventures and the hunger for stories not only in Europe but also in the Arabic and Persian world. It therefore seemed appropriate to extend the assessment of the tradition of Latin fiction through the Middle Ages until the beginning of the Early Modern period, when the humanists looked upon those texts with a new interest and inaugurated a new search for the ancient novel, hoping to find more of it in the libraries of medieval monasteries and cathedrals.

VI

The history of Latin fiction, however, did not come to an end in the sixteenth century: since Latin was the main language of politics and diplomacy, commerce and scholarship, the works of Greek literature which have come to the Latin West since the fourteenth and fifteenth centuries were soon translated into Latin and spread both in manuscripts and since the second half of the fifteenth century, also in printed editions. Sometimes a translation into Latin or the vernacular even preceded the Greek edition and made a text earlier known than the printed edition of the Greek original. This was also the case with some Greek novels which aroused the curiosity of a wider lettered readership first in translation.

The novel by Achilles Tatius on the adventures of Leucippe and Clitophon (cf. Reardon 1994), for instance, was first accessible in a Latin translation by Annibale della Croce, the first part of which was published in 1544, containing Books V–VIII, and the second part, containing Books I–IV, in 1554 (together with the already published Books V–VIII). In 1546 Ludovico Dolce translated Della Croce's Latin rendering of Books V–VIII into Italian (reprinted in 1547), and in 1551 – three years before the complete Latin version appeared – a complete Italian translation by Angelo de Coccio was published in Venice which since then has often been reprinted. In 1554 a French translation by Jacques Vincent and in 1597 an English translation by William Burton were printed, both on the basis of Della Croce's Latin and De Coccio's Italian translations, before in 1601 the first printed edition of the Greek text of Achilles Tatius was published in the Officina Commeliniana in Heidelberg by I. and N. Bonnvitius, the nephews of H. Commelinus, together with Parthenius' *Love Stories* and Longus' *Daphnis and Chloe*.

This Heidelberg edition of 1601 of Longus' pastoral romance *Daphnis and Chloe* (cf. Morgan 1994b) was the second printed edition of the Greek text and followed the first edition (Florence 1598) at an interval of three years. Here too several translations preceded the *editio princeps* of the Greek original: the first Italian translation was made sixty years earlier by Annibale Caro about 1537, but was printed in Parma and Florence as late as 1784 and 1786; later Italian translations followed in 1643 by Giovanni Battista Manziani and in the eighteenth century by Casparo Gozzi (Venice 1766,

Paris 1781, London 1792) and others (cf. Berger 1988b). A French translation by Jacques Amyot was first published anonymously in Paris in 1559 and three times reprinted (in 1578, 1595 and 1596) before the appearance of the first Greek edition. The first Latin version of *Daphnis and Chloe* was an adaptation in Latin hexameters by Lorenzo Gambara, printed under the title *Expositi* ('The Foundlings') in Naples in 1574, still thirty years before the first Greek edition, and until the eighteenth century often reprinted together with the Greek text, for the last time in the edition of B.G.L. Boden (Leipzig 1777). The first Latin prose translation appeared face to face with the Greek text in the Heidelberg edition of 1601.

Heliodorus' *Aithiopika*, that is, the story of the adventures of Theagenes and Chariclea (cf. Morgan 1994c), was first edited in the Greek original by Vincentius Opsopoeus and printed in Basel in the printing office of Hervagen in 1534, but before the second printed edition was published in the Officina Commeliniana in Heidelberg in 1596, several translations in Latin and vernacular appeared, by which Heliodorus' novel gained great popularity and fame:[19] the first translation was in French by Jacques Amyot (who later also translated Longus), published in Paris in 1547 and followed five years later[20] by the Latin translation of the young Polish scholar Stanisław Warszewicki, who had studied in Padua and Wittenberg, where he was a pupil of Philip Melanchthon. It was printed in the office of Johannes Oporinus in Basel in 1522 with an enthusiastic preface by Warszewicki's academic teacher Melanchthon. A Latin *Epitome*, an abbreviated version on the basis of Opsopoeus' Greek edition (Basel 1534), was made by the Tübingen Professor of Greek Martin Crusius (1526–1607) and published in the printing office of J. Wechel in Frankfurt in 1584, but this *Epitome* with its didactic and moralizing comments did not meet the taste of the Latin reading public and has never since been reprinted (cf. Berger 1988a). In the same year in which Warszewicki's translation was published, another Latin translation of the first Book only by René Guillon appeared in Paris in the Officina Wecheliana which however could not match the success of Warszewicki's (cf. Baliński 1992).

Of a rather late date are the first printed editions of the Greek text of the *Ephesian Stories* by Xenophon of Ephesus (cf. Konstan 1994) and the *Adventures of Callirhoe* by Chariton (cf. Egger 1994), both with facing Latin translation: Xenophon of Ephesus appeared for the first time in print in London in 1726, edited and translated into Latin by the Florentine medical doctor Antonio Cocchi,[21] Chariton in Amsterdam in 1750, edited by Jacques Philippe d'Orville (1696–1751, Professor in Amsterdam) and translated into Latin by Johann Jacob Reiske (1716–1774, since 1748 Professor in Leipzig; cf. Reardon 1998).

These few remarks may show that between the sixteenth and eighteenth centuries even the texts of the Greek novels circulated and were read in Latin and vernacular translations and thus formed part of the history of Latin fiction in the Early Modern period – just as in Antiquity and Late Antiquity certain texts of Greek fiction, for instance the *Alexander Romance*, the Trojan narratives, the Apocryphal Acts of Apostles and the Lives of Saints, were translated into Latin and read or listened to by a Latin-speaking audience in the West. The history of Latin fiction however went on: the first examples of 'modern' fiction in Latin are translations from novellas of Boccaccio by Petrarch, Leonardi Bruni and Matteo Bandelli,[22] and up to the twentieth century, along with many other literary texts, novels too, originally written in the European vernacular languages, were translated into Latin in order to make those texts accessible to scholars and a general lettered reading public which was not so well-read in English or French but was still capable of reading Latin prose quite fluently or enjoyed the exotic pleasure of reading well-known novels in Latin (cf. Grant 1954; Ijsewijn 1998: 243ff.; Hofmann 1998). As a consequence we know Latin translations of, for instance, the *Lazarillo de Tormes* (1554),[23] the *Diana Enamorada* (1564) of Gaspar Gil Polo,[24] the *Télémaque* (1699/1717) of Fénelon in both prose and hexameter,[25] the *Bélisaire* (1767) of Jean-François Marmontel[26] or the *Robinson der Jüngere* (1779/80) by Joachim Heinrich Campe,[27] and even a modern novel such as *Bonjour Tristesse* by Françoise Sagan![28]

VII

Finally, a considerable number of Neo-Latin novels by humanists and other Neo-Latin writers continued to be produced between the sixteenth and eighteenth centuries. Some of them became quite famous and had a strong influence on European literature mainly through later translations into vernacular (cf. Ijsewijn 1998: 253 ff.). To these belongs in the first place Thomas More's (1478–1535) *Utopia* (Louvain 1516),[29] a combination, in the form of dialogue, of philosophical treatise and fictional adventure narrative which in its turn provoked similar Neo-Latin utopian fiction[30] as, for instance, Antonius Legrand's *Scydromedia* (London 1669),[31] Caspar Stiblinus' (1526–1562) *Commentariolus de Eudaemonensium Republica* (Basel 1555),[32] Joseph Hall's (1574–1656, pseudonym 'Mercurius Britannicus') *Mundus alter et idem* (Frankfurt 1605),[33] Johannes Valentinus Andreae's (1586–1654) *Christianopolis* (Strassburg 1619),[34] Tommaso Campanella's (1565–1639) *Civitas Solis* (1612/20/36, last published version Paris 1637),[35] Jakob Bidermann's (1578–1639) *Utopia* (1602/4, published Dillingen 1630),[36] Samuel Gott's (1614–1671) *Nova Solyma* (London 1648),[37] or the most important and famous of all Neo-Latin utopia's since More's, the *Nicolai Klimii iter subterraneum* (Copenhagen/Leipzig 1741) by the Danish-Norwegian author Ludvig Holberg (1684–1754), a satirical novel about the travel of the young Copenhagen student Niels Klim to the subterranean planet Nazar and the fantastic adventures he experienced there – more than 120 years before Jules Verne's *Voyage au centre de la terre*! –, inspired by the rationalistic movements of the Age of Enlightenment and a vehement attack against pietism and absolutism and the exaggerated praise of scholarship and the implicit faith in science.[38]

This utopian tendency is also manifest in a number of other texts of Neo-Latin fiction, the most influential ones being John Barclay's (1582–1621) two novels *Euphormionis Lusinini Satyricon* (London/Paris 1603/7)[39] and *Argenis* (Rome 1621; cf. Isjsewijn 1983a): the first an anti-utopian criticism of contemporary society and politics in a strong satirical vein (Euphormio, a visitor from utopian Lusinia, finds himself confronted with the – from his perspective absurd and ridiculous – realities of seventeenth-century Europe and its absolutistic monarchies) which led to censure and confiscation of the first printed editions, the second a baroque combination of political treatise, historical allegory and romance of chivalry, a *roman-à-clef* about virtue rewarded and vice punished, one of the most popular books in seventeenth- and eighteenth-century Europe with more than fifty-five editions, several continuations and even an hexametrical version in Latin and translations, adaptations and abbreviated versions (the first Latin edition had 1,206 pages in 8.°) in many European languages. Barclay's influence can still be traced in Samuel Gott's *Nova Solyma* (mentioned above), in Johann Ludwig Prasch's *Psyche Cretica* (Regensburg 1685),[40] an amalgamation of Apuleius' *Tale of Cupid and Psyche*, Virgil and the *Argenis*, in François Guyet's *Gaeomemphionis Cantaliensis Satyricon* (1628),[41] Claude-Barthélemy Morisot's *Peruviana* (1644; cf. Maillard 1978), where the conflicts between Cardinal Richelieu, Maria de' Medici and Gaston d'Orléans are transplanted to South America and the characters hide under Peruvian names, and the *Eudemia* (Leiden 1637/45)[42] by Ianus Nicius Erythraeus (Giovanni Vittorio Rossi, 1577–1647) who sketches a satirical picture of seventeenth-century Rome dominated by the Barberini, which he contrasts with a community of ancient Romans from the time of Tiberius who live on the island Eudemia far out in the Atlantic Ocean.

These centuries provide us also with a number of Latin novels on the House of Habsburg and the political and personal affairs of its family members (cf. Ijsewijn 1998: 255f.), many of them written as *romans-à-clef* and still awaiting closer study and interpretation, for instance, Anton Wilhelm Ertl's *Austriana regina Arabiae* (1688), the anonymous *Aeneas Habspurgus* (1695), Andreas Dugonic's *Argonauticorum sive de vellere aureo libri XXIV* (1778), an allegorical treatment of Habsburg's *Ostpolitik*, or Christoph Friedrich Sangershausen's *Minos sive de rebus Friderici II apud inferos gestis* (1797/9). Finally, the literary genre of the Neo-Latin novel was also used, next to that of Neo-Latin epic,[43] to narrate the adventures of the discovery, exploration, conquest and exploitation of the New World: a good example of this type of Neo-Latin fiction which brings the incredible adventures on the mysterious new continent in the European reader's study is the *Argonauticon Americanorum sive Historiae Periculorum Petri de Victoria ac sociorum eius libri XV* (Munich 1647) by the Bavarian Jesuit Johann Bisselius (1601–82), who is also known as author of the satirical Latin novel *Icaria* (Ingolstadt 1637) in which he describes his own flight from Regensburg while the city was besieged by the Swedes in 1632. The *Argonautica Americana* is a Latin adaptation and translation of an originally Spanish adventurous account of the travels of the Jesuit Pedro Govea de Victoria of Seville (*c.* 1560–1630) and his companions in South America. Bisselius knew and translated this from a German translation (1622), which in its turn was based on an earlier Latin translation of Victoria's Spanish original. Like much of the Jesuit writing of that period, Bisselius' American novel, too, is a combination of history and fiction, a mixture of allegory and psychological novel which above all serves a moral purpose: 'to illustrate the vanity and futility of earthly existence' (Hill 1970: 660).

But to deal with these texts more extensively and to assess both their debts to Latin fiction of Antiquity and their importance for the history of Latin and vernacular fiction since the sixteenth century would open a new province of Latin fiction in the Early Modern period – and require another book.

Notes

1 Cf. Chapters 2 to 5 in Morgan and Stoneman 1994.

2 G. Sandy, 'New Pages of Greek Fiction', in Morgan and Stoneman (eds) 1994, 130–145. The fragments are edited by Stephens and Winkler (eds) 1995.

3 Reproductions in Hägg 1983, 19 f. and 22 f. For recent discussion see Quet 1992.

4 Cf. Perry 1927. On another group of more than 150 quotations possibly from the *Hermagoras* see Prete 1987, 46 ff.

5 Cf. Sandy 1994, 139 ff. and Stephens 1996, 669 ff.; the fragments (with translation) in Stephens and Winkler (eds) 1995, 314 ff. and 358 ff.

6 On the Metiochos–Parthenope romance see Maehler 1976; Sandy 1994, 131 f., 135 ff; Stephens 1996, 657 ff.; the fragments in Stephens and Winkler (eds) 1995, 72 ff.; on the Life of St Parthenope: Hägg 1984. On the Apocryphal Acts of Apostles and the Lives of Saints see Pervo 1994 and 1996, Perkins 1994 and Chapter 12 by G. Huber-Rebenich in this volume.

7 *Institutio oratoria* 10, 1, 93. This statement has been much discussed as to its meaning. I adhere to the interpretation given above and do not think that Quintilian accepted the existence of a Greek genre 'satire': cf. van Rooy 1965, 117 ff.

8 See the contributions by G. Anderson (Chapter 3), G.N. Sandy (Chapter 8), H.J. Mason (Chapter 6) and N. Shumate (Chapter 7) in this volume.

9 He was a rival to Septimius Severus (193–211) and usurper on the throne (195–197).

10 *Historia Augusta*, XII: *Life of Clodius Albinus* 12, 12.

11 Macrobius, *Commentary on the Dream of Scipio* 1, 2, 7 f. The translation here and in the following is quoted from Stahl 1952, 84.

12 *Rhetorica ad Herennium* 1, 12 f.; Cicero *De inventione* 1, 27.

13 Cf. Golden and Hardison 1968, 156 ff.; Rösler 1980, 309 ff.; Morgan 1993, 189 f.

14 Another negative statement occurs in a letter of Emperor Julian († 363) in which he recommends suitable reading for a priest (*Letter* 89, 301 b): not 'love stories' (*erotikai hypotheseis*), which are fiction (*plasmata*) posing as history, but the true

works of historiography. The Latin equivalent of the Greek term *hypothesis* employed by Emperor Julian is *argumentum*.

15 Morgan 1994, 4. On the problem of a 'consumer literature' in antiquity see now the contributions in Pecere and Stramaglia (eds) 1996.

16 Therefore I think that the conclusions at which Harris 1989 arrived are too optimistic: cf. the review of Vessey 1992. For the problem of literacy and the audience/readership of ancient fiction see also Hägg 1983, 90 ff.; Treu 1989; Stephens 1994; Dowden 1994; Bowie 1994 and 1996; Cavallo 1996, and the contributions in Cavallo-Chartier (eds) 1995.

17 Cf. Sandy 1997, in particular, 131 ff., 176 ff., 233 ff.

18 Recent research has shown that manuscripts of the *Metamorphoses* must have been known at least partly before the manuscript of Montecassino (now F = Laurentianus 68.2) which is now our oldest witness to the text was discovered by Zanobi da Strada and brought to Florence: see Chapter 16 by R.H.F. Carver in this volume.

19 On the history of editions and translations of Heliodorus see Rattenbury 1925–29; Mazal 1966; Berger 1984.

20 A first attempt at a Latin translation was made by Angelo Poliziano, but he did not get beyond one chapter of the tenth book (X 27) which was printed in his *Miscellaneorum Centuria Prima*, Florence 1488.

21 This *editio princeps* was also preceded by a translation in vernacular, namely the Italian translation of A.-M. Salvini, published in 'London' (in reality, in Florence) in 1723.

22 Petrarch translated the famous Griseldis story from the *Decamerone* (X 10), Leonardo Bruni *Decamerone* IV 1 (Guiscard and Sigismunda), Matteo Bandelli *Decamerone* X 8 (The friendship of Titus and Gisippus).

23 *Vitae humanae proscenium*, Cologne 1623 (a shortened version). The translator Caspar Ens was born at Lorch near Schwäbisch-Gmünd in 1568 and lived from 1603 until 1628 in Cologne where he published several Latin translations and adaptations of vernacular literature. Cf. Briesemeister 1978 and 1984 and Ijsewijn 1998, 244.

24 *Erotodidascalus sive Nemoralium libri V*, translated by Capsar Barth, Hanau 1625.

25 An anonymous hexameter translation appeared in Berlin in 1743, another one by Stephanus Alexander Viel Ludovicianus in 1808. A first prose version by Gregor Trautwein was published in Frankfurt/M. in 1744 and reprinted in Ulm in 1755, a second one by Iosephus Cl. Destouches in Augsburg in 1764. Cf. Tarnai 1979; Briesemeister 1985, 211 f.

26 Cf. Briesemeister 1985, 212. The Latin translation by Michael Horváth was published in Vienna in 1771. On him and other Latin translators from Hungary see Tarnai 1979.

27 *Joachim Henricus Campe, Robinson secundus. Tironum causa Latine vertit atque indicem Latinitatis adjiciendum curavit* Philippus Iulius Lieberkühn, Züllichau 1785. *Robinson Crusoëus, Latine scripsit* F.J. Goffaux, London 1820. Cf. Grant 1954, 154 f.; Ijsewijn 1998, 245.

28 *Tristitia salve!*, translated into Latin by Alexander Lenard, Paris: Julliard, 1963. The same translator made a Latin translation of A.A. Milne's famous children's novel *Winnie-the-Pooh* under the title *Winnie ille Pu* (London: Methuen and Co., 1960). Also Carlo Collodi's *Pinocchio* was twice translated into Latin (*Pinoculus*) by Enrico Maffacini (Florence: Marzocco, 1950, [7]1956) and Ugo Enrico Paoli (Florence: Le Monnier, 1962, repr. Zurich and Munich: Artemis, 1983).

29 Edited and translated by E. Surtz S.J. and J.H. Hexter, New Haven and London: Yale University Press, 1965 (*The Complete Works of St Thomas More*, vol. 4), and by

G.M. Logan, R.M. Adams and C.H. Miller, Cambridge: Cambridge University Press, 1995.

30 Cf. the inventories of Negley 1977 and Winter 1978 and the brief studies by Kytzler 1980, Kytzler 1982, and von Koppenfels 1981.

31 Edited with German translation and commentary by U. Greiff, Bern: Lang, 1991.

32 Edited with German translation and commentary by I.-D. Jahn, Regensburg: S. Roderer Verlag, 1994.

33 English translation with introduction and commentary by Wands 1981.

34 Edited by R. van Dülmen, Stuttgart: Calwer Verlag, 1972.

35 Edited and translated by C. Carena and L. Bolzoni, Milan, 1997.

36 Edited with German translation and studies by M. Schuster, Bern: Lang, 1984.

37 Cf. Davis 1981, 139ff. There is no new edition of the Latin text available. English translation by W. Begley (London 1902) who ascribed the work to John Milton.

38 Cf. Peters 1987. Ed. C. Peterson in Copenhagen 1931, 501–654, with commentary by A. Krogelund, 3 vols., Copenhagen 1970, and nowadays even on Internet: http: //www.kb.dk/elib/ lit/dan/old/authors/Holberg/Klim.

39 Edited and translated with introduction and notes by D.A. Fleming, Nieuwkoop: de Graaf, 1973. Cf. Berger 1991. This novel belongs to the type of Menippean Satire, i.e., prose mixed with verse. See Relihan 1993: 49ff.; Dronke 1994; Pabst 1994; de Smet 1996.

40 Edited by Desmet-Goethals 1968; cf. Ijsewijn 1983b.

41 Edited by Juliette Desjardins, Leiden: E.J. Brill, 1972. French translation by the same, Geneva: Slatkine, 1972.

42 *Iani Nicii Erythraei Eudemiae libri VIII*. Leiden: Elzevier 1637. Enlarged edition: *Iani Nicii Erythraei Eudemiae libri decem*. Coloniae Uborium: apud lodocum Kalcorium et solios (Amsterdam) 1645. A reprint was published in Cologne in 1740.

43 On this aspect see Hofmann 1994.

Bibliography

Adamietz, J. (1987) 'Zum literarischen Charakter von Petrons Satyrica', *Rheinisches Museum* 130: 329–46.

Adamietz, J. (1995) 'Circe in den *Satyrica* Petrons und das Wesen dieses Werkes', *Hermes* 123: 320–34.

Baliński, J. (1992) 'Heliodorus Latinus: Die humanistischen Studien über die *Aithiopika*. Politianus – Warszewicki – Guillonius – Laubanus', *Eos* 80: 273–89.

Baslez, M.F., Hoffman, P. and Trédé, M. (eds) (1992) *Le monde du roman grec*, Paris: Presses de l'Ecole Normale Supérieure.

Berger, G. (1984) 'Legitimation und Modell: Die *Aithiopika* als Prototyp des französischen heroisch-galanten Romans', *Antike und Abendland* 30: 177–89.

—— (1988a) 'Rhetorik und Leserlenkung in der Aithiopika-Epitome des Martin Crusius', in S.P. Revard, F. Rädle, M.A. Di Cesare (eds) *Acta Conventus Neo-Latini Guelpherbytani. Proceedings of the Sixth International Congress of Neo-Latin Studies*, Wolfenbüttel 12 August to 16 August 1985, Binghamton, NY: Medieval and Renaissance Studies, pp. 481–90.

—— (1988b) '*Longo volgarizzato*: Annibale Caro und Casparo Gozzi als Übersetzer eines problematischen Klassikers', in H. Hofmann (ed.) *Groningen Colloquia on the Novel*, vol. I, Groningen: Egbert Forsten, pp. 141–51.

Berger, G. (1991) 'John Barclay's *Euphormio*: Zur Rezeption eines neulateinischen

Bestsellers in Frankreich', in A. Dalzell, Ch. Fantazzi, R.J. Schoeck (eds) *Acta Conventus Neo-Latini Torontonensis. Proceedings of the Seventh International Congress of Neo-Latin Studies*, Toronto 8–13 August 1988, Binghamton, NY: Medieval and Renaissance Studies, pp. 231–40.

Beschorner, A. (1992) *Untersuchungen zu Dares Phrygius*, Tübingen: Gunter Narr.

Bowie, E. (1994a) 'Philostratus, Writer of Fiction', in J.R. Morgan and R. Stoneman (eds) *Greek Fiction: The Greek Novel in Context*, London/New York: Routledge, pp. 181–99.

—— (1994b) 'The Readership of Greek Novels in the Ancient World', in J. Tatum (ed.) *The Search for the Ancient Novel*, Baltimore, MD/London: Johns Hopkins University Press, pp. 435–59.

—— (1996) 'The Ancient Readers of the Greek Novels', in Schmeling, G. (ed.) *The Novel in the Ancient World*, Leiden/New York/Cologne: E.J. Brill, pp. 87–106.

Briesemeister, D. (1978) 'La difusión europea de la literatura española en el siglo XVII a través de traducciones neolatinas', *Iberoromanica* N.F. 7: 3–17.

—— (1984) '"*Hablar en buen romance*" und "*facete narrare*": Die erste neulateinische Übersetzung des *Lazarillo de Tormes*', in G. Holtus and E. Radtke (eds), *Umgangssprache in der Iberoromania. Festschrift für H. Kröll*, Tübingen, pp. 331–42.

—— (1985) 'Französische Literatur in neulateinischen Übersetzungen', in R.J. Schoeck (ed.) *Acta Conventus Neo-Latini Bononiensis. Proceedings of the Fourth International Congress of Neo-Latin Studies*, Bologna 26 August to 1 September 1979, Binghamton, NY: Medieval and Renaissance Studies, pp. 205–15.

Cavallo, G. (1996) 'Veicoli materiali della letteratura di consumo. Maniere di scrivere e maniere di leggere', in O. Pecere and A. Stragmaglia (eds) *La letteratura di consumo nel mondo greco-latino*, Atti del convegno internazionale Cassino, 14–17 September 1994, Cassino: Università degli Studi di Cassino, pp. 11–46.

Cavallo, G., and Chartier, E. (eds) (1995) *Storia della lettura*, Rome/Bari: Editori Laterza.

Davis, J.C. (1981) *Utopia and the Ideal Society. A Study of English Utopian Writing 1516–1570*, Cambridge: Cambridge University Press.

Desmet-Goethals, M.-J. (1968) 'Iohannis Ludovici Praschii Ratisponensis *Psyche Cretica*. Edition du texte avec une introduction sur le roman néo-latin', *Humanistica Lovaniensia* 17: 117–56.

Dowden, K. (1994) 'The Roman Audience of *The Golden Ass*', in J. Tatum (ed.) *The Search for the Ancient Novel*, Baltimore, MD and London: Johns Hopkins University Press, pp. 419–34.

Dronke, P. (1994) *Verse with Prose from Petronius to Dante: the Art and Scope of the Mixed Form*, Cambridge, MA and London: Harvard University Press.

Egger, B. (1994) 'Looking at Chariton's Callirhoe', in J.R. Morgan and R. Stoneman (eds) *Greek Fiction: The Greek Novel in Context*, London/New York: Routledge, pp. 31–48.

Engels, L.J., and Hofmann, H. (1997a) 'Literatur und Gesellschaft in der Spätantike: Texte, Kommunikation und Überlieferung', in L.J. Engels and H. Hofmann (eds) *Neues Handbuch der Literaturwissenschaft*, vol. IV, *Spätantike*, Wiesbaden: Aula-Verlag pp. 29–88.

Engels, L.J., and Hofmann, H. (eds) (1997b) *Neues Handbuch der Literaturwissenschaft*, vol. IV: *Spätantike*, Wiesbaden: Aula-Verlag.

Fantham, E. (1996) *Roman Literary Culture from Cicero to Apuleius*, Baltimore/London: Johns Hopkins University Press.

Gärtner, H. (ed.) (1984) *Beiträge zum griechischen Liebesroman*, Hildesheim/Zurich/New York: Georg Olms.

Golden, L., and Hardison Jr., O.B. (1968) *Aristotle's Poetics. A Translation and Commentary for Students of Literature*, Englewood Cliffs, NJ: Prentice-Hall.

Grant, W.L. (1954) 'European Vernacular Works in Latin Translation', *Studies in the Renaissance* 1: 120–56.

Hägg, Th. (1983) *The Novel in Antiquity*, Oxford: Basil Blackwell.

—— (1984) 'The Parthenope Romance Decapitated?', *Symbolae Osloenses* 59: 61–92.

Harris, W.V. (1989) *Ancient Literacy*, Cambridge, MA/London: Harvard University Press.

Harrison, S.J. (1998) 'The Milesian Tales and the Roman Novel', in H. Hofmann and M. Zimmerman (eds) *Groningen Colloquia on the Novel*, vol. IX, Groningen: Egbert Forsten, pp. 61–73.

Heinze, R. (1899) 'Petron und der griechische Roman', *Hermes* 34: 494–519. (Reprinted in Gärtner (ed.) pp. 15–40.)

Hill, H.C. (1970) 'Johann Bissel's *Argonauticon Americanorum* (1647): a Reexamination', *Modern Language Notes* 85: 652–62.

Hofmann, H. (1994) '*Adveniat tandem Typhis qui detegat orbes*: Columbus in Neo-Latin Epic Poetry (15th–18th Centuries)', in W. Haase and M. Reinhold (eds) *The Classical Tradition and the Americas*, vol. I 1, Berlin and New York: W. de Gruyter, pp. 420–656.

—— (1998) 'Point de vue sur les méthodes et perspectives des études néo-latines', *Cahiers del'Humanisme* 1.

Holzberg, N. (1996a) 'The Genre: Novels Proper and the Fringe', in Schmeling, G. (ed.) *The Novel in the Ancient World*, Leiden/New York/Cologne: E.J. Brill, pp. 11–28.

—— (1996b) 'Novel-like Works of Extended Prose Fiction II', in Schmeling, G. (ed.) *The Novel in the Ancient World*, Leiden/New York/Cologne: E.J. Brill, pp. 619–53.

Ijsewijn, J. (1983a) 'John Barclay and his *Argenis*: A Scotish Neo-Latin Novelist', *Humanistica Lovaniensia* 32: 1–27.

—— (1983b) 'Amour et Psyché dans un roman latin de 1685: la *Psyche Cretica*', in H. Zehnacker and G. Hentz (eds) *Hommages à Robert Schilling*, Paris: Les belles Lettres, pp. 337–45.

—— (with D. Sacré) (1998) *A Companion to Neo-Latin Studies. Part II: Literary, Linguistic, Philological and Editorial Questions*, Leuven: University Press.

Konstan, D. (1994) 'Xenophon of Ephesus: Eros and Narrative in the Novel', in J.R. Morgan and R. Stoneman (eds) *Greek Fiction: The Greek Novel in Context*, London/New York: Routledge, pp. 49–63.

Koppenfels, W. von (1981) '*Mundus alter et idem*: Utopiefiktion und menippeische Satire', *Poetica* 13: 16–66.

Kuch, H. (ed.) (1989) *Der antike Roman. Untersuchungen zur literarischen Kommunikation und Gattungsgeschichte*, Berlin: Akademie-Verlag.

Kytzler, B. (1980) 'Neulateinische Utopien', in J.C. Margolin (ed.) *Acta Conventus Neo-Latini Turonensis. Proceedings of the Third International Congress of Neo-Latin Studies*, Tours, Université François-Rabelais 6–10 Septembre 1976, Paris: J. Vrin, pp. 729–40.

—— (1982) 'Zur neulateinischen Utopie', in W. Vosskamp (ed.) *Utopieforschung*, vol. 2, Stuttgart: J.B. Metzler, pp. 197–209.

Maehler, H. (1976) 'Der Metiochos-Parthenope-Roman', *Zeitschrift für Papyrologie und Epigraphik* 23: 1–20.

Maillard, J.-F. (1978) 'Littérature et alchimie dans le *Peruviana* de Claude-Barthélemy Morisot', *XVIIe Siècle* 30: 171–84.

Mazal, O. (1966) 'Die Textausgaben der *Aithiopika* Heliodors von Emesa', *Gutenberg-Jahrbuch* 41: 182–91.

Merkle, S. (1994) *Die Ephemeris belli Troiani des Diktys von Kreta*, Frankfurt a.M./Bern/New York/Paris: Peter Lang.

Morgan, J.R. (1993) 'Make-believe and Make Believe: the Fictionality of the Greek Novels', in C. Gill and T.P. Wiseman (eds) *Lies and Fiction in the Ancient World*, Exeter: University of Exeter Press, pp. 175–229.

—— (1994a) 'Introduction', in J.R. Morgan and R. Stoneman (eds) *Greek Fiction: The Greek Novel in Context*, London/New York: Routledge, pp. 1–12.

—— (1994b) '*Daphnis and Chloe*: Love's Own Sweet Story', in J.R. Morgan and R. Stoneman (eds) *Greek Fiction: The Greek Novel in Context*, London/New York: Routledge, pp. 64–79.

—— (1994c) 'The Aithiopika of Heliodoros: Narrative as Riddle', in J.R. Morgan and R. Stoneman (eds) *Greek Fiction: The Greek Novel in Context*, London/New York: Routledge, pp. 97–113.

Morgan, J.R., and Stoneman, R. (eds) (1994) *Greek Fiction: The Greek Novel in Context*, London/New York: Routledge.

Negley, G. (1977) *Utopian Literature. A Bibliography with a Supplementary Listing of Works Influential in Utopian Thought*, Lawrence, KS: Regents Press of Kansas.

Pabst, B. (1994) *Prosimetrum. Tradition und Wandel einer Literaturform zwischen Spätantike und Spätmittelalter*, 2 vols, Cologne/Weimar/Vienna: Böhlau.

Parsons, P. (1971) 'A Greek *Satyricon*?', *Bulletin of the Institute of Classical Studies (University of London)* 18: 53–68.

Pecere, O., and Stramaglia, A. (eds) (1996) *La letteratura di consumo nel mondo greco-latino.* Atti del convegno internazionale Cassino, 14–17 settembre 1994, Cassino: Università degli Studi di Cassino.

Perkins, J. (1994) 'Representation in Greek Saints' Lives', in J.R. Morgan and R. Stoneman (eds) *Greek Fiction: The Greek Novel in Context*, London/New York: Routledge, pp. 255–71.

Perry, B.E. (1967) *The Ancient Romances. A Literary-Historical Account of Their Origins*, Berkeley and Los Angeles: University of California Press.

—— (1972) 'On Apuleius' *Hermagoras*', *American Journal of Philology* 48: 263–6.

Pervo, R.I. (1994) 'Early Christian Fiction', in J.R. Morgan and R. Stoneman (eds) *Greek Fiction: The Greek Novel in Context*, London/New York: Routledge, pp. 239–54.

—— (1996) 'The Ancient Novel Becomes Christian', in G. Schmeling (ed.) *The Novel in the Ancient World*, Leiden/New York/Cologne: E.J. Brill, pp. 685–711.

Peters, S. (1987) *Ludvig Holbergs Merrippeische Satire: Das 'Iter subterraneum' und seine Beziehungen zur antiken Literatur*, Frankfurt, Bern, New York: Peter Lang.

Prete, S. (1987) 'Frammenti di Apuleio o pseudo-apuleiani nel *Cornu copiae* di Niccolò Perotti', *Nuovi Studi Fanesi* 2: 39–63.

Quet, M.-H. (1992) 'Romans grecs, mosaïques romaines', in M.F. Baslez, P. Hoffman and M. Trédé (eds) *Le monde du roman grec*, Paris: Presses de l'Ecole Normale Supérieure, pp. 125–60.

Rattenbury, R.M. (1925–29) 'The Manuscripts and Editions of Heliodorus', *Classical Quarterly* 19 (1925): 177–82; 20 (1926): 36–41; 23 (1929): 100–4.
Reardon, B.P. (1994) 'Achilles Tatius and Ego-narrative', in J.R. Morgan and R. Stoneman (eds) *Greek Fiction: The Greek Novel in Context*, London/New York: Routledge, pp. 80–96.
—— (1998) 'Apographs and Atticists: Adventures of a Text', in J.P. Bews, I.C. Storey and M.R. Boyne (eds) *Celebratio: Thirtieth Anniversary Essays at Trent University*, Peterborough, Ontario: Trent University, pp. 67–75.
Relihan, J.C. (1993) *Ancient Menippean Satire*, Baltimore and London: Johns Hopkins University Press.
Rohde, E. (1876) *Der griechische Roman und seine Vorläufer*, Leipzig. (3rd edn, revised by W. Schmid, Leipzig: Breitkopf and Härtel, 1914, reprint Hildesheim/New York: Georg Olms, 1960.)
Rooy, C.A. van (1965) *Studies in Classical Satire and Related Literary Theory*, Leiden: E.J. Brill.
Rösler, W. (1980) 'Die Entdeckung der Fiktionalität in der Antike', *Poetica* 12: 283–319.
Sandy, G.N. (1994) 'New Pages of Greek Fiction', in J.R. Morgan and R. Stoneman (eds) *Greek Fiction: The Greek Novel in Context*, London/New York: Routledge, pp. 130–45.
—— (1997) *The Greek World of Apuleius: Apuleius and the Second Sophistic*, Leiden/New York/Cologne: E.J. Brill.
Schmeling, G. (ed.) (1996) *The Novel in the Ancient World*, Leiden/New York/Cologne: E.J. Brill.
Smet, I.A.R. de (1996) *Menippean Satire and the Republic of Letters 1581–1655*, Geneva: Librairie Droz.
Stahl, W.H. (1952) *Macrobius, Commentary on the Dream of Scipio*. Translated with an Introduction and Notes, New York/London: Columbia University Press (2nd edn, 1966).
Stephens, S.A. (1994) 'Who Read Ancient Novels?', in J. Tatum (ed.) *The Search for the Ancient Novel*, Baltimore, MD/London: Johns Hopkins University Press, pp. 405–18.
—— (1996) 'Fragments of Lost Novels', in G. Schmeling (ed.) *The Novel in the Ancient World*, Leiden/New York/Cologne: E.J. Brill, pp. 655–83.
Stephens, S.A., and Winkler, J. (eds) (1995) *Ancient Greek Novels: the Fragments. Introduction, Text, Translation and Commentary*, Princeton, NJ: Princeton University Press.
Stoneman, R. (1994) '*The Alexander Romance*: from history to fiction', in J.R. Morgan and R. Stoneman (eds) *Greek Fiction: The Greek Novel in Context*, London/New York: Routledge, pp. 117–29.
Tarnai, A. (1979) 'Lateinische Übersetzungen französischen Schrifttums im Ungarn des 18. Jahrhunderts', in P. Tuynman, G.C. Kuiper, E. Kessler (eds) *Acta Conventus Neo-Latini Amstelodamensis. Proceedings of the Second International Congress of Neo-Latin Studies*, Amsterdam 19–24 August 1973, Munich: Wilhelm Fink, 976–82.
Tatum, J. (ed.) (1994) *The Search for the Ancient Novel*, Baltimore/London: Johns Hopkins University Press.
Treu, K. (1989) 'Der antike Roman und sein Publikum', in H. Kuch (ed.) *Der antike*

Roman. Untersuchungen zur literarischen Kommunikation und Gattungsgeschichte, Berlin: Akademie-Verlag, pp. 178–97.

Vessey, M. (1992) 'Literacy and *Litteratura*, A.D. 200–800', *Studies in Medieval and Renaissance History* 13: 139–60.

Wands, J.M. (1981) *Another World and yet the Same: Bishop Joseph Hall's* Mundus alter et idem, New Haven/London: Yale University Press.

Winter, M. (1978) *Compendium Utopiarum. Typologie und Bibliographie literarischer Utopien*. Part 1: *Von der Antike bis zur deutschen Frühaufklärung*, Stuttgart: J.B. Metzler.

Part 1

PETRONIUS

1

PETRONIUS AND THE *SATYRICA*

Gareth Schmeling

I The author: Petronius

Tacitus (*Annals* 16.17–20) tells us a brief but famous history of a courtier of Nero who held a proconsulship in Bithynia and later became consul (AD 62), but who gained some fame or notoriety for a life-style of studied ease and natural elegance. His full name seems to be Titus Petronius Niger, and, though only a fairly close associate of Nero's literary coterie, he somehow threatened the influence of Tigellinus, Prefect of the Guard, who turned the emperor against him, and Petronius was forced – without seeming to be – to kill himself (AD 66).[1] The form of his suicide has become a model for later literary and religious writers (e.g. Jeremy Taylor, *The Rule and Exercises of Holy Dying* (1651) to Nicholas Blake's mystery, *The Worm of Death* (1961)). Our portrait of Petronius is so coloured by the power of Tacitus' rhetoric, however, that uncareful critics see Tacitus' Petronius behind various sentiments of Encolpius, the first-person narrator of the *Satyrica*. Tacitus does not mention the *Satyrica*, a fact which should not surprise us, nor does Plutarch or Pliny the Elder, each of whom briefly alludes to Petronius. Part of the attraction of Petronius and the mystery which surrounds him are due to the tantalizing bits of biographical information, the knowledge that he was close to Nero's inner circle whose sexual practices are better imagined than known,[2] and the total absence of any didactic intent in the *Satyrica* (unlike Horace's dictum in *Ars Poetica* 343, *qui miscuit utile dulci* – 'who mixes the useful with the sweet').

For many years scholars have debated about the date of the *Satyrica*, some at one extreme placing it as early as Augustus, others at the end of the second century, some even as late as the fourth century AD. The weight of evidence, however, points to the years just preceding AD 66 and to the Petronius of Tacitus, Nero's courtier, as its author.[3] In the 2,000 years since his death Petronius has developed, as it were, a second *persona*, one unattached to the *Satyrica*: he is *the* ancient author of pornography. In these many years Petronius' name has been affixed to a large number of obscene works which on their face could not have been written by any ancient author (Schmeling 1994).

II The work: the physical evidence of the *Satyrica*

The title of the novel by Petronius is most likely *Satyrica* (i.e. *Satyricōn libri* – 'books of the *satyrica*'), and is the title now preferred by scholars (Müller 1983: 491–2, 1995). It imitates (or sets) the pattern for other ancient novels, e.g. *Ephesiaca*. The meaning of *satyrica* might well be something like 'tales of satyrs', adapted to a new loose, episodic prose structure. The most significant characteristic of the extant *Satyrica* is its physical condition: it survives in an exceedingly fragmentary state. The beginning of our extant *Satyrica* appears from manuscript evidence to come from book 14, the *Cena Trimalchionis* ('Banquet of Trimalchio') (one-third of the whole), from book 15, and the last 40 or so chapters from book 16. Sullivan (1968: 36) speculates that the length of the original might have extended to 24 books (400,000 words!) in imitation of the *Odyssey* – each book possibly presented to an imperial literary gathering. All of this, of course, assumes many things not in evidence: that the manuscripts are accurate, that Petronius had a grand design at the outset for the *Satyrica*, and that he finished the work. The *Satyrica* is fragmentary for reasons which lie in the history of its transmission from antiquity, not for literary motives: Petronius did not structure his work to reflect a breakdown of Roman life, the fragmentary nature of existence. If the *Satyrica* ran to 24 books, it was a prime candidate for a copyist to write *Excerpts* from. . . . . Then too, we might have the best bits of the *Satyrica*, the other 21 books not being very successful or entertaining – or perhaps too obscene or not obscene enough to attract the mind and spirit of a few rather dull copyists who, as it turned out, controlled the life and death of the *Satyrica*. As late as the twelfth century John of Salisbury seems to have possessed a rather large amount of the *Satyrica*, and there is evidence that in the thirteenth century the *Satyrica* and *Cena* were known in bulk in Dublin and Cambridge.[4] In the fifteenth century manuscript collectors as capable as Poggio had discovered and then lost a unique copy of the *Cena*.

The surviving sections of the *Satyrica* are supported by a strange assortment of manuscripts, and the manuscript tradition relating the story of how the text arrived from the ancient to the present time is not always clear. It is conjectured that the ancient world passed down to the medieval (AD 800) only excerpts of what was originally a long work, and what was handed down came mostly from later parts of the novel. This might indicate that Petronius had no central plan in mind when composing the early books of the *Satyrica* and only in the later books did the work take on a unifying structure and hold the interest of scribes. It seems that by 800 the archetype (lost) of the *Satyrica* had been excerpted in various ways and survived in only four forms: (1) A group of manuscripts called L contains the longer narrative (racy) pieces, but these fragments often seem unrelated; (2) another group of manuscripts called O presents the shorter pieces but these are better connected and contain material in dialogue and poetry; (3) the *Cena Trimalchionis* (chapters 26–78), transmitted in a single manuscript called H, representing about one-third of the extant work, survives in its entirety; (4) florilegia, or collections of short pieces by various authors. The fact that our present text is in as good a shape as it is, is owing to a long series of exceptional editors who have slowly made order out of chaos. I cite the work of Konrad Müller who between 1961 and 1995 established the common text of today. We are not certain of course that the arrangement of the chapters of the *Satyrica* today is also that of the author. In addition to the 141 chapters of our fragmentary novel, some 50 brief fragments have also been transmitted, attributed in one fashion or another to Petronius, which editors attach as a kind of appendix to the novel proper. These 50 fragments might refer to Petronius but not necessarily to his *Satyrica*.

III The *Satyrica*: contents in outline, structure by episodes

Let us begin with several assumptions: (1) that, of the *Satyrica*'s 24 books, we have some of book 14, all of 15, some of 16; (2) that the *Satyrica* of AD 66 did not begin where we pick it up in our chapter 1 in the area around Puteoli, but far away, perhaps as far away as Massilia (frag. 1) and that the hero of the novel is moving (possibly) in a southeasterly direction toward Lampsacus, the home of Priapus, where he will atone (in some humorous fashion) for offences committed against Priapus at some early (lost) point in the novel; (3) that, based on our extant portions, the hero (and narrator) of the novel is always accompanied by his boy-love Giton and by one other person, Ascyltus (1–82) then Eumolpus (83–141), making an unstable triad; (4) that the *Satyrica* is arranged, presented, and related to the reader or audience in discrete, not always closely tied episodes; (5) that every episode is set into a literary framework of some genre, for example, many features of the *Cena* resemble the tradition of symposium literature.

The extant *Satyrica* is composed of a connected series of nine major episodes told in the first-person by Encolpius:

1–6	Debate on the decline of rhetoric/education (Puteoli)
7–11	Quarrels of love triad dissolve in fragments
12–15	Stolen cloaks and gold coins
16–26	Sexual episode with Quartilla, priestess of Priapus
26–78	Dinner with Trimalchio
79–99	Eumolpus (poet) replaces Ascyltus in triad
100–115	Aboard Lichas' ship, shipwreck (south Italy)
116–124	Journey to Croton, epic of Eumolpus

125–141 Our heroes pose as the rich beset by *captatores* ('inheritance seekers')[5]

At the core of the story are Encolpius and his comrades who live on the margin of society, stealing not working, flattering the rich, preying on the gullible, selling sex, and then move on. Though they are estranged from society, they are neither evil nor vicious,[6] but almost Damon Runyon-type thieves (incompetent often). Each scene or episode is structured to resemble, or to remind the reader of, a literary genre; for example, chapters 12–15 resemble a plot of New Comedy; 16–26 is one of the *Priapea* in prose or the kind of short story which the Parthians were amazed to find in the luggage of Roman officers (Plutarch, *Crassus* 32); 126ff. is an hilarious travesty of the Odysseus–Circe affair; 80 is a struggle between two homosexual 'brothers' but portrayed as the fatal battle between Eteocles and Polynices. The only complete episode we possess is the *Cena Trimalchionis* in which Encolpius (almost as a third-person narrator) recounts the lives of Trimalchio and his fellow freedmen, various parts of which remind the reader of Plato's *Symposium*, Horace's *Cena Nasidieni* ('Banquet of Nasidienus', *Satire* 2.8), and other works.

The *Satyrica* opens (1–6) with a lively debate between Agamemnon and Encolpius over the sad state of education. Rhetoric is a topic of much discussion in the *Satyrica* and gives an artificial tone to the entire novel, whether it is the rhetoric of the educated like Encolpius and Agamemnon who try to give meaning to their words and to say something of substance but fail, or the rhetoric of freedmen who attempt to ape the language of their betters but fail. The opening episode dissolves into fragments, and Encolpius and his friend Ascyltus return to their lodgings where they quarrel over which of them should get to enjoy the favors of the young lad Giton (7–11). The instability of the love triangle is momentarily set aside because our heroes are short of money and must sell a cloak which they had stolen (12–15). In a scene reminiscent of New Comedy Ascyltus surrenders the cloak to its owner but retrieves a tunic containing gold coins. No sooner has our triad returned home than a banging on the door causes it to collapse and to reveal Quartilla, randy priestess of Priapus, who threatens, blusters, weeps, oozes sexual scents, and accuses Encolpius of having desecrated the rituals of Priapus (16–26). Priapus is a deity represented as a wood stump to which is attached a large erect penis. What exactly his rituals entail (beyond meaningless sexual revelry) we do not know, but it seems that it would be virtually impossible to profane them. Quartilla has come with the sole purpose of continuing Priapic rituals, which include the deflowering of a 7-year-old girl observed through a key hole, and which the Roman readers would associate with stage productions of bawdy mimes.

Agamemnon has invited our triad to a banquet at Trimalchio's (26–78), a local millionaire freedman. Trimalchio is such a dominant presence at the banquet that Encolpius is forced to assume the role of reporter. The host bombards his guests with a variety of tasteless entertainments, acrobats, singers, foods, drinks, but above all with the speeches of freedmen,who tell tall tales, banter with each other, are easily insulted by our educated heroes, and complain about high prices and moral decay. The banquet comes to a sudden end when Trimalchio asks his guests to imagine him dead and to weep over him. Someone blows a funeral trumpet so loudly that the local fire brigade, believing it is a signal of a fire, rushes into Trimalchio's house.

The sixth scene (79–99) introduces Eumolpus, a mediocre poet, who replaces Ascyltus. This is a transitional scene which moves the actors from the banquet near Puteoli toward Croton in the south. After expounding on the sad state of the arts, Eumolpus tells the story of the 'Pergamene Youth', or how he seduced a rich man's son. This incongruity of outlook on the part of Eumolpus, who condemns deception only to practise the same, is a hallmark of Petronian characterization. The second triumvirate leaves the Puteoli area by boat only to discover that the captain is the man who had earlier been robbed by Encolpius and whose wife was seduced (100–115). Hopes for group sex cool the tempers of all concerned, and Eumolpus titillates everyone on board by telling the story of the 'Widow of Ephesus' or how a resourceful woman conquers death. A storm blows up, and the ship is wrecked. Shipwrecks and storm scenes are a staple of ancient narratives: from the *Odyssey* to the *Aeneid* to St Paul, shipwrecks are so common that the modern reader wonders why all ancient travellers did not walk.

In episode eight (116–124) Eumolpus amuses his comrades with a short epic version of the 'Civil War' between Caesar and Pompey, until they arrive at Croton. Our heroes are penniless, but everyone at Croton is searching for the rich who can leave them legacies for services rendered (125–141). So Eumolpus, an elderly gentleman with a lively imagination, puts forward a scheme in which he claims to be a wealthy man from Africa, shipwrecked but expecting bags of money to arrive any day: Eumolpus deceives the very people who had hoped to deceive him. Meanwhile Encolpius has an aborted (three times) love affair with Circe, because he suffers from impotency, a curse sent by Priapus. The novel breaks off as Eumolpus convinces the inheritance seekers to give him even more credit by including them immediately in his will on the condition that they eat his dead body.

The extant *Satyricon* as a whole is less well known than one part, the *Cena*, which because it is not a fragment and Trimalchio and his friends make great characters, renders the part greater than the whole – in many people's minds. In literary studies the *Cena* often overwhelms the rest of the *Satyrica*. As one-third of the extant work, the *Cena* has the great advantage of being a self-contained whole – and is consequently often published separately. The Quartilla episode (16–26) has possibilities of being completely outrageous and remains the best delineated orgy and religious ceremony passed down from the classical world. The interpolated (inset) tale of the 'Pergamene

Youth' (85–87) is perhaps a Milesian Tale as is the 'Widow of Ephesus' (111–112). These two narratives are short tales within episodes, little jewels of Latin literature which have taken on lives of their own and are often included in anthologies or examples of the best of Latin literature. After the *Cena* the episode of Eumolpus and the legacy-hunters (124–141), which includes the stories of Encolpius and Circe, Encolpius and the priestesses of Priapus, Philomela and her children, and the last will and testament of Eumolpus, is the best written.

IV Models and sources

Hallmarks of Latin literature are often considered to be its conservative nature and didactic intent. Sullivan (1968) has demonstrated how conservative Petronius is in his choice of models and sources. Imaginative Greeks, however, are credited with inventing the literary models, while Romans are relegated to making copies. This attitude extends even to the *Satyrica*: 'Natural reason long ago revealed that Petronius had a Greek model'.[7] With this observation Parsons seems to imply that the highly complex and episodic *Satyrica* with its exceedingly thick literary texture is somehow a close relative to the very fragmentary *Iolaus* (*P. Oxy.* 3010) and its ancestors.

For many years and for some critics the *Satyrica* was classified *sui generis*. By adventurous critics, however, the *Satyrica* began over time to be grouped with the diverse collection of works called the ancient novels (Apuleius' *Metamorphoses*, the *Historia Apollonii regis Tyri*, and the so-called five Greek novels) (Bowie and Harrison 1993; Perry 1967). The five complete Greek novels could all be characterized as sentimental/ideal, the *Historia Apollonii* as a sentimental family novel, the novel of Apuleius as racy/religious but in many ways similar to the realistic, at times obscene, *Satyrica*. These eight works can be housed – not always comfortably – under one large tent called the novel, the Latin examples always closer to the fringe than to the core. Since AD 400 the *Satyrica* and Apuleius' *Metamorphoses* have been most auspiciously linked by Macrobius (*Comm. in Somn. Scip.* I.2.6–12) as examples of *argumenta* ('plots') (plus the comedies of Menander) written to entertain audiences. The *Satyrica*, however, remains the black sheep in the family. Where the other novels reward the good and punish the bad, the *Satyrica* is realistic; where the others value heterosexual relationships and marriage, the heroes of the *Satyrica* are homosexual or bisexual, and marriage is an object of mockery (it appears that everything conventional is mocked); only in the *Satyrica* is the social level of each character distinguished by the level of his language. Because it often appears to stand in opposition to many elements of the other novels, perhaps the *Satyrica* could be a parody of the novel (Heinze 1889). The differences between the *Satyrica* and the other novels are consistent and intentional, however, but more in the spirit of an anti-novel, an 'other novel', than the parodic and satiric nature of something like Lucian's *True History*: its chief actor (and narrator) is thus an anti-hero, an early *picaro* (Zeitlin 1971). A problem with reading the *Satyrica* as a parody of the novel is that so little of the *Satyrica*, so few of its themes, motifs, scenes, and literary adaptations have anything to do with the extant Greek novels (if *Iolaus* is a novel, its connections to the *Satyrica* are most important) (Holzberg 1995). If the *Satyrica* is a parody, it is a parody of the established, canonical genres (i.e., the *Satyrica* is conservative) of classical literature, not of the ancient novel genre (Sandy 1994a: 1544), which seems not to have been clearly identified and defined by ancient critics (Reardon 1991), and even today resides outside the magic canon in classical literature (Bowie and Harrison 1993). The dense literary texture of the *Satyrica* offers free play for parody, but I would contend that, while the *Satyrica* is not a (wholesale) parody of the ancient novel, Petronius does expand the limits of the novel genre by constantly dipping into other genres: the *Satyrica* seems to make use of almost every known literary genre. But is Petronius' intent parody, mockery, good fun, entertainment, or an attempt to see if he could write something by borrowing from every known form of literature? Put another way, how do we interpret the *Satyrica*?[8] At 132.11 Encolpius describes his impotent member in words reproduced from *Aeneid* 6.469–470, which Virgil had employed to describe Dido's eyes. Is this parody, a daring attempt to do the impossible or unthinkable in bookish humour? Is the long epic poem on the *Bellum Civile* ('Civil War') at 119ff. a parody, an attempt to show Lucan how to write epic, a subtle pro-Caesar (anti-Senate) poem, or the normal effusion of a frustrated poet with time on his hands (entertainment for the journey to Croton) and a captive audience?

It is unfortunate for critics that Petronius entitled his work *Satyrica*: the word is just close enough to encourage them to jump from there to satire ('the thought lets itself be guided by the word'). The *Satyrica* is generally listed in literary histories under satire and included in books entitled something like 'Roman Satire'. If we wish to read (or to interpret) the *Satyrica* as satire, we really ought first to ask ourselves at least three questions: (1) what/who is being satirized, (2) who is doing the satirizing, and (3) from what standpoint is the satire realized? Could we say that the answer to question 1 for the opening chapters (1–5) of the novel is Agamemnon, education and training in rhetoric? For question 2, Petronius is the satirist? For question 3, the satire arises from Petronius' patriotic feelings, ethical objections, moral indignation, or wounded literary sensitivities? To the first question we should note that many ancient authors (Tacitus, *Dial.* 35; Quintilian 2.10.3–9) commented unfavorably about the nature and quality of rhetorical education and that such criticism was already hackneyed in Petronius' day. If this is the subject of satire, it had been done before and often. Perhaps Petronius satirizes those who had satirized rhetorical education. If we conclude this, we would judge the *Satyrica* as something unoriginal. To the second question we must note that Petronius, an adviser of Nero, is not the satirist; that would be Encolpius whose judgement of, and contact with, reality are always suspect (Schmeling 1994–95). At 1–5 Encolpius is eager to please Agamemnon and to cadge for free meals. This satirist of education, who is taken seriously by some critics, is soon tricked by an old woman into entering a brothel (7), deceived by Giton (9), made fun of by Ascyltus (10), responsible for losing his and his friends' gold coins twice (15), tricked by a youthful maid of a priestess of Priapus (20), and then generally abused by that priestess (26). If Encolpius is a satirist, he is unique: in fact, we have no satirist in the *Satyrica*. To the third question we must answer that nowhere in the *Satyrica* can we observe ethical, moral, religious indignation or wounded literary sensitivities (Sandy 1969; Schmeling 1969, 1971).

Some critics prefer to remove the hard-edge of satire from a description of the *Satyrica* and to classify it as Menippean Satire (Adamietz 1995). In recent books such as J. Relihan's *Ancient Menippean Satire* (Relihan 1993) and somewhat less in P. Dronke's *Verse with Prose from Petronius to Dante* (Dronke 1994), the authors by their own rhetoric are under pressure to find as many examples of the genre in question as they can and to include all possibilities, even remote ones, within the scope of their studies. In the search for examples of Menippean Satire researchers often discover surface similarities among works and then lump the texts together into one genre. Rather than using the genre to interpret the text, some critics use texts to fill out a genre. In the case of Menippean Satire the evidence from the ancient world that the term indicated a literary genre is unclear.[9]

I would like to suggest that, rather than displaying a dominant interest in parody or satire, Petronius is more occupied in experimenting with previous literary forms and in so doing creating something novel. And one of the earlier forms with which he experiments is Menippean Satire. The *Satyrica* is then not an example of Menippean Satire, but rather Menippean Satire is one of many forms (the *Odyssey*, Milesian tales, diatribes, symposium literature, New Comedy, etc.) which Petronius turns into grist for his mill. We should not confuse the part (Menippean Satire) with the whole (the novel). The open form of the novel encourages experimentation and development.

There seems to be a desire to equate a work which mixes prose and poetry (*prosimetrum*) with Menippean Satire, as though either term describes one and the same genre. Chariton, Xenophon of Ephesus, Apuleius, Achilles Tatius, Heliodorus, and the anonymous authors of the *Historia Apollonii* and *Alexander Romance* – to mention only novelists – all include verses with their prose, but there is little interest in describing these latter works as Menippean Satire. Therefore, if *prosimetrum* and Menippean Satire are not the same thing, and we know what *prosimetrum* is, what is Menippean Satire?

In his work on the *Apocolocyntosis* Eden provides a brief, useful description of Menippean Satire: 'Its characteristic features, imprinted on it by its eponymous originator . . . are its form, which is a mixture of prose and original verse, and its treatment, which is spoudogeloion' (Eden 1984: 13).

Varro's *saturae Menippeae*, from which not a few scholars believe that Petronius took the form, feeling and substance of the *Satyrica*, shares certain similarities with Seneca's *Apocolocyntosis* but differs in content and tone, since Varro attacks social foibles while Seneca attacks the person. Though motifs such as ascension into heaven, a council of the gods, and descent into the underworld appear in the Menippean Satire of Seneca, Lucian's *Council of the Gods* and *Icaromenippus*, and Julian's *Caesares*, these motifs do not survive in the fragments of Varro's *saturae Menippeae*.

While the *Satyrica* is a mixture of prose and verse in form like those works just mentioned, its treatment is not serious/comic: there is nothing serious in the *Satyrica*. The treatment is comic/literary: 'No classical narrative that we know of even remotely approaches the literary complexity of Petronius' (Conte 1994a: 460). In addition, works of Menippean Satire like those of Varro, Seneca, Lucian and Julian, all appear to be much briefer than the *Satyrica* with its structure of numerous episodes. The *Satyrica* offers us a representation of everyday existence, which is the realm of the novel: the plot is not traditional but original and involves daily quarrels and struggles in a literary framework, made attractive by the combination of intense animosity and complete lack of consequences enjoyed for their own sake with no feeling of need for resolution, because no harm is done. The *Satyrica* rejects the supernatural except in jest, and all meals are eaten by very common people. Where the feeling of Seneca's *Apocolocyntosis* is biting, that of Lucian is unengaged and often absurd, Varro shows us a 'mixture of crude realism and fantastic imagination, as well as the bitter . . . tone of popular preaching' (Conte 1994a: 216). In the Menippean Satire of Varro, Seneca, Lucian and Julian there is a virulent strain of satire; in the *Satyrica*, satire is benign.

So why all the poetry in a work of extended prose fiction? The simplified answer is that the *Satyrica* is full of poets and would-be poets who naturally spout poetry – only to be showered with stones (90) by those who prefer prose (these stone-throwers should be viewed as ancient critics). In his experimentation with the novel Petronius allots a much larger role to poetic inserts than do other ancient novelists and in so doing expands the open form of the novel. Astbury adduces Knoche who holds that the prosimetric form of the *Satyrica* should be linked *both* to Menippean Satire and the mixed prose and verse in the ancient novel (Astbury 1977: 30). The *Iolaus* fragment with its similarities to the *Satyrica* 'enormously strengthens the case for believing that *prosimetrum* was not alien to the Greek romance' (ibid.: 31). What distinguishes the *Iolaus* is its obscenity, prosimetric form and knowledge of a line from a frequently quoted play, *Orestes* by Euripides. The simplest of outer forms, the *prosimetrum*, should not be used to establish a genre.

In his *Genres and Readers* Conte offers a most elucidative analogy for genre study:

> In the *Dialogues of the Dead*, Lucian recounts the Cynic Menippus' meeting in the underworld with the skeleton of Thersites, the ugliest of all Greek warriors who went to Troy. Thersites points out to the philosopher the skeleton of Nireus, the fairest of all who went to Troy. But, in fact, there is no visible difference between the two skeletons. For those of us who are looking for texts and want to read them and distinguish between them, it is the flesh that makes the difference, which lets us distinguish every time between Nireus and Thersites.
>
> (Conte 1994b: 127–8)

It is not the prosimetric skeleton but the flesh of the *Satyrica* which determines the genre. Description by genre should be a basic aid in interpretation of a text and on balance be more helpful than no genre designation at all.

V The genre: novel

The *Oxford English Dictionary* defines the novel as 'a fictitious prose narrative or tale of considerable length in which characters and actions representative of the real life of past or present times are portrayed in a plot of more or less complexity'. If the name Oxford still possesses its magical powers, the argument over genre is soon settled. If we must resort to an even higher authority, let us recall the opinion of a novelist, E.M. Forster:

> Perhaps we ought to define what a novel is before starting . . . It is . . . 'a fiction in prose of a certain extent' . . . and if this seems to you unphilosophic will you think of an alternative definition, which will include *The Pilgrim's Progress*, *Marius the Epicurean*, *The Adventures of a Younger Son*, *The Magic Flute*, *A Journal of the Plague Year*, *Zuleika Dobson*, *Rasselas*, *Ulysses* and *Green Mansions*, or else will give reason for their exclusion?
>
> (Forster 1974: 3)

In the spirit of Forster I would like to be inclusive in my approach to defining the novel. If the name of a novelist is not weighty enough to persuade the jury about the open form of the novel, we must resort to the highest authority in the land, the literary critic – in this case Wayne Booth:

> The novel began, we are told, with Cervantes, with Defoe, with Fielding, with Richardson, with Jane Austen – or was it with Homer? It was killed by Joyce, by Proust, by the rise of symbolism, by loss of respect for – or was it the excessive absorption with? – hard facts. No, no, it still lives, but only in the works of . . .[10]

It is of course an anachronism to refer to the *Satyrica* as a novel. The label, however, has been used for some years by classicists, now even by a few scholars in modern languages, and seems to have stuck to its object. The *Satyrica* is a work of extended narrative prose fiction, which in today's tolerant classification system we simply call a novel – but then quibble for hours about how we define 'fiction'. Most classicists are not reluctant to refer to the *Satyrica* (also *The Golden Ass*) as a novel, while the Greek novels are still often called romances. For historical reasons, however, the classics establishment has never really accepted the novel into the classical canon (Bowie and Harrison 1993). Scholars of English literature like Ian Watt and J. Paul Hunter (Watt 1957; Hunter 1990), on the other hand, admit all classical works into the canon of literature but exclude all of ancient extended prose narrative fiction from the novel genre. Watt, Hunter, *et al.* have defined the novel in an exclusive fashion as a genre which arose in eighteenth century England: a novel should not be 'in any sense an imitation of another literary work'; language should not be used 'as a source of interest in its own right, rather than as a purely referential medium'; the novel is a product of a society so sophisticated that the best connection between writer and reader of a novel is a commercial publisher. These English guardians of the novel appear to be defending a term only.

Even in its fragmentary state we recognize that the *Satyrica* is episodic (Schmeling 1991), and it seems possible that Petronius delivered it orally in a serial fashion, which could help account for its great length. We find the *Satyrica* in written form (radical of presentation), but if Petronius presented each episode to a literary group in spoken form or acted out some parts, then the radical of presentation would be entirely different and, according to Frye (1957: 246–7), so would the genre. In the spoken/acted form Petronius would have at the same time interpreted the *Satyrica*, and what is dark to us would have been bright to his audience. For us, however, the 'implied medium' of the *Satyrica* is the written word – presented to the reader as if it were spoken.[11]

The *Satyrica* is not merely a collection of episodes and tales, whether Milesian or of some other kind, sewn together without motivation, cause/effect, or unifying characters. Nor do the *Cena Trimalchionis*, episodes at rhetorical schools, adventures at Croton belong to the sub-genre of Milesian tales. If the *Satyrica* must have an ancestor, Sullivan suggests that we look to the *Odyssey*, the ancestor of all *Reiseromanen*.[12]

The same luxuriant literary texture which makes the *Satyrica* so attractive, intriguing and endlessly fascinating is also the source of its greatest frustration: what are we to make of this new mosaic of previous literature? While Lecky calls the *Satyrica* 'one of the most licentious and repulsive works in Roman literature', and Highet and Arrowsmith term it moral,[13] Slater contends that we must consider that Petronius might have intentionally encouraged meaninglessness in his narrative and so structured the narrative voice that the end product defies interpretation: the text, he says, 'is singularly uninterpretable' (Slater 1990: 250). Perhaps, though, we would find it more profitable to follow Eagleton (1983: 205 ff.) who has concluded that the search for interpretation begins and ends with rhetoric: Petronius is clearly in love with the game of rhetoric, the creation of literary structures, the music of prose. But what of the meaning, the difficulty to interpret the *Satyrica*? Is it some kind of mystery around which Petronius has erected camouflage to mask its meaning? To discover the secret (if there is one) of the *Satyrica* would be most gratifying to an *interpres* ('interpreter') who believes that interpretation is important: a secret is after all what best explains the camouflage erected to conceal it.

Petronius employs Encolpius as a first-person narrator, a personified narrator, one with a real part in the story (intradiegetic), whose narrative thus seems to suggest very personal experiences, which reflect honesty because they include admission of failures, in short, a confession. The tone of his confession, however, is not always clear because it is coloured by a clash in understanding/misunderstanding reality: I doubt that Encolpius knows at all times what is real. I stress the point because one of the most complimentary adjectives used for the *Satyrica* is 'realistic' – so realistic in fact that Roman social historians use it as a primary source. Any information of historical value coming to us from the novel must, however, arrive via Encolpius who uses facts in the same way as an overly imaginative schoolboy brags to his mates. This novel is stocked with characters who are meant to seem real, even if they are fictional ('formal realism').[14] In ancient literary works actors are intended to seem unreal, i.e. unlike people one might meet on the street. By grasping the *Satyrica* as a confession, the reader will, I believe, obtain a relatively unbiased view of this novel. The narrator is the only element of the *Satyrica* which remains unchanged from first to last, and around which we can wrap our genre theory.

The voice of *Satyrica* is always that of Encolpius, but it is so unreliable, his perception so conditioned by his fantasies of self, his statements of facts so regularly contradicted, his contexts so steeped in literature, that we are forced to treat the whole work with caution. At the same time we function at the mercy of Encolpius to obtain all information. The 'assumed source' of the novel is the memory of the narrator (Beck 1973), who it seems, is recalling events of the past, things which had happened, which the audience is thus led to believe are factual (65.1 *quarum etiam recordatio me, si qua est dicenti fides, offendit* – 'even the memory of which . . . makes me sick'; 56.10 *quae iam exciderunt memoriae meae* – 'which have now slipped my mind'). The 'implied audience' of Petronius' first presentation could be an imperial literary circle. The narrator of the story for some reason feels that it is necessary to record for his audience some of his past life and is searching his memory: a desire to leave some record of his life? a need to defend himself by explaining his past? a response in reply to inquiries of some kind? The extraordinarily extensive and dense intertextuality means that while the subject matter is base, only highly educated readers could appreciate the riches of literary allusions.

Our narrator employs a limited quantity of free indirect speech, preferring instead to report the direct speech of the characters at centre stage. Such a decision means that at regular intervals the narrator turns over his duties to sub-narrators, who when they are freedmen, provide the reader with the only (literary) slave-level speech in Latin literature: each speaker betrays not only his social background by his level of Latin grammar, syntax, and style, but also his sense of contemporary injustice and sensitivity to societal prejudices. When the sub-narrator is an educated speaker, he not only exposes his high level of rhetorical training, as in the case of Agamemnon and Eumolpus, but each reveals his lack of moral fibre: Agamemnon (1–5) does not believe what he teaches, and Eumolpus (85) carefully styles himself a teacher in order to seduce a boy. And all in direct speech.

Our view of what is in the *Satyrica* is given meaning by our sense of what is left out. The actors are charlatans (most narrators of novels are charlatans), impostors, rogues, social climbers, figures without virtues – nevertheless amusingly portrayed. Hard-working fathers, devoted mothers, fun-loving children are nowhere to be found. The centre of society at all levels has been excluded by the margins. All descriptions, conversations and thoughts are dominated by literature: it is not a physical world, it is literary.

Notes

1 Rose 1971 has assembled an impressive array of circumstantial evidence to support the name Titus Petronius Niger and to identify the courtier of Nero with the author of the *Satyrica*. Arbiter is a descriptive term used by Tacitus; it is not part of his name.

2 Vessey 1991–93: 149, notes that Petronius would lose much glamour and appeal had he written under Vespasian.

3 Those interested in the debate would do well to consult Rose 1971.

4 Colker 1992. On the history of the re-discovery of the various fragments of the *Satyrica* see Chapter 16 by R. F. Carver in this volume.

5 For a detailed summary see Schmeling 1996a: 462–9.

6 Schmeling 1994–95; Encolpius confesses to crimes he did not commit.

7 Parsons 1971: 66; on all novel fragments see now Stephens and Winkler 1995. For a shorter interpretation see Sandy 1994 and Stephens 1996.

8 Slater 1990; and Schmeling 1994 for objections.

9 Relihan 1993: 12: 'Menippean satire is not an ancient generic term'.

10 Booth 1983: 36; Selden 1994 opposes the use of the term 'ancient novel'.

11 On the oral aspect of the *Satyrica* see Vogt-Spira 1990b and Blänsdorf 1990.

12 Sullivan 1968: 96; Walsh 1970: 8: the Greek novel is ' . . . the sole type of extended episodic fiction in Greek for which any evidence exists before Petronius.'

13 For a review of the controversy see Schmeling 1969, 1971.

14 Jones 1991 offers insightful remarks on realism.

Bibliography

Adamietz, J. (1995), 'Circe in den *Satyrica* Petrons und das Wesen dieses Werkes', *Hermes* 123: 320–34.

Astbury, R. (1977), 'Petronius, *P. Oxy.* 3010, and Menippean Satire', *Classical Philology* 72: 22–31.

Beck, R. (1973), 'Some Observations of the Narrative Technique of Petronius', *Phoenix* 27: 42–61.

Blänsdorf, J. (1990), 'Die Werwolf-Geschichte des Niceros bei Petron als Beispiel literarischer Fiktion mündlichen Erzählens', in G. Vogt-Spira (ed.) *Strukturen der Mündlichkeit in der römischen Literatur*, Tübingen: Gunter Narr, pp. 193–217.

Bodel, J. (1984), 'Freedmen in the Satyricon of Petronius', dissertation, University of Michigan, Ann Arbor.

Booth, W. (1983), *The Rhetoric of Fiction*, Chicago: University of Chicago Press (originally published in 1961).

Bowie, E. and Harrison, S. (1993), 'The Romance of the Novel', *Journal of Roman Studies* 83: 159–78.

Colker, M. (1992), 'New Light on the Use and Transmission of Petronius', *Manuscripta* 36: 200–9.

Conte, G.B. (1994a), *Latin Literature: a History*, Baltimore/London: Johns Hopkins University Press.

—— (1994b), *Genre and Readers*, Baltimore/London: Johns Hopkins University Press.

—— (1996), *The Hidden Author: An Interpretation of Petronius's Satyricon*, Berkeley/ Los Angeles/London: University of California Press.

Dronke, P. (1994), *Verse with Prose from Petronius to Dante*, Cambridge, MA.: Harvard University Press.

Eagleton, T. (1983), *Literary Theory: an Introduction*, Minneapolis: University of Minnesota Press.

Eden, P. (ed.) (1984), *Seneca, Apocolocyntosis*, Cambridge: Cambridge University Press.

Forster, E.M. (1974), *Aspects of the Novel*, London: Edward Arnold (originally published 1927).

Frye, N. (1957), *Anatomy of Criticism*, Princeton, NJ: Princeton University Press.

Heinze, R. (1889), 'Petron und der griechische Roman', *Hermes* 34: 494–519.

Holzberg, N. (1995), *The Ancient Novel: an Introduction*, London/New York: Routledge.

Hunter, J.P. (1990), *Before Novels: the Cultural Contexts of Eighteenth-Century English Literature*, New York: W.W. Norton.

Jones, F. (1991), 'Realism in Petronius', in H. Hofmann (ed.), *Groningen Colloquia on the Novel*, vol. 4, Groningen: Egbert Forsten, pp. 105–19.

Morgan, J.R. and R. Stoneman (eds) (1994) *Greek Fiction: The Greek Novel in Context*, London/New York: Routledge.

Müller, C.W. (1980), 'Die Witwe von Ephesus – Petrons Novelle und die *Milesiaka* des Aristeides', *Antike und Abendland* 26: 103–21.

Müller, K. (ed.) (1983), *Petronius, Satyrica*, Munich: Artemis.

—— (1995), *Petronii Arbitri Satyricon Reliquiae*, Stuttgart/Leipzig: B.G. Teubner.

Parsons, P (1971), 'A Greek *Satyricon?*', *Bulletin of the Institute of Classical Studies* 18: 53–68.

Perry, B.E. (1967), *The Ancient Romances: a Literary-Historical Account of Their Origins* (*Sather Classical Lectures*, 37), Berkeley/Los Angeles: University of California Press.

Petersmann, H. (1977), *Petrons urbane Prosa: Untersuchungen zu Sprache und Text*, Vienna: Verlag der Österreichischen Akademie der Wissenschaften.

Reardon, B. (1991), *The Form of Greek Romance*, Princeton, NJ: Princeton University Press.

Relihan, J. (1993), *Ancient Menippean Satire*, Baltimore/London: Johns Hopkins University Press.

Rose, K.F.C. (1971), *The Date and Author of the Satyricon* (*Mnemosyne*, Supplement 16), Leiden: E.J. Brill.

Sandy, G. (1969), 'Satire in the *Satyricon*', *American Journal of Philology* 90: 293–303.

—— (1994a), 'Apuleius' *Metamorphoses* and the Ancient Novel', in W. Haase (ed.) *Aufstieg und Niedergang der römischen Welt*, vol. II 34.2, Berlin/New York: W. de Gruyter, pp. 1511–74.

—— (1994b), 'New Pages of Greek Fiction', in J. R. Morgan and R. Stoneman (eds) *Greek Fiction: The Greek Novel in Context*, London/New York: Routledge, pp. 130–45.

Schmeling, G. (1969), 'Petronius: Satirist, Moralist, Epicurean, Artist', *Classical Bulletin* 45: 49–50; 64.

—— (1971), '*The Satyricon*: Forms in Search of a Genre', *Classical Bulletin* 47: 49–53.

—— (1991), '*The Satyricon*: the Sense of an Ending', *Rheinisches Museum* 134: 352–77.

—— (1994), '*Quid attinet veritatem per interpretem quaerere? Interpretes* and the *Satyricon*', *Ramus* 23: 144–68.

—— (1994–95), 'Confessor Gloriosus: a Role of Encolpius in the *Satyrica*', *Würzburger Jahrbücher für die Altertumswissenschaft* N.F. 20: 207–24.

—— (1996a), 'The *Satyrica* of Petronius', in G. Schmeling (ed.) *The Novel in the Ancient World*, Leiden/New York/Cologne: E.J. Brill, pp. 457–90.

—— (1996b), *The Novel in the Ancient World* (*Mnemosyne*, Supplement 159), Leiden: E. J. Brill.

Selden, D. (1994), 'Genre of Genre', in J. Tatum (ed.), *The Search for the Ancient Novel*, Baltimore/London: Johns Hopkins University Press, pp. 39–64.

Slater, N. (1990), *Reading Petronius*, Baltimore/London: Johns Hopkins University Press.

Stephens, S. (1996), 'Fragments of Lost Novels' in G. Schmeling (ed.) *The Novel in the Ancient World*, Leiden/New York/Cologne: E.J. Brill, pp. 655–83.

Stephens, S. and Winkler, J. (eds) (1995), *Ancient Greek Novels: the Fragments. Introduction, Text, Translation and Commentary*, Princeton, NJ: Princeton University Press.

Sullivan, J.P. (1968), *The* Satyricon *of Petronius: a Literary Study*, London: Faber and Faber.

Vessey D. (1991–93), 'Thoughts on "the Ancient Novel" or What Ancients? What Novels?', *Bulletin of the Institute of Classical Studies* 38: 144–61.

Vogt-Spira, G. (ed.) (1990a), *Strukturen der Mündlichkeit in der römischen Literatur*, Tübingen: Gunter Narr.

Vogt-Spira, G. (1990b), 'Indizien für mündlichen Vortrag von Petrons *Satyrica*', in G. Vogt-Spira (ed.) *Strukturen der Mündlichkeit in der römischen Literatur*, Tübingen: Gunter Narr, pp. 183–92.

Walsh, P.G. (1970) *The Roman Novel*. Cambridge: Cambridge University Press.

Zeitlin, F. (1971), 'Petronius as Paradox: Anarchy and Artistic Integrity', *Transactions of the American Philological Association* 102: 631–84.

2

THE *CENA TRIMALCHIONIS*

John Bodel

Perhaps no excerpt of classical Latin prose has benefited more, or has suffered more, from an early separation from the work in which it originally appeared than the episode of Petronius's novel known as the Banquet of Trimalchio (Petr. 26.7–78). The benefits are immediately obvious: unlike the other battered remnants of his once glorious masterpiece, the section of Petronius's *Satyrica* describing, through the jaundiced eyes of the narrator Encolpius, the extravagantly tasteless dinner party hosted by a wealthy ex-slave, Trimalchio, at his suburban villa outside a Campanian town (probably Puteoli) sometime around the middle of the first century AD has come down to us virtually intact: apart from a few minor lacunae near the start, the narrative here runs continuously for some fifty-five pages in a modern text – something that cannot be said of any other part of the work that survives.

At what point in antiquity or the Middle Ages the *Cena Trimalchionis* became detached from the rest of the novel is impossible to say, but there is no reason to distrust an inference derived from the history of the only manuscript to preserve the entire episode, the so-called *codex Traguriensis* discovered in Dalmatia around 1650 (**H**), that the *Cena* originally corresponded, in whole or in part, to book 15. Shorter and spicier titbits of Petronius's work had been circulating in Europe for nearly two hundred years before modern readers had their first taste of what has since come to be regarded as its *pièce de résistance*.[1] The gusto with which critics ever since have sunk their teeth into this meatiest part of the narrative is disproportionate to its size (about one third) within the surviving corpus, and it is from this concentration of attention, paradoxically, that the *Cena* suffers. By literary design as well as by hazard of transmission the Banquet of Trimalchio is so clearly marked off from the surrounding narrative that it is easy, in considering its merits, to lose sight of its relation to the *disiecta membra* of the whole. Even within the episode, the flood of light focused on the central figure may blind us to the virtues of Petronius's more subtle characterizations and can obscure the significance of the portrait within its larger narrative frame. It will therefore be useful to begin with a brief overview of the literary landscape that defines the contours of the episode.

I A satiric symposium

Whatever literary forms may have influenced Petronius elsewhere, when he embarked on an extended description of a dinner party he set sail on familiar waters. A rich stream of Greco-Roman banquet literature had long since divided itself into two well demarcated channels: dialogues, such as the philosophical symposia of Plato and Xenophon, in which the dinner setting serves primarily as a backdrop for the conversation of the guests, and descriptive catalogues, often derisive, of the foods and entertainment served up by a boorish host, such as the banquet satires of Lucilius and Horace and Juvenal.[2] Characteristically, Petronius drew from both traditions and found inspiration in particular specimens of each – one Greek, which he parodies and subverts, the other Roman, which he imitates and elaborates. Plato's *Symposium*, the ultimate source of all banquet literature, occupies the centre of the episode (41–46) and is prominently acknowledged in the second half of the banquet. The literary model for the vulgar host Petronius found closer to home, in Horace's *Cena Nasidieni* (*Sat.* 2.8).

Like Nasidienus, Trimalchio is a social upstart whose culinary extravagances, designed to impress, elicit only scorn from a more sophisticated narrator. Both hosts dominate the conversation with banal commentary on the food served (Hor. 2.8.44–53, Petr. 39); both favour surprise dishes (Hor. 2.8.26–30, Petr. 33.4–8, 69.8–70.3) and offer a variety of fine wines (Hor. 2.8.16f., Petr. 34.6–8, 48.1); both suffer an unexpected mishap in the staging of their gastronomical spectacles (Hor. 2.8.54–58, the collapse of an awning; Petr. 53.11–55, the fall of an acrobat); both leave the table temporarily, to the relief of their guests (Hor. 2.8.76–78, Petr. 41.9); both dissolve into tears (Hor. 2.8.58f., Petr. 72.1). The excesses of both cause their guests, at first, to suppress laughter (Hor. 2.8.63f., Petr. 47.7), then to lose appetite (Hor. 2.8.92f., Petr. 69.7), and finally to flee the scene (Hor. 2.8.93–95, Petr. 78.8).[3] In the *Satyrica* the rhetorician Agamemnon fills the role of Maecenas, the cultivated guest at Nasidienus's table; Encolpius and his companion Ascyltus play Vibidius and Servilius Balatro, the uninvited 'shadows' (*umbrae*) a significant term: see below section IV of Maecenas (Hor. 2.8.21f.); and Trimalchio's fellow freedman Hermeros plays Nomentanus, the toady in Horace's satire. These correspondences show that Petronius wrote a familiar satiric type into a recognizable literary setting; but whereas Horace's Nasidienus remains a one-dimensional figure marked by unmistakable but ill-defined social pretensions, Petronius endows Trimalchio with a specific juridical status, that of an ex-slave, and fleshes him out with a set of attitudes and social ambitions peculiarly appropriate to his station (see below section II; cf. Conte 1996: 124–31).

Plato's *Symposium*, the paradigm of a philosophical dialogue presented as dinner conversation, provided a touchstone by which the existential concerns and intellectual capabilities of Trimalchio and his friends could be measured. For Petronius it served primarily to establish, humorously and by contrast, the social background against which Trimalchio is to be viewed. The interlude toward the middle of the episode in which five of the freedmen guests, in the temporary absence of the host, deliver consecutive speeches before Trimalchio returns to dilate upon his digestion (41–47) was clearly modelled on Plato's dialogue, where, too, five speakers contribute to the discussion before the central figure delivers a crowning oration. Each group has its nostalgic defender of religious tradition (Phaedrus, *Symp.* 178a–180b; Ganymede, Petr. 44); each has its cynical advocate of moral indifference (the sophist Pausanias, *Symp.* 180c–185c; the pleader Phileros, whose name explicitly recalls the topic of discussion at Agathon's table, Petr. 43); and each has its pedantic purveyor of pseudo-scientific medical wisdom (the doctor Eryximachus, *Symp.* 185e–188e; Seleucus, Petr. 42). These correspondences, disposed chiastically, highlight the dramatic discrepancies in cultural setting, level of discourse, and sympotic decorum that characterize the two banquets. In place of Plato's sober philosophical dialogue, conducted in an orderly fashion by physicians, lawyers, and poets and leading progressively to ever more ethereal planes, Petronius gives us the drunken, down-to-earth maunderings of semi-literate ex-slaves, whose intensely self-centred monologues betray the limits of their intellectual horizons.[4]

Subsequently in the *Cena* Petronius invokes Plato's *Symposium* at the introduction of each new freedman guest, as if to mark each as belonging to the same social universe as Trimalchio, and at the end, when Trimalchio's dinner, like Agathon's, is interrupted by the sudden entry of a band of strangers (revellers at Plato, *Symp.* 223b, firemen at Petr. 78.7). Niceros's reluctance to speak lest he appear ridiculous (Petr. 61.4) recalls Aristophanes's disclaimer to Eryximachus (*Symp.* 189b) and sets up his werewolf story (Petr. 61–62: the vicious duality of man) as the antitype of Aristophanes's parable of the round hermaphrodites (*Symp.* 189c–d: the loving duality of man). Habinnas's drunken entrance late in the banquet (Petr. 65) comically evokes Alcibiades's late arrival at Agathon's home (*Symp.* 212d–e) and serves a similar structural function in introducing and prompting the final revelation of the main character.[5]

Other literary forms – notably mime and new comedy – influenced the presentation of Trimalchio's banquet, but none provides a recognizable model in the way that Horace's *Cena Nasidieni* and Plato's *Symposium* do.[6] References to the stage and theatre pervade the *Cena*, but it is not always clear, when considering their significance, whether we are dealing with literary shaping (by narrator or by author) or with Trimalchio's own self-presentation, and, if the latter, whether Trimalchio's theatrical behaviour should be seen as eccentric or normal.[7] A fine line separates verisimilitude from caricature, and we cannot always see precisely where it ought to be drawn. Discerning Petronius's intent requires that we recognize the social realities he comically distorts as clearly as the literary models he parodies and imitates – a task more easy to identify than to accomplish and one more frequently taken for granted than seriously undertaken.

II Between fact and fiction: the portrait of Trimalchio

Half a century ago a distinguished literary critic, in an influential book on the representation of reality in western literature, declared that in allowing the freedmen at Trimalchio's table to voice their own concerns in their own language, Petronius achieved the highest degree of realism of any author of antiquity (Auerbach 1953). A few years later an ancient historian, in an equally influential essay, argued that Trimalchio's biography, for all its comic exaggeration, should be taken seriously as a historical document (Veyne 1961). Though difficult to define and elusive to pin down, Petronius's realism – the impression he conveys in his representation of Trimalchio and his milieu of drawing his characters from the real world – is so vivid that many have considered this to be his finest literary accomplishment.[8] When viewed in (ancient) terms of verisimilitude, Petronius's realism (a modern critical concept) seems subversive, based as it is on an underlying leitmotif of pretence and deception (F. Jones 1991), but ancient historians have been sufficiently impressed by it to describe Trimalchio as typical – even if they have not always agreed precisely what type Trimalchio represents.[9] Literary critics, looking to historians for guidance, naturally find their assessment of Petronius's artistic aims confirmed. Some (notably Dupont 1977) see in this comfortable consensus a dangerous circularity, but it is inevitable, given the conventions of Roman satire and the social realities of early imperial Rome, that literary and historical analyses of the *Cena* should converge on the portrait of a wealthy ex-slave with pretensions to culture and should, if properly pursued, support one another. When seen as a question of alternatives, the problem of distinguishing verisimilitude from literary modelling in the *Cena* is falsely posed: Petronius's representation, though drawn with a sharp eye on reality, is shaped throughout by a powerful and disciplined imagination (Martin 1988: 232–42; Conte 1996: 174–80).

As the satiric centrepiece, Trimalchio is painted in bright colours, but with a subtle brush: transported to Italy from Asia as a boy, subsequently manumitted and instituted as heir by his wealthy master, Trimalchio multiplied his fortune by shipping goods to Rome and then withdrew to his landed estates, where self-sufficiency enabled him to live the life of a Roman gentleman (Petr. 75.10–77). Documentary and material sources confirm that many ex-slaves rose to prominence by this route during the first century AD, and our upper-class literary authorities provide ample evidence of the frictions that resulted from their rapid ascension into the upper levels of imperial society. At the heart of the problem was wealth, traditionally the base of the landed aristocracy's hold on political and social power but now piled up overnight by ambitious ex-slaves free to engage in the sort of speculative and lucrative commercial maritime ventures denied to members of the senatorial order. New money had always been a target of élite resentment and snobbery – Aristotle (*Rhet.* 2.1391a) sniffed that the newly rich generally had more and worse bad habits, owing to their 'lack of education in wealth' (ἀπαιδευσία πλούτου). What aggravated the situation in early imperial Rome was the barrier to social advancement posed by the juridical liability of being an ex-slave. The strictures of Roman law made of freedmen a class apart, and the tension inherent in Trimalchio's determined, yet futile, efforts to transcend this segregation enabled Petronius to combine a comically realistic portrait of a literary type (the boorish host) with a thematically cogent representation of a contemporary social phenomenon, the successful independent freedman.

In keeping with his outlook as an ex-slave, Trimalchio aims for the grandeur of an *eques* ('knight') rather than for that of a senator, i.e. not for the highest social rank but for the second-highest, that of the equestrian order, whose members included freedmen notorious for their abundant wealth. His social ambitions are precisely limited by the boundaries of his horizons (Veyne 1961: 240–46). Within this broadly realistic outline Petronius interlaces plausible and implausible details so artfully that it is sometimes difficult to tell where verisimilitude ends and parody begins.

HOC·MONVMENTVM·HEREDEM·NON·SEQVATVR

C·POMPEIVS·TRIMALCHIO

MAECENATIANVS

HIC·REQVIESCIT

HVIC·SEVIRATVS·ABSENTI·DECRETVS·EST

CVM·POSSET·IN·OMNIBVS·DECVRIIS

ROMAE·ESSE·TAMEN·NOLVIT

PIVS·FORTIS·FIDELIS

EX·PARVO·CREVIT·RELIQVIT·HS·CCC

NEC·VMQVAM·PHILOSOPHVM·AVDIVIT

VALE·ET·TV

Figure 2.1 Trimalchio's epitaph

Consider Trimalchio's epitaph (Fig. 2.1), as Trimalchio himself might have wished it to appear (Petr. 71.7, 12). Certain formulaic phrases (*hic requiescit*, *vale et tu*) and the heroic epithets (*pius fortis fidelis*) establish context and lend verisimilitude. The boast of financial advancement (*ex parvo crevit*) and the allusion to the *seviratus*[10] and the *decuriae* of Rome likewise fix Trimalchio's social position at the expected place. Other features, however – the placement of the clause prohibiting alienation of the tomb at the start (*ante omnia*, 71.7) rather than at the end of the epitaph, the declaration of financial assets of thirty million sesterces, and the boast never to have listened to a philosopher – by a subtle distortion of familiar tropes introduce an element of parody. The idea that the office of *sevir* was bestowed in Trimalchio's absence, the suggestion that he declined to pursue opportunities open to him at Rome, above all the misappropriation of the cognomen Maecenatianus – these details incongruously blend equestrian affectations with the distinctions of a freedman, so that Trimalchio's social pretensions, though fully consonant with his station, are subtly and humorously divorced from reality (D'Arms 1981: 108–16; Beard 1998: 95–98). This is one of the ways Petronius appealed to his original readers' knowledge of their contemporary world to further his literary goals. Another is by associating Trimalchio directly with recognizable celebrities. In this his choice of models was eclectic: a notorious ex-slave furnishes an amusing analogue for Trimalchio's path to success (Petr. 75.10–11; Pliny, *NH* 34.11–12, *CIL* I^2 1004); the affectations of an imperial governor of Syria anchor the most extravagant of Trimalchio's morbid charades – the mock funeral at the end of the banquet – firmly in the real world (Petr. 78.5–6; Sen. *Epist.* 12.8); incidental parallels with the habits of the emperor Nero comically inflate Trimalchio's pretensions and perhaps reflect a gentle teasing by the emperor's *arbiter elegantiae.*[11]

The social background against which Petronius projected this remarkable figure reveals an equally subtle palette. Even where he went further in naturalism than other authors of antiquity, as in representing faithfully the mental preoccupations and linguistic mannerisms of Trimalchio and his freedmen friends, the deft brushwork of the impressionist can always be discerned. When compared with the scribbled outpourings of real-life contemporaries at Pompeii, the hints of colloquialism worked into the freedmen's language show the author's restraint and his care to vary the speech patterns of individual characters. The same is true of the cultural tastes and social attitudes evinced by Trimalchio's freedmen guests: their views and behaviours are carefully modulated to support the characterization of Trimalchio and to conform with Petronius's broader thematic aims (see below section IV).[12] How closely Petronius manipulated the presentation of these details can best be seen from the elaborate structure he imposed upon the narrative.

III A labyrinthine feast

Petronius, like Apuleius in his novel, favours a narrative technique that combines the complementary devices of linking – by the common denominator of a shared character, by parallelism, sometimes by contrast – and framing – by setting stories within stories, by formally bracketing interpolated narratives, and by repeating significant details (Callebat 1974). Within the *Cena* these mechanisms articulate the episode into a series of concentric frames, which become apparent only gradually, as the reader proceeds through the narrative, when incidents and themes encountered in the first half of the banquet begin to recur systematically, in reverse order, in the second half.[13] As the pattern begins to emerge around the centre of the episode, the receptive reader experiences the sense of methodically retracing a path out of an intricate, box-like, maze and thus of replicating the narrator's perceptions. 'What were we poor wretches to do', Encolpius rhetorically asks late in the episode, after an unsuccessful attempt to escape Trimalchio's house, 'shut in by some new kind of labyrinth?' (*novi generis labyrintho inclusi*, 73.1).[14]

The image of the labyrinth serves as a metaphor not only for the deceptions and ambiguities of Trimalchio's self-presentation but also for the process itself of reading the *Cena*, for the outermost narrative frame does not, in fact, correspond with the end of the episode; it creates instead the false sense of a conclusion at a point where the banquet seems to be drawing to a close but in fact begins anew, apparently in a fresh direction (74.6–7).[15] The beginning of this second act not only repeats, with variation, the sequence of events at the start of the banquet, it also conforms, in smaller scale, to the same pattern of nested panels observed earlier in the episode. The details can perhaps best be illustrated with a diagram, Figure 2.2.[16] The coda (A'-A") creates in the reader a sense of being caught up in a closed narrative cycle destined to expand and contract indefinitely, like the bellows of an accordion. This structural patterning enables the narrator to shape the events he relates to reflect his experience of them at the time: Trimalchio's house was a trap from which there seemed no exit. At the same time, the labyrinthine experience of returning inexorably to the point of origin, only to begin the cycle again, reinforces a major thematic motif – that a freedman's status is self-perpetuating and inescapable (see below section IV). The narrative architecture of the *Cena* thus figures one of its principal points: the medium is the message.

IV Death and status

Trimalchio's life revolves around death: thoughts of it – his own and others' – hang like a shroud over the banquet, and images of it recur so frequently throughout the *Cena* that many have sought to view the episode, indeed the entire novel, through this lens. For Arrowsmith (1966) the morbid luxury at

A *bucinator* signals the passing of time (26.9); ball game (27) and bath (28.1); Trimalchio's funereal entrance (28.4–5)
B Encolpius enters T.'s house, past gatekeeper (28.6–8) and painted watchdog (29.1–2)
C mural ecphrasis on the young T.'s life as a slave (painted autobiography) (29.3–9)
D guests enter dining room (30.5), slaves quarrel (30.7–31.2), sing (31.5–7), tend to guests' feet (31.3–4)
E entrance of T. (cushions) (32–33.1); game-playing with slave (33.2–3); *matteae*: chicken and eggs (33.3–8)
F silver skeleton (34.8–9); T. composes doggerel (34.10)
G First course: mythological food (Pegasus and Marsyas), the carver Carpus (36)
H Hermeros exhorts Encolpius not to scorn the freedmen, describes his fellow freedmen (37–38)
I T. interrupts guests, shows off his learning with word-play (zodiac dish) (39)
J Second course: boar containing thrushes (40); E. shows ignorance, Hermeros explains; pun on 'Liber' (41)
K T. goes to the toilet (41.9)
L freedmen's speeches (a): Dama unable to speak (41.10–12)
M freedmen's speeches (b): Seleucus (pessimistic) (42) and Phileros (optimistic) (43)
M′ freedmen's speeches (b′): Ganymede (pessimistic) (44) and Echion (optimistic) (45)
L′ freedmen's speeches (a′): Echion ctd. (46); Agamemnon unwilling to speak (46.1)
K′ T. returns from the toilet (47.1–6)
J′ Third course: pig containing sausages; E. shows ignorance, T. explains (49); pun on 'Corinthus' (50)
I′ T. interrupts guests, shows off his learning with word-play (*apophoreta*) (55–56)
H′ Hermeros rebukes Ascyltus and Giton for scorning the freedmen, describes himself (verbal autobiography) (57–58)
G′ Fourth course: mythological drama (*Homeristae*), the carver Ajax (59)
F′ Niceros's werewolf story (61–62) and T.'s ghost story (63); Plocamus performs doggerel (64.5)
E′ entrance of Habinnas (65.3–7); game-playing with slave (64.5–13); *matteae*: chicken and eggs (65.1)
D′ slaves enter dining room (70.10–13), quarrel (70.4–5), sing (70.7), tend to guests' feet (70.8)
C′ tomb ecphrasis on the life of T. as a freedman (sculpted autobiography) (71)
B′ Encolpius attempts to leave T's house and is thwarted by a gatekeeper (72.10) and watchdog (72.7–9)
A′ cock crow as *bucinus* signals the passing of time (74.1–4); calisthenic games (73.4–5) and bath (73.2)
A′ cock crow signals a fire or a death in the neighbourhood; *vale Gai . . . ave Gai* ('*ave atque vale*') (74.1–7)
B″ servants depart and arrive freely; *hinc primum hilaritas nostra turbata est*; Fortunata calls T. 'dog' (74.7–9)
C″ T.'s account of his life from childhood (slavery) to maturity (freed status) (verbal autobiography) (75–77)
B‴ D″ Stichus brings funerary gear into the dining room (77.7–78.4); *ibat res ad summam nauseam* (78.5)
A″ E″ T.'s funereal exit, propped up on cushions; horn players summon firemen (78.6–8)

Figure 2.2 The structure of the Cena Trimalchionis

Trimalchio's table represented the spiritual death of a society glutted with its own excesses; for Sullivan (1968) it was a merely satiric touch, a manifestation of Trimalchio's vulgar Epicureanism. More recently Trimalchio's efforts to ward off his fear of dying with merriment have been seen as a reflection of the carnivalesque reality of contemporary imperial society (Herzog 1989, Döpp 1991) or as an image of a freedman's inverted attitude toward death (Magnani 1991). Others link the motif of games in the *Cena* to funeral contests, such as those described by Virgil in Book 5 of the *Aeneid* (Saylor 1987), or see in the leitmotif of funereal themes a systematic deployment of mythological allusions designed to represent Trimalchio as Pluto/Hades, lord of the underworld (Schlant 1991). While no single interpretation of death imagery in the *Cena* can fully explain all its various manifestations, one that draws upon the narrative architecture of the episode to link Trimalchio's fascination with death with his status as a freedman may at least serve to illustrate the complexity of the phenomenon.

Late in the episode the narrator Encolpius and his companions attempt to flee the banquet but are prevented by a watchdog, which is placated with scraps from the table, and an officious gatekeeper, who advises them that Trimalchio's guests are never permitted to leave by the same route by which they arrived (Petr. 72.7–10). As has long been recognized, Petronius here evokes Virgil's account of Aeneas's visit to the underworld in Book Six of the *Aeneid*. Just as that episode is introduced by a description of the Minoan labyrinth sculpted on the doors of the temple of Apollo at Cumae (*Aen.* 6.20–34), so the Petronian vignette is preceded by Trimalchio's narration of the scenes he wants sculpted on his tomb (Petr. 71). That ecphrasis, in turn, recalls the autobiographical mural painted in Trimalchio's portico depicting four scenes from his life as a slave and a fifth scene, set off from the others, representing his elevation to freedman status as an apotheosis ($C' \approx C$ in Fig. 2.2). In style and content this peculiar frieze is without precedent in Roman domestic decoration; parallels are found instead in funerary art, especially in the allegorical self-representations common during the first century on the tombs of ex-slaves of foreign extraction. In Trimalchio's vision, manumission is figured as a transition from the life of a slave to a blessed afterlife. Cast in another light, Trimalchio's house emerges as a home of the dead, a social underworld populated by ex-slaves, into which the narrator Encolpius enters as an outsider, as if on a catabasis (Bodel 1994).

Direct references to funerals (42.2, 65.10) and undertakers (38.14, 78.6) and the funereal processions with which the banquet begins (28.4–5) and closes (78.6–8) provide thematic continuity, but it is the mural ecphrasis at the start of the episode that establishes a fundamental connection between Trimalchio's fascination with death and his ambivalent status as an ex-slave. As a self-made man in a society that values freebirth and ancestry over personal achievement, Trimalchio naturally sees no further than his own lifetime and focuses obsessively on the end. Denied the respectability to which he feels his wealth entitles him, he lives in a peculiar social limbo, like the disembodied spirits of the underworld, who have the form but not the substance of real men. Riches bring no happiness to Trimalchio because riches cannot obviate the two unavoidable necessities for a freedman in early imperial Rome: death and status. Realism and symbolism converge in Petronius's presentation to convey this starkly bleak vision of a freedman's place in the world, and the mechanism of recognition is sprung simultaneously at two levels – the visual, through distortion of the decorative conventions of Roman art, and the verbal, through literary parody and allusion. In both cases the dislocations (sepulchral paintings on a house, Encolpius as Aeneas in the underworld) are incongruous and humorous but also symbolically potent and thematically coherent. This is how Petronius weaves complexity and richness into his carefully articulated narrative.

V The *Cena* in context

No consideration of the *Cena Trimalchionis* can evade the question of its relationship to the whole. There can be no certainty here, nor even much argument: what little evidence we have for the original scope of the *Satyrica* is of doubtful interpretation and dubious value, and reconstructions of the plot necessarily remain speculative.[17] Within a narrative of unknown scope, the *Cena* may or may not have been typical in character and length. As an episode, it seems to be unusual in the degree to which the narrator withdraws from the action and merely reports, and perhaps also in the degree to which it is isolated and self-contained. Whereas Trimalchio appears only in the *Cena*,[18] other major characters, such as Quartilla (16.3), Tryphaena (100.7), and Lichas (101.7), originally figured prominently in more than one episode, in parts of the narrative no longer extant. Others, such as Agamemnon (1–5) and Circe (126–130) engage Encolpius directly in a way that Trimalchio never does. Ascyltus (6) and Eumolpus (83.7, 90.1), his replacement as rival for Giton's affections in the triadic configuration of protagonists that Petronius seems to favor (cf. Sullivan 1968: 44), propel the story forward in concert with the narrator/actor Encolpius. Trimalchio's banquet represents an interlude in the headlong progress of the plot and provides an unusually elaborate setting for an extended cameo portrait.

Thematically the *Cena* has much in common with the only other major episode to survive, the scenes set in Croton (116–141). There too an underworld motif (centring on Encolpius's sexual impotence: Zeitlin 1971: 67–68) is linked with the representation of a sterile and closed society (inheritance hunters and their victims, 116: Fedeli 1987). There too Petronius draws upon well-known models in Roman satire and epic to establish context and theme (Herzog 1989: 131–33). In the *Cena*, as we have seen, setting and subject recall Horace's *Cena Nasidieni* (*Sat.* 2.8), and reference to Virgil's *Aeneid* (Book Six) conveys thematic point. In the Croton episode, the context –

shipwreck on an unknown shore, the view from a hill of a distant city, and a description of its inhabitants by an anonymous informant (115–116) – evokes Virgilian epic (Aeneas's arrival at Dido's Carthage), and Horace's satire on inheritance hunting (*Sat.* 2.5), pointedly set in the underworld, provides thematic continuity. Both episodes may have ended with the pseudo-death of the central figure – Eumolpus's anticipated funeral, at the point where our text breaks off, has the look of a *Scheintod* (Wesseling 1993: 89–92) – just as the intervening narrative culminates in the actual death and funeral of Lichas (115). Perhaps, as the narrator underwent a series of metaphorical descents to the underworld, Petronius punctuated large units of the narrative with the deaths (metaphorical or real) of major supporting characters. We do not know, and speculation cannot rectify our ignorance. What seems certain is that the *Cena Trimalchionis*, since the time of its discovery an outsized diamond in Petronius's crown, was originally but one illustrious gem in a richly bejewelled setting.

Notes

1 The fascinating story of **H** is told by De La Mare 1976: 239–51. A facsimile of the portion of it preserving the *Cena* was published by Gaselee in 1915. The *editio princeps* of the so-called shorter excerpts of the *Satyrica* (at Milan) dates from *c.* 1482; for the book numbers, see Müller 1995: xxi–xxiii. Cf. also Chapter 16 by R. F. Carver in this volume.

2 For the latter see Shero 1923; Martin 1931 surveys commonplaces of the Greek tradition.

3 Shero 1923: 134–38 adduces further parallels.

4 Dupont 1977: 61–89 sees the *Cena* as a sort of anti-*Symposium* characterized by the absence of a '*logos sympotikos*' (succinctly defined on p. 39 as 'une méditation du plaisir'), in which Petronius represents the freedmen's failed attempt to recreate the free speech of the democratic Athenian symposium. Bessone 1993 finds in the freedmen's speeches parody of a more conventional sort, without the moralizing overtones.

5 See Citroni 1995: 301–5 (Niceros); Cameron 1969 and Dupont 1977–79 (Habinnas). Elsewhere in the *Satyrica* Petronius recalls Plato's *Symposium* in the story of the Pergamene boy (85–87) by representing Eumolpus as a sort of Socrates *manqué* (cf. *Symp.* 217a–219d): Dimundo 1983. The fragments of a possibly contemporary Greek novel, *Metiochus and Parthenope* (Stephens and Winkler 1995: 72–94), likewise include a banquet scene modelled on Plato's *Symposium* in which the nature of Eros is discussed. Perhaps Petronius looked back to Plato through the prism of the ideal novel.

6 See Sandy 1974: 329–39. Panayotakis 1995: 52–109 gives a full survey of theatrical elements in the *Cena.*

7 For two rather different approaches to these questions, see C.P. Jones 1991: 185–94 and Slater 1990: 50–86.

8 Sullivan 1968: 151–52 believed that Petronius's sympathy for Trimalchio enabled him to transcend his originally narrow literary aim of satire.

9 For Rostovtzeff, Trimalchio was primarily a petty bourgeois capitalist; for Veyne he was a wealthy freedman; *alii alia*. The best discussion is by D'Arms 1991.

10 Already at 30.2 we learned that Trimalchio was a *sevir Augustalis*, i.e. a member

of the board of six priests – usually wealthy freedmen – 'who supervised the cult of the emperor and were granted in return various privileges and honours' (Smith 1975: 62).

11 See Bodel 1989 and Sullivan 1968: 129–32, on Calvisius Sabinus, a wealthy dilettante (Sen. *Epist.* 27.5–8). For possible allusions to Nero see Bartsch 1994: 199. According to Plutarch (*Mor.* 60e), the courtier T. Petronius chided Nero, a profligate spender, with meanness.

12 Boyce 1991 and Gaide 1995 are the most recent and most accessible of many studies of the colloquial Latin of the freedmen. Horsfall 1989 usefully surveys popular culture in the *Cena.*

13 We owe this insight to Hubbard 1986, whose attempt to trace the sequence beyond the boundaries of the *Cena* episode, however, is unpersuasive. For an alternative view, see Figure 2.2.

14 For Trimalchio's house as a labyrinthine trap, see Dupont 1977: 147–51 and Fedeli 1981: 99–109.

15 See Herzog 1989: 128ff.: 'Dieses Fest kann nicht enden' (131). Schmeling 1991 explores the phenomenon of apparent endings throughout the *Satyrica* and observes (357) a similar ring pattern of frames in the Widow of Ephesus story (111–12).

16 The main part of the figure (A–A′) is based on Hubbard 1986: 194–201 but differs in detail and orientation: Hubbard's decision to label the frames from the centre out (A–U) obscures the rhythmical pattern of the coda and seems to misrepresent the author's intentions.

17 Sullivan 1968: 34–80 gives a balanced overview of what can plausibly be surmised, but some of our surviving fragments seem to have been displaced: see Van Thiel 1971 and Chapter 1 by Gareth Schmeling in this volume.

18 Outside the *Cena* Trimalchio's existence is acknowledged only fleetingly in the transitional passage immediately following the episode (79.6).

Bibliography

Arrowsmith, W. (1966), 'Luxury and Death in the *Satyricon*', *Arion* 5: 304–31.

Auerbach, E. (1953), 'Fortunata,' Chapter 2 in *Mimesis. The Representation of Reality in Western Literature*, transl. W. Trask. Princeton, NJ: Princeton University Press, pp. 26–33.

Bartsch, S. (1994), *Actors in the Audience. Theatricality and Doublespeak from Nero to Hadrian*, Cambridge, MA.: Harvard University Press.

Beard, M. (1998), '*Vita inscripta*', in *La Biographie Antique* (Entretiens sur l'Antiquité Classique, tome XLIV), Geneva: Fondation Hardt, pp. 83–114.

Bessone, F. (1993), 'Discorsi dei liberti e parodia del "Simposio" platonico nella "Cena Trimalchionis"', *Materiali e discussioni per l'analisi dei testi classici* 30: 63–86.

Bodel, J. (1989), 'Trimalchio and the Candelabrum', *Classical Philology* 84: 224–31.

—— (1994), 'Trimalchio's Underworld,' in J. Tatum (ed.), *The Search for the Ancient Novel*, Baltimore/Los Angeles/London: Johns Hopkins University Press, 237–59.

Boyce, B. (1991), *The Language of the Freedmen in Petronius' Cena Trimalchionis* (*Mnemosyne* Supplement, 117), Leiden: E.J. Brill.

Callebat, L. (1974), 'Structures narratives et modes de représentation dans le *Satyricon* de Pétrone', *Révue des Etudes Latines* 52: 281–303.

Cameron, A. (1969), 'Petronius and Plato', *Classical Quarterly* n.s. 19: 367–70.

Citroni, M. (1975), 'Due note marginali a Petronio', *Maia* 27: 297–305.
Conte, G. B. (1996), *The Hidden Author. An Interpretation of Petronius' Satyricon*, Berkeley: University of California.
D'Arms, J. H. (1981) 'The "Typicality" of Trimalchio', Chapter 5 in *Commerce and Social Standing in Ancient Rome*, Cambridge, MA: Harvard University Press, pp. 97–120.
De la Mare, A. C. (1976), 'The Return of Petronius to Italy,' in J. J. G. Alexander and M. T. Gibson (eds), *Medieval Learning and Literature: Essays presented to Richard William Hunt*, Oxford: Oxford University Press, pp. 220–54.
Dimundo, R. (1983), 'Da Socrate a Eumolpo. Degradazione dei personaggi e delle funzioni nella novella del fanciullo di Pergamo', *Materiali e discussioni per l'analisi dei testi classici* 10–11: 255–65.
Döpp, S. (1991), 'Leben und Tod' in Petrons "Satyrica"', in G. Binder and B. Effe (eds), *Tod und Jenseits im Altertum*, Trier: Wissenschaftlicher Verlag Trier, pp. 144–66.
Dupont, F. (1977), *Le Plaisir et la loi: Du "Banquet" de Platon au "Satiricon"*, Paris: François Maspero.
Fedeli, P. (1981), 'Petronio: il viaggio, il labirinto', *Materiali e discussioni per l'analisi dei testi classici* 6: 91–117.
—— (1987), 'Petronio: Crotone o il mondo alla rovescia', *Aufidus* 1: 3–34.
Gaide, F. (1995), 'Intuitions linguistiques de Pétrone dans sa mise en scène des affranchis de la *Cena*', *Latomus* 54: 856–63.
Gaselee, S. (1915), *A Collotype Reproduction of that Portion of the Codex Paris. 7989, commonly called the Codex Traguriensis, which contains the Cena Trimalchionis of Petronius, together with Four Poems ascribed to Petronius in Codex Leid. Voss. 111,* Cambridge.
Herzog, R. (1989), 'Fest, Terror und Tod in Petrons *Satyrica*', in W. Haug and R. Warnings (eds), *Das Fest* (Poetik and Hermeneutik XIV), Munich: Wilhelm Fink, pp. 120–50.
Horsfall, N. (1989), 'The Uses of Literacy and the *Cena Trimalchionis*', *Greece and Rome* 36: 74–89, 194–209.
Hubbard, T. (1986), 'The narrative architecture of Petronius's *Satyricon*', *L'Antiquité Classique* 55: 190–212.
Jones, C. P. (1991), 'Dinner Theater', in W.J. Slater (ed.), *Dining in a Classical Context*, Ann Arbor: University of Michigan Press, 139–55.
Jones, F. (1991), 'Realism in Petronius', in H. Hofmann (ed.), *Groningen Colloquia on the Novel*, vol. 4, Groningen: Egbert Forsten, 105–20.
Kloft, H. (1994), Trimalchio als Ökonom. Bemerkungen zur Rolle der Wirtschaft in Petrons *Satyrica*', in R. Günther and S. Rebenich (eds), *E fontibus haurire: Beiträge zur römischen Geschichte und zu ihren Hilfswissenschaften*, Paderborn/Munich/Vienna/Zurich: Schöningh, 117–131.
Magnani, L. (1991), 'Paura della morte, angoscia della vita di gente comune in Petronio', in *Gli affanni del vivere e del morire*, Brescia: Grafo, 131–49.
Martin, J. (1931), *Symposion. Die Geschichte einer literarischen Form*, Paderborn: F. Schöningh.
Martin, R. (1988), 'La *Cena Trimalchionis*: les trois niveaux d'un festin,' *Bulletin de l'Association Guillaume Budé*: 232–47.
Müller, K. (ed.) (1995), *Petronii Arbitri Satyricon Reliquiae*, fourth edn, Stuttgart/Leipzig: B.G. Teubner.

Panayotakis, C. (1995), *Theatrum Arbitri. Theatrical Elements in the Satyrica of Petronius* (*Mnemosyne* Supplement, 146), Leiden: E.J. Brill.

Sandy, G. N. (1974), 'Scaenica Petroniana', *Transactions of the American Philological Association* 104: 329–46.

Saylor, C. (1987), 'Funeral Games: The Significance of Games in the *Cena Trimalchionis*', *Latomus* 46: 593–602.

Schlant, E. (1991), 'Petronius: Our Contemporary', *Helios* 18: 49–71.

Schmeling, G. (1991), 'The *Satyricon*: The Sense of an Ending', *Rheinisches Museum* 134: 352–77.

Shero, L. R. (1923), 'The *Cena* in Roman Satire', *Classical Philology* 18: 126–43.

Slater, N. W. (1990), *Reading Petronius*, Baltimore/London: Johns Hopkins University Press.

Smith, M.S. (ed.) (1975) *Petronii Arbitri Cena Trimalchionis*, Oxford: Clarendon Press.

Stephens, S.A., and Winkler, J.J. (eds) (1995), *Ancient Greek Novels: The Fragments*, Princeton, NJ: Princeton University Press.

Sullivan, J. P. (1968), *The Satyricon of Petronius. A Literary Study*, London: Faber and Faber.

Van Thiel, H. (1971), *Petron. Überlieferung und Rekonstruktion* (*Mnemosyne* Supplement, 20), Leiden: E.J. Brill.

Veyne, P. (1961), 'Vie de Trimalcion', *Annales ESC* 16: 213–47.

Wesseling, B. (1993), 'Leven, Liefde en Dood: motieven in antieke romans', Diss. Groningen.

Zeitlin, F. (1971), 'Romanus Petronius: A Study of the *Troiae Halosis* and the *Bellum Civile*', *Latomus* 30: 56–82.

3

THE NOVELLA IN PETRONIUS

Graham Anderson

Together with the examples in Apuleius' *Metamorphoses*, the inset tales in Petronius' *Satyrica* mark the high point of Latin use of an elusive literary form. The novella as a short realistic story was already well established in Greek literature. As early as the eighth book of the *Odyssey*, the tale of Ares and Aphrodite's adultery offers us a fully-fledged novella of typical subject-matter and context: an artistically-wrought and immediate anecdote, often of lust, stupidity or cunning, with a popular 'feel', and often an element of encasement and audience reaction.[1] The form is capable of a variety of moral registers, of enlivening with rhetoric and humour, and of shaping to extend the audience or readers' view of the character of the teller. It is also capable of embodying and enlivening popular or literary materials that are encountered in other genres as diverse as fable and historiography.

There are at least five fully-worked novellas inset into the extant portion of Petronius' still incomplete and enigmatic text: if the traditional book indications are correct, the first sixteen books of the *Satyrica* might have contained something in the region of twenty to thirty inset novellas, giving it a sense of a container for such materials in the same way as Apuleius' version of the ass story was to become. We should also note the tendency of individual episodes in the text to resemble novella in character, perhaps most notably the paradoxical situation where the runaways find themselves trying to buy a worthless garment with a purse sewn into it in the market place (*Sat.* 12–15), or the episode where Eumolpus describes Ascyltus' loss of his clothes at the baths (*Sat.* 92.6–10). This should not surprise us: racy storytelling at a popular level is close to the essence of the comic novel, to a far greater extent than in the case of its 'ideal' counterpart.

I Unbreakable glass and unfaithful wife (*Sat.* 51 and 111 f.)

First we might look at two novellas, one all but ignored and the other celebrated, to notice how material handled in novella form might contrast with its use in other genres. It is useful to begin with the story of the artist and the broken glass, as it suggests the bare minimum required for almost any kind of story. In Dio Cassius' version (57.21.5ff.) the story is given as follows:

> At this time too the great stoa in Rome, which had begun to subside, was restored to an upright position in an amazing way. For a certain architect, whose name nobody knows (for Tiberius, out of envy for his amazing feat, would not allow his name to be recorded) – this man, whoever he was, strengthened the foundations all round to prevent movement, and packed the rest of the structure with wool and thick matting, and secured it firmly with hawsers on all sides, propped it up by means of a huge team of men and machines, and restored it to its original position. At this Tiberius both admired and envied the man, and rewarded him out of admiration, but exiled him from the city out of jealousy. After this when the man approached him to plead his case, and at this point purposely let fall a glass vessel and rubbing it with his hands – it was dented in some way or damaged – he instantly demonstrated that it was unbroken, in the hope of securing a pardon, but Tiberius had him killed.

Here we are given materials clearly believed by Dio to be historically authentic; the first part is simply a factual account of an engineering operation; the tale of the glass is little more than an anecdotal tailpiece. The 'historical' anecdote integrates the anonymous inventor carefully into a context, into the reign of a specific emperor, with virtually no comment or embellishment. For Dio the story illustrates the none-too-benign disposition of the emperor, and that in turn accounts for the anonymous identity of the principal character.

We can now consider the material transformed into a Petronian anecdote. The host Trimalchio has been rambling on about his 'Corinthian' ware, and comes round to musing on the price of glass (*Sat.* 51):

> But there was a craftsman who made a glass cup which wouldn't break. And so he was granted an audience with the emperor with his gift <and having given it to him> he got the emperor to give it back and let it fall on the floor. Caesar was frightened out of his wits. But the fellow picked up the vessel from the floor; it was dented just like brass; then he brought out a little hammer and taking his time knocked it neatly back into shape. For this feat he expected that he would sit on Jove's own throne, then when the emperor asked 'does anyone else know how to cast glass like this?' now listen (*vide modo*): when he said no, Caesar ordered him to have his head chopped off; because if it had become known, gold would have become dirt cheap.

The operative part of the tale is now much more detailed in Petronius, with the focus on the step-by-step demonstration by the clever protagonist. The story, like that of so many novellas, is implied to be recent; the names do not matter in the same way as they do to the historian who has to account for their omission. There is nothing of the overall profession of the inventor, considerably grander than that of the mere *faber* he is here; nothing either of the previous record of antipathy on the emperor's part. Instead we have a lively blow-by-blow account, with the homely detail of the emperor frightened to death when the vessel is let drop (*Caesar non pote valdius quam expavit*), in contrast to the assured performance of the *faber* himself. Then the lively and telling detail: the workman sees himself in the seventh heaven, not realizing the calculation of the emperor or thinking through the true economic implication of his invention; nor indeed realising that he might have saved his life or played for time by wrongly claiming that his secret was well known. But most telling of all is the integration between the story and its teller. When Trimalchio is talking about ancient myth the results are horrendous: when he is talking about money, wealth, and speculation in the present he is a master narrator right on the mark.[2] His stories also have a certain appetite for violence: life is as cheap to Tiberius as it is to the often tyrannical Trimalchio himself, quite capable of crucifying a slave for a trivial reason.

There is no doubt of the story's historicity, but in terms of popular narrative it might be seen as an unusual variant on a very common tale. The popular form is that of the naive optimist who hopes for a fortune from a glass vessel or something similarly fragile, and builds on it hopes which ill-luck or carelessness will shatter. The tell-tale phrase in Petronius' story is really that the craftman, *putabat se solium Iovis tenere* ('thought he was in possession of Jupiter's throne'): in our parlance, he is building castles in Spain or castles in the air. In the *Tale of the Hunchback* in the *Arabian Nights* the dominant character is a lively sinister storyteller in a picaresque context: one of his tales is about the owner of a splendid glass bowl who hopes to make his fortune with it – only to find himself the victim of attempted murder and of an official exile.[3] In this case the 'glass of hope' is broken in the normal way: but we might be left with the suspicion that Petronius could have adapted and updated a traditional 'castles in Spain' story to take account of the latest technology: timeless folktale is succinctly transformed into topical novella.

In contrast to this curiosity, the story of the *Widow of Ephesus* well illustrates the fullest generic expectations we might have of novella.[4] This is generally felt as the defining example of 'Milesian Tale', an entertainment of pornographic tendency after Aristides of Miletus.[5] In fact there is nothing explicitly pornographic about any ancient version of this tale, though the ethos is certainly permissive. But there is also an important cultural connexion of the famous version in Petronius in a fable collection, *Appendix Perottina* 15, reconstructing a lost fable of the first-century verse fabulist Phaedrus; and we are not surprised to find a part analogue either at the conclusion of the *Life of Aesop*; the subsequent *Nachleben* of the story tends to stress the theme of the wickedness of women which Petronius seems to tone down considerably. On the other hand the ethic with which Petronius presents the story was to imbue the *Decameron* in due course: the idea that sexual meanness and public reputation are in the end false values when confronted with sexual needs and common sense. Huber's valuable study underlines the place of this tale in the repertoire of fable and exemplum (1990: 57–150): at its simplest level it underlines the same resourceful and hard-headed art of survival as so many of the animal fables.

The skeleton of fable and Petronian versions is one and the same: a widow celebrated for wifely devotion abandons her vigil over her late husband's corpse for an affair with a soldier; required to supply a substitute for the body he failed to guard, she offers her husband's. However Petronius ensures a vital difference by putting the story into the mouth of the degenerate poet Eumolpus, whose own eye for sexual opportunism suits a salacious rendition of the story (see, in particular, Beck 1979). It is an orally delivered experience, supposedly to reduce tension on a fraught sea-voyage.[6] Once more the novella character of the tale is emphasized by Eumolpus' troubling to tell us that *nec se veteres tragoedias curare aut nomina saeculis nota, sed rem sua memoria factam* ('he wasn't concerned with antique tragedies or famous names from history, but with something that took place within his own memory') (*Sat.* 110.8); and the story is given a sense of audience (*conversis igitur omnium in se vultibus auribusque sic orsus est* ('So when everyone's eyes and ears were turned to him, he began the following story.'). It is explicitly told in the context of misogynist materials, which are one suspects thoroughly ingrained in popular storytelling in any case; but as a self-consciously educated poet in his own right, Eumolpus is able to offer a sophisticated rendition. Roger Beck (1979: 249) has emphasized the degree to which Eumolpus himself is successful because of his own basis in experience: here is a practised lecher well able to delineate the exploitative side of human nature. Conte for his part underlines the alliance in the story between food and sex: *ceterum scitis quid plerumque soleat temptare humanam satietatem* ('But you know what tends to tempt the human body when it has had its fill of food') (*Sat.* 112.1) (cf. Conte 1996: 106f.). Commentators since Collignon generally underline the effect of echoes of Dido in the widow who has found a new lover: Dido's grand suicide gesture then gives way all the more stridently to commonsense self-preservation. Petronius' achievement overall is in timing as well as texture, and in the use of masterly ambiguity: the widow's substitution of her husband's corpse for that of the crucified criminal is contrived in the most natural possible way by steps quite inconsequential in themselves, and the listeners' attention is then cleverly deflected in the conclusion of the tale by the puzzle of how the new body appeared on the cross. In this last sentence the tale steers back to the sense of 'strange but true' that so readily interacts with lust and infidelity in the world of novella.

A comparison with the version from Phaedrus in Perotti's appendix[7] underlines the limitations of fable as opposed to novella; Phaedrus' original would most probably have been written several decades before the traditional date of Petronius. In the first place we find that the fable presents a widow of nowhere in particular: the Petronian novella version is specific and documentary, and there is a certain piquancy to the widow's belonging to Ephesus, a city noted for its moral self-indulgence.[8] Here, interestingly, she does not start acquiring her reputation for chastity till after she begins the vigil at the husband's tomb: comparison with Petronius shows how much his novella version is enriched and exaggerated here, with the widow a tourist attraction even while her husband is alive, a touch which will underline her fall all the more. A noticeable minor detail appears at this point in the fable version, where we are actually told why the corpses on the cross had been crucified: the reason has of course nothing to do with the widow as such; but the victims had been punished for pillaging a temple of Jupiter, and so the notion of propriety and social constraint is emphasized (*Appendix Perrottina* 15.6f.).

The treatment of the soldier is more direct and to the point in the fable: he simply asks the widow's maid for a drink of water, catches a glimpse of the widow, and sets about finding a way to seduce her. What becomes the artistic hub of Petronius' novella is given a matter of a few lines in the fable: *cotidiana capta consuetudine/paulatim facta est advenae submissior/mox artior revinxit animum copula* ('she was won over by her daily contact with the man; little by little she became more resigned to the stranger; and soon a tighter bond came to hold her heart to him'; *Appendix Perottina* 15.22ff.). Petronius' hint of sensuality is still more delicate: *nec deformis aut infacundus iuvenis castae videbatur* ('chaste as she was, she thought he was not unpleasing either in his looks or his conversation'). The widow's reaction when the corpse disappears is less pointed in the fable, though irony is retained (*at sancta mulier . . .*); but the final epimythion is carefully contrived: *sic turpitudo laudis obsedit locum* ('thus did vice besiege the place of virtue') (*Appendix Perottina* 15.31).

Petronius' version also deviates interestingly not only from the emphasis of the Phaedran version and its medieval relatives in fable and exempla, but from the clearly notable oriental form in which the widow is either accosted by the revitalized husband, who has only been testing the fickleness of women, or by a supernatural reminder of her oath. In such versions the widow herself is clearly the villain and is eligible for punishment by some kind of divine justice or by the still living husband himself (Ure 1956: 5; Bömer 1986: 139). There may be a disembodied hint of this development in Lichas' revisionist version on hearing the dénouement of Eumolpus' performance: if the emperor had been just, the widow herself should have been put up on the cross (*Sat.* 113.2).

*

Petronius' version of the story, then, remains elusive: even in isolation from its many folktale parallels and analogues it is clearly being exploited by a much more sophisticated author than Phaedrus for its ambiguity, hence the divided reactions among the audience who are listening. We should compare the dispute expected over the punishment of Glyco's adulterous steward (between lovers and outraged husbands, *Sat.* 45.7). This makes the task of constructing reader-oriented criticism all the more difficult: I am not sure I can agree with Slater (1990: 109) about the theatrical aspect of the tale: the widow is certainly a *fabula*, (111.5) but in an entirely different sense: she is story rather than drama, though indeed she is a cynosure of all around her; but the people wondering about how the husband's body went up on the cross are scarcely an audience in the same sense (or Petronius could have emphasized the point much more clearly had he wished). But Conte (1996: 105–10) is undoubtedly right to regard the episode as a microcosm of the *Satyrica* and its values overall, neatly underlining the analogy between the widow's sacrifice of the husband's body and Oenothea's recycling of the murdered goose of Priapus as a meal. The real vitality of Petronius' version is concentrated in the sudden reversion to practicality: *iubet ex arca corpus mariti sui tolli atque illi quae vacabat cruci affigi. usus est miles ingenio prudentissimae feminae* ('she ordered the body of her own husband to be brought from the coffin and nailed to the empty cross. The soldier took advantage of the quick thinking of the most sensible of women . . .'; *Sat.* 112, 8).

II The tale of the Pergamene boy (*Sat.* 85ff.)

Eumolpus' earlier major tale anticipates the theme of the widow: that modesty when roused will outstrip its assailant. This story too must clearly rank as a Milesian tale: and this time it is told in the first person by Eumolpus, introducing his credentials as a skilled paederastic seducer who almost boasts of his own virtuosity in both hypocrisy and seduction.[9] By posing as a puritan Eumolpus insinuates himself into a household where he can whisper to the son of the household three successive bribes, with the present of a dove, a pair of game-cocks, and a thoroughbred horse. Only the first two are delivered: he finally sleeps with the boy but does not pay the reward. However after initial indignation the boy himself now shows an appetite, and after a further seduction begins to wear Eumolpus out.

The action of the Pergamene boy is accomplished with the help of a threefold whispering in sleep: one might compare the story in the Italian folktale *il pecoraio a corte*, where a mysterious stranger muses in his sleep about the three gifts he will give the young boy who obliges him; [10] on the other hand the presents, or at least the first two offered are in line with the normal presents expected of an *erastes* on Greek vase-paintings. The outline may well exhibit a standard structure in folktale (a rule of three, with a significant difference third time round, and a tag line turning the tables).

But Eumolpus is also a master raconteur, of a story cleverly told against himself in the end. The ambience of the tale is very rapidly established: it takes place when Eumolpus is on the staff of a governor of Asia, and once more is established as contemporary (though some years back). Unfortunately in this case the setting is bedevilled by lacunae: it is most probably part of the picture-gallery scene, told to Encolpius under the same circumstances as Clitophon's story is told to the narrator of Achilles Tatius (1.2), but we cannot be certain. The tale works at a higher level to define quickly the side of Eumolpus' character that marks him out both as a fit companion for Encolpius and his runaways, and as a threat to the anti-hero's relationship with the young Giton. The analogy with Socrates and Alcibiades has been aptly advanced, but is not explicitly invoked by either Petronius or his narrator.[11]

III The tales of Niceros and Trimalchio (*Sat.* 61.6–63.10)

Two tales in the *Cena Trimalchionis* form a lively pair of ghost stories. One of Trimalchio's freedman guests tells a tale of how he set off to sleep with a newly widowed innkeeper's wife, Melissa of Tarentum (61.6–62.14). A companion he took on the way turns into a werewolf, attacks Melissa's livestock and is wounded by a servant, as the terrified man finds on his arrival. He is able to match the wound when the lycanthrope resumes his normal shape. Is this simply a tale made up by Petronius for the purposes of the occasion, or is it part of a larger tradition? One example may serve to warn us how often similarities occur in popular material of this kind. The distinctive feature of Niceros' tale is that it is not just a werewolf story, but an unusual combination of a tale of sex and superstition: we might call it 'The werewolf and the timid lover'. A medieval Spanish tale[12] has the portrait of a lover who is so terrified by superstitious fears on the way that his would-be mistress rejects him. One suspects we are looking at a scaled-down version of the same tale once more, but with a catalogue of terrors instead of the werewolf. Such a background would help to explain the oddity of Niceros' reception by Melissa: she seems to blame him for not arriving quickly enough to help her, and the night's excitement might entitle us to infer that he will not enjoy her favours after all.

Trimalchio's tale might also be classified as a ghost-story once more (63.3–10), but like the story of Niceros which it follows it rigorously maintains the factors essential to the feel of the novella. In the first place the context and presentation have an air of spontaneity about them. Trimalchio begins by reacting as if convinced by the previous story: *ut mihi pili inhorruerunt* ('how my hair stood on end') and he emphasizes the credibility of the narrator: *quia scio Niceronem nihil nugarum narrare: immo certus est et minime linguosus* ('because I know Niceros doesn't tell idle tales: on the contrary he's reliable and doesn't embroider). It is as if 'it really happened to him but it's nothing to what happened to me . . .'. The story happened a long time ago, but within Trimalchio's memory, and he himself was a witness. When he himself was a long-haired slave, his master's favourite slave died. The liveliness of the description in no more than a few words increases the effect of spontaneous reminiscence: *mehercules margaritum, catamitus et omnium numerum* ('a gem, my goodness, a darling boy, one in a million'). Trimalchio always has an eye for good-looking boys, and the phrases reinforce his own personal bonding with the narrative. The punch line of the tale is delivered succinctly: *subito strigae coeperunt* ('suddenly the witches started') (while the mourning was in progress). Then we are on to a still more elaborate thumbnail sketch: *habebamus tunc hominem Cappadocem, longum, valde audaculum et qui valebat*: *poterat bovem iratum tollere* ('we had at the time a Cappadocian fellow, a tall chap, a bloke with real guts and strong: he would have lifted an angry ox'). The action takes place in three movements: he does battle with a witch, but himself retires wounded; a changeling is substituted for the mourned child; and finally the witch-hunting slave dies. But Trimalchio has enlivened the tale with oral mannerisms: he begs protection for the part of himself corresponding to the part of the witch the slave wounded, but he casually lets slip that neither he nor anyone else actually saw the witches. The more 'all in the mind' the story, the more authentic as a projection of popular fear. The ironic comments of Encolpius, who obviously does not believe any of the tale, but is obliged to go along with Trimalchio's superstitious humour, rounds off the episode. The ultrasophisticated commentator maintains a nuance of embarrassment: Trimalchio, he seems to imply, is even worse than his uneducated guests. We are meant not only to enjoy the considerable artistry and entertainment of this uneducated tale, but also to savour the discomfiture of the educated listener relaying it to us. . . .

This is perhaps the best example of a minimalist story: not a great deal happens, yet lively delivery, present reference, and audience reaction all contribute to the sense of an amazing but authentic event. If not actually hot news as novella characteristically purports to be, Trimalchio's story is the next best thing.

IV Conclusion

In comparison with the novellas of Apuleius those of Petronius are better restrained, controlled and crafted to their context; they are also a good deal less improvisatory and yet in some respects no less puzzling. In each case we can at least notice either the certainty or a hint of popular tales, often with a wisdom element. A complete understanding of the significance of such episodes and their interrelationship is only likely to come after much more study of the analogues of picaresque tales, and of the overall purpose and character of the *Satyrica* itself; but the presence of fortune and 'a man and his luck' certainly looms large. Petronius' distinctive contribution has been by way of refinement and pointing of detail, and in the interaction of tales, contexts and storytellers. I let Niceros have the last word: he is downcast when Trimalchio sets him off into his story, and immediately he is a natural virtuoso in stream-of-consciousness narrative with multiple corroborative detail: [13]

> While I was still a slave, we were living in a little back street: it's Gavilla's house now. There, by the will of the gods, I began to fall in love with the wife of Terentius the inn-keeper: you used to know Melissa from Tarentum, the loveliest wench imaginable. But I swear it wasn't her body or sex I was interested in, but more because she had such a nice nature. If I asked her for anything, she never said no . . .

We never actually find out how the affair ended: is Niceros' dejection because of the opportunity he missed through his encounter with the werewolf? It is Petronius' genius to capture the inconsequences and turn them into much more. Whatever the shape of the *Satyrica* overall, the novellas illustrate his facility and genuine rapport with popular material, and his total command of detail.

Notes

1 For the materials, scope, and development of the genre in Greek literature, Trenkner 1958; Cataudella 1957: 7–172. For a general overview of the Latin materials, Pepe 1991, and the *Acta* of the Perugia interdisciplinary seminar on the Latin Novella collected as *Semiotica della novella latina* (Rome 1986).

2 Cf. Pepe 1991: 86. For further discussion, Santini 1986.

3 'The Tale of Al-Ashar the Barber's Fifth Brother', tr. N.J. Dawood, *Tales from the Thousand and One Nights*, Harmondsworth 1973: 61–68.

4 On the history of the tale tradition as a whole, see especially Huber 1990 (detailed discussion of Petronius' handling, 12–56), still supplemented by Ure 1956; commentary: Pecere 1975; further recent discussion: Pepe 1981; Cicu 1986; Conte 1996: 105–9. As a duo with 'The Pergamene Boy', Parca 1981; Sega 1986.

5 On the *Milesiaca* and their relationship to the novella tradition, Cataudella 1957: 126–64; Walsh 1970: 10–17; Pacchieni 1978; Müller 1980; Lefèvre 1997b: 15–32 (among much).

6 It may be worthwhile to note the kind of risqué sexual discussion conducted on board ship in Achilles Tatius (2.35–38).

7 For detailed discussion, Pecere 1975: 3–14; Massaro 1981; Huber 1990: 67–82.

8 One thinks of the Ephesian widow Melite in Achilles Tatius, who does not hesitate to take a lover when she finds out that she had not been widowed after all (5.27).

9 On the novella, Dimundo 1982/3, 1983, 1986; paired with the Widow, Parca 1981; Sega 1986; Lefèvre 1997a; Lefèvre 1997b: 8–15.

10 The lad made himself as small as possible so as not to disturb him, keeping perfectly still to give the impression he was sleeeping; but he couldn't shut his eyes for watching the man. Nor was the man sleeping, but mumbling to himself under the illusion the boy was asleep. 'What present can I make this boy who lined the stone for me with leaves and who's thoughtful enough to stay on his side and not disturb me? I can give him a linen napkin which unfolded produces dinner for everybody present, I can give him a little box which opened produces a gold coin. I can give him a harmonica which played sets everyone within earshot to dancing.

Italo Calvino, *Italian Folktales*, tr. G. Martin, Harmondsworth 1982, p. 203 (after Nerucci)

11 See Dimundo 1983. Much depends on how far one is prepared to accept the implication of an analogy between the arrival of Alcibiades in Plato's *Symposium* and that of Habinnas in the *Cena*, on which see Averil Cameron, 'Petronius and Plato', *Classical Quarterly* N.S. 19 (1969): 367–70 and J. Bodel, Chapter 2, this volume.

12 Brewer 1996: 42 f. (*Arcipreste de Talavera*, by Alfonso Martinez de Toledo, 1438, tr. by A. Deyermond as 'The Timid Lover's Expedition'); for extensive bibliography, Brewer, ibid. 182.

13 On Niceros' tale as an example of oral narrative see Blänsdorf 1990.

Bibliography

Beck, R. (1979), 'Eumolpus *Poeta*, Eumolpus *Fabulator*: A Study of Characterization in the *Satyricon*', *Phoenix* 33: 239–53.

Benz, L. (1997), 'Die Fabula Milesia und die griechisch-römische Novellistik', in L. Benz (ed.), *Script Oralia Romana. Die römische Literatur zwischen Mündlichkeit und Schriftlichkeit*, Tübingen: Gunter Narr.

Blänsdorf, J. (1990), 'Die Werwolf-Geschichte des Niceros bei Petron als Beispiel literarischer Fiktion mündlichen Erzählens', in G. Vogt-Spira (ed.), *Strukturen der Mündlichkeit in der römischen Literatur*, Tübingen: Gunter Narr, pp. 193–217.

Bömer, F. (1986), 'Die Witwe von Ephesus: Petron 111,1ff. und die 877. in Tausendundeiner Nacht', *Gymnasium* 93: 138–40.

Brewer, D. (ed.) (1996), *Medieval Comic Tales*, Cambridge: D.S. Brewer.

Cataudella, Q. (1957), *La novella greca*, Naples: Edizioni Scientifiche Italiane.

Cicu, L. (1986), 'La matrona di Efeso di Petronio', *Studi Italiani di Filologia Classica* 79: 249–71.

Conte, G.B. (1996), *The Hidden Author: An Interpretation of Petronius'* Satyricon, Berkeley/Los Angeles/London: University of California Press.

Dimundo, R. (1982/83), 'La novella del fanciullo di Pergamo. Struttura narrativa e tecnica del racconto', *Annali della Facoltà di Lettere e Filosofia di Bari*, 15/16: 133–78.

—— (1983), 'Da Socrate a Eumolpo: Degradazione dei personaggi e delle funzioni nella novella del fanciullo di Pergamo', *Materiali e Discussioni per l'analisi dei testi classici*, 10/11: 255–65.

—— (1986), 'La novella dell'Efebo di Pergamo: struttura del racconto', in L. Pepe (ed.) *Semiotica della novella latina, Atti del seminario interdisciplinare 'La novella latina'*, Perugia 11–13 April 1985, Rome: Herder Editrice e Libreria, pp. 83–94.

Fedeli, P. (1986), 'La matrona di Efeso. Strutture narrative e tecnica dell'inversione', in L. Pepe (ed.) *Semiotica della novella latina, Atti del seminario interdisciplinare 'La novella latina'*, Perugia 11–13 April 1985, Rome: Herder Editrice e Libreria, pp. 9–35.

George, P.A. (1966), 'Style and Character in the *Satyricon*', *Arion* 5: 336–58.

Harrison, S.J. (forthcoming), 'The Milesian Tales and the Roman Novel,' in H. Hofmann and M. Zimmerman (eds.), *Groningen Colloquia on the Novel*, vol. 9, Groningen: Egbert Forsten.

Huber, G. (1990), *Das Motiv der 'Witwe von Ephesus' in lateinischen Texten der Antike und des Mittelalters*, Tübingen: Gunter Narr.

Lefèvre, E. (1997a), 'Der Ephebe von Pergamon (Petron *c.* 85–87)', in M. Picone and B. Zimmermann (eds) *Der antike Roman und seine mittelalterliche Rezeption*, Basle/Boston/Berlin: Birkhäuser, pp. 129–35.

—— (1997b), *Studien zur Struktur der 'Milesischen' Novelle bei Petron und Apuleius*, Akademie der Wissenschaften und der Literatur Mainz, Abhandlungen der geistes- und sozialwissenschaftlichen Klasse 1997, Nr. 5, Stuttgart: Franz Steiner.

Massaro, M. (1981), 'La redazione fedriana della Matrona di Efeso', *Materiali e contributi per la storia della narrativa greco-latina*, 3: 217–37.

Müller, C.W. (1980), 'Die Witwe von Ephesus: Petrons Novelle und die *Milesiaka* des Aristeides', *Antike und Abendland* 26: 103–21.

Pacchieni, M. (1978), *La novella 'milesia' in Petronio*, Lecce: Edizione Milella.

Parca, M. (1981), 'Deux récits milésiens chez Pétrone: *Satyricon* 85–87 et 111–112: une étude comparative', *Revue belge de philologie et d'histoire*, 59: 91–106.

Pecere, O. (1975), *Petronio, La novella della matrona di Efeso*, Padua: Antenore.

Pepe, L. (1981), 'I predicati di base nella Matrona di Efeso petroniana', *Materiali e contributi per la storia della narrativa greco-latina* 3, Perugia, 411–24.

—— (ed.) (1986), *Semiotica della novella latina. Atti del seminario interdisciplinare 'La novella latina'*, Perugia 11–13 April 1985, Rome: Herder Editrice e Libreria.

—— (1991), *La novella dei romani*, Naples: Loffredo.

Perry, B.E. (1967), *The Ancient Romances: A Literary-Historical Account of their Origins* (*Sather Classical Lectures*, 37), Berkeley/Los Angeles: University of California Press.

Rastier, F. (1971), 'La morale de l'histoire: Notes sur la Matrone d'Ephèse (*Satiricon*, CXI–CXII)', *Latomus* 30: 1025–56.

Santini, C. (1986), 'Il vetro infrangibile (Petronio 51)', in L. Pepe (ed.) *Semiotica della novella latina, Atti del seminario interdisciplinare 'La novella latina'*, Perugia 11–13 April 1985, Rome: Herder Editrice e Libreria, pp. 117–24.

Scobie, A. (1969), *Aspects of the Ancient Romance and its Heritage. Essays on Apuleius, Petronius, and the Greek Romance* (*Beiträge zur klassischen Philologie*, 30), Meisenheim am Glan: Hain.

—— (1979), 'Storytellers, Storytelling and the Novel in Graeco-Roman Antiquity', *Rheinisches Museum* 122: 229–59.

Sega, G. (1986), 'Due milesie: la Matrona di Efeso e l'Efebo di Pergamo', in L. Pepe (ed.) *Semiotica della novella latina, Atti del seminario interdisciplinare 'La novella latina'*, Perugia 11–13 April 1985, Rome: Herder Editrice e Libreria, pp. 37–81.

Slater, N. W. (1990), *Reading Petronius*, Baltimore/London: Johns Hopkins University Press.

Smith, M.S. (1975), *Petronii Arbitri Cena Trimalchionis*, Oxford: Clarendon Press.

Sullivan, J.P. (1968), *Petronius' Satyricon: A Literary Study*, London: Faber and Faber.

Trenkner, S. (1958), *The Greek Novella in the Classical Period*, Cambridge: Cambridge University Press.

Ure, P. (1956), 'The Widow of Ephesus: Some Reflexions on an International Comic Theme', *Durham University Journal* 18: 1–9.

Walsh, P.G. (1970), *The Roman Novel: The* Satyricon *of Petronius and the* Golden Ass *of Apuleius*, Cambridge: Cambridge University Press.

4

REREADING THE ARBITER

Arbitrium and verse in the *Satyrica* and in '*Petronius redivivus*'

Catherine Connors

Author as arbiter

One of the rather tantalizing scraps of information we have from the ancient world is that Petronius bore the nickname Arbiter.[1] An *arbiter* is a judge, or a decision maker in a more general sense, and *arbitrium* is the exercise of this decider's will; key to these terms is a sense of autonomy of judgment and independence from external constraint.[2] Tacitus' picture of Petronius as Nero's *elegantiae arbiter* (*Annals* 16.18.2) gives a sense of a man of exquisite taste setting the fashion at the court. The *Satyrica* itself can seem the work of an arbiter, one who stands outside a situation and makes judgments about it or controls its outcome. Indeed, the text models this control for us when Ascyltos attributes his discovery of Giton in hiding under a bed to the action of 'some god, arbiter of human affairs' (*deus quidam humanarum rerum arbiter*, 98.6). Conte sees Petronius as a 'hidden author' who manipulates Encolpius' narrative voice; Barchiesi in turn compares this description of authorial manipulation with the connotations of detached judgment and control attached to the name Arbiter.[3] For these modern readers, Petronius as arbiter of the narrative stands outside the traditional limits of genre; the manipulation of many different prose and verse literary forms in the novel is a manifestation of his *arbitrium*.

One of Petronius' rare medieval readers saw connections of a different sort between the name arbiter and the text of the *Satyrica*. This unnamed author, apparently working in England in the late twelfth or early thirteenth century, composed a collection of short satirical pieces combining verse with prose. The collection has been called the work of a '*Petronius redivivus*' because some of its words and phrases seem to be taken from the *Satyrica* and because its mixture of prose and verse seems modelled on the presence of verse (some thirty short poems and two longer ones) in the *Satyrica*. An intriguing curiosity in its own right, the collection also offers a spirited 'reading' and reworking of its Petronian model. It can sharpen our perceptions of the *Satyrica* in two ways. In the first section of this essay I demonstrate that the collection's reworking of Petronian themes draws attention to manifestations of *arbitrium* as an organizing principle of the *Satyrica*. In the essay's second section I use the clear contrast between the medieval collection's verse technique and that of the *Satyrica* as a starting point for considerations of Petronius' verse. Verse in the *Satyrica* is often viewed as merely a sign of the work's possible relations to other genres (especially Menippean Satire or racy prosimetric Greek fiction). A comparison of the *Satyrica* and the medieval text can draw our attention beyond such questions of genre toward a more precise appreciation of Petronius' sophisticated verse.[4]

Although at first glance the eclectic medieval collection may not seem closely connected to the episodic narrative of the *Satyrica*, the medieval author in fact takes his central theme, which I would describe as the exercise of *arbitrium*, from his perceptions of the ancient text. In other words, a previously unacknowledged aspect of the medieval collection's imitative relationship to the *Satyrica* is its playful representation of 'judgment' in legal or extra-legal contexts. I suspect that this concern with the exercise of judgment in the medieval collection results from what the medieval author knew of the author of the *Satyrica*. As the evidence assembled by Müller makes clear, the author of the *Satyrica* was known to readers in the middle ages as Petronius Arbiter or simply as Arbiter.[5] If medieval readers did not have access to Tacitus' *Annals*, they did not have the option of identifying Petronius as Nero's *elegantiae arbiter*.[6] For medieval readers, then, the name *arbiter* would not function as a reference to scenes of Neronian decadence. Instead, the term would refer to the exercise of *arbitrium*, especially in a legal context. It thus makes perfect sense either that a medieval author would keep returning to legal issues in creating his own humorous 'Petronian' text, or (if we imagine things happening the other way around) that in assembling a set of humorous legal or mock-legal pieces he would cast them in a recognizably Petronian form – racy prose interspersed with occasional poems.

I *Arbitrium* as plot

Reading the *Satyrica* itself over this medieval reader's shoulder, we see it anew as a series of brushes with the law. Episodes often involve legal or mock-legal judgments, and even when no 'actual' court proceedings, oaths, rights, or punishments are at issue, legal metaphors or jokes keep breaking out. Whether Petronius and his audience felt any particular word (such as *litigo* or *lites* which can be used of court cases but also of quarrels more generally) to be a live and specifically legal metaphor is less important here than the fact that the medieval author could easily interpret such words as part of the Arbiter's playful manipulations of legal language and institutions.

Under the sign 'Arbiter', the story begins at Agamemnon's 'law school' (1–5). Along the way we learn of Encolpius' 'real' encounters with the law: he has committed crimes and escaped being punished (9.9, cf. 81.3, *effugi iudicium* and 130.2, *proditionem feci, hominem occidi, templum violavi*). In the market scene, Encolpius and his friends happen to see in the possession of a peasant, the tunic which had been stolen from them (with their gold apparently still sewn into its seams); they in turn are accused of possessing a cloak stolen from the peasant or the woman with him; bystanders summon officials to put legal machinery in motion to settle the dispute in court, and a *sequester* is chosen, an agent with whom both garments may be deposited until the court can convene. Faced with the prospect of court the peasant gives up the tunic and the companions retire, thinking they had obtained their money back. Next, Quartilla seeks out the companions to punish them for their 'crime' (17.6, *inexpiabile scelus*), and proposes to release them from the 'appointed case' (*constituta lite*) on the condition that they agree not to divulge what they saw of her Priapic rites. Trimalchio too is a legal joker: he begins the meal by citing the 'dinner rule' *ius cenae* (35.7, punning on *ius*, 'law' and *ius*, 'sauce') and stages the serving of a later course by giving a legal settlement (*ius*) to two disputatious slaves (*litigantes*); rejecting his judgment they smash each other's jars with cudgels and the shellfish which fall out are served to the guests (70.5).

The struggle of Encolpius and Ascyltos for the affections of Giton is repeatedly cast in legal terms. When Ascyltos proposes that Giton choose with whom to live, Encolpius says 'I put the dispute in the hands of the judge' (*commisique iudici litem*, 80.6). In the picture gallery, Encolpius phrases his reactions to the painting of gods and their beloved ones with legal metaphors. He says that the nymph would not have kept Hylas if she had believed that Hercules would challenge her claim 'by injunction' (*interdictum*, 83.5, cf. 13.4), and he sums up his argumentative reaction to the paintings by saying 'while I litigate (*litigo*) with the winds' (83.7, cf. 132.13). At their reunion, Giton hands himself over to Encolpius for punishment, recollecting their earlier parting by calling himself 'your judge' (91.2); Encolpius in turn claims not to have put 'authority over love' (*amoris arbitrium*) into the hands of another judge (*iudex*, 91.7). When strife breaks out aboard Lichas' ship, Eumolpus first produces a formal speech (*declamatio*) to appeal to Lichas (107); the conflict escalates but is finally settled by truce (108.13) and then a treaty (109.1–4).

More lawbreaking is the focus of Eumolpus' tale of the Widow of Ephesus. After the soldier discovers the body he was supposed to be guarding has been stolen he decides to 'administer justice (*dicturum ius*) with the sword for his neglect of duty' rather than 'await the decision of the judge' (*iudicis sententiam*, 112.6) before the widow bids him replace the lost body with her husband's corpse. Encolpius' hexameter prayer to Priapus centres on a legalistic appeal: 'as a poor man, exhausted by destitute circumstances, I committed the crime (*facinus . . . feci*) not with my whole body. Whoever sins (*peccat*) as a poor man is a lesser defendant (*minor est reus*)' (133.7–10). Encolpius phrases his submission to Circe in legal terms in a letter, writing that he is a confident defendant (*confidentem reum*) and that 'whatever you may order, I have deserved' (*quicquid iusseris, merui*) before listing his crimes of betrayal, murder and temple desecration (130.2). The encounter with Oenothea devolves into a plea that Encolpius be able to make financial restitution (*expiare manus pretio*) for the goose he has killed, since it is not as if he has killed a person (137.6). The peculiar provisions of Eumolpus' will (141.2), and its citation of the 'law' of cannibalism in some nations (140.3) might also have caught the eye of a legally minded reader. And of course the whole deception at Croton puts Eumolpus and his lawless companions in a vulnerable position: as Encolpius says, 'how painful it is for those who live outside the law (*extra legem*), always expecting what they deserve' (125.4).

The medieval author thus has before him in the Arbiter's *Satyrica* a text overflowing with jokes about judgment, and in response he himself creates or collects stories which turn on, or end in, an exercise of judgment. His simplest example of legal joking is the anecdote of the student in Bologna (presumably studying law, as Colker 1975: 185 observes) and the thief (6.62). The student is awakened by the thief's attempt to steal his bedclothes. After struggling sleepily with the thief he says that because he is awake the thief can't take the blankets by stealth (*furari*), though he could snatch them by force (*auferre*); amused by the law-student's humour, the thief decides to depart empty-handed. In a pattern typical of the use of prosimetric form in the collection, a concluding poem praises the student's wit in giving up the struggle and the thief's willingness to accept the joke instead of the bedclothes by celebrating humour as a liberating respite from fear and continual striving for money: 'a free life flourishes in the will of the mind' (*mentis in arbitrio libera vita viget*, 6.63).

Four longer and more complex stories tell of adulterous or lustful women as wielders of their own judgment and as objects of men's judgment. In the first the jealous husband of an adulterous wife (described as *pulchram noteque pudicicie matronam* [1.1], in terms borrowed from Eumolpus' opening of his tale of the widow of Ephesus, *matrona . . . tam notae erat pudicitiae*, *Sat.* 111.1) kills first her lover and then the woman herself. But, as the author points out, this action is not permitted under the Julian law on adultery, according to which the husband is not permitted to kill the wife, and the husband can kill the adulterous man with impunity only if he is a pimp, actor, dancer, singer or a freedman of a member of the family.[7] Thereafter, community disapproval of the husband's excessive reaction makes the husband afraid to leave his house.

Male and female decisions are contrasted in the fifth tale. Two merchants making a pilgrimage to Jerusalem in order to pray for financial recovery after a shipwreck hire a servant on the road. Because it is very difficult to judge the trustworthiness of such people (5.29, *diiudicare*), they are unable to tell that he has criminal designs on their money. Before setting off from Apulia for Jerusalem they hide their money beneath a tree on his advice, and when they return, they cannot recover it because he has stolen it and sewn it into his clothing.[8] They appeal to Robert Guiscard of Apulia for help in finding and punishing the thief. While claiming to put off an enquiry for the moment, he tells a long story about his daughter. She loved his steward, whom he sent to the king of France, meanwhile marrying the daughter to a rich man. When the husband heard about the incident with the steward, he told her he wouldn't sleep with her until she was free of her earlier obligation and sent her to her former lover in France bearing a letter explaining the situation. After a happy reunion things went sour when the steward read the letter; she departed angry with a letter of release for her husband from the steward. On the road she met robbers, one of whom wanted to marry her, but she was so resolute in refusing him that after reading the letters he let her go. Once Robert has told of his daughter's desires (first for the steward, then for the husband, then for suicide rather than the bandit), he asks his audience in turn whether they would have accommodated the daughter's desires: he asks the elder merchant if he would have let the daughter go as the husband did ('entrusted to her own will', *suo arbitrio commissam*, 5.55) and the younger merchant if he would have sent her off as the steward did, and they both say yes, they would have honourably yielded to her will. The servant is asked whether he would have let her go as the robber did, and his 'no' makes Robert conclude that the servant stole the merchants' money. Inspection of his clothing reveals the money and he is condemned to the mines. In a manner analogous to the reworking of the widow tale in the first story, the Petronian elements of theft, money in a cloak, and court decisions are recombined in such a way that transgressors are eventually punished.

In the longest story (7), Hero betrays her husband Zetus first by having an affair with his Saracen prisoner Antheus and arranging his escape, then by handing Zetus over to Antheus, and finally by handing Zetus over to a soldier, Nepos. Zetus eventually prevails and asks the community to decide what to do about Hero. They recommend death, but he decides that men should not spill female blood and marries her to his Saracen gardener.[9] The eighth tale's insatiable woman is a wife accompanying her British husband on a crusade because he so desires her. She has sex with the Saracens who enter the cave where she and her husband are spending the night, and betrays him to them. While the Saracens sleep he is able to escape from bondage and kill them, but he decides to leave his wife there instead of killing her too. The stork's tale too puts law on display: a female stork's adultery is detected by her husband, and she is tried, convicted, and executed by a jury of her fellow storks. The author concludes by offering the moral that the human 'decision to live purely' (*ad caste vivendum discretio*) has taken its process of reasoning (*argumentum*) from the natural example of the birds (9.146).

Other stories represent the exercise of judgment outside a legal framework. The account of Nero's death focuses on Nero's indecisiveness in the face of ruin (3.19); in this it differs slightly from the otherwise comparable accounts by Orosius and John of Salisbury.[10] The fourth tale tells of a certain 'I' at London who squandered his inheritance. The people who knew about him judged (*iudicabant*) it amazing that a man who seemed sensible when out in public could make such bad judgments about his patrimony; the author concludes, in phrasing that smacks of his account of the humours (10.147, esp. on *colera*), 'But I think that excess (*superfluitas*) of the table tended to change the early morning's conceived plan in the slipperiness (*lubricitate*) of his mind' (4.34). In the second tale, a wealthy man builds a beautiful house in Campania and invites a catamite (*cinaedus*) to see it. While being given the tour, the guest spits in the owner's face, and upset, the host asks the reason for the insult. The guest replies very wittily (*bellissime*) that he found nowhere more unsightly (*turpius*) in the gorgeous house where he could spit, and asserts that it is right (*fas*) to spit on the face of a man so besotted with earthly vanities (2.17). While the owner of the lavish Campanian house recalls Trimalchio, the *cinaedus* and even the spitting may build on the entrance of the *cinaedus* in the Quartilla episode, 'a man most unappealing in every way, and thoroughly worthy of that house' (*intrat cinaedus, homo omnium insulsissimus et plane illa domo dignus*, 23.2, cf. Colker 1975: 183); after singing a song he gives Encolpius a saliva-drenched kiss (*inmundissimo me basio conspuit,* 23.4).

Certainly in composing his exploration of *arbitrium* the medieval author relishes narrating crime more than punishment. Yet, the text does not indulge completely in Petronian lawlessness: where people in the *Satyrica* get away with most things, in the medieval collection the thief leaves the student his bedclothes, passionate matrons are killed or otherwise punished by being bestowed on Saracens, gold is found in the cloak and the thief punished, and the Campanian rich man gets his comeuppance. Once the classical age had passed, anthologists selected those Petronian sentiments and verses most open to a moralizing interpretation for transplantation into anthologies; here in his own much more creative way the medieval author takes on the role of arbiter himself in recasting the content of the Arbiter's text – erotic narrative, legal joking, and prosimetric form – into a new text about the exercise of judgment which is at least somewhat more likely to reinforce social norms.[11]

II Verse and the exercise of *arbitrium*

Just as the medieval text reins in Petronius' lawlessness in its meditations on *arbitrium*, so too in its use of verse it is much more restrained than its ancient model. The medieval poems are simple hexameters or elegiac couplets, and they comment on or accentuate the exercise of judgment in the narrative (no characters perform verses). So in the first tale, about the man who was harshly judged by his community when he killed his wife and her lover, concluding generalizations on the fickleness of friends are rounded off with an Ovidian elegiac couplet saying that luck brings many friends, difficulties bring solitude (1.14, quoting Ovid *Tristia* 1.9.5–6). The tale of Robert of Guiscard's accurate judgment through storytelling closes with generalizations on good judges (such as Robert) which give way to a ten-line poem contrasting good judges with faithless ones, criticizing the treacherous judge (*arbiter infidus*) who would sell his decision for a bribe. And as I have already noted, in the following tale of the thief and the student, money and judgment are viewed from a different angle, as the student's and the thief's ability to joke instead of struggling for the bedclothes is praised in a twenty-two-line poem contrasting laughter with incessant pursuit of wealth: 'he who holds wealth in contempt, is daring enough to hold luck in contempt, / laughs at the malevolence of luck and has enough' (6.63). In the immediately following tale of Hero and her husband Zetus, three short poems mark the moments of her three betrayals by describing wilful female lust (*arbitrio commissa suo vesana cupido*, 7.82, cf. 99 and 116). A fourth and final poem warns wealthy men to rein in their desires lest they harm themselves (7.127), the implication being that if Zetus had not been so eager to win glory by capturing Antheus in the first place none of this would have happened. In the eighth tale, the case of the British crusader who decides to abandon his lustful and treacherous wife to the Saracens, a final poem indicts the judgment of lustful women: such a woman does not judge lovers on appearance (*per speciem*) but on the size of their organs, and distinguishes (*secernit*) 'a slow plower' (*serum arantem*) from a 'forceful' one (*valido*, 141).

The simple and homogeneous verses in the medieval text are only 'Petronian' because they make the text prosimetric and reinforce its representations of the exercise of *arbitrium*. By not being 'Petronian' in style or scope or sophistication they put those very aspects of the verse in the *Satyrica* into high relief. Viewed from this unfamiliar angle the questions of genre which have exercised Petronius' critics begin to seem less compelling. The impulse to use the verse to diagnose the *Satyrica*'s generic affiliations arises partly because the novels we have grown up on do not use verse,[12] and partly because no other ancient author uses verse in a comparable way. To be sure, the influential writings of Bakhtin and the understandable eagerness of students of Menippean Satire to claim the *Satyrica* as a Menippean text have proposed connections between the *Satyrica*'s use of parody and prosimetric form and Menippean Satire's dizzying swoops between high and low literary registers. Yet Petronius' verse is altogether more varied in tone and in narrative framing and more revealing of character than what we see in Menippean texts. The exciting discovery of fragments of Greek novels which treat racy subjects in a comic way and include snatches of verse make it difficult to insist on an exclusively Menippean reading of the *Satyrica*, though nothing in the Greek evidence revealed by the sands of Egypt has approached the variety, complexity and sophistication of the *Satyrica*'s verse.[13] Because ancient prose fiction has no formal generic constraints (nor even a name as a genre) verse is but one tool in an ancient novelist's big toolbox, alongside letters, oracles, riddles, treaties, mime plots, brief or extended references to epic, tragedy and lyric, or elements of historical, philosophical or geographical discourse. Ancient fiction was such an open-ended and plastic form that the mere inclusion of verse in any novel would not stake a definitive generic claim. The Petronian verses are thus not an assertion of affiliation to a specific genre; instead they help constitute the encyclopaedic, experimental and open-ended quality of the *Satyrica*. In effect, verse is a better index of the affiliation of the medieval text to the *Satyrica* than it is of the *Satyrica*'s connections to particular ancient genres.

At the same time, it is also evident that Petronius uses verse as one element of the linguistic representation of the social positions of his characters (it is this characterful manipulation of verse that is most different from the verse technique of Seneca's *Apocolocyntosis*, the only surviving classical Latin example of Menippean Satire).[14] Sometimes this happens in an almost trivial way: the *cinaedus* in Quartilla's entourage performs Sotadean verses precisely because these verses were associated with *cinaedi* (23.3). Linguistic characterization is also at issue in Trimalchio's performances of poetry which is decidedly non-elite in form. He produces two unimpressive epigrams on fortune and death (34.10, 55.3) and one and possibly two, snatches of mime, a 'quotation' of Publilius Syrus, himself a born a slave (55.6), and a song from a mime called 'The Silphium Man' (35.6; because of a break in the text it is not certain who sings this, but it seems likely to be Trimalchio). Quoting mime, a form known for its wide popular appeal, is part of representing him as an uneducated man. Yet though verse can be part of a realistic-seeming characterization it is not a transparent index of social position. Tryphaena's hexameter verses rebuking her companions for arguing on board Lichas' ship probably have more to do with Petronius' wish to evoke literary models of civil strife than they do with Tryphaena's social position (108.14); Oenothea's celebration of her magic powers in hexameters owes more to literary representations of witches than it does to an attempt to represent her social position with any degree of realism (134.12).

In the case of Encolpius, the crisp and capable epigrams he produces as a witty adornment to his narrative are one element of realistically representing his literary education and his freeborn social position. His companion Ascyltos too can produce an epigram on the unfairness of law courts where money buys justice. Like Encolpius' ability to allude to epic, history and oratory, the production of offhand verses marks him as a man of some education. Giton seems not to produce verse (or much in the way of literary allusions at all), which probably indicates his lack of education. In contrast to Encolpius' status as an educated amateur, Eumolpus and Agamemnon are both literary professionals. Encolpius does not perform in public within the scenes of the novel, and his position never depends on his ability to produce appealing literary works. Agamemnon's performance of verses to Encolpius right at the beginning of the novel (5) is a lure to a potential customer rather than a private joke or entertainment. Eumolpus has moments of private verse performance but from the moment he enters the text and starts speaking in satiric hexameter verse (83.10) it is clear to Encolpius and to us that he is a professional poet – and not a greatly skilled one. By representing these public or quasi-public performances Petronius marks Agamemnon and Eumolpus as literary professionals, inhabiting a social position distinct from that of Encolpius.

Still, Eumolpus' poems on the Fall of Troy, performed in the gallery where he meets Encolpius, and on the Civil War, performed on the road to Croton after the wreck of Lichas' ship, have a length and scope that transcends their function in representing the character of a mediocre professional, and consequently, readers have often looked for some deeper meaning in them. Some have seen them as Petronius' own parodic attacks on Seneca and Lucan respectively or on bad poets generally. My own sense is that their subject matter is crucially important. Each poem represents a foundational episode for Rome: the fall of Troy, and the Civil War between Caesar and Pompey that ended the Republic and led the way to the creation of Empire. These events bring into being the world inhabited by the novel's characters; by including them Petronius allows his fiction to embrace the totality of the Roman world and to engage intensely with the monumental treatments of these themes by Virgil and Lucan. And each poem is constructed in such a way as to replicate symbolically the action of the novel's debased plot. The tragic narrative in iambic trimeter of the taking of Troy through the stratagem of a horse yields a legendary paradigm for Eumolpus' narrative of seducing the Pergamene boy (Romans could use the name Pergamum to refer to Troy) through the promise of a horse (85–87). The strife of Civil War, represented in Eumolpus' epic hexameter fragment by the simile of the storm-tossed ship (123.233–7), finds a debased parallel in the squabbling aboard Lichas' ship, and the real storm which engulfs it; the parallel is strengthened if one retrospectively views the verses that Eumolpus is composing during the storm as 'actually' his Civil War poem (115.2–5). I feel too that debased re-enactments of epic models have a special resonance in what amounts to Nero's 're-enactment' of Augustus' empire.

As such considerations reveal, rereading poems in the *Satyrica* solely as expressions of *arbitrium* will not come to grips with everything that is interesting about them: the medieval imitator is not attentive to the novel's linguistic representation of character and social position or to its intense engagements with the Roman visions of Virgil and Lucan. Nevertheless, the medieval author's obsession with *arbitrium* can be suggestive in one way: he helps us to see that the dynamics of *arbitrium* animate Petronius' verse as it does Petronius' prose: that is, characters in the *Satyrica* perform verse to express or attempt control over the unfolding action. So for example, in the attempt to recover the tunic Ascyltos forcefully rejects Encolpius' suggestion that they try to recover it in court and caps his remarks with the epigram saying that a law case is just a public auction with justice for sale to the highest bidder (14.2).[15] In a somewhat different struggle for the upper hand between Agamemnon and Encolpius, Agamemnon interrupts Encolpius' tirade on education with one of his own. Having seized the declamatory initiative, Agamemnon closes with verses on literary education (5). Encolpius listens so attentively (*diligentius*) to the verses that he does not notice the departure of Ascyltos, and, since he does not remember the way back to their lodgings accurately (*diligenter*) he is helplessly lost in the city (6.1–3). When Quartilla gets Encolpius to promise that he will not reveal what he saw in her Priapic shrine, she uses legal terms in an epigram to praise him for treating her respectfully (contempt would have provoked her revenge) and giving up his advantage over her (18.6, cf. Courtney 1991: ad loc.):

> It is shameful to be held in contempt, to relinquish one's legal claim
> is splendid:
> I love this, that I can go where I like.
> For certainly even a wise man when treated contemptuously wages
> quarrels, and he who does not go for the throat [in a court case]
> usually walks away the winner.

But Quartilla's deference to Encolpius at this point is merely a pretence, and she seizes control of the action so vigorously that he later says 'we have not committed such a great crime that we deserve death by torture' (20.1). The *cinaedus* in Quartilla's entourage sings Sotadaeans as he has his way with Encolpius (23.3). Trimalchio's performance of verse during his banquet is but one expression of his dominance over his captive audience. His short epigrams take up fate (34.10, juxtaposed with the fatalistic associations of the zodiac platter) and *fortuna* (55.3) each of which is a force limiting one's ability to exert *arbitrium* over one's own life. His longer 'quotation' from Publilius is phrased as a matter of judgment too for he is comparing Cicero with Publilius and asking 'what can be said better than these lines?' (55.6). Not long after escaping from Trimalchio, Encolpius meets the poet and plot-maker Eumolpus. In particular, the Civil War poem is an expression of Eumolpus' literary judgment (as set out in his programmatic remarks at 118) and an expression of his dominance of the narrative situation (in which Encolpius has just sworn to play the role of Eumolpus' slave in the deception at Croton), a dominance emphasized when Encolpius reasserts control: 'when Eumolpus had poured forth these things in a huge flow of words, finally (*tandem*) we entered Croton' (124.2). Other poetic utterances which function as assertions of control include Tryphaena's achievement of peace on Lichas' ship with a poetic performance (108.14), and Oenothea's announcement of her magic powers in a poem which begins 'whatever you see on earth heeds my bidding' (*paret mihi*, 134.12.1).

Although the fragmentary state of the text makes for some uncertainties, Encolpius seems to perform poems for another character only in his attempt to flatter Circe (126.18). Otherwise, he uses verse as narrator. He includes erotic verse in accounts of his disappointments with Giton and with Circe (79.8, 128.8, 131.8) and uses poetic allusions and quotations to frame his own adventures in absurdly 'epic' terms (127.9, 132.8, 11, 136.6, 139.2). Perhaps of special interest to his imitator, verses on fickle friends comment on Giton's choice (as *iudex*) to go off with Ascyltos (80.9), and once Oenothea accepts restitution for her dead goose, Encolpius celebrates with an epigram equating money with *arbitrium*, saying that the man with money 'adjusts chance to his own will' (*fortunamque suo temperat arbitrio*, 137.9.2).[16] In general, while other characters within the novel can use a poem as a kind of punch line to assert their control within a scene, Encolpius as narrator uses verse to assert before his audience a literary mastery over his squalid adventures. We may agree with Conte that in Encolpius' poetic utterances (as in his philosophical and oratorical outbursts) the *Satyricon* enacts a contest of wills between Encolpius' aspirations to the sublime ('an excess of will in the narrating protagonist, a wistful "wanting to become"') and Petronius' hidden but all-controlling insistence on exposing him as ridiculous by designing episodes which will tempt those aspirations (Conte 1996: 6).

On the whole, the simplicity of the medieval verse and its straightforward relation to the prose narrative sensitize us to the sophistication of Petronius' characterful manipulation of verse – even when his characters' poetic performances are unsophisticated. And once our eyes are drawn to the operations of *arbitrium* in the novel at large, they are evident in the performance situations of the verse as well.

As in any reception-oriented study, placing these ancient and medieval texts next to each other has illuminated features of each that might otherwise have remained in the shadows. The cultural accident that the medieval author did not know the Tacitean account of the name *arbiter* freed him to read the *Satyrica* as a fantasy on *arbitrium*. Rereading the *Satyrica* in this medieval light brings Petronius' many representations of *arbitrium* in both prose and verse into focus. Indeed, it almost begins to seem that if the author of the *Satyrica* hadn't already been given the name Arbiter (and who chose it?) we might have invented it for him ourselves.

Notes

1 See K. F. C. Rose, *The Date and Author of the Satyricon*, Leiden, 1971, 44–5.

2 See e.g. Cicero *pro Q. Roscio comoedo* 10 (distinguishing an *arbiter*'s more open-ended decision making powers from the more narrow purview of a *iudex*); Seneca

Hercules Furens 205 (Jove as *arbiter* of the universe); *Natural Questions* 2.38.3 (distinguishing between what is within one's own *arbitrium* as opposed to what is predetermined fate); *de vita beata* 6.1 (the mind as *arbiter* of luxury and pleasures).

3 G. B. Conte, *The Hidden Author: An Interpretation of Petronius's Satyricon*, Berkeley, 1996, 6; A. Barchiesi, '*Extra legem*: consumo di letteratura in Petronio, Arbitro,' in O. Pecere and A. Stramaglia (eds), *La letteratura di consumo nel mondo Greco-Latino*, Cassino, 1996, 191–208.

4 This chapter grew out of my *Petronius the Poet: Verse and Literary Tradition in the Satyricon*, Cambridge 1998, which can be consulted for lengthier discussion of individual poems and more detailed bibliography than it will be possible to include here. For the medieval text see M.L. Colker, *Analecta Dublinensia: Three Medieval Latin Texts in the Library of Trinity College, Dublin*. The Medieval Academy of America no. 82. Cambridge, MA, 1975, and his 'New Light on the Use and Transmission of Petronius,' *Manuscripta* 36 (1992), 200–9, in which he proposes that the author be identified with Elias of Thriplow (on whom see P. G. Schmidt, 'Elias of Thriplow – a Thirteenth-century Anglo-Latin Poet', *Papers of the Liverpool Latin Seminar* 3 [1981], 363–70). On 'Petronius redivivus' see also P. Dronke, *Verse with Prose from Petronius to Dante: The Art and Scope of the Mixed Form*, Cambridge, MA, 1994, 23–5, with discussion of the author's use of Boethius' *Consolation of Philosophy*. Imitations indicate the author's access both to the L tradition of manuscripts (which lack the *Cena* section) and to the *Cena* itself (represented only in H); Colker 1975: 183–5, Colker 1992 and K. Müller, *Petronius Satyricon Reliquiae*, Stuttgart, 1995, xxxv–xxxvi, list linguistic parallels. I am grateful to Brian McGing for kindly making it possible for me to examine the medieval manuscript (no. 602) in the Library of Trinity College, Dublin and to Paul Remley and Robin Stacey of the University of Washington. All references to Petronius are to Müller 1995. Translations are my own.

5 Those who cite Petronius as Petronius Arbiter or simply Arbiter include Fulgentius (Müller Test. 4a), Jerome (Müller fr. 24), and John of Salisbury (Müller Test. 16).

6 *Annals* 11–16 are preserved in one medieval manuscript written in Montecassino in the mid-eleventh century which remained there until the fourteenth century: see L.D. Reynolds (ed.), *Texts and Transmission: A Survey of the Latin Classics*, Oxford, 1983, 407–8.

7 On the provisions of the law see S. Treggiari, *Roman Marriage: 'Iusti Coniuges' from the Time of Cicero to the Time of Ulpian*, Oxford, 1991, 283–4.

8 Apulia is mentioned upon their return for the money at 5.37. Thus *appropinquant Bario* 'they approach Bari,' should probably be read rather than *appropinquant barro* 'they approach an elephant' at 5.30.

9 Since the name Antheus is derived from the Greek *anthos*, flower, Hero's punishment may be etymologically fitted to her crime; marrying Hero to the gardener perhaps also gestures toward the use of plowing as a sexual metaphor elsewhere in the collection: 8.141, 12.158. The mythical Hero is famously associated with a tower from which she lit a signal for her lover Leander (Ovid *Heroides* 19.35); the medieval Hero's first betrayal takes place in the tower where Antheus is her husband Zetus' prisoner, and this is perhaps one reason for her name.

10 Orosius, *Historiarum adversum paganos libri VII*, 7.7.6; John of Salisbury, *Policraticus* 8.18; see C. C. J. Webb, *Ioannis Saresberiensis episcopi Carnotensis Policratici sive de nugis curialium et vestigiis philosophorum libri viii*, Oxford, 1909, vol. 2 p. 362.

11 Poems and other moralizing selections from the *Satyrica* as it now stands appear in the twelfth century anthology known as the *Florilegium Gallicum*. Additional

poems unattested in our *Satyrica* fragments are transmitted in the collection known as the Latin Anthology; I discuss them in Connors 1998: 8–9; on the likely authenticity of these poems see E. Courtney, *The Poems of Petronius*, Atlanta, Georgia, 1991, 3–14.

12 Modern novels which do put verse and prose into dialogue to explore contrasting states of consciousness or world views include James Joyce's *Ulysses*, with its snatches of song and overarching allusions to epic, A.S. Byatt's *Possession*, with its investigation of the life and work of a fictional minor Victorian poet, and Pat Barker's World War One trilogy *Regeneration*, *The Eye in the Door* and *The Ghost Road* which includes the poets Siegfried Sassoon and Wilfred Owen as characters.

13 Menippean readings: M. Bakhtin, *The Dialogic Imagination: Four Essays by M. M. Bakhtin*, M. Holquist (ed.), translated by C. Emerson and M. Holquist, Austin, 1981, esp. 21–2; J. C. Relihan, *Ancient Menippean Satire,* Baltimore, 1993, 91–9; cf. Dronke 1994: 9–12. Relations to the Greek novel: S. Stephens and J.J. Winkler (eds), *Ancient Greek Novels: The Fragments*. Princeton, 1995, 358–74 (*Iolaos*), 400–8 (*Tinouphis*); G. Sandy, 'New Pages of Greek Fiction', in J. R. Morgan and R. Stoneman (eds), *Greek Fiction: The Greek Novel in Context*, London, 1994, 130–45; R. Astbury, 'Petronius, P.Oxy. 3010, and Menippean Satire', *CP* 72 (1977), 22–31. Discussion of the *Satyrica*'s differences from these forms: Conte 1996: 140–70; A. Barchiesi, 'Il romanzo,' in F. Montanari (ed.), *La prosa latina: Forme, autori, problemi*, Rome, 1991, 229–48.

14 On linguistic characterization in the *Satyrica* see further W. Martin Bloomer, *Latinity and Literary Society at Rome*, Philadelphia, 1997, 196–241.

15 L places this poem after 13.4; it was moved to 14.2 by Bücheler following Anton.

16 The final poem in the medieval collection, attached to the account of the humors, celebrates the power of money in terms quite different from the disregard for money promoted in the collection's other poems (10.148): its sentiments are perhaps influenced by this celebration of money in Petronius' text.

Bibliography

Astbury, R. (1977), 'Petronius, *P. Oxy*. 3010, and Menippean Satire', *Classical Philology* 72: 22–31.

Bakhtin, M. (1982), in M. Holquist (ed.), *The Dialogic Imagination: Four Essays by M. Bakhtin*, translated by C. Emerson and M. Holquist, Austin: University of Texas Press.

Barchiesi, A. (1991), 'Il romanzo', in F. Montanari (ed.), *La prosa latina: Forme, autori, problemi*, Rome: La Nuova Italia Scientifica, pp. 229–48.

—— (1996), '*Extra legem*: consumo di letteratura in Petronio, Arbitrio', in O. Pecere and A. Stramaglia (eds), *La letteratura di consumo nel mondo Greco-Latino*, Cassino: Università degli Studi di Cassino, pp. 191–208.

Beck, R. (1973), 'Some Observations on the Narrative Technique of Petronius', *Phoenix* 27, 42–61.

Bloomer, W. M. (1997), 'Latinity and Literary Society at Rome', Philadelphia: University of Pennsylvania Press.

Colker, M. L. (1975), 'Analecta Dublinensia: Three Medieval Latin Texts in the Library of Trinity College, Dublin', *Medieval Academy of America no. 82*, Cambridge, MA: Harvard University Press.

—— (1992), 'New Light on the Use and Transmission of Petronius', *Manuscripta* 36, 200–9.

Connors, C. (1998), *Petronius the Poet: Verse and Literary Tradition in the Satyricon*, Cambridge: Cambridge University Press.
Conte, G. B. (1996), *The Hidden Author: An Interpretation of Petronius' Satyricon*, Berkeley/Los Angeles/London: University of California Press.
Courtney, E. (1991), *The Poems of Petronius*, Atlanta, GA: Scholars Press.
Dronke, P. (1994), *Verse with Prose from Petronius to Dante: The Art and Scope of the Mixed Form*, Cambridge, MA and London: Harvard University Press.
Müller, K. (ed.) (1995), *Petronii Arbitri Satyricon Reliquiae*, Stuttgart/Leipzig: B.G. Teubner.
Relihan, J. C. (1993), *Ancient Menippean Satire*, Baltimore/London: Johns Hopkins University Press.
Reynolds, L. D. (ed.) (1983), *Texts and Transmission: A Survey of the Latin Classics*, Oxford: Clarendon Press.
Rose, K. F. C. (1971), *The Date and Author of Satyricon* (*Mnemosyne* Supplement, 16), Leiden: E.J. Brill.
Sandy, G. (1994), 'New Pages of Greek Fiction', in J. R. Morgan and R. Stoneman (eds), *Greek Fiction: The Greek Novel in Context*, London/New York: Routledge, pp. 130–45.
Slater, N. W. (1990), *Reading Petronius*, Baltimore/London: Johns Hopkins University Press.
Smith, P. G. (1981), 'Elias of Thriplow – a Thirteenth Century Anglo-Norman Poet', in *Papers of the Liverpool Latin Seminar. Third Volume 1981*, ed. F. Cairns, Liverpool: Francis Cairns, pp. 363–70.
Stephens, S. and Winkler, J. J. (eds.) (1995), *Ancient Greek Novels: The Fragments*, Princeton, NJ: Princeton University Press.
Sullivan, J. P. (1985), *Literature and Politics in the Age of Nero*, Ithaca, NY: Cornell University Press.
Treggiari, S. (1991), *Roman Marriage: Iusti Coniuges from the Time of Cicero to the Time of Ulpian*, Oxford: Clarendon Press.
Webb, C. C. J. (1909), *Ioannis Saresberiensis episcopi Carnotensis Policratici sive de nugis curialium et vestigiis philosophorum libri viii*, 2 vols., Oxford: Clarendon Press.
Zeitlin, F. I. (1971), 'Romanus Petronius: A Study of the *Troiae Halosis* and the *Bellum Civile*', *Latomus* 30: 56–82.

Part 2

APULEIUS

5

APULEIUS' *GOLDEN ASS*

From Miletus to Egypt

Gerald N. Sandy

I The author and his work

The Golden Ass has tempted many readers to make the kinds of links between the author and the protagonist, between the *auctor* and the *actor*, that generally evoke scepticism now. The practice begins with St Augustine in the fifth century. In the course of defending the reputation of Christ against the fame of Apuleius as a miracle-worker he is uncertain whether his compatriot was actually transformed into an ass or only pretended to have been (*De Civitate Dei* 18.18). The protagonist introduces himself as the offspring of a family rooted in the Greek mainland – in Attica, the Isthmus of Corinth and the Peloponnesus – and that can boast of a maternal branch that includes the famous biographer and essayist Plutarch and his nephew, the philosopher Sextus, who was one of Marcus Aurelius' mentors. Near the conclusion of the story Apuleius transfers the birthplace of the protagonist, whose mother tongue is Greek and who as a young adult acquired Latin as a second language 'by dint of hard work and without the aid of a teacher,' to the Romanized city of Madauros in the Roman province of (North) Africa Proconsularis.[1] Like Apuleius, the protagonist studied in Athens and then went to Rome and was a devotee of mystery religions.[2] These seemingly gratuitous details Greek origins and the adoption of Roman culture, philosophical heritage, *laine-vraie* Athenian education and religious immersion – and, of course, a strong interest in the supernatural inform much of the extant Apuleian corpus, including *The Golden Ass*.

Whether or not *The Golden Ass* is in part autobiographical, enough is known of Apuleius from other sources to warrant a few paragraphs on the elements of his intellectual and artistic development that have left a lasting mark on his novel. His *Apology*, which is the principal source of biographical details, is the extant written version of Apuleius' defence of himself against charges of bewitching a prosperous widow named Pudentilla, with whose son, Pontianus, Apuleius studied in Athens (*Apol.* 72.3). The trial was conducted at some point in the one-year period spanning AD 158–159 in the coastal town of Sabrata, some 60 kilometres from Oea (modern Tripoli in Libya), where the events for which he was tried are alleged to have occurred (Syme 1959: 318). He claims to have been initiated into many religious cults in Greece and adds that when he first arrived in Oea in 155/156 he gave a public address on Aesculapius, the Greek god of healing, and discoursed on his familiarity with sacred mysteries (*Apol.* 55.8–12). He later became one of Aesculapius' priests (*Fl.* 16.38 and 18.38); and according to St Augustine he was *sacerdos provinciae* (priest of the province) (Rives 1994).

Apuleius likens the process of adapting a Greek work into Latin to a circus performer leaping from one moving horse to another (*Met.* 1.1.6). His choice of the adjective '*Graecanica*' ('Grecian') instead of '*Graeca*' ('Greek') at the beginning of *The Golden Ass* conveys the notion "adapted" (into Latin) "from Greek".'[3] In fact, Apuleius devoted most of his writing career to bridging the two classical cultures, to transmitting and interpreting the cultural accomplishments of the Greek East to the Latin West. Indeed, this is one of the charges made against him:

> 'We accuse him . . . of being a handsome philosopher most eloquent,'
> – what shame! – 'both in Greek and Latin'.
>
> (*Apol.* 4.1)

The people of Carthage have heard him discourse in both Greek and Latin over a period of six years (*Fl.* 18). A fragment that appears to have become detached from the philosophical treatise *On the God of Socrates* announces that Apuleius will deliver the rest of the discourse in Greek (Beaujeu 1973: 161–8). Apuleius has adapted, in both Greek and Latin, biological treatises by Aristotle and has coined Latin words to represent Aristotle's technical language (*Apol.* 36.3–8). Likewise, he asks his readers to forgive him for the neologisms that Plato's specialized vocabulary has required him to use (*Pl.* 1.9.200).

I shall have something to say later about the qualities of the *Golden Ass* as an adaptation. At this point it is worth noting Apuleius' habitual practice, which he shared with other Romans such as Terence and Horace, the latter of whom expresses scorn for the *fidus interpres*, of modifying his models very freely.[4] Almost 44 per cent of Apuleius' *On the Universe* consists of accretions to the Greek model (Müller 1939: 133). When Apuleius announces to the courtroom in Sabrata his plan to improve on Aristotle's biological works and when he explains at the beginning of the *On the Universe* his intention to *explicare*, to explain, Theophrastus and Aristotle, he is undertaking no more or less than his Latin-speaking listeners and readers would have expected of Latin renderings of Greek works.

The label 'Platonic philosopher' is attached by St Augustine, the residents of Madauros, the manuscript tradition and Apuleius himself to Apuleius' name. He was demonstrably familiar with at least twenty-two of the thirty-six Platonic titles and exerted enough control over Platonic material to incorporate it playfully into the alien environment of *The Golden Ass*.[5] In the *Apology* Apuleius repeatedly stresses his Platonic credentials, although the only philosophical publications that he cites are completed and projected adaptations of ichthyological treatises by Aristotle, Theophrastus, Eudemus, Lyco and other *Platonis minores* (followers of Plato) (*Apol.* 36.3). As well, he bases his diagnosis of epilepsy on Plato's *Timaeus* (*Apol.* 49.1).

Substantial parts of Apuleius' extant philosophical publications fit the mould of the practices of the (Greek) Second Sophistic. Philostratus, the chronicler of the Greek sophists, in the preamble to his *Lives of the Sophists* defines his subjects as 'those who were philosophers but were thought to be sophists', that is, philosophers blessed with exceptional speaking ability and vice versa. This attitude towards philosophy as a form of eloquent discourse is evident in Apuleius' claim that Plato perfected the rudimentary philosophical doctrines of his predecessors by means of the force of his eloquence (*Pl.* 1.2.185). He refers to a large audience assembled to hear him present a 'live' philosophical discourse in the Carthaginian theatre where crowds also gather to be entertained by mimes, comedies and tight-rope walkers (*Fl.* 5 and 18.1–5). At least one of his philosophical treatises was intended for oral presentation. This work, the *On the God of Socrates*, is the best example in the Apuleian corpus of the complete fusion of oratory and philosophy. Apuleius refers to himself as an orator and to the discourse as an oration, and he repeatedly responds to his listeners' confusion over matters of Platonic demonology.[6] This discourse, which provides the fullest and most detailed account of demonology that has survived from classical antiquity, has some bearing on the tale of Cupid and Psyche in the *Golden Ass*. Cupid (Amor) is included there among the demons, as he is in Plato's *Symposium*, which is the principal source for all subsequent demonology.[7] Apuleius' other major philosophical work, the *On Plato and his Doctrine*, is a scholastic résumé of Platonic doctrine. Like *The Golden Ass*, it represents another important pattern of Apuleian composition, the consolidation and presentation of others' ideas.

Apuleius was above all a compiler and adapter. In the *Apology* he quotes his erotic poems for which he cites the poetry of the Greek philosophers Solon, Diogenes the Cynic, the Stoic Zeno and Plato as precedents (9.9–10.5). To judge by the titles, citations of passages and descriptions of the contents of Apuleian works that no longer survive, Apuleius produced a substantial number of compilations and adaptations. A work in two books known as the *On Proverbs*, possibly in verse, was almost certainly a compilation.[8] The versified aphorisms, some of them modelled on sayings of Plato and Epicurus that had previously been translated by Cicero and the younger Seneca, obviously fall into the categories of compilation and adaptation. The *Epitome of Histories* was certainly a compilation; and it seems likely that the technical treatises *On Medical Questions*, *On Agriculture*, *Astronomica* and *On Trees*, the subjects of which are consistent with the interest in ichthyology that he emphasizes in the *Apology* and the interest in astronomy that is evident in some of his other works such as the *On the Universe*, were also compilations. Finally, Apuleius' penchant both for Platonic philosophy and for interpreting Greek works to the Latin West found expression in his translations of Plato's *Republic* and *Phaedo*. Sidonius Apollinaris judged the latter translation to be less literal than Rufinus' translation of Origen, *ad verbum sententiamque translatus* (translated [less literally] word-for-word and in accordance with the sense [of the words]). In summary, all of Apuleius' extant non-oratorical works and several of his lost writings are adaptations of earlier, usually Greek publications. In two cases, the *On the Universe* and *The Golden Ass*, Apuleius' versions can be compared with the Greek models.

II *The Golden Ass*

Sources

The earliest reference to *The Golden Ass* by title cites it by the Greek title the *Metamorphoses*. During the period 395–7 an editor named Sallustius worked on the text both in Rome and Constantinople. Whenever he refers to the novel by title, he invariably uses the Greek title, for example:

> *Metamorfoseon Libri X. Explicit. Ego Sallustius legi et emendavi Romae felix.* (Book 10 of the *Metamorphoses*. The end. I Sallustius read and corrected [it] successfully in Rome.)

Some thirty years later Apuleius' compatriot St Augustine, whose knowledge of Greek was minimal, uses the Latin title *Asinus Aureus* (*The Golden Ass*) (*De Civitate Dei* 18.18). The 'golden' of the Latin title is usually explained on the basis of the younger Pliny's apparent reference to the advertisement used by professional story tellers, 'Provide a copper "penny" and get a golden story' (*Epistulae* 2.20).[9] As for the Greek title, its use some thirty years before St Augustine's use of the Latin title is not sufficient evidence of Greek origins of the novel. However, there is other, compelling evidence that Apuleius used a Greek model for at least substantial parts of it.

1 Milesian tales

'But I would like to stitch together for your benefit various tales written in the Milesian style that you favour', begins the novel. Ancient accounts of Milesian tales almost uniformly characterize them as ribald. One exception to this portrayal occurs in *The Golden Ass* itself with reference to the saccharine tale of Cupid and Psyche (4.36.2). The passage also shows that Apuleius (or the author of the Greek model) was aware of the Greek author who is credited with originating the tradition. When Psyche's father consults the oracle of the 'Milesian god', that is, Apollo at Didyma near Miletus:

> Apollo, although an Ionian Greek, gave his prophecy in Latin for the benefit of the compiler of this Milesian tale.
>
> (ibid.)

Apart from parodying the conventions of narrative in the traditional novels (Hofmann 1993b: 135), Apuleius appears here to be acknowledging Aristides of Miletus, with whom the origins of Milesian tales are associated. Only one word of his collection of *novelle* has survived, and the nine short fragments of the Roman historian Sisenna's adaptation or translation of Aristides' work do not help us to form an impression of the Greek work. Later references, however, add considerable detail.[10] Ovid attributes ribaldry to both Aristides and Sisenna:

> Aristides associated scandalous Milesian tales with himself. . . . Sisenna translated/adapted Aristides, and he did not suffer because he had woven ribald jests into his story.
>
> (*Tristia* 2.413 and 443–4)

One can also infer from this passage that Aristides, like the dramatized narrator Lucius in *The Golden Ass*, was an actor in the scandalous events that he narrated.[11] Finally, Ovid's statement suggests that, as in *The Golden Ass*, there was a framing narrative, the *historia* or story-line, into which the ribald tales were stitched. It may not be coincidental that Apuleius promises to stitch together a medley of stories for the readers' benefit (1.1.1).

The pseudo-Lucianic *Erotes* (1) adds another Milesian narrative dynamic that Apuleius may have adopted in *The Golden Ass*. One of the speakers in the dialogue thanks his companion for telling ribald stories that have provided relief from more serious matters. So beguiling were the lewd stories, he says, that he felt like Aristides being charmed by Milesian tales. This suggests that the dramatized narrator Aristides represented himself as the delighted recipient of stories told by others.

This narrative template is frequent in *The Golden Ass*. The first inset tale adheres to it. The narrator Lucius urges a fellow traveller to repeat for his benefit a story that another travelling companion has greeted sceptically (1.2.4–1.4). At its conclusion he thanks the story teller 'because he has diverted us with a charming and delightful story and because I have passed through a long and rough stretch of road without effort or boredom' (1.20.5).

In the tradition of Aristides' *Milesian Tales*, *The Golden Ass* contains a central narrative and a central narrator who transmits to the reader his own sometimes ribald adventures and the sometimes risqué experiences of companions and acquaintances and of the subjects of the stories that he overhears or that are told directly to him. Septimius Severus criticized the emperor Clodius Albinus for wasting his time on 'old wives' tales and the Punic Milesian Tales of his [compatriot] Apuleius.'[12] The pairing of old wives' tales and Milesian tales by both Apuleius and Septimius Severus suggests that the Milesian tale was not so much a formally defined literary genre like tragedy or epic as a label attached to any open-ended fictional prose narrative containing a first-person narrator and a patchwork of sometimes ribald, self-contained short stories linked by a single narrative thread.[13]

2 The Greek 'Metamorphoses'

In addition to the Greek pedigree of the narrator and of the Milesian tales Apuleius assigns a Greek derivation to the entire story, 'We begin our Grecian story' (*fabulam Graecanicam incipimus*, 1.1.6). The *fabula Graecanica*, that is, the Greek *Metamorphoses*, no longer survives, but a synopsis of its first two books has survived. It is usually called the *Onos*, the Greek equivalent of *asinus*. We also have a comparison of the abridgement with the original Greek work that the Byzantine patriarch Photius prepared for his brother in the second half of the ninth century. H. Mason's chapter in this volume (Chapter 6) deals with the confusing details of Photius' comparison. I shall single out only a few of his statements that have implications for the analysis of Apuleius' novel provided later in this chapter.

Photius' statement that the Greek *Metamorphoses* included 'the transformations of persons into other persons and into animals and back again' does not accurately reflect events in *The Golden Ass*. In the Latin novel there is only one cycle of transformations, that of Lucius into a donkey and back again into a human.[14] There is also the question of the tone of the Greek works. It is difficult to understand how the retention of 'the same words and syntax' in the epitome could transform the 'silly nonsense of old tales' in the Greek *Metamorphoses* into mockery of 'Greek superstition', as Photius claims. There is no hint of mockery in the Greek abridgement; and in Apuleius' version both those who are superstitious, as are Lucius, Socrates and Aristomenes, and those like Thelyphron who discount the power of witchcraft suffer alike at its hands.[15] The issue of tone, of whether Apuleius presents 'superstitious' tales at face value or counterbalances them with the power of the goddess Isis' grace, has important implications for the interpretation of *The Golden Ass*. To judge by Photius' reference to the 'broad expanse' of the Greek *Metamorphoses*, the original work, like *The Golden Ass*, consisted of what Photius calls 'several books/volumes' of episodes and inset tales, 'the silly nonsense of old tales', that, as Apuleius promises in the first sentence of his novel, the Greek author 'stitched . . . together'.

Adaptation

Substantial parts of Book 2 of *The Golden Ass* closely resemble, and are sometimes word-for-word translations of, material retained in the Greek *Onos*, which, according to Photius, preserves 'the . . . syntax and words' of the first two books of the Greek *Metamorphoses*.[16] At the beginning of the book Lucius wakes up on the first morning of his stay in Hypata, the very city, he reflects, in which Socrates, the subject of the first inset story, died because of his involvement with a witch. When the Lucius of the Greek epitome wakes up, he enumerates a lacklustre list of marvellous occurrences such as a person in flight or being transformed into stone that he is eager to witness. There is no corresponding earlier inset tale in the epitome to reinforce the prevalence of witchcraft in Thessaly. The 'person in flight' anticipates in both versions the magical ability of the hostesses of the two young men to transform themselves into owls (*Asin.* 12, *Met.* 3.21). The anticipated petrifaction, which also appears in the Apuleian Lucius' more flamboyant list of hoped-for magical wonders, does not actually occur in the epitome. The events that precede the realized human petrifaction in Apuleius are identical to the corresponding passage in the epitome. Either the writer of the epitome has omitted it from his abridgement of the Greek original, or Apuleius has exploited the narrative potential unrealized in one or both of the two possible Greek sources.[17] His Lucius gets his wish: he admires at his aunt's house a sculpted ensemble depicting Actaeon's transformation into a quadruped because of excessive curiosity (2.4). Apuleius thus provides thematic reinforcement and a proleptic component absent from the epitome.

The dinner party at the house of Lucius' aunt contains another good example of Apuleius' tendency to develop details absent from the epitome that serve to initiate and bolster major themes in the Latin novel. One of the guests is urged to entertain the other guests with a story about the witches in the area, who 'at the very moment of the funeral rites arrive so quickly that they prevent burial' (2.20.3). The story is about wizardly body snatching, told by the hired 'body guard' Thelyphron, whose mutilated face is living testimony to the power of witchcraft. This is one of many direct and indirect warnings about witchcraft that Lucius receives, each more immediate than the preceding one. The story about Socrates, which shares several formal and thematic features with that of Thelyphron, was about a victim of witches who was already dead. This time Lucius is face-to-face with one of their victims. As on the other occasions, his reaction to the warning is to race all the more eagerly and heedlessly into direct contact with witchcraft (Sandy 1973: 233).

Other events at Byrrhena's house, of which again there is no hint in the Greek abridgement, serve to define Lucius and his dangerous quest. She is entertaining the *flos ipse civitatis* ('the very flower of [provincial] society') (2.19.1). We have already learnt that she and her sister, Lucius' mother, are related to the distinguished family of Plutarch and that Lucius' mother has married 'better', into the senatorial class (2.3.2–3) (Mason 1983). In spite of his genteel background, when his aunt, like a representative of a visitors' bureau, enumerates the public and private amenities of her beloved provincial town, which offers 'relaxation for the person on holidays and the hustle and bustle of Rome for the commercial traveller', Lucius expresses his obsessive interest in its underbelly, 'the hidden and inescapable hot beds of the black arts' and the grave robbers (2.19.5–20.3). These seemingly incidental details reinforce the concluding theme of the novel: in spite of his blue-blooded ancestry and high level of education Lucius has reaped the fruits of his baleful curiosity (11.1.1).[18]

Book 11 appears at first glance to be an Apuleian accretion completely independent of the Greek model(s). The Greek abridgement concludes with a ribald episode that is absent from *The Golden Ass*. The former human lover of the ass Lucius violently expresses her disappointment that Lucius has exchanged his large asinine penis along with his other asinine attributes for diminutive human features (*Asin.* 56). He regained his human form by eating rose petals, as prescribed by the witch's maidservant (*Asin.* 14 and 54). In Apuleius' version the goddess Isis responds to Lucius' prayer:

> Let there be an end to my toils and perils. Strip off my appalling asinine appearance and let me be Lucius again.
>
> (11.2.4)

The goddess Isis then rises slowly from the sea and declares:

> Behold, Lucius, I am here to help you because I have been moved by your prayers. . . . I am here to offer you kind and supporting help because I have felt compassion for your misfortunes. You must now stop crying and grieving. Banish your sorrow. Because of my providence the morning of your day of salvation is brightening.
>
> (11.5.1 and 4)

She then gives him detailed instructions for obtaining the rose petals from her priest that he must eat to regain his human form. He is to draw close to the priest as though he were going to kiss his hand and once he has plucked the rose petals, 'Immediately divest yourself of the hide of that worst of beasts that I have so long detested' (11.6.2).[19] The rest of the book describes the various rites and duties that Lucius performs to qualify for initiation into Isis' mysteries and for membership in the god Osiris' College of Pastophori. Like the tale of Cupid and Psyche, the novel ends on a joyful note of everlasting fidelity, 'Wherever . . . I went I joyfully continued . . . to perform the duties of the most ancient college' (11.30.5).

Form and meaning

The *Golden Ass* is one of the three Latin novels that have survived from classical antiquity, the other two being Petronius' (fragmentary) *Satyricon* and the anonymous *History of Apollonius, King of Tyre*, both of which are discussed elsewhere in this volume. They are not, however, the only representatives of the genre. Five extant ancient Greek novels and fragments of others are available for comparison.

Until recently, the linguistic demarcation appeared to signal divergence in tone as well. The extant Greek novels tend to portray idealized love, tracing its course from sudden, unexpected beginnings ('love at first sight'), through the separation of the young lovers caused by some external agent such as pirates and their quest to be reunited, to the happy union of the pair at the conclusion of the story. The action is usually set in the distant past, and the characters belong to the upper echelons of urban society. This generalized representation of the Greek tradition, never wholly accurate, has been completely undermined by publication during the past twenty-five years of fragments of newly discovered Greek novels that do not conform to the stereotype. Low-life realism and coarse comedy, we can now see, are as much a part of the Greek traditions of extended prose narrative as they are of *The Golden Ass* and the *Satyricon*.[20]

Books 1–7

The Golden Ass is the first-person account of the picaresque-like adventures of a young Greek named Lucius. The first episode does not contribute to the announced theme of bodily transformations, but it establishes some of the ancillary themes and the methods used repeatedly by Apuleius to introduce and develop them. While travelling on business to Thessaly the narrator encounters two other travellers. One of them ridicules the story that his companion has just told 'off stage', 'Spare me those ridiculous and monstrous lies of yours' (1.2.5). Describing himself to the reader as 'thirsty for novelty', Lucius encourages the traveller named Aristomenes to resume the story by reassuring him that he wants 'to know everything or at least most things' (1.2.6). This short exchange initiates the theme of Lucius' 'ill-starred curiosity', which the priest of the goddess Isis says near the conclusion of the novel has contributed to Lucius' misfortunes (11.15.1). The story itself gives a preview of Lucius' imminent confrontation with witchcraft. Aristomenes tells the story of his friend Socrates' death at the hands of the witch Meroë and her 'weird sisters'. Socrates incurred the vindictive wrath of Meroë when he fled from her embraces while he was a guest at her inn. Similarly, Lucius is to suffer the consequences of witchcraft while a guest at the house of Milo and his wife, the witch Pamphile. Both witches employ magic to advance their erotic designs and use it against the unwilling objects of their lust (1.7–9 and 2.5).

The narrator highlights the link between Socrates' death and his own vulnerability on his first morning as a guest of Milo and Pamphile (2.1). Their household and that of Lucius' aunt Byrrhena subsequently serve as the focal point of the misfortunes that follow. Byrrhena warns her nephew that his hostess is a witch. She enumerates a catalogue of Pamphile's magical powers that matches that of Meroë (1.8–9 and 2.5). When told of Meroë's powers by Socrates, Aristomenes' reaction was to express the wish to flee as far as possible from her (1.11.1–3). Lucius, however, is all the more eager to toy with witchcraft:

> But I, ever curious, as soon as I heard the desired words 'magical art', was so far removed from heeding the warning about Pamphile that I even took it upon myself to submit to such instruction at any cost and in one quick leap to plunge headlong into the very abyss.
>
> (2.6.1)

He also plunges into the arms of his hosts' maidservant Fotis, whom he has resolved to seduce so that she will disclose the magical practices of her mistress Pamphile (2.6.4–8). After spending several nights of graphically described sex with her, Lucius, 'incited by . . . [his] customary curiosity', again expresses his desire to have the hidden works of witchcraft laid bare without realizing that he has already been its victim (3.14.1). As he was returning to his hosts' house after hearing stories of witches who transform themselves into animals and of necromancy, which his obsession with witchcraft prompted, Lucius, 'swollen with excessive wine', encounters three apparent burglars kicking vigorously at the door of his hosts' house (2.20–30). He draws his sword and plunges it into each of them 'until large multiple punctures cause them to gasp out their last breath at my feet' (2.32.5).

As Lucius is being led to court the next day to face charges of murder he notices a curious thing, 'For of the countless thousands of people who were swelling around there was not a single person there who was not bursting with laughter' (3.2.4). The trial itself is conducted so as to cause Lucius maximum dread; it includes 'victims' impact statements' and, in ordinary Greek fashion, the torture of his slave to ensure that his testimony is reliable (3.8–9). However, the trial concludes as its preliminaries began, 'Then laughter, which by design had been held in check for some time, burst out throughout the crowd' (3.2.4). Lucius has been the unwitting victim of an elaborate practical joke on the day of the annual festival of Laughter (*Risus*). The imagined burglars were in fact wine-skins made of goat hide that had responded to the smell of burning goat hair. Fotis had substituted it for the hair of a young man for use by Pamphile in a rite of sympathetic magic intended to satisfy her lust for him (3.16).

Fotis' professional incompetence on that occasion is repeated later when she makes a mistake in preparing the magical ointment that is supposed to transform Lucius into an owl as it had transformed Pamphile. Lucius rubs the ointment on his body, spreads his arms as if to fly and:

> no down or even a little feather anywhere. Instead, the hair [on my body] became coarse and bristly, my tender skin hardened into hide, at the ends of my palms my fingers lost their individuality and were all squeezed together into hooves, and from the base of my spine a huge tail extended. My face was enormous now, my mouth distended, my nostrils gaping and my lips hanging; my ears also grew grossly bristly and large.
>
> (3.24.2–5)

Lucius has become an ass, but:

> although I had become a complete ass and a beast of burden instead of Lucius, I nevertheless retained my human intelligence.
>
> (3.26.1)

Much of the rest of the story depends on Lucius' retention of his human mental and emotional faculties. Before he has an opportunity to eat the roses that will restore him to human form, robbers seize him to carry the loot that they have taken from Milo's house. Thereafter, he passes from one usually cruel master to another, reacting, in his mind at least, humanly and humanely to various outrages and castigating the humans whose depraved behaviour his seemingly dumb asinine guise allows him to witness (e.g. 9.13.3).

Lucius reports his adventures as an ass to the reader in the first person. He also overhears accounts of others' experiences, which he reports to the reader, sometimes humorously exploiting the authorial limitations imposed on him by his asinine condition, as in the tale of Cupid and Psyche (6.5.1). Similarly, in the Phaedra-like story about a wicked stepmother whose sexual advances are rejected by her stepson, the asinine narrator assumes the historiographical pose of Thucydides. The stepson, who has been falsely charged with murdering her son with the poison that was intended by her for him, is to be tried in a court imbued with the fabled gravity of the Athenian Areopagus (10.7.1–2). The asinine narrator has gleaned information about the trial that he could not attend because he had been confined to his stable from interviews and has included in his account only what he could accurately ascertain (10.7.3–4).

On other occasions the asinine narrator counts it as a blessing that Fotis' mistake has enabled him, like the Odysseus of Homer, 'the divine inventor of ancient poetry', 'to visit many cities and come to know varied peoples' (9.13.4). He adds:

> I have decided to offer to your ears the best tale of all, a charmingly

> elegant one. . . . I was consoled . . . by this one benefit of my damnable deformity, namely, because I was equipped with very long ears I could very easily hear everything, even at a distance.
>
> (9.14.1 and 9.15.6)

The 'best tale of all' turns out to be two tales of adultery exchanged by the cruel wife of the ass' new master and her friend (9.16–21). These two tales, which 'are brought to my ears', are followed by the adulterous behaviour of the master's wife, which a third tale of adultery has preceded (9.22 and 24–5). At this point the asinine narrator becomes involved in the action by exposing the lover of his master's wife (9.27.2). To try to salvage her broken marriage, the wife turns to a witch and pleads with her either to reconcile her with her husband or to invoke a demon to attack him. The narrator now steps off the pages of the novel to underscore the irony of an asinine narrator:

> But perhaps as a scrupulous reader you will criticize my account, reasoning thus: 'Although you are a clever little ass, how could you when confined to the mill know what the women did, as you insist, in secret?' Let me tell you, therefore, how I, though maintaining the appearance of a beast of burden, was curious enough to learn each detail of what was done to destroy [my master] the baker.
>
> (9.30.1–2)

These examples of Apuleius' self-conscious references to narrative modes represent a few of the methods that he uses to weave together a variety of tales. Only rarely does he resort to the perfunctory introduction of an inset story such as, 'I heard the following account of her punishment' (10.23.2). Instead, Apuleius has fashioned a complex blend of interlocked characters and events and the stories of shared experiences that bind them together.

The next major set of inset stories revolves around a young woman named Charite. It encompasses Books 4–6 and extends into Book 8. This complex of stories actually begins in Book 3 when robbers break into the house of Lucius' host and take Lucius, now an ass, to carry the booty. When they arrive at their hideout, a second gang of robbers joins them. They all devour food and wine and behave barbarously, thereby lending plausibility to the drunken boasting and insults that the two gangs exchange. A member of the second group of robbers, provoked by insults into defending the loss in action of three of its members, tells entertaining stories about their bungled robberies (4.9–21).

The robbers later break camp and return in the morning with Charite, whom they have kidnapped. She has a nightmare, and the robbers' housekeeper diverts her with 'the charming old wives' tales' of Cupid and Psyche (4.27.8). First, however, Charite tells of the preparations for her wedding that were underway when she was kidnapped (4.26). Thus the tale of Cupid and Psyche, which on one level is about the separation of an engaged couple, is appropriate for her circumstances; and her talk of the bond of long-standing love that she and her fiancé feel for each other integrates his later appearance to rescue her into the narrative texture.

Apuleius provides added plausibility to the arrival of Charite's fiancé by first representing the robbers as depleted in number because of 'a variety of bold undertakings' (7.6.1). They decide to conduct 'a draft of comrades in arms' so that 'the profile of their cohort of Mars would be restored by the conscription of new young recruits to the number of the previous detachment' (7.4.3).[21] Thus the enlistment of Charite's fiancé is all the more plausible. To earn the robbers' trust, he represents himself as the famous Thracian robber Haemus ('Blood-thirsty'), son of the equally illustrious Theron ('Hunter'/'Nimrod'). He was, he says, 'nurtured on human blood and brought up among the very squadrons of his [father's] troop [to be] the successor and equal to his father's prowess' (7.5.6). To arouse the interest of his audience, he makes an oblique reference to misfortune in the time-honoured tradition of story-telling and pauses, 'But I shall tell the story from beginning to end so that you will understand' (7.6.1).

'Haemus' becomes the robber chieftain and soon arranges for Charite's escape. He turns out to be her fiancé Tlepolemus. His identity has been kept from the narrator (and thus from the reader), which gives Apuleius the opportunity to exploit the hypothesis of the novel that the asinine narrator has retained his human mental and emotional faculties, 'At that very moment', he soliloquizes when he sees 'Haemus' and Charite kissing, 'the character of all womankind hung on the judgement of an ass' (7.10.4).

Book 8 opens with the arrival of one of Charite's slaves, who, like a messenger in a Greek tragedy, announces:

> No more is our Charite. The poor little girl by the most grievous misfortune has gone, and not alone, to the land of the dead.[22]

He continues in the fashion of a skilled story-teller and that of the self-conscious narrator Lucius:

> But so that you will know everything, I shall tell you from the beginning what happened, such events as those who are wiser and on whom Fortune has bestowed the gift of writing could unfold on the pages of a work such as a history.

He then recounts 'her destruction and that of her entire estate'.

The nexus of stories and events in which Charite figures encompasses a substantial portion of the novel. The asinine narrator rarely plays a direct role in the events. Instead, he celebrates the role of the narrator and the art of narration. This complex, like that of roughly the first three books where

Lucius is centre stage, has a high degree of cohesiveness. It derives principally from the self-contained circle of related events and characters. In subsequent books the asinine narrator passes through the hands of a number of owners, and the core of characters and events becomes distended. The diminished narrative integrity of Books 8 to 10 tends to derive from the clustering of thematic types such as adultery, that do not appear to resonate beyond their immediate context. Even in this more loosely structured part of the novel, modern scholars have detected a high degree of thematic continuity and have successfully applied the principles of narratology to the shifting points of view.[23]

Books 8–10

With rare exceptions, betrayal, violence, murder, lust and the destruction of households mark the events that follow the flight of Charite's servants from her shattered estate. The asinine narrator accompanies them in his usual role as a pack-animal and witnesses the fear and chaos of the countryside through which they pass. The events that he reports include an old man who transforms himself into a giant snake and devours a young boy and the cruel punishment of a servant whose master has him smeared with honey and left to be eaten by ants (8.20–2).

The asinine narrator's range of experiences extends beyond the previously closed circle of the households of Milo and Charite when he is sold at an auction. Cruel Fortune 'again turned her unseeing eyes towards me and found . . . a buyer remarkably matched in every way to my [previous] harsh experiences' (8.24.1). His buyer is one of a troupe of perverts who go from town to town carrying a statue of the Syrian Goddess as a ploy to solicit offerings from the gullible and indulging their homosexual lust. In his travels with the 'itinerant mendicants', 'I heard a delightful story about the cuckolding of a certain poor man that I want you to know too', and the tale follows (9.4–7).

Eventually, the priestly perverts run afoul of the law, and the ass is again sold at an auction, this time to a miller. The asinine narrator now counts it as a blessing that his transmogrification has equipped him with long ears that enable him to hear 'a good tale, better than the rest'. The miller is a good and reasonable man, but in the lottery of life has drawn 'the worst of wives, a woman much the worst of all women' (9.14.2). Although she vents her cruelty on the asinine narrator, he nevertheless is again thankful that Fotis' incompetence has blessed him with the long ears that permit him to learn of the tales and events of adultery that occupy most of Book 9 and that culminate in the destruction of the miller's household.

Another auction follows, and the asinine narrator is sold to a poor market-gardener. He witness there several supernatural prodigies such as a green frog leaping out of the mouth of a sheep dog (9.33–4). These strange events are followed by the news of the destruction of a neighbouring household that occurred when three young men died in a quarrel with their arrogant landlord, and their father committed suicide (9.35–9). The market gardener also falls victim to the violent and lawless mayhem that characterizes Book 9.

Book 10 resumes the pattern of wicked women that marks the previous book. In his new household the narrator learns of a terrible crime that 'I am adding to my book so that you too can read about it' (10.2.1). It is about a stepmother who lusts after her stepson. The narrator likens it to Euripides' tragedy about Phaedra and Hippolytus:

> Therefore, excellent reader, be informed that you are reading a tragedy rather than a tale and that the buskin of tragedy is taking precedence over the sandal of low comedy.
>
> (10.2.4)

Uncharacteristically, however, the story has a happy ending when justice and rule of law prevail. The Phaedra-like character's stepson is acquitted of all wrongdoing, and she is sentenced to exile.

This exceptional outcome gives way to the usual conclusion of a tale of domestic affliction. The asinine narrator is now sold to two slaves. They are expert chefs, and the fortunes of the ass appear to take a turn for the better as he surreptitiously dines on the leftovers of their lavishly prepared food. The 'prodigiously refined sense of taste of the ass' impresses their master, and he purchases him from his slaves (10.15–9). His new owner is a wealthy municipal official who is planning to stage a public festival to thank the people of Corinth for electing him to public office. Before it takes place another event likened to another repugnantly lustful woman of Greek legend occurs. Like Pasiphaë, who lusted for a bull, a wealthy Corinthian woman 'gradually conceived an extraordinary lust for me' (10.19.3). She bribes the asinine narrator's keeper to allow her to have sex with the ass.

In the Greek epitome the wealthy woman reappears in the concluding episode after the ass has regained his human form. She violently expresses her disappointment that he has lost his 'large . . . trailing symbol of ass[hood]' along with his other asinine attributes. In both versions of the story the owner of the ass decides to exploit his talent for fornicating with women by arranging for the ass to have sex at a public festival with a woman who has been convicted of murder. In Apuleius' version of the novel the narrator has learned 'the following story of her sentence' for murdering her husband, which he proceeds to report to the reader (10.23.2–10.28). As *The Golden Ass* now exists in the manuscript tradition, shame at the prospect of public fornication and fear of death drive the asinine narrator to flee from the public spectacle to the nearby port of Cenchreae, which was a major centre of the cult of the goddess Isis.[24]

Book 11

Book 11 literally comes out of the blue (sea), as the goddess Isis rises from it in response to Lucius' anguished prayer. Explanations of the role of Book 11 in the rest of the novel have been as varied as 'the varied [Milesian] tales' that Apuleius has stitched together for the reader's amusement.[25] Many critics see the book as a contrived religious resolution to the preceding ten books of ribaldry, as 'solemn pageantry [added] as ballast to offset the prevailing levity of the preceding ten books', analogous to Defoe's self-serving *apologia* in the preface to *Moll Flanders*:

> To give the History of a wicked Life repented of, necessarily requires that the wicked Part should be made as wicked as the real History of it will bear, to illustrate and give a Beauty to the Penitent part.[26]

Even in antiquity Macrobius relegated the *Golden Ass* to the nursery (*in nutricum cunas*) and expressed disappointment that 'Apuleius often dabbled in . . . stories filled with the fictional adventures of lovers' (*Somnium Scipionis* 1.2.8). If the original conclusion of the novel is absent in the limited manuscript tradition, Book 11 as we have it may be even more open-ended than Winkler supposed; and the curiously incomplete last word of the novel (*obibam*, 'I continued to perform my functions') could signal that the mysteries of Isis and Osiris, like the depraved activities of the perverted priests of the Syrian Goddess, were only one more example of the deception and humiliation that find expression in the cynical disillusionment at the conclusion of the Greek abridgement.[27]

Moral fable

Interpretations of *The Golden Ass* as an instructive moral fable begin with Fulgentius in the late fifth or early sixth century and continue into the Renaissance.[28] This kind of allegorical exegesis is older than many people suppose. It was especially prevalent in antiquity among Middle Platonists like Apuleius. He expresses the Middle Platonist doctrine of differentiated levels of meaning (*Apol.* 12.1). According to this view great creative writers like Homer encoded their fables with a layer of metaphysical mystery that only the pious could penetrate.[29] We see something of this in Book 11 when Lucius prepares to be initiated into Isis' mysteries. The profane are dismissed, and Isis' priest leads him 'to the innermost part of the very sanctuary' (11.23.4). He pauses:

> Perhaps, attentive reader, you are eager to enquire what was next said and done. I would tell you if I were permitted to tell; you would know if you were permitted to know. . . . Therefore, I shall relate

> only what can be revealed without the need for the uninitiated to perform expiatory rites.
>
> (11.23.5 and 7)

If *The Golden Ass* is more than a patchwork of ribald Milesian tales intended to titillate the readers' ears, the key to unlocking its theosophic enigmas is likely to found in the words of Isis' priest. He places Lucius' previous experiences *sub specie aeternitatis*:

> Driven like a slave by great suffering of all kinds and buffeted by the mighty storms and tempests of Fortune, you have come at last, Lucius, to the port of Rest and the altar of Mercy. Not your birth nor even your rank nor that branch of learning in which you excel has profited you; but having slipped down into servile pleasures on the uncertain slope of vigorous youth, you have reaped the unfortunate reward of your ill-starred curiosity.
>
> (11.15.1)

Lucius has been a slave to pleasure. When he becomes Isis' servant, he will enjoy the reward of freedom (11.15.5). Most critics understand the servile pleasures to be Lucius' prolonged sexual dalliance with the maidservant Fotis. This is reasonable in view of the large amount of graphic detail devoted to their sexual affair and Lucius' misgivings about the vow of sexual abstinence required for initiation into Isis' cult (11.19.3).

There is a major problem with this interpretation, however. Lucius turns to Fotis not because he is a slave to sexual passion but because he is unwilling to violate the marriage bed of his host Milo by having a love affair with his wife, the witch Pamphile (2.6.6). The passion that he feels is to experience witchcraft, 'For I most ardently desire first-hand knowledge of witchcraft' (3.19.4). With the guidance of Isis' priest Lucius exchanges the bonds of his obsession with discredited witchcraft for servitude to Isis.[30] He replaces devotion to the *arcana secreta* of magic with worship of the *arcana purissimae religionis secreta* (3.15.3 and 11.15.3).

III Conclusions

At the outset of the novel Apuleius promises to tickle the reader's ears with a patchwork of tales written in the Milesian style. Egypt is mentioned, but, seemingly, only as the traditional source of writing implements: 'Egyptian papyrus written on with a sharpened reed from the Nile'. The reader will marvel at 'the shapes and fortunes of people transformed into different outward appearances and then back again by a common thread of entanglements to their former selves'. 'I begin', the narrator adds, and he introduces himself with the question, 'Who is he/am I?' The so-called linear reader at the conclusion of the story might justifiably ask, 'How has he transformed a medley of typically ribald Milesian tales into a pilgrimage to redeem his soul as well as his outer appearance by grace of the Egyptian goddess Isis?'

Apuleius has anticipated that question. The religious faithful bear witness to his 'conversion', 'The majestic godhead of the omnipotent goddess has transformed him back into a human today' (11.16.3). In this way Apuleius reaffirms the initial narrative theme of transformation, this time adding to it a layer of meaning that goes well beyond the announced theme of the sense of wonder to be derived from a mélange of Milesian tales joined together by the common thread of physical transformations. Lucius 'has', the faithful add, 'earned such remarkable divine support that he has in some way been instantly reborn and pledged to compliance with the holy rites because of the innocence and faithfulness of his earlier life' (11.16). This declaration appears to add a moral dimension to the interwoven Milesian tales. Finally, Isis' priest appears to place Lucius' earlier experiences in the wider context of his need for spiritual salvation (11.15.1; quoted above, p. 16).

First-time linear readers who accept at face value these links between the beginning and the end of the novel, between the various events and adventures of the first ten books and their apparent religious resolution in Book 11, may be satisfied that they have indeed read a 'golden' tale about a reconstructed ass. Readers who read the novel a second or third time and watch for the seeds of eventual religious resolution within the various adventures and inset tales of the first ten books may feel deceived.

I have tried to make a case for interpreting the Milesian tales of the first three books as *fabulae de se*. They serve as warnings about the dangers of toying with the black arts. The tale of Cupid and Psyche also mirrors the course that Lucius follows. It is more difficult to make a case for supposing that the sometimes ribald *variae fabulae* of approximately the last third of the novel underscore Lucius' spiritual progress and contribute to the soteriological Book 11. For example, in the episode that immediately precedes the ass-narrator's desperate appeal to Isis for salvation he is to fornicate at a public spectacle with a woman who has been convicted of murder. The spectacle includes a salacious performance of the pantomime 'The Judgment of Paris' (10.30–2). As in Plato's account of Socrates' trial, he names Palamedes and Ajax as the legendary victims of venal Greek justice. Apuleius then undercuts this seemingly serious diatribe. The reader is imagined to object, 'Look, are we now to endure an ass philosophizing to us?' (10.33.4).

Winkler has been at the forefront of modern critics who question whether this type of 'self-questioning performance' permits 'a clear and final authorization'.[31] Other modern critics have found evidence of thematic and narrative resonance in the same episode. Elsom, for example, detects in Lucius' undercutting of the diatribe against the venality of Greek justice the theme of forensic rhetoric that extends from the beginning to the end of the novel (1985: 152–5). Zimmerman-de Graaf argues that the episode constitutes evidence that the 'narrating I' is reviewing past events from the perspective of his regained humanity.[32] And there is sufficient evidence that Apuleius was capable of constructing a congruous plot when he wanted to. The Festival of Laughter, for instance, is probably as unexpected to most readers as it is to Lucius (3.1–11). However, all the clues for anticipating something like it are in place for the second-time reader. Fotis' warning of an outbreak of violent mayhem in Hypata persuades Lucius to arm himself with a sword when going out at night (2.18.3–5); his aunt mentions to him in casual conversation that the people of Hypata are preparing to celebrate the festival (2.31.2–3); and his admitted drunkenness preconditions Lucius to misapprehend what he appears to see in the dark (2.31.4).

The problem remains, however, that Lucius does not provide any clues for his new-found certainty that the goddess Isis offers the promise of salvation (11.1.2) (Winkler 1985: 131). The *Golden Ass* remains a delightful blend of entertainment and parable. Apuleius' desire 'to titillate the readers' ears' prevails in substantial parts of the novel.

Notes

1 *Met* 1.1.1–4 and 11.27.9. References to *The Golden Ass* are based on the divisions used in the Budé edition, ed. D. S. Robertson (Paris: Société d'Edition 'Les Belles Lettres', 1940). The following abbreviations are used for Apuleian works: *Apol.* = *Apology*; *Fl.* = *Florida*; *Met.* = *Metamorphoses/Golden Ass*; *Pl.* = *De Platone* . . . ; *Soc.* = *De Deo Socratis*. St Augustine, *De Civitate Dei* 8.14, refers to Apuleius as 'the Platonist from Madauros'. Apuleius' name has been restored by editorial conjecture to the fragmentary base of a statue erected by the residents of Madauros in honour of a '[Pl]atonic [ph]ilosopher' (S. Gsell, *Inscriptions latines de l'Algérie* [Paris: Champion, 1922] I, 2115).

2 Studies: *Fl.* 17.4 and 20.4, *Apol.* 23.2 and *Met.* 1.24.1; mystery religions: *Apol.* 55.8–12, *Met.* 3.15.3 and 11.21.2–11.30.

3 Mason 1978: 1. See also his Chapter 6 in this volume and Mason 1994.

4 Horace, *Ars Poetica* 133. In general see Blatt 1938; Brock 1979; Russell 1990: 4–7 and Sandy 1997.

5 De Lacy 1974: 7 and Anderson 1982: 79; see, too, Trapp 1990.

6 *Soc.* 3.125, 5.129, 14.150, 20.166.

7 *Soc.* 16.154; Plato, *Symposium* 202d–203a. See Schlam 1976: 31 and Chapter 8 on the tale of Cupid and Psyche in this volume.

8 Fragments and Apuleian works cited by other writers in classical antiquity are conveniently assembled in Beaujeu 1973: 171–80.

9 Scobie 1975: 47–9. Martin 1971 relates the Latin title to the Greek *onos pyrros*, the rust-coloured ass that represented the goddess Isis' enemy Seth-Typhon. Winkler 1985: 312–8 equates the 'golden' to one of Seth's cult titles: 'golden Seth'.

10 I am indebted to Dr G. Jensson for several of the details that follow. He developed the material in his 1996 University of Toronto Ph. D. thesis on Petronius and in a lecture presented at the meetings of the Classical Association of Canada in 1997. See also Harrison 1998.

11 For example, *Met.* 2.7–11, 9.27, 10.19–22. In the *Satyricon* Encolpius is both actor in, and narrator of, lewd adventures.

12 'Life of Clodius Albinus' 12.12 in the *Historia Augusta*.
13 *Met.* 4.27.8 and 4.36.2. The Milesian tale appears to be the only geographically defined literary type that had a character independent of its geographical designation. See Theon, *Progymnasmata*, in L. Spengel (ed.), *Rhetores Graeci* (Leipzig: Teubner, 1854), II, p. 73.
14 The witch Meroë is reported to have transformed her recalcitrant lovers into a beaver, a frog and a ram in the past, but nothing is said of their regaining human form (*Met.* 1.9.1–4). The same is true of the witches who are reported to have transformed themselves into animals (2.22.2–3) and the old man reported to have become a man-eating snake (8.20–1).
15 Superstitious, e.g. 1.3, 1.9, 1.11, 2.12, 3.19.2–4; sceptical, e.g. 2.21.
16 Fuller details and bibliography in Sandy 1997: 236–41.
17 The major flaw in the attempt of Perry 1967: 242–5 to isolate Apuleian accretions is his tacit assumption of narrative perfection in the lost Greek *Metamorphoses*.
18 Fotis recognizes the same qualities in Lucius (Apuleius, *Met.* 3.15.4).
19 This passage is the principal support for the notion that Lucius' transformation into an ass is connected with Isiac cult since Isis' enemy, Seth-Typhon, is sometimes depicted as an ass. See, e.g. Griffiths 1975: 162.
20 Sandy 1994 and 1997: 241–53. Add now Alpers 1996.
21 Apuleius regularly uses military terms for the gang of robbers.
22 I have borrowed the 'no more' from J. Hanson's translation in the Loeb edition to represent the Latin '*fuit*' ('[she] has been', i.e., is no more), the first word in the announcement.
23 Dowden 1993 (on the thematic integrity of Book 8) and Hofmann 1993a.
24 On the preserved version of *The Golden Ass* see below, n. 27. On Cenchreae see Griffiths 1975: 14–20.
25 Harrison (1996: 508–9 and 511–15) and Shumate (1997: 285–328) summarize the issue and provide their own thoughtful interpretations.
26 The quoted phrase comes from Perry 1967: 244–5; see, too, Sandy 1978.
27 Winkler 1985: 223–7. Van Mal-Maeder (1997: 112–4) discusses the possibility that the original ending of *The Golden Ass* has not survived. MS Laurentianus 68, 2 (F), which is the ancestor of all or most of the extant manuscripts, does not have the subscription at the end of Book 11 that all the other books except Book 1 have (see the example quoted in section I); and the scribe has left a blank space at the end of the novel, which was the customary procedure when the exemplar was illegible or a folio or folios were missing from it. This article raises other serious questions about the seemingly religious sincerity of Book 11.
28 On Fulgentius and Renaissance interpretations of the novel see Chapter 13 by C. Moreschini in this volume.
29 See Chapter 8 on the tale of Cupid and Psyche in this volume.
30 Cf 3. 19.5 ([*me*] . . . *servilem modum addictum atque mancipatum . . . volentem*) with 11. 15. 2 and 5 (. . . *servitium deae nostrae . . . Ministerii iugum subi voluntarium. Nam cum coeperis deae servire* . . .); and see above note 25.
31 Winkler 1985: 126 and 131. Shumate 1996 and in her Chapter 7 in this volume takes account of Winkler's views.
32 Zimmerman-de Graaf 1993: 154–5. Similarly, Lucius' reference to laughter being held in check 'by design' can be taken as evidence of a 'post-narrating-I' perspective (quoted above, p. 90).

Bibliography

Alpers, K. (1996), 'Fragmente eines unbekannten Romans aus der Zeit der Zweiten Sophistik', in M. Billerbeck and J. Schamp (eds) *Kainotomia: Die Erneuerung der griechischen Tradition. Le renouvellement de la tradition hellénique*, Freiburg, Switzerland: Universitätsverlag, pp. 19–55.

Anderson, G. (1982), *Eros Sophistes: Ancient Novelists at Play* (*American Classical Studies*, 9), Chico, CA: Scholars Press.

Beaujeu, J. (ed.) (1973), *Apulée: Opuscules philosophiques . . . et fragments*, Paris: Société d'Edition 'Les Belles Lettres'.

Blatt, F. (1938), 'Remarques sur l'histoire des traductions latines', *Classica et Mediaevalia* 1: 217–46.

Brock, S. (1979), 'Aspects of Translation Technique in Antiquity', *Greek, Roman and Byzantine Studies* 20: 69–87.

De Lacy, P. (1974), 'Plato and the Intellectual Life of the Second Century A.D.', in G. Bowersock (ed.), *Approaches to the Second Sophistic*, University Park: American Philological Association.

Dowden, K. (1993), 'The Unity of Apuleius' Eighth Book and the Danger of Beasts', H. Hofmann (ed.) *Groningen Colloquia on the Novel*, vol. 1, Groningen: Egbert Forsten, vol. 5, pp. 91–107.

Elsom, H. (1985), 'Apuleius and the Writing of Fiction and Philosophy in the Second Century A.D.', PhD thesis, Cambridge University.

Griffiths, J. G. (1975), *Apuleius of Madauros: The Isis-Book (Metamorphoses, Book XI). Ed. with an Introduction, Translation and Commentary* (*Etudes préliminaires aux religions orientales dans l'empire romain*, 39), Leiden: E.J. Brill.

Harrison, S.J. (1996), 'Apuleius' *Metamorphoses*', in G. Schmeling (ed.) *The Novel in the Ancient World* (*Mnemosyne*, Supplement 159), Leiden: E. J. Brill, pp. 491–516.

—— (forthcoming), 'The Milesian Tales and the Roman Novel', H. Hofmann and M. Zimmerman (eds) *Groningen Colloquia on the Novel*, vol. 9.

Hofmann, H. (1993a), 'Die Flucht des Erzählers: Narrative Strategien in den Ehebruchsgeschichten in Apuleius' *Goldenem Esel*', in H. Hofmann (ed.) *Groningen Colloquia on the Novel*, Groningen: Egbert Forsten, vol. 5, pp. 111–41.

—— (1993b), 'Parodie des Erzählens – Erzählen als Parodie: Der *Goldene Esel* des Apuleius', in W. Ax and R. Glei (eds), *Literaturparodie in Antike und Mittelalter*, Trier: Wissenschaftlicher Verlag Trier, pp. 119–51.

—— (1997), 'Sprachhandlung und Kommunikationspotential: Diskursstrategien im *Goldenen Esel*', in M. Picone and B. Zimmermann (eds), *Der antike Roman und seine mittelalterliche Rezeption*, Basle/Boston/Berlin: Birkhäuser, pp. 137–69.

Martin, R. (1971) 'Le sens de l'expression *asinus aureus* et la signification du roman apuléien', *Revue des études latines* 48: 332–54.

Mason, H. (1978), '*Fabula Graecanica*: Apuleius and his Greek Sources', in B.L. Hijmans Jr. and R. van der Paardt (eds) *Aspects of Apuleius' Golden Ass*, Groningen: Bouma's Boekhuis, pp. 1–15.

—— (1983), 'The Distinction of Lucius in Apuleius' *Metamorphoses*', *Phoenix* 37: 135–43.

—— (1994), 'Greek and Latin Versions of the Ass-Story', in H. Temporini and W. Haase (eds) *Aufstieg und Niedergang der römischen Welt*, Berlin: W. de Gruyter, II 34.2, pp. 1665–1707.

Müller, S. (1939), *Das Verhältnis von Apuleius' "De Mundo" zu seiner Vorlage* (*Philologus*, Supplement 32.2), Leipzig: Dieterich'sche Verlagsbuchhandlung.

Perry, B. E. (1967), *The Ancient Romances. A Literary-Historical Account of Their Origins* (*Sather Classical Lectures*, 37), Berkeley/Los Angeles: University of California Press.

Rives, J. (1994), 'The Priesthood of Apuleius', *American Journal of Philology* 115: 273–90.

Russell, D.A. (1990), 'Introduction: Greek and Latin in Antonine Literature', in D. Russell (ed.) *Antonine Literature*, Oxford: Clarendon Press, pp. 1–17.

Sandy, G. (1973), 'Foreshadowing and Suspense in Apuleius' *Metamorphoses*', *Classical Journal* 68: 232–5.

—— (1978), 'Book 11: Ballast or Anchor?', in B.L. Hijmans Jr. and R. van der Paardt (eds) *Aspects of Apuleius' Golden Ass*, Groningen: Bouma's Boekhuis, pp. 123–40.

—— (1994), 'New Pages of Greek Fiction', in J. Morgan and R. Stoneman (eds), *Greek Fiction: The Greek Novel in Context*, London/New York: Routledge, 130–45.

—— (1997), *The Greek World of Apuleius. Apuleius and the Second Sophistic* (*Mnemosyne*, Supplement 174), Leiden: E.J. Brill.

Schlam, C. C. (1976), *Cupid and Psyche: Apuleius and the Monuments*, University Park: American Philological Association.

Schmeling, G. (ed.) (1996), *The Novel in the Ancient World* (*Mnemosyne*, Supplement 159), Leiden: E.J. Brill.

Scobie, A. (1975), *Apuleius Metamorphoses (Asinus Aureus) I: A Commentary* (*Beiträge zur klassischen Philologie*, 54), Meisenheim am Glan: Hain.

Shumate, N. (1996), *Crisis and Conversion in Apuleius' 'Metamorphoses'*, Ann Arbor: University of Michigan Press.

Syme, R. (1959), 'Proconsuls d'Afrique sous Antonin le Pieux', *Revue des études anciennes* 61: 310–19.

Trapp, M. (1990), 'Plato's *Phaedrus* in Second-Century Greek Literature', in D. Russell (ed.) *Antonine Literature*, Oxford: Clarendon Press, pp. 141–73.

Van Mal-Maeder, D. (1997), '*Lector, intende: laetaberis*. The Enigma of the Last Book of Apuleius' *Metamorphoses*', in H. Hofmann (ed.) *Groningen Colloquia on the Novel*, Groningen: Egbert Forsten, vol. 8, pp. 87–118.

Winkler, J. J. (1985), *Auctor and Actor: A Narratological Reading of Apuleius' "The Golden Ass"*, Berkeley/Los Angeles/London: University of California Press.

Zimmerman-de Graaf, M. (1993), 'Narrative Judgement and Reader Response in Apuleius, *Metamorphoses* 10, 29–34: The Pantomime of the Judgement of Paris', in H. Hofmann (ed.) *Groningen Colloquia on the Novel*, Groningen: Egbert Forsten, vol. 5, pp. 143–61.

6

THE *METAMORPHOSES* OF APULEIUS AND ITS GREEK SOURCES

Hugh J. Mason

The narrator of Apuleius' *Metamorphoses* closes the prologue with the phrase *fabulam graecanicam incipimus*, followed immediately by the claim *lector intende: laetaberis*. Part of the reader's pleasure, in other words, will derive from the Greekness of the tale. *Graecanicus*, 'adapted from Greek' (Mason 1978: 1)[1] is the correct term for a text in which, as in a Plautine prologue, the *argumentum graecissat* (*Menaechmi*, 11); a Greek narrator speaking in Latin impersonates Greeks speaking Greek for a Latin audience. This *uocis immutatio* causes pleasure for the attentive reader by the resulting narratological paradoxes, such as when an uneducated monolingual Greek servant parodies the opening of Cicero's *First Catilinarian* (*Met.* 3. 27). However, *graecanicus* is also an appropriate term for the content of a work in which Apuleius adapts, or rather deconstructs, also like Plautus (W. F. Anderson 1993: 4–29), a pre-existing text whose identity he does not reveal (Winkler 1985: 202).

We know this text from the work *Loukios e Onos* (hereafter *Onos*) in our manuscripts of Lucian. In *Onos*, as in Apuleius, a young man named Lucius narrates in the first person how he was transformed by magic into an ass. Since close comparison of *Onos* and Apuleius reveals several passages in which the Latin follows the Greek word for word,[2] there can be little doubt that the Roman author was using *some* version of this Greek narrative.[3]

I Loukios of Patrai

The patriarch Photios (*Bibliotheke*, 129) compared *Onos* to a work he described as the '*Metamorphoseis* of Loukios of Patrai'. We cannot therefore be certain that the Greek text which Apuleius used was the same one which we possess. Photios observed that *Onos* was the shorter of the two works, but used the same wording as the *Metamorphoseis*, and surmised that *Onos* was an abbreviation of the longer *Metamorphoseis*. Goldbacher (1872) and Bürger (1887) pointed to *lacunae* in *Onos* and argued convincingly that it was an abbreviation. Since part of their case depended on a comparison with Apuleius, there, is, however, a danger of circularity in using their conclusions as a criterion when tracing Apuleius' sources.

Exhaustive exploration of the possible relationship between the three texts has been one of the more prolific pastimes of scholarship since the first modern texts of the *Onos* and of Photios were published (Mason 1994).[4] Most scholars have concluded that the '*Metamorphoseis* of Loukios of Patrai' was the original text, abbreviated in *Onos* and adapted, translated and generally transformed by Apuleius. Some of the arguments for Apuleius' use of *Onos* have not been without subtlety and learning,[5] but they have failed to upset the prevailing view that it was the *Metamorphoseis* which were adapted by Apuleius.

According to Photios, *Onos* was at one and the same time a literal adaptation of the *Metamorphoseis* using the same words and phrases, and also different from it in tone, in that *Onos* mocked Greek superstition while the author of the *Metamorphoseis* seriously believed in 'all the idle chatter of the ancient myths'. Both of these statements cannot be true, as was observed by Courier (1818: iv). Since Werner (1918), few readers have been willing to accept Photios' view of *Onos* as a satire of Greek religion. As a result, his judgement that the *Metamorphoseis* took a serious view of magic and superstition must also be called into question (Kussl 1990). Our confidence in Photios' account of the *Metamorphoseis* is not enhanced by the fact that he identified the *narrator* 'Loukios of Patrai' as its author.[6] The Greek narrator Loukios is a believer in magic and other superstition, like Apuleius' Lucius (*Met.* 1.20.3), but this tells us as little about the *author's* attitude and the tone of the work as Lucius' various pronouncements tell us about Apuleius' beliefs or the ultimate purpose of the *Golden Ass*.

II Lucian

What is the connection of Lucian to the various versions of the Ass-story? The present Lucianic corpus certainly includes many inauthentic works, some of Byzantine date, and there are solid reasons for questioning his responsibility for *Onos*. The most important is the conviction that Lucian could not have produced a mechanical epitome of another's work, nor a text whose Greek, when it does not actually deviate from second century norms, both Attic and *koine*, 'rarely rises above the adequate' (Sullivan 1989: 591). Arguments that the style is a deliberate attempt to imitate, and so parody, the narrator's linguistic inadequacies (Schmid 1919), have not succeeded in dispelling these doubts. Both the Greek and the Latin Lucius are upper-class youths with a thorough Greek rhetorical education. Their Greek style one would project, on the analogy of Aristides, Favorinus and Herodes Atticus, to have been careful Attic with the virtuosity of the second Sophistic. Lucian, an accomplished parodist, could have easily produced a work in the baroque style of contemporary intellectuals. *Onos* is not such a work. On the other hand, if Lucian had wished to poke fun at the inelegance and solecisms of an author who did not follow Attic norms, the errors would have been more consistent, and have corresponded to the favourite shibboleths of second-century Atticists. As for Lucian's adapting another's work, we learn from an Arabic text of Galen, that he once produced a bogus work of Herakleitos to discredit incompetent critics (Strohmaier 1976). Yet this evidence of Lucian's skills as a forger and parodist does not provide a very useful parallel for his supposedly satirizing another's work by a process of not very competent excerpting. Lucian cannot have composed *Onos*.

Ben Perry, in his Princeton thesis (1920) and a series of later works, argued that Lucian was the author of the original *Metamorphoseis*. If Lucian has anything to do with the ass-story, it is more likely to be with the complete work. Perry's suggestion has been widely accepted, but his principal argument, that *Onos* is the kind of work which Lucian *might* have written, does not prove that 'Lucian was the only man known to us who wrote in that humorous or satirical spirit' (Perry 1967: 213). This claim has become less compelling as we have become more aware of the wide variety of ancient prose fiction. The linguistic character of the *Onos*, which supposedly used the same vocabulary and phraseology as the *Metamorphoseis*, differs significantly from Lucian's usual clever style. It is not at all obvious that either the process of epitomisation, or the art of parodying a supposed source, can fully explain the linguistic and stylistic differences (Hall 1981: 362–4).

We must also recognize that Lucian and Apuleius were close contemporaries, probably both born around 125 AD; if Apuleius adapted Lucian, we need to consider how a *Metamorphoseis* would fit into various proposals for the chronology of Lucian's work, and how that can be related to suggested publication dates for *The Golden Ass* (McLeod 1994: 1379–84; Walsh 1970: 248–51; Dowden 1994). More, perhaps, than other scholars, I find that such questions of relative chronology count against Lucianic authorship of the *Metamorphoseis*, which probably belongs to the first half of the second century AD (Mason 1994: 1681–5).

The case for Lucian remains unproven, and the author of the *Metamorphoseis* unidentified, since none of the alternative candidates suggested has obtained general consent. It is, however, easy to understand how versions of the ass-story have come to be assigned to Lucian. From Poggio on,[7] scholars who have written on the topic have written 'Lucius' for 'Lucian' or vice versa, and the error has not always been caught (Schlam 1971: 292).

III The content and character of the *Metamorphoseis*

Photios asserted that the *first two books* of the *Metamorphoseis* were comparable to *Onos*. There have been two interpretations of this: (1) that the entire *Metamorphoseis* dealt with the ass-story, but Photios did not bother to read more than the first two books (Winkler 1985: 256); (2) that the first two books dealt with the ass-story, and later books with other examples of metamorphosis (Hall 1981: 414–32). Debate on this topic has also been lively; a likely, but far from certain, conclusion is that Photios chose only to comment on the two books that interested him, and that these two books contained the entire ass-story. The size of the *Metamorphoseis* is important for the understanding of Apuleius' adaptation: if it was no more than five pages longer than *Onos* (Junghanns 1932: 118–9),[8] then most of Apuleius' work, five or six times the length of *Onos*, did not derive from the *Metamorphoseis*; if, on the other hand, the ass-story took up more than two books of the original *Metamorphoseis*, then large sections of Apuleius without corresponding passages in *Onos* may nevertheless be adapted from the Greek original.

There is virtually no consensus on what of Apuleius' material might have been found in the *Metamorphoseis*. Those like Van Thiel (1971) who trace substantial parts of Apuleius' work to the Greek original, probably place too much emphasis on Photios' account of the 'serious' character of the *Metamorphoseis* (Mason 1972; 1978: 3). This includes the proposal by Carl Schlam (1992: 18–28) that the *Metamorphoseis* had a religious ending comparable to Apuleius' version.

The *Metamorphoseis* in the view of most scholars resembled *Onos* in character and tone: ironic and unsentimental, with an undercurrent of satire against those who believe in and write about the marvellous.[9] It probably included some digressive material that was excised by the excerptor, but nothing on the scale of the extended secondary narratives in Apuleius' novel. There is no good reason to assume that the digressions were the same in both works.

IV Sources and subtexts

The narrator of Apuleius' prologue appealed to a *reader* and the detecting of intertextualities is essentially a reader's pleasure. Recollections of Homer and Theokritos by Virgil, of Kallimachos by Latin neoteric poets, of Greek tragedians by Seneca, all depend on the implied reader having access to the text of the Greek original. It is important, and somewhat sobering, to realize how little evidence there is that Greek fiction was known in Rome. Chariton's *Callirhoe* may be mentioned by Persius (1.134), but Lucian is mentioned in his lifetime only, so far as we can tell, by Galen. For the *Metamorphoseis* of Loukios, we can be certain only of three readers in all of antiquity: Apuleius, Photios and the creator of the *Onos* (Bowie 1996: 105). Chariton could count on his readers to appreciate his Homeric tags; Longus alluded to Theokritos and Sappho, confident that his readers had access to their texts; Heliodorus expected his audience to appreciate references to Greek tragedy and to critical terminology about it. Apuleius, on the other hand, could not assume that the Greek ass-story, whether by Lucian or not, was familiar to a learned audience in Rome, still less to a readership in North Africa without access to Roman or Alexandrian libraries.

Once again, we return to the Plautine analogy. Although it is possible for a scholar to compare a Plautine play to its Greek originals, Plautus did not expect his audience to do so. Apuleius' Plautine invitation to his readers to enjoy themselves by paying close attention to his Greek-style narrative was not meant to invite comparison with *Onos* or *Metamorphoseis*.

Apuleius was very conscious of his wide-ranging scholarship and loved to use it to dazzle his audiences; as Winkler noted in another context (1985: vii), 'Borges and Nabokov have nothing on Apuleius'. In the preface to the English edition of *King, Queen, Knave* (Nabokov 1968: x), a novel in which, as in Apuleius, the author appears in the final section, Nabokov alludes to 'my amiable little imitations of *Madame Bovary*, which good readers will not fail to distinguish', and warns of the cruel traps he has set for unwary Freudians. Apuleius expects, in much the same spirit, that attentive readers 'will not fail to distinguish' his allusions to earlier literature; but for the allusive game to be successful, the works recalled must have some familiarity.

If we have correctly understood the meaning of *graecanicus*, the *fabulae* to which Apuleius alluded were not simply Greek, but Greek works in Latin guise. Apuleius' own philosophical and rhetorical output is very much adaptation in the *graecanicus* manner, and such is also the tradition of the one genre to which he alludes specifically, the *Milesia fabula*. The term is used twice; in the phrase *sermone isto Milesio* in the preface and when Apollo, *quanquam Graecus et Ionicus* (*Met.* 4.32) gives an oracular response in Latin *propter Milesiae conditorem*. The latter gives us the perfect example of Apuleian fun with issues of language and narrative voice (Hofmann 1993: 135); Apuleius reports that Lucius heard the (Greek-speaking) *anus* say that Apollo, *quanquam Graecus et Ionicus*, gave an oracle in Latin, because of the language of the *Milesiae conditorem*. If the *conditor* is meant to be Apuleius, we have a remarkable, but not uncharacteristic, dislocation of the narrative stance; if, on the other hand, *conditor* means not 'composer of this *Milesia*' but 'founder of the genre *Milesia*', the response is in Latin because Apuleius is thinking not of Aristides of Miletus, *Graecus et Ionicus* like the god, but his Roman adapter, L. Cornelius Sisenna, *praetor urbanus* in 78 BC.

We know relatively little about Milesian tales, but the references we do have[10] suggest that they dealt with erotic themes in an ironic way. The clever ending of *Onos* (56), where Lucius-as-a-man is rejected by the woman who loved him as an ass, is entirely consistent with what we know about *Milesiae*; it is part of Apuleius' play with our generic expectations that after telling us he is composing a *Milesia*, he changes the *Milesian* punch-line of his source to a religious narrative. Aristides 'of Miletus' is unknown, and may indeed, like 'Loukios of Patrai', be the narrator or participant, rather then the author, of the story (Jensson 1997: 305–13). The Latin sources (Ovid and Fronto) make it clear that the *Milesia* was familiar to a Roman audience in Sisenna's version, so that Apuleius could count on his readers picking up the allusion. Sisenna's work is not only a *Milesia*, it is a classic example of a *fabula graecanica*.

The similarity between *Met.* 10.22 (*totum me, sed totum recepit*) and Sisenna, fr. 10 (*eum penitus utero suo recepit*) suggested to some that the ass's intercourse with a Corinthian *matrona* derived from a *Milesia*. This in turn has prompted highly speculative reconstructions of Sisenna's work, and claims that much of Apuleius derives from Sisenna. In this passage, however, Apuleius follows *Onos* fairly closely and we need seek no more complicated source than the Greek *Metamorphoseis*. The supposed derivation of this scene from Sisenna seems forced.[11] Nevertheless, if the climactic sex scene in Corinth does not derive from Sisenna, other material may; the *lepidam de adulterio fabulam* of *Met.* 9, 4–8 was witty and sexy enough to belong in a *Milesia*. It is likely that Apuleius made several allusions to Sisenna's work which we have not detected.

Not all erotic narratives which Apuleius might have used had the ironic tone of the *Milesia*. Apuleius' narrative of the death of Charite in Book 8, for example, recalls historical anecdotes in Greek authors of 'womanly virtue' reported in a serious vein, such as the tale of Kamma told most recently by Plutarch (W. Anderson 1909). Note how Romanized Apuleius' version is, with recollections of Sallust and Virgil (Walsh 1970: 164).

The other common form of 'serious' erotic narrative is the relatively sentimental Greek novel. As with the ass-story itself, however, we must note that we do not have much evidence that any given novel was known in second-century Rome, still less that they were suitable as sources for learned allusions. Sandy (1994) may be right to conclude that the connections between Apuleius and the Greek novels are relatively few, and the parallels cited by earlier scholars unconvincing. However, the case for some recollection of Chariton's *Callirhoe* is somewhat stronger. It is the novel most likely to date before Apuleius and possibly was known to Roman readers. Such features as the formal debates among the bandits (Chariton 1, 7, 10; *Met.* 7, 5, 9) and the bogus bandit 'Haemus' (*Met.* 7.5) who gives as his father's name that of the chief bandit in Chariton (1.7) suggest that Apuleius may indeed have alluded to at least this one novel (Mason 1978: 9).

Among other forms of Greek *fabula* that Apuleius may have used is the Aesopic tradition (Crusius 1889), including the *Vita Aesopi*. Apuleius was very interested in the Aesopic *fabula*, putting all his remarkable rhetorical skills into a retelling of the fable of the Fox and the Crow in the preface to *De Deo Socratis*. He deliberately reworked the direct allusion to an Aesopic tale in *Onos* 45 to include the mention of another tale, that of the *umbra asini* (*Met.* 9.42). The Aesopic tradition also qualifies as *graecanicus*, with a distinguished and clever Latin version by Phaedrus.

Comedy as reworked by the Roman dramatists is perhaps the clearest example of the adaptation of Greek material for which *graecanicus* is the appropriate term. Macrobius (*Somn. Scip.* 1.2) compared Petronius and Apuleius to Menander as authors of *fabulae* aimed only to entertain. Apuleius' rhetorical and philosophical works certainly show an interest in Comedy, but the *Metamorphoses* proves less influenced by the New Comedy of Menander and his contemporaries (fourth/third centuries BC) than its Plautine prologue would lead one to expect. Nevertheless, there may be a memory of Menander's *Perikeiromene* in the brother-and-sister tale set in Corinth (*Met.* 10.23–8); note, however, that by using the forms of a well-known comedy, Apuleius set a trap for the unwary by giving the tale a tragic conclusion. He set a similar trap at *Met.* 10.2, *scito te tragoediam non fabulam legere*. This story, which is a version of the Phaedra–Hippolytos myth, has a 'happy' ending as in a comedy or a novel (Xenophon, *Ephesiaca* 3, 5, 11); the poison taken by the stepson is only a soporific drug. Again, the term *graecanicus* is relevant; although the Phaedra myth is Greek and the defining version Euripides' play, Apuleius' narrative draws more on Virgil's Dido and Seneca's *Hippolytus* (Walsh 1995: xxviii).

Finally, what *fabula graecanica* might a *philosophus Platonicus Madaurensis* wish to suggest his readers recall as they approached his *Metamorphoses*? The translation, adaptation and general transformation of Greek ideas which Apuleius attempted in his philosophical works show marked similarities to the way he adapted the ass-story in the *Metamorphoses* (Hijmans 1987). There have been several careful studies of Platonic influence on the *Metamorphoses* (Schlam 1970; Thibau 1965; Fick 1991; Münstermann 1995); among the multiple readings that the novel encourages, a Platonic one is no more out of place than any other, although the overriding philosophical tone is cynic or sceptic (Winkler 1985: 125, n. 4). A *fabula* in Plato should mean one of the myths he used to illustrate his philosophical ideas. 'Cupid and Psyche' recalls not the closely argued philosophical discussion about the nature of the Soul, but the myths of the *Symposium* and the *Phaedrus*. Here particularly I find in Apuleius the same pleasure that I do in Nabokov. When Psyche hangs on for dear life to Cupid's leg, and prevents him from rising to heaven (*Met.* 5.2.1) an alert reader recalls Plato, *Phaedrus* 248c. Yet the recollection does not inspire confidence that Apuleius is making a serious philosophical point. Indeed, once you have read Apuleius' light-hearted narrative, it is difficult to treat the *Phaedrus* passage with the seriousness it deserves. Apuleius used Pausanias' theme of the two Aphrodites (*Symp.* 180d–181b) seriously in his *Apology* (12); but we cannot insist that he makes a serious argument about the two forms of Aphrodite in the *Metamorphoses* after his portrayal of Venus in 'Cupid and Psyche', in which Greek ideas again receive a Roman twist and become *graecanica*. When Venus offers French kisses as a reward for the recovery of Psyche (*Met.* 6.8), 'a Hellenistic conceit' (from Moschus 1.4) 'which Apuleius hopes his readers will recognize', she does so in a purely Roman setting, at the *Metae Murciae* (Walsh 1970: 211). Apuleius' Venus is a delightful and far from serious mix of Plato's *Symposium*, the opening of Lucretius' *De rerum natura*, Hellenistic epigram, Virgil's Juno, and the social behaviour of an upper-class Roman *matrona*. In the portrayal of Venus, with its mixture of Greek and Roman, its constant undercutting of serious content for the sake of dropping an allusion, we see most clearly how the *fabula Graecanica* or *Milesia* that *Metamorphoses* claims to be brings delight to an attentive reader, like a Nabokov novel or a Borges poem. There is very little of this allusive wit in the Greek versions of the ass-story; and here, rather than in the details of his use of his immediate Greek model, we see the true character of the contribution of the Sophist of Carthage to the Ass-Story.

Notes

1 Varro *L. L.* 10.70, used it to characterize Greek proper names with Latin as opposed to Greek case-endings (*Hectorem* not *Hectora*).
2 Knaut (1868: 16–17) first provided concrete examples; comparison is facilitated by the facing-page edition of Van Thiel (1971).
3 The argument against this by Hicter (1942) was not based on a close reading of the two texts.
4 Poggio published *Onos* in 1450 (Fubini 1964). Schottius (1606: 39) first noted the significance of Photios for Apuleius.
5 Notable among them are Bianco (1971), Rohde (1869) and Teuffel (1864).
6 Browne (1978) accepts the reality of an *author* Lucius of Patrae; see however Mason (1994: 1671).
7 Poggio was unaware of 'Loukios of Patrae', but entitled his edition of *Onos*, '*Lucii philosophi Syri comoedia quae "Asinus" intitulatur*' (Fubini 1964: 1. 138).
8 With these additions, *Onos* with 1088 lines of text would approach the dimensions of *True Story*, 1392 lines in two books.
9 Perry (1967: 217–20), G. Anderson (1982: 75, n.2), Holzberg (1984), Winkler (1985: 271).
10 Plutarch, *Crassus*, 32; [Lucian], *Amores*, 1.1; Ovid, *Tristia*, 2, 413, 444; Fronto, *Ad M. Caesarem* 4,3,2.
11 G. Anderson (1976: 47; 1984: 201–2); Mazzarino (1950: 77); Mason (1978: 7; 1994: 1691–2).

Bibliography

Anderson, G. (1976), *Studies in Lucian's Comic Fiction* (*Mnemosyne*, Supplement 43), Leiden: E.J. Brill.

—— (1982), *Eros Sophistes: Ancient Novelists at Play* (*American Classical Studies*, 9), Chico, CA: Scholars Press.

—— (1984), *Ancient fiction: the Novel in the Graeco-Roman World*, London/Sydney: Croom Helm.

—— (1994), 'Lucian: Tradition versus Reality', in W. Haase (ed.) *Aufstieg und Niedergang der römischen Welt*, Berlin/New York: W. de Gruyter, pp. 1422–47.

Anderson, W. (1909), 'Zu Apuleius' Novelle vom Tode der Charite', *Philologus* 68: 537–49.

Anderson, W.F. (1993), *Barbarian Play: Plautus' Roman Comedy*, Toronto/Buffalo/London: University of Toronto Press.

Bianco, G. (1971), *La fonte greca delle Metamorfosi di Apuleio*, Brescia: Paideia.

Bowie, E. (1996), 'The Ancient Readers of the Greek Novels', in G. Schmeling (ed.) *The Novel in the Ancient World*, Leiden/New York/Cologne: E.J. Brill, pp. 87–106.

Browne, Gerald M. (1978), 'On the "*Metamorphoses*" of Lucius of Patrae', *American Journal of Philology* 99: 442–6.

Bürger, K. (1887), *De Lucio Patrensi*, dissertation, University of Berlin: Berliner Buchdruckerei.

Courier, Paul-Emile (1818), *La Luciade ou l'âne de Lucius de Patras*, Paris: A. Bobée.

Crusius, O. (1889), 'Vorlage der Apuleianischen Metamorphosen', *Philologus* 47: 448.

Dowden, K. (1994), 'The Roman Audience of *The Golden Ass*', in J. Tatum (ed.), *The Search for the Ancient Novel*, Baltimore/London: Johns Hopkins University Press, pp. 419–34.

Fick, Nicole (1991), *Art et mystique dans les Métamorphoses d'Apulée*, Paris: Société d'Editions 'Les Belles Lettres'.

Fubini, R. (ed.) (1964), *Poggio Bracciolini Opera*, Turin: Bottega d'Erasmo (reprint of the 1538 edition).

Goldbacher, A. (1872), 'Über Lukios von Patrae, den dem Lukian zugeschriebenen "*Loukios e Onos*" und des Apuleius "*Metamorphosen*"', *Zeitschrift für die Österreichischen Gymnasien* 23: 323–41, 403–21.

Haase, W. (ed.) (1994), *Aufstieg und Niedergang der römischen Welt*, II 34.2, Berlin/New York: W. de Gruyter.

Hall, J. (1981), *Lucian's Satire*, New York: Arno Press.

Hicter, M. (1942), *Apulée, conteur fantastique*, Brussels: Office de publicité.

Hijmans, B.L. Jr. (1987), 'Apuleius, Philosophus Platonicus', in W. Haase (ed.), *Aufstieg und Niedergang der Römische Welt* II 36.1, Berlin/New York: W. de Gruyter, pp. 395–475.

Hofmann, H. (1993), 'Parodies des Erzählens – Erzählen als Parodie: Der *Goldene Esel* des Apuleius', in W. Ax and R. Glei (eds), *Literaturparodie in Antike und Mittelalter*, Trier: Wissenschaftlicher Verlag Trier, pp. 119–51.

Holzberg, N. (1984), 'Apuleius und der Verfasser des Griechischen Eselsromans', *Würzburger Jahrbücher für die Altertumswissenschaft* N.F. 10: 161–77.

Jensson, G. T. (1997), 'The Recollections of Encolpius as Greco-Roman Erotic Fiction', unpublished Ph.D. dissertation University of Toronto.

Junghanns, P. (1932), *Die Erzählungstechnik von Apuleius' 'Metamorphosen' und ihrer Vorlage* (*Philologus* Supplement, 24.1), Leipzig: Dieterich'sche Verlagsbuchhandlung.

Knaut, C.F.E. (1868), *De Luciano libelli qui inscribitur Lucius sive Asinus auctore*, Diss. Leipzig: A. Edelmann.

Kussl, R. (1990), 'Die *Metamorphosen* des "Lukios von Patrai": Untersuchungen zu Phot. *Bibl.* 129', *Rheinisches Museum* 133: 379–88.

McLeod, M. D. (1994), 'Lucianic Studies since 1930', in W. Haase (ed.) *Aufstieg und Niedergang der römischen Welt*, Berlin/New York: W. de Gruyter, pp. 1362–421.

Mason, H. J. (1972), Review of Van Thiel 1971, *Phoenix* 24: 313–17.

—— (1978), '*Fabula Graecanica*: Apuleius and his Greek Sources', in B. L. Hijmans and R. Th. van der Paardt (eds), *Aspects of Apuleius' Golden Ass*, Groningen: Bouma's Boekhuis, pp. 1–15.
—— (1994), 'Greek and Latin Versions of the Ass-Story', in W. Haase (ed.) *Aufstieg und Niedergang der römischen Welt*, Berlin/New York: W. de Gruyter, pp. 1665–707.
Mazzarino, A. (1950), *La Milesia e Apuleio*, Turin: Chiantore.
Münstermann, H. (1995), *Apuleius: Metamorphosen literarischer Vorlagen. Untersuchungen dreier Episoden des Romans unter Berücksichtigung der Philosophie und Theologie des Apuleius* (*Beiträge zur Altertumskunde*, 69), Stuttgart/Leipzig: B.G. Teubner.
Nabokov, V. (1968), *King, Queen, Knave*, translated by Dmitri Nabokov in collaboration with the author, New York: McGraw Hill.
Perry, B. E. (1920), *The Metamorphoses of Lucius of Patrae* (dissertation, Princeton University), New York: G. F. Stechert.
—— (1967), *The Ancient Romances. A Literary-Historical Account of their Origins* (*Sather Classical Lectures*, 37), Berkeley/Los Angeles: University of California Press.
Rohde, E, (1869), *Ueber Lucians Schrift* Λούκιος ἢ ὄνος *und ihr Verhältnis zu Lucius von Patrae und den Metarmorphosen von Apulejus. Eine literarische Untersuchung*, Leipzig: Engelmann.
Sandy, G. (1994), 'Apuleius' "Metamorphoses" and the Ancient Novel', in W. Haase (ed.) *Aufstieg und Niedergang der römischen Welt*, Berlin/New York: W. de Gruyter, pp. 1512–74.
Schlam, Carl C. (1970), 'Platonica in the *Metamorphoses* of Apuleius', *Transactions of the American Philological Association* 101: 477–87.
—— (1971), 'The Scholarship on Apuleius since 1938', *Classical World* 64: 285–308.
—— (1992), *The Metamorphoses of Apuleius. On Making an Ass of Oneself*, Chapel Hill, NC/London: University of North Carolina Press.
Schmeling, G. (ed.) (1996), *The Novel in the Ancient World* (*Mnemosyne*, Supplement 159), Leiden: E.J. Brill.
Schmid, W. (1919), 'Epikritisches zur Echtheitsfrage von Lucians *Onos*', *Berliner Philologische Wochenschrift* 39: 167–8.
Schottius, A. (1606), *Photii Myriobiblon sive Bibliotheca*, e Graeco Latine reddidit et scholiis auxit Andreas Schottius, Augsburg: Christopher Magnus.
Strohmaier, G. (1976), 'Übersehenes zur Biographie Lukians', *Philologus* 120: 117–22.
Sullivan, J. P. (1989), 'The Ass', in B. P. Reardon (ed.), *Collected Ancient Greek Novels*, Berkeley/Los Angeles/London: University of California Press, pp. 589–618.
Teuffel, W. S. (1864), 'Lukians *Loukios* und Apuleius' *Metamorphosen*', *Rheinisches Museum* 19: 243–54.
Thibau, R. (1965), 'Les *Métamorphoses* d'Apulée et la théorie platonicienne de l'Erôs', *Studia Philosophica Gandensia* 3: 89–144.
Van T. H. (1971), *Der Eselsroman. I: Untersuchungen. II: Synoptische Ausgabe* (*Zetemata*, 54: 1–2), Munich: Beck.
Walsh, P. G. (1970), *The Roman Novel*, Cambridge: Cambridge University Press.
—— (1995), *Apuleius. The Golden Ass*, translated with introduction and explanatory notes, Oxford/New York: Oxford University Press.
Werner, H. (1918), 'Zum "*Loukios e Onos*"', *Hermes* 53: 225–61.
Winkler, J.J. (1985), *Auctor & Actor. A Narratological Reading of Apuleius's 'The Golden Ass'*, Berkeley/Los Angeles/London: University of California Press.

7

APULEIUS' *METAMORPHOSES*

The inserted tales

Nancy Shumate

The recent resurgence of interest in the prose fiction of Greek and Roman antiquity has been fuelled in part by a new appreciation of the complexity of the narrative techniques employed in these texts. In the ancient novel, critics have 'discovered' a range of sophisticated strategies that seem to anticipate those widely regarded as the hallmarks of the modern novel exclusively, or generally viewed as the identifying features of modernist and post-modernist fiction (see, for example, Doody 1996). These strategies include a multiplication of perspectives that fragments the narrative's unity and vexes the reader's search for an authorized meaning; a playful self-consciousness about the text's own status as fiction; and various forms of intertextuality, including parody and elaborate networks of literary allusion. One relevant device that holds a prominent place in the ancient novelistic tradition is the 'inserted' tale, or the tale within the tale: digressions, frequently of great length, usually but not always related by one of the characters in the main narrative. In some instances, the layering of story lines can become so complex that the main narrative is altogether obscured.[1] Many recent critics have read this complexity as a means of exploring the relationship between representation and reality, and of questioning the reliability of narrators and the authority or truth value of any narrative, as we will see.

The Latin novel of Apuleius is representative of ancient fiction in this respect. The narrative teems with sub-narratives, and they begin in the very first scene. On his journey to Hypata Lucius meets two travellers, one of whom, Aristomenes, tells a tale of his recent experience with witches, hoping (correctly, as it turns out) that Lucius will be a more sympathetic audience than the sceptical third traveller. Aristomenes recalls an encounter with his long-lost friend Socrates, who in turn tells of his own affair with the witch Meroë; Aristomenes tries to rescue his friend from her clutches but is foiled when she and a minion surreptitiously steal Socrates' heart, resulting in his death and Aristomenes' exile (1.5–19). The theme of scepticism vs. credulity is replayed in Book 2 (13–14), when Lucius' host Milo tells his guest the story of how Diophanes, a soothsayer currently making the rounds in Greece, allowed his mask momentarily to drop on his last visit to Hypata and thus inadvertently exposed his own chicanery. Milo intends the story as a warning to Lucius against easy belief in the supernatural; thus the novel's first two tales establish credulity as one of the main character traits of the protagonist.

The supernatural is again the subject of the next two tales. At 2.21–30, at Lucius' aunt Byrrhena's banquet a guest named Thelyphron is called upon, apparently against his will, to tell the tale of his own encounter with the dark side. As a young man he was hired to guard a corpse against mutilation by witches. He thought he had been successful until the corpse revived to bear witness to the suspicious circumstances of its death, reveals that Thelyphron was mistaken for a dead man while he slept on guard duty and as a result had his own nose and ears stolen. Thelyphron had not realized this because the witches had fashioned wax substitutes, a practice not alluded to before this point – one of several lapses in logic and expectation that give this tale as well as others an unsettling quality typical of Apuleian narrative. Thelyphron's tale ends in his humiliation and exile, as had that of Aristomenes. Then in Book 3 (15–18), the slave girl Photis makes a lengthy confession to Lucius to ease her sense of responsibility for his suffering at the Risus festival (where he had endured a trial whose carnivalesque character is revealed only after he was thoroughly convinced he would pay the penalty for homicide). Photis feels guilty because her mistress Pamphile (who practises black magic) had animated the goatskins that Lucius had 'murdered' in the belief she was summoning a handsome young man whom she desired – a mistake that results from Photis' substituting goat hair for human when she is unable to secure the latter.

After the mock-heroic bandit's tale in Book 4 (9–21), which is told in the robbers' lair where Lucius the ass and the damsel Charite are held captive, and includes an account of the exploits of the bandit Thrasyleon disguised as a bear, we come to the tale of Cupid and Psyche (4.28–6.24). The old woman who serves as the bandits' cook offers this, the longest of the inserted narratives, to comfort the distressed Charite. In it, the extraordinary beauty of the mortal girl Psyche provokes the jealous wrath of the goddess Venus, who resolves to punish Psyche by wedding her to a hideous monster. Charged with bringing about this union, Venus' son Cupid instead spirits Psyche away to an enchanted realm and keeps her for his own wife. There the naive girl is egged on by her wicked sisters to violate her invisible husband's injunction not to probe into his identity. When her treachery is revealed, Cupid flies away and Psyche must endure a series of trials imposed by Venus. These she completes successfully with supernatural assistance, until her innate curiosity leads her again to try to look upon a forbidden sight, this time the beauty locked in a box that she had fetched from the goddess Proserpina in the underworld. But Cupid intervenes in the potentially dire consequences, and a reconciliation of all parties, mediated by Jupiter, brings the tale to a harmonious close.

Inserted tales continue to pile up in the four books of the novel between the tale of Cupid and Psyche and Lucius' conversion (7–10). Charite's betrothed Tlepolemus infiltrates the bandits' circle by posing as a renegade named 'Haemus' and gives a fictitious account of his life of crime to qualify for acceptance into the group (7.6–8). Later, after their escape, we hear of the demise of Charite and Tlepolemus from a slave of the family's household who reports the sad news to a group of fellow-slaves and herdsmen; the young man had been betrayed and murdered by his best friend Thrasyllus who wanted Charite for himself, but she foiled his plans by blinding her husband's murderer and killing herself (8.1–14). On an apparently lighter note is the intricate web of adultery tales in Book 9 (5–7, 14–31), overheard by Lucius *qua* ass and reported in his narrative; these tales are organized around the stereotype of women as promiscuous and perfidious. Returning to unrelenting mayhem, the inserted tales culminate with three accounts of the violent destruction of households: the report that Lucius and his gardener owner hear about the conflict between the three noble youths and the greedy landlord, which ends with the deaths of all four and ultimately with the suicide of the boys' father (9.35–8); and the stories heard by Lucius in Book 10 about the destruction wrought on their families by two lustful and jealous wives, one of which ends happily (an anomalous outcome in the tales), the other in cataclysm (10.2–12, 23–8).

The presence of so many highly elaborated inserted narratives raises a number of questions in the reader's mind: Why did Apuleius put them there? In what ways, if any, do they advance the plot? What is their relationship to the main narrative? Are they told purely for their value as entertainment, or are we to take them seriously in some sense? Any theorizing about the function of the tales should be informed by an understanding of the genesis of the Latin *Metamorphoses*. The evidence suggests that there were three literary narratives about a man transformed into an ass circulating in antiquity. The two extant pieces of evidence other than Apuleius' novel are, first, a short ass narrative in Greek that in its general outline resembles the Latin version, entitled *Lucius or the Ass* and known as the *Onos*; this work has been transmitted among the writings of the satirist Lucian. Second, we have a discussion by the ninth century Byzantine scholar Photius of two ass narratives that he had recently read. One is apparently the clearly satiric *Onos*; the other is another Greek work that he calls *Metamorphoseis*, written in an uncritical spirit (according to Photius) by a 'Lucius of Patrae' (*Bibliotheca*, cod. 129). Current scholarly opinion holds that this lost Greek *Metamorphoseis* preceded both the *Onos* and the Apuleian *Metamorphoses*; the former was an abridgement of 'Lucius of Patrae', the latter an expansion. The author of the lost work is generally considered to have been Lucian, whose satiric tone and critical distance from his narrator 'Lucius' were lost on the patriarch. The

Onos, then, would be an epitome of this Lucianic work, done by someone other than Lucian himself.[2]

If we know, then, that Apuleius was working from an existing text, the question that arises is this: at what points is the Latin narrative his own invention, and what passages are derived from the lost Greek *Metamorphoseis*? It is, after all, in part what Apuleius added that makes his *Metamorphoses* a work in its own right instead of a mere translation, and it is the work in its own right that must form the basis of any critical opinion about the particular aims and concerns of the Apuleian text, including the tales. Unfortunately, the epitome is all we have to go on when it comes to assessing the contents (and tone) of the lost work. Where the epitome and Apuleius correspond, the obvious explanation is that both borrowed from the common lost source at these points. A comparison of the *Onos* and the Latin text reveals parallel narrative outlines, as well as many shared motifs (magic and metamorphosis) and episodes (the eunuch priests, *Onos* 35–41, cf. *Met*. 8.24–9.10; the sadistic boy, 29–33, cf. 7.17–28; the ass's 'education' and his liaison with the Corinthian lady, 47–52, cf. 9.2–10.22).

On the other hand, a very great percentage of the Latin text is made up of material entirely absent from the epitome. This material includes all the tales enumerated above (although a tiny kernel of Charite's tale appears in the *Onos*), as well as the debate about evidence and belief that frames Aristomenes' tale, and the incident in the marketplace with the petty official Pythias and the overpriced fish in Book 1; the elaborate description of the group of statues depicting Actaeon and the goddess Diana in Byrrhena's foyer, and the scene of Byrrhena's banquet in Book 2; the entire episode of the Risus festival in Books 2 to 3; and finally, the Isisbook (Book 11) *in toto*. My premise here is that this material represents Apuleian innovation and is not derived from any literary source.[3] Even if the prototypes of these tales and episodes existed in the longer (probably Lucianic) narrative, there are good grounds for believing that their Latin incarnation represents a substantial reworking of the inherited material by Apuleius to serve his own purposes. To take the tale of Charite as a case in point, the treatment of her demise (by accidental drowning) that is suggested in the *Onos* (34) is expanded in the Latin version into a major episode involving deception, the collapse of social codes, and a descent into bestiality, all central concerns whose recurrence unites the Apuleian narrative. The tale as Apuleius tells it furthermore has an unmistakably Virgilian cast, something difficult to imagine in a satire by Lucian.[4] My point is that in all likelihood the tales with which we are concerned here are either original with Apuleius, or so extensively changed from their Greek form as to be virtually original with him. It is therefore appropriate that an analysis of the tales take place in the context of a discussion of the thematic unity of the Latin *Metamorphoses* as a whole.

How the tales have been read in the past has been determined by the critical orientation of particular readers toward the work in its entirety. There has always been a school of criticism that has taken Apuleius at his word when he appears to give instructions about how the text is to be read: *lector, intende: laetaberis* ('reader, listen: you'll enjoy yourself'), he says (1.1). These critics, typified by Perry, have considered the novel as a whole to be a compendium of pleasantly diverting stories and lascivious entertainment; this, then, is their view of the tales as well. Others have located traditional religious and philosophical preoccupations within the text, reading the *Metamorphoses* as a morality play about the dangers of pursuing forbidden knowledge in black magic and forbidden pleasures in unsanctioned sex; according to these critics, the tales reiterate this message (e.g., Vallette 1940, Walsh 1970, Tatum 1969 and 1972). More recently, Apuleian criticism has taken a turn toward the post-structuralist. Winkler was the first to argue along these lines; he proposed that the *Metamorphoses* is a 'deliberately unauthorized, self-questioning performance' whose multiplication of perspectives sabotages any tendency toward a unified meaning. No 'clear and final authorization' of any one signification for the text emanates from either narrator or author (Winkler 1985: 126, 131). A central concern with the arbitrary character of all knowledge is communicated in the series of 'hermeneutic games' that constitute the *Metamorphoses* and replay in miniature the text's overall resistance to totalizing interpretation.

Winkler views the inserted tales in particular as 'epistemological exercises' designed to expose the provisional and subjective nature of all apparent truths. Because the reliability of their narrators is often suspect, and because the way their content is construed can vary wildly depending on who the interpreter or audience is, the tales raise important questions about the truth value of stories (and by extension of any text). Through the tales, according to Winkler, Apuleius explores the endless ways in which texts can be variably read or misread, and evidence variably or wrongly interpreted. He observes in connection with the tales that repeatedly, 'what seems for the moment to be a true interpretation (of narrative or personal experience) is later shown to depend on the perspective of the interpreter'. Inevitably, the scepticism engendered in the reader by these 'exercises' must extend to the question of the reliability of the main narrator Lucius himself, especially when it comes to deciding how seriously we are to take his religious conversion in Book 11.[5]

These apparently disparate readings are in fact not mutually exclusive. Religious and hermeneutic approaches to the *Metamorphoses* can complement one another, if aspects of religious experience beyond the strictly moralistic are admitted. The novel's delectatory features, moreover, can provide the proverbial honey on the rim of a cup of medicine that makes what might have been a rather dense intellectual brew go down more smoothly. Given the dénouement in the Isisbook, it is evident that the *Metamorphoses* is a narrative of religious conversion in some sense. To the extent that the novel has been studied as such, however, the defining feature has been located in an alleged sequence of moral 'fall' and redemption on the part of the protagonist Lucius. But religious conversion can involve epistemic as well as moral rupture and reorientation, and it is in issues of epistemology that religious and hermeneutic readings of the *Metamorphoses* intersect; the difference is that in religious readings the rupture is repaired, whereas in hermeneutic readings it can never be.[6]

The basic movement of the narrative is not from a degeneration of Lucius' personal morality to moral purgation; rather it is from a disintegration of his habituated values and structures of meaning to the construction of a new system of meaning around Isis. The narrative moves, in a word, from disorder to order, at least at the level inhabited by Lucius the character who undergoes the experiences described in the *Metamorphoses*, or Lucius the *actor* in Winkler's terms. This Lucius is to be distinguished from Apuleius the author and from Lucius the narrator or *auctor*, whose hindsight commentary on events is strangely absent from the narrative. Neither Apuleius nor the second Lucius endorses the religious conclusions reached by Lucius the *actor*/convert; their aloofness, on the contrary, as well as various apparently satiric elements in the Isisbook (the insinuations about priestly venality, for example) all suggest a critique. But along the central thread of the narrative that traces the subjective religious experience of the *actor*, Books 1 to 10 represent the disillusionment with conventional values and the subsequent fragmentation of the subject's world view that often precede religious conversion. In Book 11 this instability is resolved with the convert's discovery of 'true' value in divinity, and the resulting reunification of his world. The tales, then, mirror, anticipate, and recapitulate the experience of the main character and the gradual transformation of his vision in this regard.

The crisis in values of Lucius the *actor* and the exhausted utility of his customary pursuits are expressed in the novel in ways appropriate to the genre. Classic spiritual autobiography (most famously, the *Confessions* of Augustine) incorporates a retrospective commentary on past events and their meaning for the narrator's development. In the absence of any such fictionalized commentary in the *Metamorphoses*, the confessional novel in this case offers dramatization, metaphor, and reduction to absurdity. The inadequacy of worldly objects of desire and sources of pleasure to provide true, ultimate satisfaction is a standard motif in narratives of religious conversion. This idea is conveyed in the *Metamorphoses* in a series of vivid vignettes suggesting that only empty pleasures follow the fulfilment of Lucius' many lusts. Past critics have concentrated on his longing for sexual and magical experiences in their attempts to identify his 'sin', but it is clear that his desires range indiscriminately over a wide variety of objects, from the gravely consequential to the apparently harmless. In spite of their seeming disparity, his pleasure-seeking activities are linked by means of the same vocabulary of desire and pleasure. They are thus equated as *all* representing the same syndrome of misguided casting about for some pleasure, any pleasure, that will last. Thus, the exposure of worldly values and pursuits as 'false' that is so central to narratives of conversion as a genre appears in the novel as an implied critique of Lucius' insipid strategies of gratification. By disseminating his desiderative energies impulsively and uncritically on a range of moving targets, Lucius demonstrates that, from a religious perspective, his entire cognitive orientation is incorrect; true satisfaction can come only from concentrating those energies on a divine centre.

Lucius' deluded patterns of pleasure-seeking illustrate this principle, and the tales provide a background of analogous activity. To be sure, his attraction to sex and sorcery as potential modes of gratification holds a prominent place in the narrative, especially in the first three books, which tell of his spirited affair with Photis and his machinations to gain entry into his hostess Pamphile's mysterious magical underworld. These adventures are driven by desire (*cupido*), and their intended reward is pleasure, as the diction in both episodes makes clear. But this is true also of Lucius' many miscellaneous acts of idle curiosity beyond his initial obsessive curiosity about magic. It is clear, in fact, that in the novel's calculus, curiosity is postulated from the outset as a major category of 'false' desire, that is, desire which when fulfilled cannot lead to lasting satisfaction, owing to the ephemeral character of its objects.[7] Curiosity is the desire that drives Lucius to seek momentary pleasure randomly in *any* novel sight, experience, or tale (as at, for example, 6.27, 7.13, 8.22, 9.4, 9.12, 9.14, 10.29; when the object of curiosity is a tale, we have a typically neat Apuleian twist in that the tales' content reiterates the main character's compulsive behaviours, while the tales are themselves in these cases the object of his compulsions). The recurrent image of Lucius mindlessly directing his attention wherever an amusing diversion might present itself is the novel's primary means of conveying the extent of his spiritual derailment. He accumulates an unconnected series of frivolous pleasures, but they never add up to real happiness, which eludes him as long as he remains on this misguided path. The futility of Lucius' efforts is symbolized in the seemingly endless cycle of rising expectations and dashed hopes that he must endure as an ass (3.27, 3.29, 4.2, his frustrated quest for the therapeutic roses; 7.15, 7.16, 9.1–3, 10.16, other hopes with disappointment at their heel). In religious terms, Lucius is represented as acting habitually on an unrecognized and displaced *desiderium dei*. His desire is for divinity, but he spends it on mere palliatives instead.

Numerous characters in the inserted tales are caught up in the same syndrome as Lucius; they too inhabit a world of false values and deluded pursuits, which once again are regularly formulated in terms of a wrong-headed system of desires and pleasures. In the tales, as in the main narrative, sex and magic are salient as potentially unhealthy objects of desire. Socrates' affair with the witch Meroë as related by Aristomenes in Book 1 (5–20) and the extramarital escapades of the baker's wife (9.22–31) both begin as lighthearted diversions, but end in disaster. In the tales of Charite and Thrasyllus (8.1–14) and of the treacherous stepmother (10.2–12), on the other hand, sexual passion is destructive from beginning to end. Lucius' longing to witness or experience something supernatural is also mirrored in the tales, as when, in Thelyphron's story of his own disgrace (2.28–29), he and a crowd that has gathered around the necromancer Zatchlas crane their necks for a good view. But the amorphous desire of the characters in the tales, like that of Lucius, lights on many other objects as well. In the tale of adultery that her hag friend tells to the baker's wife, the greed of the slave Myrmex for the gold of a bribe is characterized as a desire (*cupido*), and he anticipates that the money will bring him pleasure (*voluptas*) (9.19). This category of lust is clearly destructive, insofar as it corrupts the character of the previously loyal slave.

But in other instances in the tales, the negative implications of actions driven by desire, and even the status of the motivating impulse as a kind of desire, are not as immediately apparent. As with Lucius, here again the thoughtless direction of idle curiosity toward trivial objects is a less easily identifiable, but equally significant, symptom of missing the mark of one's 'true' desire (in religious terms). The syndrome is vividly epitomized in the recurrent images of idle, diversion-seeking mobs that materialize whenever an unusual sight offers the possibility of momentary amusement (as at, for example, 2.28, 4.16, 8.6, 10.12). The idiotic gaping of these crowds clearly mirrors the habitual attitude of Lucius as a man and as an ass, and captures the religious idea of the inadequacy of gratification coming from any temporal source.[8] In several instances of good fortune followed closely by disaster, the tales also reiterate the suggestion of the main narrative that when life is thus approached from the wrong angle, the most that one can expect is a mere accumulation of tenuous pleasures; real happiness will remain elusive (1.17, Aristomenes thinks that the doomed Socrates is fine and that their troubles are over; 2.26–30, Thelyphron is pleased with the apparently successful outcome of his mission, only to discover that he has been deceived; 7.13, 8.1–14, the report of Charite's demise is received shortly after her joyous return home).

A more elaborately worked out parallel movement from 'false' or deceptive values to 'true' and reliable ones can be discerned in the lengthiest of the inserted tales, the story of Cupid and Psyche (4.28–6.24).[9] Seeing such a pattern in the tale represents a refinement of the established allegorical interpretation, which reads in Psyche's trials a Platonic ascent of the soul from the degraded material realm to communion with the ideal. Within this general framework, the tale describes Psyche's habit of allowing her desire to be displaced onto 'false' objects. This habit indicates an incorrect orientation that is the cause of her separation from her true love Cupid, and which results, as it does for Lucius, in a period of trials and exile. Only when the divine becomes the sole object of her desire does Psyche at last experience enduring pleasure, symbolized by her immortal daughter *Voluptas*. The opening sequence of the tale offers a programmatic statement of the operative problem in its vivid picture of citizens as well as foreigners worshipping the mortal girl as if she were a goddess, their religious longings veering off course. Their misguided devotion is, of course, a disaster for Psyche herself, since it stirs the wrath of the real goddess Venus, who is forced to settle for 'indirect worship' (4.30, *vicaria veneratio*).

This initial glimpse of the workings of derailed desire sets the stage for the presentation of Psyche's own tendencies in that direction. Although given the opportunity to live in a state of blissful union with a god, she perversely allows herself to be seduced away from that enduring source of pleasure. Like Lucius slouching toward Isis, she repeatedly wanders off course in her quest to be reunited with Cupid, forgetting what her proper business is; and like him, she is especially susceptible to the lure of 'false' desire in the form of curiosity (5.6, 19, 23; 6.19, 20, 21). Curiosity is dangerous insofar as it is a symptom of an intellectual habit that prevents both Lucius and Psyche from concentrating on the serious business of life, as it keeps them distracted by anything, great or small, that happens to catch their interest. But Psyche is not incorrigible because, like Lucius, she is not bad, but rather misguided and naive (it is her shrill, deceitful, and covetous sisters who represent the world of false values, which she ultimately transcends, at its most treacherous and horrific). More than anything else, she and her counterpart in the main narrative are represented as simply not knowing any better in their orientation toward a 'wrong' paradigm of desire and pleasure. Their defect is epistemological: they fail to calculate correctly where 'true' knowledge and value lie. Thus, the tale of Cupid and Psyche reprises the main obstacle that Lucius must overcome in his own bumbling journey – his habits of mind and learned systems of value and meaning.

The world of the *Metamorphoses* is one utterly lacking in the cohesion imparted by a unifying, naturalized system of values that orders experience and assigns a hierarchy of meaning to its undifferentiated phenomena, since, as we have seen, it is precisely such a system of conventional values that the narrative discredits as spurious. The novel has many ways of representing the topsy-turvy quality of a pre-conversion world whose centre has disappeared and whose orienting signposts have been uprooted. Lucius' reality becomes inscrutable and unstable on every level. Established boundaries are exposed as arbitrary and transgressed with more and more frequency, and gaps open up between signs and their accustomed meanings, between appearance and reality. The world that the novel creates is a *terra infirma* whose ground is always shifting underfoot, one where old certainties and assumptions evanesce. The tales provide a mirror or counterpoint to these developments in the main narrative.

Let us consider, for example, the thematic importance of the disintegration of the social laws that regulate human behaviour. Lucius laments that *fides* has lost its force, leaving those around him to indulge their worst impulses with impunity (3. 7, 26). In the subordinate narratives, not only *fides* but also *religio* and *pietas* are cast aside (explicitly, in the tales of Charite and the two wicked women of Book 10: 8. 2, 7, 12; 10. 3, 4, 24–27). The perverse *Schadenfreude* with which the citizens of Hypata carry out their mock prosecution of Lucius at the Risus festival (3.1–13) (an experience whose dangers and humiliation are clearly real enough to the victim) can be connected to the licence to ignore the salutary constraints of the social contract that a striking number of the novel's characters seem to feel that they possess. Lucius' treatment as the butt of a joke in which he does not share, and the sense of alienation that he experiences as a result, are anticipated in the tale of Thelyphron and the circumstances surrounding its telling. His story is solicited and received at Byrrhena's banquet with similar gales of malevolent laughter, as is the relevation of his mutilation in the tale itself; and his feeling of humiliation is conveyed with equal vividness (2.20–31). These episodes have a comic side, but in the tales of Books 8 to 10, human behaviour degenerates with alarming rapidity, and there is little to mitigate the effect. In these tales, a central device in the representation of this process is the pointed attribution of animal qualities to human characters. Thrasyllus and Charite (Book 8), the greedy landlord (9), and the two female criminals in the penultimate book are especially notable for the beastly ferocity and rabid wildness with which they career toward their ruin.[10] It is in the same books that the ass confounds expectation and graduates from one human accomplishment to the next. In these instances, then, the tales provide not a mirror or reiteration of Lucius' experience, but rather a counterpoint or inverted parallel to them.

All of this action takes place against a background in which the formation of false opinions and the misconstruction of evidence are chronic. The sometimes comic and sometimes tragic, but always chaotic results of the characters' failure to question and analyse what *appears* to be true, add another layer to the picture of extreme volatility and unreliability in the social institutions and human society of the novel. False opinion can be the product of a concerted effort to deceive, or of a neutral set of facts that are incorrectly construed. Whatever its source, the frequency with which false opinion is accepted as fact in the *Metamorphoses* suggests a world where knowledge is not absolute, but provisional and subjective. Lucius is shocked when circumstantial evidence leads the people of Hypata to conclude that he plundered his host Milo's home (7.1–3); later, he himself forms an equally ill-grounded negative judgement about Charite (7.10). A series of unrelated events is taken to indicate that the ass has rabies (9. 2–4), and the wicked boy's lies about the animal's lasciviousness are accepted as truth (7. 21–8); both developments have potentially harmful consequences for the protagonist. As usual, the tales reprise this theme. A close reading of the tale of Charite, the stories of the two murderesses, and the adultery tales reveals the extent to which the action there hinges on deception and mendacity, which generate whole networks of false opinion. The latter set of stories represents a comic variation on the theme, but in all cases the impression, in philosophical terms, of epistemological instability is unmistakable. Indeed, the fluidity of the novel's world penetrates down to the gross physical reality represented in the text. Given the pervasiveness of this theme and the variegated modes of its expression, the metaphorical value of the magical plot mechanisms introduced in the main narrative and reiterated in the tales of the first three books becomes clear. As Ebel puts it, in the *Metamorphoses* 'magic is as much an expression as a cause [of the universal fact] that all appearances are unreliable and all realities transient' (1970: 163).

When, in Book 11, Isis takes centre stage in Lucius' vision, her greatest benefit is to order the disorder that had characterized his old life. She functions more as a metaphysical anchor than a moral task mistress, providing his destabilized world with a new structural centre. Lucius the convert makes contact with a divinity who presents herself as the source of natural and cosmic order, the author of a grand design, the point of origin of all things. From that source, a coherence and harmony flow into his world where before there had been a vacuum. Lucius finally finds himself on solid ground, with his previously fragmented desiderative energies concentrated on their only 'true' object – Isis; he has found a system of meaning and value upon which he can rely. All this is implied of the experiencing Lucius; what is missing is any validating testimonial from the narrator, testimonial of the sort that readers intuitively expect at the close of a confessional narrative, produced from the point of view of the present or the time of writing. The two Luciuses, in other words, are never united. The narrator's failure to endorse the conversion, along with the parodic and satiric aspects of the Isisbook that undermine the conversion's solemnity, operate to suggest a critique of religious experience imbedded in the compelling invocation of it.

It should be stressed, however, that a critique and an invocation existing alongside one another are not as contradictory as they might appear to be; one can understand the attractions of a religious world view without being able to make the leap of faith. Read as critique, Book 11 is the culminating instance of the lesson rehearsed by the tales, that all knowledge (including, now, religious knowledge) is subjective and non-authorized, that any text or experience (including religious texts and experiences) 'can only be unified by the reader's decision to see it in a certain way' (Winkler 1985: 131–2). Read as invocation, Book 11 sympathetically describes the convert's new life; the inserted tales are an integral device in representing the intolerable deficiencies of the old life that preceded it.

Notes

1 The reader can easily gain a sense of how common the devices enumerated in this paragraph are in the Greek novel by perusing Reardon 1989.

2 For brief accounts of the history of the problem of the three asses and their authorship, see, e.g., Mason 1978, 1994 and Chapter 6 in this volume; also James 1987: 7–24, Schlam 1992: 18–28.

3 For the reasoning that supports this premise, see Mason 1978: 4, Mason 1994: 1699, and in this volume, Chapter 6.

4 On the Virgilian elements in the tale of Charite, see Finkelpearl 1986, Frangoulidis 1992 and Shumate 1996b. Apuleius' reworking tendency is evident in many episodes that are not inserted tales. The sequences involving the sadistic boy (Book 7) and the eunuch priests (8), for example, while present in the *Onos*, are recast in the Latin text to stress deception, mendacity, and false accusation, and thus are incorporated into an ongoing and peculiarly Apuleian exploration of these issues.

5 Winkler 1985: *passim*. On how the tales reiterate the main narrative's concern with 'the hermeneutic game of "What is true?" (117), see his discussion of the programmatic debate about belief and disbelief between Lucius and the traveller that frames Aristomenes' tale, and its echoes in the tales of Diophanes, 'Haemus', and the wicked stepmother (1985: 27–32, 81–6; 39–42; 46–50; 77–80). For a discussion of the same question from Lucius' perspective see Van Mal-Maeder 1995.

6 Shumate 1996a argues that shifts in an individual's structures of knowledge (as opposed to moral crisis as it is usually understood) can lie at the heart of religious conversion, and accordingly can be a central concern in literary representations of this experience, including the *Metamorphoses*. The claims made here about the generic features of narratives of conversion are substantiated in the longer study through the use of extensive comparative material. See in particular the rereading of Augustine's *Confessions* as an account of the reorientation of the narrator's intellect toward a new, unitary source of meaning (1996: 204–15).

7 See Walsh 1988 for a discussion of the values (negative and positive) attached to curiosity in a range of ancient texts; for *curiositas* especially in the *Met.* see Hijmans 1995. For the connections between the theme of curiosity and Apuleius' Platonism, see De Filippo 1990 and Hijmans 1995: 376 f. In his understanding of curiosity as a symptom of general spiritual malaise, Apuleius anticipates Augustine – see Shumate 1996: 243–8.

8 Collective fascination with spectacle is a recurring motif in the ancient novel as a genre, but the larger religious framework that structures the Apuleian narrative expands the ways in which these crowd scenes can be read.

9 See on this tale, Chapter 8 by G. N. Sandy in this volume.

10 It is Apuleius' practice to intersperse comic versions of a theme or motif with more dramatic or serious treatments. In the present connection, the beastly bellowing of the cuckolded Barbarus in the third adultery tale of Book 9 (21) is a case in point. Likewise, the preoccupation with *fides* in the bandits' tales provides a comic or ironic commentary on the idea of the disappearance of trust.

Bibliography

De Filippo, J. (1990), '*Curiositas* and the Platonism of Apuleius' *Golden Ass*', *American Journal of Philology* 111: 471–92.

Doody, M. (1996), *The True Story of the Novel*, New Brunswick, NJ: Rutgers University Press.

Ebel, H. (1970), 'Apuleius and the Present Time', *Arethusa* 3: 155–76.

Finkelpearl, E. (1986), 'Metamorphosis of Language in Apuleius' Metamorphoses', dissertation Harvard University.

Frangoulidis, S. A. (1992), 'Charite's Literary Models: Virgil's Dido and Homer's Odysseus', in C. Deroux (ed.), *Studies in Latin Literature and Roman History*, vol. VI, Brussels: Latomus, pp. 435–50.

Hijmans, B.L. (1995), 'Curiositas', in *Groningen Commentaries on Apuleius*: *Book IX*, Groningen: Egbert Forsten, pp. 362–79.

James, P. (1987), *Unity in Diversity: A Study of Apuleius' Metamorphoses*, Hildesheim/New York: Olms-Weidmann.

Mason, H. (1978), '*Fabula Graecanica*: Apuleius and his Greek Sources', in B. Hijmans and R. van der Paardt (eds), *Aspects of Apuleius' Golden Ass*, Groningen: Bouma's Boekhuis, pp. 1–15.

—— (1994), 'Greek and Latin Versions of the Ass-Story', in W. Haase (ed.), *Aufstieg und Niedergang der römischen Welt*, vol. II 34.2, Berlin/New York: W. de Gruyter, pp. 1665–707.

Perry, B. E. (1967), *The Ancient Romances: A Literary-Historical Account of Their Origins* (*Sather Classical Lectures*, 37), Berkeley/Los Angeles: University of California Press.

Reardon, B. P. (ed.) (1989), *Collected Ancient Greek Novels*, Berkeley/Los Angeles/London: University of California Press.

Schlam, C. C. (1992), *The Metamorphoses of Apuleius: On Making an Ass of Oneself*, Chapel Hill, NC and London: University of North Carolina Press.

Shumate, N. (1996a), *Crisis and Conversion in Apuleius' Metamorphoses*, Ann Arbor: University of Michigan Press.

—— (1996b), "Darkness visible": Apuleius Reads Virgil', in H. Hofmann and M. Zimmermann (eds), *Groningen Colloquia on the Novel*, vol. 7, Groningen: Egbert Forsten, pp. 103–16.

Tatum, J. (1969), 'The Tales in Apuleius' *Metamorphoses*', *Transactions of the American Philological Association* 100: 487–527.

—— (1972), 'Apuleius and Metamorphosis', *American Journal of Philology* 93: 306–13.

Vallette, P. (1940), 'Introduction', in D. Robertson (ed.) *Apulée, Les Métamorphoses*, vol. 1, Paris: Société d'Edition Les Belles Lettres, pp. v–lxiv.

Van Mal-Maeder, D. (1995), 'L'*Ane d'Or* ou les métamorphoses d'un récit: illustration de la subjectivité humaine', in H. Hofmann (ed.), *Groningen Colloquia on the Novel*, vol. 6, Groningen: Egbert Forsten, pp. 103–25.

Walsh, P. (1970), *The Roman Novel*, Cambridge: Cambridge University Press.

—— (1988), 'The Rights and Wrongs of Curiosity', *Greece and Rome* 35: 73–85.

Winkler, J. J. (1985), *Auctor & Actor: A Narratological Reading of Apuleius's 'The Golden Ass'*, Berkeley/Los Angeles/London: University of California Press.

8

THE TALE OF CUPID AND PSYCHE

Gerald N. Sandy

I The tale

The longest of the many self-contained tales that are recounted by the dramatized first-person narrator Lucius to soothe the ears of the listener, the tale of Cupid and Psyche occupies the centre of Apuleius' *Golden Ass*. The narrator of the novel heard it being told to a kidnapped young woman named Charite by 'that crazy and drunken . . . old woman' who served as house-keeper for the kidnappers to comfort her after she had been awakened by a nightmare.

The first two sentences of the tale have the earmarks of a fairy-tale, 'There were in a certain city a king and queen. They had three lovely daughters.' Psyche, the youngest of the three sisters, is of such incomparable beauty that mortals abandon the worship of the goddess Venus and instead direct their admiration to Psyche. The goddess, jealous of a mortal's usurpation of her due, instructs her son Cupid to afflict Psyche with an irresistible passion for a base commoner.

Meanwhile, on earth, Psyche's father despairs of finding a husband for her because all mortals stand in awe of her divine beauty.[1] He consults the oracle of Apollo at Miletus, which instructs him to place her on a mountain peak. There, the oracle declares in Latin instead of Greek for the benefit of the author of a Milesian tale, 'dressed for funereal wedlock', she will be taken as bride by an unnamed, winged serpent that even the gods fear. The gentle West Wind wafts her to a valley. When she wakes, she sees and enters a regal palace 'built not by human hands but by divine arts'. Ethereal voices address her and incorporeal servants attend to all her needs. At the end of the day she climbs into bed, and 'her unknown husband soon was there and made Psyche his wife'.

Meanwhile, Psyche's sisters, at the urging of her grieving parents, set out to learn of her fate. Her still unnamed (and unseen) husband warns her that if she pays heed to their concerns, she will cause him great stress and bring about her own ruin. He also promises that their still unborn child will be divine if she keeps their secret from her sisters. The sisters become jealous of her wealth and divine husband and scheme to plant the seeds of marital discord by convincing Psyche that her still unseen husband is the beast foretold in Apollo's oracle. Psyche takes her sisters' advice to unmask the hidden identity of her husband. She holds an oil lamp over her sleeping husband and sees that her husband is 'the handsome god Cupid': 'Thus Psyche in her ignorance let herself fall in love with Love.'

Psyche, previously depicted as innately naive, now schemes to destroy her sisters. As well, she is advised by the god Pan to earn Cupid's favour. Meanwhile, Venus is informed that her son Cupid 'has been whoring on a mountain' and that both have fallen into disrepute on earth. She angrily leaves the sea to confront her wayward son Cupid with threats of punishment. Meanwhile, Psyche resolves to earn her mother-in-law's favour. She successfully performs difficult tasks for her. The last task requires that she go to the Underworld to fetch a flask of Proserpine's beauty for Venus. Cupid aids her in this task and 'consumed by love' pleads with Jupiter for help against his mother's spiteful intransigence. Jupiter ordains that Cupid and Psyche be wed 'legally and in accordance with civil law' and 'to them was born a child, whom we call Joy (*Voluptas*)'.

II The context

The Golden Ass lends itself to allegorical interpretations. The narrator Lucius is transformed into a beast and is redeemed both physically and spiritually by divine grace. The tale of Cupid and Psyche equally naturally invites Platonic exegesis. It incorporates elements of two of the Platonic dialogues that were best known in the second century, the figurative ascent of the soul (Psyche) and its progress towards god in the *Phaedrus* and Diotima's definition of love (Cupid) and its assimilation to immortality in the *Symposium*.[2]

Allegorical and Platonic interpretations of *The Golden Ass* and the tale of Cupid and Psyche have a long history. Adlington, in the preface to his translation of *The Golden Ass* (1566), also translated P. Beroaldus' '*scriptoris intentio*' from his commentary of 1500:

> Verily under the wrap of this transformation is taxed the life of mortal man, when as we suffer our mindes so to bee drowned in sensual lusts of the flesh, and the beastly pleasure thereof . . . that we lose wholly the use of reason and vertue . . . . So can we never bee restored to the right figure of ourselves, except we taste and eat the sweet Rose of reason and vertue.

Adlington and Beroaldus had established precedents for uncovering underlying messages. Fulgentius, of the late fifth or early sixth century, applies a mixture of Platonic and Christian allegorical interpretation to the tale of

Cupid and Psyche.[3] Exegesis of the enigmas embedded in theosophic literature was especially prevalent among Middle Platonists like Apuleius, probably an extension of Plato's 'noble lie' (*Republic* 3. 451b–c). They maintained that the great creative writers like Homer had the duty to keep hidden from the profane the religious and ethical truths intended for the eyes of only those capable of understanding them (Heine 1978; Sandy 1982). The Middle Platonist Apuleius was aware of this tradition of differentiated levels of understanding. In a passage that has special relevance to the tale of Cupid and Psyche he paraphrases Pausanias' description in Plato's *Symposium* of the twofold nature of Aphrodite, the goddess of love. He prefaces the paraphrase thus:

> For I decline to speak of those other lofty and divine Platonic doctrines that are unknown to scarcely any of the pious but are unrecognized by all the profane: that the goddess Venus is really two goddesses.
>
> (*Apol.* 12.1)[4]

The contrary notion that *The Golden Ass* has no purpose other than immediate, superficial pleasure and diversion has equally time-honoured claims. In the fourth century Macrobius dismissed it thus:

> [Mere] delights to the ear are works such as the comedies of Menander . . . and the stories filled with the fictional adventures of lovers . . . . I am surprised that Apuleius often dabbled in these stories.[5]

The 'Life of Albinus', one of the biographies in the late fourth-century collection of imperial lives from Hadrian to Constantine the Great known as the *Historia Augusta*, recounts that Septimius Severus expressed disdain for Clodius Albinus by publicly criticizing him for wasting his time with old wives' tales and the bawdy Milesian tales of his compatriot Apuleius.[6]

It is evident that conflicting reactions to the tale of Cupid and Psyche and to the entire novel derive as much from the character of various episodes within the novel, from the tarnished reputation of Milesian tales and from ancient traditions of literary exegesis as from the tale itself. Apuleius seems to offer encouragement to those who conclude that the novel 'is a mere adventure story' intended to appeal to the senses rather than the mind: [7]

> Well then, I shall stitch together for your pleasure various tales in the Milesian manner favoured by you and I shall soothe your ears into receptiveness with a charming murmur . . . so that you will marvel at

> the forms and fortunes of people transformed into different shapes and states and in turn restored back to their proper selves.
>
> (1.1.1)

The 'charming murmur' that introduces the novel and the old wives' tales castigated by Septimius Severus also introduce the tale of Cupid and Psyche, 'I shall immediately divert you with charming stories and old wives' tales' (4.27.8). Thus Apuleius appears to assign the tale of Cupid and Psyche to the large group of *lepidae fabulae* (charming stories) that are characterized as entertaining diversions. The unmistakable echoes of the first sentence of the novel and of the narrator's characterization of its first inset tale as the diversion afforded by a charming story contained in the introduction to the tale of Cupid and Psyche demand that the tale be viewed within the context of the entire novel.[8]

The words quoted above (4.27.8) are spoken by the elderly housekeeper of a gang of robbers to their kidnapped victim Charite. This part of the novel, occupying most of Books 4 to 7 and spilling over into the first fourteen chapters of Book 8, roughly a third of the entire work, can be thought of as the centrepiece of *The Golden Ass*. This nexus begins with the farrago of three overtly comical tales of inept robbers who cloak their failures with incongruously elevated language (4.9–21). It includes the infiltration of the gang by Charite's fiancé, who pretends to be the 'famous Haemus' ('Bloody'), the son of the 'equally famous Theron' ('Predator', Nimrod) (Hijmans 1978: 115–16). Its tragic conclusion is preceded by the ass-Lucius' indignant censure of Charite's apparent breech of fidelity to her fiancé (7.11.5–6). It also includes Charite's attempted escape from her kidnappers on the back of the donkey, which she likens to the commandeered animals used as escape vehicles in myths. She vows to commemorate the donkey's deeds in words apparently designed to undermine the seriousness both of the memorial and the hypothesis of the novel:

> Our unsophisticated story will be the subject of closely studied tales and will be immortalized by the pens of the learned: 'Carried on the back of a donkey, royal maiden fleeing captivity.' You too will ascend to the level of the gods honoured in marvellous old myths . . . . But if Jupiter really behaved like a bull, perhaps the appearance of a human or the likeness of the gods lies hidden somewhere in this donkey of mine.
>
> (6.29.3–5).[9]

III *Lepidae fabulae*

The *lepidae fabulae*, among them the tale of Cupid and Psyche, appear by definition to disqualify themselves and the entire novel from the ranks of 'serious' literature. In fact, however, many of the inset tales reinforce themes that are developed elsewhere in the novel. An example or two will serve in the immediate context to suggest that the tale of Cupid and Psyche may have the potential to contribute more than the momentary diversion of Charite and the reader.[10]

The first inset tale establishes a pattern. The narrator Lucius meets a fellow-traveller named Aristomenes. He urges Aristomenes to tell him the story that has aroused the disdain of the latter's travelling companion. The first listener, as the first-time reader of *The Golden Ass* may be tempted to do, has dismissed the tale as a falsehood, to be classified with the magical incantations that in popular belief are capable of overturning the laws of nature (1.2.4–1.3.1). Apuleius contributes to the minimal expectations that the first listener and the first-time reader may feel by continuing the initial promise of entertaining diversion. Like the *lepido susurro* of the first sentence of the novel, the 'charming delight of stories' can alleviate unpleasantness (1.2.6), or, as the merry Host of the Tabard Inn in the *Canterbury Tales* puts it, provide the 'most solas'. But the merry Host also places a premium on 'best sentence', on best meaning, as does the narrator Lucius:

> If you [i.e., the first listener] scrutinize these [strange and incredible] things, you will perceive that they are not only open to understanding but even readily capable of happening.
>
> (1.3.3)

The story that Aristomenes is persuaded to relate to Lucius functions as one of the many unheeded warnings about the dangerous consequences of meddling with witchcraft. Socrates, the subject of Aristomenes' story, was the victim of the jealous wrath of his hostess, the witch Meroë. She used her magical powers to transform the uncooperative objects of her passion into appropriate kinds of animals (1.9). At the conclusion of Aristomenes' story Lucius continues on his way alone to Hypata, where he becomes the guest of Milo and his wife, the witch Pamphile. In Hypata Lucius is informed that his hostess also applies witchcraft to her erotic designs and transforms unresponsive lovers into animals (2.5.7). Lucius himself unwittingly makes the link between Socrates' misfortune and the eventual transformation that he undergoes at the hands of witchcraft when he reflects that he is in the very town where Socrates suffered the consequences of witchcraft (2.1.1–2).

The *bella fabella* of Cupid and Psyche, like many of the *lepidae fabulae*, performs the function of foreshadowing and reinforcing major themes in *The Golden Ass*.[11] As in their case and as noted above, its introduction appears designed to undermine its overall importance. There are, however, hints that the tale has wider applicability than the immediate solace of Charite. In her previously quoted promise to celebrate the donkey in return for its assistance she perpetuates the pattern shared by other *lepidae fabellae* of incorporating details that take on added significance for the 'repeat' reader. The 'unsophisticated story' of a braying ass when 'closely studied' does indeed 'ascend to the level of the gods' and 'the appearance of a human . . . [does in fact] lie hidden somewhere in this donkey.'

Charite does not realize that the tale of Cupid and Psyche has special relevance to her own situation, that it is a *fabula de se*. Psyche eventually surmounts hardship and is reunited with and marries her fiancé Cupid. Psyche's success is a precursor of Charite's rescue, which leads to her reunion with and marriage to her fiancé.[12] When their love is first thwarted by others' envy and jealousy, the two women are transformed from innocent ingenués into ruthless avengers (6.28 and 8.8–14). This kind of thematic interlocking implies a degree of overarching design in the *lepidae fabulae* that is not always immediately evident to the casual reader of *The Golden Ass*.

More evident but still not always appreciated is the relevance of the tale of Cupid and Psyche to the fortunes of the eavesdropping donkey who regretted that he was unable to take note 'of such a pretty story' told by 'that crazy and drunken . . . old woman' (6.25.1). As the listener to the tale of Cupid and Psyche, Charite stands to it as Lucius stands to the unheeded relevance of what he has heard and witnessed. His whimsical denigration of the tale represents his continued denial of the thinly veiled warnings seen in earlier self-contained *lepidae fabellae*.

Psyche's curiosity is directly responsible for her misfortunes (5.6.6, 23.1 and 6.20.5). She insists on satisfying it despite Cupid's repeated warnings against doing so and suffers the consequences when Cupid 'sprang forth high into the sky on his wings' (5.24.5). She undergoes a series of trials as she goes in search of him until Jupiter is prevailed upon to intervene and decrees that they shall be joined 'in legitimate marriage in accordance with civil law' (6.23.4).

The narrator Lucius likewise undergoes a series of physically and emotionally painful trials as a consequence of his irrepressible curiosity. Despite being members of the provincial aristocracy, Psyche and Lucius become the powerless playthings of hostile supernatural powers until they are rescued by divine grace and, after undergoing spiritual 'deaths,' are united with the divine.[13] Lucius' physical and spiritual redemption culminates in the ineffable joy (*inexplicabili voluptate*) of contemplating the holy image of the goddess Isis (11.24.5). Psyche's reunion with the god Cupid concludes with the birth of their child Joy (*Voluptas*) (6.24.4).

The framework for introducing the novel and the tale of Cupid and Psyche and the filigree of interrelated characters and compositional techniques reveal that the tale of Cupid and Psyche, like other *lepidae fabulae*, is an integral part of the novel, not incidental decor. The tale underscores principal themes of the novel: loss of identity caused by unrestrained curiosity, quest for it in the face of malign Fortune and its restoration by divine grace in union with God.

IV Origins

Greek model

Because the tale of Cupid and Psyche is an integral component of the novel, we must give some consideration to the origins of the complete novel. This is a complex issue that cannot be fully developed here (Mason 1978, 1994). The major story line of *The Golden Ass* derives from a Greek novel known as the *Metamorphoseis*. This work no longer survives. However, an extant epitome of it has found its way, probably incorrectly, into the manuscript tradition of Apuleius' contemporary Lucian, where it bears the title '*Lucius or the Ass*,' usually cited as the *Onos* (Latin *asinus*, i.e., ass or donkey). We have as well the somewhat confusing comparison of it with the epitome provided by Photius in the second half of the ninth century. The two major portions of Apuleius' novel that stand out as distinct in tone and apparently in genesis from the Greek original as represented in the epitome are the tale of Cupid and Psyche and the intervention of the goddess Isis in Book 11. The components that serve to launch the tale of Cupid and Psyche, however, also exist in rudimentary form in the *Onos*: a frightened young female captive of kidnappers and their aged female housekeeper, who, as in the *Golden Ass*, could have told her the story to assuage her fears. It is impossible to state categorically whether these components are vestiges of a tale similar to that of Cupid and Psyche in the Greek original or whether Apuleius has exploited the previously unrealized potential for such a tale and has skilfully woven it into the fabric of his novel.[14]

Folk tales

Other possible sources for the tale of Cupid and Psyche are no less complex.[15] Many have been identified, but no single source accounts for the richness of the tale. The 'once-upon-a-time' opening of the story, its unnamed king and queen of an indeterminate kingdom and other elements reminiscent of Western European fairy tales and folk tales such as *Beauty and the Beast*, *Cinderella* and *Rumpelstiltskin* have attracted the attention of folklorists. No proponent of the derivation of the tale from folk tales has, however, been able to account for the two eponymous protagonists and other Olympian characters (Grimal 1963: 7–8; Kenney 1990a: 17–18). Instead, folklorists and classical scholars who rely on their collections have felt compelled to invent folk tales to account for otherwise unattested elements. Wright, for instance, who relies on the theme of 'The Supernatural Husband' compiled by J.-Ö. Swahn, avers, 'We must therefore *assume* [my emphasis] that the original folk-tale told of a hero turned into a snake and making nightly visits to his beloved during which he could not . . . be seen' (Wright 1971: 275). Recent scholarship, however, has shown that there is no place for a folk-tale version before

Apuleius and that the traditional themes of folk tales known since the Middle Ages are completely absent from his tale (Fehling 1977; Schlam 1993). Wright recognizes the wide range of potential sources, concluding, 'We have in Apuleius a folk-tale embellished with a host of literary devices borrowed from epic, love romance, satire, and, above all, Alexandrian poetry' (Wright 1971: 281).

Iconography

It is the adroit manipulation of this 'host of [antecedent] literary devices' that Kenney recognizes as Apuleius' 'astonishing feat of originality' (1990a: 21–2). He takes account as well of one of the prevalent antecedents not mentioned by Wright: the iconographic tradition that dates from at least the fifth century BC.[16] Schlam's meticulous study of the tradition shows that no known plastic representation of Cupid and Psyche before the time of Apuleius parallels the narrative pattern of Apuleius' version of the myth.[17] He demonstrates as well that the statuary and other classical representations of Cupid and Psyche carry symbolic value, especially in the sepulchral art of the Roman period, where Cupid is represented 'as a figure of divine love, as the daemon freeing the soul from the bonds of the flesh, and as an embodiment of the divine with which the soul seeks to be reunited'.[18] Apuleius himself was demonstrably conscious of the symbolic value of statuary portraying mythical events. When the aunt of the narrator Lucius welcomes her nephew into her house, she responds to his admiration of statuary depicting Actaeon's transformation into a quadruped because of his curiosity in words that function on two levels, 'Everything you see is yours' (2.5.1).

Platonism

The iconographic tradition in turn drew inspiration from the Platonic tradition, especially the *Phaedrus*. This work and the *Symposium*, among the best known of Plato's dialogues in the second century, deal with the nature of the soul and of love. The obvious equations – Cupid/Venus = love and Psyche = soul – do not do full justice to Apuleius' masterly fusion of Platonism with other creative traditions such as Alexandrian epigram and the plastic arts. Apuleius brought to the composition of *The Golden Ass* an entrenched predilection for Platonism and for the practice of combining multiple sources, usually Greek, in a single composition. As well, Apuleius shows a pronounced tendency inextricably to blend *belles-lettres* and philosophy throughout his documented writing career (Schlam 1970; Sandy 1997: 178–83).

Apuleius studied Platonic philosophy in Athens at about the same time and possibly with the same teacher as Aulus Gellius. One of Gellius' vignettes underscores the special appeal of Pausanias' eulogy of Love in the

Symposium. Gellius committed it to memory and used it as a model of Greek style (Aulus Gellius 17.20; cf. Sandy 1993: 168). Like Gellius, Apuleius translates and summarizes this famous passage:

> Venus is two goddesses . . . ; one of them is common (*vulgariam*), . . . stimulated by vulgar passion (*populari*), [having the power] to compel not only the human spirit but even farm animals and wild creatures to satisfy their lust . . . ; the other [goddess] is in fact heavenly (*caelitem*), . . . endowed with the best kind of the force of love, solicitous to humans alone and to only a few of them.

Pausanias adds that there are two Cupids, one to correspond to each of the two Venuses.

It is not an accident or artistic lapse on Apuleius' part that in the tale of Cupid and Psyche the two principal divine characters, Venus and Cupid, alternate between the dual roles assigned to them in Plato by Pausanias (Kenney 1990b). This duality is perhaps most clearly expressed in the tale when Psyche sets out to learn Cupid's identity in defiance of his orders. He discovers her violation and flees to heaven (5.24.5). Before doing so, however, he reproaches her for aspiring to 'heavenly' love and himself for succumbing to common love (5.24.3–4). Thereafter, he functions principally as an intermediary between the mortal and the divine, between vulgar and spiritual love, as, in other words, a demon, the subject of Apuleius' *On the God of Socrates*.[19]

The characterization of Venus, on the other hand, owes more to the bantering, sardonic tone of Alexandrian and derivative Roman love elegy than to Plato. Her 'aerial progress', as Kenney aptly labels her ascent from earth to heaven to seek remedies for the scandalous behaviour of her son Cupid, recalls the heavenly (*caelestis*) Venus of the majestic opening of Lucretius' *On the Nature of Things* (Apuleius, *Met*. 6.6.4; cf. Kenney 1990a: 191). Elsewhere, Venus is portrayed as the hard task mistress of love elegy. Her denigration of her would-be daughter-in-law Psyche, for instance, echoes the familiar love-elegy theme of *servitium amoris* (slavery to love) that Apuleius exploits elsewhere in *The Golden Ass* (Apuleius, *Met*. 6.8.2–3; cf. Sandy, 1978: 132).

The figuratively described 'life-cycle' of the soul in Plato's *Phaedrus* must have had special appeal to the author of *The Golden Ass* (cf. Apuleius, *Soc*. 19.163–4). The two categories of souls, those of philosophers and those of others, travel different routes to reincarnation. The souls that have not witnessed the truth pass into the life of beasts without the possibility of regaining human reincarnation. The souls that have seen the truth are able, like Lucius, to pass again from bestial incarnation to human existence (*Phaedrus* 248a–b).

More specifically, Apuleius exploits Plato's *Phaedrus* to enrich the tale of Cupid and Psyche.[20] This dialogue deals with the sophistic claim that one can construct a convincing argument without reference to the absolute truth of a topic. Socrates argues against this claim, insisting that to be persuasive a speaker must have knowledge of absolute truth and the nature of the minds (souls) to be persuaded. He recounts a myth that likens souls to horses pulling a chariot. The horses struggle to enable the charioteer to behold the Plain of Truth (248b). Souls likewise struggle to rise on wings to follow god and behold the absolute truth (248b). The souls that fail in their attempt become heavy with evil, lose their wings and fall back to earth (248c). Socrates equates love of truth, love of god and love of beauty. He represents these three longings as a person who has been smitten by the god-like beauty of another person (251a). The smitten person then experiences the madness of love, the crazed longing for the object of his or her love that renders the person a slave to Love (251–2c).

Psyche (Soul) undergoes this longing for love (Love/Cupid) when in her ignorance (*ignara Psyche*), in her failure to grasp the absolute truth, she falls in love with Love and is inflamed by crazed passion (5.23.3). In defiance of his orders she ventures to discover his identity. As Cupid flees 'from the kisses and embrace of his very unhappy wife', she seizes his right leg and is drawn by him through the clouds until, like the souls in the *Phaedrus* that fail to behold the absolute truth, she becomes exhausted and falls back to earth (5.24.1). Also like the souls in the *Phaedrus*, Psyche's crazed longing eventually compels her to surrender herself into slavery (6.6, 6.8.4) (Schlam 1976: 35).

V Conclusions

In the limited space available I have touched on only a few of the many features of the tale of Cupid and Psyche that qualify it as the centrepiece of Apuleius' novel. Introduced dismissively as an entertaining diversion, the tale is linked to other *lepidae fabulae* that on closer examination prove to be cautionary tales, *fabulae de se*, functioning as paradigms of Lucius' impetuous determination to satisfy his curiosity and his repeated disregard of warnings not to do so. The tale also performs the function of reinforcing the major theme of Lucius' fall from grace and redemption. The tale can also be viewed as a love story, about Psyche's quest for love and for her lost Love[er] (Sandy 1978: 129; Stabryla 1973: 264). At first glance *The Golden Ass* appears to be an adventure story, about Lucius' quest for physical salvation, about 'saving his skin'. Both quests prove, however, to be varieties of spiritual progress, culminating in 'the progress of the soul towards a mystical union' with a deity.[21]

Notes

1 Like Virgil, Apuleius repeatedly uses '*interea*' ('meanwhile') to shift abruptly between action in Heaven and on Earth; Kenney 1990a: 128 (on 4.32.1).

2 See De Lacy 1974 and Trapp 1990 on the place of Plato in second-century classical culture. All dates are AD unless otherwise noted.
3 *Mitologiae* 3. 6, ed. R. Helm (1898). C. Moreschini provides detailed discussion of the subject in Chapter 13 of this volume.
4 The following abbreviations are used for Apuleian works: *Apol.* = *Apology*; *Fl.* = *Florida*; *Met.* = *Metamorphoses/Golden Ass*; *Mund.* = *De Mundo*; *Soc.* = *De Deo Socratis*.
5 Macrobius *Somnium Scipionis* 1.2.8.
6 *Vita Albini* 12, in *Historia Augusta*. The author of this work and Macrobius also relegate *The Golden Ass* to the nursery: *neniis* and *in nutricum cunas*.
7 The quoted phrase come from Farquharson 1951: 99.
8 . . . *narrationibus lepidis anilibusque fabulis* . . . *avocabo* (4.27.8) and *lepidae fabulae festivitate* . . . *avocavit* (1.20.5); cf. Sandy 1978: 128.
9 The phrase '*rudis* . . . *historia*', which I translated as 'our unsophisticated story', contains a pun on the adjective '*rudis*' ('unsophisticated') and the verb '*rudo*' ('to bray') and its cognate nouns '*rudor*' and '*ruditus*' that would have been felt at this advanced stage in the story of a donkey; cf. Apuleius, *Met.* 8.29.6, *Fl.* 17.10 and *Mund.* 18.331.
10 N. Shumate provides detailed discussion of the inset tales, Chapter 7 in this volume.
11 Sandy 1973. Dowden 1993: 99–103 traces themes in Book 8 and elsewhere back to the tale of Cupid and Psyche.
12 Stabryla 1973, who otherwise sees the tale of Cupid and Psyche as decor and superficial diversion.
13 Kenney 1990a: 14–15; spiritual 'deaths': 6.13–20 and 11.23.
14 Kenney 1990a: 9 avers that it is inconceivable that Apuleius found anything like the tale of Cupid and Psyche in his Greek model(s), and this view reflects the scholarly consensus.
15 Grimal (ed.) 1963: 6–21, Kenney 1990a: 17–22 and Schlam 1992: 85–98 provide masterly surveys of various sources and models.
16 Kenney 1990a: 20–2; Schlam 1976 is indispensable on the subject.
17 Schlam 1976: 32; recently supplemented and slightly modified by Maaskant-Kleibrink 1990.
18 Schlam 1976: 31. In *Soc.* 16. 154 Apuleius includes Amor (Cupid) among the demons; cf. Habermehl 1996: 122 and 129.
19 On Apuleian demonology see Habermehl 1996 and Sandy 1997: 196–210.
20 Hooker 1955: 37–8; Kenney 1990b: 184–5; Schlam 1976: 35; Trapp 1990.
21 Kenney 1990a (ed.): 12, n. 53. On the doubts raised by Winkler 1985: 223–7 and van Mal-Maeder 1997 about the religious sincerity of Book 11 of the novel see Chapter 5 in this volume where their works are cited.

Bibliography

De Lacy, P. (1974), 'Plato and the Intellectual Life of the Second Century', in G. Bowersock (ed.), *Approaches to the Second Sophistic*, University Park: American Philological Association, 4–10.

Dowden, K. (1993), 'The Unity of Apuleius' Eighth Book and the Danger of Beasts,' H. Hofmann (ed.) *Groningen Colloquia on the Novel*, Groningen: Egbert Forsten in vol. 5, pp. 91–109.

Farquharson, A. S. L. (1951), *Marcus Aurelius, His Life and His World*, Oxford: Blackwell.

Fehling, D. (1977), *Amor und Psyche: Die Schöfung des Apuleius und ihre Einwirkung auf das Märchen. Eine Kritik der romantischen Märchentheorie*, Wiesbaden: Franz Steiner.

Grimal, P. (ed.) (1963), *Apulée: Metamorphoseis (IV, 28-VI, 24)*, Paris: Presses Universitaires de France.

Habermehl, P. (1996), 'Demonology in Apuleius' *De deo Socratis*', in H. Hofmann (ed.) *Groningen Colloquia on the Novel*, Groningen: Egbert Forsten vol. 6, pp. 117–42.

Heine, R. (1978), 'Picaresque Novel versus Allegory', in B. L. Hijmans Jr. and R. Van der Paardt (eds) *Aspects of Apuleius' Golden Ass*, Groningen: Bouma's Boekhuis pp. 25–42.

Hijmans Jr., B. L. (1978), 'Significant Names and Their Function in Apuleius' *Metamorphoses*', in *Aspects of Apuleius' Golden Ass*, Groningen: Bouma's Boekhuis pp. 107–17.

Hooker, W. (1955), 'Apuleius's *Cupid and Psyche* as a Platonic Myth', *Bucknell Review* 5: 24–38.

Kenney, E. J. (ed.) (1990), *Apuleius: Cupid and Psyche*. Cambridge: Cambridge University Press.

—— (1990b), 'Psyche and her Mysterious Husband', in D. Russell (ed.) *Antonine Literature*, Oxford: Clarendon Press pp. 175–98.

Maaskant-Kleibrink, M. (1990), 'Psyche's Birth', in H. Hofmann (ed.) *Groningen Colloquia on the Novel*, Groningen: Egbert Forsten vol. 3, pp. 13–33.

Mason, H. (1978), '*Fabula Graecanica*: Apuleius and His Greek Sources', in B. L. Hijmans Jr. and R. Van der Paardt (eds) *Aspects of Apuleius' Golden Ass*, Groningen: Bouma's Boekhuis pp. 1–15.

—— (1994), 'Greek and Latin Versions of the Ass-Story', in W. Haase (ed.), *Aufstieg und Niedergang der römischen Welt*, vol. II 34. 2, Berlin/New York: W. de Gruyter, 1665–707.

Sandy, G. (1973), 'Foreshadowing and Suspense in Apuleius' *Metamorphoses*', *Classical Journal* 68: 232–5.

—— (1978), 'Book 11: Ballast or Anchor?', in B. L. Hijmans Jr. and R. Van der Paardt (eds) *Aspects of Apuleius' Golden Ass*, Groningen: Bouma's Boekhuis pp. 123–37.

—— (1993), 'West Meets East: Western Students in Athens in the Mid-Second Century AD', in H. Hofmann (ed.) *Groningen Colloquia on the Novel*, Groningen: Egbert Forsten vol. 5, pp. 163–74.

—— (1997), *The Greek World of Apuleius. Apuleius and the Second Sophistic* (*Mnemosyne* Supplement, 174), Leiden: E.J. Brill.

Schlam, C. C. (1970), 'Platonica in the *Metamorphoses* of Apuleius', *Transactions and Proceedings of the American Philological Association* 101: 477–87.

—— (1976), *Cupid and Psyche: Apuleius and the Monuments*, University Park: American Philological Association.

—— (1992), *The Metamorphoses of Apuleius: On Making an Ass of Oneself*, Chapel Hill, NC and London: University of North Carolina Press.

—— (1993), 'Cupid and Psyche: Folktale and Literary Narrative', in H. Hofmann (ed.) *Groningen Colloquia on the Novel*, Groningen: Egbert Forsten vol. 5, pp. 63–73.

Stabryla, S. (1973), 'The Function of the Tale of Cupid and Psyche in the Structure of the *Metamorphoses*', *Eos* 61: 261–72.

Trapp, M. (1990), 'Plato's *Phaedrus* in Second-Century Greek Literature', in D. Russell (ed.) *Antonine Literature*, Oxford: Clarendon Press pp. 141–73.

Wright, J. R. G. (1971), 'Folk-Tale and Literary Technique in *Cupid and Psyche*', *Classical Quarterly* 21: 273–84.

Part 3

APOLLONIUS KING OF TYRE

9

THE HISTORY OF APOLLONIUS KING OF TYRE

Gareth Schmeling

I Interpretation of the plot

We might generalize and say that ancient novels begin with an introduction of the heroine (the most beautiful girl in the land) and the hero (the most handsome). In the opening lines of the *History of Apollonius* this expectation is not disconfirmed: the heroine is both beautiful and ripe for marriage, but the reader is a little suspicious that she has no proper name. Following her introduction, the youthful hero is expected to be presented; instead the father of the girl steps forward. Now, however, something goes seriously wrong with this ancient novel: the father Antiochus, king of Antioch, does not shelter his daughter, he rapes her. The result of the incest yields one of the most graphic scenes in ancient novels (ch. 1): the girl stands in her bedroom, while drops of her blood strike the floor.

This opening episode surely surprised and even shocked the ancient reader who expected something tamer, actions which later in the story would be open to remedial reactions. The rape of the king's daughter, unlike the *Scheintod* of Apollonius' wife or the seizure of his daughter by pirates, is irreversible; no recognition scene at the end of the novel can set the king's world into order. To keep up appearances of a good father, Antiochus entertains suitors for his daughter's hand, but each is rejected and executed when he cannot solve a riddle set as the test for the successful suitor. Enter rich and handsome Apollonius (whose name appears in the novel's title), who is well educated in all the arts and sciences by reading in his library, who has travelled by boat to Antioch, and who solves the king's riddle. But his knowledge can hardly win for himself the girl's hand: she lives (against her will) in an incestuous relationship with her father. The story cannot develop as usual: the girl cannot be the real heroine, and Apollonius' flight from Antioch is necessary to save his own life, not to keep him from committing incest with the girl. In the usual incest story the one who flees does so to avoid incest (Perry 1967: 294–324). Those who question the originality of the current structure of the novel note that the opening chapters (1–11) seem to be from a second story and to have been grafted, as it were, on to the story of Apollonius and his family, since Antiochus and his daughter disappear from the story at ch. 8, reappear only briefly at ch. 24 in an announcement of their death and again at ch. 51 where Apollonius accedes to Antiochus' throne. Those who see here not one author but several, and the last one is a seamstress and not an artist, would prefer a structure in which Apollonius is the son of Antiochus and he flees from Antioch to avoid the taboo against incest with his sister.

Let us assume, however, that something like our extant novel is what was written in the early third century. A review of the whole novel reveals that all the dominant themes and motifs of the novel are introduced in the first few chapters of the work: (1) the relationship between father/daughter is more important than that of lovers; (2) suitors for young women mark an important motif; (3) most important communications are made by riddles; (4) learning and education even for women are highly valued; (5) travel by ship is better termed travel by shipwreck; (6) successful competition in games, riddles, and art forms marks princes and princesses; (7) flowing blood is a significant symbol; (8) the key work in the novel, like a leitmotif in Wagner, is *nodus* ('knot'), a word used both for virginity and for riddles to be solved.

The plot of the novel proceeds directly enough. Apollonius flees Antioch and seeks shelter in Tarsus with friends Stranguillio and Dionysias but must soon flee thence – flight which ends in a shipwreck (ch. 11) described in hexameters out of *Aeneid* 1. He is washed ashore (like Odysseus – Holzberg 1990) in North Africa (like Aeneas) near Cyrene, impresses the king, Archistrates, and his daughter (nameless) with his learning and artistry. She is smitten by the hero in the same way (and in the same words) as was Dido. Archistrates is as good a father as Antiochus was bad: the reader is reminded of Antiochus' incest, because the author describes Archistrates' meeting with his own daughter in the same words used in the opening incest episode. The author provides a charming episode about suitors for Archistrates' daughter (ch. 21). Antiochus' incest yields no children or heirs, but Apollonius impregnates his new wife immediately. The newlyweds set sail for Antioch over which Apollonius had been named king, when Antiochus and his daughter were killed by lightning – foreshadowing the idealistic end of the novel – but the young wife dies apparently (*Scheintod*) in childbirth and is buried at sea, only to be washed up on the shore at Ephesus, to be resuscitated, and then enrolled as a priestess in the temple of Diana (ch. 27). Apollonius' wife now disappears from the story almost until the end (ch. 48), and the primary female role is taken up by the daughter born at sea and named Tarsia. Apollonius exits the stage for fourteen years (ch. 28–36), and the beautiful Tarsia dominates the story so thoroughly that she deflects all suitors from Dionysias' daughter, which causes the mother to protect her own child and get rid of Tarsia, who is eventually seized by pirates and sold to a pimp in Mytilene (ch. 33). Though confined to a whorehouse, Tarsia preserves her virginity, as Scheherazade had preserved her life, by telling stories. Like her father, Tarsia is learned, gifted, an intellectual, good at riddles. A local prince of Mytilene, Athenagoras, falls in love with Tarsia, just as Apollonius in another storm at sea is driven to Mytilene. Tarsia entertains Apollonius aboard his ship (spectre of incest?) and impresses him with a series of ten riddles (ch. 42) (Archibald 1991: 22–3; Müller 1991), but when she tries to get him to leave his ship, he pushes her away and causes blood to flow from her nose (flashback to ch. 1?). Tarsia bursts out with her life story, is recognized by Apollonius as his daughter, and is married to Athenagoras. Advised in a dream to go to Ephesus, Apollonius fetches his wife, and all return to Cyrene to Archistrates. The good people are rewarded and the guilty punished (ch. 51).

II Issues: author, title, date, language, epitome, pagan/christian

The authors of ancient novels except for Petronius and Apuleius are shadowy figures, little more than names at best. For the *History of Apollonius King of Tyre* (hereafter *History*) we do not possess even a pseudonym: Apollonius is the hero of the novel, not its author. Because he deposits a copy of his adventures in his own library and in the library of the temple of Diana at Ephesus (ch. 51), the reader might have assumed that Apollonius was the author of the *History*; or perhaps the reader is meant to believe that someone rummaging in libraries had merely copied out Apollonius' account (assumed source) and had it recopied and distributed. Such is merely the tip of the iceberg of problems with this most troublesome novel. The practice of entitling a novel a 'history' returned to fashion in the eighteenth century (Fowler 1982: 93).

Certain issues surrounding the *History* are of more than just pedantic interest: they determine our basic understanding and interpretation of the work. Our earliest external evidence[1] points to a date for the *History* to a period before the sixth century AD – without indicating how much before. Some scholars thus place the *History* to a time from the fifth to the sixth century: perhaps there was an earlier story or stories which served as a model for the later. Others working with the abundant references to relative numismatic values, styles of inscriptions and social customs in the *History* feel confident in dating it to the early years of the third century: in the period between the third and sixth centuries the text in parts was Christianized and phrases from the Bible were inserted; I would add my voice to the latter growing consensus.[2] Dating and understanding of the text's history are important because they indicate that late Christian expressions found in the text should be deleted as interpolations (Schmeling 1988: V–VIII).

Like many Latin texts the *History* contains numerous Greek words and phrases, and many of those who date the extant work to the fifth–sixth century also believe that it is a re-working from the Greek (perhaps of the third century), i.e. the original work was in Greek. If all the extant Greek novels are ideal and the Latin ones realistic, there is a kind of logic in assuming that the idealistic *History* was originally Greek. In support of my belief that the *History* was a Latin work from its origin, I cite just a few reasons. In ch. 11 we find seventeen lines of hexameter in Latin borrowed from Virgil's *Aeneid* 1.81–141; in ch. 23 there are strong echoes of Ovid, and in ch. 48 Apollonius' wife is described as a new Dido from *Aeneid* 1.496. If this were originally a Greek text, we could expect some borrowings from classical Greek authors. Since all the imitations arise from Latin authors, we can be forgiven for assuming that the work was from its original Latin.[3] I would note that all terms of endearment and little words of politeness are Latin. While attempts have been made to connect the *History* to several Greek papyri, little enthusiasm has been generated for them: the name Apollonius appearing in a narrative setting written on papyrus does not constitute a prior occurrence or textual connection.[4]

As early as 1876 Rohde had considered the *History* to be a crazy patchwork of different stories sewn together – not too artfully, and thus a kind of epitome (Rohde 1914: 435 ff.; Merkelbach 1995b). It is true that some of the narrative is skeleton-like, that the author uses summaries instead of scenes and displays a sloppiness in handling details, motivation, and story-line. The *History*, however, was enormously popular until the time of Shakespeare (Archibald 1991: 3), and its current lack of celebrity is owing to a change in taste: ' . . . the *History* . . . has now and then been taken as an unskillful abbreviation of an originally homogeneous and well-written novel. To me, however, this seems about as well founded as it would to maintain that modern detective stories or adventure films which are lacking in logic and characterization are really cut versions of more accomplished representatives of those genres' (Hägg 1983: 152–3).

The final controversy to be discussed here is whether the *History* is a pagan or Christian work. It is hard to find evidence so conclusive that it settles the question. It is my impression that the hero Apollonius seems more inclined to bear with pagan Stoicism rather than with Christian fortitude the slings and arrows of outrageous fortune. But sentiments are notoriously unreliable gauges. One could argue on the other side that Christian sentiments are highlighted in the *History*: an emphasis on virginity, a belief that slaves should be treated well, and commonplace expressions like 'they died in peace' (Hexter 1988: 188). A problem with this is that pagan writers express the same sentiments (Schmeling 1996: 532–3). While Hexter has declared the *History* to be Christian, Merkelbach (1962, 1995a) has put forward the thesis that the *History* is a cult document of Isis, a kind of ancient *roman-à-clef* 'meant to be fully intelligble only to those properly initiated into the mysteries' (Hägg 1983: 101). In the same way that the *History* cannot be a text of the Isis mysteries, so it cannot be Christian: there must be a sign. If the *History* is a Christian or Isiac work which can be recognized by the faithful, how can we explain the ordination of Apollonius' wife into the priesthood of Diana, the comparison of Apollonius with the god Apollo, frequent references to the *Manes* and Muses, the celebration of the festival of Neptune? Why, if the *History* is a bearing witness to Christ or Isis, does the author never say so? (Winkler 1985: 241). In the last chapter we read that Apollonius deposited a narrative of his adventures in the temple of Diana at Ephesus. The reader is led to believe that the work is entrusted to Diana. This novel is pagan; if the reader wishes to find a Christian novel, let him read the Pseudo-Clementine *Recognitions*.

III Physical evidence

Though the text of the *History* causes no end of trouble, the number of manuscripts (at 114) is quite large and should provide remedies to help with the text. Even with all these manuscripts, however, (or because of them) we are unable to get back in time before the sixth century to a text of the original. The best we can do today is to group the manuscripts into nine 'families' and term one of those families our 'text'. A review of the three most influential families or recensions shows that R(ecension) A is based on manuscript A, written in the ninth century in Monte Cassino; P, a fourteenth century Italian manuscript; and Va^c, a corrected twelfth century manuscript. R(ecension) B is made up of b, a ninth century manuscript from Tours, and β, a twelfth century manuscript from England. R(ecension) C, while a separate family, seems to be a combination of borrowings from RA and RB. It is believed that RA represents the earliest and best tradition of the manuscripts of the *History*, that RB derives mainly from the tradition of RA, perhaps influenced by early but no longer extant manuscripts of that family. To the fulsomeness and even wordiness of the vulgar RA, RB seems to offer remedial doses of classical restraint, to include additional information which helps to clarify situations, and even on occasion to set forward revisions in content and Latinity. It appears from time to time, however, that RB does not have as direct a line to the original *History* as does RA: for example RB fails to recognize or to preserve at ch. 11 the verses written in imitation of Virgil's storm scene from *Aeneid* 1.

A special curiosity among the manuscripts of the *History* is φ, a fragmentary tenth–eleventh century manuscript written in Germany, containing about one-third of the novel, and now housed in Budapest. This fragmentary manuscript is illustrated by a series of thirty-five drawings, which Hägg (1983: 150) refers to as 'comic strips' and which Weitzmann (1959: 103) estimates numbered about two hundred in the original, complete manuscript. Our artistic scribe follows an old custom of illustrating manuscripts with drawings: 'There is hardly another illustrated text known to us in which the scenes follow each other in such a close approximation of a cinematic narration, and it does not seem to be accidental that this should occur in an ancient romance for which the quick change of action and locality is most typical'.[5]

IV Style and language

One reason why the text of the *History* could seem to present few problems is that it is deceptively simple. The straightforward, often paratactical Latin, the use of high-frequency vocabulary, the often inartistic arrangement of words, and the lack of subtle philosophical explanations or psychological motivations all conspire to make the Latinity of the *History* appear pedestrian. Rhetoric and point for the most part seem not to have much influence on the language of the *History*, and the even flow of the narrative is rarely broken by witty or striking *sententiae* ('sentences'): sentences rarely rise to a climax or fall to a quiet paradox. Tricola when used do not really ascend or descend: ch. 1, *luctatur cum furore, pugnat cum dolore, vincitur amore*, 'he struggles against his passion, fights against his emotions, but is overcome by love', but he can play on words (ch. 7): *fugere . . . potest, sed effugere non potest*, 'he can flee, but he cannot fly'; ch. 16, *in artem musicam incidit, sed non didicit*, 'she appreciates music without knowing why'; ch. 16, *non Apollonium sed Apollinem*, 'not Apollonius but Apollo'. At times the language can be almost musical, as at ch. 34, *plus dabis, plus plorabis*, 'the more you give, the more you will groan'. Our author seems to eschew even simple metaphors and similes, but quotes and alludes to his literary predecessors, Virgil, Ovid, etc. There is a high level of clever banter between Archistrates and his daughter in ch. 18–21, between Archistrates and suitors for his daughter at ch. 19, and between a common sailor and Athenagoras at ch. 39.

What attracts the reader's sympathy and saves the story from often artless narrative scenes is poignant direct speech. At the end of ch. 20 there is an episode in which Archistrates' daughter, though hopelessly in love with Apollonius, is portrayed as so shy that she can discuss her beloved even with her own father only in a letter and then only without mentioning his name (a riddle): ' . . . best of fathers . . . I want as my husband the man who was robbed of his inheritance by shipwreck. If, father, you are surprised that a modest young girl could write so immodestly, it is because I can entrust my feeling to a letter which feels no shame . . . ' Clearly more at home with dialogue than with scenes, our author might have experience in writing for the theatre, and Perry (1967: 306–7) offers supporting evidence for this, when he states that several episodes in the *History* seem to have been prepared for the live stage.

The author of the *History* is able to orchestrate his language also for a large canvas. The *History* is replete with riddles, many of them formal – Tarsia announces that she will ask Apollonius a series of riddles – but many informal, unannounced, woven into the fabric of the narrative without alerting the reader that he must deal with a riddle. In ch. 1 Antiochus' rape of his own daughter is described with the words *nodum virginitatis eripuit*, 'he tore out the knot of her virginity'. This is graphic language, but the expression is unknown otherwise in Latin. It is clear from the context what is meant, even though the combination of words has been called un-Latin. The author could have used a common literary expression like *zonam solvere* ('to loosen her belt') or even resorted to something like *florem eripuit* ('he tore away her flower'), but he had great plans for the word *nodus* ('knot') later in the novel – perhaps it was chosen to jolt the reader with an estranging and defamiliarizing effect. The author uses the word *nodus* again at ch. 41 near the end of the novel, where Tarsia asks her father to *absolvere nodos parabolarum mearum*, 'to solve the knots of my riddles'. This is an exceedingly clever word-play because *solvere*, 'to solve', is the recognized verb in the sexual euphemism with *zonam*, 'to loosen her girdle', for which our author has substituted *nodus*. The reader's mind goes back to ch. 1 where wicked Antiochus deflowered his daughter (*nodus*) and then hid his crime by setting a riddle whose *nodus* Apollonius solved (ch. 4) to open the novel, as he solved Tarsia's *nodos* to end it (ch. 41). What does our author accomplish by his imaginative use of the word *nodus*? In the first place he binds the novel into a tight unit by ending it, as he began it. Secondly, he plays up the contrasts of good father–bad father, but does so while employing the same vocabulary. Thirdly, he can display his own gifts at word-play, and lastly, he can wrap one riddle inside another. Riddles are important throughout the *History*: the characters speak in riddles, solve riddles, often communicate in riddles, and the author uses them to anchor the structure of the narrative. At times the talent of this author sparkles.

V Sexual symmetry, family novels, and patterns

> A proper maiden (sc. like Tarsia) has no erotic interests of her own.
>
> (Konstan 1994: 103)

It is not many years ago that classicists were guilty of lumping the ancient novels together, as if cookies cut from the same mould.[6] Such oversimplification is no longer practised, not only because it was unhelpful, but also because it led to faulty conclusions. That we can appreciate that the *History* can be listed with the other ancient novels and at the same time appreciate that it has many special and even unique characteristics is owing in a significant part to Konstan's *Sexual Symmetry*.[7] After Konstan's work (1994: 112–13) we no longer place the *History* near the five extant Greek novels as an ideal, erotic novel, but as a Latin novel in origin, a form which 'is in fact cut to an entirely different pattern' (ibid.: 100) from its Greek cousins: the 'mainspring of the Greek novel' is the 'symmetrical or reciprocal enamorment' (ibid.: 101–02) of the hero and heroine, while the *History* shows us an 'unequal relationship between an older man . . . and a younger woman' (ibid.: 100).

After reviewing the corpus of ancient prose narrative fiction, the reader is struck by the great number of similar situations, for example, between the *History* on one side and the Greek novel by Xenophon of Ephesus and the Christian Pseudo-Clementine *Recognitions* on the other. A short list of common motifs shows how easy it is to connect the *History* to other works through similar situations: incest, separation of family members, brothel-keepers, pirates, *Scheintod*, physicians in Ephesus, construction of tombs, summaries deposited in the temple of Diana. What we have here, however, are only surface similarities. For the *History* to be a member of the class of canonical Greek novels it must share more than surface similarities, because, as Conte illustrates (1994: 107), genre springs from internal forces, or as he says, 'genre as generative matrix'. The efficient forces behind the *History* keep it separate from the world of the Greek novel. Even the external formalistic elements of the *History* segregate it from the literariness of the Greek novels: the want of imagery, use of simple syntax, avoidance of metaphors, and lack of self-consciousness, all conspire to keep the language of the *History* from being deformed from ordinary language to any great extent.

The *History* clearly belongs under the rubric of ancient novel (Schmeling 1996: 2, 517–51), and, while it shares many *topoi* with the Greek novel, its author is just as clearly experimenting with old approaches in the genre and developing new ones. If we focus on our author's 'strategy of literary composition', we should be able to appreciate better any contributions to the genre. For support in this procedure I again turn to the observations of Conte:

> A category of genre based exclusively upon formal features is clearly unacceptable. For example, what scholar would be willing to consider all poetry written in the Aeolic dialect as a single genre? . . . But it is just as dangerous, and more common in recent studies, to think of genre as a typology founded exclusively upon recurring contents: *topoi*, repeated themes and motifs, situations . . . In this case genre functions as a recipe, as a mechanical handbook of production, and not as a strategy of literary composition.
>
> (Conte 1994: 29)

The form of the Greek novel seems to be constructed and dependent on the mutual, equal, reciprocal and symmetrical, and eventually triumphant erotic-love of the hero for the heroine and vice versa. In the opening chapters the love of Antiochus for his daughter is incestuous, unreciprocated, and self-destructive: wrong actions taken at the beginning of the novel cannot be remediated by any *deus ex machina* at the end. What Antiochus and his daughter do establish for this novel, however, is to set a pattern: this will, against reader expectation, be a novel about fathers/daughters, not about boys/girls. The evil father/daughter, an asymmetrical relationship, is followed by the proper, though asymmetrical relationship of Apollonius and king Archistrates' daughter. Apollonius respects the princess, spends no sleepless nights thinking about her, and agrees to marry her because she is so keen to have him as a husband and because he likes her father. In fact he acts and functions toward her as a kind of older guardian, a father-figure. But this father-figure can by every acceptable rule marry the princess. She has strong feelings toward Apollonius (ch. 17; 23) and he has great emotional attachment to her (the passion of the Greek novels is absent), and at the end of the novel (ch. 49) she confesses that she fell in love with him not out of passion but out of admiration for his character. The evil father/daughter pattern set by Antiochus is corrected by Archistrates/daughter and by Apollonius/Tarsia: each is in control of himself, each is learned, and each acts with cool judgement. Stranguillio, too, has a daughter but allows his wife Dionysias to direct her upbringing, and the wife – being a woman – acts on emotions and destroys herself and him. Athenagoras has a daughter from a first marriage and, thinking of her (ch. 34; 36), realizes that he should treat Tarsia well, an action which later wins him her hand. Our author offers us two proper father/daughter examples and two improper ones: we find not only patterns but also balance.

Let us consider several other patterns. At ch. 6 Antiochus sends an agent to murder Apollonius; at ch. 31 Dionysias sends an agent to murder Tarsia, but his reluctance allows Tarsia to escape and his testimony will at the end of the novel help to sentence Dionysias to death. The pattern when applied is almost, but never exactly, duplicated. At ch. 8 a stranger named Hellenicus befriends Apollonius and warns him about Antiochus but then refuses to accept money, since he acted out of friendship. Stranguillio gladly accepts money and free grain for his city from his old friend Apollonius but later betrays him when he cannot stand up to his evil (unrestrained) wife. The good example from the pattern shows a level-headed, dispassionate, mature husband; the bad one shows a wife usurping her husband's role. The nurse of Antiochus' daughter advises the princess to yield to her father's acts of incest, and she does: the evil emanating from Antiochus taints both daughter and nurse. Tarsia's nurse (ch. 30) remains faithful: the goodness of a virtuous father influences not only daughter but also servant. The education and learning of Apollonius allow him to solve Antiochus' riddle, a good act which gets him into trouble; Tarsia's learning permits her to remain a virgin in a brothel, to pose riddles to her father, to effect a reunion with him, and then to bring the novel to an end. The suitors for the hand of Antiochus' daughter are beheaded by him so he can continue his affair with his daughter; suitors for Archistrates' daughter are treated respectfully and even democratically by the king (ch. 19); suitors for Tarsia in the brothel (ch. 34–35) are entertained by her stories, impressed by her learning, sympathetic to her plight, and contribute money to allow her to purchase her freedom. Tarsia does not let her feminism inhibit her from using her femininity.

Events, motifs, themes, and situations in the *History* are repeated, but always with variations. Motivation is often weak, if it exists at all, but the use of patterns is consistent. We could say that the plot is an arrangement of patterns. Then what can we make of this usage? Good fathers set proper examples and raise exemplary daughters; education and learning cannot be taken away like possessions in a shipwreck; good fathers make good kings and rule well over their kingdoms. Thus we do not have here a novel of love or adventure or rewards/retribution, but rather a family novel (Szepessy 1985–88). And good families have children, grandchildren, and are successful in establishing dynasties. Good families make futures for themselves.

The generic matrix is patterns. In his *An Introduction to the English Novel*, Arnold Kettle[8] comments that in producing novels writers are divided into two camps: one is eager to show 'life', i.e. an interest in the feelings/joy/ sadness of living; the other to show the 'pattern' of existence, i.e. an interpretation, point, meaning of existence.

Our author emphasizes that the significant items in life follow a structure: good fathers eventually prosper, honest slaves are rewarded, and irony seldom applies to the micromanagement of lives. We see a different bias in the *Satyrica*, for example, where Petronius develops Trimalchio into a particular individual who is unique in classical literature and who, it seems, conveys the feeling of life from AD 66. Though an individualized character, Trimalchio might nevertheless represent a particular kind of person (pattern), a type of successful entrepreneur in the early Empire who exhibits acquisitive skills (pattern), but at the same time such a 'Lust am Leben' (life) that we feel some connection to his world. In the *History*, then, the reader seems to confront a narrative more of pattern than of life.

If the author of the *History* arranges items in such a way as to represent patterns and not life, is he de-emphasizing the particular and dehumanizing the individual? While losing something in these areas, is he then able to portray characters who represent something significant, whether good or bad? There is a human morality to a patterned character: Tyche or Fortuna might be able to impede the progress of a good father, but a proper father represents the winning side; he exposes a human pattern for an abstract goodness which has no fictional beginning or end. The patterns in the *History* betray an author who sees a universe which in the end obeys laws of right and wrong. The evil characters in the *History* never deceive themselves; they always recognize that they are evil.

We perhaps no longer care for such patterned novels, but from its composition in the early third century until the seventeenth century the *History* was one of the most popular, i.e. read by people, novels in Western literature.

Notes

1 Cf. Schmeling 1988: V-VI; *De dubiis nominibus*, *Grammatici Latini*, Keil 5. 579; Venantius Fortunatus, *Carmina* 6.8.5.
2 Klebs 1899: 228–80; Perry 1967: 294–324; Duncan-Jones 1982: 252; Callu 1980: 188; Nocera Lo Giudice 1979: 273; Ziegler 1977: 57; Kortekaas 1984: 122–5; Schmeling 1988: VI.
3 Klebs 1899: 280–93; Perry 1967: 294–324; Konstan 1994: 113; Hexter 1988: 189.
4 Stephens/Winkler 1995: 391–99. For a Greek original: Kortekaas 1984: 97–131; Holzberg 1990.
5 Weitzmann 1959: 104. The manuscript which lies behind Welser's 1595 edition was also illustrated. Kytzler 1997: 480–3, includes five illustrations from fifteenth century editions.
6 And I was as guilty as any.
7 Seminal ideas also found in Archibald 1991.
8 London: Hutchinson & Co., 1967.

Bibliography

Archibald, E. (1991), *Apollonius of Tyre: Medieval and Renaissance Themes and Variations*, Cambridge: D.S. Brewer.

Callu, J. P. (1980), 'Les prix dans deux romans mineurs d'époque impériale', in *Les 'devaluations' à Rome: Epoque républicaine et imperiale*, vol. 2, Paris: De Boccard, and Rome: L'Erma di Bretschneider, pp. 187–214.

Chiarini, G. (1983), 'Esogamia e incesto nella *Historia Apollonii regis Tyri*', *Materiali e discussioni per l'analisi dei testi classici* 10–11: 267–92.

Conte, G.B. (1994), *Genres and Readers*, Baltimore/London: Johns Hopkins University Press.

Duncan-Jones, R. (1982), 'The Use of Prices in the Latin Novel', in *The Economy of the Roman Empire*, 2nd edn, Cambridge: Cambridge University Press, pp. 238–56.

Fowler, A. (1982), *Kinds of Literature: An Introduction to the Theory of Genres and Modes*, Oxford: Clarendon Press.

Frye, N. (1976), *The Secular Scripture*, Cambridge, MA: Harvard University Press.

Goolden, P. (1955), 'Antiochus' Riddle in Gower and Shakespeare', *Review of English Studies* 6: 245–51.

Hägg, T. (1966), 'Die *Ephesiaka* des Xenophon Ephesios – Original oder Epitome?', *Classica & Mediaevalia* 27: 118–61.

—— (1983), *The Novel in Antiquity*, Oxford: Blackwell.

Hexter, R. (1988), Review of Kortekaas (1984), *Speculum* 63: 186–90.

Holzberg, N. (1990), '*The Historia Apollonii regis Tyri* and the *Odyssey*', in: H. Hofmann (ed.), *Groningen Colloquia on the Novel*, vol. 3, Groningen: Egbert Forsten, pp. 91–101.

Hunt, J. (1994), Review of Schmeling (1988), *Gnomon* 66, 304–20.

Klebs, E. (1899), *Die Erzählung von Apollonius aus Tyrus*, Berlin: B.G. Teubner.
Konstan, D. (1994), *Sexual Symmetry: Love in the Ancient Novel and Related Genres*, Princeton, NJ: Princeton University Press.
Kortekaas, G.A.A. (ed.) (1984), *'Historia Apollonii regis Tyri'. Prolegomena, text edition of the two principal Latin recensions, bibliography, indices and appendices*, Groningen: Bouma's Boekhuis.
Kytzler, B. (1997), 'Fiktionale Prosa', in L.J. Engels and H. Hofmann (eds), *Neues Handbuch der Literaturwissenschaft*, vol. 4: *Spätantike*, Wiesbaden: Aula-Verlag, pp. 469–94.
Merkelbach, R. (1962), *Roman und Mysterium in der Antike*, Munich: Beck.
—— (1995a), Isis Regina–Zeus Sarapis. *Die griechisch–ägyptische Religion nach den Quellen dargestellt*, Stuttgart/Leipzig: B.G. Teubner.
—— (1995b), 'Die Überlieferungstyp "Epitome Aucta" und die *Historia Apollonii*', *Zeitschrift für Papyrologie und Epigraphik* 108: 7–14.
Müller, C.W. (1991), 'Der Romanheld als Rätsellöser in der *Historia Apollonii regis Tyri*', *Würzburger Jahrbücher für die Altertumswissenschaft* N.F. 17: 267–79.
Nocera Lo Giudice, M. (1979), 'Per la datazione dell'*Historia Apollonii regis Tyri*', *Atti della Accademia Peloritana dei Pericolanti, Classe di Lettere* 55: 273–84.
O'Sullivan, J. (1995), *Xenophon of Ephesus: His Compositional Technique and the Birth of the Novel*, Berlin/New York: W. de Gruyter.
Perry, B.E. (1967), *The Ancient Romances: A Literary-Historical Account of Their Origins* (*Sather Classical Lectures*, 37), Berkeley/Los Angeles: University of California Press.
Rohde, E. (1914), *Der griechische Roman und seine Vorläufer*, 3rd edn., ed. by W. Schmid, Leipzig: Breitkopf and Härtel.
Ruiz-Montero, C. (1983), 'La Estructura de la *Historia Apollonii regis Tyri*,' *Cuadernos de Filologia Clásica* 18: 291–334.
Schmeling, G. (ed.) (1988), *Historia Apollonii regis Tyri*, Leipzig: B.G. Teubner.
—— (1989), 'Manners and Morality in the *Historia Apollonii regis Tyri*', in F. Liviabella Furiani and A. M. Scarcella (eds), *Piccolo mondo antico*, Perugia: Edizioni Scientifiche Italiane, pp. 199–215.
—— (1996), '*Historia Apollonii regis Tyri*', in G. Schmeling (ed.), *The Novel in the Ancient World* (*Mnemosyne*, Supplement 159), Leiden: E.J. Brill, pp. 517–51.
Stephens, S., and Winkler, J. J. (eds) (1995), *Ancient Greek Novels: the Fragments*, Princeton, NJ: Princeton University Press.
Szepessy, T. (1985–88), 'The Ancient Family Novel (a Typological Approach)', *Acta Antiqua Academiae Scientiarum Hungaricae* 31: 357–65.
Weitzmann, K. (1959), *Ancient Book Illumination*, Cambridge, MA: Harvard University Press.
Winkler, J. J. (1985), *Auctor & Actor: A Narratological Reading of Apuleius's 'The Golden Ass'*, Berkeley/Los Angeles/London: University of California Press.
Ziegler, R. (1977), 'Münzen Kilikiens als Zeugnis kaiserlicher Getreidespenden', *Jahrbuch für Numismatik und Geldesgeschichte* 27: 29–67.
—— (1984), 'Die *Historia Apollonii regis Tyri* und der Kaiserkult in Tarsos', *Chiron* 14: 219–34.

Part 4

HISTORY AND ROMANCE, SAINTS AND MARTYRS

10

NEWS FROM THE PAST

Dictys and Dares on the Trojan War

Stefan Merkle

Dealing with the *Ephemeris belli Troiani* by Dictys Cretensis and the *Acta diurna belli Troiani* by Dares Phrygius in the context of 'Latin fiction' is for several reasons not without its problems. Both texts are, in dedicatory prefaces, described as translations from the Greek, but the respective Greek versions are for the most part lost. We only have two short papyrus fragments of the Greek Diktys,[1] and nothing remains of the Greek Dares.[2] It is, therefore, quite difficult to pinpoint the share of the respective translators in the extant texts. Moreover, there is no definite evidence for the time of origin of the translations or for the identity of the translators; the Latin *Ephemeris* is to be dated either to the third or to the fourth century AD, the Latin *Acta* probably to the late fifth century.[3] This complicates the determination of the texts' immediate literary environment.

However, in the last decade both texts have been increasingly commented on in scholarly surveys from different angles, and although many of these comments refer to the Greek originals or do at least not distinguish clearly between the Greek and the Latin versions, they have provided some clues that may take us closer to an understanding of the two works as part of Latin prose fiction in imperial times.

Both texts, as we have them, show close parallels. Each is prefaced with a letter by the translator which informs the reader that he has in hand sensational news from the past: a Latin translation of an eye-witness record of the Trojan War, presenting the truth about the events – the *Ephemeris* having been written by a Greek, the *Acta* by a Trojan war participant. Such a claim, of course, challenged Homer's accounts, and this is explicitly said in the Dares letter: the *Acta*, the letter concludes, allow the reader to decide if the record of Dares, the eye-witness, is true, or whether Homer's is, who lived much later and, moreover, was brought to trial in Athens for insanity.

It is on the basis of this claim to truth and the opposition to Homer that both the contents and the formal conception of the texts are to be understood. Both works contrast a plausible, rationalistic version of the events to the Homeric epic; the gods do not appear personally, and the superhuman heroism of the protagonists is reduced to human scale. And, unlike Homer's poetic shaping of the material, the texts are presented as an *ephemeris* and *acta diurna* respectively, which meant sober factual information in chronological order, conceived with little or no literary ambitions, like a *commentarius*; accordingly, both texts are written in plain, unpretentious prose. In support of the records' claim to credibility the chroniclers, Dictys and Dares, are styled as critical historians: both texts contain a kind of delayed prologue (*Eph.* 1.13; *Acta* ch. 12) and *sphragis* (*Eph.* 5.17; *Acta* ch. 44) in which the authors briefly describe their historiographical methods and provide the reader with some relevant information, cultural-historical in the *Ephemeris* and 'statistical' in the *Acta*. Apart from these passages neither Dictys nor Dares appears in the accounts, which are given throughout in the third person.[4]

Despite these parallels in the basic conception, the extant texts are remarkably different. The *Ephemeris* presents a considerably longer and more circumstantial record than the *Acta*; the *Acta*, on the other hand, deviate much further from traditional versions of the Troy material than the *Ephemeris*. Comparable differences are evident in the translators' introductory letters. While the Dictys translator provides his reader with a detailed description of the text's discovery in Dictys' grave on Crete, including the exact year (the thirteenth year of Nero's reign, i.e. AD 66) and the further fate of the work (presentation to Nero, transliteration from Phoenician letters into Greek, and storage in a library), the Dares translator, in his shorter letter, does not bother to explain why the text had been unknown for such a long time. He compensates for that through a fabrication which is analogous to the free treatment of the Troy tradition which we find in the text. He introduces himself as Cornelius Nepos and addresses his letter to Sallust, thus creating a second sensational aspect for his fifth century Latin-reading audience: not only does the text provide hitherto unknown first-hand information about the Trojan War, its Latin version moreover represents a work of the famous biographer and historian, a work nobody has ever heard of before.[5] The Dictys translator, on the other hand, apparently gives his real name: L. Septimius. These correspondences between the introductory letters and the respective translations raise the question of how much of the extant texts' shape is due to a re-elaboration by Septimius and 'Nepos'.

I 'Cornelius Nepos' and his Latin *Acta*

Ironically, much more scholarly effort has been invested so far in answering this question for the *Acta*, although there is no single trace left of the Greek original.[6] The results of the respective surveys have been, however, basically negative. Regarding the abruptness and brevity of the extant text as the result of an epitomization, scholars have combed the work for passages which in their view were abbreviated or heavily mutilated by the translator. If their observations are correct, the contribution of 'Nepos' was mainly the destruction of a quite respectable Greek text.

Such an approach, however, is not without its problems. What we consider 'acceptable' in a text depends to a high degree on very subjective criteria. Thus, in the two most exhaustive of these surveys (Körting 1874; Schetter 1988) we find a total of thirty-two 'incoherent' passages, but of these only four appear in both surveys. Therefore, many of the arguments relating to this point have been challenged, and there have been scholars, admittedly only a few, who regard the extant text as complete, pointing to certain structural and narrative consistencies in the account.[7] Although these observations can neither explain every riddle the *Acta* pose[8] nor really prove the text's integrity,[9] they have, implicitly at least, shed a more positive light on the work of 'Nepos'.

Moreover, we have one strong indication that 'Nepos' was himself very well aware of the spareness of his Latin version. In his introductory letter he claims: *optimum ergo duxi ita ut fuit uere et simpliciter perscripta, sic eam* (sc. *historiam) ad uerbum in Latinitatem transuertere* ('Therefore I thought it best to translate the work the way it was written, truly and simply, word by word into Latin'). The combination of *uere* and *simpliciter* indicates that he apparently regarded his version's lack of stylistic *finesse* as an apt device to convince his reader of the reliability and genuineness of the text. This passage, which has not been taken into account in discussions on this point, in my view confirms at least for the Latin *Acta* that the simplicity of the text is the consequence of a rigorous attempt to style the work as a *commentarius*.

However, whether 'Nepos' actually rendered his Greek model '*ita ut fuit . . . ad uerbum*', or reshaped it according to his own idea of the genre, is something that, in my view, we cannot definitely decide. Moreover, there is a third possibility we should keep in mind. Since (as indicated in note 2), none of the arguments put forward to back the common assumption of a Greek Dares is really conclusive, we cannot be sure that there was any such Greek text at all; in other words, 'Nepos' may not have been the translator, but the author of the *Acta*.[10] Instead of two forgers – Pseudo-Dares and Pseudo-Nepos – there would be only one, an author who was very much determined to deviate from traditional facts of literary history, both Greek and Latin, and who was convinced that a lack of literary elaboration would add to his work's credibility as a historical document. If this was indeed the case, his forgery was remarkably successful. Although we do not know if anybody ever believed in his claim to be Cornelius Nepos, we do know that in medieval times the *Acta* were indeed taken for what they pretended to be, a most reliable source for the Trojan War;[11] and even nowadays there is still one statement in the introductory letter which is commonly believed to be true: *optimum . . . duxi eam* (sc. *historiam*) *. . . in Latinitatem transuertere*.

II L. Septimius and the *Ephemeris*

While 'Nepos' is still suspected by many scholars of having more or less heavily distorted a stylistically and conceptually better original, Septimius has been rehabilitated from the same accusation after the publication of the first fragment of the Greek text in 1907. Surprisingly, it turned out that the Latin *Ephemeris* is stylistically superior to the original and easier to understand. The second, shorter, papyrus and a comparison between the prologue and Septimius' dedicatory letter (cf. note 1) confirmed this result. These observations allow us to sketch Septimius' method of translation. We can assume that in Books 1 to 5 which contain the war events proper, Septimius on the whole kept the structure and contents of the original, but allowed himself to alter some details. Stylistically he improved his model. Book 6, on the other hand, is a different problem. It is, as Septimius states in his letter, an abbreviated version of four (or five) books presenting the *Nostoi* of the Greeks. Accordingly, scholars have approached the *Ephemeris* to a large extent differently than the *Acta*, taking Books 1 to 5 of the Latin text basically as a direct reflection of the Greek original; a differentiation between the original and the translation has for the most part not seemed particularly important.

Looking at the work in the context of Latin fiction, however, I will focus now on specifically Roman elements in the translation. There are two aspects of the text which seem significant in this respect. (1) It has long been noted that Septimius' translation is distinctly reminiscent of Sallust's style, the parallels being so numerous that before the publication of the first papyrus they constituted an important argument for those scholars who doubted the existence of a Greek original. Two functions of this *imitatio Sallusti* have been determined so far. On the one hand, it served to raise the stylistic level of the text. On the other hand, it emphasized the presentation of the chronicler as a historian.[12] (2) Only recently Knut Usener has pointed to the occurrence of specifically Roman political terminology in the Latin *Ephemeris*, referring to such words as *curia* (2.24), *populares* (1,8; 1,10; 2,20; 5,1; 5,7; 5,10) and *senatus* (5,4; 5,8; 5,10). Since these political terms, Usener emphasizes, were known to Septimius' Latin-reading audience from the times of the late Republic, their use had at the same time both a familiarizing and a distancing effect. On the one hand Septimius made the events of the Trojan War clearer and more comprehensible for his readers. On the other hand he transported these events to remote 'Roman' times, thus creating a historical gulf between the reader and the text. This association between Trojan and Roman times, however, was not intended to provide a concrete chronological clue for the reader; Septimius, Usener states, rather set up a 'Zeichen für eine lang zurückliegende Zeit, in der andere politische Zustände herrschten, nämlich republikanische' (1994: 113).

I would like to add a further suggestion to these observations. It seems to me that both devices, the imitation of Sallust and the use of political terminology pointing to the Late Republic, provide in combination a set of associations for the reader which lend a more intense and specific Roman colour to the text than has been recognized so far.

There is one important aspect of Septimius' use of Roman political terms that Usener raises only implicitly: such terms refer almost exclusively to Troy, very rarely to the Greeks.[13] Thus, there is a specific association between the political conditions in Troy and those in Late Republican Rome. This association is both confirmed and modified where Septimius clearly alludes to definite Sallustian places.

The first such passage is the lengthy description of the Greek legation to Troy immediately after Helen's abduction (1,6–11). In this passage the Trojans are introduced to the reader, and, as throughout the account, they are presented very negatively. Troy is divided in two camps. On the one side there are the people of Troy and some aristocrats, who detest Paris' deed, on the other side the sons of Priam, who do their utmost to prevent Helen's return, even going so far as to kill fellow citizens and to attempt to assassinate the Greek legates. Hecuba too fights to keep Helen in Troy, while Priam responds to the situation with increasing helplessness.

Two comments by the chronicler on crucial events in this passage are quotations from Sallust. After the Priamids violently break up the assembly of the Trojan people to prevent them from making a decision in favour of the Greeks, we read: *ita infectis rebus populus contemptui habitus non sine pernicie sua domum discedit* ('Thus . . . without having reached their goals, the people went home, held in contempt and not without some losses' [1,8]). Later, when Hecuba through a dramatic performance reassures her wavering sons who are about to give in to the people's will, Dictys/Septimius sums up: *ita . . . bonum publicum materna gratia corruptum est* ('Thus .. the public welfare was sacrificed to maternal interests' [1,10]). The two corresponding Sallustian sentences are to be found in the first third of the *Bellum Iugurthinum*.[14] Sallust comments here on comparable events in Rome: in both cases legations were in Rome, and corrupt Romans had foiled attempts to take measures against Iugurtha.

Moreover, the Priamids are introduced in this passage with Sallust's words. It is their lust for Helen's treasures and her beautiful companions that motivates their refusal to return Helen. Dictys/Septimius describes them as *nihil pensi aut consulti patientes* ('impatient of careful thought or consideration' [1,7]); this calls to mind Sallust's *nihil pensi neque moderati habere* ('they were utterly thoughtless and reckless') of *Cat.* 12,2, where Sallust describes the disastrous moral state to which *auaritia* and *luxuria* have brought the noble youth of Rome.

These clear allusions to Sallust's monographs suggest that what happens in Troy in the preliminaries to the Trojan War resembles in essential points the clashes in Rome in the preliminaries to the Jugurthine War, with the immorality of the dominating and selfish princes reminiscent of the depraved Roman nobility of Catilina's times. Thus, the association Troy/Rome is more specific than Usener has assumed. Troy, as Septimius introduces it to his readers, shows exactly the negative sides of the doomed Roman Republic which Sallust has described in his two monographs. In the course of the account Septimius reminds his reader repeatedly of the similarity between Troy and Rome, more generally by using the above-mentioned political terms, more specifically by creating verbal links to Sallustian passages.[15] Never does he suggest a parallel between Troy and a clearly positive aspect or figure of Sallust's Rome.

This is different with the Greeks. When Agamemnon is unanimously elected commander of the army, we read: *magnus atque clarus habebatur* ('he was considered great and glorious' [1,16]); the same is said by Sallust about Cato (*Cat.* 53,1) and Marius (*Iug.* 92,1). The following preparations of armaments remind the reader of the first well-ordered measure the Romans take against Iugurtha: *arma, tela, equi, naues atque haec omnia toto biennio praeparabantur* ('arms and weapons, and horses and ships, all this was prepared within two years' [1,16]) echoes *Iug.* 43,3: *arma, tela, equos et cetera instrumenta militiae parare* ('he [sc.Metellus] got together arms and weapons, and horses and other instruments of war'). These allusions suggest that the Greeks have on their side what the Trojans have not: the positive potential of the Late Roman Republic.[16]

The Greeks, however, have an additional 'Sallustian' facet. Some of their protagonists resemble aspects of Sallust's Iugurtha-figure. Above all Achilles, when introduced in a detailed characterization (1,14), is closely associated with the Numidian prince, showing similarities in physical appearance, in his outstanding ambition and skill in military exercise, but also in his inclination towards behaving unpredictably.[17] On the 'Sallustian level', thus, the Trojan War is introduced as a war between the weaknesses of the late Roman Republic on the one hand, and a combination of its strength and Iugurtha's virtues and failings on the other.

Finally, there is a third string of allusions to Sallust in the presentation of the Greeks. Some Greek leaders and, subsequently, the Greek army as a whole are at certain points linked by verbal clues with negative Roman characters or actions in Sallust's works. This string starts in Book 2, where fierce problems arise in the Greek camp, and supersedes the two other aspects from the beginning of Book 3. Thus, the assassination of Palamedes by Odysseus and Diomedes is associated with Catilina's conspiracy,[18] and Agamemnon with his obstinacy in the Chryseis-episode is paralleled to Catilina himself.[19] In Book 3 the description of Achilles' serious inner conflict because of his love for Polyxena, which motivates his following brutal and most unheroic behaviour towards the Trojans, calls to mind the picture of Lepidus in Sallust's *Historiae*.[20] In Book 4 Septimius creates a link between the bloody victory of the Greeks over the Aethiopians and Sulla's massacres in Rome,[21] and in Book 5 the slaughter of the Trojans at the sack of the city is associated with the murder of Romans who were killed *foede* and *inulti* in

Rome after fighting for the interest of the people.[22] Finally, when Ajax is found killed after his famous quarrel with Odysseus, and Agamemnon, Menelaus and Odysseus are believed to be guilty of his assassination, we read that the Greeks insult the Atrides, *quippe quis magis libido desideriumque in femina quam summa militiae potiora forent* ('because they cared more for their lust for a woman than for their high command' [5,15]). This recalls Sallust's reference to Roman *nobiles, quibus divitiae bono honestoque potiores erant* ('nobles who cared more for riches than for virtue and integrity' [Iug. 8,1]).

With this string of allusions to Sallust, Septimius has marked important stages of the gradual loss, by the Greeks, of their clear moral superiority over their enemies. Recent analysis of the *Ephemeris* has detected this decline, but has not noticed the Sallustian references. The development starts with the serious conflicts within the Greek camp in Book 2, is focused on Achilles in Book 3, where Achilles kills Hector deceitfully in an ambush and mutilates a captured son of Priam's, and reaches its peak at the Sack of Troy and the disastrous events within the Greek camp after the war, which form a striking contrast to the picture of harmony and unity given at the beginning of the account (see Merkle 1989: 234–37).

Most recently, Joachim Latacz has suggested that this moral decline of the Greeks might be due to the Latin translator (1994: 80, n. 52), and our observations could serve to back up this assumption. However, the Greek fragments provide no indication that Septimius decisively changed the account's contents, and therefore I would still maintain that this development was part of the original; it seems that Septimius caught on to what may have been only implicit in the Greek, and chose to emphasize it in his Latin version. He may, thereby, have increased the moral impact of the account.

What, then, was the function of the clear allusions to Sallust's works? I think they could work on different levels, depending on the reader's education. A reader who could not identify them could still enjoy the aesthetics of Sallustian phrasing. On a reader who was able to recognize parts of the construction they may have had a similar effect as the use of Roman political terms: the respective characters and events seemed somehow familiar and therefore more plausible and realistic. To those readers who recognized most or all of the parallels, Septimius in my view offered a challenging, strictly Latin intertextual game. On the one hand the allusions emphasized the current state of characters and events, and created signposts foreshadowing coming developments; on the other hand they provided in a quite sophisticated manner what a Roman reader might have missed in the account: a connection between the Trojan War and Rome.[23] The conclusions such a reader could draw were, however, not very flattering. The Trojans, he could learn, were indeed surprisingly similar to the Romans; the same negative powers that ruined the Roman Republic had caused the complete destruction of Rome's predecessor. Given that the translation was presented to Romans in imperial times, some of these Romans may have had an uneasy feeling noting the basic difference between Sallust's Rome and Troy: Troy was a monarchy.

III Dictys and Dares, and their literary environment

The picture the *Ephemeris* draws of the Trojan War is, in any case, a very pessimistic one; there seem to be no winners at the end. The *Acta* are quite different. Although they present much more radical alterations of the tradition than the *Ephemeris*, they are closer to Homer in one respect: Greeks and Trojans are more or less equal, both in military skill and in moral regard. Unlike Dictys, Dares, the 'Trojan', does not disparage the 'enemy'; he even consistently dispenses with the traditional negative actions of the Greeks like the assassination of Palamedes, the quarrel between Odysseus and Ajax, and the cruelties at the Sack of Troy. Despite the similarities in the basic conception and the contrasting viewpoints of the alleged chroniclers, then, the two texts do not relate like mirror images to each other, disproving each other point by point; they rather tell two very different 'true stories' of the Trojan War. Nevertheless, it is the basic similarities outlined above which strongly suggest that one author knew the other's work; supposing that a Greek Dares did exist, we can hardly decide who came first.[24]

What we do know quite precisely is the time of origin of the Greek *Ephemeris*: between AD 66 (given in the prologue of the text) and about AD 200 (the dating of the older papyrus). Most recently Glen W. Bowersock (1994: 23) called the Greek text 'entirely a fabrication of the Neronian period', on the assumption that it was actually presented to the emperor in AD 66. This seems highly improbable to me; the πρόλογος of the Greek version (cf. note 1) suggested not only that the text was originally written in Phoenician, but also that Nero accepted it in precisely that form. Since a reference to a king or emperor is a common *topos* in forged *Fundgeschichten* (cf. Merkle 1989: 73–80), Nero's appearance is most probably part of the fiction, and therefore a somewhat later dating within the given period seems preferable.

Moreover, scholars have outlined the position of the Greek text(s) within the literature of the first and second centuries AD. On the one hand they have pointed to the general increase of Homeric revisionism during this time, and to the occurrence of alleged eyewitness reports on the Trojan War in works of different genres and of different purposes: in the eleventh speech of Dio Chrysostom, in Philostratus' *Heroicus*, and in ch. 17 of Lucian's *Cock* (the latter presenting a condensed parody of such constructions).[25] On the other hand the works have been discussed in the context of the ancient novel. There they find their place at the fringe of the genre, in the vicinity of fictional biographies (*Vita Aesopi*, Alexander Romance) and novels in letters, which also present basically 'historical events in pseudo-historical form'.[26]

For the Latin versions, the literary environment is somewhat less clearly discernible. Alan Cameron and Edward Champlin have suggested a dating of the Latin *Ephemeris* to the beginning of the third century AD, connecting the text with the sphere of archaizing Latin writers like Gellius and Fronto. Although this seems not impossible, the lack of closely comparable Latin texts in that period in my view rather suggests the fourth century when a growing and widespread interest in historical topics is indicated by a great number and variety of Latin works and translations from the Greek, as for instance the adaptations of the Alexander material, the *Breuiaria* of Festus and Eutropius, the *Historia Augusta*, and the *Corpus Aurelianum*. As narrative in the form of a historical source, the *Ephemeris* seems to respond to this interest, and similar conditions have been assumed for the fifth century *Acta*.[27]

If this is correct, the Latin texts may for that period exemplify what Latacz (1994: 78, n. 50) calls a gradual 'Verlust des kritisch-historischen Sinnes in der Spätantike'. We noted strong differences between the two Latin versions in their literary elaboration: Septimius' efforts to achieve clarity and allusiveness on the one hand, and on the other hand 'Nepos' marked and conscious lack of concern for a literary shaping of his work. Septimius, therefore, seems to have had a somewhat more educated and critical reader in mind than 'Nepos'. We should, however, note that the extent of the deviations from the Troy tradition in the *Acta* could only be appreciated on the basis of a good knowledge of this tradition.

The general assessment of the works by modern scholars varies considerably. The extremes are constituted by the 1994 publications of Latacz and Bowersock. While the latter includes the Greek *Ephemeris* in the 'four distinct markers for the evolution of fiction' in imperial times, and credits its author with a 'rich fantasy', Latacz, pointedly reviving a common judgement of scholars of the first half of this century, calls the texts 'Machwerke' (Bowersock 1994: 22, 24; Latacz 1994: 81, n. 54). Usener, mainly referring to the Latin versions, understands the works as reflections of efforts for a rationalistic and comprehensible re-shaping of history, and concludes: 'Das Ringen um Sinn hat neue Literatur hervorgebracht in einer Zeit, der man bereits den Verfall der geistigen Kultur zugeschrieben hatte' (1994: 120). I believe that the strongly pessimistic representation of the Trojan War in the *Ephemeris*, with the moral decline of the victorious Greeks, reflects the author's view on war in general, and constitutes a kind of message of the text. Nevertheless, I would regard both works, including the translation(s), primarily as literary games, whose authors and translators enjoyed adding a new facet to the production of fiction in their times, confusing the boundaries between true and false;[28] the Latin *Ephemeris* with its Sallustian *couleur* offered its readers in addition to the various Greek subtexts a strictly Latin intertextual level. Whether a reader could see through this game, or took the texts' claim to authenticity at face value, certainly depended on the level of his education; the *Nachleben* of the texts (cf. note 12) suggests that from Late Antiquity on the readiness to believe such fabrications gradually increased.

Notes

1 P.Tebt.268, P.Oxy.2539; both in Eisenhut 1973. The *prologus*, moreover, presumably represents a quite literal Latin translation of the Greek πρόλογος added later to the text (Merkle 1989: 91–112). Furthermore, Diktys was used by the Byzantine chronographer Malalas (sixth century) as a main source for his Troy section.

2 The common assumption that a Greek Dares did exist is not really capable of being proved; see Beschorner 1992: 231–43. Cf. below note 6.

3 On Dictys see below p. 162f. Language and style of the Latin *Acta* suggest a late date; the *terminus ante* is, as Schetter 1987 has shown, Dracontius' *De raptu Helenae*.

4 In the *Acta* even the delayed prologue and the *sphragis* are given in the third person, not in the first. This, in my view, is intended to suggest the high reliability of the translation; the reader is reminded of the fact that he does not have the original in hand.

5 The alleged interest of both Nepos *and* Sallust in the work, of course, underlines its importance and its credibility.

6 The occasionally quoted references of Ptolemaeus Chennus and Aelianus to a *Phrygian Iliad* by a Trojan war participant Dares are probably no evidence for the Greek original of our *Acta*. See Schetter 1987: 213 note 4, Beschorner 1992: 231–35, and Grossardt 1998: 370f.

7 Most recently Beschorner 1992: 204–230. Cf. Merkle 1990: 511–518.

8 See, e.g., the occasional incongruency between the portraits of the protagonists given in chs.12 and 13 and the account itself; cf. Beschorner 1992: 108–124.

9 The observed consistencies could have survived an epitomization.

10 On reconsideration of the correspondences between the introductory letter and the extant text, this now seems more probable to me than it used to (cf. 1990: 521f.).

11 See, e.g., Brunner 1990.

12 Merkle 1989: 68, 118–122. Occasionally Septimius added moralizing comments to the text adapting Sallustian phrases.

13 The only example of Roman political terminology I could find on the Greek side is the term *lictores* (2,33; 2,49).

14 *ita populus ludibrio habitus ex contione discedit* (*Iug*. 34.2); *ita bonum publicum . . . priuata gratia deuictum* (*Iug*. 25.3).

15 See, e.g., *Eph*. 2,23, (p. 37, 24f.; cf. *Iug*. 8,1), *Eph*. 3,21, (p. 75, 8f.; cf. *Cat*. 18,7), and *Eph*.5,6 (p. 106, 22f.; cf. *Iug*. 41,7).

16 This is confirmed in 2,44 (p. 54, 15–17) and 2,48 (p. 57, 9–11) where Ajax, like Agamemnon in 1,16, is associated with Marius and Cato (cf. *Iug*. 114,4 and *Cat*. 53,1).

17 Cf. *Eph*. 1,14 (p. 12, 2–6) and *Iug*. 6,1–2. Others show only Iugurtha's positive sides: his outstanding military skills (Ajax and, again, Achilles: cf. *Eph*.2,12 [p. 29, 1–3]; *Eph*. 2,16 [p.32, 5–8] and *Iug*. 20,8), and his mental capacities (Palamedes; cf. *Eph*. 2,15 [p. 31, 15f.] and *Iug*. 7,6).

18 Cf. *Eph*. 2,15 (p. 31, 18f.) and *Cat*. 17,7.

19 Cf. *Eph*. 2,31 (p. 44, 14f.) and *Cat*. 26,5.

20 Cf. *Eph*. 3,3 (p. 62, 2–6) and *Hist*. 1,77,11 (or. Phil.). On the Achilles-Polyxena episode in the *Ephemeris* see Merkle 1989: 199–223.

21 Cf. *Eph*. 4, 7 (p. 87, 10–12) and *Cat*. 51,34.

22 Cf. *Eph*. 5,12 (p. 113, 24f.) and *Iug*. 31,2.

23 In the *Ephemeris*, as well as in the *Acta*, Aeneas not only plays a dubious role as participant in the abduction of Helen and as staunch supporter of the Priamids

(*Eph.* 2,26); moreover, his crossing to Italy is never mentioned. Cf., most recently, Farrow 1992.

24 For contrary views see, e.g., Beschorner 1992: 250 f. and Farrow 1992: 344; cf. 349.

25 On Hegesianax, presumably the 'father of the Troy-Romance', see most recently Farrow 1992, 349–357.

26 Holzberg 1996: 18, cf. 16, 25. See also Merkle: 1989, 248–262, 293–305; 1996: 578–580, and Bowersock 1994: 1–27, esp.11–13, 21–23.

27 For the dating of the *Acta* cf. n.3 above. For detailed discussions of this problem see Merkle 1989: 263–283 and Beschorner 1992: 254–263.

28 This view is stongly supported by Grossardt's most recent analysis which convincingly describes the Greek *Ephemeris* as being modeled after the 'Trūgreden' of Homer's Odysseūs (1998: 364–93).

Bibliography

Beschorner, A. (1992), *Untersuchungen zu Dares Phrygius* (*Classica Monacensia*, 4), Tübingen: Gunter Narr.

Bowersock, G.W. (1994), *Fiction as History. Nero to Julian*, Berkeley/Los Angeles/London: University of California Press.

Brunner, H. (ed.) (1990), *Die deutsche Trojaliteratur des Mittelalters und der Frühen Neuzeit. Materialien und Untersuchungen*, Wiesbaden: Dr. Ludwig Reichert Verlag.

Cameron, A. (1980), 'Poetae Novelli', *Harvard Studies in Classical Philology* 84: 127–75.

Champlin, E. (1981), 'Serenus Sammonicus', *Harvard Studies in Classical Philology* 85: 189–212.

Eisenhut, W. (ed.) (1958), *Dictys Cretensis Ephemeridos Belli Troiani Libri a Lucio Septimio ex Graeco in Latinum Sermonem Translati*, Leipzig: B.G. Teubner (2nd edn 1973; reprint 1994).

Farrow, J. (1992), 'Aeneas and Rome: Pseudepigrapha and Politics', *Classical Journal* 87: 339–59.

Grossardt, P. (1988), *Die Trūgreden in der Odyssee ūnd ihre Rezeption in der antiken Literatūr* (*Sapheneia*, 2), Bern: Peter Lang.

Holzberg, N. (1996), 'The Genre: Novels Proper and the Fringe', in G. Schmeling (ed.), *The Novel in the Ancient World* (*Mnemosyne* Supplement, 159), Leiden: E.J. Brill, pp. 11–28.

Körting, G. (1874), *Dictys und Dares. Ein Beitrag zur Geschichte der Troja-Sage in ihrem Übergange aus der antiken in die romantische Form*, Halle/Saale: Lippert.

Latacz, J. (1994), *Achilleus. Wandlungen eines europäischen Heldenbildes*, Stuttgart/Leipzig: B.G. Teubner.

Merkle, S. (1989), *Die 'Ephemeris Belli Troiani' des Diktys von Kreta* (*Studien zur Klassischen Philologie*, 44), Frankfurt a.M./Bern/New York/Paris: Peter Lang.

—— (1990), '*Troiani belli verior textus*: Die Trojaberichte des Dictys und Dares', in H. Brunner (ed.) (1990), pp. 491–522.

—— (1996), 'The Truth and Nothing but the Truth: Dictys and Dares', in G. Schmeling (ed.), *The Novel in the Ancient World*, pp. 563–80.

Schetter, W. (1987), 'Dares und Dracontius über die Vorgeschichte des Trojanischen Krieges', *Hermes* 115: 211–31. (Reprinted in W. Schetter, *Kaiserzeit und Spätantike.*

Kleine Schriften 1957–1992, ed. O. Zwierlein, Stuttgart: Franz Steiner 1994, pp. 295–313).
—— (1988), 'Beobachtungen zum Dares Latinus', *Hermes* 116: 94–109.
Usener, K. (1994), 'Dictys und Dares über den Troischen Krieg: Homer in der Rezeptionskrise?' *Eranos* 92: 102–20.

11

THE LATIN ALEXANDER

Richard Stoneman

Hic (sc. *quod occidit Callisthenen*) *est Alexandri crimen aeternum, quod nulla virtus, nulla bellorum felicitas redimet.*
(Seneca *Naturales Quaestiones* 6.23.2)

Alexander filius Dei.
(Legend on late fourth century contorniate medallions: see A. Alföldi, *Die Kontorniaten*, 1943)

I Introduction

The career of Alexander the Great provides a unique exception to the general rule that Latin writers of history wrote (before the Christian period) only on Roman topics. There were plenty of topics from Greek and other non-Roman history which made it into the schools and provided subjects for rhetorical exercises like the *Suasoriae* and *Controversiae* of the Elder Seneca; Alexander features with fair prominence among such themes, and provided a number of *exempla* for the rhetorician's guide to moral positioning composed by Valerius Maximus; but only he became the subject of a full-length history in Latin. And this occurred more than once.

The first Latin Alexander historian was Quintus Curtius Rufus (hereafter Curtius) who composed a lengthy and important historical account of his career, probably in the first century AD. Though there are a number of manuscripts of this work, all of them lack the first two books, so that the work as we have it begins with Alexander's campaigns in southern Asia Minor. This led some Renaissance authors to 'supplement' the lost books so that in quite a few printed editions of the sixteenth and seventeenth centuries Curtius' work is printed together with these Neo-Latin supplements. The loss of the opening means that we have lost the preface, which might have provided important clues to the identity and connections of the author, of whom we know nothing for certain.

In the fourth century there appeared four other Latin prose works devoted to Alexander: (1) the translation of the *Alexander Romance*, of Pseudo-Callisthenes by Julius Valerius; (2) the *Itinerarium Alexandri Magni* addressed to the Emperor Constantius by an anonymous author, whom some have thought to be Julius Valerius; (3) the *Epitoma Rerum Gestarum Alexandri Magni* (often known as the *Metz Epitome* from the unique codex in Metz, now destroyed, in which it was preserved); and (4) the *Liber de Morte Alexandri Testamentoque eius*, a translation of uncertain date (but very probably late fourth or early fifth century) of a lost Greek work whose origin is in the years immediately following Alexander's death in 323 BC.

One should also mention here *Alexander's letter to Aristotle about India*. This is a Latin translation of a lost Greek original which was epitomized in the Greek recensions of the *Alexander Romance*. The work cannot be dated very precisely. It may be pre-Constantinian since it uses the phrase *praefectus praetorio* with a pre-Constantinian meaning; but the first reference to the work in an independent source is in the anonymous collection *About Doubtful Words* of the seventh century (cf. Schmidt 1961; Gunderson 1980: 35). It is probable that this work was circulating at the same time as the other Alexander-texts we shall be discussing, but as its ethos is so different from these historical works, and as its importance is largely as a constituent of the medieval tradition on Alexander, I shall reserve discussion of it for the chapter on the Medieval Alexander (Chapter 15).

Of these, the *Itinerarium* is incomplete; it originally contained a second section, on the expedition of Trajan to the east. There is one manuscript of the work only, Ambrosianus 49 in Milan: in this it follows the work of Julius Valerius. The unique codex containing the *Epitome* and the *Liber de Morte* was destroyed by fire after a bombing raid on Metz in 1944, and is now known only from copies made by scholars and the nineteenth-century printed editions of Dietrich Volkmann and Otto Wagner. The three shorter works (2–4) may have been designed (though they are never found all together) as a compilation covering the whole of Alexander's career: the *Itinerarium* covers Alexander's early life and his expedition as far as his arrival at the Indus; the *Epitome* covers his career from the conquest of Asia to the arrival at Pattala; and the *Liber* is concerned with his death in Babylon.

In addition, two epitomes were made of Julius Valerius' own work, probably in the late fourth or early fifth century, for those whose reading time was limited and who, in addition, might take offence at the references to the pagan gods in the full work – for reference to the gods is almost entirely expunged from these epitomes.

All these works present themselves as historical writings, and it may seem odd to consider them in a volume otherwise devoted to fictional writing. But (1) the original of Julius Valerius, the Greek *Alexander Romance*, is in many important respects a work of literary fiction and has generic similarities to other fictional writing (Stoneman 1994b); (2) Curtius is often counted among fictional writers, despite the importance of his work for historians, because of the pronounced moral slant of his work as well as the rhetorical and dramatic colour of much of his writing (Kroll 1924: 331–51; Currie

1990); and (3) the *Liber de Morte* is plainly fictional in some sense, though perhaps only in the sense that it is propaganda and untrue. All these works, moreover, are representatives of a continuing and developing preoccupation among Roman writers, poets and thinkers with the figure of Alexander and the nature of historical causation, which carries us from, at the one extreme, the characterization of Alexander as a great hero ruined and corrupted by fortune (see the quotation from Seneca at the head of this chapter) to, at the other extreme, his acceptance not only as a great and exemplary military leader but even a lynchpin figure for the last exponents of pagan religion in the Christian Empire – a son of God.

II Quintus Curtius Rufus

The name Quintus Curtius Rufus is attached to two persons who flourished in the early Empire: the first is a rhetorician who appears in a list of names in Suetonius' *De Grammaticis et Rhetoribus*; those preceding him in the list flourished just before the turn of the era, while the next following lived under Claudius (41–54) and Nero (54–69). If this is our Curtius, we could attribute to him a career spanning the reigns of Augustus to Claudius. The other candidate is a soldier and politician mentioned by Tacitus (*Annales* 1.20.3–21.3), who became praetor under Tiberius (AD 14–37), was suffect consul in AD 43 and died as proconsul of Africa in AD 53. As Heckel writes, following Sumner (1961), 'It is difficult to resist the view that the consul and the rhetorician are one and the same'.[1] If they are, when did he write his work? Given the lack of a preface and dedication to a patron, much hangs on the interpretation of 10.9.1–6 where Curtius writes of the civil war in Macedonia:

> An empire that might have stood firm under one man collapsed while it rested on the shoulders of a number. So it is with justification that the people of Rome acknowledge that they owe their salvation to their emperor [*princeps*] who shone out as a new star in the night that was almost our last. It was his rising, I declare, and not the sun's, that brought light back to a darkened world [*caliganti mundo*] at a time when its limbs lacked a head and were in chaotic disarray . . . So our empire [*imperium*] is not merely recovering, but even flourishes. If I may be forgiven for saying it, the line of this same house will prolong the conditions of these times – forever, I pray, but at least for a long duration.
>
> (tr. John Yardley)

Who is the emperor referred to? The terms are vague enough to admit of many interpretations. Sumner argues that the phrase *caliganti mundo* is a pun on the name of Caligula and that the new emperor is Claudius, whose accession also best fits the state of confusion described. Other interpretations are possible, not least the identification of the *princeps* as Augustus, the first to adopt that name (or perhaps Tiberius, the first to succeed to the title).[2] There appear to the present writer to be strong arguments for an Augustan date for Curtius.

The first argument relates to the likely pattern of Curtius' career. He became consul in AD 43, an office to which men did not generally attain before the age of 42. He held the office of praetor (usually held in a man's thirties) between 14 and 37. He died in office, therefore presumably at a fair age, in AD 53. All this suggests that he was born not later than 1 BC and maybe up to twenty years earlier.

It is uncontroversial to describe Curtius as a Livian (though some scholars have detected *clausulae* (a type of rhetorical prose rhythm) characteristic of Silver Latin in his work). As we shall see below, there are extremely close verbal correspondences between Curtius and Livy which suggest that Curtius might have been well acquainted with that author and his work. Livy, born in 59 BC, died in AD 17, and had completed the first five books of his History by 25 BC. It would be possible to envisage Curtius as a young man learning the rhetorician's craft in his late teens and twenties perhaps around the turn of the era or a decade later, and being strongly impressed by the magisterial History of the grand old man, to the extent of deciding to develop one of his rhetorical exercises into a history in the Livian manner, into which he then poured a number of Livian ideas and phrases.

Such a setting would fit with the complex of ideas about Alexander which was developing during the reign of Augustus. The fundamental study of this subject is that of Dietmar Kienast (1969), who built on the more wide-ranging discussion by Alfred Heuss (1954), to show how Augustus' own use of Alexander in his propaganda attempted rather successfully to reconcile two quite incompatible views. On the one hand, Mark Antony had already associated himself strongly with Alexander, as an oriental potentate, using Dionysiac imagery to colour his own self-presentation as Alexander had also done. Augustus had to use this 'oriental' representation of Antony to damage his opponent. On the other hand, the figure of Alexander as a world ruler had also been current in Roman thought for some time, not least in the legends that surrounded Scipio Africanus, whose birth was alleged to have been as miraculous as Alexander's. To establish his authority in the east, it suited Augustus to present himself as a new Alexander, visiting the latter's tomb in Alexandria and honouring the city. He also used an image of Alexander as his personal seal. His plan for a Parthian War is part of this Alexander imitation. In Rome, however, he had to be more cautious: as Kienast puts it, there was no room for Alexander in the world of the *Ara Pacis*.

An anti-Alexander stance was already established in Rome by Livy's discussion of his career in Book 9.17–19 of his History. This book was composed in the late twenties BC (Braccesi 1986: 46; Luce 1977), at the very time that Augustus was claiming to have solved the Parthian problem by a great diplomatic coup (*Res Gestae* 29.2). In this discussion, Livy attacks some unnamed Greek historians (*levissimi ex Graecis*) who have sometimes been considered to be identifiable with the historian Timagenes of Rhodes – an author whom Curtius also cites only to discredit him (9.5.21). His argument was that Alexander was not in fact invincible, and that if he had encountered the military might of Rome he would certainly have been defeated. His success was due to the indulgence of Fortune in not bringing him up against a sufficiently tough enemy. The description in 9.18.1 of Alexander's corruption and decadence, brought on by an excess of good fortune, is clearly an allusion to an already familiar theme. It was this theme that induced the young Plutarch later to write his essays *On the Fortune of Alexander*, in which he attacks those (in *Roman Questions* 326AB he mentions Livy by name) who argued that Alexander had been corrupted by good fortune. Plutarch argued instead that Fortune had for much of his career been *against* Alexander. The issue had been a staple of philosophical discussions from Posidonius and Cicero onwards (Stoneman 1994a: xxx), and Curtius is the fullest exponent of the idea of the corrupting Fortune in Alexander's life. It is the leitmotif of his entire history.[3]

The suspicion that Curtius learnt his attitude and his trade from association with Livy is increased when we look at the detail of his work. There are several echoes of Livy's Alexander-excursus in Curtius' language. His description (3.3.18–24) of the luxury of the Persian army, accompanied as it was by women and eunuchs and dressed in gold and other finery, is indebted at several points to Livy (9.17.16). The description of the Dionysiac procession through Carmania (9.10.24–9) contains several verbal echoes of Livy's description of the same event (9.17.17), not least the use of the word *comisabundus* (drunk) which occurs in only one other passage (in Seneca) apart from these two.[4] Curtius draws on other passages of Livy too, such as the description of the mutilated prisoners at 3.18.3, which resembles Livy 30.29.2f.

Beyond these echoes of Livy, it is possible to find more general reflections of the Augustan scene in Curtius' attitudes. Many of these parallels have been usefully assembled by Petre Ceausescu (1974). It was common to see in Alexander's liaison with the Amazon queen Thalestris (6.6.1–6) the turning point in his corruption – just as it was Antony's liaison with the oriental queen Cleopatra that made him intolerable to the Romans. A similar point is made by Curtius *apropos* Alexander's marriage to Roxane: 'His friends were ashamed that he had chosen his father-in-law at a dinner party and from subject peoples but, with the suspension of free speech following Clitus' murder, they signified their approval with their facial expressions, the feature of a man most prone to servility' (8.4.30).[5] This almost Tacitean observation, which might be thought to argue a familiarity with the demands of the court of Tiberius, if not Nero, should be set alongside Curtius' observation on the death of Callisthenes. This execution, which Seneca (*Naturales Quaestiones* 6.23.2) described as Alexander's eternal and irremediable shame (because Callisthenes was a philosopher), is regarded by Curtius more simply as a 'barbarous act' – a crime, but not because it was directed at a philosopher (as might have been the case in a writer working under, say, Nero). Instead, Callisthenes is described as *vindex publicae libertatis* (8.5.20), which as Ceausescu points out (163) is language appropriate to the conflict between senate and tyrant (in this case Antony). Augustus himself wrote *rem publicam a dominatione factionis oppressam in libertatem vindicavi* ('I avenged the liberty of the Republic which was oppressed by the domination of a faction': *Res Gestae* 1.1; Ceausescu 158). Antony's drunkenness was another propaganda point for the Augustan position, in which he again echoed a famous characteristic of Alexander.

Curtius' treatment of Alexander, then, chimes with the anti-Antonian propaganda of the Augustan period as well as with a hostile attitude to Alexander's morals and capacity which is first spelt out at length in Roman literature by Livy. In addition, Curtius seems to embody some of the contradictions of the Augustan attitude to Alexander, for the concluding summary of Alexander's career (10.5.26–37) is nothing other than encomium: 'It is obvious to anyone [it begins] who makes a fair assessment of the king that his strengths were attributable to his nature and his weakness to fortune or his youth.' A long list of virtues follows, and Curtius ends by remarking that Fortune decided to bring his career to an end (i.e. she is against him now, as in the Plutarchan view), while 'the fates waited for him to complete the subjection of the east and reach the Ocean, achieving everything of which a mortal was capable' (10.5.36). This last phrase encapsulates a view of Alexander which was to become the dominant one in Roman culture as the philosophic opposition faded out and he became instead a model for military emperors such as Trajan, Constantius and even Julian.

Curtius' style of writing is far from that of the annalistic historians of Rome. He insists that he is writing history, and his concern for facts and his sources is expressed in the word *transcribo*. Yet he is not included by Quintilian in his list of historians. Perhaps the key is in the derivative nature of his work. For modern historians he is an important source, as the fullest representative of the tradition, known as the Vulgate, which goes back to Clitarchus, a historian whose lifetime probably overlapped with that of Alexander, unlike that of the authors of any of the extant histories. But for ancient critics he was simply descanting on a theme; his history is from one point of view a *controversia* drawn out to enormous length.

Another way of looking at Curtius is as a novelist – not, to be sure, a novelist like Mary Renault, who could compose an entire novel about a character (Bagoas) who is known to us from a few sentences in Curtius, and use that character as a peg on which to hang a narrative of Alexander's career. Harry MacL. Currie (1990) has argued that the work is something between history and biography, and has important affinities with Xenophon's *Education of Cyrus*, a work which offers an account of the life of Cyrus the Great which is in part historical (though in part it flies in the face of other historical accounts, and in part is pure invention), but offers a moral portrait rather than a conventional historical account. It is a Mirror for Princes. This is not, to be sure, a description that could well be applied to Curtius' work, though it does appear to echo contemporary moral and political concerns. But it does use many literary techniques to enhance its historical narrative.

These techniques have been well summarized by Kroll (1924). One of the most important influences on Curtius' language is Virgil. Tragic techniques are also in evidence, as is the art of the forensic debate in the long and unforgettable narrative of the conspiracy and trial of Philotas (5.5), which is so naturally dramatic that more than one later playwright has adapted it for the stage with ease.[6] Ecphrasis, particularly description of geographical regions such as India and its wonders, is important, and more notable in that, as Kroll (333) puts it, Curtius probably never saw a map! All in all, Curtius' aim was to write as entertainingly as possible. But his work is more than mere entertainment. Increasingly scholars have come to value the evidence of the Vulgate tradition as a corrective to Arrian's glowing portrait of Alexander. If it borrowed techniques of Hellenistic history writing in making history both moving and alluring, it also encapsulated a certain political mood. The moral position is constant, and the turn to encomium in 10.5, though it might represent the shift of a young writer who had been half-seduced by the glamour of his subject and who (like Julian later) could not quite make up his mind whether to be for or against Alexander, could equally be regarded as echoing the complexities of the Augustan view of Alexander, in which the oriental despot was to be reviled while the noble world ruler was to be emulated. It seems quite possible that Augustus would have been impressed by this work.

III The fourth century writers

When we turn to the Latin writers on Alexander of the fourth century we find ourselves in a different world from that of Curtius. Curtius represented the first flowering of the debate about how Alexander should be judged, which was taken up with vigour by writers like Seneca, Plutarch and Dio Chrysostom. Plutarch, in his *Fortune of Alexander*, had gone some way towards turning Alexander into a philosopher-king; while Dio, writing under Trajan – an admirer of the conqueror – composed eight books (now lost) *On the Virtues of Alexander*, as well as devoting two of his *Discourses on Kingship* (II and IV) to Alexander (Stoneman 1994a: xxxi–ii). Both of these develop the picture of Alexander as a philosopher-king, through dialogues between the king and, respectively, his father Philip and the Cynic philosopher Diogenes. These writings no doubt echo the favourable attitude to

Alexander evinced by the emperor Trajan, who acquired the reputation of a virtuous ruler and at the same time developed plans for a conquest of the east nearly as far-reaching as Alexander's.

Alexander's achievement as a conqueror had always been paradigmatic (except for Livy): it is the nub of the comparison between Alexander and Germanicus in Tacitus' *Annals* 2.73. Caracalla's enthusiasm for Alexander derived from admiration of his heroic qualities; and something like this also lay behind the emergence of 'false Alexanders' in the east in his reign – an early example of the mystical significance that came to be attached to the hero's name (see p. 181).[7] As we shall see, it is Alexander's achievement as a conqueror of the east that lies at the root of the interest that the fourth century took in him.

The philosophic debates about Alexander's character and achievements which exercised these authors are behind us as we enter the fourth century, apart from some incidental echoes in the church fathers of the Stoic characterization of Alexander as a tyrant. We shall look at the four texts in turn.

Julius Valerius

The work of Julius Valerius, entitled *Res Gestae Alexandri Macedonis translatae ex Aesopo Graeco* is certainly the earliest of them, and can be dated with some confidence.[8] The author's full name is given, in those MSS that preserve the opening, as Julius Valerius Alexander Polemius. The form of the name is unusual in that it contains two *nomina* and two *cognomina*, and it has sometimes been thought that the name is a scribal confusion of some phrase such as *Alexandrou polemoi*, Alexander's Wars (cf. the title of the second Latin recension of the *Alexander Romance*, which is known as the *Historia de Preliis*). Most scholars however have accepted this as the writer's full name, and the authors of the *Prosopography of the Later Roman Empire* identify him with the Flavius Polemius who was consul in 338 and *comes* of the East in 345. The same name is mentioned as that of one of six bishops who wrote to Athanasius encouraging him to return to Alexandria in 345/46.[9]

Some other indications enable us to date the work more precisely (Kuebler 1888). There is clear evidence of use of the work by the author of the second of our texts, the *Itinerarium Alexandri*, which is dateable to 340–45 (see below), and furthermore the work was written before the capital of the empire was moved from Rome to Constantinople in 330, as is clear from the absence of any reference to this event in I.31 where Rome is described as *domina omnium gentium*. The same paragraph also refers to some newly-built parts of Rome which must be the Aurelian Walls erected in the early 270s. The sixty years between 270 and 330 thus give us the time frame in which this work was composed.

The work is a translation of the Greek *Alexander Romance* of Pseudo-Callisthenes, but not a precise translation of any of the extant Greek texts. It is close to the A-text but contains some passages, for example the Letter of Zeuxis, which are not in the Greek. More frequent however are passages where Julius abbreviates his original, an interesting example being the description of Nectanebo's astrological calculator in I.14. It may be that he was baffled by this rather obscure passage, or it may be that he was using a Greek text which, like recensions β and γ, had already cut out much of the detail. A third possibility is that the description was deliberately attenuated because of its pagan elements, a development which is even more noticeable in the fifth-century epitomes of Julius, which omit practically all reference to pagan religion. Other less significant omissions include one of Darius' letters to Alexander and a part of Darius' dying speech; these may simply be reflections of an original that differs from our own text of A. Julius adds a few references of his own, notably the reference to the *History* of Favorinus in I.13, which obviously derives from his own reading of the second-century author. An interesting detail is his use of the phrase *dominus et deus* (not in the Greek) to describe Darius; the phrase was first introduced by Diocletian (284–305) as an imperial appellation.

There was a considerable amount of translation activity from Greek into Latin at the beginning of the fourth century (Engels and Hofmann 1997: 29–52ff.). In part this reflects a loss of facility in Greek among the inhabitants of the western empire, but it is also related to the increasing domination of Latin writing by Christian authors such as Lactantius, Tertullian and Celsus. Latin was recognized as the language of rule and of the elite (Momigliano 1963: 127) and it was important to make valued texts available to a Latin readership. Scholars have spoken in terms of a 'pagan revival' during the fourth century following the conversion of the empire under Constantine, or of a rearguard action by a pagan resistance which has been identified with the so-called 'Circle of Symmachus' in the late fourth century. (This 'Circle' is a fictitious literary construction by Macrobius: Cameron 1976.) The members of this group include Nicomachus Flavianus, the translator of Philostratus' *Life of Apollonius of Tyana* into Latin, and Vettius Agorius Praetextatus (whom Jerome described immediately after his death as 'abandoned and naked in filthy darkness': *Ep.* 23.3, Berschin 1988: 51). While the cohesion of this 'resistance' has been challenged of late (Cameron 1976; Matthews 1973), it remains true that some very prominent pagans were engaged in literary activity during the fourth century. Both pagans and Christians were equally busy with translation.[10] So Julius' work may be seen in a context of some kind of attempt to rescue parts of the classical heritage for transmission to a wider western audience, running in parallel to a Christian movement to spread Greek works among a Latin elite readership.

Jerome (347–420) was an indefatigable translator from Hebrew and Greek into Latin. His Letters 57 and 106 are valuable documents of the principles of translation he followed. In Letter 106, he insists (3) that Latin is not too limited a language to convey the subtleties of Greek, and requires that a translator should preserve as far as possible the characteristics of the original in the translation. In this respect he argues for a more rigorous approach to translation than that of earlier Latin authors such as Livius Andronicus, whose main aim had been to convey the sense. Letter 57, *de optimo genere interpretandi*, is Jerome's fullest account of his theory of translation. In this letter he upholds as the ideal a Ciceronian model which conveys the original not word for word but 'sense for sense' (5–6). There is less anxiety than in *Ep.* 106 about verbatim correspondence, and he allows that even St Mark sometimes expanded his Hebrew original when quoting Old Testament passages (7, 8), and that 'etymological' translation is often undesirable (11).

Julius' practice is less strict than that of the Biblical scholar. His approach is characterized by *amplificatio*: the often jejune Greek of the original is turned into a more flowing and orotund Latin in which the language is more expansive while not distorting the sense (Romano 1974: 45–46). Julius does make some mistakes in his translations, for example misreading the word *strateumata* (camps) (where A has *kome*, village) as the name of a place, Astrata (1.828). The River Oceanus is at one point translated as Cydnus. The name Isthmia is corrupted into *thias* (1.1626), and Lycaonia is turned into Lucania (1.780). Some errors may be explained by corruptions in the Greek text he used (e.g. in I.30 his *lunatis cornibus* seems to derive from a reading ΜΗΝΟΚΕΡΩΣ not ΜΗΛΟΚΕΡΩΣ in his original). In general Julius' is a faithful rendering of the Greek into contemporary Latin, perhaps more stylish than the original.

As an author Julius is conscious of his position in a literary tradition. His work often resonates with the classics of Latin writing, for example Virgil. There are phrases which seem to come directly from his reading of Cicero, such as the oath *medius fidius* and the echo of *In Catilinam* 1.1 at 2.94. Fassbender's (1909) exhaustive study of Julius' style identified many echoes of earlier writers, among whom by far the most prominent place is held by Apuleius. The use of single words can be over-interpreted as an author of any given period will be drawing on a common stock, but repeated phrases are a little more significant, and deliberate archaism is often apparent. In general the impression is of an artificial language; but it also contains many examples of what Fassbender calls Low Latin, of which characteristic forms are elaborate compounds with redundant elements such as *abrelegare* or doubly abstract nouns such as *proeliatio* ('battle-ation') which recall modern American coinages such as 'to burglarize' for 'to burgle'. By comparison with Christian authors like Jerome and Augustine, the style is mannered and strained. Cicero is no genuine model here as he is for Jerome's ideal, *non verbosa rusticitas sed sancta simplicitas*, 'not a verbose clumsiness but holy simplicity' (*Ep.* 57.12).[11]

There is little to be said with confidence about the author and his view of his subject. His aim is to make available a text that seemed to him for some reason important to a Latin readership. There are several indications that he was an Alexandrian – first, the unusual form of his name, and secondly several references to Egyptian features, e.g. his allusion to the Island of Proteus as '*inter nostros*', and the expansions of the details about Alexander's tomb (3.33) and the fact that his deathday is kept as a sacred day in Alexandria (3.35). We may perhaps envisage this translation as the work of a relatively young author, presenting an important tradition of his native city. Romano argues for a context after the revolt of Alexandria in 296, which was suppressed by Diocletian and in the wake of which the city was heavily romanized and the use of Latin became obligatory. The translation is thus an 'accommodation' between Alexandria and Rome. It may have served to bring Julius Valerius to imperial notice, since he became a prominent political figure and, as we shall see, may also have been commissioned to write the next work we shall look at, the *Itinerarium Alexandri*.

A Diocletianic date would explain the relative freedom with which pagan details are presented in relation to not only the later epitomes, but the *Itinerarium* itself, which reflects the stricter proscription of non-Christian activity from Constantius onwards. If Julius is indeed the Polemius referred to as a bishop in the letter of Athanasius (see note 9), it is possible to imagine that he became a Christian only after the composition of the *Res Gestae*, in response to prevailing political circumstances.

Finally we should consider the ascription of the Greek original to Aesop. What does this signify? The fables of Aesop had been translated into Latin verse in the first century, and into prose in the fourth. They had held some interest for philosophers and other writers and were quite frequently cited in the first two centuries AD (Holzberg 1992, 1993: 37). Dio Chrysostom in his seventy-second speech comes close to identifying himself with Aesop, and Apuleius (*De deo Socratis*, prologue) presents Aesop as an author whose works can convey important moral or philosophical points in a painless and pleasing manner. Though it is not possible to derive from Julius' work any obvious moral or political point, it is certainly true that it conveys its historical narrative in a pleasing and painless manner. It cannot be known whether the ascription to Aesop is the work of Julius or of a later copyist, but whichever it is, it conveys something about the acceptability of this history to its readers as a worthwhile and perhaps improving work of literature.

The Itinerarium Alexandri Magni

This work, which is preserved in a single manuscript in the Ambrosian Library in Milan, is incomplete. It is the first half of a work which in its complete form included also an account of the eastern campaigns of the emperor Trajan. It can be dated quite closely, for it is addressed to Constantius on the occasion of his departure for a campaign in the east. From paragraph 2 of the work it is clear that the emperor Constantine and his son Constantine II, Constans' elder brother, are both dead, but that Constans is not (he died in 350). The work therefore is later than 340 and earlier than 350. Constantius II had succeeded his father as Eastern Emperor in 337, and much of his reign was taken up with wars against the Persians. T.D. Barnes has argued (1985; see also Lane Fox 1997: 246) that the work is probably to be dated exactly in 340, because Constantius (b. 317) is said to be the same age as Alexander when he departed for the east; and the *Itinerarium* also refers to Constantius' installation of a Roman nominee on the throne of Armenia in 338.

The work is explicitly designed as a handbook for Constantius on his campaign. The author insists that it is not be thought of as a breviary, but specifically as an itinerary. He thus distances himself from authors of the same period like Aurelius Victor and Eutropius, who composed summaries of Roman history specifically for the use of busy emperors and administrators, and aligns himself rather with authors like Varro (whom he cites) who composed a geographical handbook for use by Pompey in his eastern campaign. If this was his aim, he seems to have failed, because the work is singularly short on reliable geographical information (though of course the lost Trajanic half may have been different) and is much more an abridged history of the campaign of Alexander in general.

From the time of Trajan onwards, Alexander had always been invoked when an emperor was planning an eastern campaign. His name was in the air whenever Rome and Persia clashed. Barnes (1985) draws attention to the *Fifth Demonstration* of Aphrahat, a Syriac Christian writer, who welcomes the prospect of a Roman campaign following the siege of Nisibis in 337 and regards the Roman Empire as the fourth kingdom predicted in Daniel 7.23 (the third having been that of Alexander). Such eschatological views of Rome and Alexander were to have a long subsequent history in the east, not least in the prophecy of Pseudo-Methodius which associated the last days with a release of the peoples Gog and Magog penned in by Alexander. We may see the *Itinerarium* as an early, and quite secular, concomitant of this kind of interest in Alexander.

The *Itinerarium* covers the period from the birth of Alexander to his decision to return from India. It follows the historical account of Arrian with few deviations and presents a broadly favourable view of Alexander. (One might imagine that the lost second part also followed Arrian as the source for the narrative of Trajan's campaigns.) It is set in a framework which has some affinities with panegyric (in which Alexander was a stock object of comparison for the addressee): in paragraph 4, Constantius' modesty is compared favourably with Alexander's vanity – a nice example of the old philosophic objection to Alexander being recycled as a motif of encomium! There are few surprises in the account, though some of the proper names have become corrupt (the text is in general very corrupt, being based on a single MS, and represents a considerable challenge to an editor), and the reference to the Amazons by the name of *Unimammae* (i.e. 'Single-breasts', 41) makes clear that the author is using a Greek source which he here translates literally ('etymologically', in Jerome's terminology). One of the main expansions of the narrative is the description of the oasis of Siwa in paragraph 20, where it becomes a veritable *locus amoenus*. The description of India in paragraph 48 also makes room for some of the fabulous beasts without which no description of India was complete, though Arrian had been more sober in his approach.

The rhapsody on Siwa might suggest an Egyptian author, and in fact Romano has argued that the *Itinerarium* might be by Julius Valerius. As a *comes* in Constans' court in 349 he was plainly linked with court circles, like Aurelius Victor who also came to notice through his work in the imperial bureaucracy and whose book *De Caesaribus* brought him to the attention of the emperor Julian on his accession in 360 or shortly after (Bird 1984). The style of the *Itinerarium* is considerably more knotty than that of the *Res Gestae*, but it is the work of a skilful author and contains some good scenes. It more than once echoes the *Res Gestae*.

Furthermore, one of the MSS of the *Res Gestae*, the Parisinus 4880, differs sufficiently from the others to be regarded as in effect a second recension of the work. Not only does it omit everything relating to the cult of the pagan gods, but it also incorporates some additions from the *Itinerarium*, as well as from Josephus and Orosius (Rosellini 1993: xxiv; see also Romano 1974). Romano has argued that this MS represents a revision of the work by Julius himself, consonant with the anti-pagan mood prevailing in the later part of his career (and perhaps resulting in his conversion to Christianity himself, as in the case of Firmicus Maternus). Such a view would not only explain the non-pagan character of this recension but would also strengthen the view that the *Itinerarium* is also by Julius: he is borrowing from his own earlier work.

If the author is Julius, this might explain why the work does not fulfil its promised purpose very well. Perhaps the work was commissioned from Julius as a known expert on Alexander; but Julius was not in fact able to provide the kind of detailed geographical and climatic information that was expected, and instead provided simply a summary history of Alexander. Perhaps that might, too, explain the relative neglect of the work thereafter. Perhaps the second part, on Trajan, was found more useful by Constantius, and taken to Persia in his baggage, and lost there. There is room for speculation, but no evidence. Lane Fox (1997) has reaffirmed the suggestion that the two works are by the same author, and proposes that a second edition of the work was prepared for the Emperor Julian in the 360s; it is indubitable that Julian would have found the little book appealing.

Both these works are characteristic pieces of late fourth-century historiography. Arnaldo Momigliano (1963) once wrote of the elusiveness, the air of reticence and mystery, that characterizes fourth-century writing on pagan topics. Its background is hard to characterize. A gulf opens in the middle of the century between pagan and Christian writing. A practice of study and teaching like that enunciated by Augustine in *De doctrina Christiana* would have preserved for us nothing more of pagan literature than is found in Isidore's *Etymologiae* (Markus 1974). Conscious of the threat to pagan learning from Christian doctrine, pagan writers presented their subjects modestly, concealing the pagan associations of their subjects, and even their own identities (as in the case of the author of the *Historia Augusta*). H.W. Bird (1984: 80) remarks that 'even non-military members of the fourth century bureaucracy were seldom really well-educated or cultured'. This comment, made *apropos* of Aurelius Victor, could be applied to Eutropius, or Festus, or the author of the *Origo Gentis Romanae* – or to the author(s) of either of the works now under discussion. But it is not just limitation of learning that engenders the jejune quality of these texts, but also an anxious defensiveness, allied to a consciousness that the elite Roman reader, busy in the imperial administration, has not much time for detail. Information is at a premium, comment – whether personal, doctrinal or historical – is at a discount. Alexander represented a bulwark against barbarism and the Persians, and that significance, rather than the philosophical qualities that the second century sought to establish in him, outweighed his negative image as a pagan.

The **Epitoma rerum gestarum Alexandri** *and the* **Liber de morte Alexandri testamentoque eius**

These two works, which take the presentation of Alexander a step further still, can be quite briefly discussed. They are found together in the Metz Codex, though versions of the *Testament* appear also in the Greek recensions of the *Alexander Romance* and this work plainly goes back to a Greek original of the fourth century BC (Heckel 1988).

The *Testament* has been thoroughly discussed by Heckel (1988), who defines it as a work of the period following Alexander's death, produced as propaganda for the Perdiccan faction and possibly composed by the otherwise obscure Holkias who is named as its scribe in the text. This will does not appear in any of the major historical sources – Arrian, Diodorus or Curtius – but it is in all the Greek recensions of the *Romance* and also in Julius Valerius. A form of the will was known to Ammianus Marcellinus (330–95) who mentions it in his *History* 23.6.7: '. . . not to mention the wars of Alexander and the passing by his will and testament of the whole nation to the jurisdiction of a single successor'. That is not quite what the *Testament* says, so the possibility remains open that Ammianus was drawing on some other tradition; but it seems more likely that he is referring imprecisely to this document. If he knew the *Testament* itself, that would imply an early fourth-century date for the Latin text. The versions of Julius and the *Testament* were made independently as their language does not coincide: the *Testament* derives from the Greek pamphlet while Julius is translating the version that had already been adapted into the *Romance* by the author of the first Greek recension. The *Testament* was collected by the compiler of the Metz Codex or its original as a complement to the *Epitome* to give a complete account of Alexander's campaigns, since the *Epitome* ends with Alexander's arrival in Pattala.

The *Epitome*, unlike the *Liber*, is an original Latin work of probably the fourth or fifth century:[12] it takes the form of a historical breviary of the type that became popular at this period (as in the works of Festus and Eutropius). It supplements all the other historical narratives at several points (for example on the siege of Massaga, and the assertion that Roxane had borne a son in 326, who died) and cannot be seen as a summary of any one of them. The author probably went back to Clitarchus for his material, for he emphasizes a number of the sensational aspects of Alexander's expedition (the story of Spitamenes, the dogs which fight lions) as Clitarchus is known to have done. He also presented a favourable image of Alexander in which the murder of Clitus and the fall of Callisthenes are treated very lightly. He includes several letters which correspond to elements of the Romance tradition, notably the exchange of letters with the Gymnosophists: this raises interesting but unanswerable questions about how much of the *Romance*'s material had its origin in Clitarchus.

The question has been raised whether the *Liber* and the *Epitome* are by the same author. Friedrich Pfister (1946: 37–9) took the view that the works were by different authors, while Lellia Ruggini (1961) has argued that they are by the same hand. The stylistic arguments are insufficient to decide the matter since many of the points raised are common to other writings of this period also: the use of archaic and compound words, the form of adverbs in *-tim*, the absence of any kind of 'Biblical' Latin. However, Ruggini's study does the valuable service of drawing attention to the closeness of these two works in their cultural ambience, even though they depend on different historical traditions. Following perhaps a generation after the *Itinerarium*, they belong to a period when the figure of Alexander was becoming increasingly widespread as a cultural emblem. In the second half of the fourth century, John Chrysostom (347–407) was inveighing against the prevalence of the use in Antioch of images of Alexander as magical talismans (πρὸς τούς μέλλοντας φωτίζεσθαι 2.5; P.G. 49, col. 240).[13] We know the kind of thing he was referring to, for there survive a large number of medallions bearing images of Alexander, or of his mother Olympias. These medallions, known as contorniates, were exhaustively studied by Andreas Alföldi (1943), who regarded them as documents of the last pagan resistance to Christianity at the end of the fourth century. The earlier ones depict on their reverses either Alexander as the New Dionysus, or as conqueror of the Amazons, or Olympias with the serpent. The latest of the contorniates, from the end of the fourth or the early fifth century, portray Alexander with the legend *Alexander filius dei*, 'Alexander the son of God'. These medallions are surely only part of a much wider recognition of

Alexander as a divine figure; the *Historia Augusta*, which was composed in the Theodosian age, includes among its many bizarre documentations of late polytheism this information about the family of the Macriani:

> An embossed head of Alexander the Great of Macedonia was always used by the men on their rings and their silver plate, and by the women on their headdresses, their bracelets, their rings and ornaments of every kind, so that even today there are still in that family, tunics and fillets and women's cloaks which show the likeness of Alexander in threads of divers colours. We, ourselves, recently saw Cornelius Macer, a man of that same family, drink the health of a pontiff from a bowl made of electrum, which had in the centre the face of Alexander and contained on the circumference his whole history in small and minute figures, and this he caused to be passed around to all the most ardent admirers of that great hero. All this I have included because it is said that those who wear the likeness of Alexander carved in either gold or silver are aided in all that they do.
> (*SHA* 'Thirty Tyrants' 14.3–6; tr. D. Magie)

While one may be suspicious of this as historical information about the Macriani, it is certainly evidence for interest in Alexander in the last years of the fourth century, and the patera with the career of Alexander portrayed in it looks as if it may have been inspired by the current vogue for Alexander narratives such as the work of Julius Valerius. That such portrayals could exist is proved by the existence of a mosaic at Soueidié-Baalbeck in the Lebanon, which can be attributed to this period by the styles of the clothing portrayed. It depicts a complex scene of the birth of Alexander (Chéhab 1957; Ross 1963). On the left-hand side, which is badly damaged, are two figures, one of whom can be identified by some letters above him as Philip: this portion is referred to as an 'annunciation' by its editor. On the right is the figure of Olympias attended by a servant, while in the foreground the infant Alexander is being bathed in a large urn by a maidservant. It is hard not to see this as some kind of pagan counterpart to the nativity scenes which by this time were becoming prevalent in Christian art.

Even if scholars today are less confident than they were of the existence of a concerted 'pagan resistance', there is no denying that the image of Alexander has now come to bear a meaning in Roman culture diametrically opposite to that it had had in the age of Augustus. The evil tyrant has become a divine figure and a magical protector. The Emperor Julian, as both a philosopher and a military commander, veered between a philosophical view of Alexander as a tyrant and a soldier's view of him as a great example (Stoneman 1994a: xxxii–iii): but in the generation after Julian, with Persian wars off the agenda for a time, it was neither the philosopher's view nor the soldier's view that held sway, but rather the image of the great conqueror as one of the most sublime representatives of the achievements of pagan culture – quite literally, a name to conjure with.

Notes

1 Heckel ('Introduction' to the Penguin translation of Curtius): 4 – see 'Editions'.
2 Atkinson 1980. Barzano 1984 argues for a Flavian date.
3 For Roman writers, history is always a struggle between *fortuna* and *virtus* (Bird 1984: 80, referring to Aurelius Victor). *Fortuna* is central in Sallust: she is the power that lets down Rome (*Bell.* Cat 8.1ff.). Heckel's pages 12–13 in the introduction to the Penguin Curtius are a neat summary of Curtius' attitude (see 'Editions'). Fortune may be seen as favouring Darius to begin with (3.2.18, 3.8.20), but at 3.11.23 she transfers her favours to Alexander (cf. 3.12.6). Alexander is corrupted by Fortune (3.12.18–20); and this point is made with particular emphasis at 6.6.1–6, the very centre of the work, at the moment of Alexander's liaison with Thalestris. Fortune also favours Alexander at, for example, 4.9.22 and 8.3.1. It is important to distinguish Fortune from Chance, for as Curtius emphatically says at 5.11.10, Chance does *not* determine our lives.
4 Another echo of Curtius in Seneca is *Ep.* 59.12, which seems to pick up Curtius 8.10.1. Lassandro 1984 argues for Seneca's familiarity with Curtius' work.
5 I find this likelier than Barzano's (1984) suggestion that the parallel is with Titus and Berenice.
6 Samuel Daniel, *The Tragedy of Philotas* (1605); Terence Rattigan, *Adventure Story* (1950).
7 Dio Cassius 78.7–8; see Millar 1964: 214–18.
8 The most authoritative and fullest treatment is that by Romano 1974, which replaces the earlier study of Kuebler 1888, and his RE article. There is a recent edition of the text by M. Rosellini (See 'Editions').
9 Athanasius, *Historia Arianorum* 22.1; Barnes 1989: 313.
10 Berschin (1988: 42ff.) lists a number of such translations from the fourth to the sixth centuries. They include, in the fourth century, the translation of Dictys Cretensis into Latin and in the fifth that of Dares Phrygius, and (if there was a Greek original) the *History of Apollonius King of Tyre*. See the contributions of Merkle and Schmeling to this volume (Chapters 9 and 10).
11 Auerbach (1965) comments on the growing universality of the *sermo humilis*, the sweet and plain style, in the Christian writers of the fourth century.
12 Baynham 1995 is a careful study; her work was preceded by the fuller treatment of Ruggini 1961.
13 For the context of the 'magical' Alexander see Maguire 1995: 4 and 56; also Russell 1995: 35–50, especially 48.

Bibliography

Editions

Q. Curtius Rufus, *Historiae Alexandri Magni*, ed. Edmund Hedicke, Leipzig: B.G. Teubner, 1912. Translation: John Yardley, with introduction and notes by Waldemar Heckel, Harmondsworth: Penguin, 1984.

Julius Valerius, *Res gestae Alexandri Macedonis*, ed. M. Rosellini, Stuttgart/Leipzig: B.G. Teubner, 1993.

Itinerarium Alexandri Magni, ed. Angelo Mai, Rome 1865.

Incerti Auctoris Epitoma rerum gestarum Alexandri Magni cum Libro de morte testamentoque Alexandri, ed. P.H. Thomas, Leipzig: Teubner, 1966.

Secondary literature

Alföldi, A. (1943) *Die Kontorniaten*, 2nd edn: *Die Kontorniat-Medaillons* I (1976) and II (1990).

Atkinson, J.E. (1980) *A Commentary on Q. Curtius Rufus' Historiae Alexandri Magni Books 3 and 4*, Amsterdam: Gieben.

Auerbach, Erich (1965) *Literary Language and its Public in Late Antiquity and the Latin Middle Ages*, London.

Bardon, H. (1947) 'Quinte-Curce historien', *Les Etudes Classiques* 15: 126.

Barnes, T.D. (1985) 'Constantine and the Christians of Persia', *Journal of Roman Studies* 75: 126–36.

—— (1989) 'Christians and Pagans in the Reign of Constantine', *Entretiens Fondation Hardt* 34: 301–37.

Barzano, Alberto (1984) 'Curzio Rufo, storico di Alessandro, e i Flavi', in Sordi (1984), 169–78.

Baynham, Elizabeth (1995) 'An introduction to the *Metz Epitome*: its traditions and value', *Antichthon* 29: 60–77.

Berschin, Walter (1988) *Greek Letters and the Latin Middle Ages*, Washington DC: Catholic University of America Press.

Bird, H.W. (1984) *Sextus Aurelius Victor: A Historiographical Study*, Liverpool: Francis Cairns.

Braccesi, Lorenzo (1986) *L'Ultimo Alessandro (dagli antichi ai moderni)*, Padova: Editoriale Programma.

Breitenbach, H.R. (1969) 'Der Alexanderexkurs bei Livius', *Museum Helveticum* 26: 146–52.

Brunt, P.A. (1980) 'On historical fragments and epitomes', *Classical Quarterly* n.s. 30, 477–94.

Cameron, Alan (1976) 'Paganism and Literature in Late Fourth-Century Rome', *Entretiens Fondation Hardt* 23: 1–30.

Ceausescu, Petre (1974) 'La double image d'Alexandre le Grand à Rome – essai d'une explication politique', *Studii Clasice* 16: 153–68.

Chéhab, M. (1957) *Mosaïques du Liban*, Bulletin du Musée de Beyrouth 15: 46–50, with plates volume (1959), plates 22, 24, 25.1–2.

Cracco Ruggini, Lellia (1965) 'Sulla Cristianizzazione della cultura pagana: il mito greco e latino di Alessandro dall'età antonina al medioevo', *Athenaeum* 43: 3–80. (See also Ruggini.)

Currie, H. MacL. (1990) 'Quintus Curtius Rufus: the historian as novelist?', in H. Hofmann (ed.), *Groningen Colloquia on the Novel*, vol. 3, Groningen: Egbert Forsten, pp. 63–77.

Engels, L.J. and Hofmann, H. (1997) 'Literatur und Gesellschaft in der Spätantike: Texte, Kommunikation und Überlieferung', in (eds.) *Neues Handbuch der Literaturwissenschaft*, vol. 4: *Spätantike*, Wiesbaden: Aula-Verlag, pp. 29–88.

Fassbender, C. (1909) 'De Iulii Valerii sermone quaestiones selectae' Dissertation, Breslau.
Gunderson, Lloyd L. (1980) *Alexander's Letter to Aristotle about India*, Meisenheim am Glan: Verlag Anton Hain.
Heckel, Waldemar (1988) *The Last Days and Testament of Alexander the Great: A Prosopographic Study* (Historia Einzelschriften 56), Wiesbaden: Franz Steiner.
Heuss, Alfred (1954) 'Alexander der Grosse und die politische Ideologie des Altertums', *Antike und Abendland* 4: 65–104.
Hoffmann, Werner (1907) 'Das literarische Porträt Alexanders des Grossen im griechischen und römischen Altertum'. Dissertation, Leipzig.
Holzberg, Niklas (ed.) (1992) *Der Äsop-Roman*, Tübingen: Gunter Narr.
—— (1993) *Die antike Fabel*, Darmstadt: Wissenschaftliche Buchgesellschaft.
Isager, Jacob (1993) 'Alexander the Great in Roman Literature from Pompey to Vespasian', in J. Carlsen, B. Due, O. Steen Due and B. Poulsen (eds) *Alexander the Great: Reality and Myth*, *Analecta Romani Instituti Danici* 20, 75–84.
Kienast, Dietmar (1969) 'Augustus und Alexander', *Gymnasium* 76: 430–56.
Kroll, Wilhelm (1924) *Studien zum Verständnis der römischen Literatur*, Stuttgart: Metzler.
Kuebler, B. (1888) 'Studi su Giulio Valerio', *Rivista de Filologia Italiana Classica* 16: 361–99.
Kytzler, B. (1997) 'Fiktionale Prosa', in L.J. Engels and H. Hofmann (eds) *Neues Handbuch der Literaturwissenschaft*, vol. 4, *Spätantike*, pp. 469–94.
Lane Fox, Robin (1997) 'The Itinerary of Alexander: Constantius to Julian', *Classical Quarterly* n.s. 47, 239–52.
Lassandro, Domenico (1984) 'La figura di Alessandro Magno nell'opera di Seneca', in Sordi (1984), pp. 155–68.
Luce, T.J. (1977) *Livy: The Composition of his History*, Princeton, NJ: Princeton University Press.
Maguire, Henry (ed.) (1995) *Byzantine Magic*, Washington, DC: Dumbarton Oaks.
Markus, R.A. (1974) 'Paganism, Christianity and the Latin Classics in the Fourth Century', in J.T. Binns (ed.) *Latin Literature of the Fourth Century*, London: Routledge and Kegan Paul, pp. 1–21.
Matthews, J.F. (1973) 'Symmachus and the Oriental Cults', *Journal of Roman Studies* 63: 175–95.
Millar, F. (1964) *A Study of Cassius Dio*, Oxford: Clarendon Press.
Momigliano, Arnaldo (1963) 'Pagan and Christian Historiography in the Fourth Century AD', in A. Momigliano (ed.) *The Conflict between Paganism and Christianity in the Fourth Century*, Oxford: Clarendon Press, pp. 79–99. (Reprinted in A. Momigliano, *Essays in Ancient and Modern Historiography*, Oxford: Blackwell, 1977, pp. 107–26.)
Pfister, Friedrich (1946) 'Studien zum Alexanderroman', *Würzburger Jahrbücher* 1: 29–66. (Also in his *Kleine Schriften zum Alexanderroman*, Meisenheim am Glan: Anton Hain 1975, pp. 17–52).
Romano, Domenico (1974) *Giulio Valerio*, Palermo: Palumbo.
Ross, D.J.A. (1963) 'Olympias and the Serpent: the interpretation of a Baalbek mosaic and the date of the illustrated Pseudo-Callisthenes', *Journal of the Warburg and Courtauld Institutes* 26: 1–21.

Ruggini, Lellia (1961) '*L'Epitoma Reerum gestarum Alexandri Magni* e il *Liber de Morte Testamentoque eius*', *Athenaeum* 39: 285–357. (See also Ruggini.)
Russell, James (1995) 'The archeological context of magic in the Early Byzantine Period', in Henry Maguire (ed.) *Byzantine Magic*, Washington, DC: Dumbarton Oaks, pp. 35–50.
Rutz, Werner (1965) 'Zur Erzählungskunst des Q. Curtius Rufus: Die Belagerung von Tyrus', *Hermes* 93: 371–82.
Schmeling, Gareth (ed.) (1996) *The Novel in the Ancient World*, Leiden: E.J. Brill.
Schmidt, P.G. (1961) *Supplemente lateinischer Prosa in der Neuzeit* (Hypomnemata 2), Göttingen: Vandenhoeck & Ruprecht.
Sordi, Marta (ed.) (1984) *Alessandro Magno tra storia e mito*, Milan: Jaca Book.
Stoneman, Richard (1994a) *Legends of Alexander the Great*, London: Everyman.
—— (1994b) 'The Alexander Romance: From history to fiction', in J.R. Morgan and R. Stoneman (eds) *Greek Fiction: The Greek Novel in Context*, London/New York: Routledge, pp. 112–29.
—— (1996) 'The Metamorphoses of the *Alexander Romance*', in G. Schmeling, (ed.) *The Novel in the Ancient World*, Leiden: E.J. Brill, pp. 601–12.
Stroux, J. (1933) 'Die stoische Beurteilung Alexanders des Grossen', *Philologus* 88: 222–40.
Sumner, G.V. (1961) 'Curtius Rufus and the *Historiae Alexandri*', *Australian Universities Modern Languages Association* 15: 30–9.
Therasse, J. (1973) 'Le jugement de Quinte-Curce sur Alexandre – une appréciation morale indépendante', *les Etudes Classiques* 41: 23–45.

12

HAGIOGRAPHIC FICTION AS ENTERTAINMENT

Gerlinde Huber-Rebenich

Translated by Richard Stoneman

> *Cor sapientium ubi tristitia est, et cor stultorum ubi laetitia.*
>
> (The heart of the wise is in the house of mourning; but the heart of fools is in the house of mirth.)
>
> Ecclesiastes vii, 4

> *Admittenda tibi joca sunt post seria quaedam sed tamen et dignis ipsa gerenda modis.*
>
> (After serious matters, some jokes may be permitted, but these too are to be presented in a dignified manner.)
>
> Hildebert of Lavardin, *Libellus de quattuor virtutibus vitae honestae*[1]

No special argument is required to assert that Christians – at least the most rigorous of them – have an uncomfortable relationship with *delectatio*, with entertainment. Since the time of the earliest Fathers, this position has been ultimately grounded in the fact that no passage of the Bible indicates that Jesus ever laughed. For the strict Christian, laughter is a sign of foolishness and sin. The rejection of fun and laughter is enshrined in countless treatises, in monastic rules, and even in church law. It is connected with a prescriptive condemnation of amusement and entertainment in general, including light literature.

Alongside the prescriptivists, however, there stand the realistic thinkers who share Aristotle's recognition that laughter is a key marker of human nature (*De partibus animalium* 673a), and thus that the need for entertainment is an anthropological constant. Accordingly there were found, even among the Christians, theoreticians who could offer justifications for enjoyment (in moderation, naturally).[2]

In the preface to his *Enarrationes in XII psalmos Davidicos* (PL 14, col. 963ff.) Ambrose of Milan comes to the conclusion that 'Entertainment is something natural' (col. 965 B). From this initial principle, he develops a positive idea of *delectatio*. His fundamental argument consists in the idea that the human soul will open itself more readily to instruction which is mediated by the *suavitas dulcedinis*, the charm of sweetness, and that it will thus also internalize more profoundly the commandments laid upon it (v. col. 969 A/B).[3]

In arguing this position, the highly educated Ambrose is basing himself on ancient rhetorical theory. There too, the work of instruction or persuasion is not included solely in *probare*, proving something; just as important is *conciliare*, disposing one's hearers favourably, and *movere*, 'touching a chord'.

Like Ambrose, other Christian thinkers who wished to justify the entertainment value of literature must willy nilly have recourse to non-Christian sources. An educated Christian was very familiar, as a result of his school lessons, with the relevant material – above all with Cicero, *De oratore* (2.216ff.) and Quintilian *Institutio oratoria* (6.3.1–112), but also with Horace, *Ars poetica* (333f.) and his motto *ridentem dicere verum* (to tell the truth while laughing, *Satires* 1.1.24). He had learnt that humour and wit, practised in moderation, correspond to the ancient ethical ideal of serious-merriment (*spoudogeloion*), that they facilitate the relaxation which helps to carry out renewed exertions, and that – in rhetoric – they make the addressee receptive and even eager for the content that is to be imparted.

And the conveying of content – to be precise, of matters of doctrine – is the chief preoccupation of every form of Christian literature. Its function is always to make an appeal, which may consist in, for example, the injunction to follow Christ or to imitate or honour a saint. Such an appeal is most likely to fall on listening ears when the method of presentation is chosen in consideration of the sense of piety, the level of education, the curiosity and the need of entertainment of the intended public. The early Christian writers were well aware of this – not only highly educated scholars like Jerome, but equally the anonymous authors or redactors of the *Apocryphal Acts of the Apostles*. In many texts we encounter, to use the expression of H.R. Jauss (^{5}1974: 178f.), an 'art of entertainment', a '"culinary" art which creates conviction and enjoyment without resistance', which:

> Requires no change of horizon, but precisely fulfils expectations raised by the prevailing of taste, by satisfying the desire for the reproduction of an accustomed beauty, confirming familiar feelings, sanctioning wish-fulfilments, making unusual experiences enjoyable as 'sensations' or posing moral problems but only in order to 'solve' them, in an edifying way, as questions whose answer has already been decided.[4]

This strategy of communication requires from the author an openness to traditional forms and motifs. So we find in the earliest Christian literature types of discourse which in form and content take up existing models, but at the same time develop or transform them further. Just as, in the pagan world, literary genres accommodate themselves to historical, economic and social changes – one need think only of the differences between Old and New Comedy – so the rise of Christianity is similarly mirrored in literary production. Despite the fundamental change of mentality, and irrespective of the programmatic condemnation of pagan authors by the Church Fathers, there is no radical break with the established tradition.[5] Even their fiery insistence on *sermo piscatorius*, the simple speech of fishermen, and their polemical attacks on heathen poetry and rhetoric do not alter the fact that the Christian writers of the first centuries had themselves grown up in a school system of pagan pattern and had internalized its content to such an extent that, as long as they lived, they could not (or did not wish to) free themselves from it. The same applies, *mutatis mutandis*, for their educated – or at least literate – public.

What expectations did the public in the first centuries after Christ hold, on the basis of its reading habits, of fiction? The favoured reading of the period included numerous novels of love and adventure, either of idealizing or of comic-realistic character, utopian travel accounts, romantic-fictional biographies as well as aretalogies of prophets and philosophers. These offered the reader something to titillate and thrill: comedy, love stories, sex and crime, excitement, adventure, fantastic tales of the marvellous, exotica and – at least in the romance – in general a Happy Ending.

In addition to the points of contact with pagan literature, it should not be forgotten that the yardstick for every form of Christian literature, the Holy Scripture, is itself a rich treasure trove of exciting and entertaining narrative motifs. If the Bible, in the first instance, announces the Word of God, yet nothing human is alien to it either: it contains erotic poetry (the Song of Songs), stories of adultery and triangular situations (Potiphar's wife; David and Bathsheba), 'biographies' of god-fearing heroes (the story of Joseph) and every kind of marvel, in the Old Testament and especially in the New. In the latter, it is Jesus himself, the leading figure of the new religion, who drives out demons, heals the sick, raises the dead to life, multiplies loaves, walks dry-footed over water and in multifarious ways makes a deep impression on his 'public'. The literary influence of this text simply cannot be overestimated.[6]

In our topic, however, the reception of traditional material from pagan antiquity must hold the foreground. Since Richard Reitzenstein's *Hellenistische Wundererzählungen* (1906), the many kinds of influence of various literary genres on early Christian literature have been illuminated from many sides. In the following, special emphasis will be given to the question of the ways in which, in different kinds of Christian texts – from the *Apocryphal Acts of the Apostles* to the *Dialogues* of Gregory the Great – elements of entertainment literature are put to the service of Christian doctrine. In this connection, it is of particular interest to consider how far existing textual models are adopted, transformed or fashioned into new forms of expression.

I Apocryphal Acts of the Apostles

Christian antiquity produced a series of writings which have as their theme the missionary journeys and activities of the apostles. Of these, only Luke's *Acts of the Apostles* was accepted into the New Testament canon; the others are considered apocryphal.[7] The oldest and most significant of them are the *Acts* of John, of Peter, of Paul, of Andrew and of Thomas. These originated towards the end of the second, and in the third century AD; with the exception of the *Acts of Thomas* they are only fragmentarily preserved. In the case of the rest we are mainly dealing with later reworkings, expansions and continuations of the above-named Acts, such as the *Martyrium beati Petri Apostoli a Lino episcopo conscriptum* (sixth century; Lipsius 1, 1891 (repr. 195: 1–22; Salonius 1926) or the *Acta Andreae et Matthiae apud anthropophagos* (sixth century; Blatt 1930).

It is a feature common to all these writings that they are marked by particular religious positions. Those most prominently represented are ascetic-encratite elements, sometimes also esoteric perspectives grounded in Gnosis. However, the religious programme is, as a rule, not carried through consistently in the individual writings; on the contrary, we frequently find a hotch-potch of differing tendencies. In contrast to the Lukan *Acts of the Apostles*, which is heavily indebted to historical writing and defends a clearly articulated theological conception, in the *Apocryphal Acts* the entertainment aspect steps firmly into the foreground. It is exemplified in a strong inclination to miracles and fantastic tales, as well as in the representation of the perversions of the opponents and in a pseudo-biographical interest in the apostles, who are styled as heroes. Important points of reference include, naturally, the canonical biblical writings, the romances of love and adventure (Söder 1932, Pervo 1987, id. 1994), and occasionally also aretalogies of missions and lives of philosophers (Goulet 1981, Junod 1981).[8]

An essential element of the *Acts of Peter* (Latin ed. Lipsius/Bonnet 1891 (repr. 1959): 45–103; cf. Bremmer 1998) is the protagonist's struggle against his arch-enemy Simon Magus. Before it comes to the big showdown between 'hero' and 'villain', each tries to outbid the other with spectacular miracles: Simon impresses the masses in Rome, the scene of the decisive contest, by arriving in airborne flight. He thus succeeds in influencing many to desert, including the senator Marcellus, in whose house he takes up residence. Peter is however able to win Marcellus back, when he has Simon summoned by a talking dog to come out into the open. Thereafter, Peter drives out a demon, which results in the smashing of a statue of the emperor;

this is however put together again by sprinkling it with water. In the meantime, the talking dog has cursed Simon in the house of Marcellus. Next, the dog prophesies to Peter that he will emerge victorious from the forthcoming contest, and dies. To persuade the bystanders fully of his miraculous powers, Peter brings a smoked tunny fish back to life, so that it may be fed with breadcrumbs. Thereupon, Marcellus has Simon driven out of his house with blows. Through the agency of an infant which speaks with a man's voice, Peter bans the magician from Rome until the following Sabbath. The final contest between the two adversaries is performed before crowded tiers of seats, which have been especially erected for the occasion. It begins with mutual provocations and escalates to a regular miracle-competition (including raisings of the dead), which Peter – how could it be otherwise? – wins. Simon, however, meets an inglorious end: he announces that he is going to ascend to heaven, and actually flies away over Rome. Peter, instead, causes him to fall, by literally praying him down from heaven. The miracle shows, which always take place before large crowds of people, offer to the Christian public, at least in fictional form, a kind of substitute theatre. These people do not take their pleasure in beast-fights and gladiatorial games in a real arena, nor in mime-performances, but – in an imaginary space – in no less sensational Christian spectacles. The new heroes perform partly as solo entertainers, partly in conflict with an opponent whom they of course vanquish. This agonal element leads to an escalation of the marvellous into the grotesque. It is no accident that such fantastic occurrences are frequently reported in connection with Simon *Magus*. Magic was a topical theme in late antiquity, which offered an occasion for numerous sensational trials, and was treated in literary form in various ways, as for example in the *Apology* and the *Metamorphoses* of Apuleius. The *Acts of Peter* seizes this popular and attractive motif in order to embed it in the aretalogy of a hero.

Probably the most famous section of the *Acts of Paul* is the *Acts of Paul and Thecla*, which was detached from its context at an early date and handed down independently. The numerous translations include no less than four Latin ones (Latin ed. Mombritius 2, ²1910, repr. 1978: 559–64; Gebhardt 1902; cf. Bremmer 1996). The *Acts of Thecla* closely resembles the love-romance in respect of its plot elements: like her pagan counterparts, Thecla falls in love at first sight with Paul. Her submission is so complete that she follows the apostle everywhere – even to prison – without a thought for former relationships. On the way she is exposed to the dangers and difficulties familiar from the secular romance: attacks on her chastity by insistent suitors and false accusations by rivals. The latter lead to imprisonment and to a sentence of death, the execution of which can only be averted at the last moment by a miracle. So, for example, Thecla is condemned to be burnt on a pyre, a motif which we find in Heliodorus' *Aethiopica* (8.9.10ff.), where the protagonist Chariclea likewise courageously faces death by burning, before a large crowd; the flames, however, do as little harm to her as they do to the

Christian heroine. Again, temporary protection by upper-class benefactors and, finally, the reuniting of the long-separated couple, are characteristics of the genre. The Happy Ending, admittedly, takes a rather different form in the *Acts of Thecla*. In the novels, the lovers end up in the safe haven of marriage and in a thoroughly conventional bourgeois existence (Frye 1957: 167). Here, by contrast, their love is on another plane: Thecla has not really fallen in love with Paul, but with God, who has made himself manifest in Paul. This love can only be a purely spiritual one, of pupil for master. It reaches its fulfilment in Thecla's being recognized by Paul as his fellow apostle, and sent out by him into the world. A further difference from the pagan love-romances consists in the fact that the attachment of the two partners is very unequal. Only Thecla is fascinated by Paul, not vice versa; only she makes the effort to overcome their separation, while he goes his way without any concern for his adept. This is not a love story in the conventional sense, but rather a 'probation' of the heroine. The radically new form – for women – of submissive love and the conscious modelling of a life beyond traditional social bonds, which the following of Christ makes possible, is here propagated by familiar means. Role models are offered which are well known from the world of everyday experience, and can thus contribute to smoothing the path to the new doctrine and the new values.[9]

The *Acta Andreae et Matthiae apud anthropophagos* (Blatt 1930) strikes a different note, which may serve as an example of secondary *Apocrypha*. Matthew is sent to the land of the Anthropophagi to convert them to the Christian faith. Before he finally achieves this, with the help of Andrew and sundry miracles, the apostle has to undergo a period of hard testing. The cannibals rob him of his sight soon after his arrival and put him in a prison, where he is to be fattened up until he is ready for slaughter. These man-eaters remind one of the ghoulish stories which feature also in the *Metamorphoses* of Apuleius (e.g. the killing of Socrates by the witch Meroë and her comrades in Book 1). Of the Latin versions of these *Acts*, that in the Codex Casanatensis 1104 particularly emphasizes such effects, expanding even to include descriptions of the instruments and vessels used for the slaughter (Blatt 1930: 7). Consideration of such 'horror scenes' apart, we are familiar from epic or prose travel accounts, and from historiography, with descriptions of strange peoples with strange customs or remarkable exteriors. One thinks of the Lotus-eaters of the *Odyssey* (9.82ff.), the Enotoceutae of Strabo (2.1.9, 15.1.57) or indeed of Herodotus' reference to the Anthropophagi (4.106). Such reports are basically there to satisfy the public's need for sensationalism and its greed for the new and unheard-of.

II The Pseudo-Clementines

The so-called *Pseudo-Clementines* represent a special case of the apostolic novel.[10] As far as content is concerned, they belong to the Acts of Apostles in as much as they narrate the missionary activity of Peter and his contest with Simon Magus. At the same time, theological instruction, through preaching and disputation, takes up a significantly greater space than in the texts previously discussed. The report of Peter's activity is placed in the mouth of his pupil Clement, later to be bishop of Rome. The framework is provided by his novel-like narrative of his own development and the various fortunes of his family.

For our purposes, only the Latin version of the material in the translation by Rufinus of Aquileia is of interest: the *Recognitiones* (Recognitions). In these, the novelistic treatment is much more fully presented than in their Greek counterpart, the *Homiliai* (Sermons).

Earlier research was primarily interested in questions of theology and of literary history, especially with the reconstruction of source-writings (Heintze 1914, Cullmann 1930), and judged the text itself as a patchwork; but recently an attempt has been made to interpret it as the bearer of a coherent message: as the description of the development of a '*Clemens naturaliter Christianus*', who even before his conversion, carried within himself, without knowing it, the true Christian faith, to a 'Clemens Romanus', the worthy successor of Peter to the see of Rome. From this viewpoint the *Recognitiones* should be understood as a kind of *Bildungsroman*, like the *Cyropaedeia* of Xenophon, in which indeed didactic speeches and – in the story of Pantheia – romance or novel-like elements are combined (Tatum 1989, Vielberg forthcoming).

Clement, a young Roman from an upper-class family, is in search, from his youth onwards, of ultimate truth. After some false starts he moves into the circle of the apostle Peter. The latter allows him to take part in his preaching missions in the cities of Phoenicia, in his battles of words with Simon Magus and in the instruction in his circle of disciples. When Clement is alone with Peter, he tells him his life story: Prompted by a dream, his mother Mattidia with her two eldest sons, twins, left Rome and disappeared at sea. In despair, his father Faustinianus went on a search for them, from which he never returned. The next day, Peter meets an old beggar woman. By clever questioning, he recognizes in her Clement's mother. He learns from her that the dream vision was only an invention to enable her to escape the importunities of her brother-in-law. Peter arranges for mother and son to see each other again. Two others of his disciples, Nicetas and Aquila, on hearing of this joyful event, reveal themselves as the lost twins Faustus and Faustinus. After the shipwreck which separated them from their mother, they were captured by pirates, sold as slaves, but then taken up by a righteous Jewess and brought up well. Eventually, the father, Faustinianus, is also revealed, in the guise of a ragged old man. The latter, however, has to be cured of his scepticism and fatalism by a series of intense disputations. On the one hand a lying astrologer had persuaded him of his wife's infidelity, on the other his brother – aggrieved by Mattidia's rejection of him – had accused her of unchaste behaviour. Peter is able to put things right, so that nothing stands in the way of a complete family reunion. It goes without saying that all the participants convert to Christianity under the impact of these events.

The narrative of the *Recognitiones* makes use of a great number of literary motifs, which in the main are borrowed from the novel, but some also from comedy (Heintze 1914: 130–38). Common to both is the basic structure, in which the protagonists are separated from each other by adverse circumstances, before they find each other or are recognized for who they really are, but only after violent upheavals and often only through the help of a *deus* (*ex machina*). While in the novel it is usually pairs of lovers who are separated, in comedy the experiences of families take up the foreground – as also in the *Pseudo-Clementines*.[11]

Normally in the novel, the protagonists are from upper-class families. The journeys (mainly by ship) which they undertake, are not infrequently set in motion by dream visions or similar revelations such as oracles (cf. Xenophon *Ephesiaca*). They often end in shipwreck, though none of the main characters comes to serious harm. The shipwreck often stands at the beginning of a concatenation of adventures and ordeals, which the participants have to undergo before fate brings them together again. Capture by pirates and sale into slavery are both suffered by novelistic figures like Anthia and Habrokomas (in Xenophon's *Ephesiaca*). Like Mattidia, the heroines often endure attempts on their chastity, but are well able to protect themselves by pretexts and feigning. The Potiphar-motif, or calumny by a rejected lover, is one of the most widespread in world literature. We know it for example from the story of Joseph in the Old Testament – to which it owes its name – but also from the Phaedra tragedies of Euripides and Seneca.

The narrative technique also exhibits analogies to the novel and the drama: we find pathetic monologues, speeches of deception, ethopoeia in the dialogues, recapitulatory narrations and sudden peripeties (reversals). In addition there is the retardation of the anagnorisis (recognition), which increases suspense. The abstract discussions which drag out the action are easier for a less theoretically oriented reader to bear as a result of their integration into the plot structure. Finally, in astrology and the belief in horoscopes we encounter matters which were familiar to the late antique public not only from literature but from the world of everyday experience. The fact that themes of great topicality were being handled, albeit with a polemical intent, certainly did nothing to diminish the interest of the text.

What function is performed by the story of recognition in the *Recognitiones*? Just as the sermons and disputations are part of the propaganda for Christian belief, so too is the immanent message of the narrative. It demonstrates powerfully the operation of a generous God, against whom even the greatest sceptic can in the end find no arguments. It thus underpins, on the narrative level, the persuasive work of the theoretical passages. Like the latter, it ultimately serves the purpose of propagating Christian belief and summoning people to conversion: the individual members of Clement's family, who are baptized one after another, are living examples of this. Through a series of motifs which are familiar from already known and loved literary types, role-models are offered to the reader who will speak more to the emotions than to the intellect, in order to bring him, by this means, to the same conclusion as the annunciation in verbal form: God directs everything for the best.

That the plot is not always tightly carried through does no harm to the message. For example, it is not easy to see why Faustinianus, if he believes the calumnies of his brother, is so despairing about the fate not only of his sons but also of his wife. Again: the twins Faustus and Faustinus embrace their newly-found mother enthusiastically, but completely ignore Clement – who is after all, the protagonist of the whole work – who is present at the same moment. Such lapses have been seen as indications of contamination of several earlier versions (Heintze 1914: 114ff., Cullmann 1930: 132ff.). These inconcinnities however – always assuming it is not simply a question of incompetence of an author or redactor – may be worked into the *Recognitiones* in order to provide a greater number of emotionally effective motifs: the author did not want just the despairing father or the slanderous brother; he wanted both. The affective content of the text is increased at the expense of consistency.

The group of 'new heroes' includes not only Biblical figures as in the *Acts of the Apostles*, but also other men and women, who accepted torture and death for their confession of Christian faith. Their sufferings were preserved in writing in the *Acts* and *Passions of Martyrs*.

III *Acta* and *Passiones Martyrum*

The contemporary reports of early Christian martyrs exhibit two forms: the account by eye-witnesses or otherwise trustworthy persons (*Martyrium*, *Passio*) and the report of a trial (*Acta*).[12] Both are in evidence from *c*. 160/170. Although they make a claim to objectivity and authenticity, they can only be regarded to a limited extent as historical documents in the true sense. The reality which is reflected in them has, even in the most modest formulation, undergone a literary stylization through the process of being written down. Furthermore, they are influenced by earlier forensic literature or reports of the courageous deaths of famous men.

The *Martyria* or *Passions* recount the events: they reproduce only the most important parts of the trials in direct speech. Since such accounts were supposed to inform other communities of the events and strengthen them in their faith, they were also written down as letters and sent out, like the *Martyrium Policarpi*, the oldest preserved report of a martyrdom, and the letter of the communities of Vienne and Lyon about the persecution of the Christians there, which is preserved in the *Ecclesiastical History* of Eusebius (5.1.1ff.).

The *Acta* provide only at the beginning and end, brief notes about the events and consist mainly of the minutes of the trial in question and answer. Here, their literary and programmatic character may often be seen in the fact that the dialogues are formulated with great point, convey central items of Christian doctrine or distance themselves fundamentally from the pagan context.

A good example is offered by the *Acts of Acacius* (Knopf/Krüger/Ruhbach [4]1965: 57–60), in which the perplexed reaction of a Roman official to Christian Latin with its incomprehensible Hebraisms is portrayed (Berschin I: 45f.). The consular Marcianus questions the faithful Acacius about the name of his God. Acacius answers '*deus Abraham et deus Isaac et deus Iacob*' ('the God of Abraham and the God of Isaac and the God of Jacob'). Marcianus simply does not understand on a grammatical level the genitive construction of the Hebrew names, which are indeclinable in Latin, and inquires whether these are three gods. But it is not only the Hebraisms of this new manner of speech which confuse the Roman official, but also the new meaning of common Latin words. 'Who is the Son of God?' he asks, and Acacius answers '*Verbum veritatis et gratiae*' ('The word of Truth and Grace'). 'Is that his name?', asks the sceptical judge; and so the misunderstandings go on. The continuation of the story shows that hilarity is one possible reaction to this linguistic confusion, for the Acts are sent to the Emperor Decius, who read them, 'was amazed at the answers given in so memorable a dispute, and laughed'. From the discrepancy between classical and Christian Latin emerges a series of misunderstandings full of a comic potential that can bear effective fruit.

The fact that many of the *Passiones* are thoroughly dramatic in form indicates that the martyr-stories were intended to impress and fascinate their audiences. This means was employed already in many passages of the *Apocryphal Acts of the Apostles* (e.g. in the miracle contests before the crowded benches). Something similar occurs also in the *Passio* of St Sebastian (Acta SS Ian.t.2, 1643: 265–78 [= PL 17, 1845: col. 1021–58]), in which other confessors appear in addition to the protagonist (Berschin I; 74ff.). An early scene takes place in a Roman jail. Here, two young confessors are sought by their relatives (mothers, fathers and wives with small children), who wish to persuade them to renounce their Christian faith at the last moment before execution. Their laments are represented in long passages of direct speech. Their gestures of despair include also the tearing of hair and the rending of garments, as well as moving appeals to the duties of sons, husbands and fathers. These emotion-laden scenes could equally well be part of a tragedy. In the text they are characterized as *spectaculum* (performance), which indicates that the effect described is a deliberate one.

Thoroughly farcical effects are exhibited by contrast in an episode of the *Passio* of the three sisters Agape, Chionia and Irene, who fell victim to the Diocletianic persecution in Thessaloniki (*Acta* SS Apr.t.1, 1675: 248–50;

Delehaye 1936: 227–35). They are handed over to the governor Dulcitius, so that he can compel them by torture to renounce their faith. Inflamed by the beauty of the girls, Dulcitius promises them their freedom if they will succumb to his will. Instead of shutting them in prison, he keeps them in a private house, in a room near the kitchen. When he sets out to find them in the night, he is overcome by confusion and embraces, instead of the girls, sooty pots and pans. In the tenth century, Hrotsvitha of Gandersheim adopted this plot for her burlesque comedy entitled *Dulcitius* after the oafish governor. Other works by Hrotsvitha, *Gallicanus* and *Sapientia*, also trace their themes to the *Passiones*. Hrotsvitha has truly recognized the dramatic situation dormant in them, and released it (Berschin I; 107f.).

Another narrative text with dramatic accents is the *Passio S. Agnetis* (*Acta* SS Ian.t.2, 1643: 351–54). Agnes is a beautiful young girl with whom the prefect's son has fallen in love. However, she rejects him with the information that she already has a lover, and describes all the treasures he has given her. One of the 'parasites' of the prefect solves the riddle: Agnes is a Christian, her lover is Christ. The prefect places the girl in a brothel. By God's grace, her hair grows so long and thick that it covers her body better than any clothing. The son of the prefect, supposing that he can now achieve his desires, dies in the brothel. Although Agnes revives him, she is brought to trial as a witch.

The particular attraction of the story for the reader consists in the erotic motifs that are employed, just as they were in the novel and to some extent in comedy: the beauty of the heroine, lustful men, the scene set in a house of pleasure, threats to chastity. These familiar models serve as foil for the new significance: Agnes herself confesses to being a 'lover', but means something quite different from the normal sense and therefore, like many of her fellow-sufferers, is at first misunderstood (like Acacius with his Christian Latin). Although the intended message lies, of course, in the overcoming of fleshly lust by the love of God, the erotic elements of the story certainly do not provoke only consternation in the reader.

Prudentius included the *Passio Agnetis* in his *Peristephanon*, a collection of epic-lyric poems about Spanish and Roman martyrs. The material of the *Passiones* here crosses the threshold of high literature. A comparable phenomenon is the epic reworking of parts of the Bible (Herzog 1975). Both contribute, even if they are not fiction in the regular sense, to the pleasure of the reader. Through an increasing literarization of Christian material the ancient authors are eventually to be banished from the taste of the educated reader. These readers ultimately preferred Virgil, purely on aesthetic grounds, to the simple Latin of the new Christian texts, which with their sophisticated taste they could not appreciate and on which they poured out mockery and derision. Poets like Prudentius made the effort to provide literary pleasure even for this readership, through beauty of form.

There is another group of texts which should not be ignored in connection with these stories of confession and martyrdom: its subject is the fictional Bishop Cyprian of Antioch and it includes in a tripartite 'magical novel' *conversio* (conversion), *confessio* (confession) and *passio* (passion) (ed. Martène/Durand 1717: 1621–50; cf. Krestan/Hermann 1957). The state of transmission of this material is notably complex. It is presumed that the original was composed in Greek and that the Latin version represents a translation from the Greek. In addition, there is a series of oriental versions. Around the middle of the fifth century the material was so popular that the highly educated Empress Eudocia honoured it with a metrical recension. The content, in brief, is as follows.

The magician Cyprian undertakes extensive journeys, during which he learns all the significant practice of the ancient occult: mysteries, divination, magic spells and astrology. Eventually he settles in Syrian Antioch, which was well-known as a centre of magic practices (cf. Eusebius, *Ecclesiastical History* 4.19). Here, a young man approaches him to help him win the love of the virgin Iustina by his magic arts. She however, being a Christian convert and a bride of Christ, rejects all appeals. Even when Cyprian himself falls in love with the girl and summons demons and the devil to win her favour, she shows herself to be proof against all the forces of evil. Cyprian recognizes the powerlessness of the spirits at his command, converts to Christianity, burns his magic books and becomes at first a priest, later bishop of Antioch. During a persecution of Christians he endures martyrdom alongside Iustina. When boiling pitch cannot harm them, they die eventually in Nicomedia by beheading. Their bodies are later buried ceremonially in Rome.

Most of the motifs combined in this fiction – magic, erotic love, the failure of reliable methods of torture or execution – have already been treated in other contexts. Here one may observe simply that love-magic is revalued, in as much as its failure to work demonstrates the impotence of the demons against Christian faith.

As soon as Christianity received toleration, and then privileges, from the State, it was no longer dangerous for the faithful to confess their God. So the martyrs gradually lost their usefulness as role-models for everyday Christians. New models had to be found to take their place and inspire emulation: the hour of the ascetics had sounded.[13] Their freely-chosen deprivations and their solitary existence were represented in countless Lives of the fathers and collections of sayings. After the *Antonius-Vita* of Athanasius had conquered the west in its Latin translation, Jerome was the first to propagate the ideal of the ascetic hermit in original Latin texts by literary means.

IV The Saint's Lives of Jerome

As a Christian educative writer Jerome[14] had already made his debut with the miracle of the *septies percussa* (the woman struck seven times) (Epist. 1). It is the story of a miscarriage of justice, which a modern reader may regard as absurd, macabre and trivial in an extreme degree. But it corresponded to the late antique taste for sensational juridical literature, which we find also in some of the martyr acts. A young man and a young woman, both Christians, are imprisoned on a trumped-up charge of adultery, tried and tortured. The man admits under torture whatever is expected of him; the woman defies the procedures, which are graphically described by Jerome. Both are condemned to death. The man is beheaded, the woman, although struck three times on the neck, is not killed. A second executioner strikes her down with four blows; she appears to be dead, but wakes up in the presence of the priests who are about to bury her. She is nursed back to health in secret. Meanwhile, the death sentence, regardless of this miracle, remains in force. Then Evagrius, the wealthy patron of Jerome, appears and obtains an amnesty from the emperor. The work was characterized by Jerome's biographer Cavallera (1922, 1: 28) as a 'final examination piece', because of its resemblance in its choice of extravagant material (the scandalous theme of 'adultery', the 'trial scene', the oft-repeated failure to carry out the execution), in its declamatory style and in its learned citations from the school authors Terence and Virgil, to a rhetor's 'five-finger exercise'.

Jerome attained mastery with his lives of monks: those of Paul, of Hilarion and of Malchus. As early as the first of these, the *Vita Pauli*, which may serve in what follows as an example of his literary technique, Jerome established his fame as an author of the ascetic-monastic movement.

The Vita S. Pauli Primi Eremitae

Jerome begins with an account of the contemporary background of Paul's youth, the persecution of Christians under Decius and Valentinian. Two examples illustrate the tortures to which the faithful were subjected. The *Vita*[15] begins, thus, in the same way as a *Passio*; that is, we are dealing with a Christian background text. Paul, an educated young Christian from a good family, withdraws, when the storm of persecution breaks out, via several intermediate stops into the lonely mountains of the Theban desert in Egypt, where he selects a cave as his dwelling. There he passes the rest of his life as a hermit – more than ninety years. One day the younger Anthony sets out to visit his colleague. On the way he meets a centaur, who shows him the way; he then receives dates from a satyr as nourishment, and finally finds the cave of Paul with the help of a she-wolf. Paul feels his end is nigh and asks the guest to bury him by employing certain ceremonies. Two lions help to dig the grave with their claws.

The *Vita* drew contemporary as well as later readers under its spell. Jerome commanded all the techniques of ancient literary art and integrated stylistic elements and narrative forms of pagan, particularly Greek, origin into his works. With a sure touch he selected predominantly those elements which would serve to entertain his public: erotic and fantastic motifs, animal stories and quotations from familiar authors. Precisely this eclectic reception of a variety of models guaranteed his contemporaries a racy read.

One example may suffice. One of the two martyr stories, which are told right at the beginning of the *Vita*, as it were to attract the reader's attention, is concerned with a young confessor in chains who is exposed to the seductive arts of a prostitute. The latter brings to bear all the means at her disposal to break down his chastity. He can only escape from her attempts to approach him by biting off his tongue and spitting it in her face. The graphic description of the seduction is richly lascivious, and has the effect of creating a voyeuristic pleasure for the public.

The Vita Malchi monachi captivi

Jerome claims to have heard the story[16] himself from Malchus during his stay in Antioch. He has his protagonist describe his fortunes in a first-person narrative. This procedure is happily employed to underline the credibility of the narrative, even in cases where the events described overstep the borderline of fantasy. It is familiar from Petronius and Apuleius, but also from the (anything but) *True Stories* of Lucian.

As a young man, Malchus enters a monastery, against the will of his parents who have arranged a marriage for him. Despite the objections of his abbot, he leaves it again to take up an inheritance. Malchus is at once punished for this abandonment of the spiritual life. On his journey he falls, with some other travellers, into the hands of Saracens, who drag him off into slavery and try to make him marry a fellow captive. The couple consider the possibility of escaping the compulsion by suicide, but then decide to enter on a marriage only in appearance: Malchus will preserve his monastic virginity, while the lady will remain faithful to her real husband. They escape, cross a river on inflated skins, are hunted down by their master and a servant, and are able only in the nick of time to hide themselves in a cave. Salvation comes in the form of a lion, which tears their pursuers to pieces.

In contrast to the lions which dig Antony's grave for him, this lion exhibits no anthropomorphic qualities. Apart from the creature's experiencing its normal need for food, and coming on its proper prey, at precisely the right moment, the scene has nothing in itself marvellous about it. Happy coincidences and improbable eventualities, which in fact have rational explanations, may also be found in New Comedy and in the romance. For example, Anthia in Xenophon of Ephesus (IV.6) is imprisoned in a ditch by two savage dogs, which however do her no harm, because a sympathetic warder feeds them well.

After surviving this danger, Malchus gives his 'wife' into the protection of nuns and himself returns to his monastery. By his constancy in time of need, Malchus has proved himself, and finally achieved the restoration of his original status.

This Life contains many elements which are already familiar from the adventure romance: kidnapping, enslavement, plans of suicide, forced marriage, protection of chastity, rescue from extreme danger and happy ending. Admittedly, in such a short text, there is no long series of episodes. Instead, Jerome concentrates on a remarkable event, a surprising peripety. This takes place, without the aid of miracles, in the sphere of the realistic or at least the probable. The Malchus-Vita shares these features with the genre of the novella, as also the handling of the frame, the telling by the protagonist of his own past (Berschin I: 142f.).

With his employment of familiar narrative motifs, literary conventions and references to the classics, Jerome is addressing himself to an educated public, and thus at this period also an influential one. This is clear too from the way in which Jerome offers, in Paul and Hilarion, figures to identify with who are themselves educated, and from the fact that a certain level of education is essential for the full understanding of his texts. With the literary form of his monks' lives he directly addresses the taste of a readership familiar with pagan literature. That was important in winning them for the ascetic-monastic life – or at least for financing it.

Two of Jerome's monks, Paul and above all Hilarion, were remarkable not only for their asceticism. Additional to this was their ability to perform miracles, which take the form of healings, raisings of the dead, the driving out of demons, the breaking of evil spells and power over wild animals. Such themes reappear regularly in the hagiographic literature of the following period also. An incalculable number of texts were composed in which memorable words and deeds of exemplary men and women were put into literary form, whether in individual lives or in collections.

V Sulpicius Severus, *Vita S. Martini*

The text which gave the decisive formative touch to the Latin saint's life in the west is the *Vita S. Martini*[17] of Sulpicius Severus, a monk's life, which, in line with the career of the protagonist, develops into a bishop's life. It is the western, Latin counterpart to the *Vita* of the desert father Anthony, with which the Patriarch Athanasius of Alexandria, soon after 356, created the new genre of the ascetic monk's biography.[18] Despite the *topoi* of modesty and the insistence of the author in the dedicatory preface that he uses the *sermo piscatorius*, the speech of simple people, the work is finely crafted from beginning to end and adapted to the reader. The Latin that Sulpicius writes is no *sermo incultus*, no unpolished style, as he would like to make us believe, but extremely sophisticated and full of classical reminiscences. The dedicatory letter, like the first chapter of the *Vita*, with its programmatic statements about style, and the meaning and purpose of the saint's life, may be regarded as an *ars poetica*, a rule of composition for Christian artistic prose or Christian biography (Fontaine 1968: 359, Berschin I: 198).

The text follows the several stations of the protagonist on his way from Roman soldier, via *miles christianus*, soldier of Christ, to *imperator Dei*, God's general, and it tells of his deeds and the miracles which he worked. The individual sections are extremely effective, exciting and lively in presentation. On one occasion Martin escapes at the last moment a club swung at him by a robber (ch. 5). On another occasion he is only able to persuade some pagan priests to cut down a sacred tree by lying down himself, in chains, in the path of its fall. The tree bends dangerously close to him, but when Martin makes the sign of the cross it moves, just in time, in the opposite direction (ch. 13). Emotional passages are also not lacking in the *Vita*. In Trier, an old man comes to Martin and begs him with tears to heal his lame daughter. The girl's sickness and the despairing words of the father are so touchingly represented that the reader cannot avoid a sense of involvement (ch. 16). In other episodes, again, the effect depends on verbal or situation comedy. Among those who oppose Martin's election to Bishop of Tours, the Bishop of Angers, Defensor, is particularly prominent (ch. 9). In the course of the proceedings, to bridge a moment of delay, a random selection from the psalms is read out. The reader begins precisely with the second verse of Psalm 8: *ex ore infantium et lactantium perfecisti laudem propter inimicos tuos, ut destruas inimicum et defensorem* (Out of the mouths of babes and sucklings hast thou ordained strength because of thine enemies, that thou mightest still the enemy and the avenger). The opponent is thus rendered harmless. The resolution of the conflict is achieved through a play on words. The culmination of the action in pointed formulae is a popular structural element in novellas too. At a higher level, there is naturally also an indication of the hand of God in this correspondence of appellative and personal name.

One day, when Martin wants to destroy a temple in the land of the Aedui, an enraged horde of pagan peasants bursts upon him (ch. 15). The boldest of them threatens him with a drawn sword. Martin stretches out his neck to the blow, and the pagan starts to swing his sword. But he overdoes it, and falls backward with his sword on the ground. The villain is represented as a buffoon, who puts himself out of action by his clumsiness. This episode is in formal terms simply slapstick. To be sure, Sulpicius does not remain in this sequence at the level of farce. The divine operation which is concealed behind the foreground events, is made manifest when the pagan, beside himself with fear of God, begs for mercy.

In the period of the episcopate occurs an episode which on the one hand has a certain entertainment value because of its burlesque elements, and on the other also reveals the subtle methods by which Sulpicius stylizes his Martin into a particular type of hero. The reference is to chapter 12 (cf. Berschin I: 202–4). Martin mistakes a peasant funeral in the distance for a pagan sacrificial ceremony and casts a spell on it. The effect is that the participants in the procession are virtually turned to stone and cannot move from the spot but can only turn around in circles in a comic manner. When

Martin realises his error, he lifts the spell: *Ita eos et, cum voluit, stare conpulit et, cum libuit, abire permisit* (So he compelled them to stand still when he wanted to, and permitted them to move when it pleased him). In this antithetical concluding formula, the exact parallelism of the clauses emphasizes the power of the bishop over the freedom of movement of the funeral cortege. But there are still more layers of meaning in this episode which we have not yet elucidated. On closer inspection, one notices a cluster of military-strategic vocabulary:

> Like a Roman general, Martin makes out the enemy in the distance [*conspicari*], hesitates [*quidnam id esset*], halts at a distance that is precisely quantified in Caesar's fashion [*quingentorum passuum intervallum erat*], tries to make out what is going on [*dinoscere*], raises his cross like a standard [*levare signum*] and gives the order [*imperat*]. With the same imperial gesture [*elevata rursum manu*] he removes the spell from the cortege.
>
> (Berschin I: 204)

The burlesque episode is therefore not simply for amusement. Rather, at the level of microstructure, choice of words is used to construct a quite specific picture of the hero: in stylizing Martin as *imperator Dei*, Sulpicius indicates that the bishop has reached the highest rank of the *militia christiana*.

VI Gregory the Great, *Dialogi*

Gregory enters the stage of world literature with his four books of *Dialogi* on the activities of Italian saints.[19] This work remained continuously on the bestseller list until the Reformation. As early as the middle of the eighth century, it became known also in the east through the translation into Greek by Pope Zacharias. The Greek text was used in the ninth and tenth centuries as the basis for translations into Church Slavonic and Arabic. Also in the ninth century, King Alfred the Great translated it into Old English – the first translation into a European vernacular, though many more were to follow: Old French, Icelandic, Anglo-Norman, Catalan, Castilian, Italian, and from the fourteenth century Middle Dutch and in the fifteenth century High German. The *Dialogi* were frequently imitated in their entirety, for example in the thirteenth century by Caesarius of Heisterbach in his *Dialogus miraculorum*, and often provided a stimulus to later literary production. So, for example, the appearance of the dead and the visions in the fourth book gave powerful impulses to the blossoming visionary literature of the twelfth and thirteenth centuries. Only in the sixteenth century did a more distanced reaction to Gregory the Great set in, which was not without influence on the reception of the *Dialogi*. The stumbling block, particularly among critical-rationalist theologians, was the extreme naïvety of many of the miracle stories, which in some passages comes close to fairy tale and is not far removed from magical ideas. It is exactly in these points that the charm of the collection must have lain for its medieval public. Add to that the narrative skill of Gregory, who tells his stories in a folk idiom, lively and unforced, sometimes even conversational, at other times in vigorous direct speech and dialogue.

Of course Gregory had a didactic purpose in view in his *Dialogi*. His aim is to encourage people to virtue by examples worthy of emulation, and to scare people off sin by examples to be shunned. The appeal to *exempla* was a favourite form of education already in antiquity. The moralizing element in Gregory is not insistently foregrounded. On the contrary, the didactic element is introduced only at the end of a story or even a group of stories, so that the flow of the narrative can unfold unimpeded.

The miraculous element, which provides the counterpoint of the whole collection, is often combined with positively grotesque and humorous traits.[20] An excellent example of this kind of representation is the story of the 'Lettuce Devil' (I.4), which takes place in a nunnery under the leadership of the Abbot Aequitius. One day, as a nun bites greedily into a lettuce in the cloister garden, without having first made the sign of the cross over it, she is possessed by the devil on the spot and thrown to the ground in a fit. When Aequitius rushes to help her, the panic upsets Satan, and he whimpers apologetically, before giving way to the stronger power: *Ego quid feci? Ego quid feci? Sedebam mihi super lactucam, venit illa et momordit me* (What did I do? What did I do? I was just sitting on a lettuce, and she came along and bit me).

The 'apology' of the devil with the repeated question 'What did I do?' and the defensive following clause are presented in an almost childish tone, which combines elements of everyday and vulgar speech. The emphatic use of the personal pronoun *ego* and the ethical dative *mihi* are barbarisms which point to the *sermo humilis* or low style. This is obviously deliberately chosen here, in order, according to the ancient rule of the three styles, *parva summisse dicere* (to express mean things simply)[21] that is, to define the operation of the devil as belonging to the realm of *parva*.

We find something similar in an occurrence which affects the priest Stephanus (III.20). On his return from a journey he thoughtlessly calls his servant to him with the words *Veni, diabole . . .* (Come on, you devil . . .), to pull off his shoes. The laces are at once undone by a ghostly hand. The wrong – or rather, the right – devil has heard him, to his horror. Of course the devil is not presented in all the tales as so harmless as he is in these. In any case, such stories contribute to the naïve and fairy-tale-like tone which clings to the whole collection.

The variety of the themes treated makes the *Dialogi* a most diverting read. Next to the obligatory raisings from the dead we find stories of animals who please God, such as the snake, who guards a monastery garden from a thief

(I.3), or the wild bear, who becomes tame in the arena (III.11). In III.10 the River Po, which has overflowed its banks, only retreats into its course after receiving a written warning from a bishop, properly sealed by a notary. At the consecration of a former Arian church for catholic service, an invisible pig runs through the rows of the faithful in search of the exit (III.30). A Jew, who is compelled to spend the night in an abandoned temple of Apollo, encounters an assembly of demons, and learns from their talk some piquant details about the carnal temptations of a bishop (III.7). These examples may suffice to illustrate a central principle of composition of the *Dialogi*, namely *Variatio delectat* (Variety delights).

If we end our consideration of hagiographic fiction with Gregory the Great, that is in keeping with the conception of this volume, which is essentially concerned with its relations to ancient literature. As may well be imagined, these are particularly emphatic in a period in which it is aiming to win a readership which still stands with both feet on the ground of classical culture. But even in the early period of Christian fiction, as we have seen, there are already influences from other sources. We may think of Hellenistic-Jewish literature and above all the Bible itself, which became the yardstick text for every Christian. In addition there are many narrative elements which occur repeatedly, wandering folkloristic motifs, which cannot easily be ascribed to a particular cultural milieu.

With the advance of time and the growing distance from antiquity, the concrete links with its literature become weaker. Christian writers can refer in ever greater degree to models from their own ranks, like Jerome or Sulpicius Severus. Even if pagan textual models can still easily be discerned in these exemplars, in the course of mediation they become ever more imprecise and diluted. Many means which are used to entertain the reader or listener, or to seize his emotions, are so universal that they cannot be attributed to a particular literary tradition.

The phenomenon of Christian fiction continues in existence, of course, throughout the Middle Ages. One may think of such humorous legends of saints as that of the drunken and companionable St Goar (MGH Merov.t.4, 411–23), who welcomes guests – even, unfortunately, the spies sent to him by the Bishop of Trier to keep an eye on his fasting practices. Brought before his head shepherd, Goar gets the chance to show himself a man of God when he persuades a newborn foundling to name his parents. The infant names the bishop . . .

In the Middle Ages, too, points of contact with the classical tradition continue to be apparent. We have already spoken of the dramas of Hrotsvitha. Here, there is a connection with antiquity in that she expressly aims to drive the pagan comedies of Terence out of the public mind with her prose dramas. In the thirteenth century, priests recommend – sometimes by appeal to ancient theoreticians – the use of anecdotal examples to shake congregations out of their boredom. Thus the prefaces which Jacques de Vitry (Ed. Crane 1890, repr. 1967: XLII) gives in the prologue to his *Sermones vulgares* culminate in a quotation from Horace's *Ars poetica* (v.343): *Omne tulit punctum qui miscuit utile dulci* (Everyone votes for the man who mixes wholesome and sweet).

If, in conclusion, we review once more the various procedures which were employed to entertain the public, we may determine that they belong to various levels and appeal to quite different needs in the reader or listener. It is one thing for an educated reader to be delighted by the recognition of classical reminiscences, and another to feel a voyeuristic pleasure in the description of spicy scenes of seduction. Both types of literary pleasure may frequently be found in one and the same text – we may think of the *Vita Pauli* of Jerome. They are as indissoluble in Christian fiction as they are in Petronius' *Satyrica*. And the reason they are not separable is that, of course, an educated reader also has 'lower instincts' and enjoys excitement and erotic stories.

The emphasis on the entertainment aspect has sometimes been adjudged a decadent phenomenon, for example by Manfred Fuhrmann (1977: 87):

> As epic and tragedy, as instruments of interpretation of the world, degenerated into the escapist genres of comedy and romance, so the world-interpreting genres of early Christianity, the Gospels and Acts, degenerated through fantasy, the autonomisation of the artistic drive and purely literary mechanisms (e.g. variation and the desire to outdo the model) into 'apocryphal' writings, that is into surrogates for the world, into trivial entertaining pap . . . Christian fiction promised religious instruction and edification, and slipped in under this disguise the function of replacing the world, the aim of mere entertainment, which is achieved by unbridled fantasy.

This evaluation overlooks the fact that the 'aim of entertainment' of Christian literature is not an end in itself, but, as was indicated at the outset, in a sense a 'rhetorical chess move' which serves the achievement of higher ends.[22] All the texts we have considered were written, ultimately, with propagandistic intention. They do not simply offer a surrogate for the world, but they create it, by winning adherents for particular Christian forms of life. If the effect of the texts was not so direct that every reader of Jerome's Lives himself went into the desert, or every reader of Gregory's *Dialogi* equalled the saints in virtue, yet they contributed to the creation of a spiritual climate in which the form of life being praised represented the accepted norm. This process has quite concrete consequences.

It is no accident that many of the writings in question are addressed to influential personalities. Jerome, for example, sent his first monk's life to the wealthy Paulus of Concordia. He could be certain that this educated man would appreciate properly the literary techniques which were employed in the *Vita Pauli*. Jerome certainly did not suppose that his aged addressee would convert to a hermit, but rather that he, as the owner of a large library, controlled the appropriate infrastructure to have the work reproduced and thus to disseminate it among his peers, the educated Christian upper class of the western half of the empire (Rebenich fothcoming). It was worth winning these as potential supporters: for even Christian projects need to be financed.

An extreme example of the way in which an apocryphal text can influence the course of history is the *Acts of Silvester*,[23] fictional account of the conversion of Constantine by Pope Silvester in Rome. This popular writing, which is transmitted in numerous versions, did more to form the image of the first Christian emperor in the Latin West than the historically reliable *Life of Constantine* of Eusebius of Caesarea. It stylized him as an adept of the Roman bishop Silvester, who is said out of respect for this holy man with his miraculous powers to have left Rome and installed the Pope there in a quasi-imperial position. The *Acts of Silvester* have been shown to have laid the foundations for the 'Donation of Constantine', which attached itself to a quite concrete formulation in this text. Thus, a literary fiction provided the basis for a forged document, which resulted in definite historical consequences over a period of centuries, namely the claims of the Popes to a certain sphere of influence, to wit the '*Patrimonium Petri*', later to be known as the 'Ecclesiastical state'. Fiction and reality often lie closer together than seems at first sight to be the case.

Notes

1 PL 171, col. 1060.

2 The tension between serious cencerns and entertainment in Christian literature is discussed comprehensively by Suchomski (1975). E.R. Curtius, in his study of 'Humour and seriousness in medieval literature', had already concluded 'that the theoretical position of the Church left open every possibility, from rigorous rejection to benevolent acceptance of laughter' (Curtius [9]1978, 423).

3 Ambrose is, in the context of his explanation of the psalms, admittedly not concerned with entertainment by jokes and laughter, but by sweet-sounding songs. However, his observations are still significant in our topic, since they go beyond the concrete example of his exegesis of the psalms and contain important reflections on the functionalization of the pleasure of reading in the interests of making instruction more palatable to the public.

4 On the phenomenon of edification in Christian fiction, the fundamental study is Kech (1977); see also Degl'Innocenti/Ferrari (1998).

5 It is in the nature of the theme, that in this chapter the aspect of the continuity of literary motifs holds the foreground. The idea that hagiography also achieved some fundamentally new insights is worked out by Judith Perkins in the volume *Greek Fiction*: 'By making its protagonists afflicted and poor, hagiography introduces new roles into cultural consciousness. Not to be represented is culturally not to exist' (1994: 266). 'Hagiography introduced new categories of subjects – the poor, the sick, the suffering, and functioned to reform the cultural notion of the human society' (1994: 267f.).

6 On the literary impact of the Bible see Dormeyer (1997).

7 For an introduction and bibliographical guide see Plümacher (1978), Charlesworth (1988), Schneemelcher (1992), Kytzler (1997: 484–86), and the relevant entries in ABD; standard editions of the *Apocryphal Acts of the Apostles* by Lipsius/Bonnet (1891–1903, repr. 1959), more recently: *Corpus Christianorum, Series Apocryphorum*, Turnhout: Brepols 1983ff.; fundamental is also Bovon *et al*. (1981). The most accessible English translation of the *Apocryphal Acts* is by Keith Elliott (Oxford: Clarendon Press 1993), which replaces the older translation by Montague Rhodes James (Oxford: Clarendon Press 1924).

8 On the provenance of the forms and motifs that are reworked in the apocryphal apostolic acts cf. Blumenthal (1933).

9 Fundamental differences between ancient novels and the accounts of the life and work of Christian heroes (especially heroines) are demonstrated by Clark (1984).

10 For introduction and bibliographical guide see Perry (1967: 291), Irmscher/Strecker (1992), Jones (1992), Kytzler (1997), 485f.; Ed. Rehm/Strecker ([3]1992, [2]1994).

11 See the contribution by G. Schmeling on the *Historia Apollinii* in this volume.

12 For introduction and bibliographical guide see Berschin I: 33–110 and Fontaine (1989), 517–35; Hofmann (1997), 443–57; standard editions include Lazzati (1956), Knopf/Krüger/Ruhbach (4th edn 1965), Musurillo ([2]1972), Lanata (1974); Bastiaensen *et al*. ([2]1990).

13 On the function of holy men in late antiquity see the fundamental study by Brown (1971).

14 See Kech (1977), Fuhrmann (1977), Berschin I: 133–44; Kytzler (1997), 487f. For the Latin text see still Migne PL 23, 17–62.

15 Commentaries: Hoelle (1957), Camisani (1971: 219–35); see Bauer (1961), Hamblenne (1993), Rebenich (forthcoming).

16 Ed Mierow (1946).

17 Ed Halm (1866: 107–37), Fontaine (1967; commentary: 1968f.); see Ghizzoni (1983), Stancliffe (1983), Berschin I: 195–211.

18 See Pervo (1994) and Hofmann (1997), 447–50. On the two subsequent Latin translations of the *Vita Antonii* by an unknown author around 360 and by Evagrius of Antioch around 370 see Fontaine (1989), 535–39.

19 Ed Moricca (1924, 2nd edn 1966, 3rd edn 1990), Vogüé (1978–80); see Brunhölzl I: 50–59, Berschin I: 305–24 and Clark, F. (1987), who defends the theory that Gregory is the pseudo-author of the *Dialogi*.

20 The arguments of Auerbach (1958: 72–7) put literary evaluation of the *Dialogi* on the right course; the following examples are taken from him. His arguments have recently been taken up by Berschin I: 305–21, esp. 308–10.

21 Cf. Cic. *Orator* 101. On the doctrine of the three stylistic levels cf. Quadlbauer (1962).

22 That the functions of *docere imitationem* (to educate to imitation), *movere ad admirationem* (to move to admiration) and *delectare* (to entertain) can perfectly well work together in one and the same hagiographic work to a psychagogic effect is emphasized by J. Fontaine by reference to Ambrose's theory of *bona delectatio*, pleasure with positive value (see above, p. 188), cf. *Christianisme et formes littéraires*, 98f. (discussion) and Fontaine (1976, I: 141).

23 Ed.: Mombritius (2nd edn 1910, reprinted 1978, 2: 508–31) = Latin composite version; secondary literature: Pohlkamp (1992), with indications of older literature.

Bibliography

Auerbach, E. (1958) *Literatursprache und Publikum in der lateinischen Spätantike und im Mittelalter*, Bern: Francke.

Bastiaensen, A.A.R. *et al.* (^{2}1990) *Atti e passioni dei martiri*, testo critico, commento, tradizione, Milan: Mondadori.

Bauer, J.B. (1961) 'Novellistisches bei Hieronymus Vita Pauli 3', *Wiener Studien* 74: 130–37. (Reprinted in *Scholia biblica et patristica*, Graz: Akademische Druck- und Verlagsanstalt, 1972, pp. 215–23.)

Berschin, W. (1986) *Biographie und Epochenstil im lateinischen Mittelalter*, vol. 1, Stuttgart: Hiersemann.

Blatt, F. (1930) *Die lateinischen Bearbeitungen der Acta Andreae et Matthiae apud anthropophagos*, Gießen: Alfred Töpelmann.

Blumenthal, M. (1933) *Formen und Motive in den apokryphen Apostelgeschichten*, Leipzig: J.C. Hinrichs'sche Buchhandlung. (*Texte und Untersuchungen zur Geschichte der altchristlichen Literatur. Archiv für die griechisch-christlichen Schriftsteller der ersten drei Jahrhunderte* (4th series, vol. 3, part 1, Leipzig/Berlin.)

Bovon, F. *et al.* (eds) (1981) *Les Actes apocryphes des apôtres: Christianisme et monde païen*, Genf: Labor et Fides.

Bremmer, J. (ed.) (1996) *The apocryphal acts of Paul and Thecla*, Kampen: Pharos.

—— (ed.) (1998) *The apocryphal acts of Peter: magic, miracles and agnosticism*, Leeuven: Peters.

Brown, P. (1971) 'The rise and function of the holy man in Late Antiquity', *Journal of Roman Studies* 61: 80–101. (Reprinted in *Society and the Holy in Late Antiquity*, Berkeley/Los Angeles: University of California Press, 1972, pp. 103–52.)

Brunhölzl, F. (1975) *Geschichte der lateinischen Literatur des Mittelalters*, vol. 1, Munich: Fiak.

Camisani, E. (1971) *Girolamo, Opere scelte*, Turin: Unione tipograficoeditrice torinese.

Cavallera, F. (1922) *Saint Jérôme. Sa vie et son oeuvre*, 2 vols, Louvain/Paris: Champion.

Charlesworth, J.H. (1988) 'Research on the New Testament Apocrypha and Pseudepigrapha', in W. Haase and H. Temporini (eds) *Aufstieg und Niedergang der römischen Welt*, Berlin: De Gruyter, II.25.5, pp. 3919–68.

Clark, E. (1984) *The Life of Melania the Younger: Introduction, Translation and Commentary*, New York: Edwin Meller Press.

Clark, F. (1987) *The Pseudo-Gregorian Dialogues*, 2 vols, Leiden: Brill.

Crane, T.F. (ed.) (1890) *The Exempla or Illustrative Stories from the Sermones Vulgares of Jacques de Vitry*, London: Hult. (Reprinted Nendeln/Liechtenstein: Kraus Reprint, 1967.)

Cullmann, O. (1930) *Le problème littéraire et historique du roman pseudo-clémentin. Etude sur le rapport entre le gnosticisme et le judéo-christianisme*, Paris: Jouve.

Curtius, E.R. (1978) *Europäische Literatur und lateinisches Mittelalter*, 9th edn, Bern/Munich: Francke.

Degl'Innocenti, A. and Ferrari, F. (eds) (1998) *Tra edificazione e piacere della letteratura: le vite dei santi in età medievale*, Università degli Studi di Trento.

Delehaye, H. (1936) *Etude sur le Légendier Romain (Subsidia Hagiographica 23)*, Brussels: Société des Bollandistes.

Dormeyer, D. (1997) 'Literarische Aspekte der Bibel', in L.J. Engels and H. Hofmann (eds) Neues Handbuch der Literaturwissenschaft, vol. 4, Spätantike, Wiesbaden: Aula-Verlag, pp. 122–49.

Engels, L.J. and Hofmann, H. (eds) *Neues Handbuch der Literaturwissenschaft*, vol. 4, Spätantike, Wiesbaden: Aula-Verlag, pp. 122–49.

Fontaine, J. (1967–69) *Sulpice Sévère. Vie de Saint Martin*, vol. 1: 1967, vols 2–3: 1968–69, Paris: Editions du Cerf. (Sources Chrétiennes: 133–35.)

—— (1976) 'Prose et poésie: L'interférence des genres et des styles dans la création littéraire d'Ambroise de Milan', in G. Lazzati (ed.) *Ambrosius Episcopus*, vol. 1, Milan: Vita e pensiero, pp. 124–70.

—— (1989) 'Hagiographische Literatur: Märtyrerberichte und -akten von 280 bis 370 n. Chr.', in R. Herzog (ed.) *Handbuch der lateinischen Literatur der Antike*, vol. 5: *Restauration und Erneuerung. Die lateinische Literatur von 284 bis 374 n. Chr.*, Munich: Beck, pp. 517–39.

Frye, N. (1957) *Anatomy of Criticism*, Princeton, NJ: Princeton University Press.

Fuhrmann, M. (1977) 'Die Mönchsgeschichten des Hieronymus. Formexperimente in erzählender Literatur', in *Christianisme et formes littéraires de l'Antiquité tardive en Occident*, Genf/Vandoeuvres: Fondation Hardt, pp. 41–99.

Gebhardt, O. von (1902) *Passio S. Theclae virginis. Die lateinischen Übersetzungen der Acta Theclae*, Leipzig: G. Hinrichs. (*Texte und Untersuchungen zur Geschichte der altchristlichen Literatur. Archiv für die griechisch-christlichen Schriftsteller der ersten drei Jahrhunderte*, vol. 22, part 2, Leipzig/Berlin.)

Ghizzoni, F. (1983) *Sulpicio Severo*, Rome: Bulzoni/Parma: Istituto di lingua e letteratura latina.

Goulet, R. (1981) 'Les vies de philosophes dans l'antiquité tardive et leur portée mystérique', in F. Bovon *et al.* (eds) *Les Actes apocryphes des apôtres: Christianisme et monde païen*, Genf: Labor et Fides.

Halm, C. (ed.) (1866) *Sulpicii Severi Opera*, Corpus scriptorum ecclesiasticorum latinorum, vol. 1.

Hamblenne, P. (1993) 'Traces de biographies grecques "païennes" dans la Vita Pauli de Jérôme?', in *Cristianesimo Latino e cultura Greca sino al sec. IV. XXI Incontro di studiosi dell'antichità cristiana*, Rome: Institutum patristicum Augustinianum, pp. 209–34.

Heintze, W. (1914) *Der Klemensroman und seine griechischen Quellen*, Leipzig: J.C. Hinrichs'sche Buchhandlung.

Herzog, R. (1975) *Die Bibelepik der lateinischen Spätantike. Formgeschichte einer erbaulichen Gattung*, vol. 1, Munich: Fink.

Hoelle, P. Ch. (1957) 'Commentary on the Vita Pauli of St Jerome', dissertation, Ohio State University.

Hofmann, H. (1997) 'Die Geschichtsschreibung', in L.J. Engels and H. Hofmann (eds) *Neues Handbuch der Literaturwissenschaft*, vol. 4, *Spätantike*, Wiesbaden: Aula-Verlag, pp. 403–67.

Irmscher, J. and Strecker, G. (1992) 'The Pseudo-Clementines' in W. Schneemelcher (ed.) *New Testament Apocrypha*, (rev. edn, tr. and ed. by R. McL. Wilson) Cambridge: James Clarke.

Jauss, H.R. (1974) *Literaturgeschichte als Provokation*, 5th edn, Frankfurt: Suhrkamp.

Jones, F.S. (1992) 'Clementines, Pseudo-', in *The Anchor Bible Dictionary*, chief ed. D.N. Freedman, New York: Doubleday, 1, 1061–62.

Junod, E. (1981) 'Les vies de philosophes et les actes apocryphes des apôtres poursuivent-ils un dessein similaire?', in F. Bovon *et al.* (eds) *Les Actes apocryphes des apôtres: Christianisme et monde païen*, Genf: Labor et Fides.

Kech, H. (1977) *Hagiographie als christliche Unterhaltungsliteratur. Studien zum Phänomen des Erbaulichen anhand der Mönchsviten des Hieronymus*, Göppingen: Alfred Kümmerle.

Knopf, R., Krüger, G. and Ruhbach, G. (eds) (1965) *Ausgewählte Märtyrerakten*, 4th edn, Tübingen: Mohr.

Krestan, L. and Hermann, A. (1957) 'Cyprianus II (Magier)', in *Reallexikon für Antike und Christentum*, ed. by T. Klauser, Stuttgart: Hiersemann, vol. 3, cols 467–77.

Kytzler, B. (1997) 'Fiktionale Prosa', in L.J. Engels and H. Hofmann (eds) *Neues Handbuch der Literaturwissenschaft*, vol. 4, *Spätantike*, Wiesbaden: Aula-Verlag, pp. 469–94.

Lanata, G. (ed.) (1974) *Gli atti dei martiri come documenti processuali*, Milan: Giustrè.

Lazzati, G. (1956) *Gli sviluppi della letteratura sui martiri nei primi quattro secoli*. Turin: Società editrice internazionale.

Lipsius, R.A. and Bonnet, M. (eds) (1891–1903) *Acti Apostolorum Apocrypha*, 2 vols in 3 parts, Leipzig: Hermann Mendelssohn. (Reprinted Darmstadt: Wissenschaftliche Buchgesellschaft, 1959.)

Martène, E. and Durand, U. (eds) (1717) *Thesaurus anecdotorum*, vol. 3, Paris, cols 1621–50.

Mombritius, B. (ed.) (1475–80) *Sanctuarium seu Vitae Sanctorum*, 2 vols, Paris: Fontemoing. (2nd edn 1910; reprinted Hildesheim/New York: Georg Olms, 1978.)

Moricca, U. (ed.) (1924) *Gregorii Magni Dialogi*, Rome: Tipografia del Senato. (2nd edn, Turin: Erasmo, 1966; 3rd edn, Rome Tipografia del Senato, 1990.)

Musurillo, H. (ed.) (1972) *The Acts of the Christian Martyrs*, Oxford: Clarendon Press.

Perkins, J. (1994) 'Representations in Greek Saints' Lives', in J.R. Morgan and R. Stoneman (eds) *Greek Fiction*, London/New York: Routledge, pp. 255–71.

Perry, B.E. (1967) *The Ancient Romances: A Literary-Historical Account of their Origins*, Berkeley/Los Angeles: University of California Press.

Pervo, R.I. (1987) *Profit with Delight: The Literary Genre of the Acts of the Apostles*, Minneapolis, MN: Fortress.

—— (1994) 'Early Christian fiction', in J.R. Morgan and R. Stoneman (eds) *Greek Fiction*, London/New York: Routledge, pp. 239–54.

Plümacher, E. (1978) 'Apokryphe Apostelakten', in *Paulys Realencyclopädie der classischen Altertumswissenschaft*, supplement 15, cols 11–70.

Pohlkamp, W. (1992) 'Textfassungen, literarische Formen und geschichtliche Funktionen der römischen Silvester-Akten', *Francia*, 19 (1): 115–96.

Quadlbauer, F. (1962) *Die antike Tradition der genera dicendi im lateinischen Mittelalter*, Graz/Vienna/Cologne: Böhlau.

Rebenich, St. (forthcoming) 'Der Kirchenvater Hieronymus als Hagiograph. Die Vita S. Pauli primi eremitae', in Elm, K. *et al.* (eds) *Beiträge zur Geschichte des Paulinerordens*, Berlin: Duncker und Humblot.

Rehm, B. (1957) 'Clemens Romanus II (PsClementinen)', *Reallexikon für Antike und Christentum*, ed. by T. Klauser, Stuttgart: Hiersemann, vol. 3, cols 197–206.

Rehm, B. and Strecker, G. (eds) (^{3}1992/^{2}1994) *Die Pseudoklementinen*, 2 vols (1. Homiliai, 2. Recognitiones), Berlin: Akademie-Verlag.

Reitzenstein, R. (1906) *Hellenistische Wundererzählungen*, Leipzig: Teubner. (Reprinted Darmstadt: Wissenschaftliche Buchgesellschaft, 1963.)

Salonius, A.H. (ed.) (1926) *Martyrium B. Petri apostoli a Lino episcopo conscriptum*, Abh. Helsinki Akad. Buchhandlung.

Schneemelcher, W. (ed.) (1992) *New Testament Apocrypha*, rev. edn, tr. and ed. by R. McL. Wilson, Cambridge: James Clarke.

Söder, R. (1932) *Die apokryphen Apostelgeschichten und die romanhafte Literatur der Antike*, Stuttgart: Kohlhammer.

Stancliffe, C. (1983) *St Martin and his Historiographer. History and Miracle in Sulpicius Severus*, Oxford: Clarendon Press.

Suchomski, J. (1975) *'Delectatio' und 'utilitas'. Ein Beitrag zum Verständnis mittelalterlicher komischer Literatur*, Bern/Munich: Francke.

Tatum, J. (1989) *Xenophon's Imperial Fiction*, Princeton, NJ: Princeton University Press.

Vielberg, M. (forthcoming) Clemens in den Pseudo-Clementinischen Rekognitionen. Studien zur literarischen Form des spätantiken Romans, Berlin: Akademie-Verlag.

Vogüé, A. de (ed.) (1978–80) *Grégoire le Grand, Dialogues*, vol. 1–3, Paris: Editions du Cerf. (Sources Chrétiennes 251, 260, 265.)

Part 5

THE HERITAGE OF LATIN FICTION

13

TOWARDS A HISTORY OF THE EXEGESIS OF APULEIUS

The case of the 'Tale of Cupid and Psyche'

Claudio Moreschini

Translated by Coco Stevenson

Uniquely among all the Greek and Latin 'novels', Apuleius' *Metamorphoses* has been considered by the greatest part of modern criticism to be a work which encloses a 'second' meaning, apart from that which reveals itself at first reading. An 'allegorical' reading has also been applied to the so-called 'Tale of Cupid and Psyche', which stands out from the *corpus* of the narrative on account of its amplitude and its excellence. In fact, few and far between were those critics who saw something in the *Metamorphoses*, and in the 'Tale of Cupid and Psyche', which corresponded exclusively to that which Goethe calls 'die Lust zu fabulieren': untrammelled and unadulterated entertainment. This second, deeper meaning, about which we are speaking, both in the *Metamorphoses* and in the tale within it, is generally of a philosophical calibre, and more precisely, is derived from an interpretation in Platonic terms, or else it may be of a religious nature. When we speak of 'a second meaning' or 'another meaning', the essence of what we mean is suggested in the Greek word *allegorein*, meaning 'to say another thing' other than that which is understood in the text.

An 'allegorical' interpretation is, therefore, a constant feature in the criticism of Apuleius' *Metamorphoses*. Is such an interpretation justified? With regard to this problem Dowden (1982: 337) wrote:

> If interpretation is allowed, there is also the question of its intensity. At one extreme is the point for point allegory of Bunyan's *Pilgrim's Progress*. . . . Point for point allegory is usually considered a crude and less enriching form of art and in addition it has often been practised

> in remarkably erroneous interpretations of classical literature, in particular of Homer. It is not, therefore, surprising that the most general attitude to *Cupid and Psyche* recently has been to admit its Platonic overtones . . . but to hold that 'to interpret the tale of Cupid and Psyche as a precise philosophical allegory does violence to Apuleius' literary art'.[1]

I Late Antiquity

The allegorical interpretation of the 'Tale of Cupid and Psyche' emerged parallel to the allegorical reading of the *Metamorphoses* in their entirety relatively early on. However, allegorical interpretation began in Late Antiquity, and not before. Although a theory sustained by Dowden, I am in no way convinced that the tale related by Apuleius constituted a Platonic myth, nor that this was already recognized as such by Plotinus, as *Enneads* 3.5, would indicate. In reality, the discussion which Plotinus conducts in that treatise is based on the myth of the *Symposium*. Even less convincing is the allusion that (as Dowden observed) Bréhier would propose as the union of the individual with the Whole, as described in *Enneads* 6.9.9. No other commentators of this Plotinian treatise say anything about such a view.

As a matter of fact, allegorical interpretation proper shows itself only in the last centuries of antiquity. Fundamentally, this corresponded to the typical cultural characteristics of that time, which tended to see a more profound significance in certain figures or certain texts of the past, not dissimilar to that which occurred with the contemporary allegorization of Virgil and, in the Greek world, of Homer.

In relation to the *Metamorphoses*, we can consider Augustine's comment as evidence of a certain way of reading the novel. In the *De Civitate Dei* 18.18, he considers that the novel ought to be viewed not only as a fantastical invention of Apuleius, but as a proper autobiographical novel:

> *sicut Apuleius in libris, quos Asini Aurei titulo inscripsit, sibi ipsi accidisse, ut accepto veneno humano animo permanente asinus fieret, aut indicavit aut finxit.*

> Like Apuleius, in his books inscribed with the title *The Golden Ass*, reported or pretended to report had happened to him: after having taken a potion he became an ass, without losing his human soul.

Certainly, Augustine did not introduce an allegorical interpretation of the *Metamorphoses*, but nevertheless can be seen as a predecessor of future critics who considered it as a novel of edification.

Instead, we can find much more regarding the 'Tale of Cupid and Psyche'.

This tale must have seemed as strange to the reader of Late Antiquity as it does to us. It comprises a story of mythological characters, and it presents itself as the vicissitudes of a fall, owing to an error and a transgression against a divine command. This transgression leads to the need to brave a series of tests, which result in the redemption of the protagonist, thanks mainly to the intervention of a god. The twists and turns of the story conclude with the deification of the protagonist.

The presence, in the tale, of the traditional divinities and their presentation in human terms, indeed, often in absurd poses, did not prevent a more meaningful interpretation, as it did not prevent an analogous interpretation of the Homeric gods. The culture of Late Antiquity was, in fact, inclined to accept the presence of traditional divinities, because it was preoccupied with applying to them an allegorical or, in any case, a philosophical interpretation. A clear example of their new function is provided in a text emblematic of Late Antiquity, the *De Nuptiis Mercurii et Philologiae* by Martianus Capella. This work presents some interesting points for the history of the criticism of the 'Tale of Cupid and Psyche'.

According to Martianus Capella, Psyche is one of the daughters of the Sun and of Endelechia, wanted in marriage by Mercury, after he had realized that he could not unite himself with another divine woman (i.e. one of the allegorical personifications):

> *voluit saltem – sc. Mercurius – Endelechiae ac Solis filiam postulare, quod speciosa quam maxime magnaque deorum sit educata cura; nam ipsi ιψνχγ natali die dii ad convivium corrogati multa contulerant.*
>
> *De Nuptiis*, 1,7

> Mercury decided to ask for the hand in marriage of the daughter of the Sun and of Endelechia, since she was beautiful beyond all others and brought up with the greatest diligence by the gods; indeed, the gods, invited to a banquet on the day of Psyche's birth, had brought her many gifts.

But in spite of what Mercury desired, Virtue reported to him that Psyche 'had been wrested from her company and had been made a prisoner to Cupid and was being restrained by him with adamantine chains'. As a consequence Mercury had to find himself another bride, and there is no further mention of Psyche in the *De Nuptiis*. Of all these briefly mentioned points, one thing only should be considered: that according to Martianus Capella, Psyche was the daughter of the Sun and of Endelechia, that is to say,[2] the daughter of the eternal cosmic movement of the soul. This detail, as we will see, will later be recovered by medieval writers, although it is true that Martianus Capella did not explicitly link the Psyche, about whom he spoke and whom Mercury requested as his bride, with the Psyche of the Apuleian tale.

On the basis of our brief considerations above, one can understand that an allegorical interpretation of the Apuleian tale would not have appeared ridiculous given its historical and cultural context. The main representative of such an interpretation is Fulgentius, and the first complete allegory dates from the sixth century. But it is reasonable to think that interpretations of this kind could have been in circulation even before this time. Fulgentius is still an obscure character: it is unclear whether he should be identified with the Christian bishop of Ruspe (530).[3] Fulgentius lived in Africa, in a region which was at that time still rich in the Classical tradition.[4] Fulgentius, in his short works, displays a series of uniform interests, totally centred on the philosophical-allegorical interpretation of the Classics, in particular of Virgil (in the *Expositio Virgilianae Continentiae*). There exists, then, a coherence in the exegetical activity of this scholar which deserves our attention. The Apuleian tale, he says,[5] can not be understood literally: at face value it is none other than a *falsitas*, a lie. According to Fulgentius, Apuleius narrated a huge jumbled mass of lies (Helm 1898: 68, 21–22); and, for Fulgentius, the blame for these lies rested with the creator of the novel, a certain Aristophon of Athens. This critical attitude towards Apuleius seems to be an isolated example in Fulgentius, who does not show such an attitude towards other writers.[6] The purpose of his work is announced to the writer himself by Calliope at the end of the long and enigmatic proem (Helm 1898: 14, 20). If Fulgentius places his trust in the Muses, Calliope says, he will receive glory, not like Nero did, thanks to some poetic eulogies, but like Plato received, thanks to his mystic doctrines. Fulgentius' interpretations, then, should be *misticae rationes*, and he should reason in the same way that Plato did. Fulgentius' interest in Apuleius seems confirmed also by the fact that the myth of Cupid and Psyche is one of the few wherein Fulgentius refers to a specific writer – Apuleius – as his source. Moreover, Fulgentius also alludes to Psyche in his preface (Helm 1898: 4, 1 and 11, 8).

Briefly, here is the allegorical interpretation of the story, as it is proposed by Fulgentius, who contrasts it with the *falsitas* of Apuleius and of his source (if it ever existed), Aristophon of Athens (Helm 1898: 69, 2–4). The city in which the king and the queen reigned suggests the world, while the king and the queen are God and Matter. The three daughters are Flesh, Free Will and the Soul (the Soul being Psyche). The Soul is the youngest of the three sisters, because the Soul is inserted into the body only at a later moment, after its creation from Matter. This doctrine could be evidence of the Christian education of the author. Furthermore, Psyche is the most beautiful daughter, because she is superior to Free Will and more noble than Flesh. Venus is *libido*, who sends Cupid, that is to say, desire, to destroy Psyche. But desire can be directed towards good as much as towards bad, and Cupid therefore unites himself with the Soul. Cupid tries to convince the Soul not to want to gaze upon his face, that is to say, not to want to learn the delights of pleasure. In the same way Adam, although he could see that he was naked, did not understand that he was naked (Genesis, 2.18), that is to say he did not realize the evil in the sin he had committed, until he ate from the Tree of Desire, as Fulgentius terms it.[7] Likewise Psyche ought not to follow the advice of her sisters, Flesh and Free Will, to satisfy her curiosity by gazing upon the face of Cupid. But Psyche, convinced by her sisters, takes the lantern,[8] that is to say, unveils the flame of desire concealed in her breast and, having seen it, in all its sweetness, she loves it and desires it. With these words, Fulgentius seems to confuse the revelation of desire, which is within Psyche, with the revelation of Cupid, who is outside Psyche, unifying the two senses of *cupido*, which are 'desire' and the 'object of desire'. This confusion continues also in the next sentence, opening with the relative pronoun *quam* (sc. *desiderii flammam)*, meaning the flame of desire, if one follows the literal meaning of the text, and Cupid, if one follows its logical meaning:

> *Quam ideo lucernae ebullitione dicitur incendisse, quia omnis cupiditas quantum diligitur tantum ardescit et peccatricem suae carni configit maculam*
>
> Psyche therefore burns him with the boiling hot oil of the lamp. In fact, every desire, the more it is loved, the more it burns and pierces the stain of sin into the flesh

Fulgentius' interpretation here is overtly Christianizing. As a direct result of her disobedience Psyche is banished from the enchanted palace.

Here the allegorical interpretation stops. Fulgentius urges the reader to apply such a method, which he considers to be the only valid method, in order to interpret the rest of the Apuleian text (although not actually cited by Fulgentius) in the same way. Such an interpretation possesses all the typical elements of antique allegory, particularly of Christian allegory, which tries to investigate a more noble and moral significance, which lurks in the depths of the text, and does not correspond to that which is gleaned from a literal reading. Having accepted this meaning in its general lines (in our case, a cosmic and anthropological meaning of the fortunes of Psyche), the allegorist reader has to identify the individual details and insert them into the frame of the allegorical interpretation founded a priori, whether they fit into it easily or not. A similar method characterized the pagan and Christian exegesis, for instance that of Iamblichus and Gregory of Nyssa, which identified first of all the *skopós*, the purpose contained in the text to be commented on, and then subordinated the text itself to such a *skopós*. As a consequence, every detail and not just the text as a whole has to be allegorized. Sixth-century Christians had for a long time already been accustomed to practising (or simply encountering) this type of exegesis; indeed Fulgentius himself, in his interpretation of the *Virgiliana continentia* (i.e. the theme which is present in all of Virgil's works) behaves in exactly the same way.

II Boccaccio

The allegorical interpretation of Fulgentius provided the scheme for that of Boccaccio. He was a typically medieval scholar and yet still estranged from the Humanist tradition, which instead developed from his contemporary Petrarch. Boccaccio was able to read the *Metamorphoses* at Montecassino, where the most important manuscript of the novel, (now F = Laurentianus 68, 2) was located at the time. This manuscript was taken away soon after and carried to Florence by Zanobi da Strada. It is also known that Boccaccio procured a copy of the Montecassino manuscript for himself (now known as the Laurentianus 54, 32) and that some famous stories from the *Metamorphoses*, such as the Lover in the Cask (*Metamorphoses*,9.5ff.) and the hidden lover who betrays himself through sneezing (*Metamorphoses*,7.2 and 5.10) were revived in his *Decameron*.[9]

Boccaccio's attitude towards the Apuleian novel is twofold and according to our way of reading a text, contradictory. On the one hand, he was animated by the very same 'joy of story-telling' that is characteristic of Apuleian artistry, and as a consequence revived some stories from Apuleius, as just stated. On the other hand, his scholarly attitude prompted him to see an allegorical significance in the tale of Cupid and Psyche. His interpretation of the tale is found in a learned work, the *Genealogiae Deorum Gentilium*,[10] and constitutes a part of a work, which, as its title announces, traces the genealogy of the gods of pagan myths from the ancient sources. In doing so, Boccaccio not only elucidates the Apuleian narrative, but explains who all the different Cupids that we meet in Classical literature were. The writer, therefore, wants to identify a first Cupid who was the son of Mars and fathered *Voluptas* (9.4). The source of this piece of information, he says, is Cicero who had stated that this Cupid was a refined and lascivious god.[11] As testimony to this piece of information, Boccaccio cites a passage of the Apuleian tale (5.22) where Cupid is described sleeping, whilst Psyche gazes upon him.

> *cum videt capitis aurei genialem caesariem ambrosia temulentam, cervices lacteas genasque purpureas crinium globos decoriter impeditos, alios antependulos, alios retropendulos, quorum splendore nimio fulgurante iam et ipsum lumen lucernae vacillabat. Per umeros volatilis dei pinnae roscidae micanti flore candicant, et quamvis alis quiescentibus extimae plumulae tenellae ac delicatae tremule resultantes inquieta lasciviunt. Ceterum corpus glabellum atque luculentum et quale peperisse Venerem non poeniteret*

> On his golden head she saw the glorious hair drenched with ambrosia: wandering over his milky neck and rosy cheeks were the neatly shackled ringlets of his locks, some prettily hanging in front, others behind; the lightening of their great brilliance made even the lamp's light flicker. Along the shoulders of the winged god white

> feathers glistened like flowers in the morning dew; and although his wings were at rest, soft and delicate little plumes along their edges quivered restlessly in wanton play. The rest of his body was hairless and resplendent, such as to cause Venus no regrets for having borne this child.[12]

Straight after this (9.5) Boccaccio speaks of *Voluptas*, who is the daughter of Cupid, as is revealed in the last sentence of the Apuleian tale (6.24). The significance of that *Voluptas* is understood by Boccaccio in a fairly obvious manner, in the sense that she indicates the pleasure which is experienced when one obtains the object of one's desire. Boccaccio, with good reason, considers *Voluptas* to be sensual pleasure, in conformity with what Cupid himself says in *Metamorphoses*, 5.11, namely that, if Psyche respects the secret of their marriage, a divine child would be born, whereas if she violates the secret the baby would be mortal. On the basis of the successive events and Psyche's failure to obey the command of Cupid, we have to conclude that the *Voluptas* born from Cupid and Psyche is mortal.

More broad and exacting is the interpretation of the Apuleian tale in its entirety (*Genealogiae*, 5.22), which is conducted following the exegetical criteria introduced by Fulgentius, that is to say an interpretation which is purely allegorical. But while in method Boccaccio's explanation follows that of Fulgentius (as this allegorical method had, by that time, become well established in medieval culture), as far as the contents are concerned, it follows also that of Martianus Capella, by developing the few allusions mentioned above, that is to say, the belief, also for Boccaccio, that Psyche is Apollo's and Endelechia's daughter (*Genealogiae*, 5.22). Boccaccio gives an elucidation of this genesis of Psyche. He states that he lacks the space to explain the whole tale, and therefore he will limit himself to explaining only three points: (1) why Psyche is said to be the daughter of Apollo and Endelechia, (2) who Psyche's sisters were, and (3) why Psyche was made the wife of Cupid. Psyche is the daughter of Apollo, the Sun, that is to say, of that God, who is the true light of the world. Indeed, only God has the power to create a rational soul. The interpretation of Endelechia is extracted from the *Commentary on the Timaeus* by Chalcidius, one of the fundamental texts for medieval philosophy and for the medieval knowledge of Plato. According to Chalcidius, says Boccaccio, Endelechia signifies 'entelechy', the 'perfect state' or the Aristotelian condition in which a potentiality has become an actuality:

> *hanc ergo speciem qua formantur singula generaliter Aristoteles entelechiam,* id est absolutam perfectionem, *vocat.*
>
> *Commentary on the Timaeus*, c. 222[13]

> Therefore Aristotle calls this form, by which the individual things are shaped, generally entelechy, *this is: absolute perfection.*

The rational Soul is therefore daughter of this 'entelechy' or 'perfect state'. It is true that we receive the rational soul from 'the Father of the Light' (an allusion to Genesis 1,17) in the womb of the mother, but his creations appear only in perfect state, because we are, before that moment, guided by natural instinct, rather than by the judgement of reason. Once entelechy is completed, we begin to operate with reason. It is therefore appropriate that Psyche is called the daughter of Apollo and Endelechia. Her two sisters are the vegetative and the sensitive soul and they are older because they both develop before the rational soul. Psyche, nevertheless, is the most beautiful of the three, because, while we share the vegetative soul with plants and the sensitive soul with brute animals, we share the rational soul with the angels and with God, who is the most beautiful being of all. And since the first two souls are linked from the beginning to the functions of the body, for this reason it is said that the first two sisters married first. The wedding of the rational soul is instead reserved for someone of divine origin, that is to say, to pure love, i.e. to God himself. The soul is placed among the delights of God, by Zephyr, the vital spirit which is holy, and joined in marriage with God himself. God forbids his wife to look upon him, if she does not want to lose him, that is to say, that the soul must not seek the secrets which conceal the reasons of the eternity of God, because they are known only to him, and neither must she seek the reasons for the causes of things and for his omnipotence. Indeed, every time that man seeks to uncover these things, he loses the right pathway and loses God, or rather he loses himself. The sisters, at times, reach the height of Psyche's pleasures and obtain something of her treasures, as the vegetative soul carries out her work much better if she lives close to reason, and equally, sensitive virtues are more pure and last longer if they are in the company of the rational soul. Certainly the sisters experience envy for Psyche, because it is well known that sensuality is in direct contrast with reason. They seek to persuade reason to gaze upon her husband, that is to say, to see with her reasoning power that reality which she loves and not to recognize it through faith alone. At the same time they fill Psyche with fear, by telling her that in reality her husband is a terrible snake which will devour her. This happens every time that sensuality seeks to put reason to sleep. When the soul, in turn, foolishly pays heed to the demonstrations coming from the sensual condition, and seeks to gaze upon that which is denied to her, she is ready to kill, if the form of the things does not correspond to her desire. She sees the outward appearance of her husband, which is very beautiful, but it signifies only the external works of God. Yet the true form, God himself, she cannot see, because no one has ever seen God. And when the soul wounds God with a spark, that is to say, when she strikes him with arrogant desire, she becomes disobedient and listens to sensuality. So the soul loses the good of the contemplation and divorces herself from the divine matrimony. Thus, finally Psyche, repentent but still in love, astutely procures the ruin of her sisters, in the sense that they no longer have any power against reason. Then, through pain and suffering purified of her presumptuous pride and disobedience, she wins the good of love and contemplation of God and joins herself with him for a second time in eternity. While abandoning transient things, she is led to eternal glory and there gives birth to Pleasure from Love, that is to say to sempiternal delight and joy.

We have dwelled for a long time on this interpretation of Boccaccio, because even if compared to that of Fulgentius it is not substantially new, it is nevertheless complete, because it takes into consideration the whole novella, contrary to what had been done by the ancient critic. Moreover, by means of this mixture of elements taken from Martianus Capella and Fulgentius, Boccaccio's interpretation imposed itself on the successive allegorical exegesis of the writers of the Renaissance, when they considered it appropriate to return to this interpretation.

According to Boccaccio (*Genealogiae*, 9.4), the poet Ausonius in the *Eclogae ad Gregorium* refers to a tale about Cupid, derived from Apuleius. In fact, in a little poem, dedicated to his son Gregorius, the *Cupido Cruciatus*, and not in the *Eclogarum Liber* (in which the poet speaks to his son Drepanius and not Gregorius[14]), Ausonius describes a picture which he had seen in Trier (Augusta Treverorum) portraying mythical heroines who, in keeping with what Virgil had said in *Aeneid*, 6.422ff., had tragically died in the pursuit of unhappy love and found themselves in the infernal regions reserved for them where they nailed Cupid to a cross. As if by method of retribution, they in turn crucified Cupid by whom they had been crucified (*excruciatae*) with love when they were still alive. It appears that Boccaccio knew the little poem of Ausonius well. He cited its introduction and the story and thought that this myth of the torments of Cupid, which is actually an over-elaborate and extravagant poetic invention by Ausonius, had been derived from Apuleius. Perhaps Boccaccio was also led to this hypothesis by the fact that in the Ausonian poem Venus too grieves over the insults received from Cupid, employing some expressions that recall the reprimands which Venus directed at Cupid in the episode in the tale of Cupid and Psyche (5.29–30). In reality, excepting the very general similarities in the title, Ausonius' little poem does not derive at all from Apuleius, as Boccaccio thought.

III Renaissance

However, in the Renaissance, voices of dissent about the allegorical interpretation of the tale began to emerge. The Humanist imitations of Apuleius were practised primarily on a stylistic and literary level, as in the case of Antonio Codro Urceo. The commentators do not resort to allegory, like Giambattista Pio. They even reject it a priori, like the commentator Filippo Beroaldo, who, while being aware of the Fulgentian interpretation of the tale of Cupid and Psyche, excludes it categorically, and maintains that allegorical interpretations are the duty of philosophers, not of commentators, and he is a commentator. Therefore he states,

> But I, in the explanation of this tale, will not seek allegories, but rather the historical significance, and I will explain the interpretation of the unknown things and of the words, so as not to appear to be a bad philosopher, rather than a commentator.[15]

There are, however, some exceptions to the above. In the fervid Humanistic circle of Ferrara, we still find echoes of an allegorical interpretation, which is, however, no longer as rigorous in identifying correlations in the details, but limits itself to the general significance of Psyche, understood, naturally, as the 'soul' of man. A refined and capricious writer, like Celio Calcagnini resorts to it, but by this time it is in a way which is wholly 'modern', in the sense that allegory is an element for a poetic reading. One of his *Apologi* is entitled *Somatia*, that is to say, with a title that is simultaneously Greek and Latin, meaning 'the city of the body'. It is dedicated to the cardinal Ippolito d'Este and appears to have been written during the carnival, which Calcagnini named, with a Latin word, 'Saturnalia'. During this festival slaves could speak freely to their patrons, so now Calcagnini will allow himself to speak freely to his protector, the cardinal.[16]

In Calcagnini's fantastical reconstruction, he dwells especially on the vicissitudes of the human soul, which he generally calls 'Psyche', although one should not think that because of this the writer had the Apuleian tale in mind, given that in his *Apologus* (written in the manner of Lucian, an author much esteemed in the Renaissance), it seems that the description of the human soul was revived from the famous myth in Plato's *Phaedrus*. But Lilio Gregorio Giraldi, another humanistic writer from Ferrara and a contemporary of Calcagnini, writing in Ferrara, revived the allegorical interpretation of the tale from Fulgentius. According to Giraldi, Fulgentius had interpreted the tale *ex Graecis auctoribus*: 'from Greek authors'. Perhaps he attributed its allegorical interpretation to Aristophon of Athens, whereas Fulgentius had attributed the plot of the tale itself to this unknown Aristophon from whom it had allegedly been taken over by Apuleius. Moreover, Giraldi repeats Martianus Capella's remark that Psyche is the daughter of Apollo and Endelechia, probably deriving this information from Boccaccio.[17]

It is probable that Fracastoro was also aware of the allegorical significance of the myth of Psyche, even if he is not concerned with the various vicissitudes of it, but merely with the identification of Psyche with the human soul. In a dialogue entitled with the name of its author, *Fracastorius sive de anima*, the writer presents himself as a character in the dialogue, and introduces[18] a not particularly elegant poem entitled *Psiche*. In this, Psyche is represented invoking Cupid. She says both are from the same fatherland, that is to say, heaven. This signifies that the writer has in mind spiritual, celestial love, in the

Neoplatonic style, which is characteristic of Renaissance culture. The soul, because of its celestial origin pours the good and the beautiful into the breast of man, whereas love gives birth to the flame of the desire to obtain them. Psyche says *amoris amore exarsi*: 'I am consumed by the love of love', recalling the expression of Apuleius in the tale,

> *sic ignara Psyche sponte in Amoris incidit amorem*
>
> *Metamorphoses*, 5.23
>
> thus Psyche, unknowing and without prompting fell in love with Amor/Love

and she desires that Cupid/Amor does as much. Psyche prepares an embroidered bandage for him, on which all his exploits are depicted: he crosses the sea and the clouds, he subjugates men and the animals to his dominion, not even the gods are spared, as we read in the *Metamorphoses*, in the famous prophecy in which there is an allusion to the power of Cupid (4.33): also Psyche will be his slave.

However, in the Italian sixteenth century, the usual procedure of interpreting the 'Tale of Cupid and Psyche' allegorically (and that is to say, according to Christian doctrine) grows weak, owing to the greater weight given by critics to explaining ancient texts mainly from a literary point of view. Allegories were not completely abandoned however; usually both methods were resorted to, in the sense that the scholar accepted the allegory and placed it before the text, when referring to the context of the Apuleian tale, although re-elaborating it in a literary and poetic way. The most significant example of this approach is provided by Giovan Battista Marino, who in the fourth canto of the *Adone*, reworks with great freedom the 'Tale of Cupid and Psyche'. He adheres to the new sensitivity of the seventeenth century, but in any case, precedes his octaves with a summary, which contains, once again, an allegory based on that of Fulgentius, for the main part, and on that of Boccaccio, for the part where the Fulgentian interpretation had stopped. The poet observed that the tale of Psyche represents the state of man. The city in which she is born, stands to signify the world, the king and the queen are God and Matter (therefore not Endelechia, as stated by Boccaccio and Martianus Capella.) The three sisters are Flesh, Free Will and the Soul. The Soul is the youngest of the three sisters, because she is inserted last after the body has been completed. Finally, in the part derived from Boccaccio, we can observe that Psyche, after her disobedience, pushed by Fortune through various dangers, after much toil and persecution and re-united with Cupid, is the 'type' (a word from allegorical interpretation) of the soul itself, that after having experienced many sufferings, arrives finally at perfect joy.

But we cannot talk at any more length about these allegorical interpretations of the tale that we have presented here, through examples taken from writers of late Antiquity, such as Martianus Capella and Fulgentius, through to writers of the Middle Ages, such as Boccaccio, up until writers of the sixteenth century, among whom the chief is Marino. Even in later times, the tale suggested an allegorical interpretation, even if by that time, such interpretation was detached from that of Fulgentius, which must have appeared improper, given its definite Christian character. So, according to Leopardi, still in the first decades of the nineteenth century, the myth of Psyche stands to signify that man was not made for knowledge and that all knowledge is dangerous to him. Furthermore philologists, like Hildebrand, who, in commenting on the whole of Apuleius in 1842, had seen a religious significance in the *Metamorphoses* and an allegorical significance in the principal tale of the novel; and so on up until modern interpretations.

To return to the initial point: does attributing to the tale (or to the Apuleian novel in its entirety) a significance different from that which emerges at first reading, not imply to allegorize, even if such an 'allegory' is philosophical in content? According to one of the most well-balanced Apuleian scholars, P.G. Walsh, the novella represents the Platonic myth of the genesis and the destiny of the soul, of her life in the celestial world and of her fall into the material world (Walsh 1970: 195, 220–1). The Platonic interpretation was revived a few years ago in an essay by E.J. Kenney, which displayed great finesse and acute literary criticism.[19] Whichever way one understands these modern interpretations, whether one accepts or rejects them, they stand to demonstrate the vitality of an apparently elusive but always original text, which is, in its ambiguity, certainly unparalleled by any other work of Latin literature.[20]

Notes

1 Quoted from Schlam, 1976: 34.

2 This Psyche has been identified by some with the Apuleian Psyche, but Shanzer did not agree and invested the reference in Martianus Capella with a wider cosmological context: Cf. Shanzer, 1986: 69–70.

3 I, personally, do not believe that this is possible, notwithstanding the philologists's dread of the duplication of names and of persons. An example of this kind of attitude is constituted in the case of the exegete and theologian Origen, where the existence of both a pagan and a Neoplatonic Origen is still in dispute today.

4 On the personality and the literary production of Fulgentius, cf. the brief outline by Bertini, 1985.

5 The exposition and the interpretation of the tale is found in R. Helm's Teubner edition, 1898 pp. 66–70.

6 About this person we know as much now as one knew in the past, that is to say nothing, because he is named only in the present passage. According to Fulgentius the tale of Cupid and Psyche had been told by this Aristophon '*in libris qui disarestia nuncupantur*', that is to say in books entitled *About Dissatisfaction.* These books, Fulgentius tells us, had been composed with enormous verbosity ('*inormi verborum circuitu*'). This information has a definite air of being a

Fulgentian invention; in any case, supposing that he had not made it up, it serves little purpose, because we ought to limit ourselves to analysing what Fulgentius himself said.

7 Fulgentius, *Mitologiarum* 3,6,16–17, '*concupiscentiae arbore comedat*'.

8 The text says '*desub modio eicit*' (Helm 1898: 69,20). The '*modium*' has got nothing to do with anything, neither in the tale of Cupid and Psyche nor in its interpretation. It is probably just an echo of the Gospel of Matthew (5.15). Cf. Helm 1898: 68,8 and 68,10.

9 On the re-discovery of the *Metamorphoses* in the thirteenth century see Chapter 16 by R.A. Carver, this volume.

10 Cited from V. Romano's edition, Bari 1951. On Boccaccio's treatment of the tale of Cupid and Psyche see also Hijmans, 1981, pp. 30–45.

11 As a matter of fact, Cicero in *De Natura Deorum*, 3.60 enumerates only three different Cupids, sons of respectively Mercury and the first Diana, Mercury and the second Venus and Mars and the third Venus, but he says nothing as to his qualities.

12 Apuleius, *Metamorphoses*, volume I, edited and translated by J. Athur Hanson (Loeb, Harvard University Press 1989).

13 Cf. Plato Latinus. Edidit R. Klibansky, volumen IV: *Timaeus a Chalcidio translatus commentarioque instructus*, in societatem operis coniuncto P. J. Jensen edidit J.H. Waszink, editio altera, Londini et Leidae 1975.

14 Boccaccio's mistake could perhaps be justified in the following way: it is true that the *Cupido Cruciatus* was not part of the *Eclogae*, but Ausonius called this work *Ecloga*.

15 Beroaldo's statement appears in the note to IV, 28.

16 The *Apologus* is printed in Caelii Calcagnini Ferrariensis Protonotarii Apostolici, *Opera aliquot* . . . , Basileae 1544, pp. 610–13.

17 Cf. Lilii Gregorii Gyraldi Ferrariensis *Operum quae extant omnium* . . . tomi duo . . . , Basileae, per Thomam Guarinum, I, 1580, p. 390, 22–25.

18 Cf. Hieronymi Fracastori Veronensis *Opera omnia* . . . accesserunt Andreae Naugerii, Patricii Veneti *Orationes duae carminaque nonnulla* . . . Venetis, apud Iuntas, 1555, p. 216ab.

19 Cf. Kenney, 1990a, and his commentary on the tale of Cupid and Psyche, (Kenney, 1990b).

20 Last of all, see my own study: Moreschini, 1994.

Bibliography

Apulei Platonici Madaurensis opera quae supersunt Vol. I. Metamorphoseon libri XI, ed. Rudolf Helm, Bibliotheca Teubneriana 1898.

Apuleius, *Metamorphoses* Volume I, edited and translated by J. Athur Hanson, Loeb, Harvard University Press 1989.

Bertini, F. (1985) 'Fulgenzio', *Enciclopedia Virgiliana*, Rome.

Boccaccio, G., *Genealogiae deorum gentilium libri*, ed. Vincenzo Romano, Bari 1951.

Caelii Calcagnini Ferrariensis Protonotarii Apostolici, *Opera aliquot* . . . , Basileae 1544.

Dowden, K. (1982) 'Psyche on the Rock', Latomus 41 (2): 336–52.

Hieronymi Fracastori Veronensis *Opera omnia* . . . *accesserunt* Andreae Naugerii, Patricii Veneti *Orationes duae carminaque nonnula* . . . Venetis, apud Iuntas, 1555.

Fulgentio, F.P. (1972) *Expositio Virgilianae Continentiae*, eds T. Agozzino and F. Zanlucchi, Padova.

Lilii Gregorii Gyraldi Ferrariensis *Operum quae extant omnium . . . tomi duo . . .* , Basileae, per Thomam Guarinum, I, 1580.

Hijmans, B.L. (1981) 'Boccaccio's *Amor and Psyche*' in B.L. Hijmans and V. Schmidt (eds) *Symposium Apuleianum Groningarnum*, Groningen.

Kenney, E.J. (1990) 'Psyche and her Mysterious Husband', in D.A. Russell (ed.) *Antonine Literature*, Oxford: Oxford University Press.

—— (ed.) (1990b) Apuleius, *Cupid and Psyche*, Cambridge.

Moreschini, C. (1994) *Il Mito di Amore e Psiche in Apuleio*, Napoli.

Plato Latinus. Edidit R. Klibansky, volumen IV: *Timaeus a Chalcidio translatus commentarioque instructus*, in societatem operis coniuncto P. J. Jensen edidit J.H. Waszink, editio altera, Londini et Leidae 1975.

Schlam, C.C. (1976) *Cupid and Psyche: Apuleius and the Monuments*, University Park, PA.

Shanzer, D. (1986) *A Philosophical and Literary Commentary on Martianus Capella's De Nuptiis Philologiae et Mercurii Book I*, Berkeley/Los Angeles/London.

Walsh, P.G. (1970) *The Roman Novel*, London: Cambridge University Press.

14

APOLLONIUS OF TYRE IN THE MIDDLE AGES AND THE RENAISSANCE

Elizabeth Archibald

It is now widely accepted that the *Historia Apollonii*, which in its present form dates from the late fifth or early sixth century, is derived from a longer Greek original composed perhaps in the early third century AD; but no fragments of text or allusions survive to bear witness to the existence and reception of the story in the classical period.[1] The classical source is a shadowy ghost, which paradoxically precedes the flesh and blood *HA*: the popularity of the story throughout the Middle Ages and into the Renaissance is attested by abundant evidence, in the form of both texts (copies, translations and adapations) and allusions. Ben Jonson famously dismissed it as 'a mouldy tale': it was certainly old by his time, but still very much to the public taste. His reaction seems to have been a case of sour grapes; he was irritated by the success of Shakespeare's version of the story, *Pericles*, in contrast to the hostile reception of his own play about family separation and reunion, *The New Inn*.[2] *Pericles* begins with a speech by Gower (author of an earlier version of the story), who acts as Chorus: he calls the tale of Apollonius 'a song that old was sung', and one that offers more than mere entertainment value:

> It has been sung at festivals,
> On ember-eves and holidays,
> And lords and ladies in their lives
> Have read it for restoratives.
> The purchase is to make men glorious,
> *Et bonum quo antiquius eo melius.*
> [a good thing improves with age]
> (*Pericles* I Chorus 5–10)

By the time that Shakespeare was writing, the story was extremely well known all over Europe. Versions of the Latin text continued to be produced throughout the Middle Ages, and were among the first fictional texts to be printed; and the story was translated or adapted in almost every European vernacular. I shall deal first with the Latin tradition and then with the vernacular, treating each group more or less chronologically.[3]

The oldest extant manuscripts of *HA* date from the ninth century, but there are earlier references to manuscripts now lost; and casual allusions in a poem by Venantius Fortunatus, in a guide to the Holy Land by Theodosius, and in a treatise on grammar indicate that educated readers in the sixth and seventh centuries were expected to be familiar with the story of Apollonius. These readers included both the clergy and the laity: an eighth-century French abbot included a copy of *HA* among the theological books he bequeathed to his monastery library, and a ninth-century Italian marquis left a copy to his daughter. *HA* survives in six manuscripts produced before the twelfth century. In the tenth century some erudite scholar composed the *Gesta Apollonii*, an elaborate verse rendering of the first eight chapters of *HA* including some very obscure Grecisms to show off his linguistic skills. A short abstract or *Compendium* survives in a manuscript from the eleventh century (and also in one from the fifteenth). A fragment of three and a half leaves written in the tenth or eleventh century (Budapest, Országos Széchényi Könyvtár lat. 4) contains a remarkable series of thirty-five pen and ink illustrations; illustrated fictional narratives from this period are very rare, so this manuscript bears witness to the distinctive status of *HA* in the early Middle Ages. Evidence of a different kind is provided by an allusion in the late eleventh-century Italian *Chronicon Novaliciense*: describing the shocking behaviour of King Ugo of Lotharingia, who seduced his virgin daughter-in-law and was subsequently struck by a thunderbolt, the chronicler compares the incestuous Ugo with the fictional Antiochus, '*ut in Acta legitur Apollonii*' ('as we read in the story of Apollonius').

But it was in the twelfth and thirteenth centuries, a time of increasing stability, prosperity and literacy in western Europe, that the story began to circulate much more widely, in Latin and also in the rapidly developing vernaculars. Kortekaas (1984: 15–22) lists at least thirty-nine extant manuscripts of *HA* which were produced in the twelfth and thirteenth centuries. They include the two basic forms of the standard text known as RA and RB, variant versions (Rα and Rβ), and mixtures of the two main forms (RC). Freer versions were also produced: Godfrey of Viterbo included an idiosyncratic one in his *Pantheon*, a world history in verse written between 1186 and 1191 (he situates the story between the time of Alexander and the wars of the Maccabees).[4] Allusions to Apollonius occur in a wide range of texts at this time. Several writers mention *HA* as an example of an improving text with significant moral value. For instance Geoffrey de Vigeois in the preface to his *Chronicon Lemovicense* remarks that although *HA* is a shocking story, nevertheless it contains a moral for the pious Christian; he invokes the classical proverb that gold can be found even in a dungheap ('*in sterquilinio aurum*'). *HA* may have acquired a new appeal in the age of the Crusades, when cities with strong biblical associations like Tyre became significant in European politics; in the twelfth and thirteenth centuries several crusade chronicles mention Apollonius as a famous inhabitant of Tyre, as do travel guides describing the Holy Land.

In the age of the so-called 'rise of romance' one would also expect some interest in *HA* as a love story, in Latin as well as the vernaculars (see below). In the short lyric '*O Antioche, cur decipis me?*' preserved in the early thirteenth-century *Carmina Burana* collection, the first five stanzas are a first-person description by Apollonius (unnamed) of his adventures up to the fostering of Tarsia, with much emphasis on his shift from woe to joy: '*doleo . . . lugeo . . . doceo . . . amo . . . gaudeo*!' (I grieve . . . I mourn . . . I teach . . . I love . . . I rejoice!). The rest of the story is telescoped into the remaining five stanzas of the poem (all the recognition scenes at the end are reduced to a single stanza). This poem would have been incomprehensible to anyone not already familiar with the story of Apollonius; since many of the proper names are garbled, it was probably derived from versions at several removes from *HA* (possibly orally transmitted).

In the fourteenth century *HA* was included in at least one text of the very influential *Gesta Romanorum*, a collection of exemplary tales drawn from both classical and medieval sources which circulated very widely in Latin and was also translated into many European languages. According to Oesterley, the Apollonius story appears in only one of the hundreds of manuscripts of the *Gesta Romanorum* (though it is found in most of the vernacular translations – see below). The rubric in this manuscript mentions only Antiochus and his incest, yet the story is told in full. The rubric printed by Oesterley presents the story as an example of temporal tribulation; but although the other stories in the collection are all given Christian moralizations at the end, the Apollonius story alone has no such didactic epilogue. Apparently the Christian value of the story was thought to be self-evident, though in fact the traditional story is hardly Christianized here at all.

When printing was invented in the second half of the fifteenth century, *HA* was an early choice for the new technology – a further tribute to its lasting popularity. An undated Latin edition was produced about 1470, and more Latin and vernacular versions soon followed (see below). It was also printed as part of larger collections, in the 1475 edition of the *Gesta Romanorum*, and later in the 1559 edition of Godfrey's *Pantheon*. One of the most innovative versions of the story appeared in a printed edition in 1578: Jacob Falckenburg's *Britannia, sive de Apollonica Humilitatis Virtutis et Honoris Porta*. Here the story of the fictional Apollonius is ingeniously intertwined with that of the biblical Apollonius, son of Menestheus, who appears in *Maccabees* (this connection was not made by earlier writers, to my knowledge). But the standard *HA* text was not forgotten. It was copied in manuscript as late as the sixteenth century, and in 1595 Markward Welser produced the first critical edition with introductory comments, based on a text which he found in a monastery in Augsburg (now lost). Like Geoffrey de Vigeois so many centuries earlier, he used the metaphor of gold in the dungheap to defend the value of the story, though he admitted that the plot was absurd and the style barbarous. He also argued from details of vocabulary and style that the original text must have been in Greek, though he believed that the author was a Christian.

As for the vernacular tradition, the earliest representative is the Old English version of *HA* preserved in an eleventh-century manuscript, though perhaps composed about the year 1000. It has been suggested that *HA* was translated into Old English because of its similarity to the Wonders of the East texts popular at the time, but Raith has argued persuasively that its appeal is more likely to have been its similarity to the theme of exiled wanderers popular both in secular and hagiographic texts in Anglo-Saxon England (Raith 1956: 49ff.). It is noteworthy that in the Old English version no attempt is made to Christianize the story; the author struggled with the unfamiliar details of the gymnasium scene (the oiling and massage become a game with a hoop!), and omitted the lovesickness of the princess and Tarsia's experiences in the brothel.

Although no other vernacular version of *HA* from before the thirteenth century survives, there was probably a flourishing oral tradition by the later twelfth century, and as we have seen, the story was circulating widely in Latin. Apollonius's name crops up frequently in troubadour lyrics and in early romances as a well-known hero in the world of love and adventure, whose story should be in the repertoire of jongleurs and lovers; little detail is given in these allusions, indicating that the audience is expected to be quite familiar with the plot – Apollonius is sometimes mentioned in the same breath as Tristan. In the Occitan romance *Flamenca* (*c.* 1260), the story of Apollonius is mentioned as part of the courtly entertainment (here and in numerous other allusions it is associated with the Alexander legend). In didactic texts, it is sometimes mentioned disapprovingly, as a frivolous waste of time compared with a good sermon or moral tale.

Part of the appeal of the story no doubt came from its flexibility: it could be interpreted as a courtly romance, or as a moral exemplum. Vernacular adaptations from the later Middle Ages illustrate both these approaches. There is no complete French version earlier than the fourteenth century, but a thirteenth-century fragment (ed. Lewis 1915: 272–3) suggests a courtly version emphasizing love, and this description certainly fits two slightly later French versions, the fourteenth-century Brussels Redaction (ed. Lewis 1915: 46–147) and the fifteenth-century Vienna Redaction (ed. Zink 1982), both of which considerably expand the parts of *HA* dealing with love and war. The fourteenth-century German poet Heinrich von Neustadt borrowed episodes from Wolfram von Eschenbach's *Parzival* for his twenty-thousand-line version, *Apollonius von Tyrland*, which includes battles against Gog and Magog, and three marriages for Apollonius (one to a black queen who bears him a parti-coloured son, an incident borrowed from the history of Parzival's father), before the story returns to the conventional *HA* ending. On the other hand, the moralizing aspects of the story are heavily stressed in the Spanish *Libro de Apolonio* (thirteenth-century), in John Gower's version in his *Confessio Amantis* (VIII: 271–2008 – the last, and longest, exemplum in his collection, which was later translated into Portuguese), and in the fifteenth-century Greek *Diegesis polupathous Apolloniou tou Turou*.

Many other vernacular versions were produced, in French, German, Italian, Greek, Czech, and Hungarian, which did not vary enormously from the traditional story, though some include details derived from folklore or the Bible. Many writers seem to have had difficulty with classical elements in the plot, notably the gymnasium scene, which was sometimes replaced by more typically medieval courtly activities. Classical details were systematically removed in the French prose version of Garbin (printed 1482), but they were retained, and indeed more were added, in the later versions of Corrozet (1530) and Belleforest (1582); as one might expect, interest in the classical context reappeared in the Renaissance. One or two writers attempted to iron out some major problems in the plot, notably Timoneda in the version in his *Patrañuelo* (1576); he ties up loose ends and thriftily doubles up some of the minor characters. Allusions to the story are found in a wide range of vernacular texts, including romances, saints' lives, and chronicles, and it appears in manuscripts in similarly mixed company.

Vernacular versions of *HA* appeared very early in the history of printing: Steinhöwel's German version was printed in 1471 (and frequently reprinted), and the story appears in vernacular editions of the *Gesta Romanorum* in Dutch, French and Polish. Many other versions were printed individually in the late fifteenth century and throughout the sixteenth century. *HA* certainly had a long history, as Shakespeare makes his Chorus remark in *Pericles*; its appearance in so many collections of popular stories, from the *Gesta Romanorum* to Belleforest's *Histoires Tragiques*, indicates that Jonson was quite wrong in thinking it stale. Although there are few surviving English texts from the Middle Ages (apart from the Old English version and Gower's tale, there is only a late fourteenth-century fragment), there is ample evidence for the popularity of the story in England in the early Renaissance. Latin and French printed versions would have been available, as well as Copland's *The Romance of Kynge Apollyn of Thyre* (1510 – a translation of Garbin's French version) and Laurence Twine's *The Patterne of Painefull Adventure* (c. 1576). The Shakespearean dramatization *Pericles* was clearly a success: the quarto was printed six times between 1609 and 1635, and a prose rendering was published in 1608 by George Wilkins.[5] The change of the hero's name from Apollonius to Pericles may have been due to the exigencies of metre (in *Coriolanus*, for instance, the hero's full five-syllable name is rarely used); there are precedents in earlier French versions of the story for Apollonius assuming the name Perillie, or being referred to as 'le perilliers de mer' ('he who has been endangered/wrecked at sea'), in reference to his misadventures (Archibald 1991: 215). But the name Pericles also conveys a certain classical *gravitas* which cannot have been lost on the Elizabethan audience. Throughout the play there is an emphasis on the theme of kingship; this is of course present in the standard *HA* narrative, which involves so many kings and compares their behaviour. But in *Pericles* this theme is strongly emphasized – as in many of Shakespeare's other plays. One might also argue that a story involving so many pairs of fathers and daughters would have appealed to Shakespeare, since this theme is present in so many of his plays, and especially in the so-called romances of his final period (see Archibald 1989a).

We can only speculate about the reasons for the remarkable survival and evergreen popularity of *HA*; the other ancient romances or novels were unknown in the medieval West, and resurfaced only in the Renaissance.[6] Why was this 'mouldy tale', with its manifold illogicalities and its shocking opening scene of father–daughter incest, so popular? At one level it is a quintessential romantic adventure story, involving such hardy perennials as a falsely accused hero, shipwreck, a lovesick princess, a wicked fostermother, pirates, an ordeal in a brothel for an innocent heroine, and a satisfying series of recognitions and reunions for the finale; there are clear parallels with the classical romances, and with medieval ones too (see Frye 1976). But the story could also be read at a more serious level, and clearly was. *HA* includes references to an unspecified but potentially Christian '*deus*' ('god'); Antiochus is killed by '*dei fulmine*' (c. 24: 'god's thunderbolt'), and at the end Apollonius is directed to Ephesus and reunion with his wife by a vision of '*quendam angelico habitu*' (c. 48: 'someone who looked like an angel'). Some medieval versions, as we have seen, were heavily Christianized, though by no means all; Fortune is a more pervasive force than the Christian God. The story is clearly presented as an exemplum in the *Gesta Romanorum*, and even more explicitly in Gower's *Confessio Amantis*. Apollonius becomes an Everyman figure, undeservedly buffeted by Fortune, who resists a variety of temptations to vice; his virtue is finally rewarded in the happy ending (he is compared with Job in several versions, both Latin and vernacular (Archibald 1991: 93)). The flexibility of this story of 'temporal tribulation' constructed out of archetypal adventure story themes seems to provide at least part of the explanation for its remarkable popularity all over Europe for more than a thousand years.[7] But no doubt the incest theme also contributed to its success. In the later Middle Ages this theme was much used in cautionary tales, where it was the supreme example of a monstrous sin which could be expiated by contrition and divine grace, or punished by divine retribution; near-miss incest is also an important catalyst for the adventures of the protagonist in a wide range of romances (see Archibald 1989b). *HA* seems to have been well ahead of the fashion for this literary theme, which first becomes noticeable in twelfth-century texts. It is striking that although moral writers were shocked by the initial incest episode, no medieval or

Renaissance version omits it. It is crucial to the symmetry of the story and to the happy ending, as is made clear in Gower's summary at the end of *Pericles*:

> In Antiochus and his daughter you have heard
> Of monstrous lust the due and just reward.
> In Pericles, his queen and daughter, seen,
> Although assail'd with fortune fierce and keen,
> Virtue preserv'd from fell destruction's blast,
> Led on by heaven, and crown'd with joy at last.
> (*Pericles* V. iii. 85–90)

Notes

1 See the comments of G.A.A. Kortekaas, the pre-eminent *Apollonius* scholar, in the introduction to his magisterial edition (1984: 97–120). For other views, see Schmeling 1996: 529 ff. and Chapter 9 of this volume. The *Historia* will be cited hereafter as *HA*. Bibliographical details of primary texts are listed by author, or if anonymous by title, under 'Editions' (in cases where there is no standard title, they are cited by editor).

2 Jonson, 'On *The New Inn*: Ode to Himself', 11. 21–30. There is considerable debate about the authorship of *Pericles*; as no one doubts that Shakespeare had a hand in it, I treat him here as the author, though he may have had at least one co-author.

3 There are so many versions of the story and allusions to it that it is impossible to consider them all individually here. For more detailed discussion see Archibald (1991); the Latin and vernacular texts are discussed in Appendix I, and all the allusions known to me are printed (with translations) in Appendix II. See also the earlier studies of Klebs (1889), Singer (1895), and Smyth (1898).

4 The *Cronica de Apollonio* is omitted from the edition of the *Pantheon* in *Monumenta 'Germaniae Historica'*, *Scriptores* XXIII; but it is printed by Singer, 1895: 150–77.

5 There is much debate about the relationship between play and novel: although Wilkins' version does not follow the play as we know it in all respects, it uses the same names for all the characters. For further discussion and bibliography see editions of *Pericles*, and Archibald 1991: 211–13.

6 See Gesner 1970, Hägg 1983, and R.H.F. Carver, Chapter 16 of this volume.

7 The same could be said for the stories of Alexander and Arthur, both enormously popular in the Middle Ages, and both reworked with varying emphasis, sometimes as moral examples, sometimes as pure entertainment. For Alexander see R. Stoneman in this volume, Chapter 15.

Bibliography

Editions

Archibald, Elizabeth (ed. and trans. 1991), *Apollonius of Tyre: Medieval and Renaissance Themes and Variations*, Cambridge: D.S. Brewer, pp. 109–81.

Belleforest, François de, *Histoires Tragiques*, Rouen, 1603–4, vol. VII, pp. 109–206.

Carmina Burana, eds A. Hilka and O. Schumann, 2 vols, in 3 parts, Heidelberg: Winter, 1941, vol. I. 2, pp. 125–8.
Chronicon Novaliciense, ed. C. Cipolla in *Monumenta Novaliciensia vetustiora*, 2 vols. Rome: Forzani, 1898–1901, vol. II, pp. 5–305.
Copland, Robert, *The Romance of Kynge Apollyn of Thyre*, facsimile, ed. Edward Ashbee, London: Roxburgh Club, 1870.
Diegesis polupathous Apollonious tou Turou, ed. A.A. Janssen, as *Narratio neograeca Apollonii Tyrii*, Grave: Verhaak, 1954.
Falckenburgh, Jacob, *Britannia, sive de Apollonica humilitatis, virtutis et honoris porta*, London, 1578.
Flamenca, ed. Ulrich Gschwind, 2 vols, Berne: Francke, 1976.
Garbin, Louis, *Le romant de Apollin roy de Thir*, Geneva, *c.* 1482.
Geoffrey de Vigeois, *Chronicon Lemovicense*, ed. P. Labbé, in *Nova bibliotheca manuscriptorum*, 2 vols, Paris, 1657, vol. II, pp. 279–342.
Gesta Apollonii, ed. E. Dümmler in *Monumenta Germaniae Historica*, *Poetae Latini Aevi Carolini*, 4 vols, Berlin: Weidmann, 1884, vol. II, pp. 483–506.
Gesta Romanorum, ed. H. Oesterley, Berlin: Weidmann, 1872, pp. 510–32.
Godfrey of Viterbo, *Cronica de Apollonio*, ed. S. Singer (1895), pp. 150–77.
Gower, John, *Confessio Amantis*, ed. G.C. Macaulay, 4 vols, Oxford: Oxford University Press, 1899–1902, vol. IV, pp. 386–440.
Heinrich von Neustadt, *Apollonius von Tyrland*, ed. S. Singer, Berlin: Weidmann, 1906, pp. 3–328.
Historia Apollonii, ed. G.A.A. Kortekaas, Groningen: Bouma's Boekhuis, 1984.
Lewis, Charles B. (ed.) 'Die altfranzösischen Prosaversionen des Apollonius-Romans', *Romanische Forschungen* 34 (1915): 1–277. [Old French fragment and Brussels Redaction]
Libro de Apolonio, ed. M. Alvar, 3 vols, Madrid: Fundaciōn Juan March, 1976.
The Old English Apollonius of Tyre, ed. P. Goolden, London: Oxford University Press, 1958.
Raith, Josef, *Die alt-und mittelenglischen Apollonius-Bruchstücke mit dem Text der* Historia Apollonii *nach der englischen Handschriftengruppe*, Munich: Huber, 1956.
Shakespeare, William, *Pericles Prince of Tyre*, ed. F.D. Hoeniger, Arden edn., London: Methuen, 1963.
Twine, Lawrence, *The Patterne of Painefull Adventures*, ed. G. Bullough in *Narrative and Dramatic Sources of Shakespeare* VI, London: Routledge and Kegan Paul, 1966, pp. 432–82.
Wilkins, George, *The Painefull Adventures of Pericles Prince of Tyre*, ed. G. Bullough in *Narrative and Dramatic Sources of Shakespeare* VI, London: Routledge and Kegan Paul, 1966, pp. 492–548.
Zink, M. (ed.) (1982) *Le roman d'Apollonius de Tyr*, Paris: Union générale d'editions [Vienna Redaction].

Secondary literature

Archibald, Elizabeth (1989a) 'Fathers and Kings in *Apollonius of Tyre*', in M.M. Mackenzie and C. Roueché (eds), *Images of Authority: Papers presented to Joyce Reynolds*, Cambridge: Cambridge Philological Society, Supplementary Volume no. 16, pp. 24–40.

—— (1989b) 'Incest in Medieval Literature and Society', *Forum for Modern Language Studies* 25: 1–15.

—— (1990) 'Apollonius of Tyre in Vernacular Literature: Romance or *Exemplum?*', in H. Hofmann (ed.), *Groningen Colloquia on the Novel*, vol. III, Groningen: Egbert Forsten, pp. 123–37.

—— (ed. and trans.) (1991) *Apollonius of Tyre: Medieval and Renaissance Themes and Variations*, Cambridge: D.S. Brewer.

Frye, N. (1976) *The Secular Scripture*, Cambridge, MA: Harvard University Press.

Gesner, Carol (1970) *Shakespeare and the Greek Romances*, Lexington: University Press of Kentucky.

Hägg, T. (1983) *The Novel in Antiquity*, Oxford: Blackwell.

Klebs, E. (1889) *Die Erzählung von Apollonius aus Tyrus: eine geschichtliche Untersuchung über ihre lateinische Urform und ihre späteren Bearbeitungen*, Berlin: Reimer.

Kortekaas, G.A.A. (ed.) (1984) *Historia Apollonii Regis Tyri*, Groningen: Bouma's Boekhuis.

—— (1990) 'The Latin Adaptations of the *Historia Apollonii regis Tyri* in the Middle Ages and the Renaissance', in H. Hofmann (ed.) *Groningen Colloquia on the Novel*, vol. III, Groningen: Egbert Forsten, pp. 103–22.

Schmeling, G. (1996) '*Historia Apollonii regis Tyri*', in G. Schmeling (ed.) *The Novel in the Ancient World* (*Mnemosyne*, Supplement 159), Leiden: E. J. Brill, pp. 517–51.

Singer, S. (1895) *Apollonius von Tyrus: Untersuchung über das Fortleben des antiken Romans in späteren Zeiten*, Halle: Niemeyer.

Smyth, A.H. (1898) *Shakespeare's Pericles and Apollonius of Tyre*, Philadelphia: MacCalla.

15

THE MEDIEVAL ALEXANDER

Richard Stoneman

I The *Historia de Preliis*

The root of the medieval romance tradition about Alexander is a single manuscript, written in South Italy about the year 1000 and now held in the Staatliche Bibliothek in Bamberg (E.iii.14). This contains a number of works in Latin – the *Letter of Alexander to Aristotle about India* (of which an earlier Latin translation from the Greek had been made before 700); the *Commonitorium Palladii*, a brief account of the life of the Brahmans, translated from a Greek text which also became interpolated in the A-recension of the *Alexander Romance*; the *Collatio Alexandri cum Dindimo* or exchange of letters between Alexander and the Brahman king, not otherwise known in Greek; and, most importantly, a version of a translation of the Greek *Alexander Romance* made a few years previously by Leo the Archpriest.

Leo was in the service of Duke John III of Naples, of whom Domenico Comparetti wrote

> It is not without surprise that, in the gloom of the tenth century, we encounter in this medieval Naples, of which we know so little, a duke such as John III, who, full of noble instincts, appears, like a miniature Charlemagne, as the patron of letters, and even Greek, collecting together from every place, even from Constantinople, works both sacred and secular in both languages.
>
> (Comparetti 1895: 283)

One of John's chief agents was Leo who, as he tells us in the preface to his translation, was sent to Constantinople for the specific purpose of collecting Greek manuscripts, and when he returned, translated some of them into Latin. Among these was the *Alexander Romance*. It is plain that the late antique translation by Julius Valerius was unknown in tenth century Naples. Like Julius', Leo's translation was made from an α-version of the Greek (Stoneman 1996). The manuscript we have is not Leo's original but it is close to it. It follows the Greek original faithfully in an approachable Latin with the characteristics of the period (simple syntax, vocabulary derived from the Vulgate – *concupiscentia* – or from contemporary speech – *caballus* for *equus* – and other features). It is notable that Leo in his prologue stresses the value of a knowledge of pre-Christian history, a view which at John's court surely needed no defending, though it might have been problematic in the later fourth century (see my Chapter 11, this volume).

Leo's translation, unlike Julius', spawned an immense progeny. Another partial copy of the manuscript survives, in Lambeth Palace; but of far greater importance is the succession of reworkings known collectively as the *Historia de Preliis*, the History of Alexander's Battles [see Pritchard 1992 (Introduction); Stoneman 1996]. There are three major recensions, and each in turn had its impact on contemporary and later writing in parallel genres. The first recension (known as J^1) was made in the eleventh century, and incorporates elements known to us from the later recensions of the Greek text; so its compiler must have been working not only with Leo's text but with at least one other Greek text. This text was not any of the Greek recensions known to us but was closer to the lost recension, δ*, whose content is known to us from the Syriac translation. Characteristic of this recension are episodes such as Alexander's visit to Jerusalem, his ascent in the basket borne by eagles and his descent in the diving bell, and the episode with the prophetic trees. This recension also incorporates the correspondence with the Brahman king Dindimus, which was in the Bamberg MS, with some additions and alterations.

J^2 was composed in the twelfth century and is sometimes known as the Orosius-recension because it incorporates a number of episodes drawn from the *Historiae adversum paganos* (AD 417) of Orosius, a friend of Augustine. It also includes material from the overtly Judaeo-Christian recension, γ, namely the enclosure of Gog and Magog, but it omits the stories of Alexander's ascent and descent. This is the more surprising since the ascent was one of the most popular themes of medieval cathedral art and architecture and is known from a wide variety of locations: it seems to have represented at one and the same time a type of Christ's ascension and an allegory of man's overweening pride (Settis-Frugoni 1973; Schmidt 1995).

J^3 is of the twelfth or early thirteenth century and expands the earlier version of J^2 without adding any new material. It is of particular interest as the direct source of a long epic poem in Latin elegiac distichs by Quilichinus of Spoleto, which appeared in 1236 (Kirsch 1971). Quilichinus, a jurist associated with the court of Frederick II (1194–1250), may have had an eye on his monarch's ambitions to rule east and west in choosing to compose this long and fluent epic. It became an admired work, and was soon translated into Italian by Domenico Scolari (the MS is dated to 1355), a younger contemporary of Dante's, and into Middle High German by an unknown Bavarian poet (completed in 1397).

This literary tradition might in itself seem long and impressive enough, for the story of a heathen king of the fourth century BC; but in describing the succession of the texts of the *Historia de Preliis* we do no more than scratch the surface of the impact of Alexander on the Middle Ages. In the three centuries from 1100 when vernacular literature was being composed, the *Historia de Preliis* was translated more times than any other text except the Gospels. The ground had been prepared for this extraordinary valuation of the legend of Alexander not just by the Romance tradition, but by his gradual incorporation into chronicles, into Biblical scholarship, and into geography and cartography. This process took place in the Latin literature of the tenth to thirteenth centuries. The subject of this chapter is not the vernacular texts, but it will help to understand the impact of the Latin texts if we note the point at which each began to develop an independent life in a vernacular language. The beginning of this development takes us back to the Bamberg MS.

The *Letter of Alexander to Aristotle about India* was, perhaps not surprisingly, the earliest work to catch the eye of a vernacular translator. It was translated already in the tenth century into Old English; it is incorporated in the unique codex which also contains *Beowulf*, the *Marvels of the East*, and the story of St Christopher. It seems that whoever commissioned this manuscript had a particular interest in monsters, since this is the one feature which all these texts have in common! The author of *Beowulf* drew on these Grand-Guignol inventions as well as German ideas to create something far more profound in his conceptions of Grendel and of the dragon (Niles 1991: 139).

At about the same time the first full-blown vernacular *Alexander Romance* was composed, in Irish.[1] This contains a full range of episodes including the visit to Jerusalem, the talking trees, and the encounter with Dindimus; the author explicitly refers among his sources to Orosius and Josephus (whose *Antiquitates Judaicae* had been translated into Latin in the circle of Cassiodorus in the sixth century) (Berschin 1988: 78, 302, nn. 25–26).

Around 1100 two continental vernacular works also appeared; the first was the now-largely-lost Alexander poem of Alberic of Besançon, which was the main source of the *Alexanderlied* of Pfaffe Lamprecht (1125). Alberic used the fifth century *Epitome* of Julius Valerius. The second work was the *Chronicle* of Frutolf of Michelsberg which uses the version of the Romance made by Leo. Frutolf's work was revised and continued by Ekkehart of Aura,[2] and it seems to have been a combination of his work with the second recension of the *Historia de Preliis* that supplied most of the lore that goes up to make the *Letter of Prester John* (Slessarev 1959; Silverberg 1972; Marshall 1993: 118–41), that extraordinary document which persuaded half Europe of the existence of a mythical Christian king somewhere in Ethiopia; embassies were even sent to him for help against the Mongols.

The early date at which these texts were translated into the languages of the British Isles is remarkable; and in the case of the Irish Romance, it is useful to observe which classical sources are already being cited for the full history of Alexander. As we shall see in considering the Latin texts of the twelfth to fourteenth centuries, it was regularly the aim of the authors to blend information from the Romance tradition and from Orosius, Josephus and the chronographer Eusebius.

It is also striking that Quintus Curtius Rufus does not feature at all at this stage of the development of the Alexander legends. Curtius springs suddenly to our attention with the appearance of Walter of Chatillon's *Alexandreis* in the 1170s: this Latin hexameter epic is a versification of Curtius' history, but it is extensively epicized, with a full divine apparatus involved in the action and a long description of Hell in book X. The 'Christian' figure of Lucifer is as prominent as the pagan gods and the Virgilian personifications of such figures as Treachery and Slander – not to mention the Seven Deadly Sins. At X. 348 ff. the narrator in Walter's poem asks 'For what crime, O gods, did Alexander forfeit your favour in such a brief life, when he had been marked out beforehand by so many prodigies?' The passage signals a recurrence of the old 'philosophical' approach which stressed Alexander's corruption by Fortune (see my Chapter 11, this volume); the idea is out of key with the development of the medieval conception of Alexander, though it appealed to the Renaissance (McKendrick 1996).

Walter's poem was in turn the model for the very extensive treatments by two German authors, Rudolf von Ems (1220–54) and Ulrich von Eschenbach (1270), as well as for the Spanish *Libro de Alexandre* of the thirteenth century (though this last incorporated some material from the *Alexander Romance* as well).

II Peter Comestor

The first important step in naturalizing Alexander within the Christian scheme of things was taken by the twelfth century Latin writer Peter Comestor, who was Dean of Troyes from 1147–64 and died about 1179 (see Smalley 1952; Daly 1957). Comestor's *Historia Scholastica* is a complete account of sacred history from the Creation to the end of the Book of Acts. It is essentially a re-telling of the Biblical narrative as a consecutive history. Peter draws on a wide range of learning (much of it mediated through Jerome) to provide an account of the Biblical events in a fuller framework of secular history. His account of Alexander follows his summaries of the stories of Ezekiel, Daniel, Judith and Esther. The history of Esther is set in the reign of Artaxerxes, who, Comestor notes, also banished a number of the tribes of the Jews to a place near the Caspian Sea. A war of the Romans and Gauls is also noted, as is the death of Plato, and then with the accession of Darius there is the beginning of the story of Sanballat's secession from the Temple in Jerusalem, from Josephus. This story concluded, the story of Manlius Torquatus' execution of his son is noted; and then begins the story of Alexander.

The narrative opens with Alexander's birth as son of Nectanebo (Notanabus) and his adoption by Philip. The next event is his invasion of Darius' empire in order to conquer Syria. This leads immediately to continuation of the story of Sanballat (whom Comestor calls Saraballa) and his construction of the rival temple on Mt Gerizim, with Alexander's blessing. Then follows the story of Alexander's visit to Jerusalem and his homage to the High Priest. Comestor skims over (*nos sub silentio pertransimus*) the conquest of Porus, the visit to the Trees of the Sun and Moon and *caetera admiratione digna* which are included in the *Letter about India*, in order to reach *ea quae circa populum Dei gesta sunt*. The next section is concerned with the embassies from the Ten Tribes of Israel who have been enclosed behind the Caspian Gates; but Alexander only shuts them in more firmly, with God's help, and announces that they will only re-emerge at the end of the world. Alexander's death is briefly dealt with, and the successor kingdoms are then enumerated, as a lead-in to the story of Maccabees, followed by the Gospels and Acts, where Comestor ends.

Comestor's major source for this account is the second recension of the *Historia de Preliis*, from which he selects the episodes that are of particular interest to him. It does not seem that he drew directly on any other sources, except in one enigmatic detail. The story of the enclosure of the peoples behind the Caspian Gates originated in a seventh century apocalypse by an author known as Pseudo-Methodius, and was incorporated into the later recensions of the Greek Romance (Lolos 1976; Aerts abd Kortekaas 1998). However, in this work it is the Unclean Nations of Gog and Magog who are so enclosed, and who it is said will re-emerge at the end of time. Comestor has made these people the lost Ten Tribes of Israel, and has introduced them by his earlier mention of their expulsion by Artaxerxes, which is not mentioned at this point in the narrative of Josephus (*Antiquitates Judaicae*, xi.297–300). For Josephus (*Bellum Judaicum*, vii.7) these people were identified with the Alans, and for Jerome (*Ep.* 94) they were the Huns. The connection of the Ten Tribes of Israel with the enclosed nations seems to go back to the Apocryphal Book IV Ezra (13.40ff.), but is not found in any medieval author earlier than Comestor. Comestor is thus responsible for an important development in the figure of Alexander as a part of sacred history.[3]

More generally, Comestor's work is the first to take the Romance tradition about Alexander and to treat it as a part of world history. Its origins as a romantic tale forgotten, the Alexander material begins to become something much more pregnant, one of the culture myths of the Middle Ages.

III Godfrey of Viterbo

A very similar treatment of Alexander is found in the *Pantheon* of Godfrey of Viterbo (*c.* 1125–*c.* 1196), a cleric who was employed at the court of Frederick Barbarossa (1152–90) and, later, Henry VI (1190–98) (Mulder-Bakker 1983:

183–240). His *Pantheon* is a world chronicle in Latin verse (in the unusual form of triplets consisting of two hexameters followed by a pentameter), with some prose passages (mostly excerpted from Otto of Freising). It covers the same ground as Comestor with the omission of some of the doctrinal discussions, but continues the story through Roman, Merovingian and Carolingian times to his own day. His treatment of the visit to Jerusalem is briefer than Comestor's, but he incorporates a full version of the *Letter to Aristotle* as well as the correspondence with Dindimus, and the visit to the Trees of the Sun and Moon. Godfrey takes over from Comestor the identification of Gog and Magog with the Lost Tribes of Israel: Alexander, by being brought into this relation, becomes a type of the 'Last Emperor', who will usher in the end of the world and the reign of Christ. (Mulder-Bakker 1983: 236 argues that Barbarossa may have seen himself as a forerunner of the Last Emperor.) Alexander, the instantiation of the problematic role of the world-ruler, stands between the evil of God and Magog and the ineffectuality of the Brahmans (see below) as an emblem of active virtue, and ideal king (Mulder-Bakker 1983: 238).

IV Vincent of Beauvais

This development of the figure of Alexander continues in the later successors of Comestor in world history writing, the first of whom is Vincent of Beauvais. Vincent (1190–1264) composed his *Speculum Historiale* ('Mirror of History') under the rule of Louis the Pious. It is much more extensive than Comestor's work; in fact it is more than three times as long as the Bible itself. It covers the history of the world from the creation, but includes not just Biblical history and Alexander, but the story of Troy, the history of Rome, and the more recent history of the Carolingians and the Crusades, as well as excursuses on the lives of saints and scholars.[4] It was designed as much for reference as for reading; it begins with a very full index of topics. The account of Alexander takes up the whole of Book 4 and follows the order of events in the *Alexander Romance* (including the jumbled geography of the campaigns in Asia Minor and Greece). Vincent also cites other sources, notably Josephus, Justin and Orosius, as well as Valerius Maximus. Keeping to a chronological framework, he interrupts the account of Alexander's early years with information about Plato and his influence (including Apuleius and Plotinus) and on Isocrates. Ch 31 is a digression headed '*De luxuria Alexandri et superbia*', indicating an adherence to the ancient philosophical judgment of Alexander's character; but this does not deeply inform the rest of the narrative.

Recent research has indicated that an important source for Vincent in general was the obscure writer Hélinand of Froidmont (Bunt 1982), but Vincent is more than a copyist. While reproducing sources *in extenso*, he has also aimed to weld them together into a coherent encyclopaedic history.

Vincent's influence was very considerable. The work was translated into French by Jean de Vigny (1322) and into Dutch (*c.* 1285) by Jacob van Maerlant (d. *c.* 1292–1300). In his *Spiegel Historiael* Maerlant considerably abbreviates Vincent, turning the material into a more manageable narrative which might be read for pleasure rather than for reference. The case of Maerlant is instructive, since Maerlant's earliest work, *Alexanders Geesten* (*c.* 1260), was a free translation of Walter of Chatillon's *Alexandreis* and thus has a completely different historical content. Maerlant himself states that the narrative of the *Spiegel* is closer to history than the 'fables' of *Alexanders Geesten*. For example, in the latter work Antipater is in league with the devil when he poisons Alexander; no such elaboration is present in the *Spiegel* (van Oostrom 1996: 336–7). This is an intriguing reversal of the modern evaluation of the respective historical merits of the Curtian tradition and that of the *Romance*!

V Ranulph Higden

The third of the great Latin chronicles which incorporates the Alexander story is the *Polychronicon* of Ranulph Higden. Higden (d. 1364) entered St Werburgh's Abbey in Chester in 1299 and composed his universal history in the 1320s. Like the other universal histories we have looked at, it began with the creation: the first five books took the narrative to the conversion of the emperor Constantine, and the last two books are devoted to British history (with special reliance on the work of Geoffrey of Monmouth: cf. Taylor 1966: 44).

Higden's coverage becomes very sketchy in his own century. The book as a whole is on a far larger scale than Comestor's and fills several volumes in its modern edition. It soon established itself as an authoritative history, and was translated into English not long after Higden's death by the Cornish scholar John Trevisa (in the 1380s).

As might be expected from its scale, Higden's history drew on many sources, not just one. Though John Taylor argued that his primary source for antiquity was Vincent of Beauvais, G.H.V. Bunt (1982) has made it clear that, besides abbreviating the frame narrative which he derived from Vincent, Higden also drew on many other sources, some of them contradicting Vincent's account. Higden himself cites a number of authorities including not only Comestor but ancient authors like Justin, Josephus, Pompeius Trogus and Eutropius. (As usual, Curtius Rufus is conspicuous by his absence.) In addition he includes some anecdotes from the philosophical tradition about Alexander, for example citing Valerius Maximus for the story of the man who asked Alexander for a penny and was given a city: when he protested that the gift was too great, Alexander replied that he had an eye not to what it was appropriate for the man to receive, but what it was appropriate for himself to give. Into the frame of the usual *Romance*-based narrative Higden also incorporates the correspondence with the Brahmans, and takes over from Comestor the identification of the enclosed nations with the lost tribes of Israel. More interestingly, he is the first chronicle author to include the story of the wonderstone, which had begun to circulate in Latin in the eleventh century (see section 7).

This is also the first of the chronicles to include the remarks of the philosophers gathered at the tomb of Alexander, who utter a series of apophthegms on the theme of the brevity of life and the transience of human achievement. This paragraph has a long ancestry: a work entitled 'Sayings of the Philosophers' was first composed in Syriac in the sixth century; a longer Arabic version was composed by Hunayn Ibn Ishaq (809–873) the distinguished scholar-translator, and a still longer one by al-Mubashshir ibn Fatiq (who also wrote a book about Alexander) around 1053. Hunayn's version was translated into Spanish under the title *Los buenos proverbios* before 1400. Mubashshir's work was translated into Spanish (the *Bocados de Oro*) in the late thirteenth century; it also entered the *Disciplina Clericalis* of the twelfth century author Petrus Alfonsi, and thence entered the third recension of the *Historia de Preliis* (Stoneman 1994: xii). This last was Higden's immediate source, but the development of the text is a striking example of the complex evolution of the medieval picture of Alexander.

VI The *History Bibles*

The chronicles in their turn became the major sources for the *History Bibles* which were produced in German, Dutch and Swedish in the early fifteenth century. Their coverage is very much the same as that of the universal chronicles, beginning from the creation and incorporating pieces of ancient history to fill out the continuous Biblical narrative; but of course they end with the last book of the Bible, Revelation, and do not cover later history. Of the historical insertions, the Alexander story is by far the largest. In many of the examples the Alexander story (and indeed the rest of the book) is plentifully illustrated with coloured miniatures. As a result, Alexander became an integral part of sacred history, and his story was made known, through the illustrations, even to those whose ability to read the vernacular (let alone Latin) was limited.[5]

VII The *Iter Alexandri Magni ad Paradisum*

The *Historia de Preliis* and the chronicles are two of the most comprehensive channels of Alexander lore into the Middle Ages; but there are also several other Latin works which were important in building up the picture of Alexander which was inherited by the High Middle Ages. I mentioned above the story of the wonderstone: this is the key episode of a work known as the *Iter Alexandri Magni ad Paradisum* ('Alexander the Great's Journey to Paradise').[6] Though it cannot be dated precisely, it was known to Pfaffe Lamprecht who incorporated it in his Middle High German Alexander poem of 1175, and it probably belongs to the eleventh century. However, its origins are much older. The second element of the story, the parable of the eye, is found in the Babylonian Talmud and thence in the Hebrew versions of the *Alexander Romance*. Who first translated it into Latin we have no idea; perhaps a Jew writing in Muslim Spain? The story describes how Alexander travelled to the east until he reached a city with high moss-covered walls, in which there was just one small window. When Alexander sent messengers with a request for submission, a man leant out from the window and gave the messengers a stone resembling an eye. The curious property of this stone was that, when it was placed in the pan of a balance, no amount of gold could outweigh it; but, if a little dust was sprinkled on it, even a feather would drag the opposite pan down. Eventually an old man (in some versions a Jew) in Alexander's entourage explains that the eye is the life of man, which as long as it lives is never satiated with acquisition; but once the dust of death covers it, it weighs as nothing. The parable is clearly directed at Alexander's insatiable desire for conquest and exploration; its universal applicability turns Alexander into an Everyman figure who represents a universal truth that was perhaps particularly emphasized by the Christian Church as the inheritor of Jewish wisdom.

The story of the journey to Paradise is an elaboration of the Jewish core of the story and is another element of Alexander's incorporation into the Christian world view. The medieval imagination pictured the world as a circle with Jerusalem in the centre and the Earthly Paradise in the Far East. Many examples are known of the T-O map (as it is called), which portrayed this geographical view, and they seem to go back to the map prepared by Agrippa for Augustus in the early years of the Christian Era.[7] One of the most familiar – though not the earliest – is the Hereford *Mappa Mundi* of about 1300. The *Mappa Mundi* seems to be a particularly (though not exclusively) English phenomenon; a well-known German map, the Ebstorf World Map, which was destroyed in the Second World War, closely follows the design of the Hereford map. It has been argued that the link is to be found in the person of Gervase of Tilbury (born in Essex in about 1160) (Hahn-Woernle 1987: 83–7). Gervase was the author of the *Otia Imperialia*, a book of interesting lore about the marvels of the earth, written for the Emperor Otto IV. He may be identical with Provost Gervase of the Monastery of Ebstorf and thus author of the map which incorporates the wonders which were associated with the Alexander tradition – and, in particular, the location of Paradise on the eastern rim of the world. If Paradise was indeed within the world (and most authorities stated that it was)[8] then it was to be expected that Alexander, who had reached the Land of the Brahmans, the most easterly point before Paradise, would at least have tried to go to Paradise too. The geographical views that the Middle Ages followed made it inevitable that this adventure would be added to Alexander's repertoire.

VIII Alexander and the Brahmans

The Indian sojourn was the spring, as we saw earlier, of two freestanding works about Alexander, both concentrating on his interview with the Brahman king Dindimus. There are three separate Latin translations of the Greek work by Palladius, 'On the Life of the Brahmans', one of which was included in the Bamberg MS. This was an abridgement of a longer version (the Vatican MS); a third, attributed to St Ambrose, is probably the work of a humanist (Wilmart 1933). This work describes the ideal existence of the Brahmans, their abstinence and vegetarianism, as a contrast to the acquisitive drive represented by Alexander. Much of it takes the form of a sermon delivered by Dindimus to Alexander, undeterred by the fact that Alexander apparently leaves the scene at paragraph 40!

The 'Correspondence of Alexander and Dindimus', which is preserved in Latin only, cannot be dated, though it was known to Alcuin who sent a copy to Charlemagne in the eighth century. It is based on the same general picture of the life of the Brahmans, but takes the form of an alternating presentation of two opposed forms of life, a kind of early Allegro and Penseroso. Unusually for a text of the kind, Alexander not only has the last word but seems to win part of the argument: one of his last remarks is 'I insist that your life is not blessedness but punishment', and this is nowhere gainsaid. The relatively complex moral sensibility thus expressed by the author of this work makes it in some ways a better aid to thought than the sermonizing of Dindimus; it obviously struck a chord for it was regularly translated, the latest new version being a chapbook of 1683.[9] As noted above, it was incorporated in the *Historia de Preliis* from the second recension onwards; it was thus included in Quilichinus' Latin poem and also in the longer chronicle versions of Vincent (out of narrative sequence, after Alexander's death) and of Higden (in its proper position in the narrative). This debate between the active and contemplative lives, which might seem an excellent expression of the dilemma of a Christianity which honoured both the monastic life and the career of a crusader, gave Alexander something of an edge as in effect a warrior for Christ (which he clearly became in the French *Roman d'Alexandre*).

IX The *Secreta Secretorum* and the *Gesta Romanorum*

This brings us to the end of our survey of the influence and development of the Latin Alexander texts deriving from the Romance tradition. However, it would be wrong to close without mentioning another key work of medieval Latin literature which also makes the figure of Alexander the Great central: this is the *Secreta Secretorum* or 'Secret of Secrets' attributed to Aristotle and presented as a letter of advice on kingship from the philosopher to his young pupil (Ryan and Schmitt 1982). It contains much advice on royal behaviour, but also an extensive section on medical matters and the preservation of health and, in its longer version, on astronomy, the lore of stones and talismans and on physiognomy. A form of this work was originally composed in Syriac and was translated into Arabic by a Christian Arab, Yahya Ibn Batrik (900–950). This was translated into Spanish and into Latin in the twelfth century, and a little later into Hebrew. The Latin version was by Johannes Hispalensis (fl. 1135–42). A second version, from an enlarged Arabic text, was made in the first half of the thirteenth century by Philip, a cantor and later archdeacon of Tripoli (Manzalaoui 1982: 56). Though the version of Philip was the one which made most impact – it is the source of all the French translations, for example – the earlier version was also well known. The work became the inspiration for a large number of works of a similar kind which did not involve the figures of Alexander and Aristotle; but the Latin version was also translated several times in part or in its entirety, the first version being that of Jacob van Maerlant for his patron Count Floris V, the *Heimelijkheid der Heimelijkheden* of 1266 (van Oostrom 1996: 243, 415). Some parts were put into English verse by John Gower and John Lydgate in the mid-fourteenth century.[10]

One notable story from this work which is not known from the romance tradition is that of the Poison Maiden.[11] Aristotle warns Alexander against accepting the gifts of the Queen of India, which include a beautiful girl whose property is to kill instantly anyone who kisses her. Forewarned, Alexander is able to evade the danger by resisting the seductive approaches of the girl. This story had an immense progeny, with elaborations such as Alexander's testing her bite on a condemned prisoner; in some versions it is said that the queen raised the girl by placing her as a baby in the egg of a snake. The story is not in the earlier translation by Johannes Hispalensis, but the appearance of it in Philip of Tripoli's version won it instant dissemination. Its first appearance may be that in Jacob van Maerlant's *Alexanders Geesten*, which as noted above in general follows the version of Walter of Châtillon; Jacob inserts the story after Alexander's contest with Nicolaus of Acarnania, another event from the *Romance* tradition. It is also in Jacob van Maerlant's *Heimelijkheid der Heimelijkheden* (van Oostrom 1996: 432).

The story of the Poison Maiden is also one of a number of Alexander anecdotes included in the great medieval compilation, the *Gesta Romanorum* (datable somewhere between 1362 and 1473). This, one of the last of the great Latin language collections, drew on a wide range of sources, not only the classical Latin authors but also the *Disciplina Clericalis* of Petrus Alfonsi. Another story found here but not in the regular tradition is that of Alexander's stratagem to neutralize that dangerous creature, a basilisk, which the defenders of a city had mounted on their walls to destroy the attackers. His philosophers advise him to raise up a mirror to reflect its image on the defenders. This successful trick draws forth the concluding moral: 'My beloved, look into the glass of reflection, and, by remembrance of human frailty, destroy the vices which time elicits' (*Gesta Romanorum* 1959:

244–5, no. cxxxix). This rather trivial piece of magic is thus dignified with a Christian moral application.

Even more striking is another story in the *Gesta Romanorum* (xcvi, p. 168 f):

> King Alexander placed a burning candle in his hall, and sent heralds through the whole kingdom, who made the following proclamation: 'If there be any under forfeiture to the king, and he will come boldly into his presence, while the candle burns, the king will forgive the forfeiture. And whosoever is in this predicament, and comes not before the expiration of the candle, he shall perish by an ignominious death.' Many of the populace, hearing the proclamation, came to the king and besought his mercy. The king received them kindly; but there were many who neglected to come; and the very moment in which the candle expired, they were apprehended and put to death.
>
> Application. My beloved, Alexander is Christ, the burning candle is the life present, and the heralds are the preachers.

The story has no source in the historical or Romance traditions. It seems to be unique to this work. There could be no better example of the way in which Alexander has been fully adopted into the world view of medieval Christianity; the great conqueror, whom the ancient philosophers reviled as a luxurious tyrant, has made his pilgrimage through the medieval cosmos. He has learnt the virtues of humility and austerity from the Brahmans, but tempered their ineffectualness with a positive valuation of the gifts of the earth and the diversity of human nature. He has received the lesson of the vanity of earthly existence from the old man at the Gate of Paradise. He has shut up the evil hordes until the end of time and been presented as the type of the universal king. He has been stripped of all the negative attributes the classical tradition attached to him and has become a type of Christ himself. Such a figure could not only carry weight as a chivalrous knight and warrior against the Saracens in the vernacular romances; more fundamentally, his sacralization seemed to represent hope for Everyman.

Notes

1 The Irish text is not noted in Cary 1956. It is dated to the tenth century by Erik Peters (1967) and to the eleventh century by Stokes and Windisch (1887). Both these publications include complete translations of the Irish text into German.

2 Ross 1963, n. 242, with further citations. See also Mulder-Bakker 1983: 111–23 on Ekkehard, 35–110 on Frutolf.

3 Comestor's invention of this identification is also argued by Ross 1963, 35. From Comestor it got into Quilichinus (3299), who did not find it in his main source, the *Historia de Preliis*, third recension.

4 There is a useful summary of Vincent's narrative in Van Oostrom 1996: 308 ff. On Vincent see in general Aerts *et al.* 1986.

5 On History Bibles see Merzdorf (1870); there is a useful orientation on German popular sacred literature in Kalinke (1996: 16). I have myself examined the following Dutch History Bibles: The Hague Koninklijke Bibliotheek, 78D38II and 78D39, and the German History Bible; Staatsbibliothek zu Berlin, MS Germ. fol 565.
6 Translated in Stoneman 1994; and see Introduction, xxii–xxiii.
7 Wiseman 1992: 22–42. For the later developments of the *Mappa Mundi* see Harvey (1996) and Hahn-Woernle (1987).
8 For the controversy see Stoneman (1994).
9 Reproduced in Stoneman 1994: 93–101.
10 Gower, *Confessio Amantis* vii; John Lydgate, *Secrees of Old Philisoffres* [sic], ed. Robert Steele (London: Early English Text Society e.s. 66, 1894). There is a survey of other translations on pages xii–xiii of the latter work.
11 W. Hertz, 'Die Sage vom Giftmädchen', in his *Gesammelte Abhandlungen* (Stuttgart/Berlin 1905), 156–277. The motif is the basis of Nathaniel Hawthorne's story, 'Rapaccini's Daughter'. For an anthropological view of the motif see Penzer (1952: 3–71).

Bibliography

Editions

Der Brief Alexanders an Aristoteles über die Wunder Indiens: Synoptische Edition, ed., Michael Feldbusch Meisenheim am Glan: Verlag Anton Hain, 1976.

Comestor, Petrus, *Historia Scholastica*, in *Patrologia Latina* ed. J.P. Migne, vol. 209, cols 1496 ff.

Gervase of Tilbury, *Otia Imperialia*, ed. G.W. Leibnitz (1707).

Gesta Romanorum, *editio princeps* printed by Keteklaer and De Leempt, Utrecht, n.d. but between 1472 and 1475; second edition printed by Ulrich Zell, Cologne, n.d. but before 1475. (The quotations in this article are taken from the translation by Charles Swan and Wynnard Hooper, *Gesta Romanorum or Entertaining Moral Stories*, London 1876; reprinted New York 1959.)

Godfrey of Viterbo, *Pantheon* in *Monumenta Germaniae Historica: Scriptores*, vol. 22 (1872) (abridged).

Higden, Ranulph, *Polychronicon*, Rolls series 1865–1886. (This edition includes also John Trevisa's English translation on facing pages.)

Historia de Preliis, synoptic edition of the three recensions, ed. H.-J. Bergmeister, Meisenheim am Glan: Verlag Anton Hain, 1975.

Iter Alexandri ad Paradisum, ed. A. Hilka, in L.P.G. Peckham and M.S. La Du, *La Prise de Defur et le Voyage d'Alexandre au Paradis terrestre*, Elliott Monographs 35; Princeton, NJ: Princeton University Press, 1935.

Kleine Texte zum Alexanderroman nach der Bamberger HS, ed. F. Pfister, Heidelberg: Winter, 1910.

Leo Archipresbyter, *Historia Alexandri*, ed. F. Pfister (1913).

Quilichinus of Spoleto, *Historia Alexandri Magni*, ed. W. Kirsch, Skopje: Živa Antika 1971.

Vincent of Beauvais, *Speculum Historiale*. There is no modern edition. (I have used an edition of 1494 in the British Library – IB 22010.)

Walter of Châtillon, *Alexandreis*, ed. M.L. Colker (Padua 1978). (Also in Migne, *Patrologia Latina* vol. 209, cols. 459–574.)

Translations

Alexander's Letter to Aristotle about India, trans. Lloyd L. Gunderson, Meisenheim am Glan: Verlag Anton Hain 1980.

Gesta Romanorum: or, Entertaining Moral Stories, trans. Charles Swan, revised by Wynnard Hooper, London, 1876; reprinted, New York, 1959.

Legends of Alexander the Great, edited and translated by Richard Stoneman, London: Everyman, 1994.

The History of Alexander's Battles: Historia de Preliis, – the *J*[1] *version*, trans. with introduction and notes by R. Telfryn Pritchard, Toronto: Pontifical Institute of Medieval Studies, 1992.

Secondary literature

Aeres, W.J. and Kortekaas, G.A.A. (1998) *Die Apokalypse des Pseudo-Methodius: die ältesben grieschschen und lateinischen Übersetzungen*, 2 vols, Louvrain: Peerers (csco 97–98).

Aerts, W.J., Smits, E.R. and Voorbij, J.B. (1986) *Vincent of Beauvais and Alexander the Great*, Groningen: Egbert Forsten.

Berschin, W. (1988) *Greek Letters and the Latin Middle Ages*, Washington, DC: Catholic University of America Press.

Bunt, G.H.V. (1982) 'Alexander and the universal chronicle', in Peter Noble, Lucie Polak and Claire Isoz (eds) *The Medieval Alexander Legend and Romance Epic: Essays in Honor of David J.A. Ross*, Millwood, NY: Kraus, pp. 1–10.

Cary, George (1956) *The Medieval Alexander*, Cambridge: Cambridge University Press.

Comparetti, D. (1895) *Virgil in the Middle Ages*, trans. E.F.M. Bencke, London: Swan Sonnenschein.

Daly, S.R. (1957) 'Peter Comestor: Master of histories', *Speculum* 32: 62–73.

Hahn-Woernle, Birgit (1987) *Die Ebstorfer Weltkarte*, Ebstorf: Kloster Ebstorf. (2nd edn published 1993.)

Harvery, P.D.A. (1996) *Mappa Mundi: The Hereford World Map*, London: British Library.

Hertz, W. (1905) 'Die Sage vom Giftmädchen', in his *Gesammelte Abhandlungen*, Stuttgart/Berlin.

Kalinke, Marianne A. (1996) *The Book of Reykjaholar: The Last of the Great Medieval Legendaries*, Toronto: University of Toronto Press.

Lolos, A. (ed.) (1976) *Die Apokalypse des Pseudo-Methodios*, Meisenheim am Glan: Verlag Anton Hain.

Lydgate, John (1894) *Secrees of Old Philisoffes* [sic], ed. Robert Steele, London: Early English Text Society, e.s. 66.

McKendrick, Scot (1996) *The History of Alexander the Great*, Malibu: J.P. Getty Museum. (A facsimile edition of a manuscript of Vasco da Lucena's translation of Curtius.)

Manzalaoui, M.A. (1982) 'Philip of Tripoli and his textual methods', in Ryan and Schmitt (1982).

Marshall, Robert (1993) *Storm from the East*, London: BBC Books.

Merzdorf, J.F.L. Theodor (1870) *Die deutschen Historienbibeln des Mittelalters I–II*, Tübingen: Literarischer Verein in Stuttgart.

Mulder-Bakker, A.B. (1983) 'Vorstenschool: Vier geschiedschrijvers over Alexander en hun visie op het Keizerschap', dissertation, Groningen.

Niles, John D. (1991) 'Pagan survivals and popular belief', in M.M. Godden and M. Lapidge (eds) *Old English Literature*, Oxford: Blackwell, pp. 126–44.

Oostrom, Frits van (1996) *Maerlants Wereld*, Amsterdam: Prometheus.

Penzer, N.M. (1952) *Poison-Damsels and Other Essays in Folklore and Anthropology*, London.

Peters, Erik (1967) 'Die irische Alexandersage' Zeitschrift für *Celtische Philologie* 30: 71–264.

Ross, D.J.A. (1963) *Alexander Historiatus: a Guide to Medieval Illustrated Alexander Literature*, London: Warburg Institute Surveys I.

Ryan, W.F. and Schmitt, Charles B. (1982) *Pseudo-Aristotle: The Secret of Secrets: Sources and Influences*, London: Warburg Institute Surveys IX.

Settis-Frugoni, Chiara M. (1973) *Historia Alexandri elevati per gryphos ad aerem*, Rome: Studi Storici, pp. 1–362.

Schmidt, Victor M. (1995) *A Legend and its Image: the Aerial Flight of Alexander the Great in Medieval Art*, Groningen: Egbert Forsten.

Silverberg, Robert (1972) *The Realm of Prester John*, New York: Doubleday. (Reissued by Ohio University Press, 1997.)

Slessarev, Victor (1959) *Prester John: The Letter and the Legend*, Minneapolis: University of Minnesota Press.

Smalley, Beryl (1952) *The Study of the Bible in the Middle Ages*, 2nd edn, Oxford: Clarendon Press.

Stokes, W. and Windisch, E. (1887) *Irische Texte*, Leipzig.

Stoneman, R. (1994) 'Romantic ethnography: Central Asia and India in the *Alexander Romance*', *Ancient World* 25: 93–107.

—— (1996) 'The Metamorphoses of the Alexander Romance' in Gareth Schmeling (ed.) *The Novel in the Ancient World*, Leiden: E.J. Brill, pp. 601–12.

Taylor, John (1966) *The Universal Chronicle of Ranulph Higden*, Oxford: Clarendon Press.

Wilmart, A. (1933) 'Les textes latines de la lettre de Palladius sur les mœurs des Brahmanes', *Revue Bénédictine* 45: 29–42.

Wiseman, T.P. (1992) 'Julius Caesar and the *Mappa Mundi*' in his *Talking to Virgil*, Exeter: University of Exeter Press.

16

THE REDISCOVERY OF THE LATIN NOVELS

Robert H. F. Carver

The Fates are notoriously capricious when it comes to the transmission of ancient texts: most of us would happily forgo the whole of, say, Macer Floridus' herbal for another fragment of Cornelius Gallus' poetry. But there were particular factors which militated against the survival of Latin fiction: it was not a reputable genre (arguably, not a genre at all); and because of its dependence upon feigning, it offended pagans of a Platonic cast of mind as much as it did the Fathers of the Early Church. Saint Paul, in his First Letter to Timothy (4: 7), laid the basis for later Christian attacks in his exhortation to 'avoid foolish old wives' tales' (*ineptas autem et aniles fabulas deuita*); and in his fifth-century *Commentary on the Dream of Scipio* (I. 2), Macrobius expressed amazement that so notable a philosopher as Apuleius should have indulged (like Petronius) in mere fictions, a species of discourse fit only for the 'cradles of wet-nurses' (*in nutricum cunas*).

So however deeply we regret the loss of Varro's *Menippean Satires*, Sisenna's *Milesiae* (not to mention the Milesian tales of Clodius Albinus), Apuleius' *Hermagoras*, and as much as nine tenths of Petronius, we ought to be grateful for what has survived: significant fragments of the *Satyricon*, all (or very nearly all) of *The Golden Ass*, and the *History of Apollonius, King of Tyre*. The last of these – a Latinized Greek romance rather than a Roman novel proper[1] – was well known to the Middle Ages and is hence excluded from the present discussion, having become, by Ben Jonson's day, a very 'mouldy tale' indeed (it serves, through several intermediaries, as the ultimate source of Shakespeare's *Pericles*). Readers interested in its reception are referred to Chapter 14 in this volume by E. Archibald.

I Petronius

The history of the *Satyricon*'s reception is neatly encapsulated in the qualified endorsement of Petronius (and Martial) given in a twelfth-century school syllabus attributed to Alexander Neckam: 'Both contain much that is useful, but likewise things unworthy of hearing.'[2] The fragmentary state of Petronius' text is partly the result of the excerptors' different responses to these contradictory qualities. The process of dismemberment may have begun very early indeed, and was certainly well under way by the sixth century when the compiler of the *Anthologia Latina* in Vandal Africa included at least twenty-eight poems that had been pillaged from the *Satyricon* (Müller 1995: III).

The Carolingian Renascence: the lost archetype (ω)

The earlier books of the *Satyricon* seem to have vanished almost completely, but in the middle of the ninth century the monks at Auxerre evidently had access to a substantial fragment which appears to have preserved the text of at least Books XIV to XVI in a far more complete form than we enjoy today. Regrettably, this manuscript – considered the archetype (ω) of all subsequent texts – was never copied in full before it was lost, readers preferring, rather, to quarry the work according to individual needs and tastes. Scholars have identified four main traditions (generally designated O, L, H, and φ) which descend from this broken archetype and feed into the surviving manuscripts and early printed editions.

The earliest witness to O (the *excerpta vulgaria* or 'shorter excerpts') is the ninth-century codex Bernensis 357 (B) which, Müller suggests, may have been written by Heiricus (d. 876), a monk (and poet) of Auxerre. But whoever was responsible for O had little interest in narrative (except as a frame for dialogue) and none at all in pederasty (though he does include the 'marriage' of Giton and Pannychis from chs 25–6). Instead, he preserves virtually all the poems he could extract, to function, Müller posits, as copybook examples for learned monks inflamed by a very Carolingian urge to versify.

Fortunately for modern readers, someone else (Λ) read the Auxerre archetype (ω) with rather different eyes, preserving the disreputable adventures of Encolpius and his crew through a preference for 'narrative no matter how sordid', thus laying the basis for the *excerpta longiora* or 'longer excerpts' (L).[3] Most importantly of all, the tradition of H preserved the *Cena Trimalchionis*. Drawing on all three of these traditions was the *Florilegium Gallicum* (φ), compiled at Orléans in the mid-twelfth century and privileging *sententiae* and commonplaces above everything else. In addition, sections such as the 'Widow of Ephesus' (Pecere 1975; Huber 1990) and the *De bello ciuili* circulated independently as well as within the other groups.

Medieval humanists

By the twelfth century, the state of Petronius' text is, to say the least, confused, but John of Salisbury (d. 1180) – perhaps the greatest of medieval humanists – shows awareness of all three of the major strands, O, L, and H. It was doubtless his connections with Chartres (as student and, later, as bishop,

1176–80) that allowed him to break what seems to have been a French monopoly on Petronius; but John was not unique in his knowledge of the *Satyricon*. Martin L. Colker (1975) has demonstrated that the fourteen prose narratives contained in an early thirteenth-century manuscript now housed in Trinity College, Dublin, draw heavily on L as well as showing knowledge of the *Cena* (H). And he has more recently suggested (1992) that they may be the work of Elias Rubeus of Thriplow (near Cambridge) whose named writings also show Petronian influence.[4]

The Italian Renaissance

So when we credit that most illustrious of Renaissance bookhunters and eroticists, Poggio Bracciolini (1380–1459), with the 'rediscovery' of the *Satyricon*, we should really be lamenting the extent to which knowledge of Petronius managed to contract during the thirteenth and fourteenth centuries. In or around 1420, Poggio unearthed a 'fragment' (*particula*) of Petronius which he sent from England to Niccolò Niccoli.[5] This Petronius (δ) was a thin fellow indeed, belonging to the O tradition of 'shorter excerpts' which represents only a third of our current text. Poggio's second find – at Cologne in 1423 – was potentially more dramatic. This was a text of H, the 'fifteenth book of Petronius' containing the *Cena Trimalchionis* (Harth 1984: 65; Gordan 1974: 79; Müller 1995: xxxviii). Neither Poggio nor Niccoli, however, seems to have recognized its full significance. Niccoli, moreover, was proverbially slow in processing the wealth of manuscripts that Poggio sent back to him in the course of his peregrinations. In a letter dated 13 December 1429, Poggio complains that Niccoli has still not managed to copy or return the Petronius which he had sent him more than seven years previously (Harth 1984: 89; Gordan 1974: 154).

In fact, both of Poggio's Petronian finds had been copied by this stage, though the mere transcription of a text did not ensure its resurrection. The copying of Poggio's *particula* (δ) allowed manuscripts of the 'shorter excerpts' (O) to proliferate, thus providing the basis for the *editio princeps* of the *Satyricon* which Franciscus Puteolanus (Francesco dal Pozzo, d. 1490) produced at Milan around 1482; subsequent editions of the same material appeared at Venice in 1499 and Paris in 1520. Poggio's *Cena* was also copied, probably at Florence in the period 1423–5, by 'a careful scholar' who appended it to a transcription of the 'shorter excerpts', so bringing together the traditions of H and O. The copy itself spawned no descendants, however, disappearing instead into Dalmatia where it lay, apparently unsung, for another two hundred years.[6]

Reunification

The fifteenth to seventeenth centuries witness the bringing together of the different textual traditions, but the process is not a smooth one. We know, from Petronian references in a commentary on Justinian by Jacobus Cuiacius (Jacques Cujas), that the longer excerpts (L) had resurfaced by 1562 (Müller 1995: xiii). But the new Petronius who emerged was potentially as embarrassing to humanists as he was compelling. France's Royal Reader in Greek, Adrianus Turnebus (Adrien Turnèbe, 1512–65), describes in his *Adversaria* how Enricus Memmius (Henri de Mesmes) kept his Petronius 'under lock and key' (*sub sera et claustra*), 'lest this obscene and lascivious writer corrupt anyone outside with his filthy wantonness' (*ne quem foris obscoenus et lascivus scriptor impura sua petulantia contaminet*) (Sochatoff 1976: 318). And a one-time student of Turnebus', Petrus Pithoeus (Pierre Pithou the Younger, 1539–96), boasts of keeping his Petronius 'condemned in his dungeon' (*privato carcere . . . damnavi*) – a boast which subsequent editors have had cause to rue since, while Pithoeus was able to produce (in 1577 and 1587) important editions of Petronius (as well as contributing significantly to the celebrated *Satire Ménippée* of 1594), the manuscript he used has disappeared (Müller 1995: xiii). Renaissance humanists, alas, seem to have been as proficient at losing manuscripts as they were at finding them, particularly once a copy had been made or an edition printed.

The longer excerpts did eventually see the light of day, and by drawing on L as well as O, sixteenth-century editors such as Joseph Justus Scaliger (1540–1609) and Johannes Tornaesius (Jean Detournes the Younger, *c.* 1539–1615) were able to double the size of the *Satyricon.*[7] But in assessing the literary influence of Petronius during the Renaissance, in particular, the production of such works as John Barclay's *Euphormionis Satyricon* (1603), we need to remember that the *Cena Trimalchionis* (H) was known only in fragmentary form until about 1650 when a jurist and scholar named Marinus Statileus (Marino Statileo de Trau) entered the library of Nicolaus Cippicus in Trogir (Trau) in Dalmatia and found the manuscript now known as Codex Parisenus lat. 7989 olim Traguriensis (H) (Sochatoff 1976: 319; Grafton 1990).

But even this great 'discovery' met with a mixed response. The *Cena* (H) was incorporated into Paolo Frambotto's edition at Padua in 1664 only to be denounced as spurious: many scholars were unwilling to believe that their 'elegant' Petronius would permit even freedmen to speak such unclassical Latin. Its authenticity was only established by comparing the recovered text with the fragments of the *Cena* preserved in O and L (Sochatoff 1976: 319).

If so substantial a narrative as the *Cena* could resurface, what was there to prevent further grand discoveries? In his *Discourse on Satire* (1693), John Dryden assigns the chief place amongst the imitators of Varro to 'Petronius Arbiter, whose satire, they say, is now printing in Holland, wholly recovered, and made complete. When 'tis made public, it will easily be seen by any one sentence, whether it be supposititious, or genuine' (Kinsley and Parfitt 1970: 244). It now seems clear that the supplements had actually been composed around 1673 as a form of intellectual amusement by one Pierre Linage, but had then come into the hands of François Nodot whose edition of 1691 claimed to be based on fragments discovered at Belgrade in 1688 (Stolz 1987). Critical suspicions were raised immediately, but for all its spuriousness, the edition itself, and the translations it generated, enjoyed a remarkable longevity, largely because they answered a need for a continuous narrative.

Petronius, indeed, has been almost as great a gift to interpolators as to epitomists. It is an irony which the Arbiter himself might have appreciated that the one passage of Petronius which today's general public is most likely to know is the so-called 'Reorganization forgery' (inexplicably attributed to 'Petronius Arbiter – 210 BC') which has been doing the rounds of offices since the 1940s: 'We trained hard but every time we were beginning to form up into teams we would be reorganized. I was to learn later in life that we tend to meet any new situation by reorganizing . . . and a wonderful method it can be for creating the illusion of progress while producing confusion, inefficiency and demoralisation'.[8] And when Fellini needed additional material to fill the *lacunae* in his film of the *Satyricon*, he turned, quite naturally, to Apuleius.

II Apuleius

The Golden Ass hung, throughout the Middle Ages, by an even thinner thread than the *Satyricon*, but at least it escaped dismemberment. Apuleius' rhetorical extravagance attracted the attention of a certain Sallustius who edited the text under the eye of the Christian rhetor Endelechius in Rome in 395 and at Constantinople in 397, thus ensuring that it cleared one of the first major hurdles facing any ancient text – the transfer from roll to codex (see Pecere 1984). His abstruse diction made him attractive to grammarians like Priscian and Fulgentius who have preserved the tantalizing fragments of Apuleius' other supposed novel, the *Hermagoras*; but there was little in the work (besides 'Cupid and Psyche') to appeal to the epitomator or the compiler of florilegia, and almost nothing in the way of edifying *sententiae*. While the philosophical works made their way north, to be welcomed, ultimately, by the Carolingian renascence, the *Metamorphoses* (together with the *Apologia* and the *Florida*) maintained a shadowy subsistence in the Mediterranean, well known to the likes of Augustine, Macrobius, Sidonius Apollinaris, Martianus Capella, and Fulgentius, but disappearing into the maw of what we used to call the Dark Ages at some time towards the end of the sixth century.

Traces of Apuleius' fiction were preserved in Martianus Capella's *Marriage of Mercury and Philologia*; and the story of 'Cupid and Psyche' – the subject of C. Moreschini's contribution (Chapter 13) in this volume – maintained some circulation in an epitome (with exegesis) which Fabius Planciades Fulgentius (wrongly, but helpfully, identified with the Bishop of Ruspe) included in his *Mitologiae* in the late-fifth or early-sixth century.

Asinus redivivus

We have to wait half a millennium, however, for the novel itself to resurface at Monte Cassino where a copy is made in Beneventan (i.e. South-Italian or 'Lombardic') script at some point during the eleventh century.[9] The orthodox view, propounded most cogently by D.S. Robertson, is that all the surviving manuscripts of the *Metamorphoses*, the *Apologia*, and the *Florida* descend from this copy (Laur. 68.2 or F) (Robertson 1924, 1940; Marshall 1983). Because of the method used to prepare the parchment, the ink quickly began to flake off the flesh side of manuscripts written at Monte Cassino in the eleventh century. Many were retouched during the thirteenth century, and some were copied. The second oldest MS of the *Metamorphoses*, *Apologia*, and *Florida* (Laur. 29.2 or φ) was written in Beneventan script 'about the year 1200' and, in Lowe's opinion, remained at Monte Cassino until both manuscripts were removed to Florence in the fourteenth century (Lowe 1920: 155).

The honour of liberating Apuleius from the confines of Monte Cassino was traditionally conferred upon Giovanni Boccaccio (e.g. Walsh 1970: 232), whose visit to Monte Cassino (usually dated to 1355) is described by Benvenuto da Imola in his commentary on Canto XXII of Dante's *Paradiso*. Drawn by the fame of the place and the books it was fabled to hold, Boccaccio had arrived at the monastery and humbly asked a monk if he would open up the library for him. The monk motioned him rudely towards a high staircase: 'Go on up. It's open.'[10] Climbing eagerly, he entered to find a doorless ruin – grass on the windows, priceless books in the dust, spoiled and mutilated. He ran out weeping and, on meeting a monk in the cloister, asked how such a terrible thing could have happened. He was told that some of the brothers, for the sake of a few soldi, cut up the parchment to make psalters for schoolboys and breviaries for ladies. If Boccaccio left with tears running from his eyes, he has also been supposed by later scholars to have left with some of the manuscript treasures tucked under his cloak, one of them being the codex containing Apuleius.[11] It is a dramatic scenario – the great humanist rescuing, from the dust and decay of mediaeval avarice and ignorance, one of the seminal texts of the Renaissance. The facts, sadly, do not quite measure up to the legend.

Boccaccio may well have been involved in removing some of the books from Monte Cassino (Lowe 1929/1972: 296), but it now seems clear, on chronological and codicological grounds, that F was not one of them (Coulter 1948). Zanobi da Strada (1315–61 or 1312–64) is currently the favoured candidate, Billanovich (1953) having identified his hand in annotations to F, φ, and C, the ten surviving leaves of an eleventh-century manuscript of the *Apologia* found at Assisi in 1942. Zanobi was certainly well placed, having met Petrarch in Florence in 1350 and being also a friend of Boccaccio. In 1352, he became secretary to Niccolò Acciaiuoli, Grand Seneschal of the Kingdom of Naples; in 1359, the Bishop of Monte Cassino made him Vicar

General; and shortly afterwards, he was appointed Prothonotary and Papal Secretary of Briefs by Innocent VI at Avignon (Cosenza 1962).

It is a mistake, however, to confuse (as distinguished scholars continue to do)[12] the removal from Monte Cassino of the oldest manuscript of *The Golden Ass* with the rediscovery of the novel itself. If Zanobi was the 'discoverer' of *The Golden Ass*, then the earliest he could have conveyed the manuscript to the Florentine humanists was 1355 (the same date given by Walsh, 1970: 232 for Boccaccio's 'discovery' of the novel). Yet the *Decameron*, which contains three tales from Apuleius, appeared in 1353;[13] and Coulter tells us (on the basis of apparent echoes of Apuleian diction in letters composed by Boccaccio in 1339) that 'Boccaccio had certainly read the *Metamorphoses* of Apuleius before he left Naples in 1340.'

We do, indeed, possess Boccaccio's autograph copy of *The Golden Ass* (Laur. 54.32 or L1), variously dated to around 1350 and 1338 (Coulter 1948: 223; Marchesi 1912/1978: 1010). L1, however, is a copy neither of F, the oldest extant manuscript, nor of φ, the oldest surviving copy of F. Robertson allots it to a group of manuscripts designated as Class I – manuscripts descended (he conjectures) from a copy (now lost) of F made before F was torn (i.e. before the copying of φ in about 1200). Moreover, B1 (a fourteenth-century MS now held in the British Library as Add. MS 24, 893 and a direct copy of A1 – i.e. Bibl. Ambros. N.180 sup.) is an ancestor of L1, though between B1 and L1 lies another lost manuscript and there is evidence of contamination from φ. Since A1 belongs, by Robertson's dating, 'au début du XIVe siècle' (1940: lxiv), it is clear that by the time Boccaccio made his own copy (which abounds, as Marchesi puts it, in 'distorted words and disordered and incomprehensible phrases'), a complex textual stemma had already evolved (Marchesi 1912/1978: 1010).

The Prehumanists

Responsibility for the rediscovery of *The Golden Ass* may in fact rest with scholars consigned to that somewhat unsatisfactory category of 'Prehumanists'. Knowledge of Apuleius' novel evidently took a long time to percolate from Monte Cassino, slowed perhaps by the difficulties of the Beneventan script which was far less legible than Caroline minuscule. Those in the thirteenth century whom we would most expect to show acquaintance with *The Golden Ass* know little or nothing of the work. For example, the library of Richard de Fournival – a man famed for his knowledge of the classics – can boast the presence of the *De deo Socratis*, the *De dogmate Platonis*, the *Asclepius* and the *Peri hermeneias*, but the catalogue of 1250 contains no trace of the novel (Vleeschauwer 1965: 525, 527, 530). Vincent of Beauvais (who died in about 1264) knows the title of *The Golden Ass* thanks to Augustine;[14] but the only works he has found are the *De deo Socratis* and the *De dogmate Platonis*.[15]

In the early part of the *Trecento*, however, the picture begins to change. In the *Historia de moribus et vita philosophorum* (composed between 1312 and 1322), Benzo d'Alessandria (*c.* 1260 to *c.* 1330) trumps Vincent of Beauvais' catalogue, claiming to have actually read (*legi*) the *Florida* and to have 'learnt of' or 'discovered' (depending upon one's interpretation of *comperi*) 'another book of this same man which is entitled, *The Golden Ass*; or, according to others, *The Metamorphoses of Lucius Apuleius the Platonist of Madaura*' (*alium quoque librum eiusdem comperi qui intitulatur ‹Asini aurei› vel secundum alios sic: ‹Lucii Apulei platonici Madaurensis Methamorfoseos liber›*).[16]

By 1332, Thomas Waleys – a Dominican, and a student of Oxford, Bologna, and Avignon – can claim to have seen five works, including the *De magia* (i.e. the *Apologia*) and *The Golden Ass* 'which is also called the *Metamorphoses*' (*qui et metamorphoseos appellatur*).[17] In glossing Augustine's *De ciuitate dei*, VIII. 19, Waleys is able to quote the opening words of the *De magia*; and his description of the contents and his use (like Benzo) of alternative titles suggest at least some direct contact with a manuscript of the novel:

> *Apuleius etiam in libro quem fecit de asino aureo / dicit de seipso quod artem illam libentissime didicerit / scilicet male sibi cessit ex hoc vt narrat. quia dum artem illam volebat discere / in asinum vt sibi videbatur conuersus est: & de hoc loquitur augustinus infra lib. xviiij. ca. xviij.*[18]
>
> Apuleius also says of himself, in the book which he made about *The Golden Ass*, that he learned that art most willingly, that is to say, he wickedly gave in to himself on this count, as he tells us: because while he was trying to learn that art, he was changed, as it seemed to him, into an ass. And Augustine speaks about this below in Book XVIII, ch. xvii [sc. xviii].

The importance of Waleys' testimony was recognized by his successors. Boccaccio's disciple, Benvenuto da Imola, includes him among the list of authorities with which he prefaces his own copy of Apuleius' works: *de Isto Apuleio / thomas Wayleys Anglicus . . . sic scribit . . . .*[19] In his *Liber de vita ac moribus philosophorum poetarumque veterum*, Walter Burley (1275–1337 or 1345) provides a description of the philosophical treatises followed by this account:

> *Item alium quem in duodecim libros distinxit quem asinum aureum intitulauit. vbi scripsit sibi accidisse quod accepto veneno a quadam muliere sibi dato: humano animo permanente visum illi fuit quod in asinum fuisset mutatus a qua illusione postmodum est curatus.*[20]
>
> Also another which he divided into twelve books which he entitled *The Golden Ass* where he wrote that it happened to him that on taking poison given to him by a certain woman, it seemed to him

> that (though his mind remained human) he had been transformed into an ass. He was afterwards cured of this illusion.

The most striking aspect of this passage is its reference to twelve books. Is this a simple slip? The result of indirect reporting? Or evidence of an abnormal book division or the incorporation of other material (say the *Florida*) as additional books at the end of the novel? (Carver 1991: 119). Danielle van Mal-Maeder (1997) has dared to think the unthinkable: extrapolating from Oronzo Pecere's observation that Book XI appears to be incomplete (since it lacks a *subscriptio* and the scribe of F seems to have indicated a hiatus after XI. 30), van Mal-Maeder tentatively suggests that in Burley's day a manuscript may have been circulating which contained a whole extra book of *The Golden Ass*. It is a beguiling thesis, but rather spoiled by the fact that Burley has clearly not read the novel: his account is drawn entirely from Augustine. But Burley's entry for Apuleius remains intriguing, particularly in its inclusion of an extended quotation from chapter 18 of the *Apologia*, where Apuleius answers Pudens' charge that he is poor (and so, by implication, married Pudentilla for her money) with an encomium on Poverty.

Avignon is the most likely source of the texts known to Waleys and Burley since it was a point of exchange in a network which, at various times, included Petrarch, Boccaccio, Acciaiuoli, and Zanobi da Strada, though it is impossible to match the references to a single manuscript in the papal collections.[21] The testimonies of Benzo, Waleys, and Burley all point, however, to a significant (and usually unremarked) aspect of the textual tradition of Apuleius. The tradition of F and almost all its descendants is trinitarian – the *Apologia*, the *Metamorphoses*, and the *Florida* descend together in a single block.[22] Benzo has read the *Florida* and knows about the *De asino aureo*/*Metamorphoses* but not the *De magia*. Burley and Waleys know the *De magia* in some detail and at least the name of the *De asino aureo*/*Metamorphoses*, without having heard of the *Florida*. In some fourteenth-century manuscripts, the *Metamorphoses* and the *Florida* are fused into a single work, so that the declamations seem to form a continuation of the novel; but this cannot account for all the discrepancies, and it is clear that towards the beginning of the fourteenth century, the *Apologia*/*De magia*, the *De asino aureo*/*Metamorphoses*, and the *Florida* were circulating in Italy individually or in pairs, rather than as a tripartite unit.

These early receptions lend weight to recent attacks on the primacy of F.[23] Pecere (1987) hypothesizes that Class I descends, not from a lost apograph of F (untorn), but from the lost archetype of F and C (the Assisi fragments). He exploits the discrepancy between Lowe's two dates for F (middle and end of eleventh century) and the fact that Lowe felt, on his initial observation in 1956, that C, if anything, seemed older than F. The MSS in Class I, moreover, show a marked preference for the marginal variants in F, suggesting descent not from F but from its ancestor.

But whatever stemmatic model we follow, our conclusions on at least one point must be the same: while F may constitute our best surviving witness to Sallustius' fourth-century recension, it was not, in itself, the manuscript that initiated the revival of the novel's fortunes at the beginning of the fourteenth century. We need to replace the romanticized Cassinese scenario of a single, discrete discovery with a more complex (if more prosaic) picture. Lowe imagined that, after the copying of φ, both manuscripts remained in Monte Cassino until their removal to Florence in the fourteenth century. But, even if this is true, the Cassinese manuscripts were not entirely lost to view. Robertson's model presupposes the escape of at least one manuscript (the lost archetype of Class I) before 1200; and Class II (which includes both Petrarch's manuscript and a manuscript copied in 1345) derive 'd'une seule source, aujourd'hui perdue, séparée de F par plusieurs intermédiaires' (1940: XLVI). To this skein we must add the possible influence, either of an ancestor (or collateral relative) of F or (a remote possibility, admittedly) of manuscripts independent of the Sallustian tradition represented by F.[24]

Humanist responses

Boccaccio was happy to pillage *The Golden Ass* to construct his *Decameron* and to marshall Apuleius to his defence of fiction in the final books of his *Genealogy of the Gods* (White 1977). Petrarch's attitude was rather more ambivalent. In a letter of 1359, he claims only to have read Apuleius 'once' (*semel*), 'snatchingly, hastily, making no delay except, as it were, for other ends' (*raptim, propere, nullam nisi ut alienis in finibus moram trahens*), gathering the odd excerpt into the 'forecourt of the memory' (*memorie uestibulo*) as he went along.[25] But this is disingenuous. Petrarch's manuscript of Apuleius' collected works (MS Vat. Lat. 2193) preserves notes to the *Metamorphoses* in Petrarch's own hand bearing the dates 1348, 1349, 1350, 1353, 1359, and 1369, suggesting prolonged and repeated exposure to the novel.[26] Some seventeen quotations from Apuleius feature among the marginalia to Petrarch's books, and (*pace* Ullman 1973: 127) there are frequent allusions to *The Golden Ass* in his own works.[27] In his *Invectives Against a Certain Doctor*, for instance, Petrarch plays upon the theme of the 'philosophizing ass', invoking the 'celebrated Platonist Apuleius' (*praeclarus Platonicus Apuleius*) in his most sustained defence of poetry.[28]

An even more vivid dramatization of the confrontation between scholastic and humanist tastes is given in an exchange of letters (written at some time after 1371 and before 1375) between a cleric, Stefano Colonna, and Simon de Brossano, Archbishop of Milan (Coville 1935). Stefano's own *De viris illustribus* is modelled on Burley's *Liber de vita ac moribus philosophorum poetarumque veterum*, and it may have been Burley who first prompted his interest in Apuleius (Sabbadini 1911: 833). Stefano had written to the Archbishop at Avignon, asking him for a copy of *The Golden Ass* which Simon had said was held there.[29] The book had not been received and when Stefano repeated his request he received only a rebuke. 'I do not cherish', says the Archbishop, 'the adulation expressed in your letter for the book of Apuleius' (*ambitionem tamen libri Apuleij literis tuis impressam non amplector*). The desire for such a work threatens not merely 'ignorance' (*ignorantia*), but 'mental aberration' (*alienatio mentis*), 'crippling of the faculties' (*sensuum debilitas*), and 'weakness of reason' (*infirmitas rationis*). He asks him how he can strive 'for the fabulous and the feigned which the Holy Spirit shuns' (*quomodo ergo fabulosum & fictum ambis, quem spiritus sanctus effugit?*), reminding him of St Paul's prohibition (1 Timothy 4: 7) on the reading of old wives' tales (*saltem addere debeas, ut secundum Apostolum ad fabulas non fiat conuersio*). Stefano, Simon warns, has crossed that fine line between the acceptable and the reprehensible use of pagan authors: 'I believed that you were going to this book as a scout; now, it appears, as a deserter' (*sed credebam te ad hunc librum, ut exploratorem transire, nunc apparet quasi transfugam*). There is, however, in Master Nicholas of Sicily – a reliable theologian of the old school – some 'hope of a remedy, of an expiation of this vice' (*huius tamen uitij expiationis est remedij spes*). It will be Stefano's 'safest defence and wholesome refuge, to drink from his fount and to eat crumbs beneath his table' (*tutamen tuum tutissimum erit, & salubre profugium, de fonte eius haurire, et sub mensa micas edere*).

Printed editions

Fortunately for European culture, the archbishop's views did not prevail. The printing-press reached Italy in 1465, and Apuleius was among the first authors to be published, the *editio princeps* of his works appearing (without commentary) at Rome in 1469.[30] The folio was edited by the Bishop of Aleria (in Corsica), Johannes Andreas of Buxis, printed by the German firm of Conrad Sweynheim and Arnold Pannartz, whose editor (corrector) he was, and dedicated to no less a personage than Pope Paul II, a collector of antiquities and patron of humanism.

Andreas' success in bringing together in a readable form the complete works of Apuleius is indicated by the appearance of new editions in 1488, 1493, and 1497; but the need remained for a commentary to tackle Apuleius' strange diction and convoluted syntax. That need was met in 1500 with the publication at Bologna of Filippo Beroaldo's monumental folio edition of *The Golden Ass*.[31] In the *editio princeps*, Andreas had made *The Golden Ass* his starting-point for the *Opera omnia*, 'as though it were a pamphlet in a greater work' (*Ab ea ego: uti a maioris opere libello: initium feci*) – an elegant way to introduce the writings of a learned and distinguished Platonist. Beroaldo, however, devotes his critical attentions entirely to *The Golden Ass*, marking the beginning of the shift away from the medieval notion of Apuleius as pre-eminently a philosopher, towards the modern view of him as a literary artist and shaper of fictions.

New editions[32] and translations were quick to follow. By the time that William Adlington came to translate the book into English in 1566 (following the French not of Guillaume Michel – as critical opinion has always held – but that of Jean Louveau), *The Golden Ass* was famous throughout Europe. In the course of the Renaissance it permeated the consciousness of writers as diverse as Boccaccio and Petrarch; Erasmus and Cervantes; Sidney, Spenser, and Shakespeare. Western literature would never be the same again.

III Epilogue

It is difficult not to romanticize the humanists of the fourteenth and fifteenth centuries. To book-hungry men such as Petrarch and Boccaccio, Poggio and Niccoli (to mention only the most famous), we owe the survival of a significant portion of Classical learning. But as we have seen, the notion of the 'Rediscovery of the Latin Novels' as a linear sequence of discrete and dramatic 'finds' is something of a chimera: 'recovery' and 'appropriation' are more accurate terms for the complex of processes by which little-read texts become widely known. And even that term 'Latin Novels' – the product of a modern world that privileges fiction over every other form of literary discourse – is problematic in the context of transmission and recovery. The French monks who excerpted, when they might have transcribed in full, would not have considered that they were desecrating a 'novel', nor even a piece of 'literature', but preserving, instead, what was most useful in an *auctor*. Moreover, what seems to us an egregious failure on the part of fifteenth-century humanists to capitalize on the recovery of the *Cena* may tell us something about relative values.

This chapter is not closed. We can probably look forward, for instance, to more elucidations of Petronian influence in the twelfth and thirteenth centuries; and much work remains to be done on the textual history of Apuleius. But the chimera of 'rediscovery' is perhaps a necessary fiction: we still need to believe that someone, somewhere, might once again stumble upon 'infinite riches in a little room'.

Notes

1 Scholars' opinions are still divided on this point: see Chapter 9 by G. Schmeling in this volume.

2 Walsh 1970: 230. The following account of Petronius' transmission makes no claims for originality. For a detailed exposition of this complex textual tradition the reader is referred to the expert studies of Reeve 1983; Richardson 1993; and Müller 1995. It would be perverse, in a diachronic study such as this, to use the more 'correct' title, *Satyrica*.

3 Reeve 1983: 300. L, the hypothesized parent of important twelfth-century MSS (the *Benedictinus* and the *Cuiacianus*) which were known (and lost) in the Renaissance, is based on Λ but shows, in addition, partial conflation of O and φ.

4 See Chapter 4 by C. Connors in this volume.
5 Harth 1984: 65; Gordan 1974: 80, 154; Müller 1995: XXXVIII. De la Mare 1976: 220, however, notes other early MSS annotations which seem to be Italian dating from the fourteenth century.
6 De la Mare (1976: 244–5) suggests that the person responsible for taking the manuscript to Dalmatia may have been Georgius Begna (d. 1437), a friend of its ultimate recipients, the Cippico family.
7 Scaliger (Codex Leidensis Scal. 61); Tornaesius (Lyon, 1575).
8 See *PSNL* 12.2–13 (1982): 5; 18.1and 2 (1988): 3; 24 (1994): 5.
9 The copying is generally associated with the abbacy of Desiderius (1058–87), though Lowe 1929/1972: 294 casts doubt on this dating.
10 Latin text in Coulter 1948.
11 For example, Sabbadini 1914/1967: II. 202 (but see 29 for a more cautious view).
12 For example, Weiss 1964: 30; Kenney 1990: 8.
13 Coulter 1948: 223. Tale V. 10 reworks Apuleius' story of the baker's wife (IX. 22–8). Tale VII. 2 derives from Apuleius' tale of the tub (IX. 5–7). Tale VIII. 8 adapts elements from both stories.
14 *Speculi maioris Vincentii Burgundi praesulis Beluacensis . . . tomus primus* (Venice, 1591), lib. II, cap. CV, *De falsis transmutationibus.*
15 *Speculum historiale*, IV. 7, in *Speculi maioris . . . tomus quartus*, fol. 41^{v}.
16 MS Ambros. B.24, fol. 280, reproduced by Sabbadini 1914/1967: II: 202. Benzo (or Bentius Alexandrinus) may have studied at Bologna before taking up successive positions in Milan, Como and Verona (where he was in the service of the Scaligers from 1325–9 and where he died in about 1330). See Cosenza 1962; Carver 1991: 115–16; Reeve 1991.
17 Smalley 1960: 90. In his commentary on *De ciuitate dei* (IV. 2) earlier in the fourteenth century, Nicholas Trevet – also a Dominican friar and student of Paris as well as of Oxford – can name only three works of Apuleius, the *De moribus et vita Platonis*, the *De deo Socratis* and the *De mundo*. Of these, he has seen only the first. Smalley 1960: 64.
18 Quoted from Thomas Waleys, *Divi Aurelii Augustine . . . de Giurate dei* . . . cum commentaris Thomae Valois et Nicolai Triueth, Basel: Adam Perri IBIS.
19 Bibilotheca Apostolica Vaticana, MS Vat. Lat. 3384, fol. IV.
20 *Liber de vita ac moribus philosophorum poetarumque veterum* (Cologne, after 1469), fol. 61r. The table of contents refers to *Apuleus* {sic} *Atheniensis*. Burley studied at Merton College, Oxford, and then at Paris, *c.* 1304–1307. He was at Avignon in 1327 and 1330 (*DNB*).
21 According to Smalley 1960: 75 6, Waleys was at Avignon in 1318 and from late 1331 to the New Year of 1333. Wilkins 1953 tells us that Petrarch was living at Avignon from his father's death in 1326 until 1337 and at Vaucluse and Avignon in the years 1337–41, 1345–7 and 1351–3. Faucon 1886–7: II. 31 records a *libellus Luci Apuleyi Madaurensisse de asino aureo* in the *Inventarium librorum qui solebant esse in camera Cervi Volantis, nunc vero sunt in magna libraria turris*. And the catalogue of the Library at Peñiscola in Catalonia (to which the papal collection was moved) records in 1409: *Item Asinus aureus Apulei, et liber de deo Socratis, et liber quartus ejusdem qui dicitur floritor{i}um et liber ejusdem de magia Apulei*. See Faucon 1886–7: II. 129, no. 927.
22 There are a few exceptions – V6 (copied at Bologna in 1345) contains only the *Metamorphoses.*
23 For a re-affirmation of F's primacy, see Dowden 1980.
24 Augustine (who uses the title *De asino aureo*) and Fulgentius (who knows both titles) probably had access to a pre-Sallustian recension of the text (F preserves Sallustius' single title of *Metamorphoses*). It is conceivable that traces of the

earlier recension survived. There remains the enigma of the so-called *spurcum additamentum* ('obscene interpolation'), a seventy-seven word rhapsody on fingers, unguents, and genital excitation added (again, *teste* Billanovich, in Zanobi's hand) to φ's description of the asinine Lucius' love-making with the Roman *matrona* (X. 21). The *spurcum additamentum* is evidently a medieval *jeu d'esprit* in the Apuleian style (Mariotti 1956 and 1994), but it would be interesting to have the manuscript from which Zanobi copied it.

25 *Familiarum rerum libri*, XXII. 2, 11. Ullman 1973: 115.

26 Nolhac 300–1; Ullman 1973: 130. Tristano 1974 demonstrates that Petrarch may have gained possession of the novel as early as 1343–5 or even 1341–3.

27 For example, *De remediis utriusque Fortunae* and *Familiarum rerum libri*, I.1.12; I.4.4; I.10.3; IX.10.4; IX.13.27; and *Francisci Petrarchæ Florentini . . . Opera quæ extant omnia* (Basel, 1554), 808. Scobie 1978: 212.

28 *Opera omnia*, 1209, 1213.

29 Petrarch, *Opera omnia*, 1233–6.

30 *Lucii Apuleii platonici madaurensis philosophi metamorphoseos liber: ac nonnulla alia opuscula eiusdem: necnon epitoma Alcinoi in disciplinarum Platonis desinunt* (Rome, 1469).

31 *Commentarii a Philippo Beroaldo conditi in asinum aureum Lucii Apulei* (Bologna, 1500). Beroaldo had been a student of Petronius' earliest editor, Puteloanus.

32 Most notably the first and second Juntines (Florence, 1512 and 1521), the Aldine (Venice, 1521), Colvius' Plantin (Leiden, 1588), Wower's Froben (Basel, 1606), Elmenhorst's (Frankfurt, 1621), John Price's (Gouda, 1650), the Delphine (Paris, 1688), and the great Variorum of Oudendorp (Leiden, 1786–1823).

Bibliography

Billanovich, G. (1953), *I primi umanisti e le tradizioni dei classici latini*, Fribourg: Edizioni Universitarie.

Carver, R.H.F. (1991), 'The Protean Ass: The *Metamorphoses* of Apuleius from Antiquity to the English Renaissance', D.Phil. thesis, Oxford.

Colker, Marvin L. (1975), *Analecta Dublinensia: Three Medieval Latin Texts in the Library of Trinity College, Dublin*, Cambridge, MA.

—— (1992), 'New Light on the Use and Transmission of Petronius', *Manuscripta* 36: 200–09.

Cosenza, M.E. (1962), *Biographical and Bibliographical Dictionary of the Italian Humanists and of the World of Classical Scholarship in Italy, 1300–1800*, Boston, MA: Hall.

Coulter, Cornelia C. (1948), 'Boccaccio and the Cassinese Manuscripts in the Laurentian Library', *Classical Philology*, 43: 217–30.

Coville, A. (1935), 'Une correspondence à propos d'Apulée, 1371–1375', *Humanisme et Renaissance*, 2: 203–15.

De la Mare, A.C. (1976), 'The Return of Petronius to Italy', in: J.J.G. Alexander and M.T. Gibson (eds), *Medieval Learning and Literature: Essays Presented to R.W. Hunt*, Oxford: Clarendon Press, pp. 220–54.

De Smet, Ingrid A.R. (1996), *Menippean Satire and the Republic of Letters 1581–1655*, Geneva: Librairie Droz.

Dowden, Ken (1980), 'Eleven Notes on the Text of Apuleius' *Metamorphoses*,' *Classical Quarterly*, n.s. 30: 218–26.

Faucon, Maurice (1886–7), *La librairie des Papes d'Avignon: sa formation, sa composition, ses catalogues (1316–1420) d'après les registres de comptes et d'inventaires des archives vaticanes*, Paris: Payot.

Gagliardi, D. (1993), *Petronio e il romanzo moderno: la fortuna del 'Satyricon' attraverso i secoli*, Florence: La Nuova Italia.

Gordan, Phyllis Walter Goodhart (1974), *Two Renaissance Book Hunters: the Letters of Poggius Bracciolini to Nicolaus de Niccolis*, New York: Columbia University Press.

Grafton, Anthony (1990), 'Petronius and Neo-Latin Satire: The Reception of the *Cena Trimalchionis*', *Journal of the Warburg and Courtauld Institutes* 53: 237–49.

Harth, Helene (ed.) (1984), *Poggio Bracciolini: Lettere. I: Lettere a Niccolò Niccoli*, Florence: Olschki.

Huber, Gerlinde (1990), *Das Motiv der 'Witwe von Ephesus' in lateinischen Texten der Antike und des Mittelalters*, Tübingen: Gunter Narr.

Kenney, E.J. (ed.) (1990), *Apuleius: Cupid and Psyche*, Cambridge: Cambridge University Press.

Kinsley, James and George Parfitt (eds) (1970), *John Dryden: Selected Criticism*, Oxford: Clarendon Press.

Lowe, E.A. (1920), 'The Unique Manuscript of Apuleius' *Metamorphoses* (Laurentian. 68.2) and its Oldest Transcript (Laurentian. 29.2)', *Classical Quarterly*, 14: 150–5.

—— (1929/1972), 'The Unique Manuscript of Tacitus' *Histories* (Florence Laur. 68.2)', in his *Casinensia: Miscellanea di studi Cassinesi*, Monte Cassino, 1929, pp. 257–72, repr. in his *Palaeographical Papers 1907–1965*, ed. Ludwig Bieler, vol. I, Oxford: Clarendon Press, pp. 289–302.

Marchesi, C. (1912/1978), 'Giovanni Boccaccio e i codici di Apuleio', *Studi italiani di filologia classica*, 19 (1912), repr. in his *Scritti minori di filologia e di letteratura*, Florence: Olschki, ??.

Mariotti, Scevola (1956), 'Lo *spurcum additamentum* ad Apul. *Met.* 10, 21', *Studi italiani di filologia classica* 27–28: 229–50.

—— (1994), *Scritti medievali e umanistici*, 2nd edn, Roma: Edizioni di storia e letteratura.

Marshall, P. K. (1983), 'Apuleius: *Apologia, Metamorphoses, Florida*', in L.D. Reynolds (ed.), *Texts and Transmission*, Oxford: Clarendon Press, pp. 15–16.

Moreschini, Claudio (1977), 'Sulla fama di Apuleio nel medioevo e nel rinascimento', in Giorgio Varanini and Palniro Pinagli (eds.), *Studi filologici letterari e storici in memoria di Guido Favati*, Padua: Antenore, pp. 457–76.

—— (1978), *Apuleio e il Platonismo*, Florence: Olschki.

Müller, Konrad (ed.) (1995), *Petronii Arbitri Satyricon Reliquiae*, 4th edn, Stuttgart/Leipzig: Teubner.

Pecere, Oronzo (1975), *Petronio: La novella della matrona di Efeso*, Padua: Antenore.

—— (1984), 'Esemplari con subscriptiones e tradizione dei testi latini l'Apuleio Laur. 68.2', in Cesare Questa and Renato Raffaelli (eds.), *Atti del convegno internazionale: Il libro e il testo (Urbino, 20–24 settembre 1982)*, Urbino: Edizioni Quattro Venti, pp. 111–38.

—— (1987), 'Qualche riflessione sulla tradizione di Apuleio a Montecassino', in G. Cavallo (ed.), *Le strade del testo*, Bari: Adriatica Edizioni, pp. 97–124.

Reeve, M.D. (1983), 'Petronius', in L.D. Reynolds (ed.), *Texts and Transmission*, Oxford: Clarendon Press, pp. 295–300.

—— (1991), 'The Rediscovery of Classical Texts in the Renaissance', in Oronzo Pecere (ed.), *Itinerari dei testi antichi*, Rome: L'Erma di Bretschneider, pp. 115–57.

Richardson, Wade (1993), *Reading and Variant in Petronius: Studies in the French Humanists and their Manuscript Sources*, Toronto: Toronto University Press.

Robertson, D.S. (1924), 'The Manuscripts of the *Metamorphoses* of Apuleius', *Classical Quarterly*, 18: 27–42, 85–99.

—— (ed.) (1940), *Apulée: Les Metamorphoses*, vol. I, Paris: Société d'Editions 'Les Belles Lettres'.

—— (1956), 'The Assisi Fragments of the *Apologia* of Apuleius', *Classical Quarterly*, n.s. 6: 68–80.

Sabbadini, Remigio (1911), 'Giovanni Colonna biografo e bibliografo del sex. XIV.' *Atti della Reale Accademia delle Scienze di Torino*, 46: 830–60.

—— (1914/1967), *Le scoperte dei codici latini e greci ne' secoli xiv e xv: Edizione anastatica con nuove aggiunte e correzioni dell'autore a cura di Eugenio Garin*, Florence: Sansoni.

Sanguineti White, Laura (1977), *Boccaccio e Apuleio: caratteri differenziali nella struttura narrativa del Decameron*, Bologna: Edizioni Italiane Moderne.

Scobie A. (1978), 'The Influence of Apuleius' *Metamorphoses* in Renaissance Italy and Spain', in B.L. Hijmans and R.Th. van der Paardt (eds.), *Aspects of Apuleius' Golden Ass*, Groningen: Bouma's Boekhuis, pp. 211–30.

Smalley, Beryl (1960), *English Friars and Antiquity in the Early Fourteenth Century*, Oxford: Blackwell.

Sochatoff, A. Fred (1976), 'Petronius Arbiter', in F.E. Cranz (ed.), *Catalogus Translationum et Commentariorum: Medieval and Renaissance Latin Translations and Commentaries*, vol. 3, Washington DC: Catholic University of America Press, pp. 313–39.

Stolz, W. (1987), *Petrons Satyricon und François Nodot (ca. 1650–1710): Ein Beitrag zur Geschichte literarischer Fälschungen*, Mainz: Franz Steiner.

Tristano, Caterina (1974), 'Le postille del Petrarca nel Vaticano Lat. 2193 (Apuleio, Frontino, Vegezio, Palladio)', *Italia Medioevale e Umanistica*, 17: 365–468.

Ullman, B.L. (1973), *Studies in the Italian Renaissance*, Rome: Edizioni Storia e Letteratura.

van Mal-Maeder, Danielle (1997), '*Lector, intende: laetaberis*: The Enigma of the Last Book of Apuleius' *Metamorphoses*', in H. Hofmann and M. Zimmerman (eds.), *Groningen Colloquia on the Novel*, vol. 8, Groningen: Egbert Forsten, pp. 87–118.

Vleeschauwer, H.J. de, (ed.) (1965), *La Biblionomia de Richard de Fournival du Manuscrit 636 de la Bibliothèque de la Sorbonne: Texte en facsimilé avec la transcription de Léopold Delisle*, Pretoria: University of South Africa (*Mousaion: Boek-en Biblioteekwese, Books and Libraries*, 62).

Walsh, P.G. (1970), *The Roman Novel*, Cambridge: Cambridge University Press.

Weiss, Roberto (1964), *The Spread of Italian Humanism*, London: Hutchinson University Press.

Wilkins, Ernest H. (1953), 'Petrarch's Ecclesiastical Career', *Speculum*, 28: 754–75.

INDEX

CW01464462

Anti-terrorism, citizenship and security

MANCHESTER
1824

Manchester University Press

Anti-terrorism, citizenship and security

Lee Jarvis and Michael Lister

Manchester University Press

Published by Manchester University Press
Altrincham Street, Manchester M1 7JA, UK
www.manchesteruniversitypress.co.uk

British Library Cataloguing-in-Publication Data is available

ISBN 978 0 7190 9159 9 *hardback*
ISBN 978 1 5261 3381 6 *paperback*

First published by Manchester University Press in hardback 2015

Typeset by JCS Publishing Services Ltd, www.jcs-publishing.co.uk

For Aya & Ami

and

Tamsin & Jessica

Contents

Acknowledgements

This book draws on material from an ESRC-funded research project that was initially conceived back in 2009. Over the course of the five years in which we have since worked on this project we have benefitted hugely from the help and assistance of a large number of individuals. We would like to take a moment here to acknowledge these and offer our sincere apologies to anyone we have omitted.

Firstly, we are particularly grateful to all of those people and organisations that arranged, hosted or participated in our focus groups. These included the African Community Centre in Swansea, Facilitators for a Better Jamaica in London and the Workers' Educational Association in Llanelli, all of whom organised facilities as well as helping to recruit participants for our research. We are also deeply grateful to Parveen Akhtar, Justin Gest, Gauri Kaskbekar-Shah, Miriam Smith, Rukhsana Bibi, Alison Crotch-Harvey and Marie Wiswell for their time and help with this research.

In the process of working on ideas in this book, we have also benefitted from the advice, comments, feedback and other help of a large number of academics whom we gratefully acknowledge. Drafts of material contained here were presented at conferences, including events organised by the International Studies Association and the Political Studies Association, as well as in departmental events at Oxford Brookes University, Swansea University and the University of East Anglia. Our thanks go to our colleagues and friends in our current and former departments and to Richard Jackson, Matt McDonald, Ben O'Loughlin, Basia Spalek and all those who attended our dissemination events in Swansea and London. Sections of the book were written during a sabbatical at the Department of Political Science in Copenhagen, for which we thank Lars Bo Kaspersen. We also gratefully acknowledge the Economic and Social Research Council for providing the funding for our research (RES 000-22-3765). At Manchester University Press we are indebted to Anthony Mason for his interest in and enthusiasm for the project, as well as for the patience he showed us throughout the writing of this book.

Some of the material contained in Chapter 4 was originally published under Jarvis, L. and Lister, M. (2013a) 'Disconnected Citizenship? The Impacts of Anti-Terrorism Policy on Citizenship in the UK', *Political Studies* 61(3): 656–675 and Lister, M. and Jarvis, L. (2013) 'Disconnection and Resistance: Anti-Terrorism and Citizenship in the UK', *Citizenship Studies* 17(6–7): 727–740. Chapter 5 also contains material previously published under Jarvis, L. and Lister, M. (2013) 'Vernacular Securities and their Study: A Qualitative Analysis and Future Research Agenda', *International Relations* 27(2): 157–178. We gratefully acknowledge Wiley, Taylor and Francis, and Sage respectively for permission to reuse this material.

Finally, it is only appropriate that we thank our families and friends for all of the time, help and support they have given us in the course of this research. This book was written at a particularly eventful time in our personal lives, and we simply could not have completed it without the support of our partners, Tamsin Barber and Aya Oyama. We hope, too, that our parents, siblings and friends know how grateful we are all for their encouragement over the years: thank you.

Introduction

Few issues have attracted as much discussion in recent years as that of terrorist violence and how it should be countered. Attacks from 9/11, through to events in Bali, Madrid, London, Mumbai, Woolwich and beyond have ensured that the former is never far from the headlines. Sustained and enormous military commitments in Afghanistan and Iraq, prisoner abuse scandals, high-profile assassinations, the restructuring of security bureaucracies, vast financial expenditure and much else besides have served similarly to keep the latter at the forefront of political debate. Within the UK, but beyond this as well, a concerted attempt to uprate and enhance existing anti-terrorism[1] powers has formed a major part of this dynamic, with four separate Acts of Parliament introduced between 2001 and 2008 alone. These Acts built upon substantial existing legal apparatuses in this policy area, not least the Terrorism Act of 2000,[2] and have included such measures as the (now repealed) power of detention without charge for foreign nationals, increased pre-charge detention periods, a control orders regime now replaced by a framework of Terrorist Prevention and Investigation Measures (TPIMs), greatly enhanced powers of surveillance and data retention, and a spread of new criminal offences such as glorifying terrorism and attending places of terrorist training. Whatever we think of Tony Blair's (2001) claim that '9/11' was a 'turning point in history' (see also Jackson 2005; Jarvis 2009a), it is difficult to argue that little has changed in this policy context in the years that have now passed since those attacks.

Innovations such as these have not passed without controversy. Advocates of still more muscular anti-terrorism initiatives have tended to invoke a need to revisit the always-precarious balance between liberty and security in times of extreme national duress (for example, Meisels 2005). The UK's former Lord Chancellor, for instance, referred to the importance of 'striking the right balance – between security on the one hand and liberty on the other', arguing that 'Getting that balance right is the common challenge we face – on both sides of the Atlantic' (Falconer 2006). David Blunkett (2004), former UK Home Secretary, spoke similarly of 'striking the balance between the security and liberty of the many and the rights of the individuals'. Critics of this logic and the powers it helped render possible (e.g. Cole 2003; Sivanandan 2006; Waldron 2003) have pointed, in contrast, to the pernicious implications of such measures for fundamental principles of democratic life, decrying those agitating for their sacrifice in a misguided quest for greater security.

Why citizenship? Why security?

For a book concerned with the development and experience of anti-terrorism powers in the UK since 9/11, raising the issue of why we focus on citizenship and security may seem unnecessary. It is tempting to suggest that the connection between anti-terrorism, citizenship and security is obvious. Whilst, to some extent, this is the case, their relations merit explicit exploration. In the first instance, anti-terrorism is, at some basic level, about enhancing the security of citizens: or, at least, this is how it is typically justified. In 2009, for example, then Prime Minister Gordon Brown stated: 'The first priority of any Government is to ensure the security and safety of the nation and all members of the public' (HM Government 2009: 6). Furthermore, the aforementioned 'balancing' of liberty and security draws an implicit connection between the rights and freedoms citizens enjoy (and thus the formal content of citizenship) and the quality or level of security experienced. Taken together, these two points – that the first duty of government is to protect, but that the freedoms citizenship entails create security challenges – point to an ambivalent, and perhaps dichotomous, relationship between the two phenomena. It seems that citizenship may entail both a right to security but also a threat to security.

This point is picked up by Guillaume and Huysmans (2013a). Emphasising a longstanding view of security as a right of citizenship (evidenced, for them, in documents such as the 1789 Declaration of the Rights of Man and the 1948 United Nations Declaration of Universal Rights), they identify a tension, asking: 'Is it a right to protection by the state, or a right to be saved from oppression, including from the state? ... Declaring security as a right of citizens, and humanity more generally, opens up various ways in which security is connected to citizenship, implying tensions that require negotiation' (Guillaume and Huysmans 2013a: 3).

Guillaume and Huysmans also note that academic literature, and certainly Security Studies as a discipline, has shied away from examining these tensions, preferring instead to focus either on the security of states (and not citizens) or on how particular issues become seen as ones of security (see Chapter 2). There is thus (and perhaps surprisingly) a relative lack of consideration of the interrelationship of security and citizenship in both a theoretical and empirical sense. Recent theoretical contributions (Nyers 2009; Guillaume and Huysmans 2013b) have sought to address this lacuna. This volume complements this work with an empirical probing of how citizens themselves think about these phenomena and their relations in the context of anti-terrorism. We thus aim to consider the impact upon citizenship of the UK government's attempts to provide security from terrorism. And we aim to examine the extent to which faith in citizenship and its protections underpins a sense of security from the force of (anti-)terrorism.

To do this, the book concentrates on findings from a series of focus groups we conducted with different communities across the UK, identifying some of the ways in which anti-terrorism powers are understood and evaluated within 'everyday' life. This, in turn, leads us to reflect on the implications of these attitudes for social and political relations; not least, the horizontal relations between different communities in a time of anxiety and suspicion, and the vertical relation between state and citizen in a time of expanding governmental powers. Our reason for attempting to do this is a long-held view that far too much academic and policy debate in this area (and, indeed, beyond it) has been framed in such a way so as to omit – or worse, to preclude – the voices of 'ordinary' people on the dramatic transformations in security politics characterising the post-9/11 period. That this omission may be indicative of more pervasive academic conceits (see Sylvester 2013) is further reason still for researching these otherwise much-studied areas. Our hope, in short, is that this book helps to bring non-elite experiences and understandings of the 'global war on terror' into the centre of discussion thereof.

The chapters that follow seek to do this via an exploration of four related questions. First, and most simply, this book sets out to ask: How are contemporary anti-terrorism powers understood, assessed and discussed by different publics across the UK? Is there, for instance, opposition or support for particular or general measures within this policy area, and can we identify demographic or identity-based dynamics to help explain differences of opinion? Similarly, what types of argument or evidence do people turn to in discussing these powers, and how entrenched are such views in the face of challenge by empirical evidence or counter-argument?

The book's second overarching question is: How do anti-terrorism powers impact on the experience of citizenship within the United Kingdom? Are such powers linked to erosions of civil liberties (for all, or for some), and are other aspects of citizenship – such as the ability to participate in public life – impacted at all by recent initiatives to combat the ostensible terrorist threat? Third, we ask, how do anti-terrorism powers impact on security in the UK? Do publics feel more or less secure because of anti-terrorism measures, and, if so, why? And how is a complex term such as security even understood within such assessments? Finally, the book seeks to tie these different questions together by exploring how claims about citizenship and security connect to evaluations of anti-terrorism powers. For instance, do people who feel more secure – or more secure in their status as citizens – feel more or less sympathetic towards developments in this area? And how do these three phenomena interact in the everyday life of different UK publics (in their eyes, and in their words)? We thus explore the relations between anti-terrorism powers, citizenship and security as understood and experienced by those potentially subject to the former.

For reasons detailed in the chapters that follow, none of these questions has a straightforward answer that might be applied universally across different publics within the UK. Indeed, the overarching argument we develop is that the relationships between security, citizenship and public policy are far more complex than is frequently recognised in academic debate, irrespective of whether contributors thereto are supportive or critical of anti-terrorism developments. As we attempt to show, while transformations in anti-terrorism frameworks undoubtedly impact on public experiences of security and citizenship, they do not do so in a uniform, homogeneous or predictable manner. At the same time, public understandings and expectations of security and citizenship themselves also seem to shape how developments in anti-terrorism frameworks are discussed and evaluated. In other words, the relationships between these entities are co-constitutive rather than unidirectional. They are also, importantly, multiple, rather than singular. Anti-terrorism powers generate both security and insecurity within different publics; whilst variable feelings of (in)security have variable effects on how such powers are seen. Anti-terrorism powers also, it seems, both diminish and enhance attachment to citizenship across the UK, just as diverse commitments to citizenship shape levels of tolerance to changes to the content or exercise of such powers. To make matters more complicated still, a spread of intervening factors also appear to impact on these relations, including one's prior contact and experience with the state and its policing and legal machineries. Recognising this complexity is vital, we argue, because this illustrates that public support for, dissent toward, or acquiescence in the face of anti-terrorism initiatives is affected by a host of differing experiential, cultural, discursive and other resources. Whether citizens accept, tolerate or resist anti-terrorism powers and changes therein is, in other words, an outcome of active political negotiation.

Underpinning these arguments (and our research questions) are two assumptions which we make explicit at the outset. The first assumption is that while evaluating the workings or impact of anti-terrorism powers is undeniably difficult – not least given the challenge of accessing relevant information – any assessment thereof requires far more than a balance sheet of successful and thwarted attacks designated 'terrorist'. In other words, any study of the effectiveness or desirability of recent UK attempts to counter terrorism needs to do more – indeed, perhaps needs to do other – than simply tally up or estimate their role in reducing the occurrence and costs of this form of violence. It is vital, we argue, to undertake a 'first and second order critique' (Jackson 2009a: 68) of anti-terrorism powers, in order to develop both an 'internal' and 'external' assessment of their working. This involves engaging, first, in a critical analysis of anti-terrorism on its own terms: asking whether it achieves its purported ends. And, at the same time, reflecting on 'the broader political and ethical consequences – the wider ideological and historical-material effects' (Jackson 2009a: 68) of such powers and their implementation. This critical ethos explains our interest in the impact of anti-terrorism powers on both security and citizenship: an attempt to investigate whether they achieve what they promise, and (if they do so) at what cost.

Our second starting assumption is that the impacts of anti-terrorism powers on security, citizenship or beyond cannot be known objectively. Security and citizenship have a discursive and experiential existence that is neither purely 'real' and material nor wholly subjective and limited to the mind of any individual citizen (see Buzan and Hansen 2009: 32–35). Instead, both of these much-discussed entities are better approached, we believe, as articulated, experienced and embodied phenomena. They are brought into being through the perceptions, ideas, language and practices of individual subjects. And, at the same time, these perceptions and ideas are themselves conditioned and made possible by broader social, cultural, political and economic contexts. This is important because it implies that the effects of anti-terrorism powers (or other political frameworks) cannot be known simply by identifying and assessing changes to them (although these are, of course, important). Instead, it is vital, we argue, to engage with those who are, or who might be, or who believe themselves to be, subject to such powers. In seeking to do this, our ambition is to work towards the co-creation of opportunities for those individuals to discuss those impacts – on themselves and on others – in their own terms, and with their own terms of reference.

By exploring these questions, this book attempts to make three broad contributions to contemporary academic debate around anti-terrorism, security and citizenship to which we return at different points in the analysis that follows. In the first instance, the book seeks to add a qualitative depth and complexity to existing studies of anti-terrorism powers and their impact on public opinions and attitudes. As outlined in Chapter 2, such studies have tended, in the main, to employ quantitative research techniques including survey and polling data, in an attempt to investigate the conditions underpinning support for, or opposition to, specific anti-terrorism measures (for example, Huddy et al. 2002; Davis and Silver 2004; Johnson and Gearty 2007; Joslyn and Haider-Markel 2007). Without diminishing the importance of research of this sort, our approach seeks instead to detail how publics discuss and make sense of developments in this policy area. This, we hope, contributes an empirical richness to existing knowledge that is simply not possible in large-scale statistical exercises. The sacrifice, of course, is any ability to generalise about UK public opinion, or indeed causal relations, within the dynamics we discuss.

Second, this book seeks also to extend recent literature on anti-terrorism policy and citizenship by conceptualising the latter in a far broader manner than existing work in this area. Studies of these two phenomena tend to make two (implicit) assumptions: perhaps for methodological as much as meta-theoretical reasons. The first is that citizenship is associated primarily (or even exclusively) with the possession and exercise of certain rights and liberties that are enshrined and protected within legal frameworks. The second assumption is that transformations in citizenship can be deduced by changes to legal frameworks. Taken together, these assumptions help explain why a straightforward erosion of citizenship is frequently identified in the context of contemporary anti-terrorism powers by critics thereof. Whilst there is much to be lauded in a lot of this work, our approach is one that sees citizenship as an experience that derives from the negotiation of rights but also from the making, meeting or refusal of identity claims, obligations and participation in public spaces (see Delanty 2000). As such, in order to explore the anti-terrorism/citizenship nexus it is vital that publics are offered the chance to describe their own experiences in their own terms, even if these fit poorly with established liberal or republican models of 'the citizen' detailed in Chapter 2. Indeed, as we demonstrate in Chapter 4, for many people in the UK it seems that anti-terrorism powers have impacted upon aspects of citizenship such as participation in public life far more dramatically than they have affected the status of formal rights.

Third, the book also attempts to contribute to debate around the security implications of anti-terrorism policies by exploring these at the relatively unstudied level of the individual citizen, rather than with reference to national security. As detailed in subsequent chapters, our attempt to do this is inspired by often unrelated efforts to recast the referent and status of security within discussions emanating from Security Studies and International Relations. This means that – for us – just as citizenship is something articulated rather than 'given', so too is security. Security, we suggest, is not a material condition traceable to particular conditions or attributes, as is frequently assumed. It is instead an experience that is given meaning (and again made sense of) through the interpretation of (in the case of this book) ordinary people. Hence, understanding whether 'we' are more or less secure because of contemporary anti-terrorism initiatives involves asking, first, whether citizens feel more or less secure because of these initiatives, and, second, what security means in this context. As we argue in Chapter 6, public conceptions of security are fundamental to the ways in which anti-terrorism powers are understood and evaluated, impacting the terrain upon which they are discussed.

Book organisation

The book begins, in Chapter 1, by sketching the parameters and historical development of UK anti-terrorism policy, comparing its efforts to those of other 'Western' states. The chapter explores controversies associated with earlier campaigns – especially in relation to Irish republicanism – as well as the extent to which the recent impetus for renewed anti-terrorism legislation derives from widespread claims that al-Qaeda and associated movements present a radically new form of terrorist threat. Our argument is that the UK's anti-terrorism experience – especially in relation to its use of legal frameworks – is relatively distinctive in that it is characterised by hasty, repeated and continuous activity in which terrorism is approached as a distinct security problem of exceptional significance (Neal 2012; Lister and Otero-Iglesias 2013). Moreover, whilst the UK is by no means alone in pursuing new powers to counter terrorism, it does represent something of a 'market leader' in terms of anti-terrorism legislation around the world (Roach 2007).

This backdrop to the subsequent discussion of our empirical findings is important for three reasons. First, by showing that the UK's approach differs from that of comparable countries, it becomes clear that there is a politics at work in the area of anti-terrorism. Choices and decisions are continuously made about how to confront this threat (although these are often couched as necessary or self-evident), which renders engaging with their implications and impacts – upon people and communities – an even more urgent task. This is compounded, we suggest, by the robust nature of UK initiatives and the potential they have for particular communities and citizens. Second, the UK's history of anti-terrorism is also sometimes connected by analysts to citizen expectations in relation to this policy context: the repetitive legislating against terrorism is often seen as a response to public demands upon their executives. Engaging with citizen understandings of (anti-)terrorism, then, offers an opportunity to explore such claims in descriptive detail as a way of assessing the appetite for particular kinds of governmental initiative. Third, this sketch of the UK's anti-terrorist framework also helps clarify the content of the focus group discussions that we explore in subsequent chapters. Although many of our research participants discussed anti-terrorism in general terms, others did make reference to particular powers therein. As such, there is value in being clear on what these are from the outset.[3]

The book's second chapter introduces the concepts of security and citizenship that underpin our study and establish its guiding rationale. Beginning with security, we argue that its traditional 'home' for analysis in the field of Security Studies has been radically transformed by important recent interventions within two strands of broadly 'critical' literature. The first concerns efforts to position the individual, rather than the state, as security's referent. The second is a focus on the discursive or socially constituted nature of security, insecurity and security threats (evident, for example, in constructivist and poststructuralist debate). We argue that these interventions, approached together, present a powerful call to take seriously citizens' own efforts to articulate security. Doing so, we suggest, facilitates engagement too with self-consciously critical approaches which seek to move Security Studies beyond its traditional elitism.

We then turn to a parallel, yet largely separate, debate around the concept of citizenship and its contemporary 'health' within academic and policy circles. Three general trends relating to the politics of citizenship with particular relevance for understanding anti-terrorism powers are highlighted here. The first concerns political efforts to foster and govern citizenship,[4] as well as recent academic debate around the responsibilisation (Garland 1996) of citizens. The second concerns claims to the ostensible erosion of citizenship today (for example, Somers 2008; Wacquant 2009) and arguments surrounding the retreat of the state from certain roles and functions. The third refers to questions around heterogeneity, diversity and difference associated (in particular, although not exclusively) with discussions of multiculturalism and the impact thereof upon citizenship. Our aim in considering these debates is to emphasise that in order to assess the effects of anti-terrorism on citizenship, we must situate such measures in prior social, political and economic context. As we show, citizenship, for many authors, has been subject to transformations (which are frequently seen as negative erosions of the category) concerning obligations and rights as well as membership. Thus anti-terrorism powers impact upon a citizenship which, for many authors, is already in the process of being eroded.

Our claim in this chapter is that these developments and the debates they have engendered render an analysis of citizens' understandings of security mechanisms both pressing and urgent, despite the lack of existing research on this (although see Noxolo and Huysmans 2009; O'Loughlin and Gillespie

2012). It is important, we argue, to explore how citizens think about, enact or disrupt citizenship and its associated obligations in their engagement with public policy in areas such as anti-terrorism. This is particularly so if we think that citizenship has a performative and enacted character, such that the erosion of formal rights cannot be taken as a straightforward erosion of citizenship, however pernicious it may be (Isin 2008; Nyers 2010). As we argue, the state–citizen relationship should be understood as a dynamic of negotiation, contest and change to which citizens themselves bring agency. We conclude Chapter 2 by outlining the research design and focus group methodology that underpinned the collection of the empirical 'data' on which this book focuses. This includes discussion of epistemological issues surrounding focus group conversations, as well as of the mechanics of how our data was co-constructed with our participants.

Chapter 3 begins the exploration of our empirical findings and reports on the diversity of ways in which citizens evaluate anti-terrorism powers. Sources of scepticism towards these powers include: concerns that they contribute to wider climates of fear, worries that they might drive the alienation of minority communities, questions about their effectiveness, doubts over whether they address the 'root causes' of terrorism, suspicions that they are little more than a performative exercise in 'security theatre', civil liberties concerns and worries around their application in practice, such that they might be misused by 'bad apples' within the police forces or elsewhere. We also, in this chapter, detail more specific public concerns about particular aspects of the anti-terrorism framework including stop and search powers, pre-charge detention and inchoate offences around the glorification of terrorism. The chapter concludes by outlining a range of less-sceptical stances our research uncovered. These included: relief or contentedness that the state is 'doing something' to address the threat of terrorism, a perception that robust mechanisms are necessary given the ruthlessness and unpredictability of contemporary terrorism, a sense that sufficient safeguards are in place to prevent abuses of these powers, and ambiguity towards the capacity of 'ordinary' citizens to even evaluate such mechanisms.

Chapter 4 builds on Chapter 3 by focusing more closely on the impact of anti-terrorism measures on how citizens understand and enact their citizenship. The chapter begins by arguing for a broad and inclusive approach to citizenship that is characterised by two key features. First, that citizenship is an outcome of the interaction between rights, duties, identity and participation (Delanty 2000). And, second, that it is also subjective and performative, as much as a status that exists formally in law. As Nyers (2010: 96) argues, 'to understand citizenship it is not sufficient to despair over citizenship's exclusions; equally important is to investigate the claims about rights, membership and belonging made by excluded populations'.

What emerges from our analysis, we suggest, is a variegated picture. Citizens from a range of ethnic minority backgrounds believe anti-terrorism measures have directly curtailed and diminished their citizenship. This goes beyond simple infringements of rights, to include a retreat from political engagement (or a perception that one's voice does not matter), a declining sense of identification with British citizenship and a lessening sense of duties and obligations to the UK and one's fellow citizens (justified, sometimes, in terms of the British state not upholding its own responsibilities to its citizens). This is in contrast to white participants who, whilst not untroubled about the impact of these measures, generally viewed this as a concern distanced from their everyday lives. This suggests that anti-terrorism measures may be contributing to a condition of 'disconnected citizenship' in the UK. Some individuals enjoy greater confidence in their rights, appear relatively unaffected in terms of their participation and identity, and are content to take up particular duties. For others, in contrast, the perception of diminished rights and targeting by the state contributes to the limiting of political engagement and a declining sense of belonging. The chapter concludes by pointing to several important examples of resistance towards such powers and their impacts that speaks to an exercise of political agency even amongst those who believe themselves targeted by such measures. This further emphasises that, whilst some pernicious effects of anti-terrorism on citizenship can be identified (and were by many of our participants), citizenship is also a category which affords, for some, opportunities and justifications for contesting anti-terrorism measures.

In Chapter 5 we turn to the impact of anti-terrorism policy on public experiences of security within the UK. The chapter begins by reiterating the widespread public scepticism identified in Chapter 3. Reviewing the reasons for this, we argue that a major factor was a pervasive view that security has not been enhanced by recent initiatives in this area. Indeed, some individuals – primarily from ethnic minority communities – believed that their security has been directly diminished by the introduction of new anti-terrorism powers. Understanding this scepticism, we argue, requires a deeper engagement with public understandings of security itself. To demonstrate the importance of this, the chapter explores six distinct ways that participants in our research discussed the concept of security. Here, security was linked to notions of survival, belonging, hospitality, equality, freedom and insecurity, respectively.

Chapter 6 then continues this discussion of the anti-terrorism/security/citizenship nexus. In it, we argue that individuals' underlying conceptions of security have implications for whether they are likely to see security as having been enhanced by anti-terrorism measures. Of greater significance was that the conception of security with which individuals operated strongly influenced the conceptual and linguistic terrain in which they discussed such measures. Thus, security acted as a frame for discussions of anti-terrorism policy. Those who understood security in terms of social belonging, for example, were primarily interested in the impacts of anti-terrorism measures on community cohesion. This is in contrast to those who conceived of security as 'survival', who discussed anti-terrorism more in terms of effectiveness. Similarly, those who saw security as 'freedom' sought to discuss anti-terrorism measures in terms of whether they enhanced or diminished civil liberties. Thus, in this final chapter, we re-emphasise the interconnections between anti-terrorism, security and citizenship, arguing that security is not simply an end state delivered or otherwise to citizens.

The book's conclusion reviews our findings, arguing that the complex relationships uncovered in the preceding chapters are suggestive of a set of research priorities different to the 'problem-solving' approaches frequently prevalent in research on terrorism. By placing the citizen at the heart of debates around anti-terrorism powers, and by acknowledging the diverse experiences of different citizenships and securities (and the interaction between these), we might move beyond simple binary debates (what is the correct balance between liberty and security; does anti-terrorism policy increase security?) which our research suggests are over-simplifications. In other words, the challenge is to move beyond considering 'how to respond', and instead to ask how anti-terrorism functions, what effects it has, and how experiences of citizenship, security and related phenomena play a significant role in how different publics think about and relate to such powers.

Notes

1 Throughout the book, we use the term 'anti-terrorism', rather than 'counter-terrorism'. Whilst there is considerable overlap between the two (and in some instances, they are used interchangeably), we understand the former to refer to defensive, reactive strategies to combat terrorism, and the latter to more proactive, aggressive (often military-led) interventions. The exception to this is if we are citing an author who explicitly uses the term 'counter-terrorism'; in such instances, we preserve the author's original usage.

2 These are, in chronological order: 2001 Anti-Terrorism, Crime and Security Act; 2005 Prevention of Terrorism Act; 2006 Terrorism Act and 2008 Counter Terrorism Act.

3 As detailed further in Chapter 2, our research design included providing participants in our research with an information sheet detailing controversial aspects of the UK's post-9/11 anti-terrorism framework.

4 Examples include the introduction of citizenship classes in schools to arrest phenomena such as falling electoral turnouts, and the publication of the Cantle Report following civil unrest in northern towns in the summer of 2001: a report designed to promote social cohesion between ethnic groups. As recently as 2007, the government green paper, the Governance of Britain, also invoked citizenship as a means of enhancing and strengthening British identity and values.

1

Anti-terrorism policy in the UK: historical trends and contemporary issues

> This is not a temporary emergency requiring a momentary remedy, this will last far beyond the term of my life. (Sir Vernon Harcourt, 1883, speaking of the threat from Fenian terrorism, cited in Staniforth 2013: 3)

Despite the recent – and particularly post-9/11 – upsurge of academic, political and public interest, the issue of terrorism, of course, has a much longer heritage. Indeed, it is now commonplace to note that the term itself derives from the experience of the French Revolution of 1793–94 (Gearson 2002; Chaliand and Blin 2007a): a thoroughly modern invention, perhaps, born of humanity's growing confidence in its own agency to affect socio-political change (Gray 2003).[1] Yet, as another commonplace reminds us, it is also possible to point to a much deeper history of actions, behaviour and situations that might be called 'terrorist', even if the term was not around at the time of their occurrence. The activities of groups from the first century onward, including the Sicarii, Zealots, Thuggee and Ismaili Fedayeen are all regularly discussed in such a way (see Laqueur 2001; Gearson 2002; Chaliand and Blin 2007b; Bobbit 2008) – even if such groups and their violences remain more widely invoked than studied (Rapoport 1984: 659). As Terry Eagleton (2005: 2) puts it: 'In a broader sense of the word, to be sure, terrorism is as old as humanity itself. Human beings have been flaying and butchering one another since the dawn of time'.

As violences describable as terrorist have a considerable history, so too do governmental efforts to combat, prevent and respond thereto. Our argument in this chapter is that understanding the significance of the UK government's recent anti-terrorism efforts requires locating these in historical and geographical context. This involves exploring previous anti-terrorism campaigns, as well as contrasting them with the responses of other countries to this ostensible threat. Such an exercise might seem gratuitous given this book's focus on how citizens think about, articulate and respond to anti-terrorism mechanisms. These 'vernacular' conceptions and constructions of anti-terrorism policy might have limited, if any, connection to the geographical and historical trends explored below. Yet, if the UK's responses to the (perceived) terrorist threat in the early twenty-first century were entirely commensurate with its past responses, or entirely consonant with those of other countries, there would be far less need to consider the public voice. In other words, if there was nothing distinctive about the UK's anti-terrorism activities since 2001 in particular, there would be far less of note on which to consult British citizens.

As we will argue below, the UK's response to recent terrorist attacks has been distinctive. Certainly this is the case in comparison with that of similar states, although this is not to suggest that others have not also responded dramatically. The reasons for this are rooted in the UK's historical experience of countering terrorism, which extends back at least until the late nineteenth century. A good deal of the present-day approach is informed by these struggles in which may be found much of the modern anti-terrorist paraphernalia, including internments, assassinations and far-reaching surveillance programmes (see Hewitt 2008). And yet, despite these continuities, the post-9/11 period, we suggest, has seen both an intensification and extension of these past strategies.

A brief note on terrorism

Defining terrorism is a notoriously problematic enterprise about which a few words here will suffice. As Richard Jackson (2009b: 172) notes, it is almost a 'cliché' to point to the essential contestability of the term, and the numerous definitions which abound thereunto. The first edition of the most widely known discussion of this concept (Schmid and Jongman 1988) identified over one hundred definitions nearly thirty years ago. A more recent contribution (Easson and Schmid 2011) listed over two hundred and fifty. Away from the (typically over-complicated) efforts of academia (see Badey 1998), international governmental organisations (IGOs) have also long struggled to formulate their own working definitions (Jarvis 2009a: 7). The United Nations, in particular, is regularly criticised for its failings here, although post-9/11 Conventions, including those on the financing of terrorism, have made some headway in comparison to previous attempts (Harmon 2008: 154).

Part of the challenge with defining terrorism, as Jackson et al. (2011: 101–103) note, is the concept's pejorative connotations. Terrorism, for the most part, is not a term by which people refer to their own violences. It is, instead, one reserved almost exclusively for 'what the bad guys do' (Richardson 2006: 19). Or, as Chomsky (2002: 131) puts it: 'the term applies only to terrorism against us, not the terrorism we carry out against them'. Winkler (2006) goes further, arguing that terrorism functions as a 'negative ideograph': an absolute form of otherness symbolising the negation of everything associated with 'our' (here, American) culture. These connotations – and the inconsistency they encourage in the term's usage – help explain why the question of state terrorism remains so hotly disputed (see Blakeley 2007, 2009; Jackson 2008, 2009a; Stohl 2012; Wight 2012; Jarvis and Lister 2014). While some respond to this contestability by arguing that we should move the terrorism debate beyond the definitional question altogether on meta-theoretical (Jarvis 2009a) or pragmatic (e.g. Laqueur 2003: 238) grounds, others seek instead to identify key characteristics of this phenomenon. An obvious starting point here is that terrorism seems to concern violence, or the threat thereof. A second might be terrorism's instrumentality, such that the unfortunate individuals ensnared by terrorist violence are killed or maimed to achieve another goal, generally a symbolic or communicative one. As Jackson et al. (2011: 116) argue, 'Terrorism is an act of exemplary or symbolic violence designed to send messages to a range of audiences.'

This instrumentality is connected to understandings of terrorism as involving the mobilisation of fear to advance goals, whether political, social, ideological or religious. Indeed, Goodin (2006) argues that this – rather than the targeting of civilians, for instance – constitutes terrorism's distinctiveness, in that its 'essence lies in its attempt to frighten people for political advantage' (Goodin 2006: 31). And, if the creation of fear might be thought of as terrorism's means (Goodin 2006), its desired end is almost always the bringing about of some coveted change in the world. Fromkin (1975: 693–4) makes this point clearly:

> Terrorism is violence used in order to create fear; but it is aimed at creating fear in order that the fear, in turn, will lead somebody else – not the terrorist – to embark on some quite different program of action that will accomplish whatever it is that the terrorist really desires ... The terrorist is like a magician who tricks you into watching his right hand while his left hand, unnoticed, makes the switch ... [As such, there is a danger of] concentrating too much attention on preventing terrorist actions and too little attention on foiling terrorist purposes.

If a central aspect of terrorism is the creation of fear for instrumental purposes (see also Rapin 2009), then a reasonable argument may be made that anti-terrorism should, in some way, seek to lessen or reduce fear. An anti-terrorism strategy which either fails to reduce, or worse, heightens, fear should not, perhaps, be considered appropriate or effective. English (2009: 120–121), for example, argues that a key aspect of responding to terrorism involves 'learning to live with it' and recognising it as an enduring part of our political reality. Mueller (2005: 496) makes a similar claim in his characteristically forthright terms, arguing, 'Policies designed to deal with terrorism should focus more on reducing fear and anxiety as inexpensively as possible than on objectively reducing the rather limited dangers terrorism is likely actually to pose'. As he continues, 'Since the creation of insecurity, fear, anxiety, and hysteria is central for terrorists, they can be defeated simply by not becoming terrified and by resisting the temptation to overreact' (Mueller 2005: 497).

Despite its longevity, this definitional debate was reanimated in the early twenty-first century by those positing a recent profound qualitative change in the nature of terrorism. This potential transition between 'old' and 'new' terrorism was widely debated (for an overview, see, *inter alia*, Duyvesteyn 2004; Neumann 2009; Jackson et al. 2011: 165–170; Bolanos 2013; Duyvestyn and Malkki 2013), in which transformations in the objectives, organisation and violences of terrorist groups were explored (e.g. Simon and Benjamin 2000). Although it was given new urgency by 9/11, the idea that we may be experiencing a 'new' terrorism actually came to the fore before that date, particularly in light of mass casualty attacks such as Aum Shinrikyo's release of sarin gas on the Tokyo underground and the 1998 US embassy bombings in Kenya and Tanzania. In contrast to the nationally organised 'old' terrorism, 'new' terrorism is often portrayed as transnational in focus; where 'old ' terrorism was perpetrated by hierarchical organisations, 'new' terrorism is seen as the product of looser organisational structures, such as networks. The two most defining characteristics of 'new' terrorism, however, are first that it is religiously rather than politically motivated (on this, see Gunning and Jackson 2011); and, second, that 'new' terrorism demonstrates a desire for high victim counts *contra* the more limited violence of 'old' terrorism. Thus, it is often argued that 'new' terrorism works to alter Jenkins' (1974: 4) aphorism that 'terrorists want a lot of people watching, not a lot of people dead' such that 'new' terrorists want a lot of people watching *and* a lot of people dead.

Whilst many have critiqued the 'new' terrorism thesis (Duyvesteyn 2004; Burnett and Whyte 2005; Spencer 2006; Jackson et al. 2011: 166), this conception of dramatic, qualitative change has undeniably proved attractive to politicians making the case for new and extended anti-terrorism powers (Jarvis 2009b: 65–79). Former UK Prime Minister Tony Blair (2001), for example, referred to 9/11 as a 'turning point in history' ushering in 'new and frightening threats' such that 'the kaleidoscope has been shaken, the pieces are in flux'. As he subsequently argued at the Bush Presidential Library: 'the most obvious lesson' of 9/11 was that there was simply 'no escape from facing ... and dealing with' problems such as people using 'scientific and technological advances' who 'have the capacity to destroy' (cited in Holland 2012: 85). In many ways, this British debate both echoed and complemented that taking place across the Atlantic, and indeed elsewhere (e.g. Holland 2010). There, then National Security Advisor, Condoleezza Rice (2001) had argued, 'We commonly hear the refrain that everything changed on September 11th. In many ways that is true.' And, as President Bush (cited in Jarvis 2009a: 74) subsequently put it:

> we learned on that fateful day that America is now a battlefield. It used to be that oceans would protect us. We didn't have to take certain threats seriously. We could say, well, we can deal if we want to deal with them. But we learned a tough lesson, that the old ways are gone, that the enemy can strike us here at home, and we all have new responsibilities.

In short, and as we should expect, conceptions and problematisations of terrorism are central to the creation and justification of proposed mechanisms for resolving this problem (Doty 1993; Holland 2013). As Crelinsten (2009: 7) argues, 'How people talk about problems, frame them and conceptualize them often determines what they do about them'.

Countering terrorism

Anti-terrorism, at its most basic level, concerns attempts to oppose, block, prevent and mitigate the damage done by terrorism. Importantly, given the above definitional contestabilities, the majority of literature on anti-terrorism focuses – rather narrowly – on attempts by states or IGOs to prevent attacks by non-state groups. A common feature of this literature is the construction of typologies that differentiate state activities in this area. Art and Richardson (2007: 16–17), for instance, distinguish between political measures such as negotiations, socio-political reforms and increasing international cooperation; legislative and judicial measures, including emergency or 'temporary' legislation to detain suspects and access information; and security measures such as military deployments, new organisational structures to disrupt terrorist attacks and measures to 'harden' targets.

Crelinsten (2009: 12–14) makes a different distinction between soft and hardline counterterrorism or, as he terms them September 10th thinking and September 12th thinking. The former is seen to work within the law, emphasising legal and diplomatic resolutions to complex phenomena, whilst the latter emphasises military responses, which might be unilateral and emphasise pre-emption instead of deterrence and containment. In his more recent work, he further differentiates between coercive, proactive, persuasive, defensive and long-term approaches to countering terrorism, arguing that a comprehensive approach to this threat would take advantage of all five of these logics (Crelinsten 2014). Focusing on policing, yet using similar language, Spalek (2012) distinguishes similarly between 'hard' counter-terrorism, predicated on surveillance, and 'softer' approaches encouraging community engagement. Paul Wilkinson (1977) in his *Terrorism and the Liberal State* took a similar approach, advocating a 'hardline approach' for the liberal state to deal with terrorism, one comprising a combination of politics and diplomacy, the use of law enforcement and the criminal justice system, along with deployment of military power. As he later claimed, this 'offers a multipronged approach aimed at enabling a liberal democratic state to combat terrorism effectively without undermining or seriously damaging the democratic process and the rule of law, while providing sufficient flexibility to cope with the whole range of threats' (Wilkinson 2011: 75).[2] Silke (2011: 3), finally, identifies special legislation, the creation of specialist counter-terrorism units, repression, military intervention(s), special incarceration and detention, media management and negotiations as amongst the panoply of available anti-terrorism options.

As the above suggests, legislative frameworks constitute an important – and in the UK's case, a common – technique for seeking to counter the threat posed by terrorism (see also, *inter alia*, Haubrich 2003; Rees and Aldrich 2005; Roach 2011; Lister and Otero-Iglesias 2012; Foley 2013). Whilst this might be more desirable than the recourse to military power, assessing the efficacy of these frameworks – and, indeed, all forms of anti-terrorism (see Lum et al. 2006) – is more difficult than we might expect. Although non-state terrorism 'virtually always fails' (Cronin 2009: 206), the reasons for this are varied and the pathways toward failure disparate. Because of this, the specific contribution or value of particular governmental initiatives towards the ending of terrorism might be opaque for several reasons. First, because the diversity of terrorist campaigns, states and legislative frameworks renders generalities difficult. Second, because terrorist campaigns frequently change in ways that make it hard to determine whether they have even ended: this includes splintering into smaller groups, imploding due to internal factors, changing name, or otherwise evading detection (Legrand and Jarvis 2015). Third, as Wilkinson (2011: 94) argues, terrorism by definition makes 'war on legality', hence in many cases the authority of the law has limited purchase (also Cronin 2009: 199). And, fourth, the law itself is a complex and flexible instrument with many functions: prevention, deterrence, symbolic and so forth.

As Wilkinson (2011: 92–93) correctly argues, anti-terrorism law can be introduced for a variety of reasons. These include attempting to deal with underlying grievances, deterring would-be terrorists or sympathisers, upgrading the tools at the disposal of law enforcement officials, reassuring the public that something is being done and expressing public revulsion. This raises the question of whether terrorism should be pursued through the 'normal' criminal law or through exceptional measures. Interestingly, while the introduction and use of the latter has been a prominent, and much discussed, feature of the post-9/11 period (for example, Boukalas 2014), Crelinsten (2009: 52) notes that the former was traditionally prioritised. This was because of the capacity of criminal law to delegitimise the terrorist as nothing more 'glamorous' than the ordinary criminal:

> By criminalizing the acts that terrorists commit, emphasis is placed upon their criminal nature and not on their political or ideological motive. In this way, the terrorist's claim to be acting in the name of a higher purpose is undermined and the means by which s/he attempts to achieve these higher goals is stigmatized. (Crelinsten 2009: 52)

This book will go on to characterise the raft of anti-terrorism measures introduced in the UK, and, in subsequent chapters, to assess the impacts of these upon 'ordinary' citizens and their experiences of security and citizenship. It is, though, briefly worth noting two arguments about the UK's post-9/11 measures, to which we return in greater detail below. First, as Walker (2002) argues, the very existence of so much legislation should itself be seen as some form of failure. As he suggests, one of the aims of the 2000 Terrorism Act was to put UK anti-terrorism law on a permanent, stable, footing. That such a significant piece of legislation as the 2001 Anti-Terrorism, Crime and Security Act (ATCSA) was introduced so soon thereafter can therefore be seen to indicate its predecessor's failure. In other words, the Terrorism Act was flawed because 'it was not successful in averting the passage of the Anti-terrorism Crime and Security Act in 2001 ... [T]he design of the Terrorism Act is at fault for failing to deliver a comprehensive package of laws' (Walker 2002: 7). Walker argues this is in part because its content is 'mainly traceable to the legislation which it replaces', incorporating many of the flaws of prior efforts (Walker 2002: 4). The same point can be made in relation to other, subsequent, pieces of UK legislation, and the swiftness with which these were followed by additional laws.

A second issue concerns the use of the legal apparatus itself. In the period that concerns us here, the UK's New Labour government adopted what critics described as a 'frenzied' approach to law-making: establishing more than three thousand criminal offences – or one per day – between 1997 and 2006 alone (Morris 2006). This apparent faith in the law to get things done – or as a mechanism by which to be seen to be getting things done – may therefore simply have manifested itself in the context of anti-terrorism as much as in other policy areas. At the same time, the New Labour administration was acutely aware of the varying functions – symbolic and otherwise – of security legislation. Indeed, former Prime Minister Tony Blair (2010) used his autobiography to describe the communicative role of legislation intended to extend the period of detention without charge to a maximum of ninety days thus: 'I wanted the power both in its own right but also to send a strong signal out that Britain was going to be a severely inhospitable place for terror groups to operate' (Blair 2010: 583). This emphasis on the symbolic rather than instrumental value of anti-terrorism law is given further credence by Haubrich's (2010: 204) analysis of 130 terrorism-related trials between September 2001 and September 2005. Haubrich found that that nearly all of these were brought under the 2000 Terrorism Act rather than its successors – legislation that was already on the statute books prior to 9/11. Indeed, Haubrich does not find a single charge, let alone conviction, under the 2001 ATCSA in this period. This clearly raises the question as to whether the legal apparatus installed after 2000 is of much use (in prosecuting terrorists, at least), if those convicted of terrorist offences are convicted under pre-existing law.[3]

Before sketching the post-9/11 anti-terrorism apparatus in a little more detail, we turn now to the UK's historical context in order to better situate contemporary developments. As argued above, the post-9/11 approach both builds upon, and is indebted to, the anti-terrorism strategy and measures which preceded it, while also extending and deepening core aspects thereof.

Terrorism and anti-terrorism in the United Kingdom

The modern conception of terrorism derives in large part from the campaigns of violence marking the end of the nineteenth century. Anarchist and national liberation struggles alike sought, at this time, to make use of new technologies such as dynamite and new ideas such as the 'propaganda of the deed', attributed to and popularised by revolutionaries such as Kropotkin (Hubac-Occhipinti 2006), and Pisacane (Hoffman 2006). The first modern terrorist organisation is often identified as Narodnya Volya ('The People's Will'), a Russian group responsible for a number of attacks on the Tsarist regime between 1878 and 1881, culminating with the assassination of Tsar Alexander II in 1881 (Laqueur 2001). Such actions inspired the 'Golden Age of Assassination' in Rapoport's terms (2004: 52), or the 'Decade of Regicide', where 'more monarchs, presidents and prime ministers were assassinated than at any other time in history, before or since' (Jensen 2006: 370). Anarchism is often regarded as a significant driver of such movements (for a review see Hubac-Occhipinti 2006), although the causal relationship between ideas and membership of clandestine organisations is, at best, tenuous (Stevens 2011). As Jackson et al. (2011: 160) argue in the context of religious terrorism, a 'key problem with typologies is that they tend to slip from pure description – "this group is inspired by religion" – to causal inference – "this group is violent *because* it is religious" – even if such an explanation is not supported by empirical evidence'.

Whilst the actions of groups such as Narodnya Volya were significant, other authors such as Clutterbuck (2004) argue the 'dynamite campaign' mounted by the Irish Republican Brotherhood and Clan na Gael between 1881 and 1885 has greater significance for modern terrorism. 'It was from this source, not the Russian revolutionary movement, that so many of the concepts, strategy, tactics and techniques of terrorism originated' (Clutterbuck 2004: 176; see also Hoffman 2006: 8–11). Halliday (2002: 76) similarly locates this period as the conclusion of terrorism's 'pre-history', identifying the assassinations of Tsar Alexander II and Archduke Ferdinand of Austro-Hungary in 1914 as the events bookending the 'high point' in this phase of terrorism.

Despite the importance of these campaigns, the origins of political violence in the UK that we might refer to as terrorism lie slightly earlier still. From the mid-nineteenth century onward, disaffected Irish nationalists, the Irish Republican Brotherhood (IRB), or Fenians, as they were known, began to challenge British rule. Much of this activity originally took place in Ireland, but from the mid-1860s they became active in mainland Britain. The two most noteworthy incidents both occurred in 1867: the armed hijacking of a prison van bearing two IRB members in Manchester, which resulted in the death of a police officer; and the massive explosion in Clerkenwell, in another attempted prison break, which was ultimately responsible for the deaths of twelve people (see Jenkins 2008). Whilst authors such as Gearty (1991) deny that the Fenian campaign should be seen as terrorism – not least because the Clerkenwell explosion, brutal though it was, was likely a miscalculation unintended to cause the degree of damage it did – it was a noteworthy precursor to the types of politically motivated violence now commonly understood as terrorist.

Moving forward to the 'dynamite campaign' of 1881–85, this is often seen as a more straightforward instance of terrorism. The campaign was the product of two, sometimes feuding, US-based republican groups: the IRB and Clan na Gael. Clutterbuck argues that the first bombing, of the Salford barracks (where the 'Manchester Martyrs', those deemed responsible for the death of the police officer in 1867 were later executed) represents a significant shift from previous Fenian violence. 'For the first time, in the name of a political cause and with the intention of coercing a government, terrorists had made an explosive device, placed it against their target, and escaped before it exploded' (Clutterbuck 2006: 100). Other bombs were detonated in Glasgow and Liverpool as well as in London. In violences now evocative of others much later, there were also explosions on the London Underground, as well as at Victoria Station, the House of Commons, and the offices of *The Times* newspaper (Hoffman 2006; Whelehan 2012).

The reaction of the British state to these campaigns was complex. On the one hand, the response to the Fenian insurrection in Ireland made use of quite exceptional measures. Ireland, to some extent, had always been 'a place apart' in the eyes of the British government, and limits on press freedoms and the repeated suspension of *habeas corpus* throughout the nineteenth century were introduced as seemingly legitimate responses to the violences there (Whelehan 2012: 18; also Jenkins 2006). This, however, was not the initial response, for, as Porter (1987: 3) argues, the mid-nineteenth-century Victorian state viewed political and social stability as a product of free and open societies. The corollary of this was that widespread public dissatisfaction was seen as an outcome of repressive regimes:

> Laws and agencies created in order to repress subversion had the very opposite effect. They made people aggrieved, and consequently rebellious. They would not be aggrieved – would have nothing to be aggrieved about – if they were left (as the Victorians liked to put it) 'free'. This was the answer to the problem of subversion, which was really not a genuine problem in the mid-Victorians' eyes. Political societies and systems were best defended – paradoxically – by having no defences at all. (Porter 1987: 3)

Jenkins also argues that the response of the British state to the Fenian violence of the mid-nineteenth century 'generally met the test of liberal acceptability in Britain' (Jenkins 2006: 331). Indeed, when in 1867 Disraeli (among others) pondered the suspension of *habeas corpus* in mainland Britain, the cabinet majority countered that Parliament would not consent to 'so serious an infraction of the liberty of the whole people for the sake of punishing a few desperate conspirators' (cited in Jenkins 2006: 168).

Yet, despite these liberal sensitivities, the 'dynamite campaign' was also seen as different to its precursors and requiring, as such, a different response. Porter argues that dynamite itself led to a rethinking of liberal optimism and the belief that democratic societies were best protected through asserting liberal values. Previously, liberal politicians had argued that any threat from subversives came from insurrection requiring large numbers of people. Thus, if the state could maintain its benevolent face, such large numbers would be unlikely to move to a rebel cause. But the invention of dynamite, according to Porter (1987: 24), meant that 'small groups of men and women, provided they were unscrupulous enough, had a potential for destruction out of all proportion to their numbers; which itself had rendered many of the old liberal safeguards against political subversion, which depended on *majorities* remaining unsubverted, inoperable'. Importantly, despite this increasing circumspection towards liberal values, these remained largely upheld in response to the violence of 1881–85. The main changes concerned the passing of restrictions on explosives in the 1883 Explosive Substances Act and, for the first time in the UK, the creation of a secret political police, which became Special Branch in 1887 (Porter 1987; also Clutterbuck 2006; Hewitt 2008: 12).

Substantial changes to the legal code were not seen in the UK until the period of violence surrounding the partition of Ireland. In some ways, a key legislative intervention and the precursor for much of the subsequent UK legislation (at first in relation to Northern Ireland, but later more widely) was the 1922 Civil Authorities (Special Powers) Act (known as the Special Powers Act or SPA).[4] This gave the Northern Ireland Executive broad powers to:

> impose curfews; close premises, roads, transportation routes; detain and intern individuals; and proscribe organisations. It gave the government the right to censor newspapers and radio and to ban meetings, processions and gatherings, and the use of cars. The legislation altered the court system. The SPAs granted extensive powers of entry, search and seizure, and in a Draconian catch-all phrase, empowered the civilian authority 'to take all necessary steps and issue all such orders as may be necessary for preserving the peace and maintaining order'. (Donohue 2007: 19)

This latter provision was the means by which internment was introduced in Northern Ireland on four separate occasions: 1921–24, 1938–46, 1956–62 and most famously, perhaps, 1971–75. The SPAs were introduced to deal with paramilitary violence following partition, and were justified by a Unionist member of the Northern Ireland assembly at the time in now-familiar language: 'This is an exceptional time and requires exceptional measures' (cited in Donohue 2006: 295). The SPA provisions were later repealed, although many were reintroduced in the 1973 Northern Ireland (Emergency Provisions) Act, or EPA.

There are a number of recurring issues with legislation of this sort in the UK experience. One is the frequent justification of such measures by exceptionalist arguments in which the situation's urgency – or the threat's potential severity – is invoked to justify powers that would otherwise be considered unacceptable and potentially illegal (see also Buzan et al. 1998). A second is the repeated use of 'temporary' legislation: a product of the exceptionality argument, Parliament initially renders anti-terrorism laws temporary, as they are seen to be out of the norm with conventional legal provisions. Yet such measures have a way of either being made permanent, or finding their way into permanent legislation. A third issue concerns the recurrence of efforts to circumvent normal legal processes and make use of executive powers. This is seen particularly with regard to detention without trial, or internment. The act of suspending *habeas corpus* has been one to which the British government has routinely turned over the last two centuries. Whelehan (2012: 18) points to seven suspensions of *habeas corpus* in Ireland in the nineteenth century and, as noted below, Donohue (2007) identifies four periods in the twentieth century. If we add to those Section IV of the 2001 Anti-Terrorism, Crime and Security Act, which allowed for indefinite detention without trial of foreign nationals, and perhaps even the control orders regime (considered, by one Law Lord, 'akin to detention in an open prison'; see BBC News 2008), then we might point to thirteen instances where the UK government has sought to detain its enemies without access to due legal process.

In 1939, the UK anti-terrorism experience developed further as the paramilitary Irish Republican Army (IRA) embarked on a bombing campaign in mainland Britain. Between January and July of that year alone, 127 attacks took place, resulting in one death and over fifty injuries (Hewitt 2008: 15). In response, the Westminster Parliament passed the Prevention of Violence (Temporary Provisions) Act. This gave the Home Secretary the power to require all Irish people living in the UK to register with the authorities, the power to expel from the UK and the power to detain those suspected of terrorist offences for forty-eight hours and, with special authorisation, a further five days (Donohue 2007: 21; Hewitt 2008: 15). The onset of the Second World War meant this legislation was short lived, although another recurrent feature – hastiness – of UK anti-terrorism legislation can also be seen here, given that it took five days for Westminster to pass this Act and seven for it to become law (Donohue 2006).

The arrival of 'the Troubles' in the late 1960s saw further attempts to make use of the law in the fight against terrorism. As mentioned above, many aspects of the repealed SPAs resurfaced in the 1973 Emergency Provisions Act, or EPA, making available a similarly broad range of powers of detention, search and seizure, along with provision for non-jury trials (Donohue 2007). Following the spilling over of violence from Northern Ireland to the mainland, seen particularly in the Birmingham pub bombings of 1974, new legislation was introduced, in the form of the Prevention of Terrorism (Temporary Provisions) Act of 1974. This revived many of the powers of the 1939 Prevention of Violence (Temporary Provisions) Act, including proscription of organisations deemed to be terrorist in nature, and introduced exclusion orders (which banned persons from entering certain parts, or the entirety, of Northern Ireland and/or the United Kingdom), as well as extended powers of arrest and detention (see Bonner 1992; Donohue 2007). This legislation, introduced only four days after the Birmingham bombing, was law within a further three. Described by the then Home Secretary as 'draconian' and 'unprecedented in peacetime' (cited in Walker 1986: 22), the legislation was intended to be temporary and was therefore subject to sunset clauses and renewals. Yet it remained in force twenty years later. Roy Jenkins, the Home Secretary responsible for its introduction, later commented, 'I do not regret having introduced it. But I would have been horrified to have been told at the time that it would still be law nearly two decades later ... [I]t should teach one to be careful about justifying something on the ground that it is only for a short time' (cited in Donohue 2000: 6).

In the late 1990s as the peace process in Northern Ireland started to bear fruit, there emerged a need to reconsider and re-evaluate anti-terrorism legislation. Indeed, Walker (2002: 2) suggests that reviewing anti-terrorism measures was itself an important element of the peace process. The Lloyd Report had begun reviewing anti-terrorism legislation to establish how this might be put on a permanent footing, and much of this was accepted into law in the form of the 2000 Terrorism Act. This broad piece of legislation, which marks the first time in the UK that anti-terrorism law was established on a permanent basis, contained a number of provisions, such as detention without charge of up to fourteen days, powers of search and seizure, and proscription (see Walker 2002).

Walker (2002: 4) suggests that, as it was unlike previous legislation 'which had too often been hastily drafted in circumstances of crisis', the 2000 Terrorism Act offered a chance for more considered reflection. Yet, as noted above, this Act failed to prevent the passage of another substantial piece of anti-terrorism legislation the following year. Introduced in the wake of 9/11, the ATCSA is perhaps most well-known for the Part IV powers which allowed for indefinite detention of foreign nationals *suspected of* terrorism. This was later declared illegal as the derogation from the Human Rights Act under Article 15 was deemed incompatible with the 1998 Human Rights Act (see Walker 2006: 1143). The government responded by introducing the 2005 Prevention of Terrorism Act, which sought to deal with those persons previously detained under Part IV of ATCSA by instituting a system of control orders. Control orders, unlike Part IV of ACTSA which focused on foreign nationals, could also be applied to UK citizens. Individuals subject to these faced a range of restrictions, including electronic tagging, residency constraints, limits on how many hours they could be out of their home (seen by many as a form of house arrest) and with whom and by what means they could communicate. The orders could be issued by the Home Secretary if the individual was suspected of involvement in terrorism. Although approved by a judge, the hearings took place in the absence of the individual (or their counsel) subject to the order; neither were the individuals entitled to see all of the evidence presented against them (see Zedner 2007). Control orders were subsequently replaced by the Terrorism Prevention and Investigation Measures (TPIM) regime introduced in the 2011 TPIM Act. *Contra* control orders, TPIMs are subject to a maximum of two years' duration and – for the UK's independent reviewer of terrorism legislation (Anderson 2013: 4) – are more rights-compliant than their predecessor, imposing less onerous restrictions on their subjects.

Further legislation followed after the July 2005 '7/7' bombings in London in the form of the 2006 Terrorism Act. The most prominent adaption here was the extension of the maximum period for which individuals could be detained without charge. This was increased from fourteen to twenty-eight days, although the government had initially appealed for a ninety-day limit. Further innovations included the creation of an offence to incite or directly or indirectly encourage or glorify terrorism, and an offence to receive terrorist preparation or training (see Walker 2006). Despite this being the fourth major piece of anti-terrorism legislation since 2000, the government was not quite finished and in 2008 introduced the Counter Terrorism Act, which is perhaps most notable for its failed attempt to extend pre-charge detention to forty-two days. It also allowed for some alterations to police and investigative procedures, including in relation to post-charge questioning.

In addition to these major legislative changes, the UK government also introduced an overarching anti-terrorism framework in the form of the UK Home Office's CONTEST strategy. First published in 2003, with further iterations in 2006, 2009 and 2011, CONTEST was organised around four alliterative workstreams: 'Protect', 'Prepare', 'Pursue' and 'Prevent' (Home Office 2011). Intended to integrate intelligence, homeland security and conciliatory approaches to anti-terrorism (Jackson et al. 2011: 224–229), the strategy aims to 'reduce the risk to the UK and its interests overseas from terrorism' (Home Office 2011: 9). Key mechanisms to this end included hardening key infrastructure against attacks, improving post-attack recovery, enhancing detection and prosecution of suspected terrorists and introducing measures to bolster communities' resilience to 'violent extremism'. As the UK's Annual Report of April 2014 put it:

> The Government has continued to provide the police and the security and intelligence agencies with the powers and capabilities they need to do their job. These powers are necessary and proportionate and subject to close oversight and scrutiny. We have a sustained cross-Government effort to deal with the new and wider range of terrorist threats we now face overseas. (HM Government 2014: 17)

Of CONTEST's four workstreams, the counter-radicalisation emphasis within 'Prevent' has proven most controversial (see Baker-Beall et al. 2015). Originally titled 'Preventing Violent Extremism', Prevent aims to be a locally oriented and community-focused 'hearts and minds' based anti-terrorism approach (Lowndes and Thorp 2010: 123; Thomas and Sanderson 2011: 230). The strategy is targeted at 'increasing the resilience and addressing the grievances of communities, and ... identifying vulnerable individuals, as well as challenging and disrupting ideologies sympathetic to violent extremism' (Thomas 2010: 444).

Controversy followed Prevent's initial focus on areas within the UK with disproportionately high numbers of Muslim residents. This drew criticism for its inefficient allocation of scarce resources, its blurring of security and community cohesion politics, its emphasis on religion and religious identities, and its stigmatisation of a heterogeneous and varied demographic as 'suspect' (Stevens 2009, 2011; Thomas 2009, 2010; Lowndes and Thorp 2010). Prevent-related activities are also, moreover, largely pre-emptive, with the policy and discourse of radicalisation attracting additional condemnation for targeting those 'at risk of becoming risky' (Heath-Kelly 2013: 397; also Martin 2014) before they have engaged in any behaviour related to 'extremism'. The 2010–15 coalition government acknowledged these problems, terming previous incarnations of Prevent 'flawed' (Home Office 2011: 6). Some shifts in policy have followed, including attempts to separate the integrative and anti-extremism functions, but many problems persist, such as its focus on 'British' values (see Jarvis and Lister 2011).

There are four things to take from this brief history of the development of anti-terrorism powers within the UK. The first is to show that despite the recent surge in anti-terrorism legislation, attempts to alter the legal framework and its provisions have been an important part of the British struggle against terrorism since the nineteenth century. In this sense, this surge might be seen as an acceleration of a pre-existing dynamic: a quantitative, rather than qualitative, change. The second is to show that many of the contemporary powers revive or build upon previous measures. As Donohue argues, the 'counter terrorist assault' (Donohue 2007: 17) after 9/11 represents the, 'continuation of trends that had already been underway prior to the attacks ... Powers used under the Terrorist [sic] Act predated the attacks and embodied a century of counterterrorist initiatives. The ATCSA drew on these and introduced provisions that had been considered or used previously' (Donohue 2007: 46). Haubrich (2003: 23), too, identifies 'a seamless (yet hardly insignificant) continuation of a string of liberty-curtailing anti-terrorism measures that had been legislated previously'.

Third, the above highlights the regularity with which the UK Parliament passes anti-terrorism legislation. Since 1974, the UK Parliament has passed major anti-terrorism legislation ten times,[5] and this excludes legislation passed prior to 1974 such as the 1939 Prevention of Violence Act and the hundred plus pieces of relevant legislation passed in Northern Ireland since 1800 (Donohue 2000: 5). Landman (2007: 81), indeed, puts this figure higher still, identifying twenty pieces of legislation pertaining to terrorism between 1967 and 2006 alone. Thus in the UK different executives have made legislating against terrorism offences a major plank of their broader anti-terrorism strategy.

Fourth, as might be suggested by this deluge of anti-terrorism law, such legislation is frequently introduced in direct response to particular events.

The PTA was passed in the aftermath of the Birmingham bombings; the 2001 ACTSA followed 9/11; and the Terrorism Act 2006 did so with 7/7. How conducive this is to 'good' law making is beyond the scope of this book, but the hastiness with which such legislation passes through Parliament – both upper and lower houses – may obviate careful consideration of some of the likely impacts of such measures on the wider citizenry.

The UK in comparative perspective

As demonstrated above, a number of recurrent themes in the brief history of British anti-terrorism legislation may be identified. Perhaps less well understood, however, are the reasons for these continuities. Before turning to these – and the implications thereof for citizenship and security – it will be useful briefly to locate the UK experience in geographical context. For, if anti-terrorism policy and legislation evolved in similar ways in different countries – in a 'spiral' (Donohue 2008: 15) of increasingly restrictive and 'draconian' measures – then this trajectory might be explained simply as a terrorist/anti-terrorist 'dance', whereby states always respond to political violence with more muscular or visible legislative frameworks. As Tsoukala (2006: 608) points out, 'most liberal democratic governments presume that they cannot be effective against the threat unless they sacrifice some of their democratic substance'. Yet, as we shall see, the UK experience of such frequent legislation in this area is not one repeated in other liberal democratic states (except, perhaps, Australia). This is the case even in states with comparable or similar experiences of terrorism, such as Spain and France.

To begin by briefly considering the particularities of the UK context, Landman (2007) points to this country's paradoxical position with regard to law, security and civil liberties. On the one hand, the UK has a long (albeit far from unblemished) history of championing civil liberties, going back to the signing of Magna Carta in June 1215. It was also one of the authors of the 1950 European Convention for Human Rights. And yet the lack of a written constitution, along with a system of Parliamentary sovereignty combined with executive dominance, has reduced the 'horizontal accountability' (Landman 2007: 76) or checks and balances that can, as we shall see, be identified in other states. Thus, 'On the one hand, Britain has been a beacon of liberty to the world ... On the other hand, in dealing with domestic and international terrorism it has established the strongest and most draconian set of restrictions on its citizens in Europe' (Landman 2007: 77).

Spain represents an interesting comparative case (see Serrano 2015). Like the UK, Spain has a long history of fighting terrorism within its own borders, especially in the form of Euskadi Ta Askatasuna (ETA), the Basque separatist group active from the late 1950s until its permanent ceasefire in 2010. It also has direct experience of al-Qaeda-inspired terrorism in the form of the Madrid train bombings of March 2004 in which almost 200 people were killed. Yet, in many ways, Spain's approach to dealing with terrorism is very different from the UK's (see Lister and Otero-Iglesias 2012 for a full comparison). Much of this has to do with the historical legacies of the two countries. Spain's initial anti-terrorism approach was formed under the Franco dictatorship, and had little regard for human rights and civil liberties. The transition to democracy, begun in 1978, saw changes to this framework to make it more acceptable to liberal democratic norms, although some practices, such as incommunicado detention periods, were retained.

The major difference from the UK is that Spain does not have special or distinctive anti-terrorism law. Rather, it is part of the Criminal Code and the Procedural Criminal Code, and Spain has been criticised by many different international bodies for this (see FRIDE 2008; Barrenechea 2009). Under this approach, any crime can become terrorism if authorities can prove that there is a link between the crime (kidnapping, murder, bombing etc.) and membership of a terrorist group (Lister and Otero-Iglesias 2012: 571–572). Thus Spain does not make use of 'exceptional' legal measures which list specific terrorist crimes, but can potentially link any breach of the criminal code to terrorism. Thus, the Spanish system for fighting terrorism, based on permanent law, has been seen, by some, as 'the most impressive in Europe' (Guittet 2008: 267). This is, perhaps, a major reason why we do not see the same flurry of legislative activity as we have done in the UK. Indeed, unlike in the UK, there was no significant new anti-terrorism legislation introduced in Spain after 9/11 or after the 2004 Madrid bombings. The only legislative changes introduced were minor reformulations to deal with explosives (Reinares 2009: 376–377) which more strongly echo the UK's nineteenth-century experience. Other non-legislative changes concentrated on enhancing intelligence capability, improving coordination between government agencies, attempts to combat 'radicalisation' and efforts to firm up protection of infrastructure targets (Alonso 2008: 212). Yet, amidst these changes, Colás (2010: 327) points to the 'virtual absence of institutional or legislative reform in the face of jihadist terrorism', arguing that Spain has instead been host to 'an attempt to deepen the reach of existing judiciary/law enforcement agencies and to tighten up co-ordination among relevant counter-terrorist departments of the state'.

There is, perhaps, a slight irony in that Spain's authoritarian legacy may be responsible for the relative legal restraint shown by Spanish governments in relation to the countering of terrorism. For many commentators, the legacy of the Franco regime makes stringent restrictions on liberties unpalatable. Spain's anti-terrorism law was born in the dictatorship, and the grafting of terrorist crimes onto existing criminal law has resulted in a situation where civil liberties are subsequently better protected against further restrictions (Lister and Otero-Iglesias 2012). Spain's written constitution of 1978 plays a role too, but the key point to emphasise is that how anti-terrorism law is initiated, as well as the institutional makeup of a state, has a significant impact on its future trajectory.

The importance of institutional and normative traditions within national anti-terrorism frameworks is identifiable elsewhere, too. In Germany, for example, the reconstruction of democracy following the Nazi era renders sweeping restrictions on civil liberties more difficult to enact. These protections are embedded in the German constitution, or Basic Law, which begins with the statement, 'The dignity of the Human Person is inviolable', and contains within it certain fundamental rights which cannot be overturned or altered (Heinz 2007: 159). During the Red Army Faction's (RAF) operative years in the 1970s, German law was changed to incorporate broader powers concerning affiliation with violent groups and to enable a focus on 'criminal intent rather than criminal behavior' (Katzenstein 2003: 741). Other changes were also introduced, although these mainly dealt with trial and prison procedures and, aside from provisions concerning incommunicado detention, most of these were generally seen to operate within the existing framework of German law, rather than serving as examples of its stretching (Heinz 2007).

In response to 9/11, the German government introduced two new anti-terrorism laws: Security Package I and II in 2002. These included provisions for border control and enhancing data sharing between domestic authorities, to protect aviation and infrastructure and to ban the activities of extremist associations (Katzenstein 2003: 749–751; Heinz 2007: 163–168). For Haubrich (2003: 10), these provisions together represented 'The most wide ranging package of laws directed at civil liberties in the history of the German Republic'. Despite this, Heinz (2007: 174) argues that the legacy of Nazism, a greater parliamentary and judicial influence on the executive than that of most European states and a wish to act in accordance with international norms have 'favoured a general commitment to national and international human rights norms'. This is a view endorsed by Capoccia (2010: 317), who states, 'The institutional safeguards incorporated into the Basic Law to avoid "excessive" centralisation of power ... are still firmly in place'. Thus, there is a relative lack of 'exceptional' anti-terrorism law or, indeed, new anti-terrorism provisions making large-scale alterations to the German legal framework (see also Katzenstein 2003). This, though, has not prevented Germany being placed, by human rights groups, in the top five of the 'name and shame' list of countries responsible for curbing civil liberties after 9/11 (see Haubrich 2003: 7). The point, therefore, is not that Germany has not introduced legislation restricting citizenship and civil liberties. Rather, a considerable difference of degree separates the alteration thereof in comparison to the sweeping changes adopted by the UK.

This picture of the shape, structure and intensity of anti-terrorism measures being limited, conditioned and influenced by institutions, history and (political) culture – a picture which shows the UK to be amongst those states most engaged in the most widespread alteration of legal frameworks – is further illustrated by the case of France. France is widely portrayed as having a strong and flexible approach to dealing with terrorism, primarily through the system of investigating magistrates (see Shapiro and Suzan 2003; Shapiro 2010). This system makes use of relatively elastic anti-terrorism powers in a, for some, more draconian way than the UK (Foley 2013: 3). As with the UK and Spain, France also has a long history of dealing with terrorism in recent years, both from the political left and right, and also related to Islamic fundamentalism (and specifically Algeria). Legislation was introduced in 1986, in response to a bombing campaign from the militant group Committee for Solidarity with Near Eastern Political Prisoners (CSPPA). This extended the period for pre-charge detention from twenty-four hours to four days (six days in exceptional circumstances; Shapiro 2008) and instituted the regime of investigating magistrates (Shapiro and Suzan 2003: 71–78). Further legislation followed in 1995 and 1996 in response to violences from the Armed Islamic Group (GIA), which made conspiracy to commit acts of terrorism a terrorist offence (Shapiro and Suzan 2003: 82). This also, importantly, allowed investigating magistrates to conduct 'sweeps' – large-scale arrests – in order to pre-empt terrorism. In two separate operations in 1993 and 1995, 93 and 131 people respectively were arrested and detained (most released without charge), leading to criticism from French human rights groups. Indeed, the term '*rafle*' was used in French, which has connotations of the actions taken against Jews during the German occupation (Shapiro and Suzan 2003: 84). In response to 9/11, further anti-terrorism measures were introduced, which led to enhanced powers of stop and search (including to private security guards) and electronic data surveillance (Haubrich 2003: 11–13). Thus, although lacking the volume of legislation and extent of legislative adaptation that we have seen in the UK, the French approach to anti-terrorism is viewed as 'fairly effective, though controversial' (Shapiro and Suzan 2003: 68), with some arguing that the public voice on these issues is less deferential to civil liberties than in the UK (Tsoukala 2006; Foley 2013).

Of course, other Western, non-European countries, including the United States, Canada and Australia, have also reformed their domestic provisions to deal with terrorism. The United States famously passed the USA PATRIOT Act in the aftermath of 9/11. Despite the considerable criticism it attracted, some authors argue only a few sections (concerning surveillance and deportation) of this lengthy – 352-page – Act are truly controversial, depicting much of it as, 'an amalgam of often unrelated pieces of authority, most of which simply amend existing laws, and the larger share of which are unremarkable complements to existing authority' (Banks 2005: 492; see also Etzioni 2008). Indeed, one might argue that the more recent National Defense Authorization Act of 2012, with its provision for indefinite detention of terrorism suspects represents a more significant challenge to civil liberties (see Turley 2012) than much of that contained within its better-known forebear. The comparative absence of the sorts of restriction introduced in the UK might be explained, in part, by the American experience of terrorism as an external rather than internal security threat. As Colin Powell (cited in Jarvis 2009b: 66) put it a little under two weeks after the 9/11 attacks: 'It's deeply moving to know that, one, we had this kind of vulnerability and that there were people *out there* who we knew were out there but never really had a sense of how determined they were to strike us in this way' (emphasis added). Thus, despite the obvious exception of the Department of Homeland Security, many of the US's most significant recent anti-terrorism initiatives have taken the form of overseas military interventions (as in Iraq and Afghanistan) or exceptional initiatives such as the use of military commissions and the holding of 'enemy combatants' at Guantanamo Bay.

Moving beyond the US, the Canadian case merits mention for its use of immigration law in the struggle against terrorism (Roach 2005, 2007). Yet, in the context of this discussion, it is perhaps the Australian experience which is most interesting. Prior to 2001, Australia did not have a single federal anti-terrorism law (Williams 2005: 538). Whilst seemingly some way from the front line of the 'war on terror' – although the 2002 Bali bombing in which eighty-eight Australians lost their lives perhaps shifted this perception (Williams 2005) – Australia has engaged in a post-9/11 anti-terrorism legislative bonanza, unmatched (in numerical terms) in the Western world. This has seen a total of forty-four different anti-terrorism laws passed between 2001 and 2007 alone (Roach 2011: 310). Although 'some of these numbers can be attributed to styles of legislative drafting', Roach (2011: 310) refers to this as 'Australia's hyper-legislation' which eclipses even the UK's legislative activism. The laws include powers for the Australian Security Intelligence Organization to detain those suspected of having information about terrorism offences. There were also measures directly drawn from, or inspired by, the UK context, including the definition of terrorism used (drawn from the UK 2000 Terrorism Act), and the establishment of a control orders regime (see Roach 2007, 2011; Lynch 2008; Macken 2010).

This comparative exercise shows us that the UK has been amongst the most active of liberal democracies in introducing new measures to combat terrorism. This does not, of course, mean that other countries are somehow 'soft' – or 'softer' – in this area; indeed, France and Spain might be seen to have a 'tougher' anti-terrorism regime than the UK (see Foley 2013 and Guittet

2008, respectively). It does, however, indicate the particularity of the UK's confrontation with the apparent threat of 'new terrorism', which has involved formal changes to its legal system with serious implications for the rights and lived experiences of citizens. On issues such as control orders, pre-charge detention, stop and search powers and indefinite detention, the UK policy legacy looks (perhaps with the exception of Australia, itself heavily influenced by the UK) distinctive as well as influential in setting international anti-terrorism agendas (Roach 2007).

Understanding the UK's approach

As the above brief survey shows, the global post-9/11 response to terrorism is marked by diversity (see also Roach 2011). There is a voluminous literature which seeks to compare the anti-terrorism frameworks of different countries, yet, surprisingly little addressing the *reasons* for differences therein. The majority of this work is either concerned with what states have done, historically, and assessing the success thereof (for example, Hoffman and Morrison-Taw 2000; English 2009; Wilkinson 2011) or with the juxtaposing of case studies against one another for comparative purposes (for example, Reinares 2000; Alexander 2002; Art and Richardson 2007).

Those authors who have directly addressed this question have tended to focus on the ability of executives to enact stringent measures, often emphasising the role of public fear and threat perception, in association with institutional and political factors (Roach 2007). Arguments concerning the UK here posit a combination of public unease, strong single-party government, a comparatively weak judiciary and political opposition and a relative lack of interest group mobilisation (see Haubrich 2003: 28). These factors clearly have importance in terms of what executives can do, but not all of the variation is explained by veto points, nor the executive's (in)ability to get things done. As the above indicates, it is not the case that all states desire more stringent measures yet vary in their capacity to enact them (Lister and Otero-Iglesias 2012). Rather, historical experiences at least partly shape the ways in which parliamentarians and other politicians conceive of what is appropriate and desirable.

Rather than all states responding, or seeking to respond, in the same fashion to a perceived common threat, states have distinctive and different institutional and policy legacies. This is in spite of tendencies that would push towards uniformity, such as the United Nations Security Council Resolution 1373, with its exhortations to introduce specific counter-terrorism measures (Bianchi 2006). This Resolution was passed on 28 September 2011 – a little over two weeks after the 9/11 attacks – under Chapter VII of the UN Charter, rendering its provisions mandatory for UN member states (Romaniuk 2010: 65). Although, in part, a consolidation of existing norms (Romaniuk 2010: 68), the wide-ranging 1373:

> requires states to implement counter-terrorism measures in such areas as financial regulation, migration and customs controls, travel document security, movements of arms, explosives and nuclear, chemical and biological materials, and the use of communicative technologies. In addition, the resolution calls for bilateral, regional and international cooperation on law enforcement, administrative and judicial matters, in extradition proceedings, and as regards the exchange of information regarding terrorism. (Romaniuk 2010: 67)

That national differences emerged amidst these pushes for conformity is a reflection, for Katzenstein (2003), of different country-specific policy, institutional, political and historical legacies. He argues that 9/11 was 'like a strong beam of light that gets filtered by national lenses, of different self-conceptions and institutional practices, which create distinctive political responses' (Katzenstein 2003: 732).

The insight that history matters is hardly new, although, as Pierson (2004: 2) notes, it is an insight 'often-invoked but rarely examined'. Historical institutionalist explanations focus on how seemingly common pressures can result in divergent outcomes in different states, owing to the different institutional and ideational legacies of the past. Or, as Thelen (1999: 397) puts it, 'why common international trends frequently have such different domestic consequences, disrupting previously stable patterns in some countries while washing over others seemingly without effect'. Hall's work (1993) on policy paradigms is relevant here, which he defines as 'a framework of ideas and standards that specifies not only the goals of policy and the kind of instruments that can be used to attain them, but also the very nature of the problems they are meant to be addressing' (Hall 1993: 279). As, from a different tradition, is the notion of 'security cultures', which operate as:

> patterns of thought and argumentation that establish pervasive and durable security preferences by formulating concepts of the role, legitimacy and efficacy of particular approaches to protecting values. Through a process of socialization, security cultures help establish the core assumptions, beliefs and values of decision-makers about how security challenges can and should be dealt with (Williams 2007: 256).

What these – and related explanations including 'regimes of truth' – highlight is that distinctive policy paradigms might follow the filtering of historical events through the experience of previous policy, creating shared 'cognitive filters' or discursive frameworks. These frameworks reflect and reproduce shared understandings of the social and political world, the problems requiring attention therein and the solutions available to the policymaker. Thus, as Hay and Wincott put it of historical institutionalist ideas such as path dependency:

> The order in which things happen affects how they happen; the trajectory of change up to a certain point itself constrains the trajectory after that point; and the strategic choices made at a particular point eliminate whole ranges of possibilities from later choices while serving as the very condition of existence of others (Hay and Wincott 1998: 955)

In the UK context, the trajectory of past policies influences, shapes and limits the policy response at any given moment. As we saw above, its paradigm is one where Parliament routinely legislates on terrorism, using 'temporary' measures. Likewise, history matters in different ways elsewhere, such as the decision to graft terrorism offences to 'normal' criminal offences in Spain. Anti-terrorism legislation in the UK is, then, constant and repetitive, with ten major pieces passed between 1974 and 2008. These continuities, moreover, tell only part of the story whereby, because the Prevention of Terrorism Act was itself 'temporary', it was subject to annual Parliamentary approval between 1974 and 1997, as were the Northern Ireland (Emergency Provisions) Acts. This initial 'temporary' status was a product of their reading by politicians at the time as being draconian but regrettably necessary. Ironically, this impulse – designed, one might reasonably assume, to limit the scope and duration of such powers – has created a habit of Parliament legislating on anti-terrorism. Thus, a measure designed to limit anti-terrorism law might have inadvertently created a context for its furtherance and development.

The fact that much British legislation has been problematic and, in some instances, incompatible with the law has meant that its passage also sowed the seeds of future legislation. For example, Part IV of the ATCSA, allowing for indefinite detention of foreign nationals, can be seen as directly leading to the 2005 Prevention of Terrorism Act and control orders regime. Similarly, the fact that anti-terrorism legislation prior to 2000 applied only to Northern Ireland meant that when political violence rose up from other sources, new legislation would be needed (Walker 1986). In contrast to a more flexible system of law like Spain's, furthermore, because the UK designates specific terrorist offences, new legislation is constantly required to keep pace with new terrorist offences. As Andrew Neal argues:

> Each time there is a terrorist event, security appears as a new and urgent problem to legislators. The response of legislating in a rushed, reactive, and repetitive manner is well established and almost automatic ... Although security problems appear new, the legislative response is not. Although the threats, suspect groups, governments, and legislators themselves may change over the years, the same response is repeated. And although the content of new security laws may sometimes be innovative, the legislative process always suffers from the same problems of rushed, reactive, and repetitious action. (Neal 2012: 361)

Neal (2012) notes also that Parliament is heavily subordinate to the executive on matters of security (even more than normally, in the UK's majoritarian system), although this does not mean that it simply acquiesces to the executive's whims (witness the rejection of the ninety-day pre-charge detention provision in 2006).

Invoking Bourdieu's notion of habitus to explain this legislative activism, Neal suggests that not only is Parliament mostly deferential to the executive on security matters, but that its prior legislative responses, in part, may have created their own expectations among citizens. In other words, as Parliament has responded to terrorist attacks in the past with new legislation, Parliamentarians may perceive that this is what people expect them to do in the present. Neal (2012: 365) cites a House of Lords inquiry that heard that 'very often in the aftermath of a terrorist atrocity, politicians must be seen to be doing something, and there is a public mood that demands that'. He continues, 'Politicians seem to know how they are expected to respond to terrorist attacks, which suggests that responses to terrorism are historically institutionalized and manifested as convention' (Neal 2012: 365). Thus Parliament is virtually socialised into '"emergency" legislation, whilst also being hampered by certain difficulties (such as lack of access to reliable information), which militate against effective executive scrutiny' (Neal 2012: 364–366). As a result, it has traditionally come up with poor legislation that requires constant amendment, thereby further entrenching and embedding the recurrence of anti-terrorism legislation.

This argument that history and institutional and policy legacies in particular shape national anti-terrorism activities (see also Lister and Otero-Iglesias 2012; Foley 2013) incorporates within it the importance of public attitudes. Katzenstein (2003: 734), for example, notes: 'In a political analysis of terrorism and counterterrorism, what matters most are processes that shape how groups and governments conceive of the use of violence, how publics perceive and interpret insecurity, and how threats are constructed politically.' Thus, as well as a state's institutional makeup and its historical policy legacies, broader social and cultural norms and values play their role. As discussed above, Porter (1987) argues that declining confidence in liberal values played a role in the creation of Special Branch in the 1880s. Foley (2013: 5) similarly argues that 'At the level of society or the political community, norms concerning security and liberty have a strong influence on national responses to terrorism'. Thus how publics themselves understand key values such as security and insecurity – as well as perceptions of the role of the state – is critically important in shaping how states respond to security threats such as terrorism. It is perhaps surprising, therefore, that the voices and views of the public, and their positions on and understandings of crucial issues around anti-terrorism, are neither prominent nor well understood in literature on these dynamics.

Conclusion

This chapter has sought briefly to characterise UK anti-terrorism policy and to place it in both temporal and spatial context. It does so in order that we may better appreciate the ways in which the UK government has responded to recent terrorist activity, acting as a backdrop to the chapters that follow which consider how citizens think about and articulate such policy initiatives. As outlined above, the UK context is one which is distinctive in both the volume of domestic anti-terrorism measures (and particularly changes to the legal code), and the reach or extent of these. As an example of the latter, in the UK the current pre-charge detention period is fourteen days, down from the high of twenty-eight days established in the 2006 Terrorism Act. Whilst exact comparisons between different legal systems are complex, Liberty (2010) suggests that this is by far the highest; with France at six days, Spain at five and Germany at two. In addition, stop and search powers have been extensively used in the UK. Between 2007 and 2009, for example, nearly half a million people were stopped and searched under Section 44 of the 2000 Terrorism Act (Human Rights Watch 2010). Whilst these changes do have historical precedent, and the history of UK policymaking in this area is a key factor in explaining its contemporary shape and trajectory, they have both built upon and moved beyond the policies introduced to deal with the threat of Northern Ireland. As we argued, this fosters an approach towards law-making which is characterised by hastiness (in response to recent events or perceived threat at home or abroad), distinctiveness (such that terrorism is treated as a distinctive category distinguishable from 'normal' criminal activity), continuousness (in which new laws are repeatedly passed and new terrorism-related activities repeatedly generated) and repetitiveness (in which the failings of earlier laws are reproduced in their successors). How citizens view these developments, and their impact on citizenship and public experiences of security, is the focus of the remainder of this book.

Notes

1 As Terry Eagleton (2005: 1) reminds us, it is perhaps not entirely coincidental that this invention also dovetailed with the emergence of the modern democratic state.
2 Wilkinson's analysis, here, invokes the oft-discussed need to 'balance' liberty and security to which we return below.
3 However, as outlined below, other parts of ATCSA, such as Section IV powers, were widely employed.
4 The SPA was not without its precursors, including in the 1914 Defence of the Realm Act and the 1920 Restoration of Order in Ireland Act. The SPA was subsequently updated as the 1933 Civil Authorities (Special Powers) Act (Northern Ireland). See Donohue (2006).
5 The ten are: Prevention of Terrorism Acts 1974. 1976, 1984, 1989; Criminal Justice Terrorism and Conspiracy Act 1998; Terrorism Act 2000; Counter-Terrorism Crime and Security Act 2001; Prevention of Terrorism Act 2005; Terrorism Act 2006; Counter-Terrorist Act 2008 (Walker 2002, 2009).

2

Citizenship and security

In Chapter 1 we saw that the UK approach to anti-terrorism is relatively distinct from potential comparator states. This suggests that the consequences – intended and otherwise – of its framework may well be pronounced and distinctive too. Policy and legal apparatuses in the area of security and beyond impact on populations, communities and individuals in particular and (frequently) variable ways (see also Jarvis and Lister 2015a). In order to assess these impacts upon security and citizenship more specifically, this chapter offers a brief overview of our own approach to these complex and contested concepts. We begin by exploring how recent scholarship on security has sought, first, to escape the state-centrism of earlier work in this area and, second, to examine the discursive, social and enunciative dimensions of security. Taken together, these developments highlight the importance of a focus on 'vernacular' conceptions of security: a focus on the ways in which 'ordinary' people conceive of security. A second section then places questions about the impacts of anti-terrorism on citizenship within broader debates around this term. This is because, whilst anti-terrorism powers are often seen to raise issues around the decline of citizenship, the limits of multiculturalism and the nature of citizen responsibilities, these dynamics also have a considerable history. Understanding quite how anti-terrorism plays into questions of diversity and difference, for example, requires a brief examination of the broader parameters thereof. We conclude the chapter by characterising the methodological position and choices that inform the research presented in subsequent chapters.

Security and anti-terrorism

Any examination of recent literature on security cannot but note two related dynamics. The first of these is the sheer volume of contemporary work seeking to clarify and define the meaning of this concept, its political functions or operation and its relation to surrounding terms such as insecurity. Ostensibly delimited schools of contemporary security thought – Copenhagen, Wales, Paris – have been set out, attacked, defended and revisited (see, e.g. Wæver 2004); debates over the value of competing efforts to study security 'critically' continue apace (compare Krause and Williams 1997; Booth 2007; Browning and McDonald 2013; Hynek and Chandler 2013); and, for newcomers to the field, numerous textbooks now serve to introduce the parameters and contours of these primarily conceptual discussions (Peoples and Vaughan-Williams 2010; Collins 2013; Shepherd 2013; Williams 2013; Jarvis and Holland 2015). This profusion of scholarship reproduces a contemporary desire for, perhaps obsession with, security which 'saturates the language of modern politics [such that] our political vocabularies reek of it and our political imagination is confined by it' (Dillon 1996: 12). As Neocleous notes in a heavily referenced paragraph that is worth citing at length:

> This saturation of the political and social landscape with the logic of security has been accompanied by the emergence of an academic industry churning out ideas about how to defend and improve it. Security has been defined and redefined. It has been re-visioned, re-mapped, gendered, refused. Some have asked whether there is perhaps too much security, some have sought its civilisation, and thousands of others have asked how to 'balance' it with liberty. Much of this redefining, re-visioning, remapping, and so on, has come about through a more widespread attempt at widening the security agenda so as to include societal, economic and a broad range of other issues such as development or the environment. These moves have sought to forge alternative notions of 'democratic' and 'human' security as part of a debate about whose security is being studied, the ontological status of insecurities and questions of identity, and through these moves security has come to be treated less as an objective condition and much more as the product of social processes. (Neocleous 2008: 3)

A second dynamic running alongside this profusion of work on security is the extent of contestability therein. Whether or not one views this contestability as essential in nature (compare Buzan 1991 and Baldwin 1997), there currently exists nothing like an 'established paradigm' with its 'normal science' of how the study of security should proceed (see Kuhn 2012). Political realist approaches may continue their hegemony – although to a far greater extent today in the pages of some journals than others – yet realism itself has always been a loosely structured body of work that exhibits 'a family resemblance, rather than cohering into a unified theoretical structure' (Bell 2009: 3). As a consequence, there exists no agreement on absolutely fundamental questions around what security is, how it is achieved, whether it is desirable, whose security we should prioritise, what the main threats to security are, what we can know about security or how we might study it (see Jarvis and Holland 2015).

As this suggests, a complete review of security's 'bulging archives' (Huysmans 1998: 227) would be some way beyond the scope of this chapter (or, indeed, this book). Instead, in the pages that follow, we focus our attention on two impetuses within contemporary research in this area. These, we suggest, together point to the importance of exploring public understandings or articulations of security and insecurity in the context of anti-terrorism powers and beyond. They relate, in the first instance, to recent efforts to refocus security's referent away from the state. And, in the second, to conceptions of security as a social or discursive phenomenon.

Security's referents

Literature on security – particularly that emanating from its traditional homes of International Relations, Strategic Studies and Security Studies – has, overwhelmingly, prioritised the state as security's referent. The state, put otherwise, has been the traditional answer to the question: whose security should we prioritise in study and practice? The reasons for this state-centrism are manifold but include: political realism's hegemony; the continuing importance of national identities within subjective and intersubjective understandings of the world and one's own place therein; and the contestable, but widely accepted, concentration of agency and power within states, indicated, for example, by defence expenditures and resources.

Despite their dominance, these state-centric approaches have come under increasing attack in recent years from a number of different sources. One of the more prominent attempts to decentre the state emerged with the publication of the 1994 United Nations Development Programme's Human Development Report (UNDP 1994). Although not unprecedented in its effort to prioritise human rather than national concerns (see McSweeney 1999: 51), this report was groundbreaking in its popularisation of the notion of 'human security' amongst policy and academic audiences (e.g. Smith 2005: 53; Glasius 2008: 33). In it, an individual-oriented basic needs-based approach to security was offered (Newman 2001: 243) – defined in this formulation as 'freedom from want and freedom from fear' (UNDP 1994: 24). Human security, viewed thus, was as much about long-term and structural sources of harm as it was about the major disrupting violences – especially war and its threat – that had dominated studies of this concept throughout the Cold War period in particular (Glasius 2008: 32). As such, discussions around human security constituted an important part of the widening agenda referenced by Neocleous above, with this UNDP report specifying seven distinct categories of threat to indicate the plurality of potentially relevant security issues: economic, food, health, environmental, personal, community, and political.

This effort to rework state-centric conceptions of security combines an ontological claim involving the centrality of the individual (socially located) human as security's appropriate referent, with a cosmopolitan ethics grounded in the universality of human needs, including security (UNDP 1994: 22; Bellamy and McDonald 2002: 376). This strong – and frequently explicit – normative emphasis means that the value of human security as a concept is linked, for many of its advocates, to its use for critiquing state actions, as much as to any concrete policy agenda it facilitates. This critical utility, for its supporters, spans its capacity to prioritise and challenge non-traditional, non-military, violences, as well as its power for problematising views of the state as security's guarantor (Bellamy and McDonald 2002: 376; Mack 2004: 366). While critics of human security have questioned the value of a discourse that can be, and has been, so easily co-opted by states (Browning and McDonald 2013: 244; Booth 2007), the political and normative appeal of human security offers a powerful as well as a longstanding, rejoinder to statist realpolitik with roots stretching back even beyond the mid-1990s. As Reid (2006: 10) notes drawing on Mary Kaldor's work, the genealogy of debates around human security, 'extends back, at the very least, into the period of the Cold War when, consequent upon the Helsinki Accord of 1975, liberal regimes began to urge and proclaim a newfound responsibility to the security of a common humanity over and against traditional norms of state sovereignty'.

A related, yet distinct, attempt to centre individuals within the study of security can be found in what has been termed the 'Welsh School' of Critical Security Studies (CSS). Building on Ken Booth's (1991) effort to rethink security in relation to emancipation, proponents of CSS share a number of common commitments with advocates of human security. Indeed, despite his misgivings about human security, Booth (2007: 322) himself identifies several such in his *Theory of World Security* (see also Newman 2010). Amongst the most important of these include: taking concrete sources of human insecurity as a starting point for scholarship (Booth 2005: 22, 2007: 98; Williams 2007: 1024); a recognition that security contains both subjective and objective dimensions (Booth 2007: 105–106); a rejection of individualistic atomism given the significance of human relationships for the realisation of personal security (Booth 2007: 269–273); an explicitly normative stance towards security as a desirable (if, here, never fully achievable) condition (Booth 2007: 101–108); and, most importantly for this discussion, an emphasis on the proper significance of people rather than states as security's final referent (Williams 2005: 141; Booth 2007: 225–228). In contrast to discussions around human security, however, advocates of CSS tend to view security's value in primarily instrumental terms (Booth 2005: 22). Security is, here, desirable not as an end in itself, but rather as a *means* to enhancing life opportunities, especially the opportunity to choose to 'live otherwise' (Booth 2007). As Booth (2005: 22) summarises, this is because the condition or experience of security 'frees people(s) to some degree to do other than deal with threats to their human being'.

Articulating (in)security

Constructivist thought has had a major impact across myriad debates within contemporary International Relations, Security Studies and beyond (Guzzini 2000: 147). This recent yet 'seemingly inexorable rise' (Hay 2002: 15) in some ways belies the fluidity of this designation (Zehfuss 2002: 7), although a common ontological claim to the social constitution of reality and our knowledge thereof coheres different strands of constructivist work on security and elsewhere (Guzzini 2007: 24–25). Within constructivist thinking – and we use the term broadly here – there exists no immediate, unproblematic correspondence between the world of subjects, objects and institutions, and the meaning, identity or significance they are given. Instead, the world becomes meaningful through the ideas and beliefs that are imposed upon it by actors therein, often intersubjectively. Thus, where an extra-discursive, material, reality is posited in much constructivist literature, it is viewed typically as having limited independent causal impact upon social processes (e.g. Wendt 1992, 1999). Conditions of security or insecurity for constructivists are not, as such, reducible to any brute materiality; as Wendt (1999: 255) pithily illustrates: 'Five hundred British nuclear weapons are less threatening to the US than five North Korean ones because of the shared understandings that underpin them'.

Two particular strands of constructivist research on security merit specific mention, given the impact they have had upon recent debate. The first is the 'Copenhagen School' approach (Wæver 2004), which concentrates its attention on the discursive mechanisms through which issues are created as security challenges, or 'securitized' (Buzan et al. 1998: 23–26). In this influential (although diverse) framework, security is approached not as a 'thing' in itself, but a speech act (Buzan et al. 1998; McDonald 2008: 568). Security, in other words, is a 'particular kind of social accomplishment' (Williams 2003: 514) that involves the designation of existential threats (another state, environmental degradation, migrants and so on) to posited referents (the state, a community, a shared identity, and so on) by an appropriately positioned securitizing actor (a politician, a scientist, and so on). Once this securitizing act is accepted by a relevant audience, according to securitization theory, the issue is removed from the domain of normal political decision-making. Exceptional or emergency powers to counter the (constructed) security threat are thereby legitimised given that the very existence of something is at stake. As Buzan et al. (1998: 24) argue, this is because of a political reasoning that suggests, 'If we do not tackle this problem, everything else will be irrelevant (because we will not be here or will not be free to deal with it in our own way)'. This suspension of 'politics as normal' means that securitization is generally treated as an undesirable act with potentially deleterious consequences for democratic processes and outcomes (although see Roe 2012).

A second and increasingly prominent strand of broadly constructivist literature is that of poststructuralist explorations of security discourses. This literature tends to work with a broader conception of the discursive than do more traditional forms of constructivism, seeing it as fully constitutive of the social, and the identities, institutions, threats, risks, subjects and objects therein (Herring and Stokes 2011: 6). Poststructuralist analyses tend also to differ from thinner versions of constructivism in the attention they place on moments of incompleteness, ambiguity and exclusion within efforts to stabilise security discourses (Hansen 2006; Jarvis 2009b). David Campbell's (1998) work on US foreign policy offers one prominent example in which he set out to document 'the ways in which states construct and enforce boundaries between forms of life deemed normal, civilised and worthy of securing, and those forms of life deemed fearful and dangerous' (Reid 2006: 9). Lene Hansen (2006) more recently attempted something similar, exploring competing readings of Western discourses on the Bosnian war as, variously, Balkan issue or genocide. Thus, in spite of their (considerable) differences, what Copenhagen School and poststructuralist literatures share with other constructivist literatures is an engagement in what Guzzini (2007) terms 'performative' as well as 'analytical' conceptual analysis. A desire, in other words, to ask not only what security means, but, also, what it *does* when articulated.

Vernacular (in)security studies

The above brief review obviously does scant justice to several large literatures. Poststructuralist security studies as a body of work, for example, extend far beyond discursive analyses (see also Edkins 1999); one well-cited overview (Newman 2001) identifies at least four distinct approaches to human security, whilst sociological and philosophical variants of securitization theory have also been posited in a recent review of this framework (Balzacq 2011). Other equally important works associated with feminist security studies (see Sjoberg 2009 for an excellent overview) and the 'Paris School' approach (see Bigo 2013) might also have been mentioned here. We hope, however, that this overview fulfils two functions for this book's empirical analysis. The first of these is to highlight a contemporary effort, particularly prominent within the CSS and human security projects, to reorient security analysis around the everyday experiences of ordinary people. This effort is grounded, we suggest, in two shared, and powerful, arguments. The first concerns a recognition of the state's limitations as a provider of security within and outwith its borders. Here, an ontological claim about the diversity of states (Booth 2007: 45) combines with an acknowledgement of the numerous examples of state implication in violences: direct or enabling, internal or external, military or non-military (Bellamy and McDonald 2002: 374). The second argument is that scholars have a normative responsibility to amplify the voices of marginalised actors through the provision of space for people to speak about their own (in)securities. This, in its most optimistic guise, is seen to offer a means of contesting and altering oppressive structures and practices (McDonald 2009: 112) and the harms that are enabled and justified by forces such as 'patriarchy, proselytising religion, capitalism, sovereign statism/nationalism, race, and consumerist democracy' (Booth 2007: 21). Here, a cosmopolitan ethics marries with a recognition of security's discursive power for galvanising political interest in specific issues readable as 'security': traditional and otherwise (see Barnett 2001: 25).

The second ambition of the above review is to demonstrate the significance of broadly constructivist literatures for rethinking security's ontological fixity. These literatures, we argue, have been particularly important in redirecting the security analyst's gaze away from any specific content it might have, and towards its social and political production, meaning and enunciative functions. In so doing, constructivist approaches add conceptual sophistication, first, to our understanding of how security threats emerge for particular actors in specific historical contexts, and, second, to our understanding of how designations of (in)security are implicated in other social dynamics such as identity formation (individual and collective) and the (re)production of political exclusions (e.g. Campbell 1998; Mutimer 2009).

This book represents an attempt to combine this emphasis on everyday security, on the one hand, with our interest in the processes through which security and (in)security are constructed, on the other. Despite a real lack of existing empirical research attempting to do this, there is enormous value, we suggest, to be gained from exploring 'everyday' understandings of (in)security as they are articulated by different publics. Epistemologically, scholarship of this sort poses potential to broaden significantly our knowledge of security's social meanings and roles. It offers an opportunity, put otherwise, to offer a fuller genealogy of how and by whom security is spoken, performed and experienced away from the discourses of elites that typically capture constructivist attention (Dillon 1996: 14–18). In so doing, research into vernacular securities addresses the concomitant normative risk that other voices – and, ultimately, other insecurities – are marginalised, camouflaged or excluded within research paradigms that encourage a focus on the speech acts or discourses of structurally privileged actors. Here, Booth's (2007: 166; see also Hansen 2000) critique of the Copenhagen School approach may legitimately be extended to much other relevant constructivist research: 'Securitization studies therefore suffer from being elitist. What matters above all for the school is "top leaders", "states", "threatened elites" and "audiences" with agenda-making power. Those without discourse-making power are disenfranchised, unable to join the securitization game'.

As this indicates, we find this 'elitism' problematic because it cannot but produce incomplete stories of security and insecurity (see also Enloe 2001). These stories, moreover, are typically treated as having general, if not universal relevance (also Barkawi and Laffey 2006; Sjoberg 2009: 192) from which general logics of security might be derived (Browning and McDonald 2013). As Christine Sylvester (2013: 614) has stated of International Relations, 'in IR, individuals are studied using someone else's script, not their own, which might be a reason why IR is on the back foot when it comes to anticipating people as stakeholders, actors, and participants in international relations'. Thus, as Bilgin (2010: 60) puts it:

> What is needed is further insight into insecurities as experienced by people and social groups in different parts of the world, writings that treat them as subjects and not mere objects of security, and exercises in reflexive intellectual history-writing that seek to uncover the ways in which the production and employment of security knowledge has rendered peoples and social groups less secure.

Our concern in this book, then, is to offer a space for 'lay' or vernacular understandings and experiences of security (and citizenship, and public policy) to enter academic debate on the working and consequences of anti-terrorism powers. And, in the process, to explore from where these understandings derive (see also Jarvis and Lister 2015b) and how they are articulated. Although we do not follow his approach to security, his quest for definition, or his conceptualisation of security's relation to emancipation, we here agree with Ken Booth's (2007: 152) important argument that 'security is a condition that is not difficult to define; in each case, the starting-point should begin in the experiences, imaginings, analyses, and fears of those living with insecurity'. Those experiences and fears, moreover, extend across the socio-political terrain and are limited neither to the privileged or the completely disenfranchised. In this respect, our ambitions in this book share something with, yet seek to go beyond, Vrasti's initial hopes for her own ethnography, which would:

> help me repopulate IR scholarship with the voices and action of *regular people*, neither the heads of states, diplomats and military personnel usually credited with making global politics, nor the marginalized and dispossessed critical theory has discovered a fascination for, but white middle-class people not so different in their economic background, values, and tastes from those populating the academic profession. (Vrasti 2013: 60, original emphasis)[1]

Citizenship and anti-terrorism

The anti-terrorism measures outlined in Chapter 1 clearly impact on politics and society in a number of ways. In addition to their consequences for security – at individual, community, national and other 'levels' – they also raise considerable questions for citizenship, for a number of reasons. The first, perhaps most obvious, is that anti-terrorism powers affect the rights and freedoms of citizens. Whether we view this as necessary, desirable or pernicious, measures such as extended pre-charge detention or stop and search clearly have an impact upon the vertical relationship between the citizen and the state. Second, anti-terrorism measures also have major potential ramifications for questions of identity and belonging. As numerous authors have argued, and as noted in Chapter 1, the implementation of anti-terrorism measures has tended to be far more concentrated on certain sections of the population, especially those identified as South Asian or Muslim (e.g. Kundnani 2014). This raises questions of equal treatment, as well as larger issues concerning Britishness, belonging, multiculturalism and integration (see also Croft 2012). These dynamics, in turn, have potential consequences for the horizontal relationship between citizens, as issues concerning anti-terrorism policy may complicate processes of cohesion and solidarity between communities and their constituents (e.g. Thomas 2009, 2010). Finally, recent anti-terrorism measures also rely heavily upon the involvement of citizens for their operation, whether through extra vigilance at transport hubs or through informing authorities about 'suspicious' behaviours. Thus anti-terrorism measures call forth citizen participation in the fight against terrorism, attempting to enlist them as 'citizen detectives' in Nick Vaughan-Williams' (2008) nice summary (also Jarvis and Lister 2010).

Before discussing the ways in which citizenship and anti-terrorism relate to, and impact on, one another, it is important briefly to examine wider debates around citizenship. Citizenship, as Jopkke (2010: 1) argues, remains 'a notoriously polyvalent concept'. It fundamentally orients itself around questions of membership (Delanty 2000) including, but not limited to: who is a member of a particular community; what is the relationship between members therein; what is the relationship between members and the state;

what obligations do members owe to each other and the state; what rights do members have; and, similarly, what rights do non-members possess? Questions of rights, duties, participation and identity are therefore at the core of debates about citizenship. And, as Taylor-Gooby (1991: 94) notes, citizenship is at once a normative and empirical concept. It refers both to an idealised view of what the practice should involve, on the one hand, and, on the other, an analysis (and sometimes critique) of practices and statuses that we might characterise as constitutive of the citizenship of this or that community. In other words – as with related concepts such as cosmopolitanism (see Vertovec and Cohen 2002) – debates around citizenship often contain normative claims about how citizenship *should be*, alongside empirical analyses of how citizenship actually *is* in the present.

To illustrate: liberal, communitarian and republican conceptions of citizenship (to name but three of the most prominent) build upon radically different normative premises. In broad terms, liberal conceptions of citizenship emphasise individual liberties and freedoms and pay especial attention to citizen rights. Communitarian conceptions, which emerged in part out of concerns about liberal atomisation and a lack of concern for broader, collective goods, emphasise duties and obligations. Following a long tradition in political theory, republican conceptions prioritise the centrality and importance of participation to citizenship. Beyond these classic conceptions lie feminist and multicultural critiques which emphasise the exclusionary nature of citizenship as traditionally conceptualised and practised (see Lister and Pia 2008: 8–57). Beyond this, in turn, lie more recent conceptions of sexual, cultural, post-national, ecological and cosmopolitan citizenship (Isin and Turner 2003a).

These different conceptions represent the latest in a series of debates that have surrounded this concept since its first invocation in ancient Greece. Indeed, recent years have seen citizenship come under increasing fire, in part because of the consequences (real or perceived) of socio-political and economic processes such as globalisation. These processes have sparked three discussions of particular concern to our arguments in this book. The first is a set of questions centred around the 'erosion' or 'decline' of citizenship. The second is a series of issues about diversity and difference and their protection or otherwise within the citizenry. The third asks whether the relationship between citizen and state is being, or has been, recast, with citizens being called upon to take up ever more roles and responsibilities within the modern state. Our argument in what follows is that the relationship between anti-terrorism and citizenship must be placed in the context of these debates. This is, not least, because anti-terrorism frameworks accentuate and contribute to these dynamics, either due to their impact on political practice and norms (such as human rights) (see, e.g. Fenwick 2002a, 2002b; Cole 2003; Fekete 2004, 2006; Sivanandan 2006; Cole and Lobel 2007; Gearty 2007; Donohue 2008); or because of the broader ethical and philosophical issues they raise (Meisels 2008; Grayling 2010; Waldron 2012). In the following, we begin with a brief overview of these three debates, before focusing on how anti-terrorism plays into each.

Debate 1: The erosion of citizenship?

As with security, the very concept of citizenship has received increasing attention across the last twenty years or so. Kymlicka and Norman (1994: 352) cite van Gunsteren, who claimed only in 1978 that 'the concept of citizenship has gone out of fashion among political thinkers'. Sixteen years later, however, it had become something of a buzz word: a revival traced by Kymlicka and Norman (1994), and others (Heater 1991; Pattie et al. 2003; Kisby 2007) to a range of factors. One of these, ironically, is citizenship's perceived erosion in many Western states (e.g. Pattie et al. 2003: 616): a decline manifested in reduced levels of political engagement, especially voter turnout (see Lister and Pia 2008: 80–106), as well as falling social capital (compare Putnam 2000 and Stolle and Hooghe 2005). Particular concerns within the UK have arisen about young people and citizenship, stemming from perceptions of increasing anti-social behaviour and dismal levels of political engagement. In a recent report, for example, only 41% of people described themselves as certain to vote at any future election. This figure, disturbingly, fell to 12% for 18–24 year olds (Hansard Society 2013: 1). Such concerns led to the introduction of mandatory citizenship education from 2002 onwards (Hart 2009), although the conceptualisation and implementation of this has been subject to considerable criticism (Miekle 2006; Kisby 2007; Hart 2009).

Scobey (2001: 14) points also to a perceived 'crisis of citizenship', wherein 'transnational integration and subnational devolution threaten the stability of the nation-state system and civic nationalism'. As so often in modern political debates, the notion of global transformation and the shifting place of nation states is cited as a specific factor in that which stalks citizenship:

> As the geographic boundaries among nation-states have become more permeable – and with them the notional boundary between member and stranger – the figure of the citizen has lost its self-evident status as the embodiment of the nation. The new intellectual interest in citizenship thus reflects both the significance and the fragility of the category. (Scobey 2001: 15)

Others look to related transformations to explain this decline. Turner (1991), for instance, argues that fundamental economic, social and military changes have resulted in the erosion of citizenship entitlements. The decline of the male-breadwinner model, the nuclear family and the citizen-soldier have all, for Turner, diminished the traditional entitlement to citizenship's (social) protections. Taken together, these analyses point to the ways in which discrete national citizenship, based on the fulfilment of specific roles resulting in particular entitlements from the state, has been weakened. As Ong (2006: 500) puts it, in a context of global human rights norms, 'instead of all citizens enjoying a unified bundle of citizenship rights, we have a shifting political landscape in which heterogeneous populations claim diverse rights and benefits associated with citizenship'.

Focusing her attention on the US in particular (but with relevance for the UK), Somers (2008) is more strident on this decline. For her, processes of commodification and contractualisation associated with neo-liberalism have produced a situation whereby many who are formal *de jure* citizens are actually, *de facto*, stateless: 'When the state no longer carries out its role of constraining capitalism, people are left fully exposed to the unmediated market. With no meaningful participation and with only the thinnest of connections to civil and legal rights, they are, in effect, left stateless and rightless' (Somers 2008: 133).

With the aftermath of Hurricane Katrina looming large in her analysis, Somers argues that, 'By formal law, they may be citizens, but today's socially excluded are no longer rights bearing citizens. By default they have become mere denizens, who reside in the country but are for all intents and purposes stateless and superfluous people' (Somers 2008: 137). Moreover, at the same time as legal, formal citizenship is diminished, cultural or ethnic identities are increasingly asserted, such that the stateless denizens of Somers' analysis are offered 'an ever thicker fictive ethnic nationalism' (Somers 2008: 120) to compensate for their diminished status. This 'fictive ethnic' identity is a means by which those who do not conform or belong are expelled from the body politic. Thus there is a twin deracination of citizenship for Somers: a material diminishment of the status and content of citizenship rights, and, under a celebration of ethnic nationalism which offers those who belong some compensation for their loss of civic status, a narrowing of who can be considered a citizen. Thus, non-whites, immigrants, non-heterosexuals and 'those insufficiently aligned with the dominant ethnos of American nationalism and patriotism' (Somers 2008: 139) are sacrificed to mask the reality of a declining citizenship of all. It is, Somers (2008: 119) argues, the compensation for the loss of demos with an alternative of ethnos. Yet this 'compensation' cannot hide that, for 'those who take comfort in their cultural inclusion ... their social exclusion will only increase, as all the righteousness of national inclusion and identity cannot erase the fact that they have lost the right to have rights' (Somers 2008: 142).

Diminishment of citizenship rights under anti-terrorism powers

Much of the academic literature exploring anti-terrorism and citizenship builds on these discussions by arguing that legislation and policy introduced under the 'war on terror' have continued or even accelerated the latter's diminishment. Basic rights are widely deemed to have become more precarious under this security paradigm and, perhaps, conditional upon certain ways of behaving or being. This work is, perhaps, closer to the arguments of Somers than those of Turner. This is so, as the erosion identified in this context is frequently attributed to deliberate policy interventions rather than broader social, cultural and economic shifts. In other words, much of this literature posits a direct – and, perhaps, deliberate – link between recent anti-terrorism powers and the diminishment of citizenship.

Haque (2002: 175), for example, argues that anti-terrorism measures since 9/11 have created a situation of 'weak citizenship', with Huq and Muller (2008) pointing to the diminishment of due process that took place after those attacks. Cole (2003: 3) argues similarly, stating that, in the US, anti-terrorism measures have 'compromise[d] our most basic principles – commitment to equal treatment, political freedoms, individualised justice and the rule of law'. In the European context, Guild et al. (2007) note the removal of rights for those suspected of terrorism offences, outlining the significance of measures to enhance the state's surveillance powers. In the UK, likewise, Gillespie and O'Loughlin (2009: 89) argue that citizenship has become 'increasingly, fragile and precarious' as a result of developments in anti-terrorism policy and security politics. As they also note, however, changes to the experience of citizenship are likely to be both complex and contingent, whereby 'the precariousness of citizenship is articulated in different terms depending on whether one is talking from a position of relative power and privilege or from a position of relative marginalisation and financial insecurity' (Gillespie and O'Loughlin 2009: 101).

As we shall see below, there is an important literature which examines the impact of anti-terrorism measures on specific groups and communities. The importance of this work notwithstanding, others argue that specific anti-terrorism policies and discourse create wider disciplinary forces as much as they only single out specific groups and minorities. In a broadly Foucauldian analysis, some (Puar and Rai 2002; Rygiel 2006) highlight the importance of identity politics within a 'war on terror' that relies on the identification (or constitution) of particular deviant identities. This pursuit of 'deviant' identities, however, has implications not only for those deemed undesirable or unintegrated, but also for those who display unwanted character traits. Processes of 'othering' associated with anti-terrorism produce, they argue, 'docile patriots', whereby the 'figure of the terrorist' 'provides the occasion to demand and instil a certain discipline on the population. This discipline aims to produce patriotic, docile subjects through practices, discourses, images, narratives, fears, and pleasures' (Puar and Rai 2002: 130).

The use of ethnic or identity-based components of citizenship to mask the diminishment of civic aspects of this category in the context of anti-terrorism is explored further by Maira. She argues that 'being a patriotic citizen has increasingly replaced "democratic citizen" and "involved citizen" as the primary definition of "good citizenship"' (Maira 2009: 21). This leads her to focus on the concept of cultural citizenship, which – following Ong and Foucault – she defines as 'a process the state uses to discipline populations through the notion of the ideal citizen and establishment of distinctions between those considered worthy or unfit for citizenship' (Maira 2009: 84). These themes are further developed in analyses of how contemporary anti-terrorism struggles impact on governance regimes, using concepts such as bio-politics (Amoore 2006) and risk management (Aradau and van Munster 2008).

Debate 2: Diversity, difference and citizenship

As indicated above, the model of the discrete, bounded national community of mono-ethnic citizens is widely seen to be a thing of the past, if indeed it ever existed (see Scobey 2001). This is driven, in part, by processes of globalisation and regionalisation that are often believed to have weakened national boundaries. Multiculturalism came to be used both as a term to describe an increasingly heterogeneous citizenry, and as the promotion, protection and celebration of difference that came to be seen as the policy response to these conditions. In contrast to assimilationist models of citizenship with their emphasis on conformity, multiculturalism is associated with demands for recognition and equality (Taylor 1994; Kymlicka 1995; Parekh 2000). By critiquing the supposed neutrality of liberal ideas about citizenship, advocates both emphasise the wide range of competing identities within populations, and argue for the recognition, and sometimes accommodation of this plurality. Such interventions have helped institute a range of questions about who is a citizen, about the link between nation, ethnicity and citizenship, and about what special rights, or accommodations (if any) should be granted to citizens of minority groups and communities.

Despite the political gains made by advocates of multiculturalism, recent years have seen something of a backlash against it, with authors and politicians rushing to pronounce its 'death' or 'failure' (for an overview, see Joppke 2004; Meer and Modood 2009). Rather than bringing about a situation of more, or closer, integration and inter-identity, the valorisation of difference has led – for critics – to increasing social fragmentation. The Cantle Report

(2001), published in the wake of the riots that took place that year in northern UK towns such as Oldham, made the claim that people of different (ethnic) identities were leading 'parallel lives': a claim that strongly resonated with many across the UK. As Kundnani (2002: 67) argued, 'from the state's point of view, the "multiculturalist settlement", which has dominated race relations thinking in Britain for two decades, is no longer working. The riots of summer 2001 were a wake-up call. And events since September 11 have sounded the death knell for multicultural policies'. Questions of terrorism, radicalisation and extremism (violent and otherwise), particularly following the London 7/7 attacks, added piquancy to these debates in the UK especially. For some, the state's tolerance of different identities and values has led to a context where intolerance and violent extremism can thrive. As David Cameron (2011) argued:

> Under the doctrine of state multiculturalism, we have encouraged different cultures to live separate lives, apart from each other and apart from the mainstream ... This hands-off tolerance has only served to reinforce the sense that not enough is shared. And this all leaves some young Muslims feeling rootless ... Now for sure, they don't turn into terrorists overnight, but what we see ... is a process of radicalisation.

Thus, as Meer and Modood (2009: 474) note, 'multiculturalism is widely believed to have been responsible for domestic terrorism'. Grillo (2007: 980) here identifies a backlash against the celebration of diversity and the presence of communities holding values at odds with Western, secular, liberal values which threatens social cohesion and security. Meer and Modood (2009: 481) sum this up nicely, identifying a 'coupling of diversity and anti-terrorism agendas that has implicated contemporary British multiculturalism as the culprit of Britain's security woes'.

Yet, whilst some queue up to join in such requiems, others call into question much of the above. Some academics such as Heath and Demireva (2013) and Wright and Bloemraad (2012) have suggested that there is no empirical evidence to support the claim that multiculturalism has contributed to greater segregation. Others point out that most Western societies have struggled to leave behind their histories of ethnic and racial discrimination. 'Long after racism is supposed to have faded away, racial abuse, like racialised inequality, remains' (Gilroy 2012: 382). Indeed, empirical data suggest that experiences and perceptions of racial discrimination are important factors in integration (Heath and Demireva 2013). Moreover, there is also a question as to whether the UK has ever, indeed, practised 'state multiculturalism' (Gilroy 2012) and therefore whether its success or failure may even legitimately be discussed. Despite such counter-claims, it is clear that debates about citizenship, belonging, identity, diversity and difference have been heavily inflected by issues around terrorism and security. It is into this context that anti-terrorism measures have been located, and their injection of further anxiety, tension and questioning into issues of citizenship and identity is, therefore, hardly surprising.

'Suspect communities': anti-terrorism and identity/difference

The most prominent debate around multiculturalism and difference in the anti-terrorism context centres on the particular challenges experienced by Muslim individuals and groups in the UK and beyond since 9/11 in particular. The term 'suspect community' – first coined by Paddy Hillyard (1993) to describe the experience of Irish communities under the UK's Prevention of Terrorism Act – has been widely invoked to describe these experiences, and as a stepping stone towards comparative analysis with the impacts of earlier anti-terrorism campaigns.[2] In the late 1980s and early 1990s, Hillyard conducted numerous interviews with individuals arrested under, detained by, or who had otherwise experienced the powers contained within the Prevention of Terrorism (Temporary Provisions) Act (PTA), most of which, as we saw in Chapter 1, was placed on a permanent statute footing by the 2000 Terrorism Act. Hillyard argues that these measures, although general in legal specification, were aimed at a specific section of the UK population, namely Irish (im)migrants, with their operation constituting those migrants as a suspect community. As Hillyard (1993: 257–8) puts it:

> The most important feature of the operation of the PTA has been the way it has constructed a suspect community in Britain. The wide powers of examination, arrest and detention, the executive power to proscribe selected organisations, the range of specific offences under the Acts, the power to issue exclusion orders and a whole new range of provisions covering seizure and investigation, have all played their part in making the Irish living in Britain, or Irish people travelling between Britain and Ireland, a suspect community ... To the extent that the legislation is principally directed at Irish people, it is an example of institutionalised racism.

Despite the concept's widespread appeal, the means by which such a 'suspect community' is (re)produced could, perhaps, be further clarified in Hillyard's work. As Ragazzi (2015: 161) notes about Hillyard and his contemporary interpreters:

> Hillyard as well as Pantazis and Pemberton oscillate between two meanings of the word 'community'. They at times mean a group of people that is

perceived as being suspect, but also imply that suspicion generates a social identity, such that the group formed by these policies can be called a 'community'. While the first meaning of community implies that the reality of the group exists only in the categories of security professionals, in the second meaning the practices of the police are considered to be altering or reinforcing ethnocultural boundaries.

Hillyard (1993: 256–260) himself identifies three key aspects of the construction of the Irish community as 'suspect' during the 'Troubles'. The first, fairly clearly, was the operation of the PTA, which in implementation, if not formal drafting, was oriented at the Irish (particularly at ports of entry and exit where Irish individuals sought to travel between the UK and the Republic). The second was the use of PTA powers to trawl through the community for information. Thus, if one individual was arrested or detained, his or her acquaintances, however distant, were subject also to investigation, as were their acquaintances in turn, and so on. The thread linking these people was that they were, or knew someone, Irish. The third was through the invitation of the wider population to view the Irish as suspect. Noting the then widespread invocation to the 'general public' to report suspicious activities by Irish people, Hillyard (1993: 259) recounts an interview with an Irish businessman who was heard to be discussing 'bombs' in a hotel bar with two friends. That one of the party had recently come back from Colombia and was discussing the situation there did not prevent the group being arrested.

In the post-9/11 era, this concept of the suspect community has been appropriated by many to characterise the treatment of Muslim populations in Britain (e.g. Breen Smyth 2009). Hillyard (1993: 273) had earlier argued that 'A suspect community has been constructed against a backdrop of anti-Irish racism. The community has suffered widespread violation of their human rights and civil liberties.' Yet, as Said (2004: 3) notes, 'A decade later, substitute "Irish" for "Muslim" and this could easily be read as a description of the impact and operation of the Terrorism Act 2000 and the Anti-terrorism, Crime and Security Act 2001'. (Indeed, Hillyard (2005) himself, in a short piece, invoked Marx's famous aphorism that history repeats itself, the first time as tragedy, the second as farce.) In making this argument, Said identifies the differential experience of Muslim populations under recent British anti-terrorism measures, emphasising the disproportionate increase in uses of stop and search powers on Asian individuals. Pantazis and Pemberton (2009) similarly argue that the Terrorism Act 2000, with its powers of stop and search, proscription of organisations, and criminalisation by association, has been instrumental in creating a 'suspect community' of the Muslim population in the UK.[3] In this regard, the comments of the then Communities Secretary, Hazel Blears, are striking:

> Dealing with the terrorist threat and the fact that at the moment the threat is most likely to come from those people associated with an extreme form of Islam, or falsely hiding behind Islam, if you like, in terms of justifying their activities, inevitably means that some of our counter terrorist powers will be disproportionately experienced by people in the Muslim community. That is the reality of the situation, we should acknowledge that reality and then try to have as open, as honest and as transparent a debate with the community as we can. There is no getting away from the fact that if you are trying to counter the threat, because *the threat at the moment is in a particular place*, then your activity is going to be targeted in that way. (H. Blears, cited in House of Commons 2005: 46, emphasis added)

Taken together, the institution of state policies, media and public discourses that identify, isolate, target and even constitute (see Ali 2015) specific sections of the population seems to be a recurring response to political violence in the UK (also Rygiel 2008: 212). In contrast to the oft-cited 'balancing' metaphor, this work suggests that Muslim citizens (and ethnic minority citizens) may be gaining little, if any, security from their (potentially) compromised rights. In one of the relatively few examples of qualitative empirical research in this area, Gillespie noted:

> Most interviewees feel that they have become more insecure in recent years and most are more afraid of the consequences of security policy than of terrorism. These include 'casual' everyday racism, state surveillance, arrest and detention, creeping militarism and threats to civil rights and traditions of democracy and the rule of law ... A large proportion of racialised minorities base their fears on personal experience of stop and search, identity checks and temporary detention. (Gillespie 2007: 284)

Debate 3: The responsibilisation of citizens?

Beyond the perennial issues of 'redistribution and recognition' that Isin and Turner (2007: 7) argue 'structure claims to and demands of citizenship', recent years have also witnessed significant changes in the state's expectations of its citizens. Increasingly government discourses and policies emphasise that citizens are expected not simply to be passive recipients of rights, but to be active in providing their own welfare and assisting in the delivery of broader social goods such as security and (financial) well-being (e.g. Belfrage 2008; Finlayson 2009). In one sense, this could simply be seen as a reassertion of communitarian/republican emphases on the importance of duties and participation inherent within citizenship. Yet, it could also be argued that the shift, since the late 1970s, has been more about transferring responsibilities from the state to the citizen. And, as such, is less to do with citizens being active (in the sense of authoring and creating their own political subjectivities) and more to do with the performance of pre-given roles and responsibilities (see Isin 2008). Some of this move is associated with broader governance shifts, not least with the central state assuming ever less of a 'command and control' function, and seeking instead to 'steer' policy, social and political outcomes (Pierre and Peters 2000; Hooghe and Marks 2001).

In the UK context, this (re)encouragement of citizen responsibility has been visible since the Thatcher administration. Thatcher herself stated in 1980: 'The first principle of this government ... is to revive a sense of individual responsibility. It is to reinvigorate not just the economy and industry but the whole body of voluntary associations, loyalties and activities which give society its richness and diversity and hence its real strength' (cited in Rose 1999: 138). This emphasis on individual responsibility and civic associations echoes many rich themes within traditional conservative thought (Norman 2010), yet it has also gained urgency from neo-liberal reforms to the state. As evidenced by David Cameron's 'Big Society' (Lister 2014), as the state seeks to do less, so citizens are expected to fill the gap. As Douglas Hurd, the then Home Secretary, argued in 1988, active citizens are desirable not only for reasons of abstract civic virtue, but for the delivery of certain goods: 'We have to find, as the Victorians found, techniques and instruments which reach the parts of our society which will always be beyond the scope of statutory schemes. I believe that the inspiring and the enlisting of the active citizen in all walks of life is the key' (cited in Heater 1991: 140).

More recently, in the UK's New Labour era, there was a great emphasis on the responsibilities that citizens bore, both as a means to constrain the rights that citizens held ('no rights without responsibilities') and as a mechanism for delivery of social goods (Barnett 2003; Clarke 2005; 6 et al. 2010). For example, in 2003, the Prime Minister's Strategy Unit noted the need for 'new thinking on the balance of responsibility between government and citizens', pointing to 'greater personal responsibility for behaviour, [as] key in the long run to improving outcomes in health and education, welfare and the environment' (cited in 6 et al. 2010: 428).

This emergence of 'government through community' (Rose and Miller 2008: 90) or through the individual (see Ragazzi 2015), in which the public are 'urged by politicians and others to take upon themselves the responsibility for their own security and that of their families ... to take an active role in securing themselves against all that could possibly threaten the security of their chosen style of life' (Miller and Rose 2008: 100), has been an important theme for governmentality scholars. It also links to a literature on the growth of responsibilisation as a way of assuring individual well-being. Authors point to a range of areas such as health, welfare, pensions and crime in which we have seen efforts at encouraging individual provision for personal gain (Belfrage 2008; Andersen 2007; Watson 2010). As Garland (1996: 452) argues, responsibilisation here 'involves a number of new techniques and methods whereby the state seeks to bring about action on the part of 'private' agencies and individuals – either by 'stimulating new forms of behaviour' or 'stopping established habits'. Despite the short lifespan of Big Society language within the UK, the continued pertinence of its themes as the latest iteration of responsibilisation (Lister 2014) can be seen in developments such as the Immigration Act 2014 which, among other reforms, requires landlords, doctors and others to verify the immigration status of any potential tenant, creating a situation which turns 'landlords into immigration officers' (Chakrabarti, cited in Hull 2013) and 'ordinary Britons into snitches for central government' (Massie 2013).

Citizens as tools of anti-terrorism policy

This theme of citizen activation in the provision of public and personal goods again finds strong resonance in anti-terrorism literature. Here a range of authors note the ways in which anti-terrorism policy not only seeks to involve citizens in its operation, but is increasingly dependent on participation of this sort (Vaughan-Williams 2008). Rygiel (2006: 145), for example, argues that citizens have 'been enlisted as the weapons of choice' in this policy area; wherein 'citizenship policies and practices aimed at "proving and protecting identity" have become the preferred battlefield strategy'. Thus, whether under the guise of counter-radicalisation policies such as Prevent, with its emphasis on identifying 'vulnerable' yet 'risky' individuals (Thomas 2009, 2010; Heath-Kelly 2012, 2013; Martin 2014), public information campaigns – 'If you suspect it, report it' as one Metropolitan Police (2008) initiative put it – or efforts to prepare people for possible terrorist attacks (HM Government 2004), states such as the UK have sought to activate and mobilise citizens in this all-pervasive 'fight' against terrorism (Jarvis and Lister 2010). And, with political elites more willing to proclaim ignorance of actual or potential security threats (witness Donald Rumsfeld's (2002) infamous known unknowns and unknown unknowns), citizens have been also increasingly called upon to 'fill' this knowledge gap, including by reporting suspicious activities.

Whilst these developments are, in some senses, not completely novel (see Hay 2006; Amoore 2007), the scale and scope of these exhortations represent something both distinctive and significant. Such exhortations are particularly prominent for Muslim populations (as detailed further below). In April 2014, for example, the Metropolitan Police urged Muslim women to report family members intending to travel to the Syrian conflict to anti-terrorism officials due to the fears of the radicalising impact this conflict would have (Dodd et al. 2014). Such demands, however, go far beyond specific 'suspect' communities, to the extent that it has become almost a civic obligation to participate in the monitoring of others. Thus, citizens are increasingly called on to contribute to the security of themselves and those around them through activities such as surveillance. And, in so doing, they have become – at the same time – the subjects, objects and tools of anti-terrorism: that which is threatened, the potential threat and the policy response to the threat of terrorism (Jarvis and Lister 2010; also Koskela 2010, 2011).

Speaking to citizens

As we can see from the above discussion, security, citizenship and anti-terrorism are potentially connected in multiple ways. Powers introduced in this public policy area, moreover, appear to continue, and perhaps accelerate, potentially significant transformations already taking place within social and political life. While much of this has been explored at length elsewhere, the lack of engagement with the voices, attitudes or experiences of citizens and their own understandings or constructions of these potentially profound dynamics in the context of anti-terrorism is both surprising and unfortunate. As Johnson and Gearty (2007: 143) note in reporting on the British Social Attitudes data, amidst all the sound and fury that has engulfed anti-terrorism policy and civil liberties in recent years, the perspectives of citizens themselves have been largely, and unfortunately, omitted: 'In this discussion there has been one very obvious dimension lacking: the views of the public'.

This is not to say that nothing is known of citizens' *views* or opinions on certain questions concerning (anti-)terrorism. There is, for example, a reasonably extensive volume of public opinion data which suggests, amongst other things, that publics are accepting of strong, even draconian, measures to deal with terrorism. A 2004 survey in the UK, for instance, found that 62% of respondents were in favour of indefinite detention of terrorist suspects, with 66% in favour of detaining *all* immigrants and asylum seekers until they could be assessed as security threats (ICM 2004). A more recent UK YouGov (2011a) poll evidenced similar trends, finding 73% support for the use of control orders, although a differently worded question in another survey found greater support for intensive surveillance over control orders (YouGov 2011b). This interest in public opinion is reflected in much of the relevant academic literature, which has frequently focused on large-scale quantitative studies measuring public support for anti-terrorism measures (Huddy et al. 2002; Davis and Silver 2004; Johnson and Gearty 2007; Joslyn and Haider-Markel 2007).

From the perspective of this book, what this literature and data – despite its obvious importance – lacks is any form of sustained engagement with the ways in which citizens themselves *experience* and *understand* anti-terrorism powers. More than this, what is missing in quantitative, survey research is any detailed understanding of how citizens conceptualise and articulate the impact of anti-terrorism powers on themselves, on others and on core political values such as security and citizenship. As Gillespie and O'Loughlin (2009: 109) put it: 'The citizen's voice and perspective have been missing from contemporary debates about security policy and its impact upon multiculturalism: how citizenship is *felt, talked about, thought, enacted and disrupted*' (emphasis added). Thus, as Gillespie (2007: 278) suggests, the wealth of recent theoretical work on 'new paradigms of governance' that have been instituted or reproduced within the war on terror should be combined with and complemented by qualitative, '"bottom up", socially based, culturally informed, constructionist approaches to the everyday politics of security'.

This appeal for detailed, thick and 'bottom up' research that takes seriously everyday negotiations of security frameworks and their consequences resonates with the arguments of scholars for whom anti-terrorism measures do not simply 'wash over' citizens. Guillaume and Huysmans (2013a), for example, argue there is a need not only to examine the operation of particular security regimes, but to investigate their negotiation and contestation within everyday life (also Lowndes and Thorp 2010). In other words, it is not sufficient – and perhaps not even possible – simply to 'read off' or assume *a priori* diminishments of citizenship through changes in legislative or policy frameworks. Instead, we must explore how citizens themselves interpret and respond to such changes and their implications.

Conceptualising everyday citizenship

Such a project, of taking seriously the voices of citizens and 'ordinary' people, involves recognising that citizenship is not simply a legal status but a practice or experience that incorporates an important performative, lived, aspect (Isin 2008). Whilst scholars, including those noted earlier in the chapter, have focused on what forms citizenship can and should take, in some recent literature on citizenship there has been a move away from such formal conceptions of citizenship, towards a more 'bottom up' account of how citizenship is lived and experienced by citizens themselves. Behind this lies a recognition that political and legal measures impact differently on different people. Thus Miller-Idriss (2006: 542) argues: 'a nation-state's legal policies for citizenship ... cannot be automatically extrapolated to the understandings of citizenship among ordinary citizens in their everyday lives. Moreover, we cannot assume a uniform understanding of citizenship for all of the members of a single nation.'

Similar ideas have been taken up by scholars such as Maira (2004, 2009), who focuses on 'cultural citizenship' as a way to think through the ways in which the formal statuses of citizenship are mitigated and mediated by race, ethnicity, gender and so on. In particular, Maira emphasises that after 9/11 the formal rights of citizenship will struggle to capture the reality of lived experiences for many citizens. Quoting Siu, she argues that cultural citizenship 'Is comprised [of] "behaviours, discourses and practices that give meaning to citizenship as lived experience" in the context of "an uneven and complex field of structural inequalities and webs of power relations", and the "quotidian practices of inclusion and exclusion"'(Maira 2004: 222). Others too have argued for the need to focus on the practices of 'actually existing citizenship' (Desforges et al. 2005: 448).

Ruth Lister (2007) has framed her concern with the ways in which citizenship is practised, experienced and negotiated in the everyday lives of citizens as 'lived citizenship'. For her, the context in which citizenship is encountered and experienced is crucial for shaping processes and outcomes. Thus, citing Hall and Williamson, she defines 'lived citizenship' as 'how people understand and negotiate rights and responsibilities, belonging and participation and "the meaning that citizenship actually has in people's lives and the ways in which people's social and cultural backgrounds and material circumstances affect their lives as citizens"' (Lister 2007: 55).

We take such calls seriously in this book and seek to contribute to the growing literature on the lived everyday politics and experiences of citizenship. Thus, for us, citizenship is not simply a set or series of legal entitlements and responsibilities. It is, rather, a deeply contextual phenomenon, where the identifications, connections, practices, behaviours, constraints and boundaries between groups of people and political institutions are not fixed or set only by political/legal regulations and entitlements. Rather, these are formed through varying expressions, negotiations, experiences and claims upon citizenship. Such a concern also underpins our conception of security, which we approach as something both articulated and experienced at the level of the 'everyday'. As such, considering how citizens perceive and understand the effects of anti-terrorism architectures on their lives – as citizens – is of pressing importance for research in this field.

It should be noted that some scholars have sought to investigate the understanding of some citizens on issues concerning the anti-terrorism/citizenship nexus. One significant element of this research focuses on Muslim communities and the particular challenges they face in contemporary anti-terrorism frameworks and discourses (see, for example, Gest 2010; Choudhury and Fenwick 2011; Thomas and Sanderson 2011; Mythen 2012;

Mythen et al. 2013). Others, more recently, have sought also to probe both the ways in which citizens think about terrorism (Jackson and Hall 2013) and the contemporary security environment more widely (Vaughan-Williams and Stevens 2013). This book attempts to complement and extend research such as this, by contextualising the attitudes of Muslims or South Asians in relation to those of other demographics. In so doing, it asks whether such understandings and views are distinctive, or whether individuals with other identities or experiences share similar perspectives. Our hope is that this contributes, amongst other things, qualitative richness to quantitative public opinion data.

Methodology

The chapters that follow examine the findings generated in our focus group research by exploring, *inter alia*, public evaluations of anti-terrorism measures, understandings of the impact such measures have within the UK, and the importance of different understandings of threats, security and citizenship that citizens espouse when discussing such issues. Before moving to this, it is worth briefly reflecting upon some ontological and epistemological concerns raised by research of this sort. Upon this, we will say a few words about method and the limitations of our study.

Recent interventions examining citizens' knowledge of terrorism and security (Jackson and Hall 2013; Vaughan-Williams and Stevens 2013) open a series of interesting questions on theory and method. Whilst these studies offer a normatively inspired effort to examine the views of 'ordinary' people on security and terrorism, they also exhibit a certain circumspection in so doing. Inflected with poststructural commitments relating to the subject's fragmentation, these approaches caution against a view which is common, if implicit, in much survey research: that preferences and attitudes expressed in research settings offer fixed, pre-existing expressions stemming from a unitary 'self'. Thus Vaughan-Williams and Stevens (2013) and Jackson and Hall (2013) emphasise the intersubjective nature of any 'knowledge' generated in a focus group environment and the importance of recognising the situated nature of the narratives and text such an event produces (see also Anthias 2002; Smith and Sparkes 2008; Flick 2009).

Authors such as these push this epistemological caution further with a broader scepticism about the fixedness of subjectivity and identity. Essentially, they argue that subjectivities are not fixed and singular, but plural, fragmented and, crucially, constituted through discourse. Citing Squire et al. (2008: 4), Vaughan-Williams and Stevens (2013), for example, suggest that 'the storyteller does not tell the story, so much as she/he is told by it'. Such a position poses challenges for the researcher – of which Vaughan-Williams and Stevens are keenly aware – as not only are produced narratives socially situated and a product of specific locations, but so too is the speaking agent or subject. Such a position, we argue, is ideal for examining the ways in which discourses about terrorism and security are constructed, consumed, contested and/or accepted. And, indeed, for thinking through the ways in which subjects take up or reaffirm specific subject positions in the act of discoursing on terrorism (or anything else).

Epistemological commitments such as these do, however, raise normative questions about the value and status of attempts – such as ours – to give voice to 'ordinary' people as anything other than carriers of discourse. Working with a fragmented poststructural sense of self, such views *and* voices lack permanence and substance: they are articulations that emerge in particular spatial and temporal contexts (in our case, living rooms, restaurants and community centres, amongst others). Not only are expressed views, or narratives, embedded within and specific to the particular conjuncture of that research environment, but so also is the subject from whom they emerge. If, as Gergen states, individuals 'do not author their lives' (cited in Smith and Sparkes 2008: 25), then the narratives produced are not those of an abstract, pre-given individual. Rather, they are an outcome of active negotiation in which broader social discourses are interpreted, engaged with, reproduced, transformed, accepted and contested, the act of which is integral to the reconstitution of the subject herself.

McNay's critique of Butler's notion of performativity emphasises the importance of this issue with regard to poststructural conceptions of the self. McNay (1999, 2004) argues that accounts such as Butler's lack a developed notion of agency, which is explicated in terms of spaces/instances of structural indeterminacy.

> Denuded of the idea of experience and attendant notions of self-hood, intention and reflexivity, poststructural work on subjectivity often finds itself without a workable concept of agency with which to animate its notions of resistance, subversion etc. Agency refers to an individual's capacity for action and cannot be simply understood as a property of unstable discursive structures. (McNay 2004: 179–80)

This critique chimes with related accounts that explore the importance of narrative in the formation of self and identity. Smith and Sparkes, for instance, posit a spectrum of positions which place differing emphases on the role of the social and the individual self, with 'perspectives that adopt a "thick individual" and "thin social relational" emphasis ... at one end, and a "thin individual" and "thick social relational" focus at the other', from psychosocial to performative (Smith and Sparkes 2008: 7). Stuart Hall (1997: 43), similarly, seeks to combine a 'de-centering' of identity and recognition of the subject's social embeddedness without necessarily eliding the agency thereof. Intersubjectivist approaches, related to social interactionism (e.g. Blumer 1969), argue likewise that individuals act on the basis of the meanings that things have for them and that these meanings emerge from social interaction with others via an interpretive process (see also Wendt 1992, 1999). Thus, whilst selves here 'emerge out of social structure and social situations' (Denzin 1969: 922), they are also possessing of agency. Thus, Goffman's conception (1990 [1956]) of the self as, in part, a performance remains keenly influential (although critiqued; see Denzin 2002). As he argues, the self is a 'collaborative manufacture', which he characterises in terms of a stage and an audience:

> There will be a back region with its tools for shaping the body, and a front region with its fixed props. There will be a team of persons whose activity on stage and in conjunction with available props will constitute the scene from which the performed character's self will emerge, and another team, the audience, whose interpretive activity will be necessary for this emergence. The self is a product of all these arrangements, and all of its parts bear the marks of this genesis. (Goffman 1990 [1956]: 245)

As Cahill (2010: 173) notes, one of the attractions of Goffman's work is that, although the self emerges out of interactions and performances with and to others, individuals also still have some control over their interactions, or agency, as: 'To perform is to control how others define and treat you. It is not simply to respond to what others do ... Together we dramatically construct one another's self and the social interactions in which we act'; thus, 'we are both actor in and co-author of our own life-story' (Prins 2006: 281).

The research underpinning this book fully embraces the social locatedness of the knowledge produced within each of our focus groups, as well as the impact of research environments upon the narratives told by individuals to us as researchers, themselves and other participants in the group. In this sense, the selves and the narratives we depict in the chapters that follow are situated within the specifics of these interactions and the context in which they took place (which included the answering of our invitations for research participants). Yet, as Plummer (1995: 170) argues, whilst acknowledging the constructed nature of narrative and self, there is also, 'somewhere, behind all this story telling ... real active, embodied, impassioned lives': albeit lives that become identitied (as Muslim, mother, citizen, and so on) within discursive contexts. As such, our approach is to the specifics of these narratives and performances as a co-constituted product of our participants' subjectivities and the specifics of the research environment in which we encountered them.

Method

To explore these issues, our own focus group methodology employed a comparative research design that concentrated upon two factors in particular. The first was self-designated ethnicity – with black, white and Asian selected as our categories. The second was geographical residence, with groups taking place in metropolitan and non-metropolitan areas. This design was produced to facilitate an analysis of differences amongst populations living in the UK. Our use of these two factors produced six distinct population groups for analysis: black metropolitan; white metropolitan; Asian metropolitan; black non-metropolitan; white non-metropolitan; Asian non-metropolitan. We ran two focus groups for each of these populations, to which we then added two further 'wild card' groups for the exploration of potentially excluded or pertinent opinions that might become apparent throughout the context of our research (Kitzinger and Barbour 1999).

Fourteen groups were therefore conducted in total in the context of this research. These were held throughout 2010, comprising eighty-one individuals in total. The metropolitan sites identified were London and Birmingham; the non-metropolitan sites were Oldham, Swansea, Llanelli and Oxfordshire. Forty-eight women and thirty-three men took part in the project; thirty-one of whom identified as Asian, twenty-eight as white and twenty-two as black. Participants were selected using a purposive sampling strategy and recruited through a combination of enumeration, snowballing and organisation sampling techniques (see Ritchie, Lewis and Elam 2003). A decision was made, as far as possible, to conduct the focus groups within the locales, settings and areas of the participants' communities. This meant that the focus groups were conducted in rooms in public libraries, school and college buildings, restaurants, the offices of charitable organisations and the homes of participants. These settings were selected as a response to potential power imbalances between the researcher and researched, with the intention of enabling individuals to feel as comfortable as such a research environment might allow. The fourteen focus groups produced nearly twenty hours of recorded material in total. This translated into over 400 pages of transcribed material, or almost 200,000 words.

Our selection of a focus group approach was due to the considerable methodological advantages this offered over competing research strategies (see Morgan 1996, 1997; Kitzinger and Barbour 1999). These include the ability to analyse group dynamics that evolve within vernacular conversations; the chance that focus groups provide to probe the rigidity or flexibility of public views on anti-terrorism powers and their impacts – for instance, whether these change in conversation or under challenge by others – and an opportunity to explore shared sources of knowledge within different communities and differences across them (see Jarvis and Lister 2015b). Each group employed a series of deliberately open-ended questions as part of our attempt to maximise the extent to which our participants' voices could come to the fore in these discussions (Morgan 1996: 137). As such, our role as moderators was – where possible – limited to introducing the core questions and guiding subsequent discussion.

The questions on which each focus group concentrated were broadly divided into two sections (see Appendix A). The first section dealt with public conceptions and constructions of security and insecurity. Although follow-up questions varied according to the particularities of conversation within each group, five core questions were used to structure this part of the discussion. These were: What kinds of security threats do people in this country face? What are the main issues or threats to your own security? In what ways do you think threats to security have changed over time, if any? What does security mean to you? Who do you think is responsible for providing security?

The questions then turned more specifically to anti-terrorism measures. We began by asking for responses to a series of recent anti-terrorism advertisement campaigns which attempted to invoke citizen assistance with anti-terrorism, of the type 'If you suspect it, report it'. The moderator subsequently provided the group with a visual aid which listed recent UK anti-terrorism measures (see Appendix B), including controversial powers relating to stop and search without suspicion (Section 44 of the 2000 Terrorism Act) and pre-charge detention. After a discussion of these measures, participants were asked to consider how they felt anti-terrorism measures impacted upon themselves, their communities and the UK more widely.

The methodological decision to categorise ethnicity in terms of black, white and Asian (in reference to South Asian populations) was a complex one and is of course open to contestation, not least because, as Tariq Modood (2009: 193) argues, 'there is no satisfactory way of conceptualising ... visible minorities'. Furthermore, this is clearly not exhaustive of ethnic diversities within the UK; nor is it intended to be. As an effort to compare the attitudes of particular demographic groups, this categorisation was both contingent upon and appropriate to our research foci. This was our attempt to enable analysis of the different imaginings or experiences of (in)security and anti-terrorism, and the significance of historical legacies (of migration, discrimination, policing, and so on) therein. Our use of a metropolitan/non-metropolitan distinction, moreover, was an attempt to explore whether the different spaces of everyday life impacted upon public conceptions of anti-terrorism. Did those living in urban metropolises, for instance, feel more or less threatened by terrorism than others, and did this have any concomitant effect on evaluations of anti-terrorism powers? Furthermore, did research participants in less metropolitan environments attach a higher or lower importance to 'community' than their metropolitan counterparts, and the role thereof in perceptions of (in)security?

Part of the justification for this approach was that much of the existing research in this area focuses, either entirely or primarily, on religious identities and especially Muslim individuals, groups and communities (see Said 2004). Where other voices are included, moreover, they are often so in terms of a blanket 'non-Muslim' category (see Choudhury and Fenwick 2011). As noted above, this work tends to find that Muslims disproportionately experience the 'sharp end' of anti-terrorism measures. Yet, while a consideration of non-Muslims may permit a degree of contextualisation of Muslim attitudes, it lacks finer grain to begin to discern whether there are differences between non-Muslim communities. Chief among these is whether non-Muslim ethnic minorities (who might also experience prejudice and racism) possess similar attitudes, and the extent to which discomfort with anti-terrorism measures is shared by the majority, white, population. Of particular interest to us was whether black communities, historically also subject to discrimination and targeting through controversial policing strategies (not least the 'Sus' laws of the 1970s and 1980s; see Gilroy 1982), feel similarly targeted by the current raft of anti- terrorism measures. A range of other factors, of course, could also legitimately have been chosen. Some, such as gender, were included as secondary criteria and are discussed as such in the analysis that follows. Others, such as socio-economic status or age were excluded for pragmatic reasons because of the trade-off between parsimony and complexity that characterises research design (Hay 2002: 29–37). On completion of our data collection, we subjected the transcripts to descriptive content analysis in order to identify the key themes emerging from these data (Ritchie and Spencer 2002: 313–314). Framework charts (see Ritchie, Spencer and O'Connor 2003) were produced for both the security and anti-terrorism branches of the questions to enable the interpretation of our findings, which – in an attempt at fidelity – are reproduced using our participants' own words as directly as possible throughout this book.

Our methodology, of course, militates against any claim to the potential representativeness of our findings. This is, first, because of the limited size of our sample – something that is encouraged by the focus group method's emphasis on small-scale conversational dynamics; and, second, because of our non-probabilistic, purposive generation thereof. This is important, because it means that our research has no way of answering questions about the pervasiveness or otherwise of any of the attitudes, understandings or narratives to which we turn in our empirical chapters. Nor, indeed, is it able to explore other potentially significant factors that may underpin or help explain the discussions to which we were party in our focus groups.

What is needed, then, is to consider the validity of our findings and analysis away from any notion of statistical significance and with reference, instead, to its coherence and persuasiveness (see, for example, Dunn 2006). Reconceptualising validity as such is a common feature of small-scale qualitative research and interpretivist work more generally.

Conclusion

This chapter has sought to situate the empirical discussion that follows by exploring recent work on, and some of the relationships between, the three themes of this book: security, citizenship and anti-terrorism powers. We argued that there is real value in seeking to understand how publics discuss and conceptualise security and insecurity in this policy context, and that so doing both contributes to, and extends, recent constructivist work on security as well as contemporary efforts to decentre the state within studies of global politics. As suggested above, this book represents an attempt to allow 'vernacular' accounts of (in)security to enter debate on the workings and implications of anti-terrorism powers. Turning to citizenship, we identified a similar contemporary contestability around this term, with three debates within scholarship thereof posing particular relevance to our purposes here. The first concerns accounts of the erosion or decline of citizenship: something that, for many, has been accelerated by the war on terror's intrusions upon established rights. The second related to heterogeneities within citizenship and concerns about the perceived failings of multiculturalism. This, we suggested, speaks to fears that contemporary anti-terrorism powers target or create 'suspect communities'. And, third, we explored the increasing willingness of states to responsibilise citizens, tracing examples of this in relation to anti-terrorism powers. This literature, combined, suggests first, that citizenship may be experiencing a number of pressures which are 'eroding' this key political category, and that anti-terrorism measures may exacerbate such pressures. This suggests, second, that there is an urgent need to consider the voices, views and experiences of 'ordinary' people on these issues. In the following chapters, we now describe and explore the empirical 'findings' generated by the research method outlined at the end of the above discussion. To do so, we begin by reviewing public support for, or opposition to, anti-terrorism powers within the UK, and the ways in which such evaluations are framed in vernacular discourse.

Notes

1 This book seeks to 'go beyond' these ambitions because our interest is not solely in 'middle-class, white' people, for reasons outlined below.
2 One might argue that similar dynamics extend far further back even than this, especially in relation to the 'Fenian panic' of the 1860s (see, for example, McFarland 1998).
3 In April 2014 the New York Police Department abandoned a programme – previously known as the Demographics Unit – that had been dedicated to the collection of intelligence on Muslim communities. As the *New York Times* reported, the unit 'never generated a single lead', despite years of information-gathering in the post-9/11 period (Apuzzo and Goldstein 2014).

3

Framing and evaluating anti-terrorism policy

There are, as we have seen, numerous reasons to take public understandings, experiences and discussions of anti-terrorism powers more seriously than has been the case to date. In the first instance, doing so offers opportunity, as argued in Chapter 1, for thinking through efficacy and impact in this particular area of security policy. It also, as outlined in Chapter 2, presents scope for exploring changes in practices and experiences of citizenship. This, we suggested, becomes especially significant if we approach citizenship as a performative, lived phenomenon rather than solely a formal legal status.

In this chapter we begin our attempt to explore these dynamics, by setting out the diversity of perspectives we encountered in relation to the UK's anti-terrorism powers. Our discussion offers a detailed account of the ways in which these perspectives are formulated, justified, discussed and reasoned through by individuals of different demographic and experiential backgrounds, pointing to some of the anchors upon which these knowledge claims rest. We begin by identifying prominent reasons for scepticism or outright opposition towards the UK's anti-terrorism assemblage. These included concerns around the creation of a climate of fear and alienation of minority communities, questions about the effectiveness of such powers, doubts over whether they address the root causes of terrorism, suspicions that anti-terrorism presents little more than an exercise in 'security theatre', civil liberty concerns, and fear about the potential for their misuse.

In a second section we turn to more specific concerns that we encountered in relation to three measures that received particular attention in our research: stop and search powers codified in Section 44 of the 2000 Terrorism Act; pre-charge detention; and inchoate offences relating to the encouragement or glorification of terrorism. The chapter's final section identifies a number of less-sceptical or dismissive views from participants in our groups, including the belief that the state is obliged to respond to the continuing (perhaps evolving) threat of terrorism, concerns over the ability of 'ordinary' citizens to assess the necessity of developments in this policy area and confidence in the existence of sufficient safeguards, checks and balances through which miscarriages of justice might be redressed. These views – dismissive and otherwise – are linked in subsequent chapters to claims about citizenship and security more specifically.

'A whole load of rubbish'[1]

One of the most frequent concerns articulated to us in our focus groups was that the UK anti-terrorism framework both contributed to and potentially perpetuated a climate of fear that 'scares people' (Oldham, Asian, Female). Discussions of anti-terrorism as a driver of anxiety were fairly widespread in our groups; one participant, for example, argued that recent developments were 'creating a complete fear culture and part of that police state kind of environment' (London, Asian, Female). Another female participant suggested that the UK's approach had created 'a culture of suspicion' (Oldham, Asian, Female). As she continued, reflecting on a Metropolitan Police poster identifying potential triggers of suspicion such as the ownership of multiple mobile telephones, photography equipment and commercial transport such as vans:

> It's the reds under the beds thing and it's come back round again and now it's aimed at the way a person looks or dresses and it's like when you're taking pictures and stuff and you're driving a white van and you've got more than one phone. I mean you're buggered then. (Oldham, Asian, Female)

Fears that this climate might become self-fulfilling were also a concern for some of our participants: 'I think that if you exaggerate the threat, as we are inclined to do in this country, then you are going to accentuate the threat; it's going to get worse' (Llanelli, White, Male). Others described their own anxieties in relation to the protection of privacy. As one male put it – in a group that was conducted before the 2013 NSA revelations:[2]

> one of the kind of things about the way terrorism is dealt with ... it has kind of led to a huge information trawl, because you get all involved in everybody's life, the amount that's known about me is kind of extraordinary and it's on so many different databases and there are so many different ways that our government organisations and other organisations can find out. And to some extent that I find just as uncomfortable in a way as any terrorist threat. (London, White, Male)

In another group a white female described her encounter with post-9/11 airport security procedures as one that 'kind of makes you feel a bit more, I don't know, uncomfortable and jumpy about things' (Oxford, White, Female). Elsewhere, this fear was linked instead to high-profile tragic errors such as the July 2005 shooting of Jean-Charles de Menezes (see also Jarvis and Lister 2015b):[3]

> when I look at that whole incident objectively, the main factor that I think I can [see is] ... the whole sense of fear that was stirred up by mainly the media around that time. You can obviously not excuse it for happening, but you can understand what would put a fallible human in that kind of position. (London, White, Male)

Other participants in our groups suggested that experiences of this climate posed potentially quite damaging consequences for political protest and dissent (hence citizenship), in that: 'you should be allowed to question your government and any measures that they bring out, especially if it affects you directly. But to do so means, you know, you're then regarded with some suspicion and you're almost, you know, setting yourself up for rendering' (Oldham, Asian, Female).

These accounts of the negative societal consequences of anti-terrorism powers were accompanied, in many of our groups, by reflection on the more specific impact of such powers on particular communities. Individuals identifying with a range of ethnic identities pointed, repeatedly, to the risk that contemporary powers – and their application – would alienate minority populations. In addition to the view that such alienation would harm community relations (see Chapter 4), we encountered a sense that this could also pose security problems, and, indeed, increase rather than decrease the threat of terrorism. As one male put it: 'It concerns me that people may be driven to terrorism, who might be law abiding and so on, by the very treatment they get by the police' (Llanelli, White, Male). Another person stated, 'we have to be careful, as a society, we're not ... driving our young, vulnerable persons into the hands of the wrong persons by the way we are structuring our laws' (London, Black, Female). The singling out of Muslim communities as especial 'stakeholders' in the provision of collective security (Jarvis and Lister 2010) was widely discussed in this context. As one Asian female demonstrated, there were very real concerns here about a weakening of the vertical relationship between citizen and state *because of* anti-terrorism initiatives:

> the security services can argue this point with the justification that for the security of the country it is necessary that we employ tactics such as going into mosques etc., using informants, you know. You can't disagree with it

> much, but in terms of the tactics they employ where they approach vulnerable children, vulnerable youngsters, and then using scare tactics like showing them photos of their families etc., basically a veiled warning, and saying, If you don't provide us with this or you don't engage in this then you know what the consequences will be. And these kinds of tactics I don't think are very productive; could be very counterproductive. (London, Asian, Female)

A male participant, speaking also in London, was more explicit still, arguing that the targeting of Asian youth in particular would likely generate support for extremist political movements:

> And this is just disenfranchising the sort of further ... the sort of Asian population, the Asian youngsters. And especially because unemployment is also highly predominant in these areas, for them the easiest thing for them to relate to is radical Islamism, extremism. ... through the policies such as this they will create a Leviathan, and then they will say and turn around and then they will say, I told you so; we told you that there was this problem. But the thing is the government is playing its orchestrating part in creating this problem. (London, Asian, Male)

These concerns over the differential and discriminatory use of anti-terrorism powers were frequently connected to anxieties of targeted surveillance by the state, its agents, or other citizens. Numerous participants in our groups discussed such panoptical fears, noting the extent to which their behaviour was altered in public and private spaces as a consequence thereof. While some posited an omnipresent state surveillance ('I'm being watched, I'm being searched, I'm a target group, I'm not safe' (Swansea, Black, Female)), others described avoiding particular types of vocabulary and behaviours, as in the following conversation which took place with a focus group moderator:

> MO: Do you feel that people ...? You said there, you know, that you wouldn't say certain words. Do you feel watched, in a sense? Do you feel surveilled?
>
> A: Not all the time, but here if we are like sitting in a public bar or something like that, even if we are talking in general, we are just discussing or joking with one another, we are worried. Because we think that if somebody might have overheard it and then they just go and inform the police, then all those ... I saw the people though, they were sitting in the bar and they were talking about bombs and everything. If something comes up tomorrow, God forbid, if something comes up tomorrow and obviously that person is going to report, Oh, I heard those two guys, they were talking about those bombs and all that. (Oxford, Asian, Female)

In another discussion, the removal of a dedicated prayer room at the university attended by one of our participants was also connected to anti-terrorism initiatives: 'And I think it is all down to this idea of having a lot of surveillance within universities and having this freedom taken away' (London, Asian, Male).

A third set of concerns focused on the ineffective nature of the anti-terrorism framework in its current formulation. One participant, discussing the irrelevance of many contemporary powers, argued, 'I don't believe that a lot of these things are necessary' (London, Black, Female); a view with which many others agreed: 'you're never going to catch the people by doing that ... you're just going to be suspecting everyone around you, which will just make ... it wouldn't work' (London, Asian, Female). Some pointed to a lack of discernible evidence for the continuation of contemporary powers: 'in most of the cases I can think of, it wasn't ... you know, we didn't stop terrorism based on these measures' (London, Black, Female). As another, similarly, put it,

> What I was going to say was like Guantanamo Bay, they locked people up without ... because they were suspected of being terrorists, or whatever, but bombings went on all over the world, you know, whilst people were in Guantanamo Bay, so it wasn't actually stopping anything so therefore, to me, it was ineffective. (Oldham, White, Female)

The lack of focus – and concomitant waste of resources – within the current framework also drew criticism. One participant from Llanelli, for example, bemoaned the lack of selectivity amongst airport security measures, where staff:

> go through your things, your hand luggage. All these things I find ... do we look like terrorists? Do we look like followers of Al-Qaeda? Answer me ... Holiday in Spain, and there were 200 people going to Majorca, some of them ... children, myself, all sorts, family; and it's strange that they should have these measures. Why can't they be more selective? (Llanelli, White, Male).

He continued – amidst challenge from other members in the group: 'I'm not racialist or whatever – but followers of al-Qaeda are basically Pakistani, Afghanistan, Iran, aren't they?' (Llanelli, White, Male).

Closely tied to these concerns were accusations of governmental overreaction, with a spread of unnecessary anti-terrorism mechanisms (often personally experienced) identified to bolster these criticisms. These included: first, airport security measures – 'I'd safety-pinned it and put a sewing kit in my bag, and they'd confiscated both safety-pin and sewing kit; such was the ridiculousness ... and I just thought that was so, extreme and pointless' (Oxford, White, Female); second, the removal of bins in public places – 'there is a, sort of, kneejerk reaction, let's get rid of all the bins or whatever because somebody might put a parcel in it and it might blow up, but it's a sign of the times, I think' (Oldham, White, Female); and, third, terrorism warning posters on public transport – 'Back to the posters, I just think that's an overreaction. I think that an awful lot of people travelling on the Tube will have at least, you know, will be suspicious by those definitions' (Oxford, White, Female).

Staying with questions around efficacy, other people pointed to the static and backward-looking nature of anti-terrorism policy, and the problem that 'terrorists come in different forms' (London, Black, Female), and, indeed, innovate:

> The problem with profiling is, as soon as you start to profile, you know, brown-skinned, you know, guys in their early thirties, that, you know, the real terrorists, if they're clever enough, will start, you know, using white women as their suicide bombers, which obviously they do. So there's a big danger in profiling. (London, Asian, Male)

A disconnect between contemporary fears and the realities of life in Britain today was also prominent in these discussions. One individual discussing the aforementioned anti-terrorism warning campaigns, for example, argued, 'that says terrorist communications, have you seen anyone with large quantities of mobile phones; my brother alone has got three. Almost every Asian man has got more than one' (Oldham, Asian, Female). In the words of another:

> I've got a friend who's got five cell phones, because they have each SIM card does different things, different minutes. Now, back in our days at school it would be like, yeah, three phones, got my three numbers, be hating it if you were trying to keep in touch with the person, but that's the way of life. But now they've said if a person has got more than one phone or is having a large number of mobile phones, let's raise an eyebrow, it could be a terrorist. And that in itself is very, very stupid actually. (London, Asian, Female)

Criticisms such as these led to reflection on life in a multicultural Britain, as well as public and political ignorance of different social and cultural expectations. As one participant put it discussing the same campaign:

> I think this is where the problem of having everyone policing one another comes in, because cultures are different. In Africa people are used to having three or four phones ... That information is so vague, if you're asking people who are in the country to call when you suspect a terrorist. So I think, like he mentioned, there is a problem with ... for us or people that live in a multicultural community. (Swansea, Black, Female)

A fourth set of criticisms focused on the utility of the criminal justice system as the appropriate field for confronting terrorist violence. As one participant put it, 'laws don't solve social problems. We have made these terrorism laws and terrorism has not gone away' (London, Black, Female). Viewed thus, the current anti-terrorism framework emerges as little more than a distraction, discouraging more penetrating analysis of the root causes beneath participation in terrorist activities. As another individual suggested in a critical discussion of the UK's approach: 'But we also don't hear why are people wanting to join a terrorism group? What do we need to do to change our Middle Eastern policies so that maybe people aren't so compelled to commit acts like this? It never seems to really look particularly deeply into it' (London, White, Female).

A fifth concern, connected to the above, was that anti-terrorism mechanisms offer little more than an exercise in security theatre by the state and its apparatuses. Here, powers such as enhanced security checks at airports were described as an effort, simply, to demonstrate that something was being done to confront terrorism. In the words of one male: 'I think I'd suspect that they're all about creating the impression that somebody's doing something' (London, White, Male). The potential beneficiaries of this performative gesture varied in these discussions. For some, they had a role in reassuring the public, such that, 'I think these measures are only put in place to almost make people feel safe' (London, Black, Female).[4] Other, more sceptical, voices argued that this sort of theatre posed value for political, military and other elites with more nefarious motives:

> God help us, there may be a terrorist attack in London, and they're expecting one any day, I gather, you know. But a lot of this is being used as cover for measures with authoritative people. The police in particular, the army too, and others as well, and God knows. (Llanelli, White, Male)

Discussions of anti-terrorism's performative power pointed to distinct, yet not necessarily unrelated, dynamics. Some highlighted the inability or unwillingness of publics to contest dominant terrorism discourses. For one participant, for example, 'If they say, But we're doing this for you, you know, we're preventing anti-terrorism, people are much more likely to say, Oh well, you have to do it' (Oldham, White, Male). For another, similarly, 'if you say anti-terrorism it is like a mantra: oh yes, we must have it. I do think we're becoming more and more of a police state' (Llanelli, White, Female). Others argued that there might be more immediate material interests at work in this area, with little connection to the prevention of terrorism: 'now they've banned fluids from going into the airports. You wonder if it's, if it's real, if it's ... if there was a real threat, or if it's a commercial reality for you to buy something when you get in the airport, as opposed to carry something in' (London, Black, Female). However explained, anecdotes to confirm this criticism were forthcoming in several of our groups. One participant, for example, recounted an encounter between the police and her husband, who had been stopped while working on the perimeter of London's Heathrow Airport. Picking up the story, in her words, he:

> was just about to drive off, when he was surrounded by three vehicles, very, very tight. They opened up, and the car was surrounded completely by officers, armed officers, all of them with their backs towards him, apart from the one right at his window, which was right up against the window, with the gun pretty much in his face, and stopped him getting out the car, and stopped him doing anything. There was another van that was a couple of foot up that he could see, in front, with the back doors open, with the dogs in. They didn't let the dogs out, but they were very clear that the dogs are there. Anyway, [my husband] explained who he was, gave them identification, got that, and in the end he was taken to one side, and said, Look, we know you're fine, but actually this is more a demonstration to other people than it is just to you. And he was like, Well, if they're half as frightened as I am. You know, [my husband's] got quite dark skin, hasn't he? (Oxford, White, Female)

A sixth source of concern focused on the civil liberty implications of anti-terrorism powers. In the words of one participant, 'Every time you legislate, you eat away into somebody's rights' (London, Black, Female). As another put it: 'Some of these powers remove that freedom of individuals, and it restricts the democracy that we live in' (Oxford, White, Female). Developments in this area were seen to have widespread impacts upon the organisation of political life in the UK, given that they raise profound questions for:

> democratic society that, you know, that we're taught from day one, you know, we're all equal, we've all got an equal chance, but you, that group, because you look a bit different, you know, yeah. It kind of questions, you know, the other policies that we have and, you know, free speech, free this, you know, like freedom of movement. (Oldham, Asian, Female)

These civil rights incursions[5] were often explained by reference to elite efforts to use, manipulate or exaggerate the threat of terrorism. One individual, for example, argued, 'We're becoming a police state, and we ought to be careful of government or the executive not using its powers through, um, in the name of terrorism, to infringe on our civil liberties' (London, Black, Female). As another pointed out, however, this may not be entirely unprecedented: 'There was certainly a campaign in place against the IRA, and against every other organisation stretching back ... it's always been something that terrorism has been ... a reason or excuse for suspending civil liberties' (London, White, Male). Several individuals sought to contest the hyperbole around the current terrorist threat, and thereby desecuritize it (see Roe 2004). As in the following examples, numerical evidence was frequently cited in such attempts:

> I think there is this pulling of the levers to severe, not so severe, high risk etc. It's just, again, it's like sort of ... because when you count the figures of the people that are arrested and the huge media hype by the tabloid newspapers when somebody is arrested, out of 100% of people who are arrested 94% are released without charge, 6% are convicted of any terrorism-related offences. So, when you sort of tally up the figures the sort of media hype really doesn't make much sense. (London, Asian, Male)

> [W]hen you look at the statistics, 0.4% of terrorist attacks have been Islamic or have been Islamic fundamentalists and the other 96% are peace-loving Muslim people, but it's just that 0.4% that is picked on by the media because the media needs that devil folklore sort of person to blame. (Oldham, Asian, Female)

Others described their suspicion of dominant constructions of this threat. One person, for instance, told us, 'I am wary of terrorism, but I'm also wary of what kind of information the government gives us that [is] almost creating fear' (London, Black, Female). Another, referring to the London suicide bombings of 7 July 2005, suggested, 'the big terrorist event that happened in London, I think, allows the government to manipulate, and the media to manipulate ... take that fear and say, Don't worry, you're secure, trust us to take care of you, and then you have an entirely different public perception' (London, White, Female).

Importantly, civil liberty concerns around anti-terrorism were rarely treated as an isolated issue divorced from wider political contexts. Many of our participants drew broader implications from developments in this area of public policy, seeing these as indicative of more general governance trends. One, for example, stated, 'I don't want to live in a Big Brother state, where every single move is being watched' (Oxford, White, Female). Another, describing control order powers, argued, 'it's almost like harking back to like that *1984* George Orwell sort of thing, isn't it?' (Oldham, Asian, Female). These oppositions, however, were far from utopian musings devoid of any sense of the challenges of managing the demands of liberty and security. Indeed, we encountered explicit acceptance amongst several of our participants of the need to live with the threat of terrorism as a far preferable alternative to pervasive efforts to control its risk. As one participant put it:

> I want to be part of the community. I want to be open. I want to be social. And what this, these kinds of anti-terrorism measures make me feel; I don't know how effective they are at preventing terrorism. I doubt they are. All that they do is that they make me feel this, you know, this closed borders thing, and I think it breeds that sense of insecurity. It breeds this disconnected citizenship. (Oxford, White, Female)

As she continued:

> I think part of being a liberal is that you accept that there are certain consequences to freedom, and there are certain negative consequences of having freedom, in that there will be nutters out there that will cause terror. And you can choose to be affected by this, and you can choose to have draconian measures that restrict everybody's freedom and lives; or you can accept that that's part of life and not let them terrorise you and get on with life, and ignore it. You can't ignore it and you should respect it, the victims, and that's not what I mean, and, but you cannot let their behaviour affect yours. (Oxford, White, Female)

A final source of concern we encountered was the possibility that anti-terrorism powers might be misused by 'bad apples' within the police or intelligence services. One participant, speaking with regard to the government's recent approach argued, 'They have to be very careful about their misuse. They have to be very, very, very careful' (London, Black, Female). Another, in a different focus group, stated, 'they all can be abused. That is one of the key factors that I'm picking up on about the anti-terrorism measures. They're important but they can be abused' (London, Black, Male). Some pointed to the need for training and safeguards such that: 'I hope the police officers have been retuned socially, so you don't have people who are ... perpetuating their own anger, resentment, violence and hatred at ethnic people. We have to be careful that it's not misused' (London, Black, Female). This might be seen as doubly important, given that 'any of those control orders, any of those can be used on the hearsay or the discretion of the police and you're never told what you've done wrong, you're never told why or how you've been detained' (Oldham, Asian, Female). This concern gained added emphasis from those identifying with minority ethnic identities who pointed to their own experiences of feeling unfairly targeted by the state: 'The police are gaining more powers, and they're backing people into a corner, and they are becoming bullies. And we don't feel safe. We're being bullied' (London, Black, Female); and 'Terrorism, as a theory, has been used to target ethnic persons' (London, Black, Female).

Within these discussions about misuse, a number of our participants spoke to two further dangers that have been explored at length in recent academic debate. First, that such powers would be used for purposes other than countering terrorism: 'the power to stop and search, that's not specifically for bombing. I don't think that's an anti-terrorism thing at all. I think that's a catch-all so they can, you know, they see three black guys in a car, they'll stop it because they think there's going to be drugs in there' (Oldham, White, Male). Second, that public ignorance of developments in this area meant that such powers would be consolidated without contestation or even recognition: 'a lot of people won't realise what happened to them until after all these laws are in place, and then one day, they will wake up and say, Oh, oh, we can't do anything now' (London, Black, Female).

'Too much of an infringement on our civil liberties'[6]

The sources of hostility towards anti-terrorism powers considered in the above discussion were, in the main, articulated in general terms. Whether viewed as a driver of public insecurity, an irrelevance, a distraction, an exercise in security theatre or an effort at social manipulation, these critiques targeted the UK's anti-terrorism framework in its entirety, often, indeed, blending it into other governmental programmes. Moving away now from general attitudes, we turn to three specific policy areas within the anti-terrorism framework that attracted particular comment across our groups.[7] These concerned: first, stop and search powers contained within Section 44 of the 2000 Terrorism Act; second, the detention of terrorist suspects before charge; and, third, the offence to glorify, incite or encourage terrorism (Section 1 of the 2006 Terrorism Act).

Stop and search

Discussion of the Section 44 stop and search powers was largely organised around three perspectives. The first, and least common, was support for the powers, with two justifications offered to this end. A first was that the existence of these alone offered sufficient evidence for their necessity, despite the potentially negative consequences that may result from their misuse. In the words of one participant: 'I don't have an issue with it. But then there are issues of racial profiling that come into this ... So, I mean, it is something necessary, most probably something that not many people can argue against' (London, Asian, Male). Others agreed, pointing to the limited direct impact of such powers upon their own lives: 'I don't mind the power to stop and search a vehicle. It doesn't bother me if they stop and search me' (Oldham, White, Male); and 'We need something like this, don't we? I mean, the power to stop and search, I think, in some ways that doesn't bother me' (Oxford, White, Female). As one woman put it: 'personally, I won't care being stopped as you say, well, I have nothing to hide, it wouldn't affect me that much' (Oxford, White, Female).

A second justification focused on the searches' perceived appropriateness, given the likely profile of potential terrorists. Participants discussing stop and search in these terms recognised their potential differential application but dismissed this either as a minor inconvenience or as evidence (again) of their necessity. In the words of one Asian female,

> if there were laws about stopping and searching and so on, yes, there may be that one particular black guy who's a Rastafarian who gets stopped every ... but it still happens just to show that he's more likely to commit a crime than everybody else. And is it really that bad that he gets stopped ... fine, once a day? (London, Asian, Female)

This individual did, however, subsequently qualify her support for the measure, emphasising the importance of her faith in the fairness afforded by the police and legal system:

> It's probably because I've never been stopped and searched. Maybe that would change if I had or if my husband's targeted ... but to me, I feel that, if I was mistakenly identified, I think I would have enough access to legal counsel and to be able to make sure that my voice was heard and that my rights would be enforced. (London, Asian, Female)

Most of our participants did not share these views, instead articulating their opposition to stop and search. In some cases, this was aimed not at the powers per se, but rather their implementation and potential for racial profiling. In the words of one individual, stop and search was targeted at 'Asian faces' (Birmingham, Asian, Female). A male participant in London noted a 'huge increase in stop and search for particular races' (London, Asian, Male), with another still arguing that stop and search is 'creating racism' as it is 'not stopping everyone, it's stopping a particular number of people' (Swansea, Black, Female). Many of those perceiving themselves unaffected directly offered similar criticism. One white participant in Llanelli, for example, suggested:

> Can I just say that when you come to the stop and search business, people who are stopped and searched are usually black, even if they come from a very respectable ... Far more proportion of black people are stopped. And, as [another] said, if anybody looks a bit funny with long hair and a beard, they stop them too. (Llanelli, White, Male)

Another – a former policewoman – argued similarly, drawing on the 'bad apple' criticism above:

> Unfortunately, in the wrong hands, you know ... I'd be concerned that it'd be every Asian stopped, every black lad stopped because black girls don't do it, you know. You know, if you look at it, you know, you don't get black girl terrorists, you don't get ... you've got the black lads who are going [to be] thieves and vagabonds and you've got the Asians who are ... the Asian lads who are going to blow up trains and stuff, so you could stop and search any of those and ... just the thoughts that they would get stopped and searched without suspicion because they are Asian or because they are black would be worrying, I think. (Oldham, White, Female)

Some critics did, in this context, argue that their support would be more forthcoming if the measure was applied less disproportionately. As one male put it:

> I believe very much the stop and search powers, I think they're good, because, yes, if you have reasonable grounds to believe someone is a terrorist or has just stolen something, or has just committed something which may lead to a terrorist act, fine, stop them. But don't pick people just because of the way they're dressed. (Swansea, Black, Male)

As the above suggests, we encountered particular concern at Section 44's 'without suspicion' clause. This clearly underpins fears about racial profiling, and the clause's capacity to conceal the use of ethnicity as a marker for suspicion. Other participants, however, expressed a broader concern that blanket stop and search powers violate fundamental citizenship rights. In the words of one male: 'if we do walk around in London or drive a car in London, we can be stopped without reason ... I think is too much of an infringement on our civil liberties ... I don't think stop and search without suspicion helps' (London, Asian, Male). Another described stop and search as 'undemocratic' and compromising people's ability to 'express themselves freely' because those with particular appearances were more likely to be stopped (Swansea, Black, Male). In the words of another:

> while the police stop and search a personal vehicle without suspicion, I believe that is one which can be abused a lot. Because now they can say, Well, we suspect terrorism, and then they use that because it's like a social worker wanting to prove that they've got the power to sort of intimidate a mother by saying. I've got the power to take away your child. (London, Black, Female)

A third perspective we encountered focused on the effectiveness of stop and search as an anti-terrorism strategy. As the following demonstrates, a number of our participants expressed support for these powers in cases with reasonable grounds for suspicion, whilst, at the same time, arguing that the absence thereof renders their efficacy questionable, at best:

A: I think like you said, if they stop somebody who is hiding something I would agree with that.
B: But the point is, how likely are they to do that? I mean the whole point here is, without suspicion, so does that mean they're just randomly stopping and searching people and hoping to find amongst the millions of people moving around that they're going to catch someone? That doesn't seem that likely. (London, White, Males)

In the words of another: 'I don't think ... I've ever heard of a case where they stopped someone and found, oh he's got a bomb in his car, you know' (London, Black, Female).

As much of the above indicates, faith in the police and criminal justice system appear crucial to public evaluations of these powers. In the words of one white male, for instance: 'That's disgraceful. It means that any member of the security forces who has a grudge or a grievance, or a dislike or a prejudice can take it out, I mean, if there is no reasonable grounds' (Swansea, White, Male). In contrast, an Asian participant (who was supportive of stop and search in principle), similarly stated, 'when it comes to the judiciary, the actual system of justice generally speaking they are, for example, people are released etc. So, for me, I do have faith in the justice system' (London, Asian, Male).

Ethnicity offered no clear predictor of perspective here, with Asian participants, in some cases, quite supportive of stop and search powers. Although many of our black participants were more sceptical often to the point of outright opposition – others qualified this hostility if equitable treatment could be guaranteed:

MO: So even though many of you have had problems with stop and search, and reasonable use of that, you would still be okay with the idea of stop and search?
A: If it's applied generally to everyone, not just picking a set of people. (Swansea, Black, Male)

Thus, in contrast to the absoluteness of opposition grounded in civil liberty principles which may be less amenable to change, concerns around the implementation of stop and search, at least in principle, could – seemingly – be potentially assuaged:

> I think I'd be more comfortable if I saw in a month five white people stopped on the road and they were being checked. So when I get stopped I'll go, Oh, they're just doing their job. But if every time I see you're checking someone it's a black young boy, or it's someone from the BME community, then I feel like you're just pointing fingers, you're trying to look for something. But if I drove past and I say, They stopped the white guy, okay. So when I get stopped, all right, go, you're doing your job. I think that's the thing for me. (Swansea, Black, Male)

Pre-charge detention

The complex and contested spread of attitudes we encountered in relation to stop and search powers was some distance from those on our second specific anti-terrorism measure: pre-charge detention. Whilst re-emphasising our proviso on the representativeness of our findings, barely a single voice articulated anything approaching support for the UK's pre-charge detention period – twenty-eight days at the time our research – or its extension to ninety days: a source of considerable political and press interest during this period. One individual in Oldham did argue:

> I don't like indefinite; definitely not. I've no worries with somebody being kept in for twenty-eight days if, at the end of it, you either say, sorry, we have got the wrong person and we had good reason to believe you were the right person, so you're free to go, or, we're going to charge you. (Oldham, White, Female)

Most of our participants, however, articulated views much closer to a black female in London for whom, 'You can't detain someone without charge. I mean, it's just blatantly wrong' (London, Black, Female).

On one level, the detention limit was seen as violating certain fundamental, and inviolable, liberties. One individual asked, 'Doesn't this go against some sort of constitutional right? I know we don't have a constitution, but does it not impede some sort of human rights?' (Swansea, White, Male). A male participant in London invoked the UK's historical use of internment, asking, 'Is this the way Britain is heading?' (London, Asian, Male). Another couched his opposition in far more forceful language, arguing, 'you need as a country to be clear on where you stand and what you believe in and ... effectively if you believe in liberty of the individual, you believe in fundamental human rights ... And something like this ... flies completely in the face of, you know, one of the fundamental tenets of being innocent without ... innocent until you are proven guilty' (London, Asian, Male). Others still expressed incredulity at the possibility of any public support for such an extended period of pre-charge detention:

> So, and the reason for that is because it's counterproductive to national security, so for them to tell you what they're charging you with is counterproductive to national security, which is, I mean, how could you, how could anyone ... I don't see that anyone with a rational mind could turn around and say that that was legitimate and a legitimate requirement, you know, for the security of the country. You'd have to be a complete maniac on well and truly the right side of this law, someone who would never be subjugated to it, or never know anyone that was going to be subjugated to it, in a state of, you know, complete panic and fear to sanction this. (Birmingham, Asian, Male)

Importantly, many participants in our research were fully aware of the arguments most commonly used in efforts to extend the detention period, especially the need for additional time to obtain, examine or analyse evidence (Horne and Berman 2012). There was, however, considerable scepticism toward the instrumentalism of these arguments and their implications for fundamental rights:

> Now, I actually understand that intelligence requires time to gather and whatnot, and, yes, maybe then we need to step up the ... put more money into intelligence-gathering or, you know, do something along that ... but I don't think you should fundamentally change certain lines that are ... that I think define who you are as a free nation. (London, Asian, Male)

As with stop and search, we also encountered concerns that pre-charge detention targets particular minorities. As one person put it:

> the only problem is the execution of these laws and the legislation ... But again when you select a few, and target a few, and then only use those laws because you think they're not from, shall I say indigenous people, and you use these laws on them ... I think that's the major problem for me. (Swansea, Black, Male)

A final set of concerns surrounded the impacts on those subject to an incarceration of this length. These spanned pragmatic considerations relating to the detrimental implications for everyday life: 'if you are completely innocent and you have a mortgage and you have a child, after these thirty days, these twenty-eight days, it can create a big challenge for you to get your life [back on track]' (London, Asian, Male). They also, however, encompassed worries around the social stigma likely to be incurred as a result of detention under terrorism laws: 'How can they come back into the community or workplace? He could be a professional, you know what I mean, and then after twenty-eight days ... If he was innocent? Well, who is going to declare his innocence?' (Birmingham, Asian, Female). For another participant, similarly, 'that's the difficulty with this one, because you can be tarnished' (London, Black, Male). And, as he continued, there is a genuine fear that the mistaken application or misuse of these powers would be met with little more than an apology and the invocation of the spectre of 'terrorism': 'the police or the authorities will just get away with it and say, I'm sorry, and terrorism. It is because of terrorism' (London, Black, Male).

The likely absence of recompense following unwarranted arrest was frequently discussed, with one individual contrasting the level of media and public interest in arrests and releases, arguing, 'They say very little when they're released. They say very little. They just say, We no longer require such and such. There's no compensation' (Birmingham, Asian, Male). As another put it, 'there's three or four people from Sheffield or Bradford or somewhere, it's frontpage news, it's on the news, and a couple of months you see [only] a little bit [of information], oh, they've been let off because there's no evidence, not enough evidence to prosecute was found' (Oldham, Asian, Female). A male in another focus group asked, 'How do you apologise to the person, okay, sorry we detained you for twenty-eight days ... How do you compensate for that?' (Swansea, Black, Male). While another, with experience of working as a prison officer, demonstrated similar concerns:

> people don't have to have that stigma, and it's very, very difficult to get rid of that, and just what prison does to you as a person. I was on the other side of the bars, and how bitter and twisted it's made me, and I didn't realise until I'd left, how it's changed me. And so I just think, Oh, I don't know, I mean, how do you say sorry for incarcerating somebody and keeping them away from their family for a month, when they've done nothing wrong? You know, you can't, you can't just say sorry. It's not acceptable. (Oxford, White, Female)

Such worries around stigmatisation, finally, were not limited to pre-charge detention; as one female put it in relation to control order powers: 'if people saw your house under house arrest, they will start to view you differently, even if you're what, entirely innocent, and it starts to make people feel suspicious of their community and of the people that they're around' (Oxford, White, Female).

Glorifying, inciting or encouraging terrorism

In contrast to pre-charge detention powers, inchoate offences relating to the encouragement or glorification of terrorism attracted mixed responses amongst our participants. Those expressing scepticism about such offences frequently did so because of their vagueness and the possibility for abuse this was seen to create. In one succinct summary:

> [Has] there been any clarification of what can be classed under incitement of terrorism or glorifying terrorism, because that's one area I think has been very much abused by the person who is implementing the rule. Have they explained? Are there any guides to what is an act glorifying terrorism? Or is it just anything a policeman or an enforcer feels is? If I shout too loud, is that going to incite terrorism ... How do you define that? (Swansea, Black, Female)

Others pointed to potential confusion between expressions of sympathy for the cause behind, rather than the actual use of, violence:

> When you talk about the conflicts going on around the world, which stance are you supposed to take? When you talk about Palestine, when you talk about the thing that happened in Bosnia or what's happening in Chechnya, and you think, well, you know, you almost have to excuse yourself and you say, No, I don't agree with the terrorists but I agree with their right to freedom and independence. But then you think, are you then directly or indirectly inciting terrorism? (Oldham, Asian, Female)

While several of our participants agreed, noting they felt 'quite uncomfortable' with the offence because 'it's very vague' (London, White, Female), others argued that 'having an incitement to terrorism on the statute books is not necessarily a bad thing', despite their fears that its present formulation may be a 'little bit broad' (London, Asian, Male). A white participant from Oldham, for example, argued that such measures should be applied irrespective of the transgressor's ideology or religion:

> I think people, if they do incite hatred of anybody, regardless of who it is they're inciting hatred of, has got to be stopped, so people coming out and, sort of, ranting and tanting about the way the Brits are continuing or people who go out and start about the Muslims, or whatever. No, stop them, absolutely. And I remember being at school and hearing a song which said man must learn love or else mankind will fail, and I've honestly tried to live my life that way, but if we don't care about each other then we're going to just blow the place to pieces. Yeah, like you say, if you're going to do something like that, lock you up until you decide that you're not going to do it. (Oldham, White, Female)

Another turned the group's attention to Abu Hamza – and solicited general agreement – arguing:

> if you're not from this country and you come over here, like Captain Hook[8] did, to spread this kind of ... it's an evil, isn't it, but you're going to spread this poison; not take them to court and spend the next five years trying to export them, just get them out, next plane, get rid of them. (Oldham, White, Male)

These offences were rarely opposed on the grounds of freedom of speech, with the following tentative statement as close to such concerns as we encountered,

> I guess, this, kind of, kind of, conflicts with the fact that we're supposed to have freedom of speech ... if you have freedom of speech, and we have free will, we should be able to listen to whatever we like and make our own decisions about what we want to do. (London, Black, Female)

They also, moreover, received some of the fullest support amongst our research sample from minority ethnic communities. In the words of one Asian participant: 'I'm not going to argue against the idea that, you know, these radicals need to be put into prison and, you know, need to be prosecuted etc, if they are actually sort of inciting racial, inciting explicit terrorist sort of notions' (London, Asian, Male).

This lack of opposition amongst many of our Asian participants may be explained, in part, by concerns that public perceptions of Muslim and Asian people are dominated by representations and fears of 'extremism'. After describing the prominent activist Anjem Choudry, founder of the now-proscribed Islam4UK as an 'idiot' (London, Asian, Male), one male explained his continuing frustration at the successes of a media-savvy fringe in shaping public opinion of Islam:

> The people who base their perspective of Islam, base it on these fringe minorities, on both ends; but we never see that they actually go out and actually find somebody from the East London Mosque or the Imam of, let's say, Regents Park Mosque. How many times have you ever seen two of the main mosques in the UK, the Regents Park Mosque or the East London Mosque, how many times have you seen representatives from these organisations representing the views? I can't remember a single incidence when they have been asked to give an opinion on a matter pertaining to Muslims in the country. (London, Asian, Male)

A final reason for support for these offences included a belief that the law is 'fundamentally right and just' (London, Asian, Female): a belief augmented, for this individual, in the challenges the UK had confronted in its efforts to deport Abu Hamza amidst fears of his likely torture:

> He used to preach in this country against this country's citizens and the way that we live our life. And he was allowed to do that in the name of civil liberties were being infringed, otherwise. We can't deport him to his homeland, because his life would be in danger. But that's where I find it fundamentally wrong; what about my ... what about my life being under threat from people that he has excited, people that he has encouraged, effectively, to wage war against this country? So, absolutely, I think those are the basic, fundamental laws that need to come. (London, Asian, Female)

As another participant put it more simply, 'People should live freely and peacefully and it's not good to say someone should die, that's not right' (Swansea, Black, Male).

'What else can you do?'[9]

The above indicates the existence of considerable, and widespread, public opposition to the UK's anti-terrorism framework and specific powers therein. This opposition, however, was neither universal nor absolute, with a number of our participants either qualifying their hostility, acquiescing to the existence of contemporary measures, or, indeed, going further and offering support for existing powers. The most prominent reason – noted already in the preceding discussion – was the argument, simply, that 'they are necessary' (London, Black, Female): that something needs to be done to prevent terrorism, even if the current mechanisms remain imperfect. In the words of one participant, 'there are people out there, aren't there, that are quite, you know, a threat. And, you know, what do you do? And, you know, what measures do you feel there should be?' (Oxford, White, Female). Another agreed, arguing: 'these terrorists are looking for loopholes to get back in. They're not pulling back, they're waiting, they are regrouping, they're in cells all over the place, waiting for a key word, when Bin Laden might get up and say ... a code, or whatever' (London, Black, Male).

Even some of those dissatisfied with the current framework registered their understanding for its existence. As one individual put it: 'I can understand as to why they are there, but I wouldn't want them to be there, if I have to be quite frank with you' (London, Asian, Male). An individual in another group argued similarly, noting, 'to me, they seem unethical, but obviously if you just read them, but for the last couple of minutes I was thinking, what else can you do? If these genuinely are the threats that the government sees in the country'

(Swansea, White, Male). The changing nature of contemporary terrorism was prominent in these conversations, with the belligerence and bloodthirstiness of 'new terrorist' organisations adding, for some, to the need for some sort of anti-terrorism framework:

> [the] IRA would say, I'm putting a bomb in Leicester Square, everybody leave Leicester Square, and they normally had that sort of secure way of doing things. These guys don't operate like that. They are, they go there and they just say, I'm going to have a seat here with you guys. Death to the infidels [*laughter*]. (London, Black, Male)

This produced, for others, however, a feeling of fatalism – or stoicism – rather than support for the UK's response: 'there's no legislation, if you like, for a suicide bomber coming right up close to you' (Oldham, White, Female).

Beyond those arguing, 'I don't have a problem with most of these measures' (Oldham, White, Male), we encountered a number of examples of qualified opposition. This was, frequently, due to a perceived lack of access to the information necessary to assess the need for, or effectiveness of, these security powers (see also Jarvis and Lister 2015b). In the words of one participant: 'I don't certainly feel any personal thing, but I can't quantify how successful these anti-terrorism measures are at keeping the nation secure, so that therefore we can focus on our daily, but you know, our daily troubles' (Oxford, White, Female). Interestingly, this was also primarily the case amongst those who felt neither targeted nor significantly affected by such measures, for instance:

> It's hard to say [if anti terrorism measures enhance security], I think, because you don't really know ... you don't really know how many ... if there are statistics published saying, oh, by the way, by virtue of these control orders we've stopped twenty-five ... then, yes, obviously it does. And then we can make a balance up and say, well, you know, how much has my liberty been affected by this? (London, Asian, Male).

In the words of another: 'The problem with terrorism is that you don't know ... what the threat is, so you don't know whether they're more effective. If they are infringements of your civil liberties but you have no idea whether they're actually doing any good or not' (London, White, Male).

Some participants were willing to cede decision-making to those with access to better information: 'I can understand why the things that MI5 and MI6 did because they appear to be important, although we don't really know what they do' (London, Black, Female). Others preferred to defer judgement until evidence was somehow forthcoming – for example: 'I don't think it is effective until we hear that it is effective; until we say, we have stopped and searched x number of people without suspicion, or whatever, and security is better ... Unless they tell us that then we couldn't possibly know, I don't think' (Oldham, White, Female).

Third, and directly related to the above, a number of our participants expressed some measure of support for the state's activities in this area – despite potential civil liberty concerns – due to the security they felt from actually witnessing 'something' being done. As one female put it:

> But I think for me personally, if I felt like if the government hadn't taken any measures or made any changes to legislation since recent terror attacks, I think I'd feel concerned. I'm glad that they're taking some measures but, you know, but there's of course issues of freedom and all of these pressures. (London, White, Female)

A black participant in Swansea argued similarly in response to a question from the group's moderator:

> MO: Do you personally feel safer as a result of these measures being introduced?
>
> A: To some extent, I feel to some extent because it gives me the impression that something is being done, and some extent it will be the same results, some bomb threats that have been failed. I think to some extent, but a lot still needs to be done, and it needs to be much more effective in a sense that ... Like I said earlier, I think it's more a community thing. (Swansea, Black, Male)

This sense of security persisted, for some, even following a direct encounter with anti-terrorism or related measures. One individual, for example, argued:

> I'm quite happy for security being in my face. If I get on a plane, I mean, you get people complaining that they've been patted down or they're being x-rayed. No, I'm happy to go through and be seen naked on that scanner if it means that I know that everybody else is, you know ... (Oldham, White, Male)

Another recounted having to disembark an aircraft in Italy due to a security alert, and the reassurance this provided: 'I would guess they had had some information that something wasn't right and maybe they even found it, we don't know, but certainly they arrived en masse, and I was glad to see them, I thought, go, boys' (Oldham, White, Female).

Support for anti-terrorism powers was also offered, by some, due to a sense that they helped safeguard British identity as well as national security. Here a number of participants supported state interventions to circumvent intolerant or inappropriate behaviour, arguing:

> if you come here then, I don't say you have to become British, not by any manner of means; I think whatever's in the mix is fantastic, you know, clothes, foods, whatever, religion, live your life the way you want to live it, but if you come here you obey the rules, absolutely. (Oldham, White, Female)

In the words of another:

> what I don't want to see is I don't want to see people on the streets at Wootton Bassett when they're bringing the soldiers home. They're, you know, calling them killers and this, that. Have a bit more respect. If you don't like it, that's what we do in this country. You've got [to] abide by the rules that we live [by]. If you don't like it, go somewhere else. (Oldham, White, Male)

At the same time, others were critical that there may be a utilitarian, and potentially pernicious, trade-off between the security of the majority and insecurity of minorities in this sort of logic:

> And, coming back to the question, do we feel safe about these laws? I understand the justification for why the laws are obviously there, they are obviously trying to protect their people, but whatever the justification is I, as a black person, still do not feel safe. Because in trying to protect their own people they are making other people feel unsafe. (Swansea, Black, Male)

Finally, as mentioned briefly above, a small number of respondents also qualified their opposition to the UK's anti-terrorism framework by pointing to the existence of sufficient safeguards that would assist in the prevention of egregious miscarriages of justice. As one individual put it:

> We live in ... the leading democracy in the world, that we don't feel that level of infringement of civil liberties. Part of it is, we know that there's sufficient counter-measures there, you know, the public voice, whether enough groups would stand up and prevent certain, you know ... certain sort of general acceptance of things where they might be going too far through anti-terrorism laws, etc. I have that security. (London, Asian, Female)

This faith in the courts and the legal system was discussed numerous times in the context of our research. One Asian respondent who had indicated a sense of feeling targeted by anti-terrorism measures argued that his faith in the justice system meant he did not feel compelled to self-censor, as justice would ultimately prevail:

> when it comes to the judiciary, the actual system of justice, generally speaking, they are, for example, people are released etc. So, for me, I do have faith in the justice system in its ... obviously the justice system has its flaws, but in terms of as a Muslim if I was to say something and I know that I was right on that matter then I would have faith in the system to know that there is something. But I'm not scared of what I say; I'm quite open about my beliefs. (London, Asian, Male)

Conclusion

There is, as the above conveys, an enormously disparate spread of public perspectives on anti-terrorism powers. Amongst our participants, we encountered far more opposition than support, although given our methodological approach, the numerical recurrence of any of the above arguments is of limited relevance. Critiques discussed in our groups included: the potential of such powers to generate public anxiety; their targeting of minority communities; their ineffective or irrelevant character; concerns that anti-terrorism powers were either overreaction or theatrical exercise; civil liberty worries; and fear of their misuse. We also encountered, moreover, specific concerns relating to particular measures, especially stop and search powers and pre-charge detention, although others – especially regarding the glorification of terrorism – were less harshly received. Less critical views focused on the threat posed by terrorism, the difficulties of evaluating security frameworks, the need for the state to 'do something' and faith in legal and other safeguards available to prevent miscarriages of justice.

Running through these discussions were varying levels of personal investment in the exercise or otherwise of the current anti-terrorism framework. Some individuals felt themselves directly (and often deliberately) targeted by these measures. Others, in contrast, felt rather more distanced from the operation of these powers, whether necessary or not. Thus, as one participant put it: 'I don't personally think about it very much, as in, hey, the personal effect on me' (Oxford, White, Female). In the following chapter, we look further into the implications of this heterogeneity by turning to the connection between citizenship and security politics in the context of anti-terrorism. As we shall argue, perceptions of variable targeting by anti-terrorism powers have contributed to distinct – and, we suggest, 'disconnected' – experiences of, and attachments to, citizenship within the UK today.

Notes

1 Swansea, White, Male.
2 These revelations – from former contractor Edward Snowden and journalist Glenn Greenwald – focused on hitherto secret surveillance programmes run by the United States National Security Agency and other intelligence agencies. For an overview, see Greenwald (2014).
3 Jean-Charles de Menezes was shot by the UK's London Metropolitan Police on 22 July 2005 at the Stockwell London Underground station following a case of mistaken identity.
4 We return to this point at the end of the chapter.
5 See Chapter 4 for more on this point in terms of the perceived impact on citizenship.
6 London, Asian, Male.
7 As detailed in Chapter 2, partway through the focus groups we introduced a guide to some of the UK's most high-profile and controversial anti-terrorism measures introduced since the 2000 Terrorism Act. The guide is reproduced as Appendix B in this book.
8 'Captain Hook' is a reference to Abu Hamza al-Masri, previously imam of the Finsbury Park Mosque in London, who has lost both of his hands. After a lengthy extradition process from the UK, Abu Hamza was found guilty of terror and kidnap charges in a New York court in 2014.
9 Swansea, White, Male.

4

The impacts of anti-terrorism on citizenship

This chapter follows the previous discussion of public evaluations of anti-terrorism powers by examining the impact thereof on citizens and citizenship more specifically. Two main findings from our research are discussed. First, that anti-terrorism powers have impacted – variably – on four key aspects of citizenship: rights, participation, identity and duties. As demonstrated below, for some – generally (but not exclusively) white individuals – this impact is limited. Others – primarily, but not exclusively, ethnic minority participants – noted a significant attenuation of citizenship in these areas. The second key finding is that, whilst an overall pattern emerges in our research of citizenship erosion amongst individuals identifying as ethnic minority in particular, this was far from a totalising or universal experience. Thus, whilst many of our participants discussed developments in anti-terrorism powers as a direct challenge to their citizenship – understood as both status and lived experience (see Chapter 2) – others responded by engaging in, or advocating, different forms of resistance. Three such engagements are explored in the latter section of this chapter: explicit expressions of opposition to anti-terrorism measures; denials of 'victim' or 'outsider' subject positions within the narrativisation of anti-terrorism measures and their consequences; and refusals to withdraw or abstain from established forms of political activity.

By exploring conversations around issues of rights, participation, identity and duties, the analysis in this chapter attempts an exploration of the anti-terrorism/citizenship nexus that extends beyond the dominant focus within existing literature on the erosion of liberties. Abstract, formal, citizen rights, we demonstrate, are undoubtedly important but do not exhaust the ways in which citizenship is lived and experienced. Indeed, for many of our participants at least, the impact of anti-terrorism powers on their ability to participate in the public sphere emerged as a more pressing challenge to the practice of citizenship. In making this argument, the discussion below also aims to add breadth to literature on the impact of anti-terrorism powers by exploring claims about ethnic as well as religious identity in this context. As argued in Chapter 2, too much debate in this area has focused primarily on religious identities and demographics.

The chapter also seeks to demonstrate that – although not framed in any explicit language of citizenship – the forms of resistance to anti-terrorism powers we explore are intensely related to the claims and conceptual terrain of citizenship (see, e.g., Delanty 2000, Lister and Pia 2008). Most obviously, each is both underscored and bulwarked by appeals to equality of treatment and the importance of political participation. This, we suggest, provides grounds for optimism that is often lacking in analyses of civil liberty reductions. Building on this continuing resonance of citizenship, we show that for those people advocating continued political engagement despite (or because of) anti-terrorism powers, mainstream political practices frequently offer the most effective means of resisting the negative consequences thereof. As demonstrated below, we encountered very few examples of novel or anomalous forms of political resistance in this context. However, whilst we believe the practices of resistance we encountered to be significant, their prominence should not be overstated. Although – again – not statistically significant, the majority of our participants viewed anti-terrorism measures either as irrelevant to their everyday lives or as contributory to the erosion of citizenship and its guarantees (see also Gillespie and O'Loughlin 2009). This is important, we argue, because these varied responses indicate the existence of dialectical tendencies in the anti-terrorism/citizenship relationship. Whilst anti-terrorism powers have an impact (often negative) on citizenship for some, for others it is the status and claims of citizenship that determine how anti-terrorism policy is both understood and resisted.

Taken together, these points add further support to one of the book's central arguments: the relationship between citizenship and anti-terrorism powers cannot simply be adduced by examining changes to legal frameworks alone. As argued in earlier chapters, there is a genuine need to complement the conceptual focus of existing debate in this area by exploring how contemporary anti-terrorism architectures affect citizenship as lived experience. Or, more specifically, to explore the ways in which anti-terrorism architectures are interwoven with citizens' own views of citizenship and its associated practices.

Citizenship and its erosion

Four key themes emerged in our research which structure the first part of our analysis here. These relate to the impact of anti-terrorism initiatives on: first, freedoms and rights; second, an individual's ability and desire to participate in the public sphere; third, an individual's relation to British identity; and, fourth, obligations and duties. As indicated above, while much existing research notes the impact of anti-terrorism policies on rights, it is important to recognise that citizenship is not exhausted by considerations of these alone. Nor, indeed, is it solely about participation or identity. Citizenship is, importantly, an *interaction* of these different dimensions (Delanty 2000). To assess what impact anti-terrorism measures have had upon individuals' conceptions of citizenship, it is important, therefore, to explore pertinent connections between the above themes in the lives of citizens. Equally, it is important to connect the discussions below with the three debates identified in Chapter 2. There we suggested that arguments about the erosion of citizenship (through-long term social/demographic changes or more deliberate political moves), multiculturalism and attempts to activate the citizenry all resonate with contemporary anti-terrorism policy. The findings in this chapter support this claim, first, as we see considerable evidence of citizen beliefs that anti-terrorism has eroded citizenship entitlements, identity and engagement. Second, because anti-terrorism powers have also, for many, stymied and complicated multiculturalism and cohesion. And third, because, although citizen participation in anti-terrorism is increasingly demanded, many citizens are reluctant to engage with these appeals to contribute to these and other political processes.

'They do impinge on our civil liberties':[1] *anti-terrorism and rights*

In the first instance, building on the analysis of Chapter 3, we encountered a general concern that anti-terrorism measures were systematically eroding rights, freedoms and liberties within the UK. In these discussions, some people simply articulated their opposition to contemporary powers, arguing: 'there are draconian measures that are coming in that no free country should have, and they are coming in under the guise of terrorism; playing to people's worst, most basic fears' (Llanelli, White, Female). Others drew on more emotional language, articulating their own anxieties about this perceived attenuation. One participant described the detention of foreign nationals, for example, as 'frightening' (Llanelli, White, Male). Another stated, 'I'm very, very nervous about the UK because, as you said, it's the erosion of civil liberties. I see it coming, you know, and I'm thinking, I don't really want to be around' (London, Black, Female). Unfavourable comparisons were also drawn with the US and its own war on terrorism:

> I'd worry about another Guantanamo Bay type thing; stick somebody in prison and forget it. I was very upset when that was being done in my name, you know, that you could just lock somebody up because you think he might

> be involved in terrorism, and would torture you and would keep you here for as long as we like. I'm not happy with that. (Oldham, White, Female)

The way in which concerns such as these were articulated varied considerably across our focus groups. Many of our white participants expressing their opposition to the impact of anti-terrorism powers on citizenship rights did so either in abstract terms or by focusing on the potential misuse of such powers (see Chapter 3). As one participant put it, 'some of these [anti-terrorism measures] go against the whole point of living in a democracy ... [they] remove that freedom of individuals, and it restricts the democracy we live in' (Oxford, White, Female). A number of individuals made reference to this erosion of 'basic' or 'fundamental' rights, but very few of our white participants expressed any concern that such measures would have an impact upon their own citizenship directly. This view, that rights had been compromised but only in the abstract, is neatly captured in the following exchange on recent anti-terrorism measures:

> A: I almost feel like my liberty is threatened by most of them.
> B: Yes, but I don't think your liberty is really going to be threatened, because you ... you haven't done anything wrong. (London, White, Female and Male)

Other white participants were considerably less sceptical about anti-terrorism measures and did not perceive a significant diminishment of rights in their wake. Indeed, some were happy to endorse quite drastic reductions of liberties:

> A: Never mind all the red tape and all the messing about, if you come here and you incite any hatred, regardless of who it's against or what it's against ...
> B: You lose any rights.
> A: You lose your rights, yeah. (Oldham, White, Male and Female)

This type of view appears to be related to the sense of distance from the exercise of such powers felt by most white participants in our groups. It is easier, perhaps, to countenance restrictions on fundamental rights if one feels confident this is unlikely to be experienced directly.

While many of our white participants were either content with contemporary restrictions on liberties or concerned about these in the abstract, ethnic minority participants frequently expressed strong fears that *their own* citizenship rights were being eroded, often deliberately. Many drew on ethnic and religious identifications in describing these fears; in the words of one participant, for instance, 'Since when is [a] Polish guy going to ... have some sort of pre-trial detention without charge? You know, it's not going to happen, is it? So, it's only going to happen if you're Muslim. All of these [anti-terrorism measures] are designed to control Muslims' (Birmingham, Asian, Male). Another, expressing similar feelings of systematic oppression, stated:

> I'm quite wary about an attack on my freedom or individual liberty, in the sense that I might walk down the street one minute, a black van might just come and I am taken away, whisked away by MI5 or MI6 ... I have to sort of [limit] what I say because of the possible repercussions. (London, Asian, Male)

Another participant – in a separate group – recalled a recent news item concerning the detention of Muslims, suggesting, 'that could be any one of us' (Birmingham, Asian, Male).

Crucially, similar perceptions were also articulated by black participants in our groups with previous experiences of racism seeming to act as a significant filter through which anti-terrorism measures were read. One individual articulated a view that anti-terrorism measures were not (*contra* the view of the above participants) aimed solely at Muslims, but were targeted at ethnic minorities more broadly:

> So, yes, we are, sort of, having the after-effects of ... because the fact people are still stopped and searched, it increases the racism. It increases the fact that ... I may not be Muslim, but people, sort of, like, think that ... somehow I've got something to do with it. So it makes our lives, as individuals, even more difficult. (Swansea, Black, Female)

Another black participant recounted the hostility she had personally encountered on an anniversary of the 7/7 bombings and the empathy this stimulated within her for other targeted or 'suspect' communities:

> It's actually gotten worse for some people. I mean, what happened to me in Swansea was because on July 7th, because it was the anniversary of the bomb blasts in London. I'm not Muslim, I'm not Asian ... and I was walking on the street and this girl just walked up to me, was just by my house, and she started staring at me and was like, go back to your country, you Muslim, you know? I was thinking, imagine how the people who actually wear the hijabs, what they go through. I've had so many incidents like that. And I felt like this, less than a human being, and I went home to cry my eyes out because I felt so ... it was bad. That was my first experience of racism, direct racism. I was running because she wanted to attack me because I was black and walking on the streets on this day. (Swansea, Black, Female)

Yet another participant articulated a specific view that her own sense of safety was compromised by such measures: 'If I weren't black, I'd feel safer because, obviously ... but I feel that I'm the victim in this, when I see all these things because everything is aimed at a group of people, so I don't feel safe with these laws' (Swansea, Black, Female).

Despite some exceptions noted below, we encountered a general broad consensus on two issues here. First, that anti-terrorism policy specifically, and security policing more broadly, were disproportionately targeted at particular ethnic or religious groups. And, second, that this differentiation of the populace was harmful to social cohesion and community relations. The stop and search capabilities under Section 44 of the 2000 Terrorism Act discussed in the previous chapter were a particular source of concern amongst black participants here. As in the following example, earlier uses of such powers – especially under what became known as the 'Sus Law' in the 1980s[2] – offered a prominent interpretative lens through which to evaluate the contemporary anti-terrorism mechanisms and the perceived unfairness (and futility) thereof:

> So, you know, are we any better off in actually having these increased stop and search? You know, because the ones that we had before, did they actually find anything out? No. Were they effective? So, why are you therefore going to increase the stop and search just to go on and aggravate people and further discriminate people who are already disadvantaged and socially excluded? (Swansea, Black, Female)

Where we encountered such arguments, anti-terrorism initiatives were not depicted as the sole, or even primary, source of racial discrimination. Rather, these were described as contributing to the singling out of minorities and thereby as exacerbating experiences of unequal treatment. As one participant put it, 'government drives the way security categorises people' (Oxford, Asian, Female).

The view that powers such as stop and search were targeted at ethnic minorities was not, of course, universally shared by all minority populations with whom we spoke. Some of our participants, including non-Muslim individuals from South Asian backgrounds, expressed abstract concern about contemporary anti-terrorism mechanisms without feeling directly targeted thereby. As one Asian male put it, 'They [anti-terrorism powers] do impinge on our civil liberties. And we don't necessarily feel them on a day-to-day basis, just because we ... if you're a good citizen going about your day-to-day life, it doesn't necessarily affect your day-to-day life' (London, Asian, Male). This confidence in the neutrality of such powers was all the more striking given that this individual had been repeatedly stopped by the UK Border Agency whilst travelling to Paris for work. As he continued in the conversation below, this experience was viewed as an annoyance – and both trivial and understandable – rather than anything more upsetting or sinister:

> A: I used to always get stopped by the ... what's now the Border Agency, but was previously the Home Office guy asking me all kinds of questions about where I'm from, what I'm doing, this and that. And, yes, obviously that's ... it's not obviously, but it's probably due to the way I look.
> MO: How did that make you feel?
> A: I don't really ... I don't really mind, because I really have nothing to hide, and I can tell someone exactly what my background is and what I'm doing here, there and everywhere. So I don't really mind, I just, sort of ... it is what it is. But ...
> B: At some level, don't you resent it?
> A: Yes, I do.
> B: Almost you're stereotyping the fact that, because I look a certain way, people will do that. (London, Asian, Male and Female)

The lack of concern about potential targeting by the state amongst non-Muslim individuals of South Asian background is noteworthy and resonates powerfully with the argument of one of our black participants noted above when she suggested that anti-terrorism initiatives 'further discriminate [against] people who are already disadvantaged and socially excluded' (Swansea, Black, Female).

The above individual's faith that being a 'good citizen' affords some measure of protection from the misuse of anti-terrorism powers contrasts sharply with the fear of guilt by association discussed by other – primarily Muslim – participants in our research. Some expressed direct concern that simply being in the wrong place or talking to the wrong person could result in the attention of the security services:

> It makes me think about what I'm going to say, and it makes me think who am I going to speak to, because that might be used against me. If I say hello to you, somebody might say, oh, he said hello to him, but he is linked to x, x is linked to y, y had a girlfriend and her brother was linked to al-Qaida, al-Qaida is linked to Osama Bin Laden. Oops. So, then I'm thinking to myself I only said hi to him. (London, Asian, Male)

Anti-terrorism powers, in other words, are here perceived as disproportionately targeting minority communities – including, but importantly not limited to, British Muslims of South Asian background. But this differential treatment is viewed – by those feeling directly targeted and others, alike – as limited to communities already experiencing some form of particular social or political disadvantage. For those identifying as British Muslims this is, perhaps, unsurprising given the introduction and justification of mechanisms such as the UK Prevent agenda, and its explicit emphasis on Muslim communities (see Chapter 2).

For individuals identifying with other minority communities, in contrast, it appears that prior experiences of discrimination as well as perceptions of security (see Chapters 5 and 6) are vital in how these mechanisms are understood. As we saw above, the post-2000 extension of stop and search powers under Section 44 are directly linked to the memory of similar powers stretching back to the 1980s by individuals within UK black communities, and to the perception of police stigmatisation that accompanied these. We encountered a general and real concern across our focus groups that the experience or perception of targeting could, in the words of one white participant, 'breed quite a bit of resentment amongst people who would be affected' (London, White, Male).

It is, however, important to note that some of this perceived targeting may not be due to specific measures within anti-terrorism policy. Indeed, these concerns may be entirely misguided and a product of conflating different governmental or non-governmental initiatives. What is clear, however, is that – despite the widespread view that anti-terrorism measures disproportionately target ethnic minorities – the impact thereof is seen differently by individuals with different ethnic and other identities. How these measures are understood depends upon the filtering role of existing and prior experiences of racism, other forms of discrimination and disadvantage, or of contact with the police and the state's various agencies. In this sense, there seem to be vicious and virtuous circles at play. Ethnic minority citizens who feel secure, describe themselves as law-abiding and possess little or no experience of racism or of the legal system, appear to feel that their liberties have been far less targeted by anti-terrorism measures. By contrast, citizens identifying with minority ethnic communities who might be more disadvantaged, have experienced racism, and/or have had problematic relations with the police or other authorities, are much more likely to believe that contemporary anti-terrorism measures are aimed at them individually. As a result, these individuals may feel increasingly alienated, disenfranchised and under surveillance, with a reduced sense of commitment to the state a possible outcome. Thus, although anti-terrorism powers tend to be framed universally, their experience and evaluation is highly variable and widely viewed as such (see Waldron 2003).

'I would rather keep my mouth shut':[3] anti-terrorism powers and participation

The differences of experience we encountered between those identifying with distinct ethnic identities in relation to the anti-terrorism/rights relationship grew more pronounced in terms of civic and political participation. Amongst those white individuals with whom we spoke, we found a very limited sense of any such impact, with anti-terrorism measures typically seen as something quite distant from everyday life. As one white male put it: 'All this is happening on a level that does not touch us' (Oldham, White, Male). However, in some instances where white participants had come into direct contact with security practices (for example, at airports), two distinct reactions of relevance were described. Some simply accepted the experience as 'something you've got to get used to' (Oldham, White, Male): an annoyance, perhaps, but far from invidious. Others, however, objected to such measures (such as being questioned by the police while taking photographs) on grounds of principle. One participant had contacted the Metropolitan Police to complain about an anti-terrorism advert, while another mentioned contacting their MP to protest. Often, in these situations, the sentiment expressed was of anger or irritation – 'I can't say I felt threatened; I was annoyed, I was angry' (London, White, Female) – that, as in the above examples, awakened a sense of agency and desire to respond.

This experience of anger rather than insecurity contrasts sharply with those of ethnic minorities in terms of participation. With a few exceptions – turned to below – we encountered a strong sense that anti-terrorism measures had dampened any desire for political engagement amongst those identifying as black or Asian. A number of participants stated that feeling observed and stigmatised meant that they tended to avoid expressing their own political identities and ideas as they would wish. This self-awareness – or even self-censorship – was justified, in large part, because of fear of the potential consequences of acting otherwise. As one Asian female put it:

> I mean, I would love to change things, which is probably why I have a passion for politics. But right now, currently, I would rather keep my mouth shut and not say anything that can be seen ... like I tell my friends as well, Don't say anything that can ... go against you. Because a lot of your phone calls, without you knowing, is monitored by MI5 anyway ... especially when you start saying things out of anger and emotion that can be about the system that we use to govern our ways of living. So, if you say anything bad about it, it is literally monitored. (London, Asian, Female)

This was a view we encountered repeatedly and which paints a worrying picture that anti-terrorism measures may well have stymied or depressed political engagement. With the exceptions considered at the end of the chapter notwithstanding, many also argued that participation within formal political life offered no prospect of genuine escape from contemporary climates of suspicion, whereby:

> Even when, you know, you come out against terrorism, you're not doing it because you're opposed to terrorism but you did it to safeguard your own position. So you're stuck in this Catch 22 and even if you condemn it you're still, you know, viewed with suspicion. (Oldham, Asian, Female)

Some of our black participants also pointed to the depoliticising effects of anti-terrorism measures, noting a similar sense of targeting and alienation. And, as with citizenship rights, previous or existing experiences of racism again tended to act as an interpretive prism through which these policies were filtered. Where racism had been experienced in the past, anti-terrorism measures were often seen to perpetuate segregation and a lack of broader community engagement:

> But as long as the government keeps ... or, you know, all these other organisations keep, sort of, pushing in a particular point ... you feel discriminated, you feel undermined, you feel less of an individual ...You are a citizen, technically, because of your status, but in terms of your participation, it just won't work. (Swansea, Black, Female)

As this suggests, a profound difference emerges between ethnic minority and white publics here. Amongst the former, anti-terrorism measures, with some exceptions, often produce a deadening, alienating effect which dampens and hampers political participation. Individuals articulating these concerns felt unable to express themselves as they would choose, for fear of immediate consequences or of (further) social stigmatisation. In some cases, this passivity is born of a tired, resigned, acceptance of one's inability to contest and counter: 'I almost expect it nowadays ... whatever I do it's always going to come back to the way I dress and the way I look, so there's no point in fighting it, I'll just go along with it' (Oldham, Asian, Female). For white participants, in contrast, where anti-terrorism initiatives (infrequently) affected participation in social life in some form, this tended to be met with a desire (and often attempt) to challenge such initiatives. Notably absent, importantly, was the sense prevalent among ethnic minorities that enacting one's political subjectivity was stymied either by fear of the consequences of so doing, one's personal inabilities, or the futility of seeking to do so.

'It doesn't make me feel part of Britain as much as I did':[4] *anti-terrorism powers and identity*

Given the above findings in terms of rights and participation, one might also expect these experiences to impact upon (and be impacted on by) issues of identity. Indeed, amongst white participants in our research, we encountered very little concern with identity in relation to anti-terrorism measures. We did hear frequently of a generalised disquiet over the fragmentation of British identity, but this was only occasionally explicitly connected to anti-terrorism measures. When it was, participants tended to express empathy with others, recognising the negative consequences of profiling on integration and community cohesion. One individual, for example, argued that anti-terrorism measures and related security practices seemed to involve a closing off or 'securing [of] myself away from the world' (Oxford, White, Female). Others were more forthright in their assertion that anti-terrorism measures had 'an extreme tinge of xenophobia' (London, White, Male) and were likely to 'breed suspicion' towards minorities who would 'probably feel quite alienated' (London, White, Male).

As noted in Chapter 3, such sentiments, occasionally expressed by white participants, were dominant within ethnic minority groups. We encountered near-unanimity that anti-terrorism measures were complicating social cohesion:

> I think people do feel alienated, and I think these kind of laws do, sort of, make people feel really suffocated and really alienated, and that's why there's problems with community cohesion, and that's why people are likely to resist the dominant culture, rather than integrate. (Birmingham, Asian, Female)

Others went further still, arguing that such measures have reversed processes of integration that had stretched across years, making them feel less British. As one second-generation migrant from Pakistan put it to us:

> It doesn't make me feel part of Britain as much as I did. The last ten years ... I used to feel like that I'm half and half, okay, because of my colour, my religion and my background. I am not white, English, okay, I know where I come from, I know my roots, but I'm here now. My father worked here, lived here, everything that I own, everything that's important to me is here now, so I should be allowed to be accepted in this country. But after that last ten years of things like that happening, the way I'm looked at, I don't feel as part of the British society, as accepted. (Oldham, Asian, Female)

Viewed in this way, anti-terrorism measures were a further driver of cultural isolationism, with certain groups becoming 'more insular because, you know, you're almost perceived as the outsider so what outsiders do is group together' (Oldham, Asian, Female). 'That's the danger of what these anti-terrorism measures are going to promote: that communities are going to become tighter' (Oldham, Asian, Female).

Beyond the problems this creates for cohesion, identity and citizenship (although see Thomas and Sanderson 2011), a concern was frequently articulated that such alienation also pushes people towards extremist forms of politics or religion (see also Chapter 3). Part of the source of this isolation is the feeling that it is one's own state or government driving these dynamics:

> I think theoretically people that are meant to be protecting you, protecting your freedom, making sure that we are secure and safe, are in some sense turning against you ... It's like the government, they're meant to be there to protect you to make sure [you] are safe, that your neighbourhood is safe, to make sure that you're not intimidated by somebody, and they make laws. But at the same time it's kind of the same government that is making you feel intimidated. (London, Asian, Male)

Other ethnic minorities, as in discussions of rights and duties, again approached the issue of belonging through the prism of prior experiences of racism. And, once more, anti-terrorism measures were seen to contribute to problems of racism and thus to make cohesion and common identification more problematic. Within this was a view that skin colour serves as an important determinant of Britishness, particularly when it comes to security and anti-terrorism measures:

> [F]or people ... who were born here, are they going to be treated as foreign nationals, because when you're stopped and searched you're not asked if you're British or not. The only thing is the colour of your skin, so will they ask you where you're born, and being born in England and having British citizenship, does that exclude him? (Swansea, Black, Female)

Although this perspective extends beyond anti-terrorism measures, many of our participants articulated the view that the pall of terrorist suspicion has made it more difficult for them to identify, and be identified by others, as British.

'Why should you help a government that doesn't want to help you?':[5] anti-terrorism powers and duties

There were two senses in which the issue of citizen duties or obligations arose in our research. The first related to the growing responsibilisation of citizens discussed in Chapter 2 and the increasing demands upon 'ordinary' publics to contribute to security governance – for example, by providing information on suspect activities, persons or packages. The second was in terms of the obligations – asserted within some, but by no means all conceptions of citizenship – for minority individuals to integrate into dominant or pre-existing communities and their associated 'ways of life'.

In terms of the first of these two connections, we again encountered something of a division across our research groups. White respondents were, generally, positive, if not enthusiastic, towards governmental requests that they report suspicious behaviour to the police or to others. This duty, though, was frequently viewed as limited to specific locations, notably transport hubs, with many people objecting to anything that might be seen as 'snooping' on their neighbours, for example. Perhaps unsurprisingly, given the degree to which ethnic minorities believed themselves targeted by anti-terrorism measures, enthusiasm for fulfilling such a role was far more muted among these populations. One individual began by noting that 'Muslims themselves need to take on the responsibility of engaging [with anti-terrorism initiatives]'. However, he continued by arguing that this was unlikely to happen on the state's terms: '[N]o mosque is going to say, yes, we have so many extremists in our area. No mosque is going to do that either because of the repercussions they'd face from the radicals or either because of the reputation [they would acquire]' (London, Asian, Male). Thus, even where individuals do recognise a duty to participate in security governance, perceived practical obstacles (such as competing loyalties, and concerns about the consequences of so doing) affect the likelihood of this happening.

A more prevalent perspective among ethnic minority participants was a sense that such demands exacerbated the suspicion they were already experiencing in a further act of political 'finger pointing' (London, Asian, Male). Indeed, we encountered within other groups an even stronger denunciation of such invocations, especially among those feeling targeted by the state. As one female asked: 'Why should you help a government that doesn't want to help you?' (Swansea, Black, Female). This raises an interesting point concerning the balance between liberties and duties which is frequently invoked in terms of the need to recognise that citizen rights imply an observance of certain responsibilities. For, as the above respondent succinctly points out, citizens may perceive another balance in the context of anti-terrorism (and perhaps other) powers, such that where states attenuate rights, citizens may well feel a diminishment in the duties they owe.

While one might argue that the duty to foster community cohesion is not strictly an anti-terrorism issue, the frequency with which it was raised in our groups means it is appropriate to explore it as such here. Many ethnic minority participants articulated a keen sense that their communities might do more to enhance social integration. This is, in other words, a duty or obligation that does appear widely felt: 'It's maybe for us to try our best, I guess, to put our point across' (Birmingham, Asian, Male). Others argued that

Muslims and other minorities needed to alter their mode of engagement to communicate their interests better: '[T]hey need to do it in a different way ... [Not] banging it up in East London and spreading all these leaflets... It's about being smart' (London, Asian, Female). One Asian male argued, 'I also accept as a Muslim that we haven't helped ourselves, in that we haven't been as vigilant and visible', while at the same time pointing out that 'integration itself is reciprocal' (London, Asian, Male). Still other participants, finally, discussed community cohesion through their desire that others recognise their right to belong in the UK:

> I would really like to belong somewhere, you know, like my house or my town or my country and be accepted and that sort of thing. I don't feel ... I've been here for forty years. I wasn't born here but I was very small when I came here, and I'm still a foreigner, I'm still an alien and my children are going to be treated like that as well. ... I don't have the security of belonging, you know, like I look at white people and hardly anybody totally accepts me. Nobody thinks of me as British. I'm a Paki middle-aged woman. That's how they see me: Paki. They don't know I've got a British passport and I've had it for such a long time, for thirty-seven, thirty-eight years or something. That still does not make me British. (Oldham, Asian, Female)

We return to sentiments such as these in our discussion of security in Chapter 5. What the above does suggest in the meantime, however, is that while there may exist considerable issues around social cohesion, many people identifying as Asian or black in the UK feel a responsibility to integrate, wanting to be viewed as British by others. As one Asian female put it: 'I think Muslims in this country like being seen as British. They don't want to just be seen as Pakistanis or Sikhs or whatever, they want to be accepted as a part of the society, but they're not. They're always classified as Muslims' (Birmingham, Asian, Female; also Thomas and Sanderson 2011). At the same time, many of our participants spoke about the barriers to this in the contemporary political climate. These are multifarious, but it was often felt that in contributing to a stigmatisation of Muslims and ethnic minorities more widely, anti-terrorism measures exacerbated the difficulties of successful integration.

Resisting the impacts of anti-terrorism

The disturbing picture of the citizenship/anti-terrorism nexus that comes through in the various anxieties explored above was not the only dynamic we encountered in our research. In the remainder of the chapter, we focus on a set of rarer, but perhaps less predictable, expressions of resistance to the impacts of anti-terrorism powers discussed by participants in our project. These, we argue, reverse the directionality implicit above and within much relevant literature (see Chapter 2), where citizenship is positioned as something upon which recent anti-terrorism initiatives act. As we demonstrate below, the experience and practice of citizenship itself also contributes to, and helps shape, the perception and understanding of anti-terrorism policy.

In a recent study, O'Loughlin and Gillespie (2012) explore a diversity of ways in which young Muslims have responded to contemporary security discourses. Whilst arguing that the 'dominant discursive framework[s]' connected Muslims to terrorism so rigidly that 'for some there appeared no possibility of escape, resulting in a sense of alienation', they also note that others 'invested hope in the improvement of normal politics through small, cumulative acts that modify "the mainstream" and its discourses from within' (O'Loughlin and Gillespie 2012: 116). Employing Maira's (2009) notion of 'dissenting citizenship' to foreground such acts, O'Loughlin and Gillespie (2012: 117) argue that some young Muslims:

> sought and found ways to hold on to their sense of entitlement to British (if not multicultural) citizenship by undertaking small, strategic everyday acts, seeking to educate their peers or co-workers, outside engagement with formal political institutions. In other words, dissenting citizenship may be rebellious, critical, angry and disappointed but the youth in our study believe in and invest in citizenship as an entitlement.

Our own research into anti-terrorism policy uncovered a number of instances of low-level dissent, or resistance, of this sort amongst Asian, black and white individuals alike. In the following, we chart three prominent examples thereof: expressions of outright opposition to anti-terrorism measures and their consequences; a refusal to accept or inhabit 'victim' or 'outsider' subject positions in the narration of anti-terrorism powers and their impacts; and a continued belief in, and refusal to withdraw from, engagement in (formal, mainstream) political life. Each of these, we argue, constitutes some form resistance in the sense of an oppositional action (see Rose 2002, Hollander and Einwohner 2004: 534) in that they are intended to contest either anti-terrorism powers or the more subtle forms of subjectification that such powers may foster.

Because our focus in this discussion is inductively derived from our empirical findings, we take no *a priori* position on whether resistance in this context is exhausted by the intended, overt actions discussed by our participants. Methodologically, dialogical research methods such as focus groups (or interviews) may indeed privilege findings of 'intentional', overt actions, overlooking, in the process, more 'covert' or 'unwitting' strategies of resistance that may be better discernible through participant observation, immersed ethnographies or similar research methods (Hollander and Einwohner 2004). It may, in other words, be that it is partly our methodology that leads to uncovering forms of resistance which emphasise mainstream engagement over, say, more radical forms of political engagement.

Yet there are reasons to think that this emphasis is not simply a methodological artefact. First, our findings resonate with those of related studies (Moss and O'Loughlin 2008) which encountered similar levels of public patience with formal channels of participation and engagement. And, second, as we shall see below, some of our participants stressed the importance of traditional avenues of political engagement or dissent precisely as a way of avoiding marginalisation or the dangers inherent in more oppositional forms of resistance. In so doing, they demonstrated, we argue, a commitment to concrete, piecemeal struggles and solutions to political problems, as well as to engagement in formal democratic channels and crucially citizenship. As Žižek (2007: 7) puts it:

> The lesson here is that the truly subversive thing is not to insist on 'infinite' demands we know those in power cannot fulfil. Since they know that we know it, such an 'infinitely demanding' attitude presents no problem for those in power: 'So wonderful that, with your critical demands, you remind us what kind of world we would all like to live in. Unfortunately, we live in the real world, where we have to make do with what is possible.' The thing to do is, on the contrary, to bombard those in power with strategically well-selected, precise, finite demands, which can't be met with the same excuse.

Voicing opposition

The first example of resistance encountered in our research concerned the explicit voicing of opposition – and the explicit expression of the need to voice opposition – to the recent anti-terrorism initiatives considered in Chapter 3. As detailed at length there, resistance was voiced in relation to a range of policy initiatives in this context, including stop and search powers, pre-charge detention and offences concerning the glorification or incitement of terrorism. It also, importantly, had numerous sources, spanning concerns around effectiveness, civil liberties and the possibility that anti-terrorism powers might be misused, amongst other things.

What is important in the context of this chapter is that these expressions of dissent indicate a genuine desire to engage with issues of contemporary public policy, a desire that signals, at the same time, an attachment to citizenship amongst our participants. Several people in our groups, for instance, refused to acquiesce to a sense of resignation borne of disillusionment in this context; a sense that nothing could be done to arrest racial profiling and other pernicious outcomes or drivers of security governance (whether real or perceived). Rather, they demonstrated an undiminished willingness to engage and negotiate with security and governance practices, despite the difficulties of so doing. Indeed, some participants went even further still and appealed directly to public officials in the course of their comments to the focus groups in which they participated:

> Our challenge to government, if this thing is going to be released to them, I challenge them with all the things that I've said, and I really hope that they look into all of the root causes of problems ... it needs a social agenda to solve the social problems. (London, Black, Female)

Individuals, in short, both can and continue to dispute key government policies despite the perceived existence of profound obstacles and risks of so doing. And this process of disputation works, we argue, to reaffirm and renegotiate their relationship to the state and its institutions.

Resisting subject positions: the 'victim' and the 'outsider'

A second example of resistance we encountered emerged in discussions of prejudice and stigmatisation both in relation to anti-terrorism powers and in wider contexts. In the course of these conversations, several ethnic minority participants refuted the frequent accusation that anti-terrorism policies (and the British state and society) were inherently and inexorably prejudiced, even racist. To do so, they combined empirical critiques of the seeming pervasiveness of discriminatory practices (frequently invoking their own experience of life in the UK) with a political critique of the impact of narratives of 'failed multiculturalism'. In the words of one individual, for instance:

> I've led a bit of a sheltered life ... by virtue of where I work and all the rest of it, what I do, I don't tend to come across it [racism], or maybe I don't notice it. I try to attune myself out of it, because I think to be burdened by it is an affliction, and then you can make it bigger in your head than it actually is, and then it holds you back. (Birmingham, Asian, Male)

Clarifying the roots of this perspective, this individual stated: 'the minute you start feeling subjugated, then that affects you' (Birmingham, Asian, Male). In the context of a focus group dominated by discussion of the persistence of UK-based racism, this was a potentially challenging position to hold, not least because so doing raised the risk of either downplaying or denying the experiences of discrimination recounted by those around him: experiences reflected and exacerbated, for others in the group, by contemporary anti-terrorism measures. Pointing to the disempowering and depoliticising implications of a 'victim' subject position, however, this individual maintained the need for, and his own experience of, an agency unencumbered by racism. And, as the conversation continued, he supplemented his stance with an additional normative demand that one should enter into encounters with others in a manner unprejudiced by prior assumptions about their intentions. The following discussion, which begins with a contribution from the above participant, is worth reproducing at length:

> A: That's very negative. I think the general population, the English indigenous population here are far more reasonable and civilised than, you know, we give them credit for.
> B: They are, but they're the ones that don't ... they're not the ones that cause the trouble. It's the, you know, sort of ...
> A: But, they can only cause you trouble if they say something to you. You're talking about someone injuring you by thinking something about you. They can't.
> B: You don't know what their thoughts are, that's the thing.
> A: Parliament's trying to do us for thought crime. We can't be guilty of the same thing ... You must give people the benefit of the doubt. (Birmingham, Asian, Male and Female)

As this participant subsequently argued: 'we can't judge everybody the same, call everybody a racist, just as other people can't judge us all the same and call us terrorists. We're guilty of exactly the same thing. You must be reasonable' (Birmingham, Asian, Male).

This individual's stance – which was, to be clear, a rare one in our groups – offers a different form of contestation to those of the previous chapter. Anti-terrorism policy and its application are not his primary focus here. Rather, it is the way in which such measures are narrated that is being resisted: that they are targeted at Muslim or Asian communities specifically, and thereby are a continuation of a systemic racism throughout British society. Our participant's refusal to recognise this narrative is grounded, ultimately, in a claim to equality and inclusion: a rejection, in other words, of social cartographies organised around simplistic binary logics of insider/outsider. As another Asian male, speaking in London, also argued:

> I don't feel like there is a them and us ... I take part in Islamic society, I do SU [student union] politics, I take part in youth work in the government

> or whatever, working for local government as well, doing various other things, so I'm participating in politics, and there isn't a them and us. If I go to a meeting and there are no other Muslims there I don't think there I'm a Muslim, there are no Muslims there; you are working together. At the weekend we did a ... Fellowship, and there were Muslims and non-Muslims. They are training us to be leaders; it wasn't a them and us that runs against the Muslims. It wasn't like that. And I think it is a psychological thing. And if you start thinking like that then that will happen ... the self-fulfilling prophecy, and if you label yourself as someone who is an outsider then that will end up happening to you. (London, Asian, Male)

The standpoint shared by these two individuals did not go unchallenged within our groups. One participant, sceptical of this stance, returned attention to the climate of suspicion that periodically befalls Muslims after terrorist attacks. In her words:

> For example, look at September 11, when that happened there was a high number of women who were wearing the headscarf being treated with discrimination, headscarves were being pulled off, calling names, being called terrorist, ninja, whatever, very negative name calling. Why? Because somebody says that's them, we are us, and we are British, and they are weird. We are British and they are weird, and they are them and we are us. (London, Asian, Female)

This scepticism notwithstanding, it is clear that a number of our participants – individuals opposed, importantly, to many recent anti-terrorism initiatives – maintain a belief in citizenship's protections and a desire to identify with, and contribute to, British identity. Thus, although unsympathetic to many recent policy mechanisms in this area, these denials of outsider status present a claim for recognition upon the body politic itself, a claim to the effect that 'I am a citizen, and demand to be treated as such'. And, as argued now below, such claims resonate powerfully with related arguments that communities must continue to participate in social and political practices, despite feelings and narratives of alienation.

Resisting withdrawal

The final assertion of, and engagement with, citizenship explored here concerned the argument of several individuals that participation in public life remained both possible and fruitful, despite the challenges posed by contemporary anti-terrorism policies. For some Asian participants, as implied above, this demand for continuing engagement was accompanied by a perceived need to rethink the modalities through which it took place. One individual in London, for example, was critical of street-level politics within Muslim communities, advocating instead greater engagement in more mainstream participatory channels:

> But there is a difference ... [L]et's go into politics, let's do my degree in politics, or let's do my conversion in politics, let me get into there. A friend of mine is a Muslim girl in a headscarf, she's actually gone into politics now ... she's working for the Conservative Party ... she's getting her voice recognised that way. And that is the way we need to do it now. I think it's not about sending leaflets and having these big Islamic talks and in ... some ways ... enhancing the negative perception, sowing the seeds of Islamism; it's about being smart. (London, Asian, Female)

Other participants echoed these comments, arguing that mainstream political channels offered the most effective opportunity for contributing to political debate and influencing social outcomes. Here, the possibility of social and political evolution, and the patience they required, offered hope to many such individuals. In the words of another Asian male, for example: 'There needs to be a shift in our psyche, a shift in our personalities to ... recognise that change happens slowly, and if we're aggrieved, there are, through these shady democratic processes, methods of redressing those, but it just takes time' (Birmingham, Asian, Male).

The validity of these views of the British political process is, of course, some way beyond the scope of this book. More important, however, is that these individuals rejected wariness toward political engagement because of the impact of contemporary anti-terrorism powers that we encountered from numerous individuals discussed above in this chapter. These dissenters, importantly, retained a sense that one can, and should, continue to make demands on, and work within, the established political order (see also Moss and O'Loughlin 2008; O'Loughlin and Gillespie 2012). Thus, whilst many in the UK (and we do not seek to underplay the extent of this) appear to feel that anti-terrorism has diminished their connection to public and political life, others have responded to developments in this area by persisting in practices of societal engagement, albeit in adapted form. This response, it seems, was made possible by an undiminished belief in one's capacity to exact preferences from the established political system and, to echo Žižek (2007), to put concrete, finite and realistic demands to those in power.

Conclusion

As described at the outset, this chapter has attempted to contribute qualitative depth to existing accounts of the anti-terrorism/citizenship relationship through reporting the perceptions of citizens themselves and exploring the significance of ethnic as well as religious identities in this context. As we have shown, it is neither uniformly, nor solely, Asians or Muslims who perceive negative effects here. Rather, a number of black participants in our research – and a smaller number of white participants – pointed also to the deleterious consequences of recent anti-terrorism measures on their own sense of citizenship, understood in terms of participation, identity, obligation and rights. By examining citizenship in this broad and interactive sense, we sought also to extend existing analyses of the (perceived) attenuation of rights under anti-terrorism initiatives. While much attention has, appropriately enough, focused on how anti-terrorism measures alter fundamental rights, it is important to consider the wider implications of these initiatives: of how changes to rights impact upon, and interact with, effects on citizen participation, identity and obligations. As we have argued, citizenship extends beyond the possession of rights alone, and a broader view is crucial to understanding how this experience is negotiated in everyday life (Delanty 2000). Indeed, as the above suggests, the diminishment of formal rights is, for some, perhaps even a secondary concern in relation to the perceived curtailment of these other facets of citizenship.

The chapter's second section, however, presented evidence to indicate that the diminishment of citizenship identified by many of our participants, and much relevant academic literature, is not as totalising as might be expected. Three strategies of resistance were explored. First, the articulation of opposition to the UK's anti-terrorism architecture. Second, a refusal of non-white individuals to recognise the subject positions of 'victim' or 'outsider' available within much narrativisation of anti-terrorism policy. And, third, a refusal to withdraw from formal and informal participation in political and everyday life. In each of these strategies, individuals continued to make claims and demands upon citizenship, reaffirming the value of this status in so doing.

The picture of citizenship that emerges from these findings is profoundly, yet perhaps not completely, troubling. In terms of the opening discussion, it is clear that many citizens of distinct ethnic and geographical demographics perceive a diminishment of citizenship that stems from anti-terrorism measures. Many ethnic minority participants in our research, both black and Asian, believed that their own rights and scope for public participation, as well as their sense of national identity and obligations, had been directly eroded by anti-terrorism policies; they felt they were becoming, in the words of one individual, 'second-class citizens' (Birmingham, Asian, Female). This picture is one where the perception of diminished rights and targeting by the state contributes to a diminished political engagement and a declining sense of belonging. This declining sense of belonging and dampened political engagement, moreover, impacts on perceptions of duties and the content of rights, producing a vicious circle of declining citizenship. In turn, this suggests that anti-terrorism may be exacerbating many of the challenges to citizenship we identified in Chapter 2.

This points to a second troubling aspect of our findings. In our research, we encountered contrasting – or 'disconnected' – experiences of citizenship in this context among white participants and those of other ethnic groups. For the former, the impact of anti-terrorism measures was frequently viewed as either limited or operating at a distance. As stated, many of our black and Asian participants, in contrast, reported a profound loss of rights, a reduced identification with the UK, an inability to participate politically and a scepticism about meeting citizenship obligations. While not all theories and conceptions of citizenship assert principles of universalism (and citizenship has always involved boundary drawing), differential treatment has generally been advocated for non-citizens (between, that is, citizens and non-citizens), or, if between citizens (for example, in multicultural conceptions), to advance particular freedoms and opportunities. The view that anti-terrorism powers may be creating – or contributing to – an experience of differential citizenship, with varied perceptions of, and attachments to, this category's core dimensions departs markedly from the emancipatory ambitions of such conceptions. It also, we argue, has the potential to weaken and fracture British citizenship more broadly.

Yet, there are attempts to resist the attenuation of citizenship and the social or political fragmentation associated with this. It is important to note that many of these efforts at resistance were not dominant, or even widespread, amongst the citizens with whom we spoke. For those who experience systemic prejudice and racism in the existence or exercise of anti-terrorism powers – whether accurately or otherwise – it is not easy to continue to believe in the promise of citizenship. Similarly, for those for whom anti-terrorism exists as only a distanced consideration, resistance appears a peripheral concern. Nonetheless, a number of individuals do continue to make citizenship demands around anti-terrorism: demands that people be treated equally, that rights be protected and for inclusion within social and political life. This suggests, we argue, that anti-terrorism measures and related security practices do not work solely, or uniformly, towards the undermining of citizenship. In the vertical relationship between citizens and the state, individuals do dissent and challenge the ways in which security governance has been practised by demanding more inclusive and equitable treatment. Moreover, in the horizontal relations between citizens themselves, there continues to exist a refusal to participate in criticisms of multiculturalism and a refusal to self-identify as an 'outsider'.

Notes

1 London, Asian, Male.
2 'Sus' here is an abbreviation of 'suspected person' and became a well-known shorthand for the police's power to stop and search citizens without evidence of any criminal activity.
3 London, Asian, Female.
4 Oldham, Asian, Female.
5 Swansea, Black, Female.

5

Less, more, or otherwise (in)secure? Anti-terrorism powers and vernacular (in)securities

The two preceding chapters focused on public understandings of anti-terrorism policy and the implications of these for the status and practice of citizenship. As we saw, and perhaps as we might expect, there is no unidirectional relationship between these entities. While many people in the UK feel that their experience of citizenship has been adversely affected by developments within anti-terrorism policy – or by decisions and discourses associated therewith – others announced themselves entirely unconcerned by recent initiatives in this area. This lack of concern was, for some, a product of the perceived distance between anti-terrorism measures and one's own everyday life. Others, however, were more willing to countenance or even actively support quite considerable restrictions on citizenship for one's self and for others in the face of the threat ostensibly posed by terrorism.

This diversity of positions raises two issues. The first is that citizenship might not be – indeed, we argue, is not – the only matter at stake here. Conceptions, articulations and evaluations of anti-terrorism frameworks are filtered through a host of political values, concerns, interests and agendas: at the level of the 'vernacular' as well as in elite political debate. One US-based cost–benefit analysis, for instance, conservatively estimated a $75 billion annual increase in homeland security expenditure after the 9/11 attacks (Mueller and Stewart 2011: 85). One might object to this expenditure as unnecessary or excessive on purely economic grounds. Alternatively, one might raise the opportunity costs of this spending and advocate for alternative priorities relating, for example, to the environment or the health system. Neither objection would require a claim about citizenship (although such claims would, of course, be possible in both cases).

The second, and related, issue is that anti-terrorism frameworks are, at least in part, about security. Measures to deter or respond to terrorist attacks are frequently justified and debated in terms of their ability to enhance national or personal security from the threat of terrorism; whether internal or external, present or future. And publics, as we saw in Chapter 3, frequently express scepticism towards the purposes and operation of security powers if no tangible increase in security is experienced or perceived. Indeed, a number of individuals with whom we spoke articulated their opposition to anti-terrorism powers precisely because they believed that their own security had been directly diminished by the introduction of new measures relating, for example, to stop and search.

It is to this relationship between anti-terrorism powers and security that we now turn. We begin – in this chapter – by taking a step back from anti-terrorism powers, in order to explore the vital (yet frequently overlooked) prior question of how publics conceptualise and discuss security and insecurity. As demonstrated below, publics in the UK are conscious of a diverse range of security threats. These include terrorism and anti-terrorism initiatives but stretch far beyond this to incorporate a wide variety of issues such as crime, social fracture and unemployment. Moreover, there is little uniformity in the extent to which such threats are experienced, in that no consistent identification or hierarchy of security threats could be identified in our work. This is important because public perceptions of particular issues as security threats depend upon and in turn help to shape understandings and articulations of security itself. As we therefore try to demonstrate, the concept of security is both varied and unstable within vernacular discourse, which helps to explain whether and how specific empirical issues are brought into this concept's orbit at different moments. In other words, people not only have different understandings of security; they also move between understandings in the context of specific conversations.

Having sketched the diversity of public conceptions and constructions of security, we then, in Chapter 6, tie these directly to the views on anti-terrorism explored in the preceding chapters. In so doing, we seek to demonstrate that public evaluations of anti-terrorism powers – and the terrain upon which such powers are debated – are fundamentally shaped by understandings of security and insecurity, as well as of citizenship. Thus, in the context of anti-terrorism – and, indeed, in all areas of security politics – any effort to understand public attitudes requires prior engagement with public understandings of core political values through which such policies are 'read'.

Vernacular insecurities

As we saw in Chapter 2, there is a vast and heavily contested contemporary literature on security, much of which bears scant resemblance to its forebears in what Stephen Walt (1991) termed the 'golden age' of Security Studies of the early Cold War era. One of the major differences between then and now is a concerted effort to broaden this field such that new issues could subsequently be understood as security matters. Although far from uncontested (Williams and Krause 1996: 233–234), this has helped locate issues, including environmental degradation, gendered violences and disease pandemics, at the centre of this field. For most, if not all, researchers working here, such matters are now as central to Security Studies as more traditional military concerns, in that 'issues such as poverty, migration, terrorism and some aspects of environmental security are prominent concerns in their own right' (Bourne 2014: 12).

That the meaning and study of security has changed so dramatically in recent years – and particularly following the end of the Cold War – should not, perhaps, be particularly surprising. As Dannreuther (2007: 13–33) points out, this was a time of great technological, structural and geopolitical shifts in the international system, encompassing major transformations in warfare, an end to the East/West rivalry's dominance and a movement away from bipolarity. In any case, the traditional articulation of security around matters of the state and its military enemies was itself something of a departure from its earlier derivation from the Latin *securitas*, and the absence of trouble or anxiety this connoted (Bourne 2014: 1). Indeed, as Glasius (2008: 31) notes, the statist approach to security is actually a relatively recent development, one that, for critics, has served to detach this concept from its original emphasis on the individual human.

Whatever we think of these broadening moves, this commitment to bringing a far more diverse sweep of issues into the rubric of security aligns very closely with the diversity of security threats identified by the publics participating in our research. In the course of our project, not one individual explicated or even implied an account of security wedded to the statist/militaristic parameters of Security Studies as traditionally constituted. Instead, as demonstrated below, a remarkably wide range of threats to one's self, community and others was identified across each of our focus groups. In the discussion of these that now follows, we posit a continuum between sociotropic and personal concerns which many of our participants invoked, if often implicitly, in the context of their conversations (on this, see, for example, Huddy et al. 2002; Joslyn and Haider-Markel 2007). Where the former refers to those threats confronting residents of one's society in general, the latter reflect individualised fears around one's own current or potential insecurity. Any distinction between the two, however, was seldom as stark as this implies. Many of our participants moved between these 'levels' in the context of their conversations, as they did in related research (for example, Vaughan-Williams and Stevens 2012).

'They say terrorism is the big threat':[1] *sociotropic insecurities*

The sociotropic concerns discussed by our participants included a large sweep of issues, with economic insecurity, environmental change and geopolitical concerns amongst those identified. In the case of the former, we encountered considerable disquiet about growing inequalities and the impact of a widening gap between communities: 'I think it's the disparity between rich and poor. The wider that gets, the more, I think, there'll be disillusionment and the more people – ... in the not-having group – will see that they want to take action to reduce that' (London, Asian, Male). Others pointed to issues of job security and 'the threat of kind of not being able to pay the bills, not being in debt, those kind of things' (London, White, Male). Or, as another put it: 'the threat of redundancies, unemployment, recession' (Oldham, White, Female). Geopolitical issues of the sort associated with traditional International Relations literature were mentioned at times, although less frequently than might be expected, with one participant pointing to the continuing importance of, 'threats from another country – say Iran or places like that' (London, White, Female). Environmental challenges, similarly, were identified rarely but – where they were – were described as a threat of growing global significance. They were also, at times, linked to related concerns around food security, for example:

> if things start going wrong, then there's only one way to go, and you can say we're as peaceful as we can, but, you know, there comes a point where that just doesn't hold up any more, and if you look at some of the facts ... there's 70 million more people a year in the world, and already we use 43% of farm land, it's already being used, and to keep up the production, we have to increase our agricultural output by three times as much. This isn't easy to satisfy. The demand is too high, and I think, will that eventually turn to a security issue? It has to be stopped now, eventually I suspect, you know, it's going to go wrong somewhere. (Swansea, White, Male)

The importance of these concerns notwithstanding, it was three issues in particular to which our focus groups repeatedly returned in their discussion: crime, terrorism and social fracture. Those identifying crime as a generalised security risk tended, simply, to catalogue the harms that may befall an individual. As one participant put it, 'every time you cross the street you could get hit by a car ... I don't know, being mugged or any kind of threat to your personal safety' (London, White, Female). High-profile issues were a common concern here, with youth crime, gang culture and the spread of firearms prominent in some of our groups. In the words of one white male participant, for example:

> you do get big gangs of youths roaming streets, really, which I think we've always had, but it's just ... I don't know, there just seems to be a bigger threat. I don't think that there's any more trouble than there ever was. It's just, I don't know, maybe the gangs are getting bigger. (Oldham, White, Male)

Contemporary terrorism was discussed with some sophistication across all of our groups. It was also, frequently, identified as a threat in which there resides a stark contrast between levels of personal and national insecurity. In the words of one participant, seeking to demonstrate the irrelevance of this threat to his everyday life: 'They say terrorism is the big threat, but you've got to think where that would be in Britain. It wouldn't be in Swansea, it wouldn't be where I live, anyway' (Swansea, White, Male). Very few dissented from this account of relative personal security in the face of terrorism, although many also agreed that it constituted a major challenge to the UK more generally. As one white female argued: 'I think it's inevitable ... there probably will be terrorist attacks in the future, for whatever reasons' (London, White, Female). Some approached terrorism as a primarily internal threat linked to social alienation: 'these young people who are becoming terrorists need a sense of belonging, and society is not giving them that ... until we can address that problem, we're not going to be safe' (London, Black, Female). Others, instead, located the origins of terrorism overseas, identifying (amongst other factors) British foreign policy as a pertinent explanatory framework: 'I think that the threat of terrorism features. I personally don't feel under threat but I do worry for the future, and I do feel that we've gone about the whole problem of the Middle East in a very unfortunate way ... I think it's served to exacerbate it' (Swansea, White, Female). Many of our participants were also keen to locate contemporary terrorism within pertinent historical contexts, with the Provisional IRA offering a regular point of comparison. This use of historical precedents worked, for some, to diminish the danger of those groups potentially active in the UK today: 'you've grown up while the IRA were blowing us to bits twenty, thirty years ago. That was a lot worse than al-Qaeda are throwing at us' (Oldham, White, Male). Others, however, put such a comparison to the opposite effect in order to highlight the exceptionality of contemporary groups. As one participant put it: 'I think the one thing that al-Qaeda have that the IRA didn't appear to have is suicide bombing ... which is again more dangerous' (Oldham, White, Female).

A third sociotropic threat to dominate discussion was that of social fracture, potentially leading to inter-cultural antagonism. Conversations about this threat focused, most frequently, on perceptions of cultural or religious cleavage. These took three distinct, but related, forms. First, and returning to themes raised in Chapter 2, a number of our participants pointed to a lack of integration across the UK, and the experience of detachment and disempowerment this engendered. This sense of 'apartism' (Gest 2010) was viewed as an immediate source of insecurity for isolated demographics. As one female put it, 'I think there are significant communities within the UK that are very disillusioned, that feel very detached from society' (London, Asian, Female). It was also seen as a concern for the social fabric more broadly: 'There isn't much social integration, and I think that is a big worry because you get ghettos ... And to a large extent it is our attitude towards multiracialism that has caused a lot of problems' (Llanelli, White, Female).

A second version focused on the threat of specific migrant communities to values and lifestyles deemed traditionally British. These societal security concerns were couched, at times, around the unwillingness of newcomers to assimilate in the UK. As one participant put it: 'I think the important thing is when they see these immigrants coming in and they appear to be above the law, this creates tensions with the native people' (Llanelli, White, Male). In other conversations it was anxieties relating to the present or future scarcity of resources that concerned people most: 'I feel like it's only a small country and I really don't want too many foreigners [to] come here' (Oldham, Asian, Female). As another put it: 'how the hell are we going to manage in this country with a population of, say, 80 million? Where are we going to get the resources from?' (Llanelli, White, Male).

A third rendering of social fracture as a security issue pointed to the insecurity likely experienced by the potential targets of hostilities and fears such as those mentioned above. Here, the rise of racism and Islamophobia within contemporary Britain were viewed as significant, and potentially enduring, concerns (on this, see Modood et al. 2006; Kundnani 2014). One white female in London, for instance, pointed to contemporary efforts to securitize immigration and the likely impact of this on the UK:

> There's certainly kind of a longer-term threat that I kind of feel ... the whole idea of a government in power that's going to clamp down on immigration and foreigners coming here, actually I find really unpleasant and quite threatening in a way and it's kind of changing the country really, it disturbs me. (London, White, Female)

In the words of a black female in Swansea – reflecting on her own attempt to seek refuge within the UK – 'They talk about immigration as some sort of disease' (Swansea, Black, Female).

'... bunch of hoodies on the corner, I'd cross over the road':[2] personal insecurities

Although viewed from rather different angles, the above indicates some level of broad public consistency in relation to the major security challenges confronting the UK. Importantly, such threats are widely seen as diverse and extending far beyond matters of military (or even national) security, with considerable emphasis placed on the importance of terrorism, crime and social fracture. Where the conversations in our groups turned more specifically to personalised insecurities, however, we encountered far less consistency. Anxieties discussed by our participants included issues as diverse as DNA collection and retention, surveillance by the state and its intelligence agencies, failures of public services to meet essential needs, and low-level anti-social behaviour that falls short of serious crime.

Matters relating to economic insecurity again figured prominently in discussion of personal threats, with the aftermath of the 2008 financial crisis felt keenly by many within the UK. Some, for example, pointed to their own risk of under- or unemployment and subsequent experiences of financial hardship. In the words of one participant: 'the only thing that I feel is a threat personally from day to day is economic threat ... not being able to pay the bills ... being in debt, those kind of things' (London, White, Female). Others pointed to the consequences of welfare restructuring on themselves and others. The following, for example, refers to the introduction of new restrictions on access to child support by the UK's coalition government that was formed in 2010:

> I see the Conservative government [sic] as a great threat to women and to mothers in particular ... [by] removing some of the universal benefits that would have been available to support my children; that means I have to work. And that's fine ... [but] I struggle with the lack of fairness in their cuts, at the moment. And that to me is the greatest threat to women, in particular. (Oxford, White, Female)

Others discussed their own experience of economic insecurity in the context of variable access to public services. Many, as in the following example, saw the providers of such services as inherently prejudiced:[3]

> there isn't security in the sense that you're facing discrimination from service providers, maybe. You know, they're so bureaucratic, they want you to produce all this paperwork, like passports, whatever it is, that you don't have. And in that sense you don't have any security because you don't have the money that allows you to feel secure and be yourself. (Swansea, Black, Female)

Moving away from economic anxieties, crime figured too as an immediate as well as sociotropic risk. Some discussed their experiences of caution or anxiety in public places: 'let's be frank about it – bunch of, you know, whether it's black or white, bunch of hoodies on the corner, I'd cross over the road on the other side' (London, Asian, Female). These personalised fears were often mirrored, moreover, by concerns about the behaviour of those responsible for reducing criminality. One black female, speaking in London, for instance, argued:

> I'm more wary of the police, you know, maybe police brutality or the way the police go about things ... For example, stop and search, that's something that I see happen quite often, especially at Stratford station where, you know, you see about twenty police all in one day stopping and searching people. (London, Black, Female)

Although this diversity of individual concerns was apparent throughout our conversations, perhaps even more so was the widespread perception that an endemic racism coursing throughout British society directly diminished the security of individuals therein. Although dissenters were very occasionally identifiable – 'I think this is one of the countries where actually people do try and provide that level ... more of a level playing field ... You have access to education ... you have a house over your head, which is a lot more than you can say for many other countries' (London, Asian, Female) – many people were keen to share their own experiences of racial or religious inequality and the personal insecurities these engendered. Such experiences were especially prominent in encounters with institutional or other barriers to formal employment. As one female put it: 'It's very difficult to access jobs if you are from the ethnic minority ... I've experienced it all the time, even if you're talking on the phone or with the local authorities' (Swansea, Black, Female). Indeed, so profound was this expectation of discrimination that measures devised to address it – such as equal opportunity monitoring forms – were invoked in multiple groups as contributory rather than amelioratory mechanisms: 'even this form that you fill: what is your ethnicity? Are you black, white, Indian? When you fill that form, what does it do? It profiles you, and you will not even get an interview. So that form ... is not being used for good. It's being used for pure evil' (London, Black, Female).

These experiences of institutionalised racism were complemented in several of our focus groups by reflection on a broader, less disaggregated, climate of suspicion that many participants experienced in their everyday lives. The following conversation, for instance, describes the perception of constant censure experienced by one female in Birmingham identifying as Muslim and Asian:

> A: Is that a tangible thing, though? Do you feel, do you feel oppressed or that someone's watching you or looking at you and making judgements against you, because you're Asian?
>
> B: Sometimes, yes.

A: And, possibly Muslim.
B: Yes. (Birmingham, Asian, Male and Female)

As in the above discussion of sociotropic threats, many again pointed to 9/11 as a turning point. Several participants, for example, noted a dramatic shift in how they were viewed after those attacks: 'Before [9/11], we were all right, we didn't feel any threat and we didn't have that sort of embarrassment. But it's only now they look at us and say, they must be terrorists, they must be related to a terrorist' (Oldham, Asian, Female). As one black participant noted, however, this experience was by no means confined to members of the UK's Asian communities: 'So for many people it has become worse especially after 9/11, after the bombings, if you carry a knapsack, nobody wants to walk by your side, because they fear you are carrying a bomb as a black person. I feel that' (Swansea, Black, Female).

The important point to take from this is the resonance of a broad understanding of threat, risk and insecurity across UK publics. As we have seen, security challenges – social and personal – are seen to span a range of issue areas, from terrorism and crime, through to racism, social fracture and financial hardship. As many of the above examples indicate, moreover, these risks are often perceived to be interconnected. Crime and terrorism are tied to the experience of social alienation; institutionalised racism is viewed as a source of economic inequality and British foreign policy is seen to impact on domestic security concerns. In this sense, at least, the considerable post-Cold War efforts to widen the agenda of security studies do seem to resonate with public interpretations of insecurity.

This breadth of insecurities is linked to security's malleability within everyday usage. As demonstrated in the following section, UK publics discuss security in very different ways, articulating this concept around ideals as diverse as survival, equality, freedom and hospitality. This malleability means that any issue capable of affecting one's life, freedom and so forth might be understood, at least in principle, as a security challenge. And, given the widespread normative appeal of security, the language of *insecurity* offers a potentially productive terminology for public condemnation of any undesirable behaviours, institutions or contexts. Thus, although this is not the place to revisit debates on the political value of securitizing non-military concerns (see Huysmans 2006: 19–26), our findings do indicate that the language of security is remarkably adaptable to a range of issues in vernacular usage. This is the case, importantly, whether such issues are widely securitized (for instance, terrorism and migration) or otherwise (for instance, ethnicity monitoring forms). In fact, no participant in any of our groups resisted the term's application to any issue raised in these discussions; including those viewed more commonly as nuisance than threat.

'Security, yes, it's such a broad ranging word':[4] vernacular accounts of Security

We encountered six very different understandings of security within our focus groups, as well as considerable movement between these by our participants as conversations unfolded and developed. The first, and most straightforward, description given to us formulated this term as a synonym for survival. In this conception, it was the individual person almost without exception that was identified as security's referent: the 'who' or 'what' that is or should be secured. Thus, in more truncated explanations security was simply redescribed as the continuation of one's existence: 'security means like to protect your life' (Oxford, Asian, Female). More detailed accounts, however, fleshed this out further by cataloguing the diversity of basic human needs – typically seen as universal – required for the continuation of life. In the words of one participant, for example: 'I think there are objective standards that everybody should have. A basic standard of water supply, and food supply ... of care, healthcare, basic standard in housing, basic standard of living ... those are what we need' (London, White, Male).

A second view of security – understood as the positive experience associated with belonging somewhere – shifted the focus of this term from the satisfaction of basic (perhaps universal) human needs to that of feeling appropriately situated in a particular spatial or human community. As one participant put it, security involves 'the ability to feel comfortable where you are ... from ... walking down the street in a city if you're safe to ... feeling comfortable with the people that you're with and in your job situation and in your life situation, with your health' (London, White, Female). For another, similarly: 'Security means feeling happy where you are, feeling that, you know, there's no one to threaten you ... you're not feeling like, oh, I can't [go] there ... I don't belong there' (Swansea, Black, Female). Discussions of security in terms of belonging were couched, by some, in positive terms, with the importance of familiarity with one's locale a prominent concern: 'It's [security is] your surroundings, though, isn't it? When you come to the local community, I mean, you feel safe' (Birmingham, Asian, Female). Other participants in our groups, in contrast, framed this understanding negatively, explaining the experience of security by means of contrast with spaces of insecurity: 'if you're living a bit outer, where maybe you've got all white or just all black [people] or whatever ... you think, there are eyes following me ... they're not going to say anything obviously, but you do feel that, kind of, sense of they're watching' (Birmingham, Asian, Female). If a little less tangible than understandings of security as survival, the importance of this experience of inclusion was profound for many of the people with whom we spoke. It is also – again in contrast to accounts of security as survival – an explicitly relational one, in that amicable or (at a minimum) disinterested interaction with others emerges as a prerequisite for achieving security. In the words of a participant in Swansea, for instance: 'For me, security is when you can be anywhere ... even if people don't welcome you and greet you, but at least you can feel comfortable in that place. That's security, I would say' (Swansea, Black, Female).

Third, a number of non-white participants, in particular, presented a more expansive account of security framed around notions of what we have called hospitality. Those discussing security in this way frequently used the term to describe the importance of having others recognise one's own right to belong in a shared social space. As one individual argued: 'I think if we feel welcome we'd probably feel more secure' (Swansea, Black, Male). This linkage of security to hospitality frequently appeared in discussions of racial prejudice or ignorance that – as seen above – were common across our groups. A particularly powerful example emerged in one individual's account of her recent relocation from London to Swansea. Following a group discussion of the extent to which racism may be seen as a security threat, this participant recounted her recurrent experience of having to define and defend moving to her new home:

> They said, Why are you here in Swansea? I said, I've just come to stay like everybody else. And he said, Are you asylum seeker? I said, no. Are you refugee? I said, no. Are you student? No. Why are you here then? ... [W]e all have names. Either you're asylum seeker, either you're a refugee, either you're a student. That's all you can live in Swansea. (Swansea, Black, Female)

A fourth conception, again more prominent amongst non-white demographics, connected security to equality. As one participant put it: 'To my own understanding, you are secure if you are treated the way others are treated without ... any preferential treatment or whatever ... if there is equality, everybody would feel secure and safe' (Swansea, Black, Male). For a male in a different group, similarly, 'security is equality, to have all the same rights. You are as a human. There shouldn't be any difference between the black, white, foreigner ... and these things. This is the meaning of security' (Swansea, Black, Male). Although equality was approached differently across these discussions – such that references were made to equality of opportunity, treatment, outcomes and so forth – its absence was a source of profound concern for several of our participants.

The penultimate understanding of security we encountered articulated this term around notions of freedom. In direct contrast to the widespread oppositional framing of these two values that has been common in discussions of anti-terrorism powers (see Waldron 2003), many of our participants identified a positive relationship at work here. In the words of one male, for instance: 'I equate it [security] ... to freedom, really; to feeling that you can do what you want and be where you want within the confines of the law ... without fear' (London, Asian, Male). Another male in London employed similar language, self-identifying as a Muslim in discussing his fear of racial profiling that was shared by a number of those participating in this group and beyond:

> I think liberty and freedom is an essential component of actually feeling secure ... I am quite wary now, especially with the sort of hype on Muslims per se, I'm quite wary about an attack on my freedom or individual liberty, in the sense that I might walk down the street one minute, a black van might just come and I am taken away, whisked away by MI5 or MI6. So, this is the sort of ... it is a fear, because I'm kind of quite outspoken in a sense, but then again I have to sort of [limit] what I say because of the possible repercussions. So, for me to feel safe I need to know that my liberty and my sort of liberty is still alive. It's a real component. (London, Asian, Male)

It is in this discussion that security's *political* significance becomes clear, where feared repercussions to one's own views are met with a self-imposed silence. Those arguing similarly – particularly in the context of contemporary anti-terrorism powers – offered numerous examples of self-censorship because of anxieties such as these. Such practices stretched from an outright withdrawal from political debate, as in the above example, to more mundane, yet frequently conscious, decisions within everyday interactions:

> If we're talking on the phone or chatting online, we avoid taking this terminology, bomb and this and that. Why? There might be someone recording that. They might be keeping an eye on it. And if we mention those terms, they'll think, yeah, they were talking about that. (Oxford, Asian, Female)[5]

A final account of security presented to us departed dramatically from the desirable connotations of each of the above understandings. Here, a number of individuals responded to our questions about the term by highlighting its negative associations and especially by voicing fears that invocations of security or insecurity may legitimise the suspension of (one's own) civil and political rights. In one group with Asian participants in Birmingham, for example, security was directly associated with martial law:

> A: Well, that's security to me, it's an affiliation with military, martial law. That's instantly what I believe [when] they say we're going to increase security. I think of martial law.

B: I see it as suspicion, from the point of view, to be secure.
C: I see it as an excuse. (Birmingham, Asian, Male, Female, Male)

When discussion in this group turned to the recent installation of surveillance cameras on the boundaries of two predominantly Muslim suburbs of Birmingham, the insecuritizing potential of such technologies became keenly discussed. As the following indicates, these cameras (funded by anti-terrorism monies) posed significant questions of the relevant security referents for those potentially subject to their gaze:[6]

A: But you guys, don't you think it's more safe and secure, they're doing that? I mean, it's our housing, isn't it?
B: No, it's an invasion of privacy.
A: It's an invasion of privacy, but there is some sense of security, because there are some loonies out there. Not the cameras, but just generally, you know, if there is tight security.
B: It's not for our security, though, it's for others. (Birmingham, Asian, Females)

Speaking also to this more sceptical view of security, finally, were related concerns over the ways in which purported security risks were reported by political, media or other elites. One individual, for example, contrasted the depiction and reality of threats such as terrorism, arguing that such risks were frequently manipulated for political gain, abetted by 'media hype' (London, Asian, Male). Another, speaking in a separate London-based group, argued similarly:

> [Y]ou can't feel secure unless you have trust for your institution and the people around you ... I mean, the one terrorist, or, well, the big terrorist event that happened in London, I think, allows the government to kind of manipulate, and the media kind of to manipulate ... [to] take that fear and say, Don't worry, you're secure, trust us to take care of you. (London, White, Female)

Those with longer memories, finally, couched their concerns over contemporary security technologies and practices by referring to relevant historical precedents:

> What concerns me with security is it gives a government that's in trouble all sorts of open-handed ways, or closed-handed ways. Now, I go back to the miners' strike. Now that we are going through the history, the whole of MI6 was mobilised to fight them. I mean, these are facts. They'll say, Oh don't be so stupid – [but] they did. (Llanelli, White, Male)

Vernacular securities and everyday life

As the above, hopefully, indicates, there exists considerable heterogeneity in the ways in which security is conceptualised by different publics across the UK. Although the numerical recurrence of these six images is of limited relevance due to our methodology, none of these was mentioned by one individual, or even by members of one group, alone. Not only, therefore, do individuals perceive or experience different security threats in the context of their everyday lives, as demonstrated at the start of this chapter. But, more significantly, the very meaning of the term security appears as inherently contested within public as within academic discourse. Moreover, as with related research, we encountered numerous examples of participants negotiating two or more of the six above images, pointing, significantly, to the term's malleability within public life (Gillespie et al. 2010).

This heterogeneity indicates the ontological (and normative) precariousness of security within everyday life across the UK. This is important because it might suggest that caution should be taken with regard to the claims to universality that run through much of the human-centred literature that was integral to the broadening of the security agenda. Unless we are to resort to a purely objective understanding of security – a comparatively rare position in contemporary debate – it is important to recognise that security means and therefore *is* a very different 'thing' for different people. In this sense, we here agree with Ken Booth's (2007: 152) analysis that the starting point for discussions about security should be the 'bottom up' experiences of people encountering insecurity. And, once we do this, our findings suggest that there exists much greater variation (at the level of the individual, at least) than is often assumed around such core questions as: how is security experienced? what is required for security's satisfaction? and even, is security a desirable phenomenon? This heterogeneity suggests that the relationship between security and anti-terrorism powers is not (and perhaps never could be) straightforward. Whilst such measures ostensibly aim at enhancing the security of citizens, the fact that security is perceived and experienced in different ways renders such initiatives ambiguous in security terms. Thus, if security policies are to be evaluated in terms of the extent to which they enhance or diminish security, then they are perhaps always doomed to 'failure'. It is hard to conceive of any policy which can satisfy such a heterogeneous range of conceptions.

A second point to note is that these rather different images of security also highlight considerable proximity between public understandings of this term and those making up contemporary scholarly discourse. Public discussions of security in terms of survival, and associated efforts to catalogue that which is needed for its satisfaction, bear striking similarity to debates around human security. Efforts to link security to freedom, on the other hand, as well as accounts of the importance of human communities for personal security, evoke CSS literatures and the emphasis on emancipation therein. Anxieties over the manipulation of security threats by political or media elites do likewise with Copenhagen School explorations of securitization, while concerns with security technologies and professionals highlight the pertinence of Paris School discussions of insecuritization. Given the diversity and malleability of the vernacular securities we encountered, it is unsurprising but important that none of these theories of security seemed to resonate more powerfully than others even within our research. However, that each of these diverse approaches to this concept is able to capture (some) public anxieties, fears and visions of the socio-political adds credibility, we argue, to their common effort to rethink security beyond its traditionally narrow parameters.

Security and positionality

Before returning to anti-terrorism policy in the following chapter, it is important, finally, to note that each of the six images discussed above does far more than 'fill' this particular signifier. The language of security – as much of the constructivist research introduced in Chapter 2 demonstrates – has important constitutive roles in everyday discourse, such that things happen when it is employed. Participants in our focus groups seemed to discuss security as a way of articulating identity claims and thereby positioning the self in relation to others and the external world. So discussions of security as survival, for instance, might be read as an attempt to locate the self as a corporeal subject in possession of somatic and (for some) extra-somatic needs. Focused, primarily, on the individual as security's referent, people invoked this understanding as a means of drawing attention to the requirements for life's continuation. In the words of one individual: 'To have security, like a family that loves you and a house to live in and a job that pays you money that you can live on it, is really important to everyone, I think' (London, White, Female). Discussions of security as belonging, on the other hand, might be seen as an exposition of ontological security;[7] an effort to articulate the need for a stable and rooted sense of identity. And, yet, as the analysis above demonstrates, this particular image was most frequently invoked by virtue of its absence than its presence: the language of security employed to express a desire, not experience. As one participant put it: 'You know, they've got this mentality that the moment they see you, you're a black person or you're from an ethnic minority, they've come here for the benefits. They're talking about this all the time. They've come for the housing, come for ... all this, which is not entirely true' (Swansea, Black, Female).

Descriptions of security drawing on notions of hospitality worked to position the self socially by reflecting on the responsibilities owed to, and legitimately expected from, others (whether those were perceived as having been met or otherwise). As with accounts of security as belonging, this language was also most frequently employed to describe security's absence; often by reference to differential treatment. As one Asian participant speaking in a focus group in Oxford told us:

> I have experience of Polish people, many Polish people. But they are most welcome because they are in Europe, they're most welcome here. They're welcome like the thousands and thousands every year; no skills at all, no qualifications at all. My parents, they are both highly qualified; they won awards. But when they applied to a school somewhere, they say, No, sorry, you're overqualified or something like that, or you have this much experience or this much experience. (Oxford, Asian, Male)

Discussions of security in the language of equality, freedom and insecurity, finally, work to position the self politically. Participants employed these images to articulate support for, or opposition to, political values or projects and their everyday implications. In the former two, security was invoked to express the need for, and desirability of, equitable treatment or the protection of civil liberties. In the latter it was invoked to concretise the undesirability of contemporary security practices, whether CCTV cameras or policing strategies.

Public expressions of security, then, are important because this language offers a particularly useful way of carving out and expressing one's relations to the external world, whether material, social or political. In vernacular usage, therefore, security seems to provide a powerful language for articulating support or opposition for political projects, for thinking through the importance and shifting nature of social cartographies, and for expressing the diversity of an individual's needs. Although under-researched, this has major implications for thinking through public responses to public policy issues in areas such as security. As Lene Hansen (2006: 1) puts it in her overview of poststructuralist work on foreign policy: 'foreign policies rely upon representations of identity, but it is also through the formulation of foreign policy that identities are produced and reproduced'.

Conclusion

As the above discussion suggests, we encountered a public willingness and ability to collocate security with a diversity of different values. Some of these

– such as survival and freedom – will be familiar to students of security of varying persuasion. Others, particularly hospitality and equality, have been far less explored in scholarly expositions of this term and its distinctiveness vis-à-vis other social or political values. This, we argue, alone indicates the value of greater engagement with public articulations for those concerned with security's appropriate conceptual, discursive and political location. And, as argued in Chapter 2, a growing literature seeking to do precisely this is beginning now to emerge, although much remains to be done (see Jarvis and Lister 2013b).

For the purposes of our discussion, however, this diversity is important because it indicates that public criticism or support for anti-terrorism powers couched in the language of security may be more complex than is often assumed. That is, whether people feel more or less secure because of developments in this policy area might mean very different things, depending upon what underpinning conception of security is being mobilised. As such, although anti-terrorism powers do likely impact in some way upon public experiences of security, it is also highly likely that public understandings of security are fundamental to evaluations of anti-terrorism powers. The relationship between the two, then, might be thought of as co-constitutive rather than linear. In Chapter 6 we now explore this further by charting the different ways in which the above conceptions of security link to the attitudes towards anti-terrorism explored in earlier chapters.

Notes

1 Swansea, White, Male.
2 London, Asian, Female.
3 For an excellent discussion of this in the context of contemporary anti-terrorism policy see Amoore and de Goede (2005).
4 London, White, Male.
5 As argued in Chapter 4, accounts such as these were not universal, and we encountered considerable evidence of public resistance to the logics, exercise and pernicious impacts of public policy in this context.
6 Following widespread public opposition to 'Project Champion', it was announced in May 2011 that the cameras would be dismantled, see BBC News (2011).
7 See Giddens (1990); Kinnvall (2004); Mitzen (2006).

6

Framing the security/anti-terrorism nexus

In preceding chapters, we explored the different ways in which citizens conceive of security and insecurity, and the ways in which anti-terrorism powers are interpreted and evaluated by UK publics, including in relation to their impacts on aspects of citizenship. In this chapter, we now bring these analyses together, examining the relationship between conceptions or constructions of security, on the one hand, and public understandings of anti-terrorism powers on the other. Our argument is that vernacular constructions of security seem to link loosely to attitudes to anti-terrorism, in that those who think (for example) about security primarily in terms of survival tend to be less sceptical about the utility of anti-terrorism measures. Those who conceive of security in more expansive terms – as freedom, for instance – tend, in contrast, to be more sceptical of the necessity of many contemporary powers.

Although this loose connection between vernacular securities and attitudes towards anti-terrorism is important, this chapter identifies a second, stronger relationship in public framings of these two phenomena. Vernacular securities, we argue, seem to serve as a lens through which anti-terrorism powers are approached; defining the parameters within which such powers are discussed beyond the normative or political evaluations made thereof by different publics. Thus, individuals who describe security in similar ways may diverge in their level of support or opposition for anti-terrorism powers, but they tend to have those discussions on similar linguistic and conceptual terrain. Those who talk about security in terms of physical survival, for example, tend to discuss anti-terrorism powers in terms of their effectiveness or otherwise, questioning whether such powers enhance protection against the terrorist threat. Those who think about security in relation to freedom do not always articulate similar levels of support or opposition towards anti-terrorism measures, but they do tend to debate on terrain organised around concerns associated with civil rights. Holders of conceptions of security closely linked to ideas of belonging, likewise, tend to orient their discussions around the impacts of anti-terrorism measures on community relations and participation within public spaces.

Investigating the relationships between constructions of core political values (here, security) and attitudes towards public policy (here, anti-terrorism powers) has significance, we argue, for a number of reasons. Not only does it add depth and detail to the quantitative explorations of public opinion and public policy explored in Chapter 2 (cf. Jarvis and Lister 2013a). More importantly, and drawing out arguments raised in the previous chapters, it also has potential to explore the influence of security constructions within social relations at levels often far removed from the elite discourses upon which much constructivist analysis has tended to focus. This, we argue, has epistemological and normative merit. Not only does it significantly broaden our understanding of security's social meanings and roles; it also offers space within debate on security for everyday – and potentially marginalised, camouflaged or excluded – constructions of this term. In short, our argument is that differing conceptions of security influence *how* people think about or discuss anti-terrorism powers. And, as such, that security is not simply an end state to be achieved, or striven towards, but a powerful force that works within horizontal and vertical social relations: elite and 'everyday'.

Explaining anti-terrorism attitudes

Whilst a good deal of research energy has been expended upon the legitimacy or otherwise of anti-terrorism measures and their consequences, rather less time has been spent investigating how non-elite individuals think and speak about this controversial area, including the significance of differing attitudes therein (although see Sullivan and Hendriks 2009). Notable, therefore, is Davis and Silver's (2004) work which points to a number of key factors here. Drawing on survey data from the US, Davis and Silver conclude that levels of trust in political elites and perceptions of threat interact with one another to influence public attachment to existing civil liberties. At the same time, they note that 'at every level of trust in the federal government, increased sense of threat leads to a greater willingness to concede some civil liberties in favour of security and order' (Davis and Silver 2004: 43). Yet, as well as the role played by fear of terrorist attack, Davis and Silver's research points also to the importance of related dynamics such as political ideology and sense of national pride in shaping public attitudes.

These findings are broadly echoed within other work (see Huddy et al. 2005) highlighting the salience of attitudes towards civil liberties (Rykkja et al. 2011) and attachment to right-wing authoritarian values (Kossowska et al. 2011) in evaluations citizens make in this context. Taken together, this literature indicates that citizens who are: (i) fearful of terrorist attacks; (ii) supportive of strong government intervention; and (iii) less strongly committed to the importance of civil liberties, are more likely to be supportive of harsher or stronger anti-terrorism measures. An interesting addition to this discussion comes from Johnson and Gearty (2007), who identify a strong decline in public attachments to civil liberties in the British context in the 1980s. This, as they note, suggests that fear of terrorism associated with the period after 9/11 may not be as central in attitudes towards anti-terrorism powers as is often supposed, at least in the UK. As they put it: 'at best, it seems that this heightened anxiety about terrorism may only explain part of the general trend away from commitment to civil liberties' (Johnson and Gearty 2007: 156).

Whilst this literature undoubtedly sheds light on some interesting factors at play in citizen responses to anti-terrorism frameworks, a deeper and more fine-grained analysis of citizens' understandings of the terms in which anti-terrorism is debated has considerable potential for advancing understanding further. As suggested in Chapter 5, evaluating public attitudes towards civil liberties or security in the context of anti-terrorism powers without exploring public understandings of the meaning of such terms risks implying that they are consistently understood. Yet, as demonstrated there, such consistency seems not to exist.

Rethinking security

As we saw in Chapter 2, there exists a growing body of work within Security Studies which has begun to explore what happens when the language of security is invoked. The performative emphasis within this literature is important because it moves security analysis beyond traditional conceptions of this term as a condition or state of existence. Security is seen here as a social practice that is *constitutive* of identities, issues and responses. David Campbell's *Writing Security*, for example, sets out to examine:

> the way in which the identity of '(the United States of) America' has been written and rewritten through foreign policies operating in its name ... Instead of asking how United States foreign policy serves the national interest, it examines how, through the inscription of foreignness, United States foreign policy helps produce and reproduce the doer supposedly behind the deed. (Campbell 1998: x)

Another way of framing this would be to suggest that the work of Campbell and others analyses the ways in which security *as a practice* impacts upon politics and thus reverses the traditional realist focus on security as the *outcome* of practice and politics: the ordered opposite to the chaotic, Hobbesian state of nature following establishment of the Leviathan (see Walker 1992). As Hansen (2006: 18) puts it: 'Security can be seen as a historically formed discourse centred on the nation state and as a particularly radical form of identity construction with a *distinct political force* that invests political leaders with power as well as responsibility' (emphasis added).

Despite this literature's importance, one frequent criticism is that it remains overwhelmingly focused on elite actors, utterances and practice. Although Hansen (2006) identifies intertextual webs which extend beyond elite discourses, Booth's (2007: 166) criticism of securitization studies as elitist may justly be applied to much other constructivist and poststructural work in this area. This focus on elite discourses, as Matt McDonald (2008: 574) argues, is normatively problematic, in that it 'serves to marginalize the experiences and articulations of the powerless in global politics, presenting them at best as parts of an audience that can collectively consent to or contest securitizing moves, and at worst as passive recipients of elite discourses'. As he continues (citing Milliken), this is not only an issue for the securitization literature but for discourse analytical approaches to international relations more widely. He concludes that this is not only a problem in normative terms, but that analytically, it 'blinds its proponents to the role of security as a site of competing discourses or images of politics' (McDonald 2008: 575).

The call to move beyond elite discourses on security resonates with Huysmans' (1998) argument that security be seen as a 'signifier', the meaning and functions of which are articulated, rather than given. Beginning from the point that, despite calls for widening the security agenda, not much attention has been paid to the meaning of security itself, Huysmans (1998: 228) calls for greater engagement with the 'wider cultural framework(s) within which security receives its meaning and which are often implied in the daily use of the label "security". To do this, we should move away from approaching "security" as a definition or as a concept and instead interpret it as a thick signifier.'

Drawing on Saussure's distinction of the sign into signifier (the sound or word used to characterise something) and signified (the image that is related), Huysmans characterises security as a signifier which receives its meaning through difference to others. Yet it is, he argues, a 'thick signifier' in that, '"Security" has a history and implies a meaning, a particular signification of social relations ... Uttering "security" articulates ... a register of meaning, which we will call a security formation' (Huysmans 1998: 228). The research agenda implied by such a conception, for him, is one which lays bare the politics that runs through these registers of meaning, as well as their contestation or transformation in specific social contexts (Huysmans 1998: 233). Importantly, for what follows, Huysmans (1998: 249) incorporates into his analysis a call for further investigation into 'the play of the signifier "security" in different contexts', as this would:

> contribute considerably to a critical awareness of what security (or most probably different securities) are about and what security policies imply ... Such an 'empirical' agenda would be a major contribution to the existing literature on the discursive formation of security in International Relations. It will raise questions such as – Does the signifier articulate a single, well-delineated structure of meaning (the discursive formation) or does it mean different things in different contexts ... Don't we risk ethno-, gender-, discipline-, or other centrisms if we generalize from the national security experience in International Relations? What are the differences and similarities between social security and societal security, internal security and external security in terms of the way they organize our relation to nature, to others and to the self? Answers to these kinds of questions could help us considerably in developing a critical understanding of (differences in) the significance and meaning of security practices. (Huysmans 1998: 244–245)

Huysmans here makes the important – yet frequently overlooked – point that security likely has different functions or logics depending, in part, on the conditions and contexts of its performance (see also Browning and McDonald 2013). While 'security' may (sometimes) be involved in demarcating differences between self and other, increasing an issue's importance or stifling dissent, it may (also, otherwise, or indeed only sometimes) do other things as well.

Bringing these diverse strands of literature together, two arguments may be made. First, that security should be considered not only as a (likely) normatively desirable end state which can be counterposed to anarchy, violence and death. Security is also a productive factor in social relations that is involved in the constitution of events, issues and identities. Second, this productive, performative power does not reside solely at the level of political (or other) elites, *qua* discussions around securitization. Whilst conceptions of security and threats clearly contribute to the play of geo-political dynamics, how individual citizens internalise, contest and conceive of these and other discourses also has vitally important implications for identity claims, dispositions and attitudes to security practice at the level of the 'everyday'.

All this suggests that public or vernacular understandings of security may contribute to public responses to, and evaluations of, anti-terrorism measures. If 'everyday' conceptions of security do exert influence on identities, attitudes and outlooks, it may be that they contribute to policy attitudes, rather than such attitudes explaining security positions (e.g. Davis and Silver 2004;

Huddy et al. 2005). Thus, if a policy is designed to increase national or public security, individuals with different understandings of security are likely to have differing views on the effectiveness or otherwise thereof. Moreover, as argued now below, different conceptions of security may also contribute to differential discursive framings of such interventions, whether in terms of their effectiveness, or impact on communities or rights.

Security and anti-terrorism: intersections and frames

In the following, we move to a consideration of the ways in which vernacular constructions of security interact with claims about political subjectivity and attitudes towards anti-terrorism specifically. In so doing, we bring together a consideration of public conceptions of security (explored in Chapter 5) with citizens' perceptions of anti-terrorism measures (assessed in Chapters 3 and 4). As noted above, we identify a broad attitudinal connection between these two in that different conceptions of security tend to correlate with different attitudes to anti-terrorism powers. Although this correlation is not exhaustive or exclusive, a stronger and clearer connection, we argue, exists between conceptions of security and the ways in which anti-terrorism powers are framed. In other words, vernacular conceptions of security seem to shape the linguistic and conceptual schema that citizens use to talk about anti-terrorism. They may not causally determine what is thought of developments in this policy arena, but they do seem to shape the types of rationale or logic deployed to explain and expound attitudes. Different conceptions may or may not exert influence on what people think, but we argue here that they do exert an influence on the terms in which people discuss public policy.

A frame, as used below, may be thought of as 'an interpretive schemata that signifies and condenses the "world out there" by selectively punctuating and encoding objects, situations, events, experiences and sequences of action in one's present or past environment' (Snow and Benford, cited in Steinberg 1998: 845). Generally, frame analysis focuses on the ways in which frames aid consensus formation and thereafter collective action, in that: 'frames provide a diagnosis and prognosis of a problem and a call to action to resolve it' (Steinberg 1998: 845). Yet, this process can be dynamic and plural. Indeed, a key claim for framing-process scholars is that individuals are 'deeply embroiled, along with the media, local governments and the state, in what has been referred to as "the politics of signification"' (Benford and Snow 2000: 613). Framing is seen as 'an active, processual phenomenon that implies agency and contention at the level of reality' (Benford and Snow 2000: 614). Conceptualising security as a discursive frame which 'enable[s] individuals "to locate, perceive, identify and label" occurrences within their life space and the world at large' (Benford and Snow 2000: 614, citing Goffman) thus enables an examination of the ways in which security contributes to and shapes social processes. The analysis that follows offers an analysis of these processes in relation to fifteen participants in our focus groups. These are chosen as their contributions contained both an explicit articulation of security *and* evidence of clear attitudes towards anti-terrorism powers. Other participants in our research either did not discuss the meaning of security, did so obliquely (we excluded statements where short agreement was made with another respondent's statement) or were less explicit in their attitude towards anti-terrorism measures (again, simple agreements with others' responses were excluded).

Security as survival and support for anti-terrorism?

As discussed in Chapter 5, a number of the participants in our focus groups adopted a view of security that was roughly coterminous with survival. For them, security related to the absence of threat and the meeting of corporeal and perhaps other needs necessary for continued existence. In the following, we examine responses of six of our participants who discussed security thus, along with their attitudes to UK anti-terrorism powers. As we shall see, these individuals do not have an identical approach to anti-terrorism; some are more sceptical than others. However, as outlined above, a clearer relationship emerges in the way in which anti-terrorism is thought about and conceptualised. We shall see how these people both establish and navigate a similar discursive terrain in their responses, one which coheres around the efficacy of anti-terrorism measures. Discourses of security, in other words, act as a prism that helps to frame the way these things are approached.

One explanation of security rooted in notions of survival and protection from external threats was articulated by a white male in London, who argued:

> it's about maintaining what you have and if you don't have very much, then security to you is about being healthy, having a roof over your head, having food to eat, and if you have more, going right up to the other end of the scale, it's about not having things stolen from you. (London, White, Male)

This individual here provides a relatively conservative understanding of security rooted in the maintenance of existing conditions, including, at the most basic level, human life. Security is here traced to the satisfaction of basic human needs: it is an end in itself that is juxtaposed to unforeseen or unwanted changes to the requirements thereof. When proceeding to discuss anti-terrorism measures, the importance he places on protecting the status quo can clearly be seen. Thus, while he was not wholeheartedly supportive of anti-terrorism measures, his scepticism centred on the effectiveness or otherwise, rather than – as for some others in the same group – their impact on fundamental citizenship rights. For example, whilst he stated a concern about stop and search, this was framed in the language of utility rather than, for instance, justice: 'I mean the whole point here is, without suspicion, so does that mean they're just randomly stopping and searching people and hoping to find amongst the millions of people moving around that they're going to catch someone? That doesn't seem that likely' (London, White, Male). This participant also expressed concerns about the limited impact of existing measures on the root causes of terrorism, as well as their capacity to alienate specific communities.

Another individual in the same focus group articulated similar sentiments. For him, security has certain basic, material foundations, as cited in the previous chapter: 'I think there are objective standards that everybody should have a basic standard of water supply, I think you were talking about, and food supply, a basic standard of care, healthcare, basic standard of housing, basic standard of living, and those are ... those are what we need' (London, White, Male). Again we see an emphasis here on the material, physical foundations of security. And, as with our earlier participant, this again correlates with a mildly sceptical view of anti-terrorism measures, one that also seems to stem from questions about their effectiveness:

> From the outside, they [anti-terrorism measures] all look like kind of huge infringements of civil liberty and invitations to prejudice ... the big problem with it is that *you don't know enough about the threat to actually kind of judge for yourself* ... it may be that there isn't any... that they don't deal with any kind of threat in any kind of way, but ... I'm not in a position to judge that, but I can understand that the kind of problem ... is that *it is actually quite difficult to release the information and allow us, the ordinary person, to judge whether it's an effective measure*, let alone whether it's a justified measure. (London, White, Male, our emphasis)

The statement begins and ends with a qualified concern about civil liberty infringements, although there is an implicit prioritisation of security's necessities here. This uncertainty stems, perhaps in a similar way to the above, from not knowing whether such measures actually *work*. Thus, there emerges here a connection between such attitudes and a specific conception of security; if something threatens 'basic standards', then measures to address such a threat may be acceptable, in spite of their implications for civil liberties.

A participant in a different group also discussed security in terms of survival, and again seemed to respond to anti-terrorism measures with a scepticism stemming from uncertainty about their effectiveness. For her, the protection and safety of her children were uppermost in thinking about security, as she put it: 'I think knowing that my children are in an environment that is protective ... at school they're in a safe environment, you know, that they're ... they're being fed things that are healthy, both mentally and emotionally' (Oxford, White, Female). She went on to emphasise security's association with basic needs by stating that, when asked about this term: 'I think of financial security; I think of having a roof over my head' (Oxford, White, Female). This participant shares the emphasis on physical safety, maintenance and endurance evident in the above examples. And, as with the above, the way she thinks about anti-terrorism indicates that this concern with physical protection filters into her thinking about anti-terrorism. For instance, when one person in the group expressed opposition to some existing anti-terrorism measures, her response was to ask, 'And you know, what do you do? [...] What measures do you feel there should be?' (Oxford, White, Female). Whilst this person did elsewhere in the conversation express concern at specific powers, she returned to her position that something needed to be done to address the terrorist threat. In her words: 'Yes we need laws. Yes we need protection, and we need that security, but it's getting that balance right' (Oxford, White, Female). This is a somewhat different position from the first two instances, but one in which a link is again made between a protective understanding of security in terms of survival and continuity, and the view that *effective* anti-terrorism measures may be necessary to ensure this.

A slightly different conception of security, but one that may also be discussed here, is the following. Asked how she understood security, one participant stated that, for her, 'It's kind of everything ... like a family that loves you and a house to live in and a job that pays you money that you can live on ... That's my first thought when I think of security and from that comes the thought of how lucky I am because a lot of people don't have those things (London, White, Female). Although security is here conceived in terms of emotional or psychological needs (family and love), also included are material possessions which are associated with comfort and survival.

For this individual, anti-terrorism measures are viewed with some scepticism, particularly for their vagueness and attendant scope for misuse. As she explained: 'if it just caught terrorists who were going to do something, great. But so many other people can fall ... within these kind of clauses, and be prosecuted for nothing' (London, White, Female). In a similar way to above participants, there is a concern again with the functioning and effectiveness of anti-terrorism measures. Moreover, this respondent described a sense in which, 'a lot of people ... in this country will, well, possibly will feel safer as a result. They might read that [list of anti-terrorism measures] and think, okay it's good to think that that's being done because something needs to be done'

(London, White, Female). Again, a connection might be made between a survival-oriented view of security as physical well-being, and tacit acceptance or support for measures which may offer protection from challenges thereto. It is, as above, in terms of effectiveness that anti-terrorism measures are being evaluated.

A similar framing was evident from yet another of our participants, for whom security refers to:

> knowing there are things you can rely on like the NHS and knowing that your doctor's not going to cost you if something happened, you know, you can rely on that, or if you need to claim Job Seeker's allowance or that things run smoothly, that you know, if the train said it's going to run at this time and you go to the train station it's there, and just the systems that are in place. (London, White, Female)

Again, whilst this is not a straightforward view of security as survival or protection, the importance that this conception places upon the meeting of material expectations renders it comparable to the others in this grouping. Yet, while for many of the people discussed above, concerns about effectiveness were accompanied by tacit acceptance of such measures *if effective*, here the support for anti-terrorism measures is more clearly stated: 'But I think for me personally, if I felt like the government hadn't taken any measures or made any changes to legislation since recent terror attacks, I think I'd feel concerned. I'm glad that they're taking some measures' (London, White, Female).

Our final example of the way in which this conception of security filters through into public evaluations of security politics shows the strongest support for anti-terrorism powers we encountered. One Asian female in a group we ran in London described security in terms of safety, stability and maintaining one's own life and position: 'it's personal; it's personal safety, not just ... not necessarily the imminent danger of threat, but it's also, sort of, having stability in your life as well ... just knowing that, okay, I can predict the next few years of my life as long as I work hard, it's okay' (London, Asian, Female). Thus, whilst security does have elements of physical survival here, it also refers to the confidence that comes from expectations about the continuity of one's future existence.

This view of security connects, for this person, to a very strong sense that anti-terrorism measures are justified and necessary. When discussing the deportation of Abu Hamza (see also Chapter 3), she rejected any notion that such individuals should be protected by human rights laws. Indeed, in her view, stringent anti-terrorism measures were justified given the threat posed to the public by those espousing extremist or radical views: 'what about my life being under threat from people that he has excited, people that he has encouraged effectively to wage war against this country? So, absolutely, I think those are the basic, fundamental laws that need to come' (London, Asian, Female).

When her personal safety is seen as directly threatened, this person is willing to justify relatively stringent anti-terrorism powers. Although there were limits to this, as her contributions elsewhere in the group made clear (with some practices seen as excessive), she did express support for other intrusive security measures:

> I know, for example, things like DNA, you know, sort of collecting DNA data ... I wouldn't want, for example, to subscribe to that; I wouldn't want to give my DNA for that. I think that's far too personal. I think there's things ... chance of things going wrong are too high as well. It is too high a risk, whereas if there were laws about stopping and searching and so on, yes, there may be that one particular black guy who's a Rastafarian who gets stopped every ... but it still happens just to show that he's more likely to commit a crime than everybody else. And is it really that bad that he gets stopped ... fine, once a day? (London, Asian, Female)

Later in the same group, she continued to argue that sufficient safeguards were probably in place to protect individuals from the state's excesses. As she put it: 'I'd feel safer with some of those laws being there than not, actually, because ... to me, they come across to be fundamentally right and just' (London, Asian, Female). Thus again we can see a discursive terrain marked by a concern with the effectiveness of anti-terrorism measures with a (sometimes tacit) acceptance of their necessity.

Freedom and hostility to anti-terrorism

In contrast to those who discussed security in terms of survival and the physical protection of themselves, their lifestyle or loved ones, others thought about security in connection with freedom and liberty. As we shall see, these individuals tended to see anti-terrorism in quite different ways to those considered above. In one sense, this is perhaps intuitive; if security is conceptualised in terms of freedom, one would likely be less sympathetic to view measures which restrict liberty (no matter what the aim or rationale for these curtailments might be) in positive terms. However, the picture is a little more complex than this and, again, we emphasise that understandings of security inflect and frame attitudes to, and discussion of, anti-terrorism powers.

One of the strongest articulations of security as freedom came from an Asian male in London who – when asked what security means – stated:

> I equate it to freedom, really; to feeling that you can do what you want and be where you want within the confines of the law, without being ... without fear ... So, if it ever came to be that I was worried about my security, I think it would be that I'm afraid of something, and that, obviously, would impinge on my feeling of liberty. (London, Asian, Male)

Perhaps unsurprisingly, for this participant, anti-terrorism measures were viewed with scepticism, if not outright hostility:

> You need as a country to be clear on where you stand and what you believe in. and if you believe in ... liberty of the individual, you believe in fundamental human rights ... all of these things can be defended ... And something like this [twenty-eight-day pre charge detention] flies completely in the face of, you know, one of the fundamental tenets of being innocent ... until you are proven guilty. (London, Asian, Male)

Similar points were made regarding stop and search powers, as he put it: 'The fact that ... if we do walk around in London or drive a car in London, we can be stopped without reason ... I think is too much of an infringement on our civil liberties' (London, Asian, Male). Later in the conversation, this person also expressed concern at the lack of due process in the control orders system as 'insane', summing up his position by saying: 'I think these things on a different scale are our "Guantanamos"; you can quote me on that' (London, Asian, Male).

There are several points of interest here, but the first is that his objections to anti-terrorism powers are based on concerns of principle. There is – in contrast to some of the sceptical views from those who viewed security in terms of survival – little sense here that these measures could ever gain this person's support. This is not because they might not be effective, or because we lack the requisite understanding to evaluate their legitimacy. For this person, such restrictions on liberty are de facto unacceptable. Given that his conception of security is organised around freedom, we can reasonably infer that, for him, anti-terrorism measures themselves are a threat to security; perhaps a greater one than that posed by terrorism. Indeed, as he argued when discussing the twenty-eight-day pre-charge detention period: 'Does that lead to greater security? No. I don't think it does ... It leads to a personal sense of insecurity' (London, Asian, Male).

A similar outright hostility to anti-terrorism measures was seen amongst many others in our research who described security in similar terms. Yet, this was not total and we also found some level of support for anti-terrorism restrictions amongst individuals with this understanding. In one focus group, for instance, a discussion about work/life balance by one participant was summarised in the following way by another:

> A: I was just wondering whether the security is a little bit about how we have ... feel about having the freedom to choose how we live, a little bit? I don't know, and to be able to trust?
>
> B: Yes, I think that's a very good ... That's articulated it very well for me. (Oxford, White, Females)

Importantly, this shared understanding of security 'worked' into attitudes about anti-terrorism in quite different ways for these two participants. For one, terrorism existed as a real threat out there, in that 'there has to be some measures' (Oxford, White, Female) with which to confront it. When discussing stop and search powers, moreover, she also expressed direct support for a measure widely seen by others to limit freedoms:

> We need something like this, don't we? I mean, the power to stop and search, I think, in some ways ... that doesn't bother me in some ways ... personally, I won't care being stopped as ... well, I have nothing to hide, it wouldn't affect me that much. (Oxford, White, Female)

In this instance, the framing of security in terms of freedom serves to support anti-terrorism powers as terrorism is understood as a real threat ('But there are people out there, aren't there?'). In such a context, terrorism may be viewed as the greater threat to freedom, leading to a countenancing of more stringent measures, especially if these are expected to befall others rather than the self. It is noteworthy, in this context, that when challenged about her support for stop and search, the participant responded by saying: 'Well, I think, if you're being stopped over and over again, that's a slightly different thing' (Oxford, White, Female). Thus, when faced with the possibility of direct, repeated experience of such powers, her support for them dwindles somewhat. In this sense, the security-as-freedom frame works to legitimise measures which enhance freedom from terrorism at the expense of others' liberties; yet, when one's own liberties appear threatened, this support appears less solid.

By contrast, the other individual in the above exchange expresses a stronger (perhaps less utilitarian) objection to anti-terrorism measures. For her, anti-terrorism measures which purport to enhance security (through, in part, restricting some liberties) actually function to increase insecurity, as they curtail freedoms:

> I feel very much about these measures ... that I ... am securing myself in, as a prisoner, and ... I'm securing myself away from the world. And I don't want that, I want to be part of the community. I want to be open. I want to be social. And what this, these kinds of anti-terrorism measures make me feel; I don't know how effective they are at preventing terrorism. I doubt that they are. All that they do is that they make me feel this, you know, this closed borders thing, and I think it breeds that sense of insecurity. It breeds this disconnected citizenship, or whatever. It just makes me feel it's a very negative way to go about improving our environment. (Oxford, White, Female)

Thus, in a similar vein to the Asian male above, security measures do not here enhance security, primarily because they entail a diminishment of liberty and freedom. It is interesting that the effectiveness or otherwise of the measures is noted and questioned, but this seems not to be the prime source of scepticism. Rather it is the closing off of self from other, and the restrictions on social life this entails, which undermine a sense of security and fuel her opposition. This objection to anti-terrorism on the grounds of liberty's violations is clearly stated: 'Some of these go against the whole point of living in a democracy ... Some of these powers remove that freedom of individuals, and it restricts the democracy we live in' (Oxford, White, Female).

A commitment to freedom as the basis for security, for this individual, means that one must accept that certain risks exist. Put otherwise, there is a sense that this respondent would rather tolerate the risk of physical harm than accept an existence overly trammelled by restrictions on liberty.

> You accept that there are certain consequences to freedom, and there are certain negative consequences of having freedom, in that there will be nutters out there that will cause terror. And you can choose to be affected by this, and you can choose to have draconian measures that restrict everybody's freedom and lives; or you can accept that that's part of life and not let them terrorise you and get on with life, and ignore it. (Oxford, White, Female)

This is a particularly explicit example of how understanding security as liberty influences thinking about anti-terrorism and, indeed, other security issues. For this individual, rather than the usual trade-off in which some liberty is exchanged for enhanced security, security (in terms of restrictive practices) should here be curtailed for a greater sense of security (understood as freedom). Also striking is the difference between this framing of anti-terrorism and that presented in the preceding section, where the point of debate seemed to be whether anti-terrorism measures were effective or not in preventing terrorism. For this individual, such concerns, whilst not irrelevant, are far from uppermost in her evaluation of public policy.

However, it should be noted that, aside from these instances where we can see how discourses of security frame anti-terrorism attitudes, there are some cases that do not fit neatly into this pattern. For example, one individual stated, 'I think liberty and freedom is an essential component of actually feeling secure' (London, Asian, Male). Yet, when discussing anti-terrorism measures, he was also reasonably content to accept restrictions on such freedoms. When discussing how the security services operate, for instance, he argued:

> I mean, on one issue, maybe it is necessary for them to do this. It is probably ... they can argue, the security services can argue this point with the justification that for the security of the country it is necessary that we employ tactics such as going into mosques etc., using informants, you know. You can't disagree with it much. (London, Asian, Male)

Of particular interest here is that, when discussing 'the security of the country', this person seems to be operating with a different understanding of security to that expressed earlier in the group. For him, it seems, 'feeling secure' may involve liberty and freedom, as can be seen in a statement discussed earlier in the book:

> I'm quite wary about an attack on my freedom or individual liberty, in the sense that I might walk down the street one minute, a black van might just come and I am taken away, whisked away by MI5 or MI6 ... I have to sort of [limit] what I say because of the possible repercussions. (London, Asian, Male)

In this context, it might be that two or more discourses of security exert rather different, and perhaps incoherent or incompatible, effects on framings and attitudes in this policy arena.

Belonging and community concerns about anti-terrorism

A final conjunction of security and anti-terrorism powers that came through in our research concerned conceptions of security in terms of belonging. Quite different to those based around physical survival and freedom, this is one which conceives of security as a product of living within and contributing to a (functioning) community. What we shall see is that whilst survival-based approaches to security shape an understanding of anti-terrorism powers which focuses on the effectiveness or necessity thereof, and vernacular understandings of security in terms of freedom lead to discussion around the impact on civil and other liberties, those who view security as communal belonging focus on the impact of anti-terrorism powers on communities and the individuals therein. One example, discussed in Chapter 5, was from an Asian female living in Oldham:

> Security is like... I would really like to belong somewhere, you know, like my house or my town or my country and be accepted and that sort of thing. I don't feel ... I've been here for forty years. I wasn't born here but I was very small when I came here, and I'm still a foreigner, I'm still an alien and my children are going to be treated like that as well ... I don't have the security of belonging, you know, like I'm not ... like, I look at white people and hardly anybody totally accepts me. (Oldham, Asian, Female)

For this person, security involves acceptance of her place within a community or collectivity that extends beyond her immediate family and friends, an acceptance which would serve to confer a sense of permanence and belonging. It is interesting, therefore, to see that her attitude towards anti-terrorism measures also concern communal belonging. When discussing the merits or otherwise of a twenty-eight-day pre-charge detention period, her scepticism stemmed not from a view of rights being violated (although this may be a supporting consideration), or from questions about the necessity of such a measure, but rather on the impact such an arrest would have on an individual's relationship with, and standing within, their community: 'What happens to somebody who gets arrested, put into jail and after twenty-eight days, no evidence, he comes out? He's probably lost his job and everything and not many people are going to trust him after that' (Oldham, Asian, Female).

The concern here is with whether personal experience of anti-terrorism powers – justified or otherwise – would lead to an individual's ostracism from the community. This was reiterated when she talked about a personal experience with anti-terrorism measures later in the group, namely a search at a UK airport: 'At the airport there were so many people, and the way they searched me was so humiliating, honestly. I really felt like I was hated and not wanted and everything and maybe I shouldn't have come back or something' (Oldham, Asian, Female). This experience is again not discussed primarily in terms of liberty violations. Rather, the concern here is how such an experience made her feel unwanted and disconnected, as well as the sense of social embarrassment/ostracism, making her feel that she does not belong: 'hated and not wanted'. The same person went on to talk in general terms about the impact of 9/11 and the various responses to it and, again, did so with a lament for the difficulties this event raised for fitting in to a wider social formation: 'But now suddenly, in the last ten years, because of those stupid men who bombed that building, it's ruined it for the rest of us Muslims. It has affected every single one of us. Our outlook and *the way other people look at us*' (Oldham, Asian, Female, emphasis added).

This influence of conceptions of security in terms of belonging can be seen from other participants too. Two individuals shared such an understanding, as demonstrated in the following exchange:

> A: To be safe, to be protected. And when I say, protection, it doesn't have to be state protection. It means having peaceful people around you and harmony, that when you have a community spirit, where everyone is living good and people are not suspicious of each other, you know, it's ... that's what it means, to feel safe.
>
> B: Yes, I agree. To feel safe, which also means to be relaxed in your environment. (London, Black, Females)

This exchange potentially blurs conceptions of security in terms of belonging, and conceptions of security in terms of survival. In so doing, it also demonstrates the fluidity of the vernacular constructions mentioned in Chapter 5. Nevertheless, what we have here is a slightly different understanding from the Asian female's above, who saw security as belonging to particular communities with a shared sense of identity. Here the emphasis is more upon *functioning* communities, which are 'relaxed' and where 'everyone is living good'. This sense of security links to anti-terrorism powers being debated in terms of their communal impacts. When discussing stop and search powers, there is a strong worry about their potential misuse: 'They have to be very careful about their misuse. They have to be very, very, very careful' (London, Black, Female). This discussion of effectiveness implies a view that the measures may be justified; indeed, this is stated clearly by the other participant in this dialogue, who then goes on to emphasise the importance of paying attention to the social aspects and impacts of policymaking in this area: 'Some of this legislation ... they are necessary. However, we have to have a campaign. Legislation on its own doesn't work. You have to have a *social* campaign' (London, Black, Female). Thus it is interesting to note the way in which anti-terrorism measures are evaluated in terms of community impact and the way in which the 'social' dimension is given prominence.

Other conceptions of security and anti-terrorism

In Chapter 5 we identified six different understandings of security encountered in our research. Thus far we have explored the relationship between three of these and associated views on anti-terrorism measures:

security as survival, freedom and belonging. As stated at the beginning of this chapter, we were limited in our sub-sample for this analysis to fifteen respondents who articulated clear positions on both security and anti-terrorism. This means, unfortunately, that we are unable to explore any relationship between security as equality and views of anti-terrorism powers, and the sub-sample contained only one respondent for security as hospitality and oppression. We report these here, but make due note that these are based on single cases alone.

One individual stated that security for her was something that referred to society's treatment of its least advantaged members: 'I guess it's how does society look after the vulnerable people, what happens to the elderly people, people without families to care for them, what happens to people with learning difficulties, how are those people looked after by the society?' (London, White, Female). This understanding of security is perhaps similar to some of those expressed earlier, which we grouped into the security as survival sub-group. We class this slightly differently as the emphasis here is not upon an individual's own material well-being, rather on how others are treated and cared for.

This participant later expressed her disagreement with 'pretty much all' of the anti-terrorism measures with which we presented the groups. Furthermore, in a discussion about whether her own freedom, individually, was threatened by anti-terrorism measures, she stated that it was not, arguing that it was '*our* liberty in the sense that we care about the wider society ... and whether they're treated well' (London, White, Female, our emphasis). This concern for the liberties of the wider society, rather than the personal, individual impacts of anti-terrorism powers reflects and is mirrored by this individual's conception of security in terms of social provision. There is clearly a connection here between a view of security which focuses on 'vulnerable people' and a concern about how anti-terrorism impacts upon how people are treated.

A final concatenation of security and anti-terrorism came from one participant who articulated a view of security oriented on its potential to create insecurity or even oppression for others. For her, security was seen as something which involved separating out, ring-fencing and excluding seemingly identifiable minorities:

> [T]here's this problem where you are securing the majority of the population, the majority of the white population, from this minority Muslim population that you have to regard with suspicion for your own safety. And for security for us, you think about it in our ways, it's us and them, not in a deliberate way but as a way of saying these people have to be in a bubble because everything about you is threatening, so we have to have security for us. It's

> not so much as we're securing you because you are part of the indigenous population, but because you are apart from it and you are the threat to it ... And it's just this idea that you're securing something and you're locking us out. You're secure in something and you're locking us out and you're putting us in this little section that is the danger, that needs to be secured from. (Oldham, Asian, Female)

This view of security in terms of oppression, with its distinction between the threatened self and threatening other, links, for this person, to a negative and discriminatory view of anti-terrorism. This individual had been stopped and searched; she stated that she felt 'like a rabbit in the headlights' (Oldham, Asian, Female), while expressing her resignation that this was a frequent occurrence, living where she does, such that she had to 'roll with the punches'. She also, moreover, articulated a strong sense of her powerlessness in the face of such processes:

> [I]t almost seems that they don't need a justification because of 9/11; there is no need for justification and you have to accept that these control measures are for your own good. And to question them questions your loyalty to this country, which I find, you know, you should be allowed to question your government and any measures that they bring out, especially if it affects you directly. But to do so means, you know, you're then regarded with some suspicion. (Oldham, Asian, Female)

Here there is a mirroring of the framing of security above, in which emerges a sense that anti-terrorism measures are being used by one section of the population against another to protect the former. She also, moreover, expresses her concern that such measures will make social cohesion more difficult and, as a consequence, produce cyclical dynamics: 'it's like a cycle of suspicion and fear and it just keeps going round in a circular motion' (Oldham, Asian, Female).

In this instance, as – we would argue – in the ones assessed throughout the chapter, the relationship between vernacular securities and evaluations of anti-terrorism powers is not a causal one. Within the different understandings of security, different positions on anti-terrorism have been noted. Some, for example, who thought of security in terms of freedom, were more persuaded of the necessity of anti-terrorism measures (perhaps to ensure their freedom). Similarly, individuals who thought of security as communal belonging had different positions on the appropriateness of the measures. But what is common between individuals who think of security in terms of either physical protection, freedom, communal belonging and hospitality and oppression is the topography of the linguistic terrain on which their arguments and attitudes sit. This, we argue, is the relationship between understandings of security and conceptions of anti-terrorism powers; how people conceive of security shapes the ways in which they frame anti-terrorism.

Conclusion

In sum, what we have identified here is a connection between how citizens think about and understand security, on the one hand. And, on the other, how anti-terrorism powers are thought about and discussed. While seeking to make no causal claims, our research points – at a very broad level – to some evidence of a link between discourses of security and attitudes towards anti-terrorism powers. Those who see security in terms of survival and physical protection tended, in our study, to discuss anti-terrorism in a more positive light. Our respondents here were by no means wholly supportive of anti-terrorism, but there was a frequent underlying acceptance that such measures might be necessary, and indeed might be justified (often), as long as certain criteria – such as effectiveness – could be satisfied. For those who thought of security in terms of freedom, such an attitude was considerably rarer. More common was a sense that anti-terrorism measures violated fundamental principles. Similarly, those who conceived of security in terms of community expressed a (sometimes qualified) scepticism about anti-terrorism measures, as did those who thought about security in terms of hospitality and oppression. But our non-experimental research design does not permit anything more than these general observations.

We do, however, argue that a stronger connection seems to exist in terms of how conceptions or constructions of security *frame* the issue of anti-terrorism (and this is something about which experimental methods might have rather less to say). Whilst vernacular constructions of security do not always correlate to the same attitude pattern, what is more common is the introduction and deployment of common frames, language and themes. Thus, for those who think about security in terms of physical protection, a key concern emerges over effectiveness: whether anti-terrorism is effective or not seems to be the key criterion by which one adjudicates it. For conceptions of security oriented around freedom, the issue becomes rights and liberties and the extent to which these are violated/protected. For belonging, the key discursive theme is the broader social impact they have, a concern with how anti-terrorism affects relationships between and within communities (however constructed). Related to this, where security was thought of in terms of hospitality and care, the frame was one of impact on the vulnerable. Finally, for security understood in terms of oppression, the language was marked by a sense of division between those to be secured and the threatening who were rendered without voice.

This, we argue, demonstrates the merit sketched above in paying further attention to the ways in which 'thick signifiers' such as security operate in organising and structuring social formations and relations. In a narrow sense, doing so contributes to an enhanced understanding of differing attitudes to and conceptions of (here, anti-terrorism) policy. In a broader sense, it contributes to those arguments and debates concerning the active role that security plays in the construction, regulation and determination of social and political life. It contributes, in other words, to a wider view of the role and function of security, illuminating 'security as a site of competing discourses or images of politics' (McDonald 2008: 575).

Conclusion

At the book's outset, we identified four research questions underpinning our exploration of anti-terrorism powers, citizenship and security in the United Kingdom. First, how are contemporary anti-terrorism powers understood, assessed and discussed by different publics across the UK? Second, how do anti-terrorism powers affect the experience of citizenship within the UK? Third, how do anti-terrorism powers impact on security in the UK? And, fourth, how do claims about citizenship and security connect to evaluations of anti-terrorism powers? We conclude our discussion here by revisiting our findings in relation to these questions, before reflecting on the broader significance of our work.

To begin with public attempts to make sense of anti-terrorism powers, the picture that emerges from our research is – obviously – a mixed one. At the most basic level, we encountered considerable scepticism towards such powers and their usage, albeit with varying reasons provided to us for this. Several of the participants in our focus groups suggested that efforts to address the terrorist threat potentially generated rather than reduced insecurity amongst the public or elements therein. As we saw in Chapters 3 and 4, many pointed to the measures' perceived targeting of specific (minority) communities, especially those already marginalised or disadvantaged within British life. Considerable question marks, therefore, seem to exist in the public eye around the capacity of contemporary powers to prevent future terrorist attacks or to address the root causes thereof. Especially sceptical publics, indeed, viewed such powers as little more than a performative, theatrical exercise purporting to demonstrate that something was being done in this context. Perhaps more troubling still, however, were anxieties about the civil liberty implications of anti-terrorism mechanisms in general, and of specific elements therein such as Section 44 stop and search powers, as well as concerns that such powers might be misused by police officers or others with pre-existing prejudices.

A couple of points might be made about these concerns. In the first instance, public efforts to make sense of the politics of anti-terrorism mobilise quite different logics and evidence. Personal experiences figured prominently in our focus groups, whether vicariously – as in the friend who owned five mobile telephones, thereby debunking terrorist warning campaigns – or directly – as in the case of the confiscation of a sewing kit when one of our participants was boarding a plane. The nature of these experiences, in these discussions, varied, of course. Some (including the above) were discrete events, such as the husband being surrounded by anti-terrorism police at London's Heathrow Airport. Others related to more generalised and often less tangible impressions of feeling constantly under surveillance by the state, its apparatuses or fellow citizens. Anecdotes, however, were not the only discursive resource turned to in these discussions. In other cases, people debated anti-terrorism powers by appealing to statistical evidence – '96% [of Muslims] are peace-loving' (London, Asian, Male) – by referencing historical cases such as the campaign against the IRA, or by invoking philosophical or normative principles, including in relation to democracy and civil rights.[1]

That publics employ different types of discursive or argumentative strategy in their evaluations of anti-terrorism powers is, perhaps, not surprising. As Atkins and Finlayson (2013: 162–163) note in a discussion of the use of rhetoric by political leaders, there is considerable diversity in 'The proofs actors bring forward in justifying claims and giving reasons for others to share them'. Such proofs, they continue, 'include those that rest on the character of a speaker (or on the citation of an 'authority'), appeals to the emotions and quasi-logical attempts to reason from contested or uncertain premises'. This is important for our purposes for its highlighting that publics do not - and are not likely to - assess the necessity or legitimacy of anti-terrorism powers purely on the grounds of efficacy or cost. A whole host of social, political and moral criteria are brought into play in these evaluations. That this is so might be connected, in part, to our argument in Chapter 5 that very few people feel themselves directly at risk from terrorism itself. As such, it might be expected that worst-case scenarios and existential threats have limited currency within 'vernacular' discussions.

At the same time, we also saw in Chapter 5 that a number of people in our research did argue that terrorism continues to pose something of a threat to the UK more generally. This, in turn, might feed into the less sceptical voices surrounding anti-terrorism mechanisms we explored. As detailed in Chapter 3, these included a belief that the state has to do something to respond to national security challenges, concerns over the capacity of 'ordinary' citizens to evaluate anti-terrorism powers (not least given limited knowledge of actual, emergent or future threats) and public confidence that there exist sufficient safeguards, checks and balances to prevent, address, or provide redress for miscarriages of justice. The final of these arguments is particularly interesting, given how far it departs from the concerns we encountered over pre-charge detention in particular, and the fear that detainees under suspicion of terrorism would be tarnished and stigmatised by their targeting.

These findings offer a deeper, although narrower, flavour of the public mood in relation to anti-terrorism policy than that provided in much of the survey research conducted in this area and explored at the book's outset. They become, perhaps, more interesting still when we turn to the connections that exist between such attitudes and the experience of citizenship – our second research question. As argued in Chapter 4, our research again provides something of a mixed picture here. On the one hand, we encountered considerable public concern that the protections or entitlements of citizenship had been directly reduced by policy in this area. This, importantly, was not limited to perceptions that civil liberties had been curtailed (although this was discussed in a number of our focus groups). It also encompassed concerns about other aspects of citizenship, including the obligations owed to other citizens and the state, experiences of identifying as British, and one's ability to participate in public life and spaces. Such findings suggest that anti-terrorism measures may be exacerbating the pre-existing dynamics identified in Chapter 2, such as the erosion and instrumentalisation of citizenship and concerns around cohesion and integration (although these also form part of the context in which anti-terrorism/citizenship discussions occur).

Without diminishing the importance of these views, we also explored two broad exceptions to these claims about the withering away of citizenship and its benefits. The first related to those people who described themselves as distanced from anti-terrorism powers and their application. Here, the impact thereof was seen as something that was taking place 'far away' from one's own everyday life (and thereby one's citizenship) and (often) in relation to those potentially deserving of the state's attentions (because of their glorification of terrorism, for example). The second, and more interesting, exception related to those who – although feeling potentially targeted by the framing and use of such powers – drew upon claims about rights and duties typically associated with citizenship to resist them. Examples of this include the voicing of direct opposition to anti-terrorism powers, a refusal to self-identify as a 'target' or 'victim' and a continued engagement with (mainstream) political life within the UK. Thus, whilst anti-terrorism powers do impact on citizenship, they do not do so in homogeneous or uniform fashion, a point to which we return below.

On our third research question, the relationship between anti-terrorism powers and security is discussed across several of the preceding chapters. As we have seen, 'vernacular' conceptions of security are fundamental to evaluations of these powers, not least given that support for, or resistance to them is frequently discussed in connection to their impact on security. This relationship, however, is once more not straightforward. Just as specific anti-terrorism powers both increase and decrease public attachments to citizenship, so they appear to increase the security of some citizens who feel reassured by the presence of security professionals and technologies, while decreasing the security of others who feel disproportionately targeted by stop and search and the like. Part of this ambiguity is likely because – as we saw in Chapter 5 – publics understand and experience security in very different ways.

The anti-terrorism/security relationship, however, does not only work in one direction such that the former either augments or diminishes (experiences of) the later. As we attempted to demonstrate in Chapter 6, vernacular conceptions of security are themselves fundamental to the *framing* of anti-terrorism powers in public discussion. If security is thought – or spoken – about in terms of survival, it appears increasingly likely that anti-terrorism powers will be assessed in terms of their perceived efficacy or otherwise. Where security is conceptualised in relation to freedom, in contrast, measures designed to confront terrorist violence are more likely to be assessed for their impact on civil liberties. And those citizens with whom we spoke who discussed security in terms of belonging tended, in contrast again, to discuss policy in this area in relation to its impact on community relations and participation in public spaces.

This led us to highlight two points. First, we argued that security should not be considered as solely an end state, but a productive factor in social and political relations. Second, the productivity of security does not only reside within the discourses of political elites or other structurally privileged actors. Our findings suggest that conceptualisations of security have important implications for the (re)creation of subjectivities, attitudes and positions in relation to security practices and their 'everyday' ramifications. Individuals with different conceptions of security may think differently in terms of whether security policies, such as anti-terrorism, are effective or legitimate.

As we have attempted to stress throughout the book, our sample and our meta-theoretical commitments restrain us from making any causal claims about these relations. It is, for instance, possible that these connections are a product of various methodological decisions we made in our research design. One obvious risk here is that asking our research participants to discuss 'security' at the start of our focus groups might have shaped the grounds upon which anti-terrorism powers were subsequently evaluated. A participant who had already reflected on security's relation to freedom, for example, might have been more likely to invoke rights, liberties and freedoms in their evaluation of anti-terrorism initiatives than one who had come into such a discussion without that prior experience. It is difficult to assess the impact of this, or of other manifestations of the 'researcher effect' that might run through the preceding pages. That is why – as detailed in Chapter 2 – we approach our findings as particular to the contexts in which they were produced, rather than as untarnished or objective expressions of pre-exisiting attitudes, let alone UK public opinion more widely.

With this caveat in mind, our research does, however, raise the possibility of a far more complex set of relations between our three foci than is often considered. For – and here we are in the terrain of our fourth research question – although anti-terrorism powers seem to influence attachments to citizenship and perceptions of security, conceptions of security and attachments to citizenship also seem to influence understandings of anti-terrorism powers. At the same time, faith in citizenship and the political system seems to influence public experiences of safety, at least in some areas, while willingness to articulate opposition to policies and to claim the benefits of citizenship are also apparently tied to perceptions of security. And, running through all of this, of course, are other dynamics, including awareness of and exposure to public policy. This book necessarily falls short of any definitive mapping of these connections. Our hope, however, is that it contributes to discussions thereof and to related debates within the academy and beyond. These include, as argued in earlier chapters, recent and important literatures on: the vernacular and (global) politics; the processes and logics through which security is constructed at different levels of the social; the decentring of the state in discussions of the politics of security; and arguments around the diminishment, inclusivity and demands associated with citizens and citizenship in liberal democratic states.

To return, finally, to themes raised in the discussion in Chapter 1 on the formulation of anti-terrorism policy in the UK, it is possible to argue that much existing work on terrorism and anti-terrorism powers has a distinctively problem-solving focus (see Gunning 2007; Jackson et al. 2011). Despite the diversity therein – and in spite of the sheer explosion of contemporary literature on this topic – much of it arguably remains dedicated to answering three questions (see Jarvis 2009a). First, what is terrorism, and how might it be distinguished from potentially related public policy problems? Second, what are the causes and drivers of terrorist campaigns and the 'radicalisation' of people therein? And, third, what might (or should) be done to prevent or respond to acts of terrorism and the threat that they pose?

This research agenda has obvious strengths, not least for those tasked with addressing the terrorist threat in the 'real world' of global politics. At the same time, it has arguably helped contribute to the lack of sustained efforts to theorise anti-terrorism policy itself: what it is, what it should or might be, and what it is for, for instance.[2] Whilst the urge to seek practical solutions is understandable, this book was (in part) motivated by a belief that academics have a responsibility to ask precisely these questions. Indeed, as we saw in Chapter 1, it is possible that a lack of debate about the purposes and consequences of anti-terrorism policy may be implicated in the frequent repetition of mistakes therein.

One way to address this – and that pursued in the preceding chapters – is via a recasting of anti-terrorism's referents. If we centre citizens within these discussions, it is possible to reflect differently and perhaps more fully on the consequences of anti-terrorism measures. This involves exploring the multiplicity and diversity of securit*ies* and citizenship*s* that exist within the UK today. Doing so helps conceptually to move discussion beyond the utilitarianism implicit in debates about a security/liberty trade-off that have, until recently, played too prominent a role in debate in this area. And, at the same time, to move beyond simple either/or analytical frameworks (does anti-terrorism policy increase security or insecurity; does it augment or reduce citizen rights, and so on), and towards more complex forms of engagement with these issues.

Further engagement with citizens' views on security and citizenship also, we argue, poses significant policy relevance. Efforts to enhance public security, in recent years, have been characterised by two trends within states such as the UK. On the one hand, there has emerged a specific focus on augmenting and expanding public *perceptions* of security; evident, for example, with the inclusion of public fear in measurements of police efficacy. On the other, there has been an increasing reliance on public participation in the provision of security itself (Vaughan-Williams 2008; Koskela 2010) – one that is justified by claims of the emergence of new unpredictable threats and associated demands for new and more active forms of participatory citizenship (Jarvis and Lister 2010). Against these two trends, qualitative research into public understandings of security, citizenship and other values facilitates assessment, in the first instance, of the potential successes of efforts to enhance public experiences of security. And, secondly, of the likely responses to demands for participation in the provision of collective security.

Attempting to understand anti-terrorism and the form it has taken, without considering these larger processes is, we argue, limited and unnecessarily restrictively focused on policy refinement. We therefore suggest that any understanding of anti-terrorism needs to shift from a straightforward consideration of 'how to respond', to include analysis of what anti-terrorism does, in as wide and as detailed a framework as possible. This includes exploring the changing contexts of security provision, as well as foregrounding public views and experiences of the impacts of such changes. Not only upon the vertical relationship between citizen and state, but also upon the horizontal relationships between citizens, and between communities. This book represents a first attempt to contribute to such explorations.

Notes

1 Elsewhere (Jarvis and Lister 2015b) we have also written about the extent to which publics draw on discursive resources such as fictional or news media in their 'everyday' knowledge of anti-terrorism.

2 There are, however, a number of useful overviews outlining either strategies of anti-terrorism (for example, Crelinsten 2009; Jackson et al. 2011: 222–248) or the diverse ways in which terrorist campaigns end (Cronin 2009).

Appendix A

Focus group topic guide

Preliminaries

Introduction

Very general introduction from all group participants (name, where from)

Security/safety

What kinds of threats do people in this country face?
What are the main issues/threats to your safety and security?
In what ways do you think threats to safety and security have changed, if any?
[approximately 15 minutes]

What does security mean to you?
National or individual?
Objective or subjective?
Individual (only) or linked to others (connected) *[prompts]*
[approximately 10 minutes]

Who do you think is responsible for security and safety?
Who provides security/safety?
How effective is the government in providing safety/security? *[prompts]*

Introduce prompt card including anti-terrorism warning poster

There have been some government attempts to encourage people to take responsibility for their own security. What do you think of these?
[approximately 10 minutes]

Anti-terrorism

Begin with prompt cards summarising recent UK counter-terrorism measures

What do you think about these measures?
Which of these measures do you support?
Which do you not support?
Why? *[prompts]*
Aware of all of these measures?
[approximately 15–20 minutes]

What is the effect of these measures on you, or those close to you, if any?
What do you think is the effect of these measures on your local community?
What do you think is the effect of these measures on the UK?
What is the effect of the these measures on the security or safety of:
    You and those close to you?
    Your local community?
    The UK?
[approximately 20 minutes]

If you were in government, what would you do about terrorism?
[approximately 10 minutes]

Appendix B

UK anti-terrorism measures

- Broadened definition of terrorism. Defined as action:
    - ‘designed to influence the government or an international governmental organisation or to intimidate the public or a section of the public, [where the] threat is made for the purpose of advancing a political, religious, racial or ideological cause’. (2000 and 2008 Acts)
- The power to stop and search a person or a vehicle without suspicion if the police are operating in a designated area under special authorisation [Greater London has been a designated area since 2001]. (2000 Act)
- Indefinite detention of foreign nationals suspected of terrorism without charge or trial [repealed and replaced with control orders]. (2001 Act)
- Control orders: Citizens and foreign nationals subject to house arrest and restrictions on movement, association and communications. (2005 Act)
    - Control order proceedings held in closed session with security-cleared ‘special advocates’ acting for accused. Lawyer and defendant have no right to see evidence against them.
- An offence to directly or indirectly incite or encourage terrorism, or to glorify terrorism. (2006 Act)
- Pre-charge detention of up to twenty-eight days for terrorism suspects. (2006 Act)

Bibliography

6, P., Fletcher-Morgan, C. and Leyland, K. (2010) 'Making People More Responsible: The Blair Governments' Programme for Changing Citizens' Behaviour', *Political Studies* 58(3): 427–449.

Adams, J. H. (2010) 'The Negotiated Hibernian: Discourse on the Fenian in England and America', *American Nineteenth Century History* 11(1): 47–77.

Alexander, Y. (ed.) (2002) *Combating Terrorism: Strategies of Ten Countries*. Ann Arbor, MI: University of Michigan Press.

Ali, N. (2015) 'Mapping the Muslim Community: Attending to the Practices of Counter-Radicalisation in the UK', in C. Baker-Beall, C. Heath-Kelly and L. Jarvis (eds.) *Counter-Radicalisation: Critical Perspectives*. Abingdon: Routledge, pp. 139–155.

Alonso, R. (2008) 'The Evolution of the Terrorist Threat in Spain', in B. Bowden and M. T. Davies (eds.) *Terror: From Tyrannicide to Terrorism in Europe*. Abingdon: Routledge, pp. 200–221.

Amoore, L. (2006) 'Biometric Borders: Governing Mobilities in the War on Terror', *Political Geography* 25(3): 336–351.

Amoore, L. (2007) 'Vigilant Visualities: The Watchful Politics of the War on Terror', *Security Dialogue* 38(2): 215–232.

Amoore, L. and de Goede, M. (2005) 'Governance, Risk and Dataveillance in the War on Terror', *Crime, Law and Social Change* 43(2–3): 149–173.

Andersen, J. (2007) 'Solidarity or Competition: Creating the European Knowledge Society', in L. Magnusson and B. Strath (eds.) *European Solidarities: Tensions and Contentions of a Concept*. Brussels: Peter Lang, pp. 293–311.

Anderson, D. (2013) *Terrorism Prevention and Investigation Measures in 2012 First Report of the Independent Reviewer on the Operation of the Terrorism Prevention And Investigation Measures Act 2011*. London: Stationery Office. Available online at https://terrorismlegislationreviewer.independent.gov.uk/wp-content/uploads/2013/04/first-report-tpims.pdf (last accessed 24 February 2015).

Anthias, F. (2002) 'Where Do I Belong? Narrating Collective Identity and Translocational Positionality', *Ethnicities* 2(4): 491–514.

Apuzzo, M. and Goldstein, J. (2014) 'New York Drops Unit that Spied on Muslims', *New York Times*. Available online at www.nytimes.com/2014/04/16/nyregion/police-unit-that-spied-on-muslims-is-disbanded.html?_r=1 (last accessed 4 November 2014).

Aradau, C. and van Munster, R. (2008) 'Taming the Future: The Dispositif of Risk in the War on Terror', in L. Amoore and M. de Goede (eds.) *Risk and the War on Terror*. Abingdon: Routledge, pp. 23–40.

Art, R. J. and Richardson, L. (eds.) (2007) *Democracy and Counterterrorism: Lessons from the Past*. Washington, DC: United States Institute of Peace Press.

Atkins, J. and Finlayson, A. (2013) '"... A 40-Year-Old Black Man Made the Point to Me": Everyday Knowledge and the Performance of Leadership in Contemporary British Politics', *Political Studies* 61(1): 161–177.

Badey, T. J. (1998) 'Defining International Terrorism: A Pragmatic Approach', *Terrorism and Political Violence* 10(1): 90–107.

Baker-Beall, C., Heath-Kelly, C. and Jarvis, L. (eds.) (2015) *Counter-Radicalisation: Critical Perspectives*. Abingdon: Routledge.

Baldwin, D. A. (1997) 'The Concept of Security', *Review of International Studies* 23(1): 5–26.

Balzacq, T. (2005) 'The Three Faces of Securitization: Political Agency, Audience and Context', *European Journal of International Relations* 11(2): 171–201.

Balzacq, T. (2011) 'A Theory of Securitization: Origins, Core Assumptions and Variants', in T. Balzacq (ed.) *Securitization Theory: How Security Problems Emerge and Dissolve*. Abingdon: Routledge, pp. 1–31.

Banks, W. C. (2005) 'United States Responses to September 11', in V. Ramraj, M. Y. M. Yew and K. Roach (eds.) *Global Counter-Terrorism Law and Policy*. Cambridge: Cambridge University Press, pp. 490–510.

Barkawi, T. and Laffey, M. (2006) 'The Postcolonial Moment in Security Studies', *Review of International Studies* 32(2): 329–352.

Barnett, J. (2001) *The Meaning of Environmental Security: Ecological Politics and Policy in the New Security Era*. London: Zed.

Barnett, N. (2003) 'Local Government, New Labour and "Active Welfare": A Case of "Self Responsibilisation"?', *Public Policy and Administration* 18(3): 25–38.

Barrenechea, L. (2009) *El respeto a los derechos humanos en la lucha contra el terrorismo en España*. Madrid: Fundación para las Relaciones Internacionales y el Diálogo Exterior (FRIDE).

BBC News (2008) 'Does England Have House Arrest?', BBC News. Available online at http://news.bbc.co.uk/1/hi/magazine/7460736.stm (last accessed 4 November 2014).

Belfrage, C. (2008) 'Towards "Universal Financialisation" in Sweden?', *Contemporary Politics*, 14(3): 277–296.

Bell, D. (2009) 'Introduction: Under an Empty Sky – Realism and Political Theory', in D. Bell (ed.) *Political Thought and International Relations: Variations on a Realist Theme*. Oxford: Oxford University Press, pp. 1–25.

Bellamy, A. J. and McDonald, M. (2002) '"The Utility of Human Security": Which Humans? What Security? A Reply to Thomas & Tow', *Security Dialogue* 33(3): 373–377.

Benford, R. D. and Snow, D. A. (2000) 'Framing Processes and Social Movements: An Overview and Assessment', *Annual Review of Sociology* 26(1): 611–639.

Bianchi, A. (2006) 'Assessing the Effectiveness of the UN Security Council's Counter-Terrorism Measures: The Quest for Legitimacy and Cohesion', *European Journal of International Law* 17(5): 881–919.

Biesecker, B. (2007) 'No Time for Mourning: The Rhetorical Production of the Melancholic Citizen-Subject in the War on Terror', *Philosophy and Rhetoric* 40(1): 147–169.

Bigo, D. (2002) 'Reassuring and Protecting: Internal Security Implications of French Participation in the Coalition against Terrorism', in E. Hershberg and K. W. Moore (eds.) *Critical Views of September 11*. New York, NY: New Press, pp. 72–94.

Bigo, D. (2013) 'International Political Sociology', in P. Williams (ed.) *Security Studies: An Introduction* (2nd edition). Abingdon: Routledge, pp. 120–133.

Bilgin, P. (2010) 'The "Western-Centrism" of Security Studies', *Security Dialogue* 41(6): 615–622.

Blair, T. (2001) 'Speech by Prime Minister Tony Blair at the Labour Party Conference', 2 October 2001. Available online at www.guardian.co.uk/politics/2001/oct/02/labourconference.labour6 (last accessed 4 November 2013).

Blair, T. (2010) *A Journey*. London: Hutchinson.

Blakeley, R. (2007) 'Bringing the State Back Into Terrorism Studies', *European Political Science* 6(3): 228–235.

Blakeley, R. (2009) *State Terrorism and Neoliberalism: The North in the South*. Abingdon: Routledge.

Blumer, H. (1969) *Symbolic Interactionism: Perspective and Method*. Englewood Cliffs, NJ: Prentice.

Blunkett, D. (2004) 'Defending the Democratic State and Maintaining Liberty – Two Sides of the Same Coin?' Available online at http://webarchive.nationalarchives.gov.uk/20130128103514/http://www.homeoffice.gov.uk/docs3/hs_speech_harvard04.html (last accessed 4 November 2014).

Bobbit, P. (2008) *Terror and Consent: The Wars for the Twenty-First Century*. New York, NY: Alfred A. Knopf.

Bolanos, A. (2013) 'The "New Terrorism" or the "Newness" of Context and Change', in R. Jackson and S. J. Sinclair (eds.) *Contemporary Debates on Terrorism*. Abingdon: Routledge, pp. 29–34.

Bonner, D. (1992) 'United Kingdom: The United Kingdom Response to Terrorism', *Terrorism and Political Violence* 4(4): 171–205.

Booth, K. (1991) 'Security and Emancipation', *Review of International Studies* 17(4): 313–326.

Booth, K. (2005) 'Introduction to Part 1', in K. Booth (ed.) *Critical Security Studies and World Politics*. London: Lynne Rienner, pp. 21–25.

Booth, K. (2007) *Theory of World Security*. Cambridge: Cambridge University Press.

Boukalas, C. (2014) 'No Exceptions: Authoritarian Statism, Agamben, Poulantzas and Homeland Security', *Critical Studies on Terrorism* 7(1): 112–130.

Bourne, M. (2014) *Understanding Security*. Basingstoke: Palgrave.

Breen Smyth, M. (2009) 'Subjectivities, "Suspect Communities", Governments, and the Ethics of Research on "Terrorism"', in R. Jackson, M. Breen Smyth and J. Gunning (eds.) *Critical Terrorism Studies: A New Research Agenda*. Abingdon: Routledge, pp. 194–215.

Browning, C. S. and McDonald, M. (2013) 'The Future of Critical Security Studies: Ethics and the Politics of Security', *European Journal of International Relations* 19(2): 235–255.

Bubandt, N. (2005) 'Vernacular Security: The Politics of Feeling Safe in Global, National and Local Worlds', *Security Dialogue* 36(3): 275–296.

Burnett, J. and Whyte, D. (2005) 'Embedded Expertise and the New Terrorism', *Journal for Crime, Conflict and the Media* 1(4): 1–18.

Butler, J. (1991) 'Imitation and Gender Insubordination', in D. Fuss (ed.) *Inside/out: Lesbian Theories, Gay Theories*. Abingdon: Routledge, pp. 307–320.

Butler, J. (1993) *Bodies that Matter: On the Discursive Limits of 'Sex'*. Abingdon: Routledge.

Buzan, B. (1991) *People, States and Fear: An Agenda for International Security Studies in the Post-Cold War Era* (2nd edition). Boulder, CO: Lynne Rienner.

Buzan, B. and Hansen, L. (2009) *The Evolution of International Security Studies*. Cambridge: Cambridge University Press.

Buzan, B., Wæver, O. and de Wilde, J. (1998) *Security: A New Framework for Analysis*. Boulder, CO. Lynne Rienner.

Cahill, S. (2010) 'Erving Goffman', in J. M. Charon (ed.) *Symbolic Interactionism: An Introduction, an Interpretation, an Integration* (10th edition). London: Pearson, pp. 164–181.

Cameron, D. (2011) 'PM's Speech at Munich Security Conference'. Available online at www.gov.uk/government/speeches/pms-speech-at-munich-security-conference (last accessed 4 November 2014).

Campbell, D. (1998) *Writing Security: United States Foreign Policy and the Politics of Identity* (revised edition). Manchester: Manchester University Press.

Cantle, T. (2001) *Community Cohesion: A Report of the Independent Review Team*. London: HMSO.

Capoccia, G. (2010) 'Germany's Response to 9/11: The Importance of Checks and Balances', in M. Crenshaw (ed.) *The Consequences of Counter Terrorism*. New York, NY: Russell Sage Foundation, pp. 285–334.

Chaliand, G. and Blin, A. (2007a) 'The Invention of Modern Terror', in G. Chaliand and A. Blin (eds.) *The History of Terrorism: From Antiquity to Al Qaeda*. Berkeley, CA: University of California Press, pp. 95–112.

Chaliand, G. and Blin, A. (2007b) 'Introduction', in G. Chaliand and A. Blin (eds.) *The History of Terrorism: From Antiquity to Al Qaeda*. Berkeley, CA: University of California Press, pp. 1–11.

Chomsky, N. (2002) 'Who Are the Global Terrorists?', in K. Booth and T. Dunne (eds.) *Worlds in Collision: Terror and the Future of Global Order*. Basingstoke: Palgrave, pp. 128–140.

Choudhury, T. and Fenwick, H. (2011) 'The Impact of Counter-Terrorism Measures on Muslim Communities', Equality and Human Rights Commission Research Report 72. Available online at www.equalityhumanrights.com/publication/research-report-72-impact-counter-terrorism-measures-muslim-community (last accessed 4 November 2014).

Clarke, J. (2005) 'New Labour's Citizens: Activated, Empowered, Responsibilized, Abandoned?', *Critical Social Policy* 25(4): 447–463.

Clutterbuck, L. (2004) 'The Progenitors of Terrorism: Russian Revolutionaries or Extreme Irish Republicans?', *Terrorism and Political Violence* 16(1): 154–181.

Clutterbuck, L. (2006) 'Countering Irish Republican Terrorism in Britain: Its Origin as a Police Function', *Terrorism and Political Violence* 18(1): 95–118.

Colás, A. (2010) 'An Exceptional Response? Security, Development and Civil Society in Spanish Policy after 11-M', *Development and Change* 41(2): 313–333.

Cole, D. (2003) 'The New McCarthyism: Repeating History in the War on Terrorism', *Harvard Civil Rights-Civil Liberties Law Review* 38(1): 1–30.

Cole, D. and Lobel, J. (2007) *Less Safe, Less Free: Why America is Losing the War on Terror*. New York, NY: New Press.

Collins, A. (ed.) (2013) *Contemporary Security Studies* (3rd edition). Oxford: Oxford University Press.

Crelinsten, R. (2009) *Counterterrorism*. Cambridge: Polity Press.

Crelinsten, R. (2014) 'Perspectives on Counterterrorism: From Stovepipes to a Comprehensive Approach', *Perspectives on Terrorism* 8(1): 1–15.

Croft, S. (2012) *Securitizing Islam: Identity and the Search for Security*. Cambridge: Cambridge University Press.

Cronin, A. K. (2009) *How Terrorism Ends: Understanding the Decline and Demise of Terrorist Campaigns*. Princeton, NJ: Princeton University Press.

Dannreuther, R. (2007) *International Security: The Contemporary Agenda*. Cambridge: Polity Press.

Davis, D. and Silver, B. (2004) 'Civil Liberties vs. Security: Public Opinion in the Context of the Terrorist Attacks on America', *American Journal of Political Science* 48(1): 28–46.

Delanty, G. (2000) *Citizenship in a Global Age: Society, Culture, Politics.* Buckingham: Open University Press.

Denzin, N. (1969) 'Symbolic Interactionism and Ethnomethodology: A Proposed Synthesis', *American Sociological Review* 34(6): 922–934.

Denzin, N. (2002) 'Much Ado about Goffman', *American Sociologist,* 33(2): 105–117.

Der Derian, J. (1998) 'The Value of Security: Hobbes, Marx, Nietzsche and Baudrillard', in R. D. Lipschutz (ed.) *On Security.* New York, NY: Columbia University Press, pp. 24–45.

Desforges, L., Jones, R. and Woods, M. (2005) 'New Geographies of Citizenship', *Citizenship Studies,* 9(5): 439–451.

Dillon, M. (2002) *Politics of Security: Towards a Political Philosophy of Continental Thought.* Abingdon: Routledge.

Dodd, V., Laville, S. and Pidd, H. (2014) 'Syria Crisis: Stop your Sons Joining War, Urges Met Police', Guardian Online. Available online at www.theguardian.com/uk-news/2014/apr/23/sons-war-syria-metropolitan-police (last accessed 4 November 2014).

Donohue, L. (2000) 'Civil Liberties, Terrorism, and Liberal Democracy: Lessons from the United Kingdom', Harvard University, USA. BCSIA Discussion Paper 2000–05, ESDP Discussion Paper ESDP-2000–01, John F. Kennedy School of Government, August 2000. Available online at http://belfercenter.ksg.harvard.edu/publication/2769/civil_liberties_terrorism_and_liberal_democracy.html (last accessed 4 November 2014).

Donohue, L. (2006) 'Emergency Powers and the Inception of the Northern State', in D. C. Rapoport (ed.) *Terrorism: Critical Concepts in Political Science II.* Abingdon: Routledge, pp. 278–318.

Donohue, L. (2007) 'Britain's Counterterrorism Policy', in D. Zimmermann and A. Wenger (eds.) *How States Fight Terrorism: Policy Dynamics in the West.* Boulder, CO: Lynne Reinner, pp. 17–58.

Donohue, L. (2008) *The Cost of Counterterrorism: Power, Politics and Liberty.* Cambridge: Cambridge University Press.

Doty, R. L. (1993) 'Foreign Policy as Social Construction: A Post-Positivist Analysis of US Counterinsurgency Policy in the Philippines', *International Studies Quarterly* 37(3): 297–320.

Dunn, K. (2006) 'Examining Historical Representations', *International Studies Review* 8(2): 370–381.

Duyvesteyn, I. (2004) 'How New is the New Terrorism?', *Studies in Conflict and Terrorism,* 27(5): 439–454.

Duyvesteyn, I. and Malkki, L. (2013) 'The Fallacy of the New Terrorism Thesis', in R. Jackson and S. J. Sinclair (eds.) *Contemporary Debates on Terrorism.* Abingdon: Routledge, pp. 35–42.

Eagleton, T. (2005) *Holy Terror.* Oxford: Oxford University Press.

Easson, J. and Schmid, A. (2013) 'Appendix 2.1: 250-Plus Academic, Governmental and Intergovernmental Definitions of Terrorism', in A. Schmid (ed.) *The Routledge Handbook of Terrorism Research*. Abingdon: Routledge, pp. 99–157.

Edkins, J. (1999) *Post-Structuralism and International Relations: Bringing the Political Back In*. London: Lynne Rienner.

English, R. (2009) *Terrorism: How to Respond*. Oxford: Oxford University Press.

Enloe (2001) *Bananas, Beaches and Bases: Making Feminist Sense of International Politics* (2nd edition). Berkeley, CA: University of California Press.

Etzioni. A. (2008) 'Toward a Progressive Approach to Homeland Protection', *Democracy and Security* 4(2): 170–189.

Falconer, C. (2006) 'Finding the Balance between Security and Liberty in the Modern World'. Available online at http://webarchive.nationalarchives.gov.uk/+/http://www.dca.gov.uk/speeches/2006/sp061003.htm (last accessed 4 November 2014).

Fekete, L. (2004) 'Anti-Muslim Racism and the European Security State', *Race and Class* 46(1): 3–29.

Fekete, L. (2006) 'Europe: "Speech Crime" and Deportation', *Race and Class* 47(3): 82–92.

Fenwick, H. (2002a) 'Responding to 11 September: Detention without Trial under the Anti–Terrorism, Crime and Security Act 2001', *Political Quarterly* 73(s1): 80–104.

Fenwick, H. (2002b) 'The Anti–Terrorism, Crime and Security Act 2001: A Proportionate Response to 11 September?', *Modern Law Review* 65(5): 724–762.

Finlayson, A. (2009). 'Financialisation, Financial Literacy and Asset-Based Welfare', *British Journal of Politics and International Relations* 11(3): 400–421.

Flick, U. (2009) *An Introduction to Qualitative Research* (4th edition). London: Sage.

Foley, F. (2013) *Countering Terrorism in Britain and France: Institutions, Norms and the Shadow of the Past*, Cambridge: Cambridge University Press.

FRIDE (Fundación para las Relaciones Internacionales y el Diálogo Exterior) (2008) 'Case Study Spain: The Ethical Justness of Counter-Terrorism Measures', Transnational Terrorism, Security and the Rule of Law, Working Paper 6. Available online at www.transnationalterrorism.eu/tekst/publications/Spain%20case%20study%20%28WP%206%20Del%2012b%29.pdf (last accessed 4 November 2014).

Fromkin, D. (1975) 'The Strategy of Terrorism', *Foreign Affairs* 53(4): 683–698.

Garland, D. (1996) 'The Limits of the Sovereign State: Strategies of Crime Control in Contemporary Society', *British Journal of Criminology* 36(4): 445–471.

Gearson, J. (2002) 'The Nature of Modern Terrorism', *Political Quarterly* 73(s1): 7–24.

Gearty, C. (1991) *Terror*. London: Faber and Faber.

Gearty, C. (2007) 'Terrorism and Human Rights', *Government and Opposition* 42(3): 340–362.

Gest, J. (2010) *Apart: Alienated and Engaged Muslims in the West*. London: C Hurst & Co.

Giddens, A. (1990) *The Consequences of Modernity*. Cambridge: Polity Press.

Gillespie, M. (2007) 'Security, Media and Multicultural Citizenship: A Collaborative Ethnography', *European Journal of Cultural Studies* 10(3): 275–293.

Gillespie, M. and O'Loughlin, B. (2009) 'Multilingual News Cultures and Cosmopolitan Citizenship', in P. Noxolo and J. Huysmans (eds.) *Community, Citizenship and the War on Terror: Security and Insecurity*. Basingstoke: Palgrave, pp. 89–112.

Gillespie, M., Gow, J., Hoskins, A., O'Loughlin, B. and Žveržhanovski, I. (2010) 'Shifting Securities: News Cultures, Multicultural Society and Legitimacy', *Ethnopolitics* 9(2): 239–253.

Gilroy, P. (1982) 'Police and Thieves', in Centre for Contemporary Cultural Studies (eds.) *The Empire Strikes Back: Race and Racism in 70s Britain*. Abingdon: Routledge, pp. 141–180.

Gilroy, P. (2012) '"My Britain is Fuck All" Zombie Multiculturalism and the Race Politics of Citizenship', *Identities: Global Studies in Culture and Power*, 19(4): 380–397.

Glasius, M. (2008) 'Human Security from Paradigm Shift to Operationalization: Job Description for a Human Security Worker', *Security Dialogue* 39(1): 31–54.

Goffman, E. (1990 [1956]) *The Presentation of Self in Everyday Life*. Harmondsworth: Penguin.

Goodin, R. E. (2006) *What's Wrong with Terrorism*. Cambridge: Polity Press.

Graeger, N. (1996) 'Environmental Security?', *Journal of Peace Research* 33(1): 109–116.

Gray, J. (2003) *Al Qaeda and What it Means to be Modern*. London: Faber and Faber.

Grayling, A. C. (2010) *Liberty in the Age of Terror: A Defence of Civil Liberties and Enlightenment Values*. London: Bloomsbury.

Greenwald, G. (2014) *No Place to Hide: Edward Snowden, the NSA and the Surveillance State*. London: Hamish Hamilton.

Grillo, R. (2007) 'An Excess of Alterity? Debating Difference in a Multicultural Society', *Ethnic and Racial Studies* 30(6): 979–998.

Guild, E., Bigo, D., Carrera, S. and Walker, R. B. J. (2007) 'The Changing Landscape of European Liberty and Security: Mid-Term Report on the Results of the CHALLENGE Project'. Centre for European Studies, Brussels. Available online at www.libertysecurity.org/article1357.html (last accessed 4 November 2014).

Guillaume, X. and Huysmans, J (2013a) 'Introduction: Citizenship and Security', in X. Guillaume and J. Huysmans (eds.) *Citizenship and Security: The Constitution of Political Being*. Abingdon: Routledge, pp. 1–17.

Guillaume, X. and Huysmans, J (eds.) (2013b) *Citizenship and Security: The Constitution of Political Being*. Abingdon: Routledge.

Guittet, E. P. (2008) 'Is Consensus A Genuine Democratic Value? The Case of Spain's Political Pacts against Terrorism', *Alternatives* 33(3): 267–291.

Gunning, J. (2007) 'A Case for Critical Terrorism Studies?' *Government and Opposition* 42(3): 363–393.

Gunning, J. and Jackson, R. (2011) 'What's so "Religious" about "Religious Terrorism"?', *Critical Studies on Terrorism* 4(3): 369–388.

Guzzini, S. (2000) 'A Reconstruction of Constructivism in International Relations', *European Journal of International Relations* 6(2): 147–182.

Guzzini, S. (2007) 'The Concept of Power: A Constructivist Analysis', in F. Berenskoetter and M. J. Williams (eds.) *Power in World Politics*. Abingdon: Routledge, pp. 23–42.

Guzzini, S. (2011) 'Securitization as a Causal Mechanism', *Security Dialogue* 42(4-5): 329–341.

Hall, P. A. (1993) 'Policy Paradigms, Social Learning, and the State: The Case of Economic Policymaking in Britain', *Comparative Politics* 25(3): 275–296.

Hall, S. (1997) 'Old and New Identities, Old and New Ethnicities', in A. D. King (ed.) *Culture, Globalization and the World System*. Minneapolis, MN: University of Minnesota Press, pp. 41–68.

Halliday, F. (2002) *Two Hours that Shook the World: September 11 2001: Causes and Consequences*. London: Saqi.

Hammersley, M. (2003) '"Analytics" are No Substitute for Methodology: A Response to Speer and Hutchby', *Sociology* 37(2): 339–351.

Hansard Society (2013) *Audit of Political Engagement 10: The 2013 Report*. London: Hansard Society.

Hansen L. (2000) 'The Little Mermaid's Silent Security Dilemma and the Absence of Gender in the Copenhagen School', *Millennium: Journal of International Studies* 29(2): 285–306.

Hansen, L. (2006) *Security as Practice: Discourse Analysis and the Bosnian War*. Abingdon: Routledge.

Haque, M. S. (2002) 'Government Responses to Terrorism: Critical Views of their Impacts on People and Public Administration', *Public Administration Review* 62(s1): 170–180.

Harmon, C. (2008) *Terrorism Today* (2nd edition). Abingdon: Routledge.

Hart, S. (2009) 'The "Problem" with Youth: Young People, Citizenship and the Community', *Citizenship Studies* 13(6): 641–657.

Haubrich, D. (2003) 'September 11, Anti-Terror Laws and Civil Liberties: Britain, France and Germany Compared', *Government and Opposition* 38(1): 3–28.

Haubrich, D. (2010) 'The Social Contract and the Three Types of Terrorism. Democratic Society in the United Kingdom after 9/11 and 7/7', in M. Crenshaw (ed.) *The Consequences of Counterterrorism*. New York, NY: Routledge, pp. 179–212.

Hay, C. (1997) 'State of the Art: Divided by a Common Language: Political Theory and the Concept of Power', *Politics* 17(1): 45–52.

Hay, C. (2002) *Political Analysis*. Basingstoke: Palgrave.

Hay, C. and Wincott, D. (1998) 'Structure, Agency and Historical Institutionalism', *Political Studies*, 46(5): 951–957.

Hay, J. (2006) 'Designing Homes to be the First Line of Defense: Safe Households, Mobilization, and the New Mobile Privatization', *Cultural Politics* 20(4–5): 349–377.

Heater, D. (1991) 'Citizenship: A Remarkable Case of Sudden Interest', *Parliamentary Affairs* 44(2): 140–156.

Heath, A. and Demireva, N. (2014) 'Has Multiculturalism Failed in Britain?' *Ethnic and Racial Studies* 37(1): 161–180.

Heath-Kelly, C. (2012) 'Reinventing Prevention or Exposing the Gap? False Positives in UK Terrorism Governance and the Quest for Pre-Emption', *Critical Studies on Terrorism* 5(1): 69–87.

Heath-Kelly, C. (2013) 'Counter-Terrorism and the Counterfactual: Producing the "Radicalisation" Discourse and the UK PREVENT Strategy', *British Journal of Politics and International Relations* 15(3): 394–415.

Heinz, W. S. (2007) 'Germany: State Responses to Terrorist Challenges and Human Rights', in A. Brysk and G. Shafir (eds.) *National Insecurity and Human Rights: Democracies Debate Counterterrorism*. Berkeley, CA: University of California Press, pp. 157–76.

Herring, E. and Stokes, D. (2011) 'Critical Realism and Historical Materialism as Resources for Critical Terrorism Studies', *Critical Studies on Terrorism* 4(1): 5–21.

Hewitt, S. (2008) *The British War on Terror: Terrorism and Counter-Terrorism on the Home Front since 9/11*. London: Continuum.

Hillyard, P. (1993) *Suspect Community: People's Experiences of the Prevention of Terrorism Acts in Britain*. London: Pluto.

Hillyard, P. (2005) 'The "War on Terror": Lessons from Ireland', European Civil Liberties Network. Available online at www.ecln.org/essays/essay-1.pdf (last accessed 4 November 2014).

HM Government (2004) 'Preparing for Emergencies: What you Need to Know'. Available online at www.direct.gov.uk/prod_consum_dg/groups/dg_digitalassets/@dg//@en/documents/digitalasset/dg_176618.pdf (last accessed 1 August 2013).

HM Government (2009) *CONTEST: The United Kingdom's Strategy for Countering Terrorism*. London: Home Office.

HM Government (2014) *CONTEST: The United Kingdom's Strategy for Countering Terrorism. Annual Report*. Available online at www.gov.uk/government/uploads/system/uploads/attachment_data/file/302155/CONTESTannualreport2013.pdf (last accessed 4 November 2014).

Hoffman, B. (2006) *Inside Terrorism*. New York, NY: Columbia University Press.

Hoffman, B. and Morrison-Taw, J. (2000) 'Governmental Policies: A Strategic Framework for Countering Terrorism', in F. Reinares (ed.) *European Democracies against Terrorism*. Aldershot: Ashgate, pp. 3–29.

Holland, J. (2010) 'Howard's War on Terror: A Conceivable, Communicable and Coercive Foreign Policy Discourse', *Australian Journal of Political Science* 45(4): 643–661.

Holland, J. (2012) 'Blair's War on Terror: Selling Intervention to Middle England', *British Journal of Politics and International Relations* 14(1): 74–95.

Holland, J. (2013) 'Foreign Policy and Political Possibility', *European Journal of International Relations* 19(1): 49–68.

Hollander, J. A. and Einwohner, R. L. (2004) 'Conceptualizing Resistance', *Sociological Forum* 19(4): 533–554.

Home Office (2011) *CONTEST: The United Kingdom's Strategy for Countering Terrorism*. London: Home Office.

Hooghe, L. and Marks, G. (2001), *Multi-Level Governance and European Integration*. Lanham, MD: Rowman and Littlefield.

Horne, G. and Berman, A. (2012) 'Pre-Charge Detention in Terrorism Cases', Commons Library Standard Note. Available online at www.parliament.uk/briefing-papers/SN05634 (last accessed 4 November 2014).

House of Commons (2005) *Home Affairs Committee: Terrorism and Community Relations*. Available online at www.publications.parliament.uk/pa/cm200405/cmselect/cmhaff/165/165.pdf (last accessed 4 November 2014).

Hubac-Occhipinti, O. (2006) 'Anarchist Terrorists of the Nineteenth Century', in G. Chaliand and A. Blin (eds.) *The History of Terrorism: From Antiquity to Al Qaeda*. Berkeley, CA: University of California Press, pp. 113–131.

Huddy, L., Feldman, S., Capelos, T. and Provost, C. (2002) 'The Consequences of Terrorism: Disentangling the Effects of Personal and National Threat', *Political Psychology* 23(3): 485–509.

Huddy, L., Feldman, S., Taber, C. and Lahav, G. (2005) 'Threat, Anxiety and Support of Antiterrorism Policies', *American Journal of Political Science* 49(3): 593–608.

Hull, S. (2013) 'Theresa May Sniggers through Nicky Campbell Interview on New Immigration Bill', *Huffington Post*, 10 October. Available online at www.huffingtonpost.co.uk/2013/10/10/theresa-may-nicky-campbell-immigration_n_4076039.html?utm_hp_ref=uk (last accessed 4 November 2014).

Human Rights Watch (2010) 'Without Suspicion'. Available online at www.hrw.org/reports/2010/07/05/without-suspicion (last accessed 4 November 2014).

Huq, A. Z. and Muller, C. (2008) 'The War on Crime as Precursor to the War on Terror', *International Journal of Law, Crime and Justice* 36(4): 215–229.

Huysmans, J. (1998) 'Security! What Do you Mean? From Concept to Thick Signifier', *European Journal of International Relations* 4(2): 226–255.

Huysmans, J. (2006) *The Politics of Insecurity: Fear, Migration and Asylum in the EU*. Abingdon: Routledge.

Hynek, N. and Chandler, D. (2013) 'No Emancipatory Alternative, No Critical Security Studies', *Critical Studies on Security* 1(1): 46–63.

ICM (2004) 'BBC Terrorism Poll', 28 May. Available online at www.icmresearch.com/pdfs/2004_may_bbc_terrorism_poll.pdf (last accessed 4 November 2014).

Isin, E. (2008) 'Theorizing Acts of Citizenship', in E. Isin and G. M. Nielsen (eds.) *Acts of Citizenship*. London: Zed, pp. 15–43.

Isin, E. and Turner, B. (eds.) (2003a) *Handbook of Citizenship Studies*. London: Sage.

Isin, E. and Turner, B. (2003b) 'Citizenship Studies: An Introduction' in E. Isin and B. Turner (eds.) *Handbook of Citizenship Studies*. London: Sage, pp. 1–10.

Isin, E. F. and Turner, B. (2007) 'Investigating Citizenship: An Agenda for Citizenship Studies', *Citizenship Studies* 11(1): 5–17.

Jackson, R. (2005) *Writing the War on Terrorism: Language, Politics and Counter-Terrorism*. Manchester: Manchester University Press.

Jackson, R. (2008) 'The Ghosts of State Terror: Knowledge, Politics and Terrorism Studies' *Critical Studies on Terrorism* 1(3): 377–392.

Jackson, R. (2009a) 'Knowledge, Power and Politics in the Study of Political Terrorism', in R. Jackson, M. Breen Smyth and J. Gunning (eds.) *Critical Terrorism Studies: A New Research Agenda*. Abingdon: Routledge, pp. 66–83.

Jackson, R. (2009b) 'The Study of Political Terrorism after 11 September 2001: Problems, Challenges and Future Developments', *Political Studies Review* 7(2): 171–184.

Jackson, R. and Hall, G. (2013) 'Knowing Terrorism: A Study on Lay Knowledge of Terrorism and Counter-Terrorism', paper presented at the Annual International Studies Association Conference, San Francisco, 3–5 April.

Jackson, R. and Sinclair, S. J. (eds.) (2013) *Contemporary Debates on Terrorism*. Abingdon: Routledge.

Jackson, R., Jarvis, L., Gunning, J. and Breen Smyth, M. (2011) *Terrorism: A Critical Introduction*. Basingstoke: Palgrave.

Jarvis, L. (2009a) 'The Spaces and Faces of Critical Terrorism Studies', *Security Dialogue* 40(1): 5–27.

Jarvis, L. (2009b) *Times of Terror: Discourse, Temporality and the War on Terror*. Basingstoke: Palgrave.

Jarvis, L. and Holland, J. (2015) *Security: A Critical Introduction*. Basingstoke: Palgrave.

Jarvis, L. and Lister, M. (2010) 'Stakeholder Security: The New Western Way of Counter Terrorism?', *Contemporary Politics* 16(2): 173–188.

Jarvis, L. and Lister, M. (2011) 'Values and Stakeholders in the 2011 Prevent Strategy', *Soundings*, 15 June 2011. Available online at http://soundings.mcb.org.uk/?p=31 (last accessed 4 November 2014).

Jarvis, L. and Lister, M. (2013a) 'Disconnected Citizenship: The Impacts of Anti-Terrorism Policy on Citizenship in the UK', *Political Studies* 61(3): 656–675.

Jarvis, L. and Lister, M. (2013b) 'Vernacular Securities and their Study: A Qualitative Analysis and Research Agenda', *International Relations* 27(2): 158–179.

Jarvis, L. and Lister, M. (2014) 'State Terrorism Research and Critical Terrorism Studies: An Assessment', *Critical Studies on Terrorism* 7(1): 43–61.

Jarvis, L. and Lister, M. (2015a) (eds.) *Critical Perspectives on Counter-Terrorism*. Abingdon: Routledge.

Jarvis, L. and Lister, M. (2015b) 'I Read it in the FT: "Everyday" Knowledge of Counter-Terrorism and its Articulation', in L. Jarvis and M. Lister (eds.) *Critical Perspectives on Counter-Terrorism*. Abingdon: Routledge, pp. 109–129.

Jenkins, B. (1974) *International Terrorism: A New Kind of Warfare*. Santa Monica, CA: Rand.

Jenkins, B. (2008) *Fenian Problem: Insurgency and Terrorism in a Liberal State 1858–74*. Quebec City: McGill University Press.

Jensen, R. B. (2006) 'The United States, International Policing and the War against Anarchist Terrorism, 1900–14', in D. C. Rapoport (ed.) *Terrorism: Critical Concepts in Political Science I*. Abingdon: Routledge, pp. 369–400.

Johnson, M. and Gearty, C. (2007) 'Civil Liberties and the Challenge of Terrorism', in A. Park, J. Curtice, K. Thomson, M. Phillips and M. Johnson (eds.) *British Social Attitudes: The 23rd Report: Perspectives on a Changing Society*. London: Sage, pp. 143–182.

Joppke, C. (2004) 'The Retreat of Multiculturalism in the Liberal State: Theory and Policy', *British Journal of Sociology* 55(2): 237–257.

Joppke, C. (2010) *Citizenship and Migration*. Cambridge: Polity Press.

Joslyn, M. and Haider-Markel, D. (2007) 'Sociotropic Concerns and Support for Counter-Terrorism Policies', *Social Science Quarterly* 88(2): 306–319.

Katzenstein, P. (2002) 'September 11 in Comparative Perspective: The Antiterrorism Campaigns of Germany and Japan', *Dialogue IO* 1(1): 45–56.

Katzenstein, P. (2003) 'Same War – Different Views: Germany, Japan, and Counterterrorism', *International Organization* 57(4): 731–760.

Kinnvall, C. (2004) 'Globalization and Religious Nationalism: Self, Identity and the Search for Ontological Security', *Political Psychology* 25(5): 741–767.

Kisby, B. (2007) 'New Labour and Citizenship Education', *Parliamentary Affairs* 60(1): 84–101.

Kitzinger, J. and Barbour, R. (1999) 'Introduction: The Challenge and Promise of Focus Groups', in R. Barbour and J. Kitzinger (eds.) *Developing Focus Group Research*. London: Sage, pp. 1–20.

Koskela, H. (2010) 'Did you Spot an Alien? Voluntary Vigilance, Borderwork and the Texas Virtual Border Watch Programme', *Space and Polity* 14(2): 103–121.

Koskela, H. (2011) 'Hijackers and Humble Servants: Individuals as Camwitnesses in Contemporary Controlwork', *Theoretical Criminology* 15(3): 269–282.

Kossowska, M., Trejtowicz, M., de Lemus, S., Bukowski, M., van Hiel, A. and Goodwin, R. (2011) 'Relationships between Right Wing Authoritararianism, Terrorism Threat and Attitudes towards Restrictions of Civil Rights: A Comparison among Four European Countries', *British Journal of Psychology* 102: 245–259.

Krause, K. and Williams, M. C. (1997) *Critical Security Studies: Concepts and Cases*. Minneapolis, MN: University of Minnesota Press.

Kuhn, T. S. (2012) *The Structure of Scientific Revolutions*. Chicago, IL: University of Chicago Press.

Kundnani, A. (2002) 'The Death of Multiculturalism', *Race and Class* 43(4): 67–72.

Kundnani, A. (2014) *The Muslims Are Coming! Islamophobia, Extremism and the Domestic War on Terror*. London: Verso.

Kymlicka, W. (1995) *Multicultural Citizenship: A Liberal Theory of Minority Rights*. Oxford: Oxford University Press.

Kymlicka, W. and Norman, W. (1994) 'Return of the Citizen: A Survey of Recent Work on Citizenship Theory', *Ethics* 104(2): 352–381.

Laing. R. D. (1965) *The Divided Self: An Existential Study in Sanity and Madness*. Tavistock: Penguin.

Landman, T. (2007) 'The United Kingdom: The Continuity of Terror and Counterterror', in A. Brysk and G. Shafir (eds.) *National Insecurity and Human Rights: Democracies Debate Counterterrorism*. Berkeley, CA: University of California Press, pp. 75–91.

Laqueur, W. (2001) *A History of Terrorism*. New Brunswick, NJ: Transaction.

Laqueur, W. (2003) *No End to War: Terrorism in the Twenty-First Century*. New York, NY: Continuum.

Legrand, T. and Jarvis, L. (2015) 'Enemies of the State: Proscription Powers and Their Use in the United Kingdom', *British Politics* 9(4): 450–471.

Liberty (2010) 'Terrorism Pre-Charge Detention: Comparative Law Study'. Available online at www.liberty-human-rights.org.uk/policy/reports/comparative-law-study-2010-pre-charge-detention.pdf (last accessed 4 November 2014).

Lister, M. (2014) 'Citizens, Doing it for themselves? The Big Society and Government through Community', *Parliamentary Affairs*, published online early, doi: 10.1093/pa/gst025.

Lister, M. and Jarvis, L. (2013) 'Disconnection and Resistance: Anti-Terrorism and Citizenship in the UK', *Citizenship Studies* 17(6–7): 756–769.

Lister, M. and Otero-Iglesias, M. (2012) 'New Problems, Old Solutions? Explaining Variations in British and Spanish Counter-Terrorism Policy', *Comparative European Politics* 10(5): 564–584.

Lister, M. and Pia, E. (2008) *Citizenship in Contemporary Europe*. Edinburgh: Edinburgh University Press.

Lister, R. (2007) 'Inclusive Citizenship: Realizing the Potential', *Citizenship Studies*, 11(1): 49–61.

Lowndes, V. and Thorp, L. (2010) '"Preventing Violent Extremism": Why Local Context Matters', in R. Eatwell and M. Goodwin (eds.) *The New Extremism in 21st Century Britain*. Abingdon: Routledge, pp. 124–141.

Lum, C., Kennedy, L. W. and Sherley, A. (2006) 'Are Counter-Terrorism Strategies Effective? The Results of the Campbell Systematic Review on Counter-Terrorism Evaluation Research', *Journal of Experimental Criminology* 2(4): 489–516.

Lynch, A. (2008) 'Control Orders in Australia: A Further Case Study in the Migration of British Counter-Terrorism Law', *Oxford University Commonwealth Law Journal* 8(2): 159–185.

McCord, N. (1967) 'The Fenians and Public Opinion in Great Britain', *University Review* 4(3): 227–240.

McDonald, M. (2008) 'Securitization and the Construction of Security', *European Journal of International Relations* 14(4): 563–587.

McDonald, M. (2009) 'Emancipation and Critical Terrorism Studies', in R. Jackson, M. Breen Smyth and J. Gunning (eds.) *Critical Terrorism Studies: A New Research Agenda*. Abingdon: Routledge, pp. 109–123.

McFarland, E. W. (1998) 'A Reality and Yet Impalpable: The Fenian Panic in Mid-Victorian Scotland', *Scottish Historical Review*, 77(204): 199–223.

Mack, A. (2004) 'A Signifier of Shared Values', *Security Dialogue* 35(3): 366–367.

Macken, C. (2010) 'The Counter-Terrorism Purposes of an Australian Preventive Detention Order', in N. McGarrity, A. Lynch, and G. Williams (eds.) *Counter-Terrorism and Beyond: The Culture of Law and Justice after 9/11*. Abingdon: Routledge, pp. 30–47.

McNay, L. (1999) 'Subject, Psyche and Agency: The Work of Judith Butler', *Theory, Culture and Society* 16(2): 175–193.

McNay, L. (2004) 'Agency and Experience: Gender as a Lived Relation', *Sociological Review* 52(2): 173–190.

McSweeney, B. (1999) *Security, Identity and Interests: A Sociology of International Relations*. Cambridge: Cambridge University Press.

Maira, S. M. (2004) 'Youth Culture, Citizenship and Globalization: South Asian Muslim Youth in the United States after 9/11', *Comparative Studies of South Asia, Africa and the Middle East*, 24(1): 219–231.

Maira, S. M. (2009) *Missing: Youth, Citizenship and Empire after 9/11*. London: Duke University Press.

Martin, T. (2014) 'Governing an Unknowable Future: The Politics of Britain's Prevent Policy', *Critical Studies on Terrorism* 7(1): 62–78.

Massie, A. (2013) 'Theresa May's Immigration Bill is Another Contemptible Piece of Legislation', *Spectator*, 10 October. Available online at http://blogs.spectator.co.uk/coffeehouse/2013/10/theresa-mays-immigration-bill-is-another-contemptible-piece-of-legislation (last accessed 4 November 2014).

Meer, N. and Modood, T. (2009) 'The Multicultural State we're in: Muslims, "Multiculture" and the "Civic Re-balancing" of British Multiculturalism', *Political Studies* 57(3): 473–497.

Meisels, T. (2005) 'How Terrorism Upsets Liberty', *Political Studies*, 53(1): 162–181.

Meisels, T. (2008) *The Trouble with Terror: Liberty, Security and the Response to Terrorism*, Cambridge: Cambridge University Press.

Metropolitan Police (2008) 'If you Suspect it Report it', Metropolitan Police campaign. Available online at: http://content.met.police.uk/Campaign/athotline (last accessed 4 November 2014).

Metropolitan Police (2010) 'If you Suspect it, Report it'. Available online at: http://content.met.police.uk/Campaign/nationwidecounterterrorism (last accessed 1 August 2013).

Miekle, J. (2006) 'Schools Poor at Teaching Citizenship, Says Ofsted', *Guardian*, 28 September. Available online at www.theguardian.com/uk/2006/sep/28/schools.ofsted (last accessed 4 November 2014).

Miller-Idriss, C. (2006) 'Everyday Understandings of Citizenship in Germany', *Citizenship Studies* 10(5): 541–570.

Mitzen, J. (2006) 'Ontological Security in World Politics: State Identity and the Security Dilemma', *European Journal of International Relations* 12(3): 341–70.

Modood, T. (2009) 'Muslims and the Politics of Difference', in R. Gale and P. Hopkins (eds.) *Muslims in Britain: Race, Place and the Spatiality of Identities*. Edinburgh: Edinburgh University Press, pp. 193–209.

Modood, T., Hansen, R., Bleich, E., O'Leary, B. and Carens, J. H. (2006) 'The Danish Cartoon Affair: Free Speech, Racism, Islamism, and Integration', *International Migration* 44(5): 3–62.

Morgan, D. (1996) 'Focus Groups', *Annual Review of Sociology* 22(1): 129–152.

Morgan, D. (1997) *Focus Groups as Qualitative Research* (2nd edition). London: Sage.

Morris, N. (2006) 'Blair's "Frenzied Law Making': A New Offence for Every Day Spent in Office', Independent Online 16 August. Available online at www.independent.co.uk/news/uk/politics/blairs-frenzied-law-making--a-new-offence-for-every-day-spent-in-office-412072.html (last accessed 4 November 2014).

Moss, G. and O'Loughlin, B. (2008) 'Convincing Claims? Democracy and Representation in Post-9/11 Britain', *Political Studies* 56(3): 705–724.

Mueller, J. (2005) 'Six Rather Unusual Propositions about Terrorism', *Terrorism and Political Violence* 17(4): 487–505.

Mueller, J. and Stewart, M. G. (2011). *Terror, Security, and Money: Balancing the Risks, Benefits, and Costs of Homeland Security*. Oxford: Oxford University Press.

Mutimer, D. (2009) 'My Critique is Bigger than Yours: Constituting Exclusions in Critical Security Studies', *Studies in Social Justice* 3(1): 9–22.

Mythen, G. (2012) '"No One Speaks for us': Security Policy, Suspected Communities and the Problem of Voice', *Critical Studies on Terrorism* 5(3): 409–424.

Mythen, G., Walklate, S. and Khan, F. (2013) 'Why Should we Have to Prove we're Alright? Counter-Terrorism, Risk and Partial Securities', *Sociology* 47(2): 383–398.

Neal, A. W. (2012) 'Terrorism, Lawmaking, and Democratic Politics: Legislators as Security Actors', *Terrorism and Political Violence*, 24(3): 357–374.

Neocleous, M. (2008) *Critique of Security*. Montreal: McGill-Queen's University Press.

Neumann, P. (2009) *Old and New Terrorism*. Cambridge: Polity Press.

Newman, E. (2001) 'Human Security and Constructivism', *International Studies Perspectives* 2(3): 239–251.

Newman, E. (2010) 'Critical Human Security Studies', *Review of International Studies* 36(1): 77–94.

Norman, J. (2010) *The Big Society: The Anatomy of the New Politics*. Buckingham: University of Buckingham Press.

Noxolo, P. and Huysmans, J. (eds.) (2009) *Community, Citizenship and the War on Terror: Security and Insecurity*. Basingstoke: Palgrave.

Nyers, P. (ed.) (2009) *The Securitizations of Citizenship*. Abingdon: Routledge.

Nyers, P. (2010) 'Missing Citizenship', *International Political Sociology* 4(1): 95–98.

O'Loughlin, B. and Gillespie, M. (2012) 'Dissenting Citizenship? Young People and Political Participation in the Media–Security Nexus', *Parliamentary Affairs* 65(1): 115–137.

Ong, A. (2006) 'Mutations in Citizenship', *Theory, Culture and Society* 23(2–3): 499–505.

Pantazis, C. and Pemberton, S. (2009) 'From the "Old" to the "New" Suspect Community Examining the Impacts of Recent UK Counter-Terrorist Legislation', *British Journal of Criminology* 49(5): 646–666.

Parekh, B. (2000) *Rethinking Multiculturalism: Cultural Diversity and Political Theory*. Basingstoke: Macmillan.

Pattie, C., Seyd, P. and Whiteley, P. (2003) 'Civic Attitudes and Engagement in Modern Britain', *Parliamentary Affairs* 56(4): 616–633.

Peoples, C. and Vaughan-Williams, N. (2010) *Critical Security Studies: An Introduction*. Abingdon: Routledge.

Pierre, J. and Guy Peters, B. (2000) *Governance, Politics and the State*. Basingstoke: Macmillan.

Pierson, P. (2004) *Politics in Time: History, Institutions, and Social Analysis*. Princeton, NJ: Princeton University Press.

Plummer, K. (1995) *Telling Sexual Stories: Power Change and Social Worlds*. Abingdon: Routledge.

Porter, B. (1987) *The Origins of the Vigilant State: The London Metropolitan Police Special Branch before the First World War*. London: Weidenfeld and Nicolson.

Prins, B. (2006) 'Narrative Accounts of Origins: A Blind Spot in the Intersectional Approach?', *European Journal of Women's Studies* 13(3): 277–290.

Puar, J. K. and Rai, A. (2002) 'Monster, Terrorist, Fag: The War on Terrorism and the Production of Docile Patriots', *Social Text* 20(3): 117–148.

Putnam, R. (2000) *Bowling Alone: The Collapse and Revival of American Community*. New York, NY: Simon and Schuster.

Ragazzi, F. (2015) 'Policed Multiculturalism in Europe: Governing Radicalisation through Partnerships', in C. Baker-Beall, C. Heath-Kelly and L. Jarvis (eds.) *Counter-Radicalisation: Critical Perspectives*. Abingdon: Routledge, pp. 156–174.

Rapin, A. (2009) 'Does Terrorism Create Terror', *Critical Studies on Terrorism* 2(2): 165–179.

Rapoport, D. C. (1984) 'Fear and Trembling: Terrorism in Three Religious Traditions', *American Political Science Review* 78(3): 658–677.

Rapoport, D. C. (2004) 'The Four Waves of Modern Terrorism', in A. K. Cronin and J. M. Ludes (eds.) *Attacking Terrorism: Elements of a Grand Strategy*. Washington, DC: Georgetown University Press, pp. 46–73.

Rees, W. and Aldrich, R. A. (2005) 'Contending Cultures of Counterterrorism: Transatlantic Divergence or Convergence?', *International Affairs* 81(5): 905–923.

Reid, J. (2006) *The Biopolitics of the War on Terror: Life Struggles, Liberal Modernity, and the Defence of Logistical Societies*. Manchester: Manchester University Press.

Reinares, F. (ed.) (2000) *European Democracies against Terrorism*. Aldershot: Ashgate.

Reinares, F. (2009) 'After the Madrid Bombings: Internal Security Reforms and Prevention of Global Terrorism in Spain', *Studies in Conflict and Terrorism* 32(5): 367–388.

Rice, C. (2001) 'New Counter-Terrorism and Cyberspace Security Positions Announced', 9 October. Available online at http://georgewbush-whitehouse.archives.gov/news/releases/2001/10/20011009-4.html (last accessed 4 November 2014).

Richardson, L. (2006) *What Terrorists Want: Understanding the Terrorist Threat*. New York, NY: Random House.

Ritchie, J. and Spencer, L. (2002) 'Qualitative Data Analysis for Applied Policy Research', in A. Humberman and M. Miles (eds.), *The Qualitative Researcher's Companion*. London: Sage, pp. 305–330.

Ritchie, J., Lewis, J. and Elam, G. (2003) 'Designing and Selecting Samples', in J. Ritchie and J. Lewis (eds.) *Qualitative Research Practice: A Guide for Social Science Students and Researchers*. London: Sage, pp. 77–108.

Ritchie, J., Spencer, L. and O'Connor, W. (2003) 'Carrying out Qualitative Analysis', in J. Ritchie and J. Lewis (eds.) *Qualitative Research Practice: A Guide for Social Science Students and Researchers*. London: Sage, pp. 219–262.

Roach, K. (2005) 'Canada's Response to Terrorism', in V. Ramraj, M. Y. M. Yew and K. Roach (eds.) *Global Counter-Terrorism Law and Policy*. Cambridge: Cambridge University Press, pp. 511–532.

Roach, K. (2007) 'A Comparison of Australian and Canadian Counter-Terrorism Laws', *UNSW Law Journal* 30(1): 53–85.

Roach, K. (2011) *The 9/11 Effect: Comparative Counterterrorism*, Cambridge: Cambridge University Press.

Roe, P. (2004) 'Securitization and Minority Rights: Conditions of Desecuritization', *Security Dialogue* 35(3): 279–294.

Roe, P. (2012) 'Is Securitization a "Negative" Concept? Revisiting the Normative Debate over Normal versus Extraordinary Politics', *Security Dialogue* 43(3): 249–266.

Romaniuk, P. (2010) *Multilateral Counter-Terrorism: The Global Politics of Cooperation and Contestation*. Abingdon: Routledge.

Rose, M. (2002) 'The Seductions of Resistance: Power, Politics and a Performative Style of Systems', *Environment and Planning D: Society and Space* 20(4): 383–400.

Rose, N. (1999) *Powers of Freedom*. Cambridge: Cambridge University Press.

Rose, N. and Miller, P. (2008) *Governing the Present: Administering Economic, Social and Personal Life*. Cambridge: Polity Press.

Rumsfeld, D. (2002) 'DoD News Briefing, Secretary Rumsfeld and Gen. Myers', US Department of Defense, 12 February. Available online at www.defense.gov/transcripts/transcript.aspx?transcriptid=2636 (last accessed 4 November 2014).

Rygiel, K. (2006) 'Protecting and Proving Identity: The Biopolitics of Waging War through Citizenship in the Post 9/11 Era', in K. Hunt and K. Rygiel (eds.) *(En) Gendering the War on Terror: War Stories and Camouflaged Politics*. Aldershot: Ashgate, pp. 145–168.

Rygiel, K. (2008) 'The Securitized Citizen', in E. Isin (ed.) *Recasting the Social in Citizenship*. Toronto: University of Toronto Press, pp. 210–238.

Rykkja, L. H., Lægreid, P. and Fimreite, L. (2011) 'Attitudes towards Anti-Terror Measures: The Role of Trust, Political Orientation and Civil Liberties Support', *Critical Studies on Terrorism* 4(2): 219–237.

Said, T. (2004) 'The Impact of Anti Terrorism Powers on the British Muslim Population', Liberty. Available online at www.liberty-human-rights.org.uk/policy/reports/impact-of-anti-terror-measures-on-british-muslims-june-2004.pdf (last accessed 1 August 2013).

Schmid, A. (2013) 'Introduction', in A. Schmid (ed.) *The Routledge Handbook of Terrorism Research*. Abingdon: Routledge, pp. 1–37.

Schmid, A. and Jongman, P. (1988) *Political Terrorism: A Research Guide to Concepts, Theories, Databases and Literature*. New Brunswick, NJ: Transaction.

Scobey, D. (2001) 'The Specter of Citizenship', *Citizenship Studies* 5(1): 11–26.

Serrano, A. (2015) 'Contemporary Spanish Anti-Terrorist Policies: Ancient Myths, New Approaches', in L. Jarvis and M. Lister (eds.) *Critical Perspectives on Counter-Terrorism*. Abingdon: Routledge, pp. 91–108.

Shapiro, J. (2008) 'Detention of Terrorism Suspects in Britain and France', Commission on Security and Cooperation in Europe, Brookings Institute. Available online at: www.brookings.edu/research/testimony/2008/07/15-terrorism-shapiro (last accessed 4 November 2014).

Shapiro, J. (2010) 'The French Responses to Terrorism from the Algerian War to the Present', in M. Crenshaw (ed.) *The Consequences of Counter Terrorism*. New York, NY: Russell Sage Foundation, pp. 255–284.

Shapiro, J. and Suzan, B. (2003) 'The French Experience of Counter Terrorism', *Survival* 45(1): 67–98.

Sheehan, M. (2005) *International Security: An Analytical Survey*. London: Lynne Rienner.

Shepherd, L. (ed.) (2013) *Critical Approaches to Security: An Introduction to Theories and Methods*. Abingdon: Routledge.

Silke, A. (2011) 'The Psychology of Counter-Terrorism: Critical Issues and Challenges', in A. Silke (ed.) *The Psychology of Counter-Terrorism*. Routledge: Abingdon, pp. 1–18.

Simon, S. and Benjamin, D. (2000) 'America and the New Terrorism', *Survival* 42(1): 59–75.

Sivanandan, A. (2006) 'Race, Terror and Civil Society', *Race and Class* 47(3): 1–8.

Sjoberg, L. (2009) 'Introduction to Security Studies: Feminist Contributions', *Security Studies* 18(2): 183–213.

Smith, B. and Sparkes, C. (2008) 'Contrasting Perspectives on Narrating Selves and Identities: An Invitation to Dialogue', *Qualitative Research* 8(1): 5–35.

Smith, S. (2005) 'The Contested Concept of Security', in K. Booth (ed.) *Critical Security Studies and World Politics*. London: Lynn Rienner, pp. 27–62.

Somers, M. (2008) *Genealogies of Citizenship: Markets, Statelessness, and the Right to Have Rights*. Cambridge: Cambridge University Press.

Spalek, B. (2012) 'Policing within Counter-Terrorism', in B. Spalek (ed.) *Counter-Terrorism: Community Based Approaches to Preventing Terror Crime*. Basingstoke: Palgrave, pp. 50–73.

Spencer, A. (2006) 'Questioning the Concept of "New Terrorism"', *Peace, Conflict and Development* 8(1): 1–33.

Squire, C, Andrews, M. and Tamboukou, M. (2008) 'Introduction: What is Narrative Research?' in M. Andrews, C. Squire and M. Tamboukou (eds.) *Doing Narrative Research*. London: Sage, pp. 1–26.

Staniforth, A. (2013) *The Routledge Companion to UK Counter-Terrorism*. Abingdon: Routledge.

Steinberg, M. W. (1998) 'Tilting the Frame: Considerations on Collective Action Framing from a Discursive Turn', *Theory and Society* 27(6): 845–872.

Stern, M. (2006) '"We" the Subject: The Power and Failure of (In)Security', *Security Dialogue* 37(2): 187–205.

Stevens, D. (2009) 'In Extremis: A Self-Defeating Element in the "Preventing Violent Extremism" Strategy', *Political Quarterly* 80(4): 17–25.

Stevens, D. (2011) 'Reasons to be Fearful, One, Two, Three: The "Preventing Violent Extremism" Agenda', *British Journal of Politics and International Relations* 13(2): 165–88.

Stohl, M. (2012) 'State Terror: The Theoretical and Practical Utilities and Implications of a Contested Concept', in R. Jackson and S. J. Sinclair (eds.) *Contemporary Debates on Terrorism*. Abingdon: Routledge, pp. 43–50.

Stolle, D. and Hooghe, M. (2005) 'Inaccurate, Exceptional, One-Sided or Irrelevant? The Debate about the Alleged Decline of Social Capital and Civic Engagement in Western Societies', *British Journal of Political Science* 35(1): 149–167.

Sullivan, J. L. and Hendriks, H. (2009) 'Public Support for Civil Liberties Pre- and Post-9/11', *Annual Review of Law and Social Science*, 5(1): 375–391.

Sylvester, C. (2013). 'Experiencing the End and Afterlives of International Relations/Theory', *European Journal of International Relations* 19(3): 609–626.

Taylor, C. (1994) 'The Politics of Recognition', in A. Gutmann (ed.) *Multiculturalism, Examining the Politics of Recognition*, Princeton, NJ: Princeton University Press, pp. 25–74.

Taylor-Gooby, P. (1991) 'Welfare State Regimes and Welfare Citizenship', *Journal of European Social Policy* 1(2): 93–105.

Thelen, K. (1999) 'Historical Institutionalism in Comparative Politics', *Annual Review of Political Science* 2(1): 369–404.

Thomas, P. (2009) 'Between Two Stools? The Government's "Preventing Violent Extremism" Agenda', *Political Quarterly* 80(2): 282–291.

Thomas, P. (2010) 'Failed and Friendless: The UK's "Preventing Violent Extremism" Programme', *British Journal of Politics and International Relations* 12(3): 442–458.

Thomas, P. and Sanderson, P. (2011) 'Unwilling Citizens? Muslim Young People and National Identity', *Sociology* 45(6): 1028–1044.

Tsoukala, A. (2006) 'Democracy in the Light of Security: British and French Political Discourses on Domestic Counter-Terrorism Policies', *Political Studies* 54(3): 607–627.

Turley, J. (2012) 'The NDAA's Historic Assault on American Liberty', *Guardian*, 2 January. Available online at www.guardian.co.uk/commentisfree/cifamerica/2012/jan/02/ndaa-historic-assault-american-liberty (last accessed 4 November 2014).

Turner, B. (1991) 'The Erosion of Citizenship', *British Journal of Sociology* 52(2): 189–209.

UNDP (United Nations Development Programme) (1994) *Human Development Report: Annual Report*. New York, NY: UNDP.

Vaughan-Williams, N. (2008) 'Borderwork beyond Inside/Outside? Frontex, the Citizen-Detective and the War on Terror', *Space and Polity* 12(1): 63–79.

Vaughan-Williams, N. and Stevens, D. (2012) 'Public Perceptions of Security: Reconsidering Sociotropic and Personal Threats', paper prepared for the Annual Elections, Public Opinion and Parties Meeting, Oxford, 7–9 September. Available online at: www.sociology.ox.ac.uk/documents/epop/papers/Stevens%20and%20Vaughan-Williams.pdf (last accessed 4 November2014).

Vaughan-Williams, N. and Stevens, D. (2013) 'The Stories People Tell: Public Perceptions of Threat and (In)Security', paper presented at the Annual International Studies Association Conference, San Francisco, 3–5 April.

Vertovec, S. and Cohen, R. (2002) 'Introduction: Conceiving Cosmpolitanism', in S. Vertovec and R. Cohen (eds), *Conceiving Cosmopolitanism: Theory, Context and Practice.* Oxford: Oxford University Press, pp. 1–22.

Vrasti, W. (2013) 'Travelling with Ethnography', in M. Salter and C. Mutlu (eds.) *Research Methods in Critical Security Studies: An Introduction.* Abingdon: Routledge, pp. 59–62.

Wacquant, L. (2009) *Punishing the Poor: The Neoliberal Government of Social Insecurity.* Durham, NC: Duke University Press.

Wæver, O. (1995) 'Securitization and Desecuritization', in R. D. Lipschutz (ed.) *On Security.* New York, NY: Columbia University Press, pp. 46–86.

Wæver, O. (2004) 'Aberystwyth, Paris, Copenhagen: New "Schools" in Security Theory and their Origins between Core and Periphery', paper prepared at annual meeting of the International Studies Association, Montreal.

Waldron, J. (2003) 'Security and Liberty: The Image of Balance', *Journal of Political Philosophy* 11(2): 191–210.

Waldron, J. (2012) *Torture, Terror, and Trade-Offs: Philosophy for the White House.* Oxford: Oxford University Press.

Walker, C. (1986) *The Prevention of Terrorism in British Law.* Manchester: Manchester University Press.

Walker, C. (2002) *Blackstone's Guide to The Counter-Terrorism Legislation.* Oxford: Blackwell.

Walker, C. (2006) 'Clamping down on Terrorism in the United Kingdom', *Journal of International Criminal Justice* 4(5): 1137–1151.

Walker, R. B. J. (1992) *Inside/Outside: International Relations as Political Theory.* Cambridge: Cambridge University Press.

Walt, S. M. (1991) 'The Renaissance of Security Studies', *International Studies Quarterly* 35(2): 211–239.

Watson, M. (2010) 'House Price Keynesianism and the Contradictions of the Modern Investor Subject', *Housing Studies* 25(3): 413–426.

Wendt, A. (1992) 'Anarchy is What States Make of it: The Social Construction of Power Politics', *International Organization* 46(2): 391–425.

Wendt, A. (1999) *Social Theory of International Politics.* Cambridge: Cambridge University Press.

Whelehan, N. (2012) *The Dynamiters: Irish Nationalism and Political Violence in the Wider World, 1867–1900.* Cambridge: Cambridge University Press.

Wight, C (2012) 'State Terrorism: Who Needs it?', in R. Jackson and S. J. Sinclair (eds.) *Contemporary Debates on Terrorism.* Abingdon: Routledge, pp. 50–57.

Wilkinson, P. (1977) *Terrorism and the Liberal State.* Basingstoke: Macmillan.

Wilkinson, P. (2011) *Terrorism vs. Democracy: The Liberal State Response.* Abingdon: Routledge.

Williams, G. (2005) 'The Rule of Law and the Regulation of Terrorism in Australia and New Zealand', in V. Ramraj, M. Y. M. Yew and K. Roach (eds.) *Global Counter-Terrorism Law and Policy*. Cambridge: Cambridge University Press, pp. 534–552.

Williams, M. C. (2003) 'Words, Images, Enemies: Securitization and International Politics', *International Studies Quarterly* 47(4): 511–531.

Williams, M. C. and Krause, K. (1996) 'Broadening the Agenda of Security Studies: Politics and Methods', *Mershon International Studies Review* 40(2): 229–254.

Williams, P. (2007) 'From Non-Intervention to Non-Indifference: The Origins and Development of the African Union's Security Culture', *African Affairs* 106(423): 253–279.

Williams, P. (ed.) (2013) *Security Studies: An Introduction* (2nd edition). Abingdon: Routledge.

Winkler, C. (2006) *In the Name of Terrorism: Presidents on Political Violence in the Post-World War II Era*. New York, NY: SUNY Press.

Wright, M. and Bloemraad, I. (2012) 'Is there a Trade-Off between Multiculturalism and Socio-Political Integration? Policy Regimes and Immigrant Incorporation in Comparative Perspective', *Perspectives on Politics* 10(1): 77–95.

YouGov (2011a) 'YouGov/Sunday Times Survey'. Available online at http://cdn.yougov.com/today_uk_import/YG-Archives-Pol-ST-results-07-090111_0.pdf (last accessed 4 November 2014).

YouGov (2011b) 'YouGov/Liberty Survey'. Available online at http://cdn.yougov.com/today_uk_import/YG-Archives-Pol-Liberty-SuspectedTerrorists-100111.pdf (last accessed 4 November 2014).

Young, J. K. and Findley, M. G. (2011) 'Promise and Pitfalls of Terrorism Research', *International Studies Review* 13(3): 411–431.

Zedner, L. (2007) 'Preventive Justice or Pre-Punishment? The Case of Control Orders', *Current Legal Problems* 60(1): 174–203.

Zehfuss, M. (2002) *Constructivism in International Relations: The Politics of Reality*. Cambridge: Cambridge University Press.

Žižek, S. (2007) 'Resistance is Surrender', *London Review of Books*, 29(22): 7.

Index

Lightning Source UK Ltd.
Milton Keynes UK
UKHW011545150819
347946UK00014B/124/P

9 781526 133816